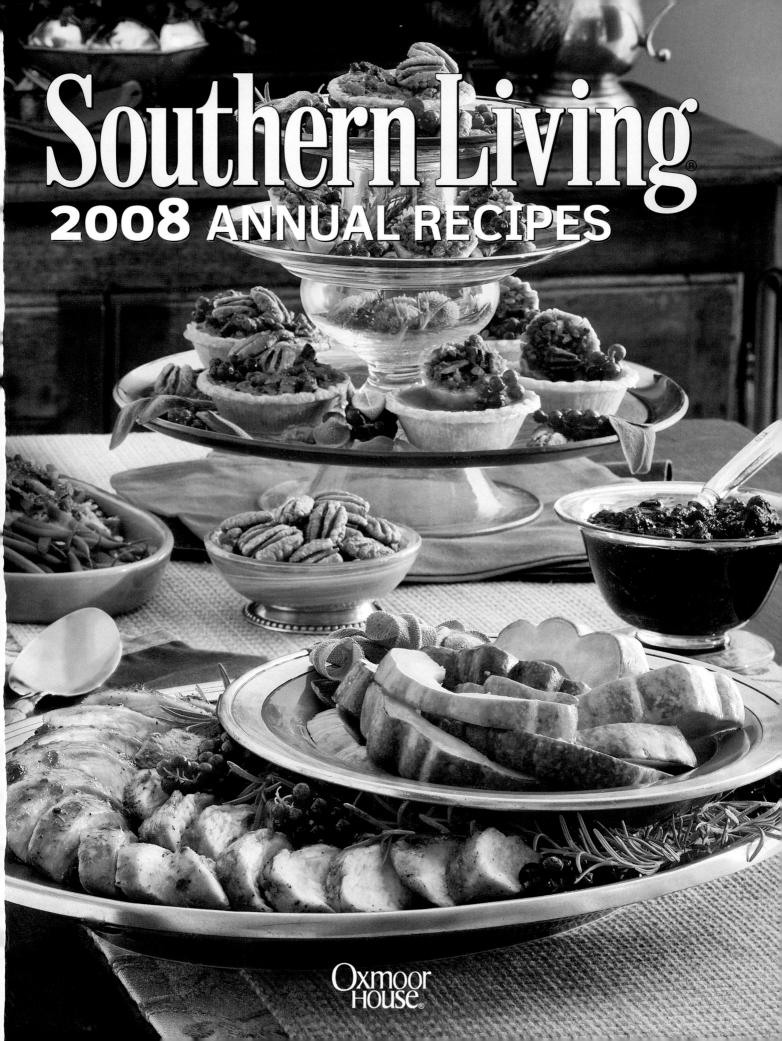

Southern Living®
2008 ANNUAL RECIPES

Oxmoor
House®

Best Recipes of 2008

Not all recipes are created equal. At *Southern Living,* only those that have passed muster with our Test Kitchens staff and Food editors—not an easy crowd to please—make it onto the pages of our magazine. Members of our Food staff gather almost every day to taste-test recipes to ensure not only that they're reliable, but also that they taste as good as they possibly can. Here we share this year's favorites.

King Ranch Chicken Casserole *(page 58)* ▶
This Texas favorite is the true definition of comfort food: soft, warm layers of chicken and tortilla with a subtle hint of green chile.

◀ Short Rib Sandwich *(page 35)*
This mouthwatering fork-and-knife sandwich boasts meat that literally falls off the bone combined with balsamic vinegar, red onion, blue cheese, and arugula.

Three-Cheese Pasta Bake *(page 28)* ▶
White Cheddar, Parmesan, and Gruyère enrich the flavor of this extra rich and cheesy dish.

▲ **Savory Baked Chicken** *(page 32)* The chicken tenderizes in a spread of garlic, salt, yogurt, and lime zest overnight, and then it roasts for over an hour in the oven to produce an unbelievable flavor sensation.

Spicy Chicken-Rice Bowl *(page 33)* ▶
Curry paste, fresh lime juice, grated ginger, and shredded Savory Baked Chicken are the secrets behind this zesty weeknight meal.

▲ **Lemon Mousse Tart (above right) and Lemon Velvet Tart (above left)** *(page 48)* The vibrant flavors of lemon and lime come alive in these scrumptious tarts, both of which include melt-in-your-mouth Lemon Curd. Easy-to-make Caramelized Sugar Spirals add a pretty presentation to the Lemon Velvet Tart.

Heavenly Angel Food Cake *(page 98)* ▶

Made from scratch in minutes with a unique two-step method for mixing the cake batter, these special little cakes are almost effortless to make up. The rich, moist texture of this divine angel food cake is unlike any other. The soft Lemon-Cream Cheese Frosting is perfect for spreading on a sheet cake.

▲ **Raspberry Tiramisù Bites** *(page 64)* This satisfying treat makes a sensible but lavish ending to any meal. Ladyfingers, raspberry preserves, and whipped cream provide a fruity twist on the traditional dessert.

◄ **Strawberry-Buttermilk Sherbet** *(page 108)* Colorful and delicious, the tang of buttermilk balances the sweetness of the berries in this cool concoction. This heavenly four-ingredient dessert requires only 15 minutes of hands-on preparation before it goes into an ice cream maker.

▲ **Gorgonzola Truffles**
(page 97) Delicious served alongside apple and pear slices and grapes, these creamy, make-ahead bites are rolled in crisp, crumbled bacon.

Raspberry Cream Tartlet (A)
Dulce de Leche Tartlet (B)
Chocolate-Hazelnut Tartlet (C)
Peach-and-Blue Cheese Bites (D)
Ginger-Brie Bite (E) *(page 112)*
Freezeable, make-ahead tartlet shells serve as the base for these elegant little bites. Guests can fill up their plates with both sweet and savory tarts. ▶

◄ **Collards with Red Onions** *(page 34)* Whether you serve it as your traditional green on New Year's Day or any other day of the year, this dish is sure to deliver on both texture and flavor. Be sure to have some cornbread on hand to soak up the vitamin-rich juices.

Rémoulade Sauce *(page 67)* Mayonnaise, yogurt, Creole mustard, and garlic are a few of the ingredients that make this sauce so irresistible.

▼ **Chicken-fried Steak and Cream Gravy** *(page 68)* With its crunchy coating, tender inside, and peppery gravy, no one will guess this dish is lightened.

▲ **First-Rate Veggie Plate** *(pages 152 to 154)* We turned to a few of our favorite chefs for some fresh vegetable recipes that are easy enough to make at home. These dishes offer hip new takes on Southern classics. No veggie plate is complete without mac 'n' cheese, and this is one of the best we've tasted. Serve Not Yo' Mama's Mac 'n' Cheese with Squash Casserole and Green Beans With Caramelized Garlic for a sensational meal.

▲ **Fish Fry Done Right** *(pages 144 and 145)* Get ready to fry up a scrumptious seafood jubilee. Serve Sweet-and-Spicy Jalapeño Poppers as a tasty appetizer. Then add Bayou Fish Fillets With Sweet-Hot Pecan Sauce; the fillets boast a cornbread mix containing sugar that causes them to fry to a deep golden brown. An unbelievable sauce is made with pantry ingredients. Pair with crisp-tender Shrimp-and-Okra Hush Puppies and your favorite fries for a soul-soothing treat.

▲ **Chocolate Marble Sheet Cake**
(page 230) This moist cake boasts a rich, creamy frosting that blends cocoa with coffee for an unbelievable dessert.

◄ **Double Apple Pie With Cornmeal Crust and Brandy-Caramel Sauce** *(page 216)* A flaky crust, 4½ pounds of apples and apple jelly help to make this one of the best apple pies that we've ever tasted.

All-Time Favorite Chocolate Chip Cookies ▶
(page 208) Crisp and buttery, rich and gooey, big batch or small—this recipe has it all.

Pecan Sugared Bacon *(page 202)* Fresh ground pepper gives an extra bite to this crispy breakfast favorite.

So-Easy Cherry Fudge Cake and Old-fashioned Oatmeal Cake *(pages 231 and 232)* These sweet treats are easy to bake and great to take to get-togethers.

▲ **Shrimp Scampi** *(page 266)* Fresh lemon juice and garlic combine to make a succulent sauce for this Italian favorite that takes just 30 minutes to make.

Coconut-Almond Cream Cake *(page 262)* Toasted almonds and coconut add to the scrumptious flavor of this melt-in-your-mouth layer cake.

▲ **Savory Blue Cheesecakes With Waldorf Salad** *(page 266)* This elegant salad transforms everyday ingredients such as apples, walnuts, celery, and raisins into a dinner party sensation.

Delta Roasted Turkey With Million-Dollar Gravy *(page 268)* With a crisp exterior and juicy meat, this bird is sure to be the cornerstone dish for any holiday meal.

Kane's Pepper Bloody Mary *(page 282)* A host of fresh herbs and lots of lemon juice make this cocktail a true standout.

Creamy Baked Sweet Onions *(page 284)* Cipolline onions and sharp white Cheddar cheese are the secret ingredients in this rich and cheesy dish that's topped with a buttery cracker crust.

Meet the *Southern Living* Food Staff

For over 40 years, the *Southern Living* Food Staff has been the trusted source of Southern cuisine. On these pages, we invite you to match the names and faces of the people who plan, kitchen-test, and write about our favorites (names correspond left to right unless otherwise noted).

▲ (seated) LYDA JONES BURNETTE, *Test Kitchens Director;* SCOTT JONES, *Executive Editor;* (standing) SHANNON SLITER SATTERWHITE, *Food Editor*

◀ (seated) REBECCA KRACKE GORDON, *Assistant Test Kitchens Director;* PAM LOLLEY *and* ANGELA SELLERS, *Test Kitchens Professionals;* (standing) MARIAN COOPER CAIRNS, *Test Kitchens Professional;* VANESSA MCNEIL ROCCHIO, *Test Kitchens Specialist/Food Styling;* NORMAN KING, *Test Kitchens Professional*

(standing) ▶
ASHLEY LEATH, *Assistant Recipe Editor;* SHIRLEY HARRINGTON, *Associate Food Editor;* MARION MCGAHEY, *Assistant Food Editor;* VICKI A. POELLNITZ *and* MARY ALLEN PERRY, *Associate Food Editors;* ASHLEY ARTHUR, *Assistant Recipe Editor;* (seated) CHARLA DRAPER, *Associate Food Editor;* DONNA FLORIO, *Senior Writer; and* NATALIE KELLY BROWN, *Assistant Food Editor*

Our Year at Southern Living®

Dear Food Friends,

2008 has been a busy and exciting year at *Southern Living*. Not only did we produce our first double issue in December (to give you even more great-tasting recipes), but we also freshened up and re-energized our pages beginning with the March issue. Our primary goal in this historic undertaking was to make the magazine easier for you to navigate and to help you get the tips, advice, and recipes you want more quickly. To quote the magazine's editor, John Floyd, "In the past 40 years, there have been significant milestones in the evolution of *Southern Living*. But one thing is still the same: We remain committed to giving you kitchen-tested recipes with our special twist." Better still, this dynamic and beautifully illustrated cookbook reflects those changes, too.

> **"We remain committed to giving you kitchen-tested recipes with our special twist."**
>
> —JOHN FLOYD

As you flip through the pages, don't miss the Test Kitchens Notebook secrets scattered throughout the chapters. This is your chance to get expert help and hints directly from our Food Staff to ensure that you have success with these tempting recipes every time. One of my favorite sections is "5-Ingredient Entertaining." We know that entertaining—both casual and special occasion—is still a very big deal in our region, and these flavor-packed treats are perfect for your busy schedule and budget.

This coming year, please allow us to set the *Southern Living* table with you in mind.
- Do you know someone who makes the "best something" you've ever tasted? Introduce us to them.
- How is the economy affecting the way you cook for family or entertain for friends? What are your favorite money-saving tips? Share them with us.
- Is there a subject you'd like us to cover? Write or e-mail us.
- Have you reinvented a favorite dish or made it healthier? Tell us about it.

We are dedicated to reflecting today's Southern kitchen and giving you more of what you want in practical and affordable ways that fit your lifestyle. Thanks for inviting us into your home, and I look forward to hearing from you and seeing more of your recipes soon.

Sincerely,

Scott Jones
Executive Editor
sl_foodedit@timeinc.com

©2008 by Oxmoor House, Inc.
Book Division of Southern Progress Corporation
P.O. Box 2262, Birmingham, Alabama 35201-2262

ISBN-13: 978-0-8487-3235-6
ISBN-10: 0-8487-3235-9
ISSN: 0272-2003

Printed in the United States of America
First printing 2008

To order additional publications, call 1-800-765-6400.

For more books to enrich your life, visit **oxmoorhouse.com**

To search, savor, and share thousands of recipes, visit **myrecipes.com**

Cover: Sugar-and-Spice Cake, page 293, and Peppermint Pinwheel Cookies, page 292

Page 1: Turkey Tenderloins With Cranberry Sauce, page 263; Roasted Winter Squash, page 285; Simple Pecan-Green Bean Casserole, page 288; and Mini Pecan Pies, page 279

Southern Living®

Executive Editor: Scott Jones
Food Editor: Shannon Sliter Satterwhite
Senior Writer: Donna Florio
Associate Food Editors: Charla Draper, Shirley Harrington, Mary Allen Perry, Vicki A. Poellnitz
Assistant Food Editors: Natalie Kelly Brown, Marion McGahey
Assistant Recipe Editors: Ashley Arthur, Ashley Leath
Test Kitchens Director: Lyda Jones Burnette
Assistant Test Kitchens Director: Rebecca Kracke Gordon
Test Kitchens Specialist/Food Styling: Vanessa McNeil Rocchio
Test Kitchens Professionals: Marian Cooper Cairns, Kristi Michele Crowe, Norman King, Pam Lolley, Angela Sellers
Editorial Assistant: Pat York
Production Manager: Jamie Barnhart
Creative Director: Jon Thompson
Design Director: Howard Greenberg
Copy Chief: Paula Hunt Hughes
Assistant Copy Chief: Katie Bowlby
Copy Editors: Stephanie Gibson, Cindy Riegle, JoAnn Weatherly
Assistant Copy Editors: Marilyn R. Smith, Ryan Wallace
Senior Food Photographer: Jennifer Davick
Photographers: Ralph Anderson, Beth Dreiling Hontzas
Senior Photo Stylist: Buffy Hargett
Photo Stylists: Rose Nguyen, Lisa Powell Bailey
Photo Services Manager: Tracy Duncan
Production Coordinators: Christy Coleman, Paula Dennis, Ryan Kelly

Oxmoor House, Inc.

Editor in Chief: Nancy Fitzpatrick Wyatt
Executive Editor: Susan Payne Dobbs
Art Director: Keith McPherson
Managing Editor: Allison Long Lowery

Southern Living® 2008 Annual Recipes

Editor: Susan Hernandez Ray
Copy Chief: L. Amanda Owens
Senior Designer: Melissa Clark
Director of Production: Laura Lockhart
Senior Production Manager: Greg A. Amason

Contributors

Designer: Nancy Johnson
Editorial Contributor: Rebecca R. Benton
Proofreader: Julie Gillis
Indexer: Mary Ann Laurens
Index Copy Editor: Jasmine Hodges
Editorial Consultant: Jean Wickstrom Liles
Editorial Intern: Anne-Harris Jones

Contents

245 Cooking School

259 November

291 December

327 5-Ingredient Entertaining

335 Appendices

338 Indexes

368 Favorite Recipes Journal

Favorite Columns

Each month, we focus on topics that are important to our readers—
from Southern classics to fast dinners to delicious menus.

Quick & Easy

■ While canned tuna has long been used in simple recipes, the aluminum pouch takes this pantry staple to an entirely new level with some flavorful dishes (page 39).

■ Cure your craving for cheesy goodness and a touch of spice with these Tex-Mex favorites that take 25 minutes or less to make (page 76).

■ Rejuvenate your supper with family-friendly Italian pies overflowing with surprising flavor (page 94).

■ Host a casual, easy get-together with bite-size treats that will wow your guests (page 112).

■ Fast and simple, a hands-off shortcut turns risotto into a scrumptious everyday meal (page 124).

■ Lasagna gets a new look when you substitute refrigerated biscuit dough, egg noodles, and frozen ravioli for traditional noodles in these creative recipes (page 193).

■ A couple of clever shortcuts make it easy to cook up a breakfast filled with hearty flavor and fresh ingredients (page 202).

■ Making your own ravioli at home has never been easier. Won ton wrappers, found in the refrigerated produce section of your grocery store, help any cook create these impressive dishes (page 242).

■ These stress-free desserts whip up in 45 minutes or less and add an elegant ending to any meal (page 267).

What's for Supper?

■ Pair pork chops with a scrumptious apple-and-potato side that will have your family clamoring for seconds (page 30).

■ Everyone will love this spaghetti dish with sausage that showcases the vibrant colors of peppers and onions (page 57).

■ This menu, starring a well-seasoned pork tenderloin, features a trio of dishes perfect for busy weeknights or company (page 95).

■ If you're searching for a speedy supper, try recipes that feature thin cuts of meat like this turkey cutlet. It pairs nicely with our ravioli made using on-hand ingredients (page 111).

■ When you're in a hurry, you'll want to try our jazzed-up one-dish meal, Shepherd's Pie. Not only does it have a few updated ingredients, but it also can be made ahead of time and frozen (page 148).

■ Bring good flavor to the table with economical chicken thighs served with chopped vegetables over mashed potatoes (page 155).

■ Spice up dinnertime with this Creole dish you can make in just one pot with a few simple ingredients, like a package of frozen vegetables, sausage, and zesty seasonings (page 199).

■ Grilled Cheese and Chili make the perfect combo for those nights when you need a quick dinner option (page 243).

■ Deliver some hearty goodness in just 30 minutes and use only two pans with our scrumptious Shrimp Scampi (page 266).

■ Try an at-home pizzeria with an unexpected Italian twist on a Southern favorite (page 300).

Healthy Living

♥ Start the new year by cooking up some nutrient-packed recipes, discovering the benefits of a favorite Southern sipper, and learning about eight ways to stay healthy over the next 12 months (page 36).

♥ Stockpile your pantry with convenient and wholesome foods, and bake up some good-for-you sweets (page 45).

♥ Let us show you why healthy eating doesn't mean giving up the foods that you love (page 66).

♥ Sneak some nutritious alternatives into your family's diet, and follow our tips for growing a great vegetable garden (page 89).

♥ Celebrate Cinco de Mayo with some traditional Mexican dishes that won't leave you feeling guilty (page 104).

♥ Entertain with a spur-of-the-moment party that features some good-for-you dishes, and discover the benefits of locally grown produce (page 129).

♥ Enjoy a guilt-free happy hour with a few of our cool cocktails (page 146).

♥ Maintain your energy throughout the day with power lunches and healthy snacks (page 158).

♥ Fall's cooler weather makes it a great time to entertain. Try a crowd-pleasing menu featuring some South American specialties. Or treat guests to an after-dinner taste of America's favorite morning drink (page 208).

♥ Making just a few small changes at mealtime could go a long way toward a lifetime of good health (page 224).

♥ Reap all the high fiber and quality protein benefits of oats by using them in some great-tasting recipes. Plus, give the gift of wellness this holiday season (page 264).

♥ These delicious down-home dishes are friendly on your pocketbook—and your waistline (page 324).

From Our Kitchen

■ Nectarines are a sweet surprise in January, when you're looking for a little taste of summer freshness. Use them to make our yummy Nectarine Tart. Also discover some tips on using Gorgonzola cheese and taking advantage of that extra oven space the next time you bake a pot roast or ham (page 40).

■ Frozen vegetables are one of our favorite time-saving shortcuts—and they're always in season. Follow our tips for selecting the best frozen varieties (page 60).

■ Spring brings out lots of new flavors and fresh ideas. Learn why Greek yogurt has become one of our favorite new treats. It's also a great time to buy watercress. And we'll discuss all the ins and outs of fresh ginger (page 80).

■ Cakes take on a creative new look when decorated with gumdrops. Follow our tips and tricks to making gumdrop rose petals and all kinds of gumdrop flowers (page 99).

■ Get ready for a good time with great party food. For spur-of-the-moment entertaining, embellish a block of feta, dress up some wrap sandwiches, or pop open a jar of jelly or jam (page 116).

■ Learn the secrets to perfectly cooked shrimp. Give shrimp a festive look with a technique called butterflying, and size up the selection (page 136).

■ You won't want to miss our versatile All-Time Favorite Chocolate Chip Cookies. We'll share various tricks for making these little gems ahead and adding some goodies to the dough to create other signature cookies (page 220).

■ A few small changes can make your kitchen eco-friendly. From recycling trash to using reusable cloth bags at the grocery checkout line, our practical ideas can lead to big results (page 244).

■ Make the best use of your freezer with our great freezing tips and tricks. And learn how to make decorative leaves that serve as a festive garnish for soups, as well as seasonal casseroles and side dishes (page 289).

■ Celebrate the season with some great entertaining ideas. Take advantage of all the tasty brews available in the late fall by hosting a beer-tasting party. And discover how to satisfy all your guests' sweet tooth with a scrumptious chocolate bar (page 326).

Cook's Chat

Our readers chat online about what they think of our recipes and how they use them. Here, they brag about some of their favorites.

Appetizers and Beverages

Bloody Mary Punch, page 44—"Really great! The Old Bay seasoning really makes it different. I served this at a brunch and used pickled asparagus as the stirrer and placed a boiled shrimp on the rim of the glass. I also made this for a neighbor who loves Bloody Marys, and I used clamato juice in place of the tomato juice. Great presentation! Thanks for sharing this recipe. I will make it again and again and again!"

Red Pepper-Black-eyed Pea Salsa, page 54—"I made this recipe to bring a little Southern to a tapas party with my New Englander friends. They all loved it. It will definitely be an addition to any parties I host where chips and dips are involved. Only change I made was using only about half the red pepper."

Fiesta Dip, page 104—"This is great for entertaining in the summer. It's nice and light and without the guilt of a bunch of excess fat."

Scarlet Margaritas, page 104—"These margaritas are so yummy, and I love that they are not high in sugar like restaurant ones. I will definitely make these again. I did not use the pomegranate seeds, but they were still good."

New South Jalapeño Pimiento Cheese, page 133—"I've made this three times since the recipe appeared in the June 2008 issue. Everyone has raved over it and requested the recipe. I followed the recipe exactly. It makes a huge batch. It is well worth the minimal effort involved to make it from scratch rather than buying from a store. Even my monthly luncheon group gave it straight 3s, the highest rating we give. We keep a batch in the refrigerator at work for those afternoons when we need a snack. We eat it on crackers."

Entrées

Spicy Chicken-Rice Bowl, page 33—"This dish was absolutely delicious! I normally am leery of exotic dishes, but this was divine! I followed the recipe, only substituting a store-bought rotisserie chicken, and it was so easy and so good. My husband does not like coconut, but since this recipe only uses a little and it blends with the other flavors, it doesn't stand out and overpower the dish. Since the dish also uses vegetables, you really don't need a side as well with it. Excellent and easy to make. Great for a new flavor!"

Shrimp and Grits, page 42—"If you are as obsessed with this very delicious Southern recipe as I am, you will love this. I make it occasionally and just devour it; my husband hardly gets any! The tang of the grits combined with the juicy shrimp mixture is amazing. This is truly one of my all-time favorite comfort foods."

Pork Chops, Cabbage, and Apples, page 50—"This was easy, quick, and all in one pan! Flavors were great and cabbage with apples—wonderful. It was best with bone-in chops, as they're more tender. My guests loved this dish, and it was easy to serve. You can serve it all by itself—no sides required, just with some bread and butter. It's a good, stick-with-you dish."

Spaghetti With Sausage and Peppers, page 57—"I was thumbing through my *Southern Living* magazines for new dinner ideas and came across this recipe—fantastic. I modified the recipe slightly with yellow pepper instead of green; left out the Parmesan and topped with Italian cheese mixture instead; and used sweet Italian sausage. My family will never eat regular spaghetti again!"

King Ranch Chicken Casserole, page 58—"Our grown children and their families come for dinner once a week. It's a bit of a challenge to make dishes that are good *and* please the various palates, but this was a hit and will definitely be made again. I used the lighter versions of both soups, added a bit more cheese and some chopped fresh mushrooms, and doubled the recipe to make 2 casseroles, one to freeze for later. Went perfectly with roasted butternut squash rings and a salad."

Basic Salmon Croquettes, page 73—"This dish was so easy, inexpensive, and used basic pantry items that allowed me to whip these up when I saw the recipe without making a special trip to the store. I did have a couple of green onions in the fridge that I added just to use them up. I made the batter early in the day and just fried them up for supper. Delicious! My husband has requested these as a once-a-week meal. We did try it with the white rice and hot sauce, and it was great. It's a definite keeper."

Hamburger Steak With Sweet Onion-Mushroom Gravy, page 93—"I like this recipe for several reasons. It was super-easy and almost foolproof for a novice cook like myself. I made it exactly as instructed but doubled the recipe. It was delicious! My hubby's only request was for more salt. I will definitely make it again and pass it along."

Tomato-Basil Meatloaf, page 115—"This Tomato-Basil Meatloaf was excellent, and I used ground turkey instead of the ground beef. Also, I warmed up some marinara and poured over the meatloaf after it was cut and put on the plates before it was served. Everyone loved it."

Bayou Fried Shrimp, page 119—"We loved this recipe! It's the best fried shrimp we have fixed at home. Light and tasty. We will definitely fix this again."

Chicken Thighs With Chunky Tomato Sauce, page 155—"This recipe is super-easy to make and very healthy! You don't have to serve the chicken over the mashed potatoes; you could substitute whole wheat pasta for a healthier alternative, but it tastes great as is. I couldn't find fire-roasted tomatoes with garlic, so I just mixed a little minced garlic with the fire-roasted tomatoes—it tasted great! I will make this again!"

Sandwiches

Open-faced Turkey Joes, page 129—"My husband and toddler loved this! We'll make this again. I used half of the French bread and sauce and then served the leftover sauce over pasta with cheese the next night. Yummy! "

Bacon-Wrapped Barbecue Burgers, page 138—"This recipe is awesome! Definitely one of the best burgers I've ever had! I would use this for special occasions or everyday meals

too. I used Sweet Baby Ray's Sweet Vidalia Onion barbecue sauce, and it worked perfectly. I served garlic French fries with them; it was a nice combo. As for hints . . . try to keep the size of the burgers a bit on the smaller side, as they will fall apart if too big. We had one that was a little bigger than the others, and it had a few cracks in it but was still very tasty. We also used fresh mushrooms instead of jarred. We didn't have any extra to put on top of the burgers after they were finished. I would probably double the sautéed mixture [onions and mushrooms] next time."

Salads

Tropical Spinach Salad With Grilled Chicken, page 52—"Delicious and light! I actually tossed my chicken into the breadcrumb mixture and grilled it on a George Foreman grill; it was perfect and the flavors were great!"

Grilled Peach-and-Mozzarella Salad, page 122— "This was absolutely delicious. I did not stack it but just made a straight salad. The dressing is very flavorful. It was a little hard to cut the peaches according to the direction size, so we cut them more in large strips."

Watermelon, Mâche, and Pecan Salad, page 142— "This salad is absolutely fantastic. I had to sign on to the Web site just so I could rave about it! I discovered it two weeks ago and have made it three times! My only recommendation is to drain the watermelon before adding the dressing. I love it! And who would have ever thought this combination could be so outstanding?"

Green Bean, Grape, and Pasta Toss, page 143—"This was very good and different. I might cut down on the amount of dressing used on the salad, but overall, a nice summer side dish. I would definitely make it again."

Sides

Three-Cheese Pasta Bake, page 28—"Wow! This is absolutely the best! I have prepared this several times now and have used quite a few different cheeses. The combination of cheeses makes this dish what it is. The cheeses in these quantities are not that expensive. Do try it with smoked Gruyère, too. It was our favorite. I paired it with applewood-smoked spicy sausages, and it made an everyday meal something special! Add some cornbread sticks or some traditional biscuits, and you can't get better than this!"

Sides (continued)

Roasted Apples and Sweet Potatoes, page 31—"The Roasted Apples and Sweet Potatoes recipe is so delicious and an excellent use of seasonal ingredients. My husband and I made these for dinner tonight and wished we had guests to share it with, because it was so delicious."

Collards With Red Onions, page 34—"What a great recipe! It's very flavorful! This just may become my staple recipe for preparing greens."

Roasted Fingerlings and Green Beans With Creamy Tarragon Dressing, page 84—"I served this at a church luncheon, and people went back for seconds, which is a rarity. I made a big batch of the Creamy Tarragon Dressing so that I can have it on hand. In fact, I'm serving this for a dinner party tonight. It is fast, easy, delicious, and a beautiful presentation. My husband suggested using asparagus next time, but everyone likes green beans, and they're cheaper than asparagus. The best part is that the entire dish cooks in the microwave."

Summer Squash Casserole, page 114—"This has been a huge hit every time! Don't leave out the water chestnuts—that crunch is the best part. Serve with grilled chicken and fresh tomato-basil salad for some color. I love this recipe!"

Basic Microwave Risotto, page 124—"I've made this recipe 5 times for both family and guests, and never have any leftovers. I've used both short-grain and Arborio rice, and both work just as well. I've used bouillon cubes, too, and that still makes an outstanding dish. A regular change I made was that I used a casserole dish with a tight-fitting lid, rather than the plastic wrap. It's easier and more eco-friendly."

Breads

Cream Cheese-Banana-Nut Bread, page 43—"Great recipe! I butter the inside of the bread pan and sprinkle sugar and cinnamon on the inside before laying the batter. Also, the peanut butter topping is fantastic on the bread (have not tried the others yet)."

Buttermilk Breakfast Cake, page 108—"Fantastic! Delicious—and so easy, too! Everyone just raved about this cake. I made it for Mother's Day brunch, and after the family gave such rave reviews I made it the next day for a birthday party at work. They're still raving about it. I will definitely make this again and again and again."

Desserts

Nectarine Tart, page 40—"I served this for a post-Christmas family get-together. It was light and refreshing after a lot of heavy eating over the holidays. Make sure the nectarines are fully ripened; if not, add a little sweetener. I will make this again in the summer with some fresh peaches."

Lemon Velvet Tart, page 48—"My sister and I made this for a barbecue. It was easy to make. It had a really good lemon flavor and was really creamy. Everyone there liked it, and people asked us for the recipe. Great summer dessert!"

Heavenly Angel Food Cake, page 98—"This cake was absolutely heavenly. I made the recipe just as it's written, used a pint of pasteurized egg whites plus 4 more egg whites. Make sure you gently fold in the sugar-flour mixture with a spatula and take your time doing this; you'll end up with a moist angel food cake—something that can be hard to find! The lemon cream cheese frosting is wonderful—I made it with reduced-fat cream cheese and it tasted great. We added fresh strawberries on the top, but this would also be great with a raspberry coulis."

Icebox Cheesecake, page 120—"This cheesecake was perfect for summer—so light and fluffy, and a great way to showcase summer berries! So easy, too . . . we made two for our Fourth of July party, and they were a hit! I will definitely make this cheesecake again!"

Candy Bar Pie, page 121—"The pretzel crust is a little different, but this recipe is yummy. The sweet and salty combination is really good. Made this for company, and the husband asked to take a piece home! A little goes a long way."

Rustic Plum Tart, page 150—"I made this using fresh cherries and cherry preserves, and it was very good."

All-Time Favorite Chocolate Chip Cookies, page 220—"I am a huge chocolate chip cookie fan, and these cookies probably rank as the best cookie I have ever had! They're super- easy to make and just perfect!"

January

Best-Ever Mac and Cheese

Impress guests by offering a fun variation of a favorite Southern spread—Macaroni-and-Pimiento Cheese Bites. Just make the mixture the night before, cut and coat as directed, and pan-fry. Keep them warm in the oven before the party starts. Or, if you're a Gouda lover, you'll want to sink your teeth into the incredible combination of cheesy noodles and smoked ham in Smokin' Macaroni and Cheese.

Find 75 more ways to reinvent this timeless classic by searching "macaroni and cheese" at myrecipes.com.

Three-Cheese Pasta Bake

MAKES 4 SERVINGS; PREP: 20 MIN.,
COOK: 7 MIN., BAKE: 15 MIN.
(Pictured on page 3)

1 (8-oz.) package penne pasta
2 Tbsp. butter
2 Tbsp. all-purpose flour
1½ cups milk
½ cup half-and-half
1 cup (4 oz.) shredded white Cheddar cheese
¼ cup grated Parmesan cheese
2 cups (8 oz.) shredded Gruyère cheese, divided*
1 tsp. salt
¼ tsp. pepper
Pinch of ground nutmeg

1. Preheat oven to 350°. Prepare pasta according to package directions.
2. Meanwhile, melt butter in a medium saucepan over medium heat. Whisk in flour until smooth; cook, whisking constantly, 1 minute. Gradually whisk in milk and half-and-half; cook, whisking constantly, 3 to 5 minutes or until thickened. Stir in Cheddar cheese, Parmesan cheese, 1 cup Gruyère cheese, and next 3 ingredients until smooth.

3. Stir together pasta and cheese mixture, and pour into 4 lightly greased 8-oz. baking dishes or 1 lightly greased 11- x 7-inch baking dish. (If using 8-oz. baking dishes, place them in a jelly-roll pan for easy baking, and proceed as directed.) Top with remaining 1 cup Gruyère cheese.
4. Bake at 350° for 15 minutes or until golden and bubbly.
*Swiss cheese may be substituted.
Note: To make ahead, proceed with recipe as directed through Step 3. (Do not top with remaining Gruyère cheese.) Cover and chill up to 8 hours. Let stand at room temperature 30 minutes. Bake at 350° for 20 to 25 minutes or until bubbly. Increase oven temperature to 400°. Top pasta mixture with remaining Gruyère cheese, and bake 10 more minutes or until golden.

Smokin' Macaroni and Cheese

MAKES 8 SERVINGS; PREP: 20 MIN.,
COOK: 7 MIN., BAKE: 30 MIN., STAND: 5 MIN.

The recipe calls for smoked Gouda, but your favorite regular or smoked cheese will work.

1 lb. uncooked cellentani pasta
2 Tbsp. butter
3 Tbsp. all-purpose flour
1 cup milk
1 (12-oz.) can evaporated milk
2 cups (8 oz.) shredded smoked Gouda cheese
1 (3-oz.) package cream cheese, softened
¾ tsp. salt
½ tsp. ground red pepper, divided
1 (8-oz.) package chopped cooked, smoked ham
2 cups cornflakes cereal, crushed
2 Tbsp. butter, melted

1. Preheat oven to 350°. Prepare pasta according to package directions.
2. Meanwhile, melt 2 Tbsp. butter in a medium saucepan over medium heat. Gradually whisk in flour until smooth; cook, whisking constantly, 1 minute. Gradually whisk in milk and evaporated milk; cook, whisking constantly, 3 to 5 minutes or until thickened. Whisk in Gouda, cream cheese, salt, and ¼ tsp. ground red pepper until smooth. Remove from heat, and stir in chopped ham.
3. Combine pasta and Gouda cheese mixture, and pour into a lightly greased 13- x 9-inch baking dish. Stir together 2 cups crushed cereal, 2 Tbsp. melted butter, and remaining ¼ tsp. ground red pepper; sprinkle over pasta mixture.
4. Bake at 350° for 30 minutes or until golden and bubbly. Let stand 5 minutes before serving.

—HEATHER MARKOWSKI, ROCHESTER, NEW YORK
Note: For testing purposes only, we used Barilla Cellentani Pasta.

Macaroni-and-Pimiento Cheese Bites

MAKES 5½ DOZEN; PREP: 25 MIN., COOK: 7 MIN.,
CHILL: 8 HR., FRY: 4 MIN. PER BATCH

Wow family and friends with easy, delicious Macaroni-and-Pimiento Cheese Bites—they make perfect party poppers. You can also bake the mixture in a casserole dish and use the breadcrumb coating as a crispy topping.

1 (8-oz.) package elbow macaroni
3 Tbsp. butter
¼ cup all-purpose flour
2 cups milk
1 tsp. salt
¼ tsp. ground red pepper
⅛ tsp. garlic powder
1 (8-oz.) block sharp Cheddar cheese, shredded
1 (4-oz.) jar diced pimiento, drained
¾ cup fine, dry breadcrumbs
¾ cup freshly grated Parmesan cheese
2 large eggs, lightly beaten
½ cup milk
Vegetable oil

1. Prepare pasta according to package directions.
2. Meanwhile, melt butter in a large skillet over medium heat. Gradually whisk in flour until smooth; cook, whisking constantly, 1 minute. Gradually whisk in 2 cups milk and next 3 ingredients; cook, whisking constantly, 3 to 5 minutes or until thickened. Stir in Cheddar cheese and pimiento until melted and smooth. Remove from heat, and stir in pasta.
3. Line a 13- x 9-inch pan with plastic wrap, allowing several inches to extend over edges of pan. Pour mixture into prepared pan. Cool slightly; cover and chill 8 hours. Remove macaroni mixture from pan, and cut into 1-inch squares.
4. Stir together breadcrumbs and Parmesan cheese in a shallow dish or pie plate. Whisk together eggs and ½ cup milk in another shallow dish or pie plate; dip macaroni bites in egg mixture, and dredge in breadcrumb mixture.
5. Pour oil to depth of 1 inch in a large skillet; heat to 350°. Fry bites, in batches, 2 minutes on each side or until golden.

—MELODY LEE, DOTHAN, ALABAMA

Golden Baked Macaroni-and-Pimiento Cheese: Preheat oven to 350°. Prepare recipe as directed through Step 2. Pour macaroni mixture into a lightly greased 13- x 9-inch baking dish; do not chill. Omit eggs and ½ cup milk. Stir together breadcrumbs and Parmesan cheese; sprinkle over mixture. Omit oil. Bake at 350° for 15 to 20 minutes or until golden and bubbly.

Caramelized Onion Macaroni and Cheese
southernliving.com favorite
MAKES 8 TO 10 SERVINGS; **PREP:** 20 MIN.,
COOK: 20 MIN., **BAKE:** 1 HR.,
STAND: 10 MIN.

Feel free to omit the pecans in this recipe. It will still taste fantastic.

1 (8-oz.) package large elbow macaroni
2 Tbsp. butter
2 large onions, halved and thinly sliced
1 tsp. sugar
1 (16-oz.) block white Cheddar cheese, shredded
1 cup (4 oz.) shredded Parmesan cheese
32 saltine crackers, finely crushed and divided
6 large eggs
4 cups milk
1 tsp. salt
½ tsp. pepper
2 Tbsp. butter, melted
½ cup chopped pecans (optional)

1. Preheat oven to 350°. Prepare macaroni according to package directions; drain and set aside.
2. Melt 2 Tbsp. butter in a large skillet over medium-high heat. Add sliced onions and 1 tsp. sugar. Cook, stirring often, 15 to 20 minutes or until onions are caramel colored.
3. Layer half each of macaroni, onions, cheeses, and cracker crumbs in a lightly greased 13- x 9-inch baking dish. Layer with remaining macaroni, onions, and cheeses.
4. Whisk together eggs and next 3 ingredients; pour mixture over macaroni mixture.
5. Stir together remaining cracker crumbs, melted butter, and, if desired, chopped pecans. Sprinkle over macaroni mixture.
6. Bake at 350° for 1 hour or until golden brown and set. Let stand 10 minutes before serving.

—KITTY FORBES, FORT VALLEY, GEORGIA

Muffin Makeover

Start with a mix, and stir in irresistible taste.

Begin any day with the amazing scent and flavor of bakeshop muffins in your own kitchen. Dried fruit adds extra moisture and a natural sweetness to no-fuss box mixes. Serve muffins fresh, or freeze them up to one month and reheat for a tasty grab-and-go snack. To make the most of breakfast on the run, simply remove the foil liner from a frozen muffin, wrap it in a paper towel, and microwave for 15 seconds or until thoroughly heated.

Tropical Banana Bread Muffins
freezeable • make ahead
MAKES 1 DOZEN; **PREP:** 15 MIN.,
BAKE: 17 MIN., **COOL:** 15 MIN.

Our editors and Test Kitchens staff loved this fruity twist on classic banana bread.

1 (17.1-oz.) package banana-nut muffin mix
1 cup dried mixed tropical fruit, roughly chopped

1. Prepare batter and muffin pans according to package directions for banana-nut muffin mix, stirring dried mixed tropical fruit into batter. Spoon batter into prepared muffin pans, filling two-thirds full. Bake and cool muffins according to package directions.
Note: For testing purposes only, we used Krusteaz Banana Nut Supreme Muffin Mix.

Creamy Berry Muffins

freezeable • make ahead

MAKES 6 MUFFINS; **PREP:** 10 MIN.,
BAKE: 17 MIN., **COOL:** 15 MIN.

1 (7-oz.) package berry muffin mix
1 (3.5-oz.) package dried blueberries
¼ cup regular or fruit-flavored cream cheese

1. Prepare batter and muffin pans according to package directions for berry muffin mix, stirring package dried blueberries into batter. Spoon batter into prepared muffin pans, filling two-thirds full. Drop 2 tsp. cream cheese onto center of batter in each muffin cup. Bake and cool muffins according to package directions.

—**VICTORIA BERRY**, ORLANDO, FLORIDA

Note: For testing purposes only, we used Martha White Wildberry Muffin Mix and Sunsweet Blueberries.

Cinnamon Streusel Muffins

freezeable • make ahead

MAKES 1 DOZEN; **PREP:** 15 MIN.,
BAKE: 18 MIN., **COOL:** 15 MIN.

1 (15.2-oz.) package cinnamon streusel
    muffin mix
½ cup dried apple pieces, roughly chopped
½ cup golden raisins
Aluminum foil baking cups

1. Prepare cinnamon streusel muffin mix according to package directions, stirring dried apple pieces and golden raisins into batter. Place foil baking cups in muffin pans. Spoon batter into cups, filling two-thirds full. Bake and cool muffins according to package directions.

Note: For testing purposes only, we used Betty Crocker Cinnamon Streusel Premium Muffin Mix.

Make Pork Chops Special

Your family will ask for second helpings after trying this meat-and-potato pair.

Pork Chops Supper

SERVES 4

Savory Herb Pork Chops

Roasted Apples and
Sweet Potatoes

Italian Tossed Salad

Dinner rolls

Recharge weeknight meals by pairing Savory Herb Pork Chops with a roasted fruit-and-vegetable side. Apple juice and Dijon mustard flavor these moist, pan-seared loin chops. Tossing Granny Smith apples and sweet potatoes with butter, brown sugar, and grated orange rind before slow roasting creates a sweet-tart side dish that spells comfort any day of the week.

Savory Herb Pork Chops

family favorite

MAKES 4 SERVINGS; **PREP:** 15 MIN.,
CHILL: 30 MIN., **COOK:** 25 MIN.,
STAND: 5 MIN.

1 cup apple juice, divided
3½ Tbsp. light brown sugar, divided
1 Tbsp. Dijon mustard
4 (¾-inch-thick) boneless pork loin
    chops
1 tsp. salt, divided
1 tsp. coarsely ground pepper, divided
2 Tbsp. vegetable oil
½ cup chopped onion
2 garlic cloves, minced
2 tsp. chopped fresh rosemary
2 Tbsp. balsamic vinegar, divided
1 Tbsp. all-purpose flour
Garnishes: thinly sliced apples, fresh
    rosemary sprigs

1. Stir together ¼ cup apple juice, 1 Tbsp. brown sugar, and mustard in a large zip-top plastic freezer bag; add pork. Seal bag, and shake well to coat. Chill 30 minutes, turning once. Remove pork from marinade, discarding marinade. Pat pork dry, and sprinkle with ½ tsp. salt and ½ tsp. pepper.
2. Cook pork in hot oil in a large skillet over medium-high heat 3 minutes on each side. Remove pork from skillet.
3. Cook onion and garlic in hot drippings, stirring constantly, 1 minute. Add remaining ¾ cup apple juice to skillet, stirring to loosen particles from bottom of skillet. Stir in rosemary, 1 Tbsp. brown sugar, 1 Tbsp. balsamic vinegar, and remaining ½ tsp. salt and pepper.

Have supper on the table in no time with these steps.
- Precut or trim meat or poultry before storing it in your refrigerator or freezer, labeled with name of item and the date you store it.
- Chop ingredients such as onions, celery, or bell peppers in advance, and store them in ready-to-use 1-cup amounts in airtight containers in the freezer up to six months.
- When making pot roast, consider cooking two at a time. You can serve one and save one for supper later. Place the second roast in an airtight container or zip-top plastic freezer bag, and freeze up to six months. Thaw the pot roast in the refrigerator 24 to 48 hours. Place it in a 13- x 9-inch baking dish, and cover it with aluminum foil. Bake at 350° for 1 hour or until hot.
- Keep frozen mashed potatoes in the freezer for an on-hand side dish.

—CHARLA DRAPER, ASSOCIATE FOOD EDITOR

4. Bring onion mixture to a boil. Reduce heat to medium low, and simmer 3 to 5 minutes or until mixture is reduced by half.

5. Add pork to onion mixture, turning to coat. Cover and cook 5 to 10 minutes or until a meat thermometer inserted in thickest portion registers 155°. Remove from heat, and place pork on a serving platter. Cover with aluminum foil. Let stand 5 minutes.

6. Meanwhile, whisk together ¼ cup water, 1 Tbsp. flour, remaining 1½ Tbsp. brown sugar, and remaining 1 Tbsp. balsamic vinegar in skillet until smooth. Bring to a boil over medium-low heat. Reduce heat to low, and simmer 1 to 2 minutes or until slightly thickened and bubbly. Drizzle sauce over pork, or serve with pork, if desired. Garnish, if desired.

—BONNIE COOPER, CARROLLTON, GEORGIA

Roasted Apples and Sweet Potatoes
family favorite
MAKES 4 SERVINGS; **PREP:** 20 MIN., **BAKE:** 35 MIN.

This oven-roasted side is flavored with a hint of orange. If you'd like your apples crisp rather than tender, you can bake them for a little less time.

3 lb. sweet potatoes (about 5 medium-size sweet potatoes), peeled
2 large Granny Smith apples, peeled
2 Tbsp. butter, melted
2 Tbsp. light brown sugar
1 tsp. grated orange rind
1 tsp. kosher salt
½ tsp. coarsely ground pepper

1. Preheat oven to 400°. Cut peeled sweet potatoes into 1-inch cubes. Cut peeled apples into ½-inch-thick slices.
2. Stir together melted butter, brown sugar, and grated orange rind in a large zip-top plastic freezer bag until blended. Add cubed sweet potatoes and sliced apples. Seal bag, and toss to coat.
3. Place potato mixture in a single layer in a lightly greased aluminum foil-lined 15- x 10-inch jelly-roll pan. Sprinkle with salt and pepper.
4. Bake at 400° for 30 to 35 minutes or until potatoes and apples are tender and lightly browned.

Italian Tossed Salad
southernliving.com favorite
MAKES 4 SERVINGS; **PREP:** 10 MIN.

This quick recipe is perfect for any weeknight supper.

1 (5-oz.) bag mixed salad greens
½ cup (2 oz.) shredded mozzarella cheese
1 (2.25-oz.) can drained sliced ripe black olives
8 quartered baby carrots
1 sliced green onion
Balsamic vinaigrette salad dressing

1. Toss together mixed salad greens, shredded mozzarella cheese, and next 3 ingredients. Drizzle with bottled balsamic vinaigrette or your favorite Italian salad dressing.

—MELISSA QUIÑONES, EUSTIS, FLORIDA

Downright Delicious

Take it from us, you'll make these often—our Food staff does.

At our table, we never shy away from telling it like it is when tasting recipes. (Sound familiar?) So, it was only after some lively scrutiny that we deemed our new roasted chicken recipe ideal for cozy meals in '08. Our Test Kitchens pros offer up all their tips to ensure perfect results. And, for good measure, they came up with an equally great-tasting next-day dish easily made by doubling up on the baked chickens.

We spill the secrets to help you make a delicious Savory Baked Chicken. To get even browning on the chicken, coat it with vegetable cooking spray before baking. "We tried melted butter," says Test Kitchens Specialist/Food Styling Vanessa McNeil Roccio, "but the skin dried out too quickly after baking."

Savory Baked Chicken
freezeable • make ahead
MAKES 4 SERVINGS; **PREP:** 20 MIN.,
CHILL: 8 HR., **BAKE:** 1 HR., 10 MIN.,
STAND: 10 MIN.

If you don't have a food processor, place garlic cloves on a cutting board and sprinkle with 1 tsp. salt. Rub ingredients on the board with the flat side of a chef's knife blade until smooth. Janet Anjaz of Kent, Washington, gave us the idea to use yogurt as a marinade. (Pictured on page 4)

10 garlic cloves
1½ tsp. salt, divided
1 cup plain low-fat yogurt
1 Tbsp. grated lime rind
1 (4½-lb.) whole chicken
3 fresh cilantro sprigs
Vegetable cooking spray
½ tsp. coarsely ground pepper
Garnishes: fresh cilantro sprigs, steamed
   green beans

1. Process garlic and 1 tsp. salt in a food processor 2 seconds or until smooth, stopping to scrape down sides as needed. Remove and reserve 1 Tbsp. garlic mixture. Stir together remaining garlic mixture, yogurt, and lime rind.
2. If applicable, remove giblets from chicken, and reserve for another use. Rinse chicken, and pat dry. Loosen and lift skin from chicken with fingers (do not detach skin); spread reserved 1 Tbsp. garlic mixture evenly underneath the skin. Place cilantro sprigs underneath skin. Carefully replace skin, and secure with wooden picks. Spread yogurt mixture over chicken and inside cavity. Cover and chill 8 hours.
3. Preheat oven to 375°. Wipe excess yogurt mixture from outside of chicken with a paper towel. Place chicken on a lightly greased wire rack in an aluminum foil-lined broiler or jelly-roll pan. Coat chicken with cooking spray, and sprinkle with pepper and remaining ½ tsp. salt.
4. Bake at 375° for 45 minutes; cover loosely, and bake 25 more minutes or until a meat thermometer inserted into thickest portion registers 165°. Let chicken stand 10 minutes before slicing. Garnish, if desired.

Roasted Chicken Hints

- To get flavor into the meat and not just on the skin, lift up the skin and rub the garlic mixture right on the chicken. Keep disposable plastic gloves on hand for this prep step.
- To prevent the skin from shrinking while cooking, use wooden picks to hold it back in place over the breast meat.
- Yogurt acts as a marinade to tenderize the chicken and make it moist. It does inhibit browning, though, so be sure to wipe excess yogurt from skin and coat the skin with cooking spray.
- Tie the ends of the legs together with kitchen string. This will help the chicken hold a better shape while baking.
- Bake on a wire rack in an aluminum foil-lined pan. It's all about not letting the chicken lounge in the drippings. Use a broiler pan with a rack, or place a rack in a pan that has at least 1-inch sides, such as a jelly-roll pan.

• TIP •

On Another Night Have Spicy Chicken-Rice Bowl on the table in 35 minutes with smart planning. Bake two Savory Baked Chickens in the oven at once (you don't need to adjust the bake time). Serve one, and shred the second for this dish. Let chicken stand 30 minutes or until cool enough to handle. It will come off the bone easily, and you get less fat because it's still melted. Freeze shredded chicken in a zip-top plastic freezer bag up to four weeks.

Spicy Chicken-Rice Bowl
family favorite
MAKES 6 SERVINGS; **PREP:** 25 MIN.,
COOK: 10 MIN.

If you want this tasty dish to be a little bit hotter, simply add more red curry paste. (Pictured on page 5)

1½ cups uncooked long-grain rice
2 Tbsp. butter
1 Tbsp. all-purpose flour
1¼ cups chicken broth
½ cup milk
½ cup light coconut milk
3 Tbsp. red curry paste
2 Tbsp. fresh lime juice
2 tsp. grated fresh ginger
½ tsp. salt
1 Savory Baked Chicken, shredded
  (about 3 cups)
1½ cups fresh steamed green beans, cut
  into 1-inch pieces
½ red bell pepper, cut into thin
  strips
¼ cup chopped fresh cilantro
Lime wedges

1. Prepare rice according to package directions.
2. Meanwhile, melt butter in a heavy saucepan over low heat; whisk in flour until smooth. Cook, whisking constantly, 1 minute. Gradually whisk in chicken broth, milk, and coconut milk. Cook over medium heat, whisking constantly, 2 minutes or until mixture is thick and bubbly.
3. Stir in curry paste and next 3 ingredients. Stir chicken, green beans, and red bell pepper strips into curry mixture; cook 2 minutes or until thoroughly heated. Stir in 2 Tbsp. chopped cilantro. Serve chicken mixture over rice. Sprinkle with remaining chopped cilantro. Serve with lime wedges.

Heavenly Chicken Lasagna
southernliving.com favorite
MAKES 8 TO 10 SERVINGS; **PREP:** 20 MIN.,
COOK: 10 MIN., **BAKE:** 50 MIN.

One roasted whole chicken or six skinned and boned cooked chicken breast halves yield about 3 cups chopped meat.

1 Tbsp. butter
½ large onion
1 (10 ½-oz.) can reduced-fat cream of
  chicken soup, undiluted
1 (10-oz.) container refrigerated reduced-fat
  Alfredo sauce
1 (7-oz.) jar diced pimiento,
  undrained
1 (6-oz.) jar sliced mushrooms,
  drained
⅓ cup dry white wine
½ tsp. dried basil
1 (10-oz.) package frozen chopped spinach,
  thawed
1 cup cottage cheese
1 cup ricotta cheese
½ cup grated Parmesan cheese
1 large egg, lightly beaten
9 lasagna noodles, cooked
2 ½ cups chopped cooked chicken
3 cups (12 oz.) shredded sharp Cheddar
  cheese, divided

1. Preheat oven to 350°. Melt butter in a skillet over medium-high heat. Add onion, and sauté 5 minutes or until tender. Stir in soup and next 5 ingredients. Reserve 1 cup sauce.
2. Drain spinach well, pressing between layers of paper towels.
3. Stir together spinach, cottage cheese, and next 3 ingredients.
4. Place 3 lasagna noodles in a lightly greased 13- x 9-inch baking dish. Layer with half each of sauce, spinach mixture, and chicken. Sprinkle with 1 cup Cheddar cheese. Repeat procedure. Top with remaining 3 noodles and reserved 1 cup sauce. Cover and chill up to 1 day ahead.
5. Bake at 350° for 45 minutes. Sprinkle lasagna with remaining 1 cup Cheddar cheese, and bake 5 more minutes or until cheese is melted. Let lasagna stand 10 minutes before serving.
Note: For testing purposes only, we used Cantadina Light Alfredo Sauce, found in the dairy section of the supermarket.

quick & tasty banana pudding

MAKES 1 SERVING; **PREP:** 10 MIN.

If you're serving a crowd, simply prepare the recipe as many times as needed. (Pictured on page 161)

1. Cut half of 1 small banana into slices; keep other half in the peel, and save for another use. Layer 1 (5-oz.) glass with 1 Tbsp. thawed nondairy whipped topping, one-fourth of banana slices, 1 Tbsp. prepared vanilla pudding, another fourth of banana slices, and 1 vanilla wafer. Repeat. Dollop with 1 Tbsp. thawed non-dairy whipped topping.

Note: For testing purposes only, we used Hunt's Snack Pack Vanilla Pudding. One (3.5-oz.) pudding cup yields 6 Tbsp. pudding.

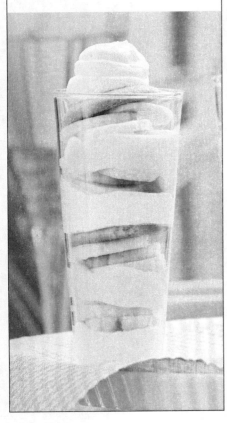

A Warm Pot of Greens

Enjoy this Southern staple packed with fresh flavor.

It's a tradition in many homes to serve greens on New Year's Day as a symbol of keeping money in your pocket. But whatever day you choose to serve it, this dish delivers on both flavor and texture. Be sure to check out more than 60 delicious and nutritious collard greens recipes by searching "collards" at myrecipes.com.

Collards With Red Onions

MAKES 8 SERVINGS; **PREP:** 20 MIN.;
COOK: 1 HR., 20 MIN.
(Pictured on page 9)

3 (16-oz.) packages fresh collard greens
2 medium-size red onions, finely chopped
2 Tbsp. vegetable oil
2½ cups vegetable broth
¼ cup cider vinegar
2 Tbsp. dark brown sugar
1½ tsp. salt
½ tsp. dried crushed red pepper

1. Trim and discard thick stems from bottom of collard green leaves. Thoroughly wash collard greens.
2. Sauté onions in hot oil in a Dutch oven over medium-high heat 8 to 10 minutes or until tender. Add broth and next 4 ingredients.
3. Gradually add collards to Dutch oven, and cook, stirring occasionally, 8 to 10 minutes or just until wilted. Reduce heat to medium, and cook, stirring occasionally, 1 hour or until tender.

—MARCY GERHART, FAIRHOPE, ALABAMA

Nana's Collard Greens

southernliving.com favorite
MAKES 6 TO 8 SERVINGS; **PREP:** 20 MIN.;
COOK: 1 HR., 15 MIN.

"My late grandmother, Cora Meadows, always used carrots to sweeten the greens," says Designer/Illustrator Christopher Davis, who updated the recipe by using fat-free chicken broth and balsamic vinegar. We think these greens would be great over grits too.

4 bacon slices
1 large carrot, chopped
1 large onion, chopped
2 garlic cloves, minced
2 to 3 Tbsp. balsamic vinegar
4 (1-lb.) packages fresh collard greens, washed, trimmed, and chopped
1 ½ cups low-sodium, fat-free chicken broth
½ tsp. dried red pepper flakes
½ tsp. salt
¼ tsp. pepper

1. Cook bacon slices in a Dutch oven until crisp. Remove bacon, and drain on paper towels, reserving 2 Tbsp. drippings. Crumble bacon.
2. Cook carrot in hot bacon drippings in Dutch oven over medium-high heat, stirring occasionally, 5 minutes. Add onion, and cook, stirring occasionally, 5 minutes or until carrot and onion begin to caramelize. Add garlic; cook, stirring constantly, 30 seconds. Add balsamic vinegar, and cook 30 seconds. Add collards, crumbled bacon, broth, and remaining ingredients. Bring to a boil; cover, reduce heat, and simmer 1 hour or until collards are tender.

Ultimate Comfort Meal

Long, slow cooking yields exceptionally tender and moist meat.

On a cold winter day, nothing smells more inviting than the rich aroma of braised beef. Short ribs make a terrific and economical choice for this slow-cooking method because of their wonderful flavor and fat marbling. When baked in a Dutch oven for hours with a small amount of liquid, Red Wine Short Ribs brings big flavor and meat that literally falls off the bone.

Make these dishes a day ahead for easy entertaining; the flavor improves with chilling overnight.

For an unexpected twist, try our delicious open-faced Short Rib Sandwiches. To create the ultimate comfort meal, serve braised ribs over polenta, mashed sweet potatoes or risotto. Visit myrecipes. com for some wonderful sides that will pair great with these saucy ribs.

Red Wine Short Ribs
make ahead

MAKES 4 SERVINGS; **PREP:** 20 MIN.,
COOK: 40 MIN., **BAKE:** 4 HR., **STAND:** 30 MIN.

Make this a day ahead, and chill it so you can easily remove the solidified fat from the top of the strained gravy before reheating the ribs.

6 lb. beef short ribs
½ tsp. kosher salt
½ tsp. freshly ground pepper
6 garlic cloves, pressed
2 carrots, coarsely chopped
2 celery ribs, coarsely chopped
1 onion, coarsely chopped
1 (14.5-oz.) can Italian-style diced
  tomatoes
2 cups dry red wine
1 cup chicken broth
1 fresh rosemary sprig
1 fresh thyme sprig
1 fresh oregano sprig

1. Sprinkle ribs evenly with ½ tsp. salt and ½ tsp. pepper. Cook ribs, in batches, in a large ovenproof Dutch oven over medium-high heat 4 to 5 minutes on each side or until browned. Remove ribs to a large bowl, and drain Dutch oven.
2. Preheat oven to 350°. Reduce heat to medium; add garlic and next 3 ingredients to Dutch oven. Cook, stirring occasionally, 6 to 7 minutes or until vegetables are tender and browned. Stir in tomatoes and next 5 ingredients. Return ribs to Dutch oven, and bring to a boil; cover tightly with heavy-duty aluminum foil and lid.
3. Bake at 350° for 3½ to 4 hours or until ribs are very tender. Remove ribs and herbs. Discard herbs; keep ribs warm.

4. Drain vegetable mixture though a fine wire-mesh strainer into a large bowl. Pour gravy into an 8-cup glass measuring cup. Let stand 30 minutes, and skim fat from gravy. Add strained gravy and vegetables back to Dutch oven. Return to a boil over medium-high heat, and cook, uncovered, 20 minutes or until thickened. Serve gravy over short ribs.

Short Rib Sandwiches

MAKES 4 SERVINGS; **PREP:** 20 MIN.,
COOK: 6 MIN., **STAND:** 5 MIN., **BROIL:** 10 MIN.

These mouthwatering fork-and-knife sandwiches—with balsamic vinegar, red onion, blue cheese, and arugula—received our highest rating. (Pictured on page 2)

1 large red onion, thinly sliced
2 Tbsp. balsamic vinegar
1 (12-oz.) sourdough French bread loaf
3 Tbsp. stone-ground Dijon mustard
3 cups shredded Red Wine Short Ribs
  (see recipe at left)
½ cup gravy from Red Wine Short Ribs
2 oz. blue cheese, crumbled
3 cups firmly packed arugula

1. Sauté sliced onion in a lightly greased nonstick skillet over medium-high heat 6 minutes or until tender. Remove from heat, and stir in balsamic vinegar. Let mixture stand 5 minutes.
2. Cut bread into 4 pieces. Cut each piece in half lengthwise, cutting to but not through opposite side. Place bread pieces, cut sides up, on a wire rack in a broiler pan.
3. Broil 6 inches from heat 3 to 4 minutes or until lightly toasted.
4. Spread cut sides of bread evenly with mustard. Stir together meat and gravy; spoon evenly onto bread. Sprinkle with cheese.
5. Broil 6 inches from heat 4 to 6 minutes or until cheese is melted. Toss together onion mixture and arugula; top sandwiches with mixture.

Healthy Living®

Jump-start your New Year with doable resolutions. These fabulous recipes and great tips will help you reach your goals.

Power Meals for Your Family

Give your repertoire a boost of flavor with these simple recipes—they're 100% wholesome.

It's easy to eat well when you stock up on nutritious recipes that deliver big flavor. Add these main-dish ideas to your weeknight plan. (And guess what? They're vegetarian.)

Mark and Kelly Leishear of Milton, Delaware, engage in a more healthful lifestyle by cutting out much of the saturated fat and cholesterol found in animal products. Bella (age 6) and Liam (age 4) eat organic dairy and eggs but no meat. "It's easier than you think," explains Kelly. "I've found many great protein substitutes at the grocery, and my kids don't know the difference."

All these suppers received high marks in our Test Kitchens.

Healthy Benefits

- Some research studies suggest that there is a specific link between a diet low in animal fat and the prevention and recurrence of breast cancer.
- Disease-fighting antioxidants are found in all fruits and vegetables, whether they're fresh, frozen, or canned.

Slow-Cooker Veggie Chili
MAKES 15 SERVINGS; **PREP:** 25 MIN.; COOK: 8 HR., 18 MIN.

Add a dash of hot sauce to your bowl for extra heat.

2 large carrots, diced (1 cup)
2 celery ribs, diced (½ cup)
1 medium-size sweet onion, diced
Vegetable cooking spray
2 (8-oz.) packages sliced fresh mushrooms
1 large zucchini, chopped (1½ cups)
1 yellow squash, chopped (1 cup)
1 Tbsp. chili powder
1 tsp. dried basil
1 tsp. seasoned pepper
1 (8-oz.) can tomato sauce
3 cups tomato juice
2 (14½-oz.) cans diced tomatoes, undrained
4 (15-oz.) cans pinto, black, great Northern, or kidney beans, rinsed and drained
1 cup frozen whole kernel corn

1. Sauté first 3 ingredients in a large nonstick skillet coated with cooking spray over medium-high heat 10 minutes or until onion is translucent. Add mushrooms, zucchini, and squash; sauté 3 more minutes. Add chili powder and next 2 ingredients, and sauté 5 more minutes.
2. Stir together tomato sauce and tomato juice in a 6-qt. slow cooker until smooth.

Stir in diced tomatoes, next 2 ingredients, and carrot mixture. Cover and cook on LOW 8 hours.
Note: Cool leftovers, and freeze in plastic freezer containers or zip-top plastic freezer bags for up to 2 months.

Per 1½-cup serving: Calories 124; Fat 0.8g (sat 0.1g, mono 0.1g, poly 0.2g); Protein 7.4g; Carb 24.5g; Fiber 7g; Chol 0mg; Iron 2mg; Sodium 566mg; Calc 63mg.

Tomato-Spinach Penne
MAKES 6 SERVINGS; **PREP:** 20 MIN., COOK: 30 MIN.

8 oz. uncooked multigrain penne pasta
1 medium-size yellow onion, chopped
1 (10-oz.) package meatless Italian sausage, sliced
1 Tbsp. olive oil
2 garlic cloves, minced
2 (14.5-oz.) cans diced tomatoes
1 (6-oz.) package fresh baby spinach leaves, thoroughly washed
2 Tbsp. chopped fresh basil
¼ cup shredded Parmesan cheese (optional)

1. Prepare pasta according to package directions.
2. Meanwhile, sauté chopped onion and sliced sausage in hot oil in a large nonstick skillet over medium-high heat 4 minutes or until tender. Add minced garlic, and sauté 1 minute. Add tomatoes, and bring to a boil; cover, reduce heat to low, and simmer, stirring occasionally, 20 minutes. Add spinach and basil; cook 5 more minutes.
3. Place pasta in a large bowl. Add onion mixture, and toss to combine. Sprinkle with Parmesan cheese, if desired.

Per serving (including cheese): Calories 315; Fat 11.7g (sat 1.4g, mono 2.1g, poly 0.6g); Protein 16.1g; Carb 39.7g; Fiber 8.5g; Chol 2mg; Iron 4.2mg; Sodium 648mg; Calc 163mg.

Peanut-Broccoli Stir-fry

MAKES 6 SERVINGS; **PREP:** 30 MIN.,
STAND: 55 MIN., **COOK:** 10 MIN.

1 (16-oz.) package firm tofu
2 cups uncooked brown rice
½ tsp. salt
1½ cups vegetable broth
1 Tbsp. light brown sugar
2 Tbsp. fresh lime juice
2 Tbsp. sweet chili sauce
2 Tbsp. creamy peanut butter
1 Tbsp. lite soy sauce
1 tsp. grated fresh ginger
¾ tsp. cornstarch
1 Tbsp. peanut or vegetable oil
1 tsp. dark sesame oil
2 cups fresh broccoli florets
1 cup carrot sticks
2 Tbsp. chopped peanuts
Garnish: lime wedges

1. Place tofu between 2 flat plates.
Weight the top with a heavy can. (Sides
of tofu should be bulging slightly but
not cracking.) Let stand 45 minutes;
discard liquid. Cut tofu into ½-inch
cubes.
2. Prepare rice according to package
directions, adding ½ tsp. salt.
3. Meanwhile, combine vegetable broth
and next 7 ingredients in a medium
bowl, stirring well. Add tofu, and
toss to coat. Let stand 10 minutes.
Remove tofu from marinade, reserving
marinade.
4. Heat oils in a nonstick skillet or wok
over high heat 1 minute. Add tofu, and
stir-fry 4 to 5 minutes or until browned.
Remove tofu. Add broccoli and carrot
sticks; stir-fry 2 minutes. Add reserved
marinade, and bring to a boil. Cook,
stirring constantly, 2 minutes or until
thickened; stir in cooked tofu. Serve
over hot cooked rice. Sprinkle with
chopped peanuts. Garnish, if desired.

Per serving: Calories 400; Fat 13g (sat 2.1g, mono 3.8g,
poly 2.7g); Protein 15.3g; Carb 58g; Fiber 5.8g; Chol 0mg; Iron 2.4mg;
Sodium 633mg; Calc 188mg.

Tofu Techniques

- Chances are you've tasted tofu
  at your favorite Asian restaurant,
  either in a soup or a stir-fry. It's a
  complete protein, low in fat and
  calories, and easy to cook. Plus,
  it absorbs tons of flavor. Look for
  it in the produce or natural foods
  section of larger supermarkets.
- We recommend a firm block of
  tofu for Peanut-Broccoli Stir-fry,
  but degrees of firmness may vary
  among brands. Do a press test
  at the grocery store to avoid the
  softer products.
- It's important to drain tofu
  before cutting it into cubes. A
  canned good from your pantry is
  just the right amount of weight
  needed to press the moisture
  out. Simply place the unwrapped
  block of tofu between two
  plates, add the weight, and let
  stand about 45 minutes for best
  results. (Softer tofu may need to
  drain longer.)
- Store unused, uncooked tofu
  covered in cold water in the
  refrigerator up to two days; drain
  before using.

Veggie Frittata

southernliving.com favorite
MAKES 8 SERVINGS; **PREP:** 20 MIN.,
COOK: 13 MIN., **BAKE:** 15 MIN.,
STAND: 3 MIN.

1 medium-size yellow onion, chopped
½ (8-oz.) container sliced fresh
    mushrooms
1 Tbsp. olive oil
1 (6-oz.) bag fresh baby spinach*
4 large eggs
6 egg whites
½ (8-oz.) block 2% reduced-fat sharp
    Cheddar cheese, shredded (about 1 cup)
¼ cup freshly grated Parmesan cheese
2 Tbsp. fat-free milk
½ tsp. pepper
¼ tsp. salt
¼ tsp. ground nutmeg
Garnishes: chopped fresh parsley

1. Sauté onion and mushrooms in hot
oil in an ovenproof nonstick 10-inch
skillet over medium-high heat 10 minutes or until tender. Stir in spinach, and
sauté 3 minutes or until water evapo-
rates and spinach wilts. Remove from
heat, and set aside.
2. Whisk together 4 large eggs, 6 egg
whites, Cheddar cheese, and next 5
ingredients.
3. Pour egg mixture into skillet with
onion mixture, stirring to combine.
4. Bake at 350° for 12 to 15 minutes or
just until set. Let stand 3 minutes. Cut
into wedges. Garnish, if desired.
*1 (10-oz.) package chopped frozen
spinach, thawed and well drained, may be
substituted.

Per Serving: Calories 139; Fat 8.5g (sat 3.7g,mono 2.2g,poly 0.5g);
Protein 12.5g; Carb 3.9g; Fiber 0.9g ; Chol 119mg; Iron 1.3mg;
Sodium 231mg ; Calc 202mg

Tea Time

Heat some water, kick up your feet, and drink your way to health

Southerners are no strangers to tea—but what may be less familiar is the bounty of health benefits in every sip. The beverage is downright good for you.

Find Your Cup of Tea

Black tea—This common tea, found in most homes and restaurants, often forms the base of iced tea. Black tea can lower cholesterol, help prevent heart attacks, slow the progression of Parkinson's disease, and increase the body's ability to handle stress. Chai tea is black tea flavored with spices. Be aware, though, that the popular powdered versions often contain large amounts of sugar and artificial ingredients.

Green tea—This pale tea is a health powerhouse. Studies show that it may reduce the risk of cancer, cardiovascular disease, Alzheimer's, hypertension…the list goes on and on.

White tea—A more delicate tea, white provides large amounts of cancer-fighting antioxidants.

Oolong tea—A rare and more expensive tea, oolong contains polyphenols, which act as antioxidants that can block bad cholesterol.

Herbal tea—This category includes any brew not made from the *Camellia sinensis* plant, such as rooibos, chamomile, mint, and lemongrass. They are 100% caffeine free and can be used to treat a number of ailments, such as headaches, anxiety, insomnia, and more.

Tea or Teasing?

Not all teas are created equal when it comes to health benefits. A hot, freshly brewed cup of plain tea remains the recommended way to reap its goodness. Iced tea can be just as healthful if consumed shortly after brewing to retain its antioxidant power. Bottled teas have a lower antioxidant level due to their long shelf life.

Chai Tea Mini Biscuits
southernliving.com favorites
MAKES 2 DOZEN; PREP: 15 MIN.,
COOK: 3 MIN., STEEP: 5 MIN., BAKE: 7 MIN.,
STAND: 5 MIN.

1 cup 2% reduced-fat milk
3 regular-size chai tea bags
3 Tbsp. granulated sugar
¼ tsp. ground cinnamon
2 cups self-rising flour
¼ cup chilled butter, cut into small pieces
½ cup powdered sugar

1. Preheat oven to 400°. Cook milk in a small nonaluminum saucepan over medium-low heat, stirring once, 2 to 3 minutes or just until bubbles appear (do not boil); remove from heat. Add tea bags; cover and steep 5 minutes. Remove and discard tea bags from milk, squeezing gently.
2. Stir together granulated sugar, cinnamon, and flour in a large bowl. Cut in butter with a pastry blender or a fork until crumbly. Add ¾ cup milk mixture, stirring just until dry ingredients are moistened. Reserve remaining milk mixture for later use.
3. Turn dough out onto a lightly floured surface; knead lightly 4 to 5 times with floured hands. Pat dough to ¾-inch thickness; cut with a 1½-inch round cutter. Place on lightly greased baking sheets.
4. Bake at 400° for 6 to 7 minutes or until golden. Let stand 5 minutes. Whisk together reserved 1 Tbsp. milk mixture and powdered sugar until smooth. Drizzle over warm biscuits.

Per serving: Calories: 74; Fat: 2.2g (sat 1.3g, mono 0.6g, poly, 0.1g); Protein: 1.4g; Fiber: 0.3g; Chol: 6mg; Iron: 0.5mg; Sodium: 151mg; Calc: 48mg

Eight for '08

1. The Dish on Goodness Fruits and vegetables increase your intake of cancer-fighting antioxidants, says Shannon Sliter Satterwhite, M.S., R.D. Fiber-rich foods boost satiety, which helps with weight loss.

2. Snooze and Win Consider a midday nap. The reduction of stress may help lower your risk of heart attacks.

3. Run From the Sun Switch to a moisturizer with sunscreen. Your healthiest glow will be from having clear, soft skin for years to come.

4. Laugh It Up "No matter what makes us laugh, it's the closest thing to exercise when it comes to working the abs," says Connie Tyne, executive director of the Cooper Wellness Program in Dallas. "It releases serotonin and dopamine that enhance our sense of well-being."

5. Broaden Your Palette Lift your spirits by adding color to your life. "It can inspire you to love your surroundings," Connie says.

6. Less Stress, More Happiness Ongoing stress can lead to all sorts of problems, such as sleep trouble, headaches, and lack of energy. Get a grip on tension: Find what relaxes you, and then do it.

7. Work It Out Make strength training part of your exercise routine to improve bone density, muscle strength, and overall fitness. Aim for 15 to 20 minutes on alternate days three times a week.

8. Take Charge It's up to you. Connie advises: "Know what makes you happy and sad, and steer your life in the direction you choose instead of being blown about by everyone else. Break the mold. Create your future on purpose, not by default!"

Perk Up a Pantry Staple

These delicious offerings prove that versatile tuna in a pouch definitely deserves your attention.

Canned tuna has long been for fast, simple recipes, but the aluminum pouch has taken this familiar product to a whole new level. Pouches not only seal in flavor and freshness, they also don't require a can opener or any draining. They've spawned new flavors that dress up old standbys. Try these dishes, and see for yourself.

Mediterranean Tuna Salad

fast fixin's • make ahead
MAKES 4 CUPS; **PREP:** 20 MIN.

We love how arugula pairs with this fresh tuna salad. Stir 2 cups shredded arugula into the salad, and serve it on crackers.

1 (12-oz.) aluminum foil pouch light tuna chunks in water
1 (15-oz.) can chickpeas, rinsed and drained
⅓ cup chopped pitted kalamata olives
¼ cup olive oil
1 shallot, finely chopped
1 Tbsp. drained capers, chopped
2 tsp. grated lemon rind
1 to 2 Tbsp. fresh lemon juice
1 tsp. minced garlic
1 tsp. Dijon mustard
½ tsp. salt
½ tsp. pepper
Assorted flatbread or pita wedges
Arugula
Feta cheese

1. Stir together first 12 ingredients in a large bowl. Cover and chill until ready to serve. Serve with flatbread, arugula, and feta. —RENEE POKORNY, VENTURA, CALIFORNIA
Note: For testing purposes only, we used StarKist Flavor Fresh Pouch Chunk Light Tuna In Water.

Tuna Cornbread Cakes

MAKES 4 SERVINGS; **PREP:** 15 MIN.,
BAKE: 15 MIN., **COOL:** 5 MIN.,
COOK: 6 MIN. PER BATCH

Cornbread crumbs add a Southern touch to these tasty cakes.

1 (6-oz.) package buttermilk cornbread mix
⅔ cup milk
2 Tbsp. mayonnaise
3 green onions, thinly sliced
3 large eggs, lightly beaten
2 Tbsp. chopped fresh parsley
1 tsp. Old Bay seasoning
1 tsp. Worcestershire sauce
2 (5-oz.) aluminum foil pouches herb-and-garlic-flavored light tuna chunks
3 Tbsp. butter
3 Tbsp. vegetable oil
Lemon Aïoli

1. Preheat oven to 425°. Stir together cornbread mix and milk. Pour batter into a lightly greased 8-inch square pan.
2. Bake at 425° for 15 minutes or until golden brown. Cool on a wire rack 5 minutes or just until warm.
3. Stir together mayonnaise and next 5 ingredients in a large bowl.
4. Crumble cornbread to equal 2 cups. Reserve remaining cornbread for another use. Fold cornbread crumbs and tuna chunks into mayonnaise mixture until well blended. Shape tuna mixture into 8 (3- to 3½-inch) patties.
5. Melt butter with vegetable oil in a large skillet over medium-high heat. Add tuna patties, and cook, in batches, 2 to 3 minutes on each side or until golden brown; drain on paper towels. Serve cakes with Lemon Aïoli.
Note: For testing purposes only, we used Martha White Buttermilk Cornbread Mix and StarKist Tuna Creations Herb & Garlic Chunk Light Tuna.

Lemon Aïoli:

fast fixin's • make ahead
MAKES ¾ CUP; **PREP:** 10 MIN.

¾ cup mayonnaise
2 garlic cloves, minced
1 tsp. grated lemon rind
1 Tbsp. fresh lemon juice
¼ tsp. salt
¼ tsp. pepper

1. Stir together all ingredients. Cover and chill mixture up to 3 days.

—SHERRY LITTLE, SHERWOOD, ARKANSAS

Test Kitchens Notebook

Pouched tuna is a good choice because it's firmer and fresher since it doesn't go through the long canning process. These recipes use tuna chunks, which is different from flaked tuna that's fairly broken apart.

—MARION MCGAHEY, ASSISTANT FOOD EDITOR

Fresh-Picked Ideas For Winter

This time of year Chilean peaches and nectarines are a sweet surprise. Left on the counter to ripen in a loosely closed paper bag, they become fragrant and juicy—perfect for eating out of hand or topping off the creamy custard-filled tart (at right) when you're looking for a little taste of summer freshness.

Like peaches, nectarines are most flavorful at room temperature, so add them to the tart just before serving. For a lighter option, omit eggs, and prepare custard as directed using 1 cup egg substitute and low-fat milk.

Blue Heaven

Rich and creamy Gorgonzola is one of Italy's most famous cheeses and a popular ingredient in many of our recipes. You may be familiar with the small containers of crumbled Gorgonzola, but it's also available from specialty markets in foil-wrapped wedges. A reddish-brown crust develops beneath the foil as Gorgonzola ages, and the flavor becomes sharper and more pronounced. Firm and crumbly Gorgonzola piccante is aged for much longer than the soft and sweet Gorgonzola dolce. For more than 50 incredibly easy and delicious ways to use this versatile cheese, visit myrecipes.

Dinner on the Double Take advantage of that extra oven space the next time you bake a pot roast or ham.

Baking a long-simmering spaghetti sauce, chili, or stew in a Dutch oven is an easy way to coax out flavor and tenderize meats without a lot of stove-top stirring. And you'll have another dinner ready for later in the week.

Prepare your favorite recipe as directed, sautéing the meat and vegetables and adding any remaining ingredients. Bring to a boil; remove from heat, and cover with a tight-fitting lid or a double layer of heavy-duty aluminum foil. Transfer to a 325° to 350° oven to finish simmering.

Nectarine Tart

MAKES 8 SERVINGS; **PREP:** 20 MIN., **BAKE:** 12 MIN., **COOL:** 20 MIN., **COOK:** 10 MIN., **CHILL:** 4 HR.

½ (15-oz.) package refrigerated piecrusts
¾ cup sugar
2 cups milk
⅓ cup all-purpose flour
4 large eggs
½ tsp. almond extract
3 nectarines, cut in wedges
¼ cup honey

1. Preheat oven to 425°. Fit piecrust into a 9-inch tart pan with removable bottom; trim off excess piecrust along edges. Line crust with aluminum foil, and fill with pie weights or dried beans.
2. Bake at 425° for 8 minutes. Remove weights and foil, and bake 3 to 4 more minutes or until golden brown. Remove from oven, and cool on a wire rack 20 minutes or until completely cool.
3. Whisk together sugar and next 3 ingredients in a heavy saucepan. Cook over medium-low heat, whisking constantly, 8 to 10 minutes or until thickened. (Mixture should be a chilled-pudding-like thickness and will just begin to bubble and be thick enough to hold soft peaks when whisk is lifted.) Remove from heat; whisk in almond extract, and immediately spoon into cooled tart shell. Cover with plastic wrap touching the surface, and chill 4 hours.
4. Arrange nectarine wedges decoratively over top of tart.
5. Microwave honey in a microwave-safe bowl at HIGH 15 seconds or until warmed; brush evenly over nectarines.

February

A Better Approach to Brunch

Indulge in the lighter side of comfort food with this casual menu.

Mid-Morning Menu

SERVES 4 TO 6

Shrimp and Grits

Baked Pears With Oatmeal Streusel Topping

Cream Cheese-Banana-Nut Bread

Bloody Mary Punch

Unbelievable flavor and easy prep make this midmorning meal perfect for entertaining. Just ask our food-loving friends on Chincoteague Island, Virginia, who are always happy to gather for good food. "This is my favorite part of the day," says homeowner Regina Hall as she lounges with her daughter, Amoreena Shenefelt, visiting from Decatur, Georgia. "It's a time to eat well, enjoy each other's company, and be inspired."

We shared a lightened spin on some of our best breakfast and brunch recipes with these friends and received rave reviews. "Everything looks so fresh and yummy," says Amoreena. "I especially like the touch of honey in the baked pears—they're not too sweet, and the streusel topping gives a nice crunch."

Try these dishes, and see for yourself how scrumptious they are. Your friends will be just as impressed as ours were—guaranteed.

Shrimp and Grits

chef recipe

MAKES 4 TO 6 SERVINGS; **PREP:** 20 MIN., **COOK:** 21 MIN.

The original recipe is from Bill Smith, executive chef at Crook's Corner, the landmark Southern restaurant in Chapel Hill, North Carolina. (Pictured on page 162)

2 bacon slices

1 lb. unpeeled, medium-size raw shrimp

⅛ tsp. salt

¼ tsp. pepper

¼ cup all-purpose flour

1 cup sliced fresh mushrooms

2 tsp. canola oil

½ cup chopped green onions

2 garlic cloves, minced

1 cup low-sodium, fat-free chicken broth

2 Tbsp. fresh lemon juice

¼ tsp. hot sauce

Cheese Grits

1. Cook bacon in a large nonstick skillet over medium heat 10 minutes or until crisp; remove bacon, and drain on paper towels, reserving 1 tsp. drippings in skillet. Crumble bacon.

2. Peel shrimp; devein, if desired. Sprinkle shrimp with salt and pepper; dredge in flour.

3. Sauté mushrooms in hot drippings with oil in skillet 5 minutes or until tender. Add green onions, and sauté 2 minutes. Add shrimp and garlic, and sauté 2 minutes or until shrimp are lightly browned. Stir in chicken broth, lemon juice, and hot sauce, and cook 2 more minutes, stirring to loosen particles from bottom of skillet. Spoon shrimp mixture over hot Cheese Grits; sprinkle with crumbled bacon.

Cheese Grits:

MAKES 4 TO 6 SERVINGS; **PREP:** 15 MIN., **COOK:** 15 MIN.

1 (14-oz.) can low-sodium fat-free chicken broth

1 cup fat-free milk

½ tsp. salt

1 cup uncooked quick-cooking grits

¾ cup (3 oz.) shredded 2% reduced-fat sharp Cheddar cheese

¼ cup freshly grated Parmesan cheese

½ tsp. hot sauce

¼ tsp. ground white pepper

Test Kitchens Notebook

Quicker Shrimp

Shrimp and grits has long been a Southern breakfast staple, especially in the Lowcountry of South Carolina. To make this shrimp-and-grits recipe even quicker, you can purchase shrimp that has already been peeled and deveined. Or, to do it yourself, simply pull off the head, if it's still on. Then pull off the legs on the inside curve of the shrimp and peel off the shell. Begin at the top by running your thumb under the section of the shell located between the legs. The tail shell may be left on the shrimp for show, if desired. Using a small knife or shrimp deveiner, make a slit down the back of the shrimp, and remove the sand vein.

—**SHANNON SLITER SATTERWHITE,** FOOD EDITOR

1. Bring first 3 ingredients and 1⅓ cups water to a boil in a medium saucepan over medium-high heat; gradually whisk in grits. Reduce heat to low, and simmer, stirring occasionally, 10 minutes or until thickened. Stir in Cheddar cheese and next 3 ingredients.

Baked Pears With Oatmeal Streusel Topping

MAKES 6 SERVINGS; **PREP:** 20 MIN., **BAKE:** 30 MIN., **COOK:** 3 MIN.
(Pictured on page 163)

⅓ cup slivered almonds
6 Bosc pears
2 Tbsp. honey
2 Tbsp. lemon juice
⅓ cup sweetened dried cranberries
½ cup orange juice
Oatmeal Streusel Topping

1. Preheat oven to 350°. Place slivered almonds in a shallow pan, and bake 4 to 5 minutes or until toasted and fragrant, stirring after 2 minutes. Increase oven temperature to 375°.
2. Peel pears, and cut 1 inch off stem end. Remove core from stem end, and scoop out about 2 Tbsp. pulp from top of each pear, using a small spoon, to form a cup. Cut about ¼ inch from bottom of pears, forming a flat base. Place pears in an 11- x 7-inch baking dish.
3. Combine honey and lemon juice in a small saucepan. Heat over medium-low heat until warm. Stir in toasted almonds and cranberries.
4. Spoon honey mixture into pears. Pour orange juice into baking dish.
5. Bake, covered with aluminum foil, at 375° for 15 minutes. Uncover and bake 10 more minutes. Sprinkle each pear with 1 Tbsp. Oatmeal Streusel Topping.

Oatmeal Streusel Topping:

fast fixin's
MAKES 1 CUP; **PREP:** 5 MIN., **BAKE:** 16 MIN.

1 cup uncooked regular oats
2 Tbsp. light brown sugar
1 Tbsp. butter, melted

1. Preheat oven to 350°. Combine oats and sugar. Add butter, tossing to coat. Place mixture in a shallow pan, and bake 14 to 16 minutes or until lightly toasted, stirring after 7 minutes.

Cream Cheese-Banana-Nut Bread

freezeable • make ahead
MAKES 2 LOAVES; **PREP:** 15 MIN.; **BAKE:** 1 HR., 15 MIN.; **COOL:** 40 MIN.

The original recipe was sent to us by Willie Monroe from Homewood, Alabama. For more tasty variations, turn to page 59. To get perfect slices, let the bread cool 30 minutes and then cut with a serrated or electric knife. If desired, you can make a glaze by stirring together ½ cup powdered sugar, ½ tsp. orange zest, and 2 Tbsp. fresh orange juice to drizzle over warm bread. (Pictured on page 163)

1¼ cups chopped pecans, divided
¼ cup butter, softened
1 (8-oz.) package ⅓-less-fat cream cheese, softened
1 cup sugar
2 large eggs
1½ cups whole wheat flour*
1½ cups all-purpose flour
½ tsp. baking powder
½ tsp. baking soda
½ tsp. salt
1 cup buttermilk
1½ cups mashed very ripe bananas (1¼ lb. unpeeled bananas, about 4 medium)
½ tsp. vanilla extract

1. Preheat oven to 350°. Place ¾ cup pecans in a single layer on a baking sheet, and bake 12 to 15 minutes or until toasted and fragrant, stirring after 6 minutes.
2. Beat butter and cream cheese at medium speed with an electric mixer until creamy. Gradually add sugar, beating until light and fluffy. Add eggs, 1 at a time, beating just until blended after each addition.
3. Combine whole wheat flour and next 4 ingredients; gradually add to butter mixture alternately with buttermilk, beginning and ending with flour mixture. Beat at low speed just until blended after each addition. Stir in bananas, ¾ cup toasted pecans, and vanilla. Spoon batter into 2 greased and floured 8- x 4-inch loaf pans. Sprinkle with remaining ½ cup pecans.
4. Bake at 350° for 1 hour or until a long wooden pick inserted in center comes out clean and sides of bread pull away from pan, shielding with aluminum foil during last 15 minutes to prevent excessive browning, if necessary. Cool bread in pans on wire racks 10 minutes. Remove from pans to wire racks. Let bread cool 30 minutes.
Note: To make ahead, proceed with recipe as directed through Step 4. Cool loaves completely, and tightly wrap with plastic wrap. Wrap again with aluminum foil. Freeze up to 1 month.
*If you've never worked with whole wheat flour, accurate measuring is everything. Be sure to spoon the flour into a dry measuring cup (do not pack) rather than scooping the cup into the flour, and level it off with a straight edge. Expect a denser bread with this recipe. It won't rise as much as traditional breads, and the texture will be very moist. (If you use frozen, thawed bananas, you might experience more wet patches throughout the bread.) We liked this version at the taste-testing table, but if you prefer a less dense bread with a little more rise and slightly lighter texture, then double the baking powder but leave the baking soda the same.

Bloody Mary Punch

MAKES 1½ QT.; **PREP:** 5 MIN.

Instead of stirring all the ingredients together, serve optional shots of vodka on the side, and let guests add it or not. (Pictured on page 163)

1 (46-oz.) container low-sodium
    vegetable juice, chilled
1 Tbsp. freshly ground pepper
3 Tbsp. fresh lime juice
1 Tbsp. hot sauce
1 Tbsp. Worcestershire sauce
½ tsp. Old Bay seasoning
½ cup vodka (optional), chilled
Celery sticks (optional)

1. Combine vegetable juice, next 5 ingredients, and, if desired, vodka in a punch bowl or a pitcher. Serve over ice in glasses. Serve with celery sticks, if desired.
Note: For testing purposes only, we used V8 Low Sodium 100% Vegetable Juice.

Delicious From the Freezer

Whether baked in parchment paper or broiled in a pan, frozen fish yields moist and yummy results.

Dishing up an amazing seafood dinner at home couldn't be easier. Simply start with a package of frozen fish from your local grocery store. Then add bold seasonings to enhance the seafood's natural sweetness.

Lemon-Dill Tilapia

MAKES 4 SERVINGS; **PREP:** 15 MIN.,
BAKE: 25 MIN.

Parchment paper keeps the fish tender by sealing in the juices. Aluminum foil can be substituted.

4 (5-oz.) frozen tilapia fillets, thawed
    according to package directions*
1 tsp. salt
½ tsp. pepper
Parchment Paper
2 lemons, sliced
¼ cup shredded carrot
2 Tbsp. fresh dill
2 Tbsp. fresh parsley
2 Tbsp. butter

1. Preheat oven to 375°. Sprinkle fillets with salt and pepper.
2. Cut parchment paper into 4 (13- x 9-inch) rectangles. Place 3 lemon slices crosswise in center of 1 parchment rectangle. Top with 1 fillet. Repeat with remaining lemon slices, fillets, and parchment paper rectangles. Sprinkle fillets evenly with carrot, dill, and parsley. Top each fillet with ½ Tbsp. butter. Fold 1 side of parchment paper over fillets; tuck excess parchment under fillets, pressing folds to form a crease.
3. Bake at 375° for 20 to 25 minutes or until fish flakes with a fork. Serve tilapia immediately.
*4 (5-oz.) fresh tilapia fillets may be substituted.

Mustard-and-Soy-Glazed Salmon

fast fixin's

MAKES 4 SERVINGS; **PREP:** 10 MIN.,
COOK: 5 MIN., **BROIL:** 10 MIN.

¼ cup pepper jelly
¼ cup soy sauce
2 Tbsp. country-style Dijon
    mustard
2 (12-oz.) packages frozen salmon fillets,
    thawed according to package directions
¼ tsp. pepper

1. Bring first 3 ingredients to a boil in a medium saucepan over medium heat; reduce heat to low, and simmer 5 minutes. Remove and reserve half of pepper jelly mixture.
2. Place salmon fillets on a greased wire rack on an aluminum foil-lined baking sheet. Sprinkle fillets with pepper, and brush with remaining pepper jelly mixture.
3. Broil fillets 5 inches from heat 8 to 10 minutes or to desired degree of doneness. Remove from oven, and brush with reserved pepper jelly mixture. Serve immediately.

Creole Baked Fish

MAKES 4 SERVINGS; **PREP:** 20 MIN.,
COOK: 19 MIN., **BAKE:** 25 MIN.

½ red bell pepper, chopped
½ green bell pepper, chopped
1 small onion, chopped
1 Tbsp. olive oil
2 garlic cloves, chopped
¼ cup dry white wine
1 (28-oz.) can diced tomatoes
1 Tbsp. Cajun seasoning, divided
½ tsp. pepper
2 tsp. hot sauce (optional)
2 (12-oz.) packages frozen cod fillets, thawed
    according to package directions

1. Preheat oven to 350°. Sauté bell peppers and onion in hot oil in an ovenproof skillet over medium heat 5 minutes or until tender. Add garlic, and sauté 1 minute. Add wine, and cook 3 minutes or until liquid is absorbed. Stir in tomatoes, 1 tsp. Cajun seasoning, pepper, and, if desired, hot sauce. Cook, stirring occasionally, 10 minutes. Remove from heat.
2. Sprinkle 1 side of cod fillets evenly with remaining Cajun seasoning. Place fillets, seasoned sides up, on top of tomato mixture in skillet. Bake at 350° for 25 minutes or until fish flakes with a fork. Serve immediately.

Healthy Living.

February is a great month to get organized. It's also a great time to bake up some delicious, good-for-you sweets.

Good-for-You Pantry

Stockpile these convenient and wholesome foods to save time in the kitchen.

Choose Good Grains
• Keep fiber-packed grains, such as brown rice, whole wheat pastas, oatmeal, and cereal, in airtight containers for up to six months.
• Look for terms such as "whole grain" and "whole wheat."

Perfect Produce
• Potatoes, garlic (unpeeled), winter squash, and onions are low calorie, fat free, and shelf stable.
• Store in a cool, dry place to maintain optimum flavor.

Use Heart-Healthy Fats
• Get more of the good fat by using canola, olive, or nut oils to sauté veggies. Store oils for one to two months.
• Nuts and peanut butter are good sources of monounsaturated fat.

Grab a Can or Jar
• Opt for reduced-sodium broths, soups, and vegetables.
• Choose fruits packed in natural juices, avoiding those with heavy syrup.
• Watch out for dented cans and lids, and follow expiration dates.

Add Easy Flavor
• Dried spices and seasonings offer zest without extra fat and calories. Store for up to six months.
• A dash of low-sodium soy sauce or flavored vinegar goes a long way, and both keep up to a year.

Snack Smart
• Choose nutrient-rich foods that are filling, such as popcorn, granola bars, nuts, and trail mix.
• Get your carbonation fix by replacing sugary sodas with sparkling water.

Healthy Benefits
• Rinsing canned beans and vegetables in a strainer under cold water can reduce nearly half of their sodium content.
• Traditional fish from a can or pouch (such as salmon and tuna) contains more calcium than the same amount of freshly cooked fish.

Our Favorite Finds
Test Kitchens Professional Marian Cooper Cairns found these tasty surprises at our local supermarket.
• Pomegranate vinegar rich in antioxidants
• Silky dark chocolate, such as CocoaVia, enriched with cancer-fighting nutrients
• 100 Calorie Packs of cookies and cakes for a sweet splurge
• Seasoned almonds loaded with heart-healthy flavor
• Kashi granola bars for a quick source of fiber

Storage Solutions
• Containers with airtight lids keep spices, seasonings, and dried fruits fresh longer. Use larger containers for pastas and grains.
• Store pantry produce with style. Simple galvanized or wooden baskets allow fruits and vegetables to breathe. Keep onions and garlic separate from potatoes—they will cause the potatoes to sprout.
• Forget the jumbo bags of chips—they take up a lot of storage space and tempt you to overeat. Maintain portion control by keeping individually packaged snacks on hand.
• Oatmeal-Pecan Snack Cookies (see recipe on page 46) stay just-baked fresh in well-sealed tins. Take them to work, school, or a potluck party.

Oatmeal-Pecan Snack Cookies

make ahead • freezeable

MAKES ABOUT 4 DOZEN; **PREP:** 20 MIN.,
BAKE: 14 MIN. PER BATCH,
COOL: 10 MIN.

These nutritious cookies taste great with a cup of cold low-fat milk for breakfast on the go. You can store them in zip-top plastic freezer bags or plastic containers in the freezer for up to one month.

1¾ cups all-purpose flour
1¼ tsp. pumpkin pie spice
½ tsp. salt
½ tsp. baking soda
¼ cup butter, softened
6 oz. reduced-fat cream cheese,
　softened
1½ cups firmly packed dark brown
　sugar
½ cup egg substitute
1 tsp. vanilla extract
3 cups uncooked regular oats
¾ cup dried cherries
Vegetable cooking spray
½ cup chopped pecans

1. Preheat oven to 350°. Combine flour, pumpkin pie spice, salt, and baking soda.
2. Beat butter, cream cheese, and sugar at medium speed with an electric mixer until fluffy. Add egg substitute and vanilla, beating until blended. Gradually add flour mixture, beating at low speed just until blended after each addition. Stir in oats and dried cherries.
3. Drop dough by rounded tablespoonfuls onto baking sheets coated with cooking spray; gently flatten dough into circles. Sprinkle about ½ tsp. chopped pecans onto each dough circle, gently pressing into dough.
4. Bake, in batches, at 350° for 13 to 14 minutes or until a wooden pick inserted in centers comes out clean. Remove cookies from baking sheets to wire racks, and let cool 10 minutes.

Per cookie: Calories 97; Fat 2.6g (sat 1.2g, mono 0.9g, poly 0.5g); Protein 2g; Carb 16g; Fiber 1g; Chol 4mg; Iron 0.7mg; Sodium 68mg; Calc 17mg.

Carrot-Oatmeal-Pecan Snack Cookies: Prepare dough as directed through Step 2, stirring in 2 grated carrots with oats and cherries. Proceed with recipe as directed.

Per cookie: Calories 99; Fat 2.7g (sat 1.3g, mono 0.9g, poly 0.5g); Protein 2.1g; Carb 16.1g; Fiber 1g; Chol 5mg; Iron 0.7mg; Sodium 70mg; Calc 18mg.

Chocolate-Oatmeal-Pecan Snack Cookies: Prepare cookies as directed through Step 4. Break 4 (0.87-oz.) dark chocolate bars into pieces. Microwave chocolate pieces in a small microwave-safe bowl at HIGH 45 seconds to 1 minute or until melted and smooth, stirring at 15-second intervals. Spoon chocolate into a small zip-top plastic bag. Snip 1 corner of bag with scissors to make a tiny hole. Drizzle chocolate onto cookies. Let stand 1 hour or until set.
Note: For testing purposes only, we used CocoaVia Original Chocolate Bars.

Per cookie: Calories 109; Fat 3.1g (sat 1.7g, mono 0.9g, poly 0.5g); Protein 2.2g; Carb 17.1g; Fiber 1.1g; Chol 5mg; Iron 0.8mg; Sodium 68mg; Calc 17mg.

Sweet & Sinless

Fall in love with these sensational desserts, rich in flavor without all the calories.

Nobody can resist desserts as luscious as these—even when they're lightened. Dark Chocolate-Bourbon Torte is soufflé-like in texture and abundant in heart-healthy antioxidants. Best of all, it cures any chocolate craving. Cherry Bread Pudding puts a guilt-free spin on a classic dessert.

Dark Chocolate-Bourbon Torte

MAKES 10 SERVINGS; **PREP:** 20 MIN.,
BAKE: 45 MIN., **COOL:** 30 MIN.

Don't worry if the torte cracks while baking—that's part of its charm. Just sprinkle it with powdered sugar and cocoa for an easy, elegant look.

Vegetable cooking spray
½ cup dark chocolate morsels
¼ cup butter, softened
¾ cup granulated sugar, divided
1 tsp. vanilla extract
1 large egg
¼ cup fat-free milk
2 Tbsp. bourbon (optional)
¼ cup Dutch process cocoa
2 Tbsp. all-purpose flour
4 egg whites
¼ tsp. cream of tartar
½ cup thawed reduced-fat whipped
　topping
1 Tbsp. powdered sugar
1 Tbsp. unsweetened cocoa

1. Preheat oven to 300°. Coat bottom and sides of an 8-inch springform pan with cooking spray.

2. Microwave chocolate morsels in a small microwave-safe bowl at MEDIUM (50% power) for 1 minute or until chocolate is melted and smooth, stirring at 30-second intervals.

3. Beat butter and ½ cup granulated sugar at medium speed with an electric mixer until well blended (about 2 minutes). Add vanilla and egg; beat 1 minute. Add milk and, if desired, bourbon; beat 1 minute. (Mixture will look curdled.) Add melted chocolate, beating just until blended. Gradually add ¼ cup cocoa and flour, beating at low speed just until blended.

4. Beat egg whites and cream of tartar at high speed with an electric mixer until foamy. Add remaining ¼ cup granulated sugar, 1 Tbsp. at a time, beating until stiff peaks form. Fold one-fourth of egg white mixture into batter; gently fold in remaining egg white mixture. Spoon batter into prepared pan.

5. Bake at 300° for 45 minutes or until set. (A wooden pick inserted in center will come out with just a few crumbs on it.) Remove torte from oven; immediately run tip of a small knife around edge of torte. Let cool on wire rack 30 minutes. (Torte will rise to top of pan while baking but will sink while it cools.) Remove sides of springform pan.

6. Spoon whipped topping into a zip-top plastic freezer bag. (Do not seal.) Snip 1 corner of bag to make a small hole. Pipe dollops of whipped topping around base of torte. Sprinkle torte with powdered sugar and 1 Tbsp. cocoa.

Note: For testing purposes only, we used Hershey's Special Dark Chocolate Chips.

Per serving: Calories 204; Fat 8.8g (sat 5.2g, mono 1.5g, poly 0.3g); Protein 3.4g; Carb 30g; Fiber 1.2g; Chol 34mg; Iron 1mg; Sodium 67mg; Calc 18mg.

Healthy Benefits

- Chocolate is good for your complexion after all. New studies suggest that the nutrients in cocoa can help protect against damaging UV rays and improve overall skin appearance.
- Tart cherries can help boost melatonin in the brain to regulate natural sleep patterns and ease jet lag.

Cherry Bread Pudding

MAKES 6 SERVINGS; **PREP:** 25 MIN., **STAND:** 40 MIN., **BAKE:** 35 MIN.

Bread pudding will rise to the top of ramekins as it bakes and may overflow. It will deflate once it's removed from the oven. Add some toasted slivered almonds for a crunchy garnish, if you wish.

1 (8-oz.) French bread loaf, cut into 1-inch pieces
Vegetable cooking spray
2 cups fat-free milk
½ (12-oz.) can fat-free evaporated milk
¾ cup no-calorie sweetener
¾ cup egg substitute
¼ cup sugar
1 Tbsp. butter, melted
1 tsp. vanilla extract
½ tsp. ground cinnamon
¼ tsp. ground nutmeg
Cherry Sauce

1. Preheat oven to 350°. Place bread pieces in 6 (8-oz.) ramekins coated with cooking spray. Place ramekins on a baking sheet.

2. Whisk together milk and next 8 ingredients until blended. Pour milk mixture over bread in ramekins; let stand 30 minutes, pressing bread to absorb mixture after 15 minutes.

3. Bake at 350° for 30 to 35 minutes or just until a knife inserted in center comes out clean. Let stand 10 minutes. Spoon Cherry Sauce over bread pudding.

—**PHILLIP HEIN**, BURLINGTON, WISCONSIN

Note: For testing purposes only, we used Splenda No Calorie Sweetener, Granular. Instead of ramekins, place bread pieces in an 11- x 7-inch baking dish coated with cooking spray, and proceed with recipe as directed. (No need to place on baking sheet.) Bake at 350° for 30 to 35 minutes or just until a knife inserted in center comes out clean. Let stand 10 minutes.

Per serving (including sauce): Calories 306; Fat 4.6g (sat 2.1g, mono 0.9g, poly 0.7g); Protein 12.7g; Carb 51.4g; Fiber 1.9g; Chol 8mg; Iron 2.9mg; Sodium 388mg; Calc 196mg.

Cherry Sauce:

MAKES ABOUT 1 CUP; **PREP:** 5 MIN., **COOK:** 18 MIN.

1 (15-oz.) can pitted tart cherries in water
3 Tbsp. light brown sugar
2 Tbsp. cherry-flavored liqueur

1. Combine all ingredients in a small saucepan. Cook over medium-high heat, stirring occasionally, 16 to 18 minutes or until most of the liquid is reduced.

Note: For testing purposes only, we used Kirsch Cherry Liqueur.

Per serving: Calories 81; Fat 0g (sat 0g, mono 0g, poly 0g); Protein 0.7g; Carb 18.5g; Fiber 1.2g; Chol 0mg; Iron 1.2mg; Sodium 5mg; Calc 11mg.

Easiest Citrus Tarts

Dazzle your taste buds with the vibrant flavors of lemon and lime.

Lemon Velvet Tart

make ahead

MAKES 8 SERVINGS; **PREP:** 25 MIN., **FREEZE:** 20 MIN., **BAKE:** 15 MIN., **COOL:** 20 MIN., **CHILL:** 4 HR.

Drizzle Raspberry Sauce (see recipe on opposite page) over your slice, if you wish. (Pictured on page 6)

½ (15-oz.) package refrigerated
    piecrusts
2 (4-oz.) white chocolate bars, chopped
1 (8-oz.) package cream cheese, softened
Lemon Curd (see recipe at right)
8 lemon candies
Caramelized Sugar Spirals
    (recipe on opposite page)

1. Fit piecrust into a lightly greased 9½-inch tart pan with removable bottom; press into fluted edges. Fold any excess dough over outside of pan, and pinch to secure to pan. (This will keep piecrust from sliding down pan as it bakes.) Generously prick bottom and sides of piecrust with a fork, and freeze 20 minutes.
2. Preheat oven to 425°. Place piecrust on a baking sheet, and bake 15 minutes or until light golden brown. Cool on a wire rack 20 minutes or until completely cool. Gently tap excess crust from sides of pan, using a rolling pin.
3. Microwave white chocolate in a small microwave-safe bowl at HIGH 1½ minutes or until melted and smooth, stirring at 30-second intervals.
4. Beat softened cream cheese at medium speed with an electric mixer until light and fluffy. Add melted chocolate, and beat until blended, stopping to scrape down sides. Add Lemon Curd, and beat until blended.
5. Spoon into prepared crust. Smooth filling with a spatula. Chill 4 hours.
6. Arrange lemon candies evenly on top of tart. Prop Caramelized Sugar Spirals against lemon candies.
Note: For testing purposes only, we used Lemon Drops candies.

Lime Velvet Tart: Substitute Lime Curd (see recipe at right) for Lemon Curd, and prepare recipe as directed.

Lemon Mousse Tart: *(Pictured on page 6)* Prepare recipe as directed through Step 4. Beat 2 cups heavy cream at high speed with an electric mixer until soft peaks form. Gently fold into lemon mixture. Spoon mixture into prepared crust, mounding mixture in center of tart. (Mixture will be about 2 inches higher than top edge of crust.) Chill 4 hours. Garnish with lemon curls and fresh raspberries, if desired.

Lime Mousse Tart: Substitute Lime Curd for Lemon Curd, and proceed with Lemon Mousse Tart recipe as directed.

Lemon Curd

make ahead

MAKES ABOUT 1⅓ CUPS; **PREP:** 10 MIN., **COOK:** 15 MIN., **CHILL:** 3 HR.

This melt-in-your-mouth soft custard is a traditional English favorite. Serve this tart-and-tangy, five-ingredient curd with sweet gingersnaps, scones, cupcakes, or warm biscuits.

1 cup sugar
1 Tbsp. lemon zest
1 cup fresh lemon juice
4 egg yolks, lightly beaten
½ cup butter, cubed

1. Bring sugar, zest, and juice to a boil in a heavy nonaluminum 3½-qt. saucepan over medium-high heat. Remove from heat, and gradually whisk about one-fourth of hot juice mixture into egg yolks; add egg yolk mixture to remaining hot juice mixture, whisking constantly until well blended.
2. Place saucepan over medium heat, and cook, whisking constantly, at least 10 or up to 12 minutes. (Mixture will be a pudding-like thickness.)
3. Add butter, in 6 batches, whisking constantly until butter melts and mixture is well blended after each addition. Remove from heat, and pour mixture through a wire-mesh strainer into a bowl. Place plastic wrap directly on warm curd (to prevent a film from forming); chill 3 hours.

Lime Curd: Substitute lime zest and lime juice for lemon zest and lemon juice. Proceed with recipe as directed.

Test Kitchens Notebook

Lemons are available year-round, and their juice and zest can be used in sweet and savory recipes. One large lemon usually yields 2 to 3 Tbsp. zest. Get double-duty from lemons by removing the zest before squeezing the juice. To remove the zest, use a special zester or fine grater. Or, you can peel the lemon, being careful to remove as little of the white pith as possible, combine it with a little sugar in a food processor, and pulse to make a fine zest. Once the zest or peel is removed, the remaining fruit can be refrigerated up to a week. Whole lemons themselves can be stored at room temperature for about a week. For longer storage, place in plastic bags, and refrigerate up to a week.

—MARION MCGAHEY, ASSISTANT FOOD EDITOR

Caramelized Sugar Spirals

MAKES ABOUT 44; **PREP:** 20 MIN.,
COOK: 30 MIN., **STAND:** 3 MIN.,
COOL: 10 MIN.

Easy-to-make Caramelized Sugar Spirals add to an impressive presentation. The secret: crushed lemon candies.

2 cups sugar
½ cup light corn syrup
Crushed lemon candies

1. Stir together sugar, corn syrup, and ½ cup water in a 3½-qt. heavy saucepan until blended. Place pan over medium-high heat, and cook, without stirring, until a candy thermometer registers 305° to 315° or until mixture begins to turn a golden caramel color (about 25 to 30 minutes). Remove from heat, and stir just until color is evenly distributed, using a clean wooden spoon. Carefully place bottom of saucepan into cold water to stop the cooking process. Remove from water, and let stand 2 to 3 minutes or until slightly thickened.

2. Sprinkle crushed lemon candies over a piece of parchment paper. Carefully spoon about 1 Tbsp. hot syrup over candies in a circular motion, creating 3-inch discs. (If syrup gets too thick, place saucepan back over heat for 3 to 4 minutes or until syrup slightly melts. Use a clean spoon to continue making spirals.) Let cool 10 minutes or until completely cool. (Mixture will harden as it cools.)

GET INSPIRED

Have a Heart

Take the gift of chocolate to a whole new level with this tasty Valentine offering. For more delicious—and guilt-free—desserts, see "Sweet & Sinless," beginning on page 46.

Grilled Chocolate Sweetheart

1. Place 2 (0.375-oz.) good-quality chocolate squares between 2 white bread slices and cut into heart or other shape as desired; brush both sides of sandwich with 1½ tsp. melted butter. Cook in a hot non-stick skillet over medium-high heat 30 to 60 seconds on each side or until chocolate is melted and bread is golden brown. Dust with powdered sugar. Garnish with raspberries, if desired. **MAKES** 1 SERVING. PREP: 5 MIN., COOK: 2 MIN.

Note: For testing purposes only, we used thin squares that would melt quickly and evenly, such as Ghirardelli 60% Cacao SQUARES Dark Chocolate, Ghirardelli Milk Chocolate With Caramelized Almonds SQUARES, and Lindt Excellence 70% Cocoa Dark Chocolate Extra Fine Squares.

Variations: Other good fillings include raspberry jam, marshmallow cream, toasted pecans, peanut butter, and sliced bananas.

Raspberry Sauce

make ahead

MAKES ABOUT 1½ CUPS; **PREP:** 10 MIN.,
COOK: 15 MIN., **CHILL:** 2 HR.

2 (12-oz.) packages frozen
    raspberries
¾ cup sugar

1. Cook raspberries and sugar in a 3½-qt. saucepan over low heat, stirring occasionally, 5 minutes or until sugar is melted. Increase heat to medium, and cook, stirring occasionally, 10 minutes. Remove from heat, and pour through a fine wire-mesh strainer into a bowl, pressing with back of a spoon. Discard solids. Chill 2 hours. (Mixture will thicken as it cools.)

Skillet Suppers

One pan is all you need to make and serve your family a mouthwatering meal.

When you're looking for a simple meal-in-one, pull out a skillet. Most will go from cooktop to oven to table, making them a great choice for weeknight dinners *or* entertaining. This casual serving piece holds a dual advantage—not only will you have minimal cleanup, but a meal served in a skillet is warmly inviting. Your guests will feel like family.

A skillet meal doesn't have to be run-of-the-mill though. These recipes possess flavor and flair, as well as appealing presentation. They also are doable for a busy cook. Once you've completed the short preparation time required, you slide Lima Bean Cassoulet into the oven, leaving you free for other activities. It emerges fragrant, bubbling, and full of stick-to-your-ribs comfort.

Creole Fried Rice and Pork Chops, Cabbage, and Apples are both cooked entirely on the stovetop to deliver great taste, eye appeal, and freshness. In fact, the festive appearance and Louisiana style of the fried rice make it a fine choice to serve at a Mardi Gras party this month.

Pork Chops, Cabbage, and Apples
family favorite
MAKES 6 SERVINGS; PREP: 20 MIN., COOK: 49 MIN.

A bottle of dark beer enriches this dish for a soul-soothing combination. Apple cider makes a delicious substitute for the beer. Pork and cabbage are a classic combination, as are pork and apples. Put the three together, and you get something really delightful. (Pictured on page 167)

3 tsp. paprika, divided
2 tsp. chopped fresh or 1 tsp. dried thyme, divided
2 tsp. kosher salt, divided
1½ tsp. freshly ground pepper, divided
2 tsp. chopped fresh or 1 tsp. dried sage, divided
6 (½-inch-thick) pork loin chops
2 bacon slices
1 head cabbage (about 2 lb.), coarsely chopped
2 medium onions, thinly sliced
1 large Granny Smith apple, peeled and sliced
1 Tbsp. tomato paste
1 (12-oz.) bottle lager beer*

1. Combine 2 tsp. paprika, 1 tsp. fresh or ½ tsp. dried thyme, 1 tsp. salt, 1 tsp. pepper, and 1 tsp. fresh or ½ tsp. dried sage; rub evenly over pork chops.
2. Cook bacon slices in a large, deep skillet over medium-high heat 6 to 8 minutes or until crisp; remove bacon, and drain on paper towels, reserving drippings in skillet. Crumble bacon.
3. Cook pork in hot drippings 3 minutes on each side or until browned and done; remove pork from pan, and keep warm.
4. Add cabbage, onions, and apple to pan. Cover and reduce heat to medium; cook, stirring occasionally, 15 minutes or until cabbage begins to wilt. Add tomato paste, beer, bacon, remaining 1 tsp. paprika, 1 tsp. fresh or ½ tsp. dried thyme, 1 tsp. salt, ½ tsp. pepper, and 1 tsp. fresh or ½ tsp. dried sage, stirring to loosen particles from bottom of skillet. Cover and cook 15 minutes or until cabbage is tender and liquid is slightly thickened. Add pork, and cook, uncovered, 5 minutes or until thoroughly heated.
*1½ cups apple cider may be substituted.
Note: For testing purposes only, we used Samuel Adams Boston Lager.

Lima Bean Cassoulet
family favorite
MAKES 8 SERVINGS; PREP: 15 MIN., COOK: 15 MIN., BAKE: 30 MIN.

Enjoy down-home comfort in this cassoulet, a Southern take on a classic French casserole. If your skillet doesn't have an oven-proof handle, wrap the handle in layers of aluminum foil to protect it. (Pictured on page 167)

3 garlic cloves, thinly sliced
1 Tbsp. olive oil
1 small onion, coarsely chopped
¾ cup diced carrots
1 (8-oz.) package cooked cubed ham
1 (16-oz.) can large butter beans, drained
½ (16-oz.) package frozen butter peas
2½ cups low-sodium fat-free chicken broth
2 tsp. chopped fresh rosemary
Cornbread Crust Batter

1. Preheat oven to 400°.
2. Sauté garlic in hot oil in a 10-inch ovenproof skillet over medium heat 1 minute. Add onion and carrots; sauté 3 to 4 minutes or until tender. Add ham; cook 3 minutes. Stir in beans, peas, and next 2 ingredients; bring to a boil, and cook 5 minutes. Remove from heat;

pour Cornbread Crust Batter over ham mixture.

3. Bake at 400° for 28 to 30 minutes or until golden brown and bubbly.

Cornbread Crust Batter:
fast fixin's
MAKES ABOUT 1½ CUPS; **PREP:** 5 MIN.

1 cup cornmeal mix
½ cup buttermilk
¼ cup sour cream
1 large egg
½ tsp. chopped fresh rosemary

1. Combine all ingredients; use batter immediately.

Creole Fried Rice
family favorite
MAKES 6 SERVINGS; **PREP:** 20 MIN.,
COOK: 36 MIN., **COOL:** 30 MIN.

Cold rice works best in this recipe. If possible, make the rice a day ahead, and store it in the fridge. Making the rice the day before and chopping the ingredients ahead will let you have this dish on the table in nothing flat. If you're in a hurry, follow Step 1 to cool it on a baking sheet. (Pictured on page 166)

1 cup uncooked long-grain rice
2 cups chicken broth
1 lb. skinned and boned chicken thighs
1½ tsp. Creole seasoning, divided
2 Tbsp. vegetable oil
½ lb. andouille or smoked sausage, sliced
½ small onion, chopped
½ small green bell pepper, chopped
2 garlic cloves, chopped
1 cup frozen sliced okra, thawed
3 plum tomatoes, chopped
2 green onions, sliced (green part only)

1. Cook rice according to package directions, substituting chicken broth for water. Spread cooked rice in a thin layer on a baking sheet. Let cool 30 minutes or until completely cool.

2. Cut chicken thighs into 1-inch pieces, and toss with 1 tsp. Creole seasoning.

3. Cook chicken in hot oil in a large skillet over medium heat 3 minutes; add sausage, and cook 3 to 4 minutes or until lightly browned. Add onion, bell pepper, and garlic, and cook 5 minutes or until onion is tender. Stir in okra and remaining ½ tsp. Creole seasoning.

4. Increase heat to high; add rice, and cook, stirring constantly, 4 minutes or until thoroughly heated.

5. Stir in tomatoes. Sprinkle with sliced green onions, and serve dish immediately.

Pick a Pan

A great skillet is an indispensable piece of cookware. Choosing the right one is a highly personal process though. You don't need to shop expensively for a skillet that performs well, but quality definitely pays off in the long run. Here are some things our Foods staff recommends you look for when shopping, along with a few of our favorite selections. Cookware often goes on sale in April, so if you got a gift certificate for Christmas, you may want to hang onto it until spring.

- The best **stainless steel** skillets have a heavy bottom with a layer of aluminum and/or copper for good heat distribution. Cuisinart, Emerilware, and most of the professional-quality pans offer this feature. Executive Foods Editor Scott Jones favors All-Clad's 10-inch skillet. "It's more expensive but worth every penny," he avows. Associate Food Editor Mary Allen Perry finds that Martha Stewart's Tri-Ply offers good value for the money.
- Opinions vary among the Food staff regarding **nonstick** skillets, though we agree they provide good browning with very little oil. Most like a heavy skillet with a nonstick lining, but others of us find a light, inexpensive pan to be a good choice. Test Kitchens Professional Vanessa McNeil Rocchio says, "Every three years or so I buy a cheap nonstick to use for eggs." She likes the discount store-quality skillets because they heat up quickly. They're good for browning items that cook fast, such as crab cakes or fish fillets.
- Test Kitchens Professional Norman King swears by Calphalon's **infused anodized aluminum** pan for beautiful browning. "There's not a better pan for searing meat," he says. "And the stay-cool handle is a nice addition." These pans are oven- and broiler-safe, letting you brown the meat on the cooktop and finish it in the oven.
- **Cast iron** still reigns supreme for certain tasks, such as making roux, frying, and baking cornbread. It's inexpensive and virtually indestructible as well. **Enameled cast iron** offers some advantages over the original. It's great for braised meats and stove-top casseroles, which require browning and then longer cooking. Because it's enameled, the iron doesn't react with tomatoes and other acid ingredients and offers even cooking on the cooktop and in the oven.

Grab a Bag of Spinach

Treat yourself to a quick fix of garden-fresh flavor with this convenience product.

Packaged spinach makes a speedy start for many of our favorite winter salads. The tender but hearty texture pairs perfectly with warm toppings, such as pan-fried chicken or sautéed mushrooms.

When steaming or sautéing spinach, take full advantage of the price you pay for freshness. Cook it only until the leaves are wilted; the color should still be bright green. A 10-ounce bag shrinks to about 1½ cups of cooked spinach, which is a little more than a 10-ounce package of frozen.

Use spinach on sandwiches and burgers, or stir a handful into hot soup or pasta just before serving. It's a great way to sneak extra goodness into the foods you love.

Spinach-Mushroom Sauté

fast fixin's

MAKES 2 SERVINGS; **PREP:** 10 MIN.,
COOK: 5 MIN.

1 Tbsp. butter
1 Tbsp. olive oil
1 (8-oz.) package fresh mushrooms,
   sliced
½ small onion, finely chopped
1 garlic clove, minced
¼ tsp. salt
1 (10-oz.) package fresh spinach, thoroughly
   washed
2 Tbsp. fresh lemon juice

1. Melt 1 Tbsp. butter with 1 Tbsp. oil in a large skillet over medium-high heat; add sliced mushrooms and next 3 ingredients. Sauté 3 to 5 minutes or until tender; gradually add spinach, stirring to coat with mushroom mixture. Remove from heat, and toss spinach mixture with 2 Tbsp. lemon juice.

—TRACEY FERRELL, NASHVILLE, TENNESSEE

Pan-Fried Chicken-and-Spinach Salad

family favorite

MAKES 4 SERVINGS; **PREP:** 20 MIN.,
COOK: 10 MIN., **STAND:** 5 MIN.

It's hard to beat this dish for a satisfying, last-minute supper.

4 skinned and boned chicken breasts
¼ cup all-purpose flour
1 large egg, beaten
⅔ cup Italian-seasoned breadcrumbs
¼ cup olive oil
1 (6-oz.) package fresh baby spinach,
   thoroughly washed
1 large apple, thinly sliced
½ cup walnut pieces
1 (8-oz.) jar poppy seed dressing
½ cup sweetened dried cranberries
½ cup crumbled blue cheese

1. Dredge chicken in flour; dip in egg, and dredge in breadcrumbs.
2. Cook chicken in hot oil in a large skillet over medium heat 3 to 5 minutes on each side or until done; remove from skillet, and let stand 5 minutes. Cut chicken diagonally in ½-inch-thick slices.
3. Toss together baby spinach, apple slices, and ½ cup walnuts, and divide between 4 serving plates; top with cooked chicken.
4. Stir together poppy seed dressing, cranberries, and blue cheese; serve with salad.

—DEB RIORDA, ST. CHARLES, ILLINOIS

Note: For testing purposes only, we used Maple Grove Farms of Vermont Fat Free Poppyseed Dressing.

Garlic-Parmesan Spinach

fast fixin's

MAKES 4 SERVINGS; **PREP:** 10 MIN.,
COOK: 8 MIN.

For a tasty twist, substitute crumbled feta cheese for Parmesan, and sprinkle with a few kalamata olives.

4 large garlic cloves, finely chopped
3 Tbsp. olive oil
1 (20-oz.) package fresh spinach,
   thoroughly washed
¼ cup chopped fresh basil
½ tsp. salt
¼ tsp. pepper
½ cup shaved Parmesan
   cheese

1. Sauté chopped garlic in hot oil in a large skillet over medium-high heat 2 to 3 minutes or until golden. Gradually add spinach, stirring until spinach is wilted and coated with garlic mixture (about 5 minutes). Remove from heat, and stir in chopped basil, salt, and pepper. Transfer spinach mixture to a serving dish, and sprinkle with ½ cup Parmesan cheese.

—STEPHANIE MARCY, WEST HOLLYWOOD, CALIFORNIA

Tropical Spinach Salad With Grilled Chicken

southernliving.com favorite

MAKES 6 SERVINGS;. **PREP:** 20 MIN.,
CHILL: 1 HR., **SOAK:** 30 MIN., **GRILL:** 8 MIN.,
STAND: 10 MIN.

You can omit the chicken and serve this recipe as a side salad.

6 skinned and boned chicken breast halves
Citrus Marinade
2 (6-oz.) bags fresh baby spinach
2 mangoes, peeled and sliced
1 medium-size red onion, sliced
1 (3-oz.) package goat cheese,
   crumbled
1 cup fresh raspberries
½ cup chopped pistachio nuts
Fresh Basil Vinaigrette

1. Preheat grill to 350°. Place chicken in a large zip-top plastic freezer bag, and add Citrus Marinade. Seal and shake to coat. Chill 1 hour.
2. Remove chicken from marinade, discarding marinade.
3. Grill, covered with grill lid, over medium-high heat (350° to 400°) 4 minutes on each side or until done. Let stand 10 minutes before slicing.
4. Arrange baby spinach on a large serving platter. Top evenly with mango slices, onion slices, and sliced chicken. Sprinkle with crumbled goat cheese, raspberries, and chopped pistachio nuts. Serve with Fresh Basil Vinaigrette.

Citrus Marinade:

MAKES 1 CUP; **PREP:** 5 MIN.

¾ cup fresh orange juice
2 Tbsp. chopped fresh basil
2 Tbsp. lime juice
2 Tbsp. extra-virgin olive oil
1 garlic clove, crushed
½ tsp. dried crushed red pepper
¼ tsp. salt

1. Whisk together all ingredients.

Fresh Basil Vinaigrette:

MAKES 1 CUP; **PREP:** 5 MIN.

¼ cup chopped fresh basil
¼ cup raspberry vinegar
1 tsp. Dijon mustard
1 garlic clove, chopped
¼ tsp. salt
¼ tsp. pepper
¾ cup extra-virgin olive oil

1. Process first 6 ingredients in a blender until smooth. With blender running, gradually add oil in a slow, steady stream; process until smooth.

Sensational Salsa

Treat your party guests (and your chips) to these fresh, flavor-packed dips.

Whether you're hosting a Super Bowl bash or simply need a few low-fuss party ideas, these fantastic salsas—developed by Test Kitchens Professional Marian Cooper Cairns—will deliver big impact. Most can be made ahead, and they all show off this traditional dip in tasty new ways.

Try serving a variety of salsas and chips for a salsa bar, or use some of the dips here to round out an appetizer menu. Tame the heat with a dab of guacamole and one of the thirst-quenching beverages we've included.

Test Kitchens Notebook

Salsa Secrets
Some people shy away from homemade salsa because of time-consuming chopping, but many of these recipes involve little or no chopping. For the recipes that do, you can use a food processor to chop the tomatoes. If you use your food processor to chop herbs and garlic, chop them before you do the tomatoes. For other types of ingredients, it's best to chop them by hand so that you have better control of the size and shape of the pieces. Dice onion by hand, as food processors release so much of the juices that they become overpowering.

—**MARION MCGAHEY,** ASSISTANT FOOD EDITOR

Bacon-and-Greens Salsa
make ahead
MAKES 4 CUPS; **PREP:** 15 MIN.,
COOK: 22 MIN.

Warm salsa? You bet. It's just right for chilly weather. We loved the salsa with pork rinds and sweet potato chips. It's also tasty over cream cheese (a great idea for leftovers). You can prepare the recipe up to a day ahead—just reheat before serving.

8 bacon slices
1 (16-oz.) package frozen mixed greens, thawed and drained
½ medium-size sweet onion, chopped
1 tsp. minced garlic
1½ cups frozen corn, thawed
1 serrano chile pepper, minced
¼ tsp. salt
¼ tsp. pepper
2 Tbsp. cider vinegar
Pork rinds
Sweet potato chips
Hot sauce

1. Cook bacon in a large skillet over medium-high heat 7 to 9 minutes or until crisp; remove bacon, and drain on paper towels, reserving 2 Tbsp. drippings in skillet. Crumble bacon.
2. Sauté greens, onion, and garlic in hot drippings 7 to 10 minutes or until tender. Stir in corn and next 3 ingredients, and cook 3 minutes or until thoroughly heated. Remove from heat, and stir in vinegar. Sprinkle with bacon. Serve warm with pork rinds, sweet potato chips, and hot sauce.

Red Pepper-Black-eyed Pea Salsa

fast fixin's • make ahead

MAKES 3 CUPS; **PREP:** 20 MIN.

This salsa is terrific with your favorite tortilla chips. It's also a tasty, good-for-you topping to spoon over grilled chicken or fish for an impressive presentation.

1 (15.8-oz.) can black-eyed peas, rinsed and drained
1 (12-oz.) jar roasted red bell peppers, finely chopped
3 green onions, thinly sliced
1 Tbsp. chopped fresh parsley
1 Tbsp. chopped fresh oregano
2 Tbsp. lemon juice
1½ tsp. hot sauce
¾ tsp. ground cumin
¼ tsp. salt
¼ tsp. pepper

1. Stir together all ingredients in a large bowl. Cover and chill until ready to serve.

Two-Ingredient Guacamole

fast fixin's

MAKES 2½ CUPS; **PREP:** 5 MIN.

2 (8-oz.) packages refrigerated guacamole
¾ cup refrigerated salsa

1. Stir together both ingredients. Serve immediately.
Note: For testing purposes only, we used AvoClassic guacamole and Garden Fresh Gourmet Jack's Special Medium Salsa.

Fast Fix-ups for Jarred Salsa

Tropical Salsa: Stir together 1 (17.5-oz.) jar fire-roasted salsa, 1 cup finely chopped pineapple, ½ cup canned black beans, and ½ tsp. ground cumin. Makes 3 cups. Prep: 10 min.

Smoky Salsa: Process 1 (16-oz.) jar medium salsa with ¼ cup firmly packed fresh cilantro leaves, 1 to 2 chipotle peppers in adobo sauce, and 1 Tbsp. lime juice 10 seconds or until smooth. Makes 1½ cups. Prep: 5 min.

Chunky Salsa Verde: Stir together 1 (11.5-oz.) jar salsa verde; 1 avocado, diced; ½ cup chopped green tomato; and ¼ cup chopped fresh cilantro. Makes 2 cups. Prep: 10 min.

Pico de Gallo

fast fixin's • make ahead

MAKES 3 CUPS; **PREP:** 20 MIN.

If you make ahead, stir in the salt just before serving. This will keep the salsa from becoming too watery.

6 plum tomatoes, chopped
½ cup finely chopped sweet onion
¼ cup chopped fresh cilantro
2 Tbsp. fresh lime juice
1 jalapeño pepper, seeded and minced
1 garlic clove, minced
½ tsp. salt

1. Stir together all ingredients. Cover and chill until ready to serve.

Pico Queso: Cook 1 lb. torn white American cheese slices and ¾ cup whipping cream in a nonstick saucepan over low heat, stirring often, 6 to 8 minutes or until cheese is melted and smooth. Stir in 1¾ cups Pico de Gallo and 1 to 2 Tbsp. hot sauce. Serve immediately, or keep warm over low heat, stirring often, for up to 30 minutes. **MAKES** 3½ CUPS. Prep: 10 min., Cook: 8 min.

Avocado-Mango Salsa

MAKES 3 CUPS; **PREP:** 20 MIN., **CHILL:** 30 MIN.

This colorful recipe is best when made no more than four hours ahead.

1 cup diced jarred mango
¾ cup diced red bell pepper
½ cup diced jicama
½ cup thinly sliced red onion
¼ cup chopped fresh cilantro
2 Tbsp. fresh lime juice
½ tsp. ground cumin
½ tsp. chili powder
Salt and pepper to taste
2 avocados, diced

1. Combine first 8 ingredients in a large bowl. Stir in salt and pepper to taste. Gently fold diced avocado into mango mixture. Cover and chill 30 minutes before serving.

Raspberry-Beer Cocktail
fast fixin's
MAKES 6 SERVINGS; **PREP:** 5 MIN.

¾ cup fresh raspberries*
3½ (12-oz.) bottles beer, chilled
1 (12-oz.) container frozen raspberry
    lemonade concentrate, thawed
½ cup vodka

1. Using the back of a spoon, mash raspberries in a bowl; transfer to a pitcher. Stir in remaining ingredients. Serve over ice.
*¾ cup thawed frozen raspberries may be substituted.

Southern Shandy
fast fixin's
MAKES 6 TO 8 SERVINGS; **PREP:** 5 MIN.

3 (12-oz.) bottles beer (not dark), chilled
4 cups lemonade, chilled
½ cup peach brandy

1. Stir together all ingredients. Serve over ice.

Zesty Santa Fe Salsa
southernliving.com favorite
MAKES 4½ CUPS; **PREP:** 15 MIN.,
COOK: 20 MIN.

Top an ordinary baked potato with this salsa, sour cream, and cheese for a super Tex-Mex meal.

1 large onion, thinly sliced
4 garlic cloves, minced
2 Tbsp. vegetable oil
1 (14.5-oz.) can petite diced tomatoes with
    chilies
½ jalapeño pepper, seeded and minced
1 tsp. chopped canned chipotle peppers in
    adobo sauce
2 tsp. adobo sauce (from canned chipotle
    peppers)
1 (15-oz.) can black beans, rinsed and
    drained
½ cup frozen whole kernel corn
¼ tsp. salt
¼ cup chopped fresh cilantro
2 Tbsp. lime juice
Garnishes: jalapeño pepper, seeded and
    sliced lengthwise, forming a fan
Tortilla or corn chips

1. Sauté onion and garlic in hot oil in a large saucepan over medium-high heat 5 minutes or until tender. Add tomatoes and next 3 ingredients; bring mixture to a boil. Reduce heat to medium low, and cook, covered, 10 minutes, stirring occasionally.
2. Process 1 cup tomato mixture in a blender until smooth, stopping to scrape down sides; return to saucepan.
3. Stir in black beans, corn, and salt; cook 3 minutes or until thoroughly heated. Stir in cilantro and lime juice. Garnish, if desired. Serve with your choice of chips.

Plenty of Pot Roast

Make the most of your slow cooker, and prepare two meals at once.

Double your dining pleasure by preparing two roasts at one time with Slow-cooker Pot Roast. Use one for supper the first night, and shred the second roast for hearty Cheesesteak-Style Sandwiches later in the week. You can also freeze the meat for up to two months to have on hand for supper anytime. And be sure to try the Italian Pot Roast, one of our favorite SouthernLiving.com recipes.

Cook's Notes

You can freeze these flavorful roasts. When you're ready to serve, thaw in the refrigerator for one to two days before reheating. To reheat, place roasts in a 13- x 9-inch baking dish. Cover with aluminum foil, and bake at 350° for 1 hour or until hot.

Slow-cooker Pot Roast
freezeable • make ahead

MAKES 4 TO 6 SERVINGS; **PREP:** 15 MIN.;
COOK: 12 HR., 10 MIN.

2 (2¼- to 2½-lb.) eye-of-round roasts,
   trimmed
2 tsp. salt
1 tsp. freshly ground black pepper
1 Tbsp. vegetable oil
1 (1-lb.) package baby carrots
1 (14.5-oz.) can petite diced tomatoes
1 cup chopped celery
1 cup beef broth
½ cup dry red wine
4 garlic cloves, chopped
1 tsp. dried thyme leaves
½ tsp. dried marjoram

1. Rub roasts evenly with 2 tsp. salt
and 1 tsp. pepper.
2. Brown roasts on all sides in hot oil
in a Dutch oven over medium-high heat
(about 10 minutes). Place roasts, side by
side, in a 6-qt. slow cooker. Add carrots
and remaining ingredients.
3. Cook, covered, on LOW 10 to 12
hours or until tender. Remove roasts
from slow cooker; shred 1 roast, and
serve with 2 cups vegetable-and-gravy
mixture. Shred remaining roast. Store
remaining roast and 2 cups vegetable-
and-gravy mixture in separate airtight
containers in refrigerator up to 3 days
or freeze up to 2 months.
— SHERI CASTLE, CHAPEL HILL, NORTH CAROLINA

Slow-cooker Chuck Roast:
Substitute 1 (3¼- to 3¾-lb.) chuck
roast, trimmed, for eye-of-round roasts;
reduce salt to 1 tsp.; dried thyme leaves
to ½ tsp.; and dried marjoram to ¼ tsp.
Prepare recipe as directed through Step
2. Cook, covered, on LOW 10 to 12
hours or until tender. Remove roast and
vegetables, and shred meat. Pour gravy
mixture from slow cooker into a 4-cup
measuring cup or fat strainer, and let
stand 15 minutes. Spoon or pour fat out
of gravy mixture in cup or fat strainer,
and discard. Serve gravy with shredded
roast and carrots.

Cheesesteak-Style Sandwiches
family favorite

MAKES 5 SERVINGS; **PREP:** 10 MIN.,
COOK: 15 MIN., **BROIL:** 3 MIN.

*Turn one of the slow-cooked roasts into
a sandwich supper. The reserved gravy
makes a great dipping sauce.*

1 medium-size sweet onion, sliced
1 small red bell pepper, sliced
1 small green bell pepper, sliced
½ tsp. vegetable oil
½ tsp. Creole seasoning
1 Tbsp. Worcestershire sauce
1 cooked and shredded Slow-cooker
   Pot Roast
5 (6-inch) hoagie rolls, split
10 provolone cheese slices (about 6 oz.)
2 cups Slow-cooker Pot Roast gravy
Potato chips
Garnish: banana peppers

1. Sauté first 3 ingredients in hot oil in
a large nonstick skillet over medium-
high heat 15 minutes or until golden
brown. Sprinkle with Creole seasoning
and Worcestershire sauce.
2. Spoon shredded pot roast and bell
pepper mixture evenly onto bottoms
of split rolls, and top with provolone
cheese; replace tops of split rolls. Place
sandwiches on a baking sheet.
3. Broil 6 inches from heat 2 to 3 minutes or until cheese is melted and tops
of rolls are toasted.
4. Microwave Slow-cooker Pot Roast
gravy in a glass measuring cup at HIGH
1 to 1½ minutes or until thoroughly
heated. Serve sandwiches with gravy
for dipping and potato chips. Garnish,
if desired.

Italian Pot Roast
southernliving.com favorite

MAKES 6 SERVINGS; **PREP:** 15 MIN.;
COOK: 6 HRS., 40 MIN.

*Chuck roast is one of the most economical
cuts of beef for pot roast, but it is a high-
fat choice. Substitute eye of round (which
is more expensive) or English shoulder
roast for a lower fat choice.*

1 (8-oz.) package sliced fresh mushrooms
1 large onion, halved and sliced
1 (2½- to 3-lb.) boneless beef chuck roast,
   trimmed
1 tsp. pepper
2 Tbsp. olive oil
1 (1-oz.) envelope dry onion soup mix
1 (14-oz.) can beef broth
1 (8-oz.) can tomato sauce
1 tsp. dried Italian seasoning
3 Tbsp. tomato paste
2 Tbsp. cornstarch
Hot cooked egg noodles

1. Place mushrooms and onion in the
bottom of a 5½-qt. slow cooker.
2. Sprinkle roast with pepper. Brown
roast on all sides in hot oil in a large
Dutch oven over medium-high heat.
Place roast on top of mushrooms and
onion in slow cooker. Sprinkle onion
soup mix evenly over roast. Pour beef
broth and tomato sauce over roast.
Cover and cook on HIGH 5 to 6 hours
or until meat shreds easily with a fork.
3. Remove roast from slow cooker, and
cut into large chunks; keep warm.
4. Skim fat from juices in slow cooker;
stir in Italian seasoning and tomato
paste. Stir together cornstarch and
2 Tbsp. water in a small bowl until
smooth; add to juices in slow cooker,
stirring until blended. Cover and cook
on HIGH 20 to 30 more minutes or
until mixture is thickened. Add roast
pieces back to slow cooker. Cover and
cook until thoroughly heated. Serve
over hot cooked egg noodles.

Spaghetti's On

Add these no-fuss weeknight staples to your family's stash of best recipes.

Good news! You can make Spaghetti With Sausage and Peppers in about 40 minutes, including prep time. Instead of chopping and blending the recipe's vegetables into the sauce, our reader's version showcases the vibrant colors and textures of the peppers and onions. Plus, if you have a picky eater in the family, the veggies are easy to remove.

Round out your menu with a side of steamed broccoli or assorted salad greens served with your favorite vinaigrette. And don't forget to include that big basket of warm garlic-cheese bread.

Spaghetti With Sausage and Peppers

family favorite • freezeable

MAKES 4 SERVINGS; **PREP:** 20 MIN.,
COOK: 20 MIN.

8 oz. uncooked spaghetti
1 (1-lb.) package mild Italian sausage, casings removed
1 medium onion, cut into eighths
1 medium-size green bell pepper, cut into strips
1 medium-size red or yellow bell pepper, cut into strips
2 to 3 garlic cloves, minced
1 Tbsp. olive oil
1 (28-oz.) can diced tomatoes with basil, garlic, and oregano
¼ tsp. salt
¼ tsp. pepper
½ cup grated Parmesan cheese

1. Prepare pasta according to package directions.

2. Meanwhile, cook sausage in a large Dutch oven over medium-high heat 8 to 10 minutes or until meat is no longer pink, breaking sausage into pieces while cooking. Remove sausage and drippings from Dutch oven, and drain well on paper towels.

3. Sauté onion and next 3 ingredients in hot oil in Dutch oven over medium-high heat 5 to 6 minutes or until vegetables are crisp-tender. Stir in tomatoes, salt, and pepper; cook 4 minutes or until thoroughly heated. Stir in sausage, pasta, and cheese. Transfer mixture to serving platter, and serve immediately.

—**RUDETTE GELISH,** PLAYA DEL REY, CALIFORNIA

Note: To freeze, prepare recipe as directed. Cool 30 minutes. Place pasta mixture in a 13- x 9-inch baking dish. Cover tightly with plastic wrap and aluminum foil. Freeze up to 2 months. Thaw in refrigerator 24 hours. Preheat oven to 350°. Remove and discard plastic wrap and aluminum foil. Cover with aluminum foil, and bake at 350° for 40 to 45 minutes or until thoroughly heated.

Turkey Spaghetti With Sausage and Peppers: Substitute 1 (1-lb.) package Italian turkey sausage for mild Italian sausage. Remove and discard casings from sausage. Increase olive oil to 2 Tbsp. Cook sausage in 1 Tbsp. hot oil as directed in Step 2. Discard any drippings in Dutch oven. Proceed with recipe as directed, sautéing onion and next 3 ingredients in remaining 1 Tbsp. oil.

Look Past the Ground Beef

Try fresh Italian sausage instead. It adds extra flavor to recipes, and you can find it in the meat case at your supermarket. If you're trying this sausage for the first time, cut through the casing lengthwise on one side of each sausage. Remove the meat, and place it in a large nonstick skillet or Dutch oven, discarding the casings. Cook the sausage over medium-high heat for a few minutes, stirring frequently, until the meat is no longer pink.

Broccoli Parmesan

southernliving.com favorite

MAKES 6 SERVINGS; **PREP:** 5 MIN.,
COOK: 16 MIN.

1 (16-oz.) package fresh broccoli flowerets
2 Tbsp. butter or margarine
3 Tbsp. chopped onion
2 Tbsp. all-purpose flour
1 tsp. chicken bouillon granules
1¾ cups milk
½ cup freshly grated Parmesan cheese
½ tsp. salt
½ tsp. pepper
½ tsp. dry mustard
¼ tsp. ground marjoram
Parmesan cheese (optional)

1. Steam broccoli, covered, in a steamer basket over boiling water 5 minutes or until crisp-tender. Keep warm.

2. Melt butter in a heavy saucepan; add onion, and sauté until tender. Add flour and bouillon granules, stirring until blended. Cook, stirring constantly, 1 minute. Gradually add milk; cook over medium heat, stirring constantly, until thickened and bubbly. Stir in ½ cup cheese and next 4 ingredients; pour over broccoli. Sprinkle with additional cheese, if desired.

—**MARILYN M. FALLIN,** ORLANDO, FLORIDA

Our Favorite Casserole

Fall in love with the ultimate comfort dishes of Texas.

Assistant Food Editor Marion McGahey admits, she's never been a huge casserole lover. While living in Texas, she was always mystified by the popularity of this Lone Star favorite. After our resident Texan and Test Kitchens Professional Vanessa McNeil Rocchio shared her family's from-scratch King Ranch Chicken Casserole recipe with our staff, she finally got it. This is the true definition of comfort food: soft, warm, cheesy layers of chicken and tortilla with a subtle hint of green chile to remind us of its origins. We even offer an equally delicious lightened version.

Pair it with your favorite salad or try Easy Spicy Caesar Salad, a tried-and-true favorite on southernliving.com.

King Ranch Chicken Casserole

family favorite •make ahead

MAKES 8 TO 10 SERVINGS; **PREP:** 30 MIN.;
COOK: 1 HR., 19 MIN.; **COOL:** 30 MIN.;
BAKE: 1 HR.; **STAND:** 10 MIN.
(Pictured on page 2)

1 (4½- to 5-lb.) whole chicken
2 celery ribs, cut into 3 pieces each
2 carrots, cut into 3 pieces each
2½ to 3 tsp. salt
2 Tbsp. butter
1 medium onion, chopped
1 medium-size green bell pepper, chopped
1 garlic clove, pressed
1 (10¾-oz.) can cream of mushroom soup
1 (10¾-oz.) can cream of chicken soup
2 (10-oz.) cans diced tomatoes and green chiles, drained
1 tsp. dried oregano
1 tsp. ground cumin
1 tsp. Mexican-style chili powder*
3 cups grated sharp Cheddar cheese
12 (6-inch) fajita-size corn tortillas, cut into ½-inch strips

1. If applicable, remove giblets from chicken, and reserve for another use. Rinse chicken.
2. Place chicken, celery, carrots, and salt in a large Dutch oven with water to cover. Bring to a boil over medium-high heat; reduce heat to low. Cover and simmer 50 minutes to 1 hour or until chicken is done. Remove from heat. Remove chicken from broth; cool 30 minutes. Remove and reserve ¾ cup cooking liquid. Strain any remaining cooking liquid, and reserve for another use.

3. Preheat oven to 350°. Melt butter in a large skillet over medium-high heat. Add onion, and sauté 6 to 7 minutes or until tender. Add bell pepper and garlic, and sauté 3 to 4 minutes. Stir in reserved ¾ cup cooking liquid, cream of mushroom soup, and next 5 ingredients. Cook, stirring occasionally, 8 minutes.
4. Skin and bone chicken; shred meat into bite-size pieces. Layer half of chicken in a lightly greased 13- x 9-inch baking dish. Top with half of soup mixture and 1 cup Cheddar cheese. Cover with half of corn tortilla strips. Repeat layers once. Top with remaining 1 cup cheese.
5. Bake at 350° for 55 minutes to 1 hour or until bubbly. Let stand 10 minutes before serving.
*1 tsp. chili powder and ⅛ tsp. ground red pepper may be substituted for Mexican-style chili powder.

Lightened King Ranch Chicken Casserole: Reduce butter to 1 Tbsp. Substitute reduced-fat soups for regular and 2% reduced-fat cheese for regular. Prepare recipe as directed through Step 4. Bake, covered, at 350° for 50 minutes; uncover and bake for 10 to 15 minutes or until bubbly. Let stand 10 minutes before serving.
Note: For testing purposes only, we used Cracker Barrel 2% Milk Natural Sharp Cheddar Cheese.

Quick-and-Easy King Ranch Chicken Casserole: Substitute 1 (2-lb.) skinned, boned, and shredded deli-roasted chicken for whole chicken, 3 cups coarsely crumbled lime-flavored white corn tortilla chips for corn tortillas, and ¾ cup chicken broth for cooking liquid. Omit celery, carrots, and salt. Prepare recipe as directed, beginning with Step 3.

Easy Spicy Caesar Salad

southernliving.com favorite
MAKES 8 SERVINGS; **PREP:** 20 MIN.

Cut rather than tear the romaine into strips; it's a technique called chiffonade. Use a vegetable peeler to cut or shave thin slices from a wedge of Parmesan cheese.

1 head romaine lettuce, cored
1 ¼ cups creamy-style Caesar dressing
1 jalapeño pepper, quartered and
    unseeded
1 Tbsp. fresh lime or lemon juice
⅔ cup shredded Parmesan cheese
1 (5.5-oz.) package gourmet Caesar
    croutons
Garnish: Parmesan cheese shavings

1. Separate lettuce into leaves; wash and pat dry with paper towels. Stack 5 leaves, and roll up tightly, beginning at 1 long end; cut crosswise into 1-inch pieces, making strips.
2. Process Caesar dressing, jalapeño pepper with seeds, and lime juice in a blender until smooth, stopping to scrape down sides. Cover and chill until ready to serve.
3. Place romaine strips and ⅔ cup shredded cheese in a large bowl; drizzle with dressing mixture, and gently toss until coated. Sprinkle with croutons, and serve immediately. Garnish, if desired.
Note: For testing purposes only, we used Wishbone Creamy Caesar dressing for a sweeter flavor and Ken's Steak House Creamy Caesar dressing for a tangier flavor. For the gourmet croutons, we used Cardini's Gourmet Cut Caesar Croutons.

—**JULIA MITCHELL**, LEXINGTON, KENTUCKY

Warm Breakfast Bread

Cozy up to hearty slices of this Southern favorite without guilt.

Great flavor doesn't have to mean full fat. The secret to these lightened banana-nut breads is reduced-fat cream cheese beaten with a little butter for a moist bite every time. Use the recipe for Cream Cheese-Banana-Nut Bread (featured on page 43) as a starting point for these tasty combinations, and enjoy the goodness.

Toasted Coconut-Cream Cheese-Banana-Nut Bread: Reduce pecans to 1 cup. Prepare recipe as directed through Step 1, toasting (on page 43) all pecans. Remove and reserve ¼ cup toasted pecans. Proceed as directed through Step 3, omitting pecans sprinkled over batter. Bake as directed. Meanwhile, cook ¼ cup fat-free evaporated milk, 2 Tbsp. granulated sugar, 2 Tbsp. brown sugar, and 1 Tbsp. butter in a small saucepan over medium heat, stirring constantly, 3 to 4 minutes or until bubbly. Remove from heat. Stir in ¼ cup sweetened flaked coconut, reserved toasted pecans, and ½ tsp. vanilla extract. Remove bread from oven; immediately spread tops lightly with coconut mixture. Broil 5½ inches from heat 2 to 3 minutes or until topping starts to lightly brown. Cool in pans on wire racks 20 minutes. Remove from pans to wire racks; cool 30 minutes before slicing.

Cinnamon-Cream Cheese-Banana-Nut Bread: Prepare recipe (on page 43) as directed through Step 3, omitting pecans sprinkled over batter. Stir together ¼ cup firmly packed brown sugar, ¼ cup chopped pecans (not toasted), 1½ tsp. all-purpose flour, 1½ tsp. melted butter, and ¼ to ½ tsp. ground cinnamon. Lightly sprinkle mixture over batter in pans. Bake and cool as directed.

Peanut Butter-Cream Cheese-Banana-Nut Bread: Prepare recipe (on page 43) as directed through Step 3, omitting pecans sprinkled over batter. Combine ¼ cup all-purpose flour and ¼ cup firmly packed brown sugar in a small bowl. Cut in 2 Tbsp. creamy peanut butter and 1½ tsp. butter with a pastry blender or fork until mixture resembles small peas. Lightly sprinkle mixture over batter in pans. Bake and cool as directed.

Always in Season

Frozen vegetables are one of our favorite time-saving shortcuts. Neatly trimmed and perfectly chopped, they offer consistent quality year-round. Processed soon after harvest, frozen vegetables often exceed the nutritional value of fresh.

The trick to preparing fresh-tasting frozen vegetables is all in the timing. Regardless of the method, it's important not to overcook them. The flavor and texture of the new steam-in-bag frozen vegetables (that go from freezer to microwave to table in less than five minutes) received top ratings in our Test Kitchens. Quickly sautéing frozen vegetables in a teaspoon of hot oil in a large skillet over medium-high heat also helps keep their color and crunch.

In this speedy recipe, the natural sweetness of fresh pears transforms frozen green beans into a spectacular side dish.

Sautéed Green Beans and Pears: Prepare 1 (12-oz.) package frozen steam-in-bag whole green beans according to package directions. Meanwhile, sauté 2 peeled and sliced pears with 2 Tbsp. each of melted butter, brown sugar, and balsamic vinegar in a large skillet over medium-high heat 5 minutes or until crisp-tender. Stir in hot green beans, and sprinkle with salt and freshly ground pepper to taste. **MAKES** 6 SERVINGS;. PREP: 10 MIN., COOK: 5 MIN.

Citrus Power This month, we begin using the term "zest" instead of "grated rind" in our ingredient lists. Most of you already know that zest is the grated outermost layer of citrus fruit, and we agree it's a culinary term that deserves its place on our pages. Thanks for changing with us.

Fast and Healthy

Create your own flavorful medley of fresh or frozen vegetables with the new microwavable steaming bags from Ziploc and Glad. Instructions are printed right on the bag; just fill, cook, and serve.

Steaming vegetables in the microwave requires little, if any, extra liquid, allowing the nutrients to remain in the food rather than leach out into the water, as they do when cooked conventionally. Try combining fresh-cut carrots and sweet potatoes with a few pieces of sliced ginger. Discard the ginger after steaming, and mash the mixture together with a little butter, brown sugar, and cinnamon.

Choosing Sides

Keep these tips in mind the next time you buy frozen vegetables.

- Read nutritional labels. Some frozen vegetable medleys contain additives or artificial flavors. They can also be deceptively high in fat, calories, and sodium.
- Frozen vegetables labeled Grade A by the USDA are the most tender and flavorful. Less expensive Grade B vegetables are more mature but still a quality buy. Super-thrifty Grade C vegetables are best used in long-simmering soups or stews.
- Most frozen vegetables are blanched during processing so there's no need to precook them before adding to casseroles. Just place them in a colander, and run under cold water to thaw.
- Frozen vegetables are a terrific addition to salads. Steam only until crisp-tender; immediately plunge into ice water to stop the cooking process, and drain well. To prevent the color of green veggies from fading, season with lemon juice or vinegar just before serving.

Take the Party Outside

Welcome the season with a doable yet impressive menu.

We think an outdoor supper is the way to celebrate the first pleasures of spring. Start with tangy, no-cook Avocado Soup, and then fire up the grill to prepare a succulent pork tenderloin and fabulous side dish of Grilled Fennel and Radicchio. You may be new to this vegetable combination, but after tasting it, you'll rush back for seconds. The rich, nutty flavor of Creamy Gruyère Grits is the perfect accompaniment to these savory items. And last but not least, Strawberry-Orange Trifle will bring lots of applause. All the recipes have short prep times (15 minutes or less), and some can be made ahead.

Avocado Soup With Marinated Shrimp

MAKES 8 TO 10 APPETIZER SERVINGS;
PREP: 15 MIN., **CHILL:** 1 HR.,
STAND: 15 MIN.

This dish is a cinch to prepare because it requires no cooking. Instead of bowls, consider using martini glasses or other fun glassware for serving.

3 large avocados, cut into chunks
2 (14-oz.) cans vegetable broth
¼ tsp. ground red pepper
1 tsp. salt, divided
½ cup buttermilk
4 Tbsp. fresh lemon juice, divided
¼ cup off-dry white wine (Riesling) (optional)
½ lb. medium-size peeled, cooked shrimp
1 Tbsp. olive oil
1 tsp. lemon zest
Garnish: chopped fresh chives

1. Process first 3 ingredients and ¼ tsp. salt in a blender until smooth, stopping to scrape down sides.
2. Transfer avocado mixture to a bowl; stir in buttermilk, 3 Tbsp. lemon juice, and, if desired, wine until smooth. Place plastic wrap directly on soup, and chill at least 1 hour or up to 4 hours.
3. During last 15 minutes of chill time for avocado mixture, combine shrimp, olive oil, lemon zest, and remaining 1 Tbsp. lemon juice and ¾ tsp. salt, and let stand 15 minutes.
4. Ladle soup into small bowls, and top each with shrimp. Garnish, if desired.

—**SHARON WOOD**, DALLAS, TEXAS

Grilled Honey-Mustard Pork Tenderloin

make ahead

MAKES 8 SERVINGS; **PREP:** 10 MIN.,
CHILL: 2 HR., **GRILL:** 30 MIN.,
STAND: 10 MIN.

The longer you marinate the pork, the more flavor it will absorb. Don't marinate it for more than 8 hours or the marinade may begin to break down the texture of the meat.

2½ lb. pork tenderloin
½ cup chopped fresh parsley
½ cup red wine vinegar
¼ cup olive oil
¼ cup honey
3 Tbsp. country-Dijon mustard
2 garlic cloves, minced
1 Tbsp. kosher salt
1½ tsp. coarsely ground pepper

1. Remove silver skin from tenderloin, leaving a thin layer of fat covering the tenderloin.
2. Stir together chopped parsley and next 7 ingredients until blended. Pour mixture in a large, shallow dish or zip-top plastic freezer bag; add pork, cover or seal, and chill at least 2 hours or up to 8 hours, turning occasionally. Remove pork, discarding marinade.
3. Preheat grill to 350° to 400° (medium-high). Grill tenderloin, covered with grill lid, 8 to 10 minutes on all sides or until a meat thermometer inserted into thickest portion registers 150° to 155°. Remove tenderloin from grill, and let stand 10 minutes before slicing.

—**JAN DOWNS**, SHREVEPORT, LOUISIANA

Creamy Gruyère Grits

fast fixin's

MAKES 8 SERVINGS; **PREP:** 10 MIN., **COOK:** 20 MIN.

1 tsp. salt
1¼ cups uncooked quick-cooking grits
1 (8-oz.) block Gruyère cheese, shredded*
½ cup half-and-half
1 Tbsp. butter
¼ tsp. pepper

1. Bring 5¼ cups water and 1 tsp. salt to a boil in a medium saucepan over medium-high heat; gradually whisk in 1¼ cups grits, and bring to a boil. Reduce heat to medium-low, and simmer, whisking occasionally, 12 to 15 minutes or until thickened. Whisk in shredded Gruyère cheese and remaining ingredients until cheese is melted and mixture is blended.
*1 (8-oz.) block Swiss or white Cheddar cheese, shredded, may be substituted.

Grilled Fennel and Radicchio

MAKES 8 SERVINGS; **PREP:** 15 MIN., **STAND:** 5 MIN., **GRILL:** 16 MIN.

4 fennel bulbs
3 heads radicchio
½ cup orange juice
2 garlic cloves, minced
1½ tsp. sugar
½ tsp. freshly ground pepper
¾ tsp. salt
½ cup extra virgin olive oil
Vegetable cooking spray

1. Cut fennel bulbs lengthwise into ½-inch-thick slices, keeping core (root end) intact. Cut radicchio into eighths, keeping core (root end) intact. Place fennel and radicchio in a single layer in an aluminum foil-lined jelly-roll pan.
2. Whisk together orange juice, next 3 ingredients, and ½ tsp. salt. Gradually whisk in oil. Reserve ½ cup vinaigrette for later use. Drizzle remaining vinaigrette over fennel and radicchio,

and sprinkle with remaining ¼ tsp. salt. Let stand 5 minutes.
3. Coat cold cooking grate with cooking spray, and place on grill. Preheat grill to 350° to 400° (medium-high). Place fennel on cooking grate, and grill, covered with grill lid, 5 to 7 minutes on each side; remove fennel. Add radicchio, and grill, covered with grill lid, 1 to 2 minutes. Toss fennel and radicchio with reserved ½ cup vinaigrette.

—**ANN MARIE CALLAHA**, ARVADA, COLORADO

Strawberry-Orange Trifle

make ahead

MAKES 8 TO 10 SERVINGS; **PREP:** 15 MIN., **STAND:** 10 MIN., **CHILL:** 1 HR.

This tasty dessert starts with no-cook custard enriched with store-bought lemon curd.

1 qt. strawberries, halved
4 oranges, sectioned and halved
2 cups orange liqueur or orange juice
3 Tbsp. sugar
1½ cups whipping cream
1 (11.3-oz.) jar lemon curd
1½ sleeves shortbread cookies, crushed
Garnish: fresh mint sprigs

1. Toss together first 4 ingredients, and let stand at room temperature 10 minutes.
2. Meanwhile, beat whipping cream and lemon curd at low speed with an electric mixer until blended. Gradually increase mixer speed, beating until medium peaks form.
3. Layer one-third each of fruit mixture and curd mixture in a large bowl. Top with half of crushed cookies. Repeat layers once. Top with remaining one-third fruit mixture and curd mixture. Cover and chill at least 1 hour or up to 8 hours. Garnish, if desired.
Note: For testing purposes only, we used Keebler Sandies Simply Shortbread cookies.

GET INSPIRED

Easy Flatbread

MAKES 8 SERVINGS; **PREP:** 15 MIN., **BAKE:** 12 MIN.

Try these yummies. They'll be great with your next pasta dish or dinner salad.

Parmesan-Parsley Biscuit Flatbreads: Preheat oven to 400°. Separate 1 (16.3-oz.) can refrigerated jumbo biscuits into individual rounds. Pour 2 Tbsp. olive oil onto a baking sheet. Dip both sides of each biscuit round in oil, and arrange on baking sheet. Using fingertips, press each biscuit into a 4-inch free-form flat circle. Sprinkle each flattened biscuit with 1 Tbsp. freshly grated Parmesan cheese, 1½ tsp. chopped fresh parsley, and a pinch of kosher salt and freshly ground pepper. Bake at 400° for 10 to 12 minutes or until golden brown. Cut into strips.

Rosemary-Garlic Biscuit Flatbreads: Omit the Parmesan cheese and parsley, and then prepare the recipe as directed. Sprinkle the biscuits evenly with 2 tsp. chopped fresh rosemary and 2 minced garlic cloves.
Note: For testing purposes only, we used Pillsbury Homestyle Buttermilk Grands! Refrigerated Biscuits.

Tempting Two-Bite Desserts

End your meal on a sweet but sensible note with these lavishly satisfying treats.

Chocolate-Coffee Cheesecake Tartlets

make ahead

MAKES 15 TARTLETS; **PREP:** 30 MIN., **BAKE:** 12 MIN., **CHILL:** 2 HR.

If you plan to make these ahead, save the plastic tart shell packaging for storing the prepared tartlets.

2 Tbsp. slivered almonds
1 (2.1-oz.) package frozen mini-phyllo pastry shells, thawed
2 Tbsp. heavy cream, divided
½ tsp. instant espresso powder
1 (3-oz.) package cream cheese, softened
3 Tbsp. powdered sugar
2 Tbsp. light brown sugar
1 oz. bittersweet chocolate

1. Preheat oven to 350°. Place almonds in a single layer in a shallow pan. Bake at 350°, stirring occasionally, 5 to 7 minutes or until lightly toasted and fragrant.
2. Place thawed pastry shells on a baking sheet, and bake at 350° for 3 to 5 minutes or until crisp.
3. Stir together 1 Tbsp. cream and ½ tsp. espresso powder in a small microwave-safe ramekin or cup. Microwave at HIGH 10 seconds; stir until espresso is dissolved.
4. Beat cream cheese and sugars at medium-high speed with an electric mixer until smooth. Gradually add espresso mixture, and beat 30 seconds or until creamy and light. Spoon 1 rounded teaspoonful into each phyllo shell.
5. Microwave chocolate and remaining 1 Tbsp. cream in a small microwave-safe ramekin or cup at HIGH 20 seconds, stirring after 10 seconds and at end until smooth. Spoon ¼ tsp. chocolate mixture over each tart. Top immediately with almonds. Cover and chill 2 hours or up to 24 hours.

—RECIPE DEVELOPED BY **MARIAN COOPER CAIRNS**

Raspberry Tiramisù Bites

make ahead

MAKES 8 SERVINGS; **PREP:** 30 MIN., **CHILL:** 2 HR.

There are crisp Italian cookies also called ladyfingers, but be sure to use soft ones in this recipe. Look for them in the bakery or produce section of your supermarket. (Pictured on page 7)

3 Tbsp. seedless raspberry preserves
1 Tbsp. orange liqueur
1 (3-oz.) package cream cheese, softened
¼ cup sugar
½ cup heavy cream
8 ladyfingers, halved crosswise
8 fresh raspberries
Garnish: fresh mint sprigs

1. Microwave raspberry preserves in a small microwave-safe bowl at HIGH 20 seconds. Stir in liqueur.
2. Beat cream cheese and sugar at medium speed with an electric mixer until creamy (about 1 minute).
3. Beat heavy cream with an electric mixer until soft peaks form. Fold into cream cheese mixture. Spoon into a zip-top plastic bag. (Do not seal.) Snip 1 corner of bag with scissors to make a hole (about ½ inch in diameter).
4. Press 1 ladyfinger half onto bottom of 1 (1½-oz.) shot glass. Repeat procedure with 7 more shot glasses. Drizzle about ½ tsp. raspberry mixture into each glass. Pipe a small amount of cream cheese mixture evenly into each glass. Repeat procedure with remaining ladyfingers, raspberry mixture, and cream cheese mixture. Top each glass with 1 raspberry. Cover and chill 2 hours. Garnish, if desired.

— **STEPHANIE HAWKINS,**
CHARLESTON, SOUTH CAROLINA

Test Kitchens Tips

- A hand mixer works great for these small desserts, so you won't need to pull out the heavy equipment.
- Store tightly wrapped leftover ladyfingers in the freezer. Or toast them, and top with ice cream and fudge sauce for a spur-of-the-moment dessert.
- Toast more almonds than you'll need for the tartlets. Store extra almonds in a plastic container in the freezer.

Scout-Approved Sweets

Save a few extra boxes of these seasonal cookies, and create desserts galore.

Leftover Girl Scout cookies are a rare find, but it turns out those crumbs can create some pretty terrific desserts. You'll want to make sure you save some for these exciting recipes developed by Test Kitchens Professional Kristi Michele Crowe.

Samoas Ice-cream Truffles

family favorite • make ahead

MAKES 16 TRUFFLES; **PREP:** 25 MIN., **STAND:** 15 MIN., **FREEZE:** 30 MIN.

1 pt. vanilla ice cream
Parchment paper
8 coconut-chocolate cookies

1. Let ice cream stand at room temperature 15 minutes to soften.
2. Meanwhile, line a baking sheet with parchment paper, and place in freezer.
3. Process cookies in a food processor 1 minute or until mixture resembles coarse crumbs. Pour cookie crumbs into a shallow dish.
4. Scoop ice cream into small balls using a 1¼-inch ice-cream scoop, and roll in cookie crumbs. Arrange on prepared baking sheet in freezer. Freeze truffles at least 30 minutes or up to 24 hours.
Note: For testing purposes only, we used Girl Scout Samoas cookies.

Trefoils Ice-cream Truffles: Substitute 1 sleeve (21 cookies) old-fashioned shortbread cookies for coconut-chocolate cookies. Proceed with recipe as directed. **Makes** 22 Truffles. Prep: 25 min., Stand: 15 min., Freeze: 30 min. **Note:** For testing purposes only, we used Girl Scout Trefoils cookies.

Do-Si-Dos Ice-cream Truffles: Substitute 1 sleeve (11 cookies) peanut butter-cream cookies for the coconut-chocolate cookies. Proceed with recipe as directed. **Makes** 22 Truffles. Prep: 25 min., Stand: 15 min., Freeze: 30 min. **Note:** For testing purposes only, we used Girl Scout Do-Si-Dos cookies.

Using a food processor is the best way to crush cookies into crumbs. All cookies, except coconut-chocolate cookies, can also be crushed in zip-top plastic bags using a rolling pin.

Peanut Butter-Chocolate Tagalongs Milk Shakes

family favorite • fast fixin's

MAKES 4 SERVINGS; **PREP:** 15 MIN.

Freeze the cookies before crushing to prevent chocolate from melting and making the crumbs stick together.

1 qt. chocolate ice cream
1 cup milk
1 (7-oz.) package chocolate-covered peanut butter cookies, frozen and crushed
Chocolate-Peanut Butter Sauce

1. Process ice cream and milk in a blender 15 to 20 seconds or until smooth, stopping to scrape down sides, if needed. Remove and reserve 1 cup crushed cookies. Fold remaining crushed cookies into ice-cream mixture.
2. Pour ice-cream mixture evenly into 4 serving glasses. Drizzle each with 2 Tbsp. Chocolate-Peanut Butter Sauce. Sprinkle with reserved crushed cookies. Serve immediately.
Note: For testing purposes only, we used Girl Scout Tagalongs cookies.

Vanilla-Banana Tagalongs Milk Shakes: Substitute vanilla ice cream for chocolate ice cream. Proceed with recipe as directed, processing 1 banana with milk and ice cream.

Chocolate-Peanut Butter Sauce:
MAKES ABOUT ½ CUP; **PREP:** 5 MIN., **COOK:** 2 MIN.

¼ cup milk
½ cup bittersweet chocolate morsels
1½ Tbsp. creamy peanut butter
2 tsp. sugar

1. Combine milk and morsels in a small saucepan. Cook over low heat, whisking constantly, 2 minutes or until smooth. Remove from heat, and whisk in peanut butter and sugar until well blended.

Thin Mints Cheesecake

family favorite • make ahead

MAKES 16 SERVINGS; **PREP:** 25 MIN.; **BAKE:** 1 HR., 15 MIN.; **COOL:** 1 HR.; **CHILL:** 8 HR.; **STAND:** 30 MIN.

Aluminum foil
1 (10-oz.) package thin mint cookies, crushed and divided
¼ cup butter, melted
4 (8-oz.) packages ⅓-less-fat cream cheese, softened
1 (8-oz.) container light sour cream
1 cup sugar
1 tsp. vanilla extract
4 large eggs
½ cup semisweet chocolate morsels

1. Preheat oven to 325°. Line bottom and sides of a 9-inch springform pan with aluminum foil, allowing 2 to 3 inches to extend over sides. Stir together 1½ cups cookie crumbs and butter; press firmly onto bottom of prepared pan.
2. Beat cream cheese at medium speed with an electric mixer until smooth. Add sour cream, sugar, and vanilla, beating well. Add eggs, 1 at a time, beating at low speed just until blended after each addition. Pour into prepared crust.
3. Microwave chocolate morsels in a microwave-safe glass bowl at HIGH 1½ minutes or until smooth, stirring at 30-second intervals. Pour melted chocolate onto center of cheesecake batter. Swirl chocolate into batter using a small spatula. (Do not overstir.)
4. Bake at 325° for 1 hour and 10 minutes to 1 hour and 15 minutes or until center is almost set. Cool on a wire rack 1 hour or until completely cool. Cover and chill at least 8 hours or up to 24 hours. Gently run a knife around outer edge of cheesecake to loosen; remove sides of pan and foil. Let stand for 30 minutes before serving. Sprinkle with remaining cookie crumbs.

Healthy Living®

Enjoy some light fare to keep you feeling
your best.

Fry With a Clear Conscience

If you think healthy eating means giving up the foods you love,
grab a plate and taste what you've been missing.

Healthy Benefits

- Catfish is one of the best sources of vitamin D, a vital nutrient that helps your body absorb and retain calcium, promoting bone health.
- Beef is a good source of nine essential nutrients. The leanest cuts, such as those used for cubed steak, average just 1 more gram of saturated fat per serving than a skinless chicken breast.
- Low-calorie, high-fiber potatoes offer vitamins C and B6 and potassium. Mashed potatoes are a favorite (especially with Chicken-fried Steak, page 64), but skip the butter, and stir in a few spoonfuls of fat-free cream cheese instead. The cheese adds richness and calcium and lowers the glycemic index of the potatoes.

Pecan-Crusted Chicken Tenders

family favorite

MAKES 8 SERVINGS; **PREP:** 15 MIN.,
BAKE: 20 MIN.

*These plump and juicy chicken tenders
are supereasy to cook for a crowd and
always a hit. A quick flip during the last
few minutes of baking ensures all-around
crispness. Don't turn them too soon, or the
coating will stick to the rack.*

16 saltine crackers, finely
    crushed
¼ cup pecans, ground
2 tsp. paprika
½ tsp. salt
½ tsp. pepper
1 egg white
Vegetable cooking spray
Parchment paper
1½ lb. chicken tenders
¼ cup all-purpose flour

1. Preheat oven to 425°. Stir together crushed crackers and next 4 ingredients.
2. Whisk egg white just until foamy.
3. Place a wire rack coated with cooking spray in a parchment paper-lined 15- x 10-inch jelly-roll pan.

TIP

Dredging food in flour or cornstarch before dipping in a binder and crumb coating seals in the moisture and adds extra crispnes to the finished product. We prefer to use all-purpose flour rather than whole wheat for dredging, which is heavier and absorbs moisture less readily.

4. Dredge chicken tenders in flour; dip in egg white, and dredge in saltine mixture. Lightly coat chicken on each side with cooking spray; arrange chicken on wire rack.
5. Bake at 425° for 18 to 20 minutes or until golden brown, turning once after 12 minutes.

Per serving: Calories 152; Fat 4.3g (sat 0.3g, mono 1.6g, poly 0.7g); Protein 19.5g; Carb 8g; Fiber 0.8g; Chol 46mg; Iron 1.2mg; Sodium 494mg; Calc 9mg

Coconut Shrimp

MAKES 4 SERVINGS; **PREP:** 20 MIN.,
BAKE: 12 MIN.

*This oven-fried favorite tops our list of
fabulous party food. Paired with a savory
sauce, it's too tempting to resist.*

1½ lb. unpeeled, large raw shrimp
Vegetable cooking spray
2 egg whites
¼ cup cornstarch
1 Tbsp. Caribbean jerk seasoning
1 cup sweetened flaked coconut
1 cup Japanese breadcrumbs (panko)
1 tsp. paprika

1. Preheat oven to 425°. Peel shrimp,
leaving tails on; devein, if desired.
2. Place a wire rack coated with cooking spray in a 15- x 10-inch jelly-roll
pan.
3. Whisk egg whites just until foamy.
4. Stir together cornstarch and jerk seasoning in a shallow dish. Stir together
coconut, Japanese breadcrumbs, and
paprika in another shallow dish.
5. Dredge shrimp, 1 at a time, in cornstarch mixture; dip in egg whites, and
dredge in coconut mixture, pressing
gently with fingers. Lightly coat shrimp
on each side with cooking spray;
arrange shrimp on wire rack.
6. Bake at 425° for 10 to 12 minutes
or just until shrimp turn pink, turning
once after 8 minutes.

Per serving: Calories 363; Fat 8.9g (sat 5.4g,
mono 0.7g, poly 1.2g); Protein 39g; Carb 28.8g; Fiber 2.6g; Chol 259mg;
Iron 4.5mg; Sodium 601mg; Calc 93mg

TIP

**Choosing the right ingredient
and technique** for a recipe is
important. A binder made with lightly
beaten egg whites works magic with
oven-fried foods. The light, coarse
texture of Japanese breadcrumbs
(panko) and crushed saltine crackers
maximizes the crunch factor of coating mixtures. After dredging, firmly
press any loose crumbs from the
coating mixture onto the food.

Rémoulade Sauce

fast fixin's • make ahead
MAKES 10 SERVINGS; **PREP:** 5 MIN.

½ cup light mayonnaise
½ cup plain nonfat yogurt
3 green onions, minced
2 Tbsp. Creole mustard
2 garlic cloves, minced
1 Tbsp. chopped fresh parsley
¼ tsp. ground red pepper

1. Stir together all ingredients until
blended. Serve immediately, or cover
and chill up to 3 days.

Per 2-Tbsp. serving: Calories 50; Fat 4g (sat 0.8g, mono 0g, poly
0g); Protein 0.7g; Carb 2.9g; Fiber 0.2g; Chol 4mg; Iron 0.2mg;
Sodium 165mg; Calc 22mg

Tartar Sauce: Omit mustard, garlic,
and parsley. Prepare recipe as directed,
stirring in ¼ cup sweet pickle relish
and 2 tsp. lemon zest.

Per serving: Calories 55; Fat 4.04g (sat 0.8g, mono 0g, poly 0g);
Protein 0.6g; Carb 4.3g; Fiber 0.2g; Chol 4mg; Iron 0.1mg; Sodium 153mg;
Calc 19mg

Honey-Mustard Sauce

fast fixin's • make ahead
MAKES 10 SERVINGS; **PREP:** 5 MIN.

*Pair this quick-to-fix dip with Coconut
Shrimp or Pecan-Crusted Chicken
Tenders.*

½ cup plain nonfat yogurt
¼ cup coarse-grained mustard
¼ cup honey
2 Tbsp. horseradish

1. Stir together all ingredients. Serve
immediately, or cover and chill up to
3 days.

Per serving: Calories 32; Fat 0g (sat 0g, mono 0g, poly 0g); Protein 0.6g;
Carb 8.2g; Fiber 0.2g; Chol 0mg; Iron 0mg; Sodium 85mg; Calc 18mg

Hooked on Flavor: Here's a terrific little recipe for pan-frying fish without a skillet full of oil. Natural sugars in paprika and cornmeal caramelize to a deep golden brown, creating a paper-thin crust that seals in the juices. We used catfish fillets, but any mild-flavored fish will be just as tasty. Amp up the flavor by replacing the salt and pepper with a spicy seasoning blend such as Creole or Caribbean jerk. Don't overcrowd the pan. If your skillet isn't large enough to hold all four fillets, just cook the fish in two batches.

TIP

The secret to pan-frying is a heavy skillet hot enough to sear the food as soon as it hits the pan. Monitor the heat, turning it down or lifting the skillet away from the burner for brief intervals, if the food is browning too quickly.

TIP

Lightly coating the food rather than the skillet or baking pan with vegetable cooking spray allows the oil to evenly cover the surface for optimum browning.

Light-and-Crispy Catfish
fast fixin's
MAKES 4 SERVINGS; **PREP:** 5 MIN.,
COOK: 8 MIN.

4 (6-oz.) catfish fillets
Salt and pepper to taste
⅓ cup yellow cornmeal
1 Tbsp. paprika
Vegetable cooking spray

1. Sprinkle catfish fillets evenly with desired amount of salt and pepper. Stir together cup yellow cornmeal and paprika in a shallow dish. Dredge catfish fillets in cornmeal mixture; coat fillets on each side lightly with vegetable cooking spray.
2. Cook in a hot skillet over medium heat 3 to 4 minutes on each side or until fish begins to flake and is opaque throughout.

Per serving: Calories 275; Fat 13.7g (sat 3.1g, mono 6.2g, poly 2.8g); Protein 27.5g; Carb 8.6g; Fiber 1.3g; Chol 80mg; Iron 1.4mg; Sodium 95mg; Calc 19mg

Chicken-fried Steak
MAKES 6 SERVINGS; **PREP:** 15 MIN.,
COOK: 8 MIN. PER BATCH
(Pictured on page 9)

6 (4-oz.) cubed steaks (1½ lb.)
½ tsp. salt
½ tsp. pepper
¼ cup all-purpose flour
½ cup egg substitute
45 saltine crackers, crushed (1 sleeve plus
    7 crackers)
Vegetable cooking spray
Cream Gravy

1. Sprinkle steaks with salt and pepper. Dredge steaks in flour; dip in egg substitute, and dredge in crushed crackers. Lightly coat steaks on each side with cooking spray.
2. Cook steaks, in batches, in a hot nonstick skillet over medium heat 3 to 4 minutes on each side or until golden, turning twice. Transfer steaks to a wire rack in a jelly-roll pan. Keep warm in a 225° oven. Serve with Cream Gravy.

Per serving (not including gravy): Calories 315; Fat 11.9g (sat 3.9g, mono 5g, poly 1.1g); Protein 29.3g; Carb 20.3g; Fiber 0.9g; Chol 65mg; Iron 4.1mg; Sodium 369mg; Calc 43mg

Cream Gravy:
family favorite • fast fixin's
MAKES 6 SERVINGS; **PREP:** 5 MIN.,
COOK: 5 MIN.

You can find jars of soup base next to the soups and bouillon cubes at the grocery store.

1½ cups 1% low-fat milk
¼ cup all-purpose flour
1 Tbsp. low-sodium jarred chicken soup
    base
½ tsp. pepper

1. In a small saucepan, gradually whisk milk into flour until smooth; cook over medium heat, whisking constantly, 3 to 5 minutes or until mixture is thickened and bubbly. Whisk in soup base and pepper.

Per ⅓-cup serving: Calories 55; Fat 0.9g (sat 0.5g, mono 0.2g, poly 0.1g); Protein 3.2g; Carb 8.3g; Fiber 0.2g; Chol 4mg; Iron 0.3mg; Sodium 126mg; Calc 77mg

Take-Out Treats

Warmer weather invites you to step outside and enjoy these healthful snacks.

Make the most of the season, and get outdoors with these nutritious and portable goodies. Grape-Mint Salsa travels easily in a large Mason jar or any container with a lid. Consider an airtight tin to keep Sugared Pita Chips from breaking. Both are perfect for picnics, camping, or a casual afternoon on the porch.

You can serve salsa chilled or at room temperature.

Healthy Benefits

- Flavonoids in grapes may help lower bad cholesterol and the risk of cardiovascular blood clots.
- Hot peppers, including jalapeños found in Grape-Mint Salsa, are a good source of vitamin A, folic acid, and vitamin C.
- Getting outside and breathing fresh air can make you feel rejuvenated and can boost your mood.

Grape-Mint Salsa
make ahead
MAKES 8 SERVINGS; **PREP:** 15 MIN.,
CHILL: 1 HR.

Serve leftover salsa over grilled meats or fish. The flavor combination makes it a versatile topping.

2 cups green seedless grapes, coarsely chopped
2 cups red seedless grapes, coarsely chopped
2 Tbsp. chopped fresh chives
2 Tbsp. chopped fresh mint
1 Tbsp. fresh lime juice
1 whole jalapeño pepper, seeded and finely chopped
Sugared Pita Chips

1. Combine first 6 ingredients in a medium bowl; cover and chill at least 1 hour. Serve with Sugared Pita Chips.

Per ½-cup serving (including chips): Calories 180; Fat 0.7g (sat 0.1g, mono 0.1g, poly 0.3g); Protein 4.6g; Carb 40.2g; Fiber 1.8g; Chol 0mg; Iron 1.6mg; Sodium 230mg; Calc 49mg

Sugared Pita Chips
fast fixin's
MAKES 8 SERVINGS; **PREP:** 10 MIN.,
BAKE: 18 MIN.

These crunchy chips are great for dipping into Grape Mint Salsa.

1 (12-oz.) package pita bread rounds
Vegetable cooking spray
1 Tbsp. sugar

1. Preheat oven to 350°. Split each pita round horizontally into 2 rounds; stack rounds, and cut into 8 wedges to make 96 triangles. Arrange triangles in single layers on baking sheets.
2. Spray pita triangles lightly with cooking spray. Sprinkle evenly with sugar.
3. Bake at 350° for 16 to 18 minutes or until crisp. Let cool completely before storing in an airtight container.

Per serving (12 pieces): Calories 123; Fat 0.5g (sat 0.1g, mono 0g, poly 0.2g); Protein 3.9g; Carb 25.3g; Fiber 0.9g; Chol 0mg; Iron 1.1mg; Sodium 228mg; Calc 37mg

• T I P •

Easily cut pita rounds into wedges for chips using kitchen shears. Split each pita into 2 rounds, stack them, and then cut stack into 8 triangles.

A Cut Above

These staff favorites deliver big flavor and value.

The supermarket meat case is full of new cuts. The meat industry is trying to deliver more value by developing moderately priced choices suited for weeknight meals. Poultry companies are also making more products available as year-round options to the big holiday bird. But learning what to buy and the best ways to cook them is a challenge. Our Food staff has been in the same boat, so we did some research to help demystify meat counter secrets. We looked to our reader files to see how you are cooking with these popular new choices and found more ideas than we can fit in one story. We had great fun at the tasting table sampling tender, juicy main dishes and swapping tips about our finds.

Pan-Seared Flat Iron Steaks

family favorite • fast fixin's

MAKES 4 SERVINGS; PREP: 10 MIN.,
COOK: 10 MIN., STAND: 5 MIN.

4 (6- to 8-oz.) flat iron steaks
1 Tbsp. dried Italian seasoning
2 tsp. lemon pepper
1 tsp. salt
1 tsp. garlic powder
½ tsp. paprika
2 Tbsp. olive oil

1. Trim steaks, if necessary. Combine Italian seasoning and next 4 ingredients; rub over steaks.
2. Heat oil in a large nonstick skillet over medium heat. Add steaks, and cook 4 to 5 minutes on each side or to desired degree of doneness. Let stand 5 minutes.

Lemon-Garlic Sirloin

family favorite • make ahead

MAKES 6 TO 8 SERVINGS; PREP: 10 MIN.,
CHILL: 5 HR., BROIL: 15 MIN.,
BAKE: 35 MIN., STAND: 5 MIN.

Sirloin is readily available in the meat section, but for a thicker portion, such as the one called for in this recipe, check with your butcher to see if you'll need to preorder it. Marinate the steak the night before for an easy entrée. This rich thick-cut steak cooks up like a premium roast and delivers a great bang for the buck.

1 (1¼-inch-thick) boneless beef top sirloin steak (about 2 to 2½ lb.)
2 garlic cloves, pressed
2 Tbsp. lemon zest
1 Tbsp. kosher salt
1 Tbsp. olive oil
1 tsp. coarsely ground pepper
1 Tbsp. finely chopped fresh flat-leaf parsley

1. Trim steak, if necessary. Combine garlic and next 4 ingredients; rub over steak. Place steak in a large, shallow dish or 2-qt. zip-top plastic freezer bag. Cover or seal, and chill at least 5 hours or up to 8 hours.
2. Remove steak from marinade, discarding marinade. Place steak in a heavy-duty aluminum foil-lined jelly-roll pan.
3. Broil 6 inches from heat 15 minutes; reduce oven temperature to 375°, and bake 30 to 35 minutes or to desired degree of doneness. Remove from oven; let stand 5 minutes before slicing. Sprinkle with 1 Tbsp. chopped parsley.

● TIP ●

Test Kitchens Professional Pam Lolley says, "I use beef shoulder tender a lot—it has a great flavor, is very tender, and is perfect for the grill. You can also buy it marinated, which is convenient." For a recipe using this cut of beef, try Honey-Balsamic Broiled Steaks (below).

Honey-Balsamic Broiled Steaks

family favorite • make ahead

MAKES 4 SERVINGS; PREP: 15 MIN.,
CHILL: 8 HR., BROIL: 16 MIN.,
STAND: 5 MIN.

1¼ to 1⅓ lb. shoulder petite tender steak
¼ cup balsamic vinegar
2 Tbsp. canola oil
1½ Tbsp. honey
2 garlic cloves, pressed
1½ tsp. chili powder
½ tsp. kosher salt
½ tsp. dried crushed red pepper
½ tsp. freshly ground pepper

1. Trim steak, if necessary, and cut into 2-inch medaillons.
2. Stir together balsamic vinegar and next 7 ingredients in a large, shallow dish or zip-top plastic freezer bag; add medaillons, turning to coat. Cover or seal, and chill 8 hours, turning once after 4 hours.
3. Remove medaillons from marinade, discarding marinade. Place on a lightly greased wire rack in a heavy-duty aluminum foil-lined roasting pan.
4. Broil 6 inches from heat 6 to 8 minutes on each side or to desired degree of doneness. Remove steaks from oven, and let stand 5 minutes.

— JESSICA JOHNSON, GREENVILLE, SOUTH CAROLINA

Maple-Mustard Broiled Steak

make ahead

MAKES 4 SERVINGS; PREP: 10 MIN.,
BAKE: 7 MIN., CHILL: 8 HR., STAND: 35 MIN.,
COOK: 10 MIN., BROIL: 20 MIN.

¼ cup chopped pecans
⅔ cup maple syrup
⅔ cup balsamic vinegar
⅓ cup Dijon mustard
3 Tbsp. fresh thyme leaves
1 (1-lb.) flat iron steak
1 tsp. kosher salt
1 tsp. ground pepper
3 oz. crumbled blue cheese

1. Preheat oven to 350°. Place pecans in a single layer in a shallow pan, and bake, stirring occasionally, 5 to 7 minutes or until toasted and fragrant.
2. Whisk together syrup and next 3 ingredients; remove and reserve half of syrup mixture. Add remaining half of mixture to a large, shallow dish or zip-top plastic freezer bag. Trim steak, if necessary, and add to dish or zip-top plastic freezer bag, turning to coat. Cover or seal, and chill 8 hours, turning once after 4 hours.
3. Remove steak from marinade, discarding marinade. Sprinkle steak with salt and pepper. Let stand at room temperature 30 minutes.
4. Cook reserved half of marinade in a small saucepan over medium heat 10 minutes or until reduced by half.
5. Place steak on a lightly greased wire rack in a heavy-duty aluminum foil-lined jelly-roll pan. Broil 6 inches from heat 8 to 10 minutes on each side or to desired degree of doneness. Remove from oven; let stand 5 minutes before slicing. Arrange steak slices on serving platter. Spoon sauce over steak, and top with toasted pecans and blue cheese.

— DIANE SPARROW, OSAGE, IOWA

MEATY FACTS

Your favorite cut may have an alias. We've included the basic name, along with names that may be used to identify the same cut of meat.

NAMES	MEAT FACTS	COOKING GUIDELINES
Traditional Cut Flat Iron Steak • Boneless Top Blade Steak • Beef Chuck Top Blade Steak • Book Steak • Butler Steak • Lifter Steak	This tender cut is considered the second-most tender beef cut after tenderloin. A thin line of connective tissue runs through the center of each steak when it is cut in the traditional manner.	It is very flavorful, but after cooking you must cut away the connective tissue that runs through the center of the steak after cooking.
New Cut Flat Iron Steak • Beef Shoulder Top Blade Steak	This steak is trimmed with the new cutting method to remove the tough connective tissue. It is sometimes cut into smaller rectangular steaks.	Steaks can vary in thickness from ¾ to 1¼ inch and are great for family or informal entertaining. They can be grilled, pan-broiled, broiled, stir-fried, or cut into pieces for kabobs.
Shoulder Petite Tender • Shoulder Petite Tender Roast • Shoulder Cut Petite Tender Steak	This boneless portion is lean, flavorful, and similar in appearance to tenderloin, only smaller. It can be cut crosswise into ½- to ¾-inch-thick medaillons.	Remove any gristle from the edge before cooking. It is best when sautéed, pan-seared, roasted, or grilled and is a good choice for entertaining.
Boneless Beef Top Sirloin Steak • Boneless Sirloin Butt Steak	Cut from the sirloin, these steaks are lean, boneless, and versatile.	This thick-cut steak is a terrific alternative to premium roasts. You may grill, pan-broil, broil, or stir-fry it.
Turkey Tenderloins	This cut is all-white breast meat sliced from the inside center of the turkey breast. It's lean, boneless, and skinless.	Tenderloins may be sautéed, roasted, broiled, stir-fried, or grilled. Do not overcook, or the meat will be dry and rubbery.
Turkey Drumsticks	This all-dark meat cut is sold bone-in or boneless.	Drumsticks are best braised, roasted, or grilled. They are not as tender as the tenderloin, so you'll need to cook them longer.

Turkey tenderloins are the perfect option for quick-to-fix meals. This lean choice can be cooked in a variety of ways (see "Meaty Facts" on previous page), making it ideal for just about any occasion. Remember, this is a lean cut of meat, so you'll want to cook it just until it's no longer pink in the center. You can store cooked turkey in a zip-top plastic freezer bag in the freezer for up to three months—it's on hand to add to prepared pasta, salads, or soup.

Turkey Medaillons With Parsley Sauce

family favorite • make ahead

MAKES 4 SERVINGS; **PREP:** 20 MIN.,
COOK: 30 MIN.

To get a head start on this recipe, prepare the turkey as directed in Step 1. Place turkey in a zip-top plastic freezer bag, and chill 24 hours.

1 lb. turkey tenderloins
Heavy-duty plastic wrap
5 Tbsp. butter, divided
2 garlic cloves, minced
1 cup whipping cream
2 Tbsp. dry white wine
½ tsp. salt
½ tsp. pepper
¼ cup shredded Parmesan cheese
2 Tbsp. chopped fresh parsley

1. Cut turkey into ½-inch slices. Place medaillons between 2 sheets of heavy-duty plastic wrap, and flatten to ⅛-inch thickness, using a rolling pin or flat side of a meat mallet.
2. Melt 2 Tbsp. butter in a large skillet over medium-high heat. Add turkey; cook, in batches, 2 to 3 minutes on each side or until lightly browned. Remove turkey from skillet, and keep warm. Reduce heat to medium.

3. Melt remaining 3 Tbsp. butter with garlic in skillet over medium heat; cook 1 minute or until lightly browned. Stir in cream and next 3 ingredients. Bring to a boil, and cook, stirring occasionally, 10 to 12 minutes or until reduced by half. Stir in cheese. Spoon sauce over turkey. Sprinkle with parsley, and serve immediately.

— JEAN HART, NEW BERN, NORTH CAROLINA

Oven-Barbecued Turkey Drumsticks

family favorite

MAKES 4 SERVINGS; **PREP:** 15 MIN.;
COOK: 15 MIN.; **BAKE:** 1 HR., 30 MIN.

Turkey drumsticks are a favorite with kids. For family suppers, plan on one drumstick for two youngsters and a drumstick apiece for teenagers or adults. Serve them with curly fries for a simple, kid-friendly dinner.

1½ cups ketchup
½ cup lite soy sauce
¼ cup firmly packed brown sugar
2 tsp. Worcestershire sauce
2 garlic cloves, pressed
1 bay leaf
2 tsp. hot sauce
4 fresh turkey drumsticks (about 3 lb.)

1. Preheat oven to 350°. Stir together ketchup and next 6 ingredients in a 1-qt. saucepan over medium-high heat. Bring to a boil; reduce heat to low, and simmer, stirring occasionally, 10 minutes.
2. Place drumsticks in an 11- x 7-inch baking dish. Pour 1 cup ketchup mixture evenly over drumsticks. Bake, covered, at 350° for 1 hour; uncover, top with remaining 1 cup sauce, and bake 30 more minutes or until fork tender.
Note: To make ketchup sauce ahead, prepare as directed in Step 1. Cool sauce, pour into a 1-qt. airtight container, and chill for up to 2 days.

Grilled Turkey Drumsticks

southernliving.com favorite

MAKES: 8 SERVINGS; **PREP:** 15 MIN,
GRILL: 1 HR., 30 MIN; **CHILL:** 8 HR.

4 turkey drumsticks
¼ cup butter or margarine, melted
⅓ cup vegetable oil
⅓ cup dry sherry
⅓ cup soy sauce
1 garlic clove, minced
¼ cup chopped onion
¼ cup chopped fresh parsley
¼ tsp. salt
¼ tsp. pepper

1. Place turkey drumsticks in a large shallow dish or heavy-duty zip-top plastic bag.
2. Combine butter and next 8 ingredients, stirring well. Pour over drumsticks; cover or seal, and chill 8 hours, turning occasionally.
3. Drain drumsticks, reserving marinade. Wrap each drumstick and ¼ cup marinade in heavy-duty aluminum foil.
4. Grill, covered with grill lid, over medium heat (300° to 350°) about 1 hour, turning turkey after 30 minutes. Remove foil, reserving marinade. Return drumsticks to grill, and continue cooking 20 to 30 minutes, basting frequently with reserved marinade.

Try These Skillet Cakes

Salmon is the key ingredient that makes them irresistible. They were devoured at our tasting table.

Salmon patties—you may know them as the slightly rounder croquettes—are among Senior Writer Donna Florio's favorite casual entrées. They offer simplicity, health benefits, and economy. Reader Kathy Reeme took basic croquettes to new heights with cornmeal mix and buttermilk, as well as an easy drop-and-fry cooking method. The crunchy and delicious results can be on the table in 25 minutes—assuming your family doesn't eat them all first.

Basic Salmon Croquettes

MAKES 4 TO 6 SERVINGS; **PREP:** 10 MIN.,
FRY: 6 MIN. PER BATCH

You can mix up the batter a few hours before you plan to cook these. Serve them with grits or cooked white rice and hot sauce. Or you can pair them with Lemon-Caper Cream as appetizers or with salad and a starch for a laid-back supper.

1 (14-oz.) can pink salmon
1 large egg, lightly beaten
⅓ cup cornmeal mix
½ cup buttermilk
2 Tbsp. self-rising flour
⅛ tsp. garlic salt
2 cups vegetable oil
Lemon-Caper Cream

1. Drain salmon; remove skin and bones, and flake. Place salmon in a medium bowl. Stir in egg and next 4 ingredients until blended. (Batter will be wet.)
2. Drop salmon mixture by table-spoonfuls into hot oil in a large skillet over medium-high heat, and slightly flatten with a fork. Fry, in batches, 2 to 3 minutes on each side or until golden. Drain on paper towels. Keep warm on a wire rack in a jelly-roll pan in a 200° oven. Serve with Lemon-Caper Cream.

—KATHY REEME, VILLA RICA, GEORGIA

Lemon-Caper Cream:
MAKES 1 CUP; **PREP:** 10 MIN.

1. Stir together ¾ cup light sour cream; 2 Tbsp. capers, drained; 2 Tbsp. mayonnaise; ½ tsp. lemon zest; and 1 tsp. lemon juice. Season with salt and pepper to taste. Store in an airtight container in refrigerator up to 2 weeks.

Salmon Beignets With Red Pepper Rémoulade
MAKES 6 MAIN-DISH OR 12 APPETIZER SERVINGS; **PREP:** 25 MIN., **COOK:** 12 MIN., **STAND:** 20 MIN, **FRY:** 4 MIN. PER BATCH

Save money by substituting 1 (14-oz.) can pink salmon, drained, with skin and bones removed.

½ cup finely chopped sweet onion
¼ cup finely chopped green onions (about 3 green onions)
2 garlic cloves, minced
½ tsp. salt
½ tsp. ground red pepper
1 Tbsp. vegetable oil
1 lb. skinless salmon fillets
2 cups all-purpose baking mix
2 large eggs
¾ cup milk
2 cups vegetable oil
Red Pepper Rémoulade

1. Sauté first 5 ingredients in 1 Tbsp. hot oil in a medium skillet over medium heat 3 minutes or until onion is tender. Place onion mixture in a bowl.
2. Add salmon to skillet; cook, covered, 9 minutes or until almost done. Remove to a plate, and let stand 20 minutes. Flake salmon; stir into onion mixture.
3. Whisk together baking mix, eggs, and milk in a large bowl just until blended; stir in salmon mixture.
4. Drop salmon mixture by tablespoonfuls into hot oil in a large skillet over medium-high heat. Fry, in batches, 2 minutes on each side or until golden. Drain on paper towels. Keep warm on a wire rack in a jelly-roll pan in a 200° oven. Serve with Red Pepper Rémoulade.

Red Pepper Rémoulade:
make ahead
MAKES ABOUT 1¼ CUPS; **PREP:** 10 MIN.

In small amounts, anchovy paste provides a nice, non-fishy depth of flavor.

⅔ cup light mayonnaise
½ cup jarred roasted red bell pepper strips, drained
2 Tbsp. lemon juice
2 Tbsp. chopped dill pickle
1 Tbsp. capers, drained
1 Tbsp. Worcestershire sauce
1 Tbsp. Dijon mustard
2 garlic cloves, minced
1 tsp. anchovy paste (optional)

1. Process first 8 ingredients and, if desired, anchovy paste in a food processor or blender 15 seconds or until smooth. Store in an airtight container in refrigerator up to 5 days.

—DEVON DELANEY, PRINCETON, NEW JERSEY

Keep-It-Casual Italian

Let your kitchen be the dining room for this laid-back get-together.

Invite guests to slip onto barstools, put their elbows on the island, and help themselves to refreshing Lemon-Basil Antipasto. This way, you won't miss a thing as you prepare the veggie main dish of Creamy Tortellini Primavera while friends chat over the first course.

Arrange-and-serve Lemon-Basil Antipasto is fun to eat and beautiful. Place ingredients on the platter in a decorative arrangement. Cover with damp paper towels and plastic wrap, and refrigerate up to four hours. Just before guests arrive, uncover, drizzle with olive oil and lemon juice, and sprinkle on basil, salt, and pepper.

Wrap up the night in the living room with coffee or espresso and Carrot Cake Sandwich Cookies or your favorite purchased brownies or cookies.

Lemon-Basil Antipasto
fast fixin's • make ahead
MAKES 4 SERVINGS; **PREP:** 20 MIN.

Antipasto means "before the meal." Each ingredient is called an "antipasti." Provolone is usually packaged in half-moon shapes and found on the specialty cheese aisle. We prefer the taste and texture of provolone cheese labeled "sharp" (or "piquant") over low-sodium choices. We also like the mildly seasoned Genoa salami over smoky hard salami.

½ lb. sharp provolone cheese, cut into
   8 wedges
1 small zucchini, thinly sliced
8 pepperoncini peppers
4 radishes, cut into quarters
½ cup pitted kalamata olives
12 thin Genoa salami slices
2 Tbsp. extra virgin olive oil
½ medium lemon
2 Tbsp. chopped fresh basil*
¼ tsp. kosher salt
¼ tsp. freshly cracked pepper
Breadsticks, crackers, or sliced
   Italian bread

1. Arrange provolone cheese and next 5 ingredients on a serving platter; drizzle with olive oil. Squeeze juice from lemon over antipasto, and sprinkle with next 3 ingredients. Serve immediately with breadsticks, crackers, or sliced Italian bread.
*2 Tbsp. chopped fresh parsley may be substituted.

Creamy Tortellini Primavera
MAKES 4 SERVINGS; **PREP:** 15 MIN.,
COOK: 17 MIN.

Our Test Kitchens tried this pasta cooking method several times. By draining and rinsing with cold water, the tortellini will not stick together while you prepare the sauce. Pasta cooked just until firm to the bite is called "al dente."

1 (10-oz.) package refrigerated reduced-fat
   Alfredo sauce
2 Tbsp. dry white wine
¼ tsp. dried crushed red pepper
1 lb. fresh asparagus
1 (20-oz.) package refrigerated cheese-
   filled tortellini
3 garlic cloves, minced
2 Tbsp. olive oil
1½ cups sliced fresh mushrooms
½ tsp. salt
1 cup halved grape tomatoes
¼ cup freshly grated Parmesan cheese

1. Stir together first 3 ingredients. Snap off and discard tough ends of asparagus; cut into 1-inch pieces.
2. Bring 5 qt. of salted water to a boil; add tortellini, and cook 6 minutes or just until tender. (Pasta should still be firm to bite.) Drain; rinse with cold water, and drain well again. Place in a serving bowl.
3. Sauté garlic in hot oil over medium-high heat 1 minute or until garlic is lightly browned. Stir in mushrooms, asparagus, and salt; sauté 3 to 5 minutes or until asparagus is crisp-tender. Reduce heat to medium, and stir in Alfredo sauce mixture. Cook 5 minutes or until thoroughly heated.
4. Pour sauce mixture over cooked tortellini; toss gently. Sprinkle with tomatoes and Parmesan cheese. Serve immediately.

—**BRYAN LEATH**, BIRMINGHAM, ALABAMA

Note: For testing purposes only, we used Buitoni Light Refrigerated Alfredo Sauce and Buitoni Three Cheese Tortellini.

Carrot Cake Sandwich Cookies

MAKES 1 DOZEN SANDWICHES; **PREP:** 15 MIN.,
BAKE: 18 MIN., **COOL:** 15 MIN.

¾ cup grated carrots (about 2 medium
    carrots)
2 Tbsp. firmly packed dark brown sugar
½ tsp. ground ginger
½ tsp. ground cinnamon
⅓ cup raisins
1 (16.5-oz.) package refrigerated sugar
    cookie dough
Cream Cheese Icing

1. Toss together first 4 ingredients in a
large bowl. Stir raisins into carrot mixture.
2. Tear cookie dough into pieces, and stir
into carrot mixture until well combined.
3. Drop cookie dough mixture by
tablespoonfuls, 2 inches apart, onto
lightly greased baking sheets. (Dough
should make 24 cookies.)
4. Bake at 350° for 15 to 18 minutes or
until edges are crisp. Cool on baking sheets
5 minutes. Remove to wire racks, and cool
10 minutes or until completely cool.
5. Turn half of cookies over, bottom
sides up. Spread each with 1 Tbsp.
chilled Cream Cheese Icing. Top with
remaining cookies, bottom sides down,
and press gently to spread filling to
edges of cookies.

Cream Cheese Icing:

MAKES 1 CUP; **PREP:** 10 MIN., **CHILL:** 30 MIN.

5 oz. cream cheese, softened
¼ cup unsalted butter, softened
1 cup powdered sugar
½ tsp. fresh lemon juice
¼ tsp. vanilla extract

1. Beat cream cheese and butter at
medium speed with an electric mixer
until creamy.
2. Add remaining ingredients, beating
until smooth. Cover and chill 30 minutes or until spreading consistency.
Note: For testing purposes only, we
used Pillsbury Create 'n Bake Sugar
refrigerated cookie dough.

Lunch Date

Enjoy a leisurely afternoon with your friends by serving these
delicious make-ahead recipes.

Make-Ahead Lunch

SERVES 6

Spinach Lasagna Rollups

Three-Tomato Salad

Southern Sweet Tea

Spinach Lasagna Rollups

make ahead

MAKES 6 SERVINGS; **PREP:** 1 HR.,
COOK: 43 MIN., **BAKE:** 25 MIN.,
STAND: 5 MIN.

*Rolling the lasagna noodles rather
than layering them in a rectangle lends
flair. To make this dish ahead, make the
rollups through Step 5 up to 24 hours
ahead. Cover and store in the refrigerator. Let stand at room temperature 30
minutes before baking.*

14 uncooked lasagna noodles
1 large onion, finely chopped
2 tsp. olive oil
2 garlic cloves, minced
3½ Tbsp. all-purpose flour
3½ cups 1% low-fat milk
1¾ tsp. salt, divided
½ tsp. freshly ground pepper, divided
⅛ tsp. ground nutmeg
1 (16-oz.) bag frozen cut-leaf spinach,
    thawed
1 (24-oz.) container small-curd cottage
    cheese
1 cup grated part-skim mozzarella cheese
1 large egg
¼ cup freshly grated Parmesan cheese

1. Cook 7 lasagna noodles according to
package directions; remove with tongs
or a slotted spoon to a large bowl of cold
water. Repeat with remaining noodles.
Drain noodles, and arrange in a single
layer on clean kitchen towels. Cover with
plastic wrap.
2. Cook onion in hot oil in a saucepan over
medium heat, stirring occasionally, 8 minutes or until onion is caramel colored.
Add garlic, and sauté 1 minute. Reserve
¼ cup onion mixture. Whisk flour into
remaining onion mixture in saucepan,
and cook, whisking constantly, 1 minute. Gradually whisk in milk. Cook over
medium heat, whisking constantly, 8 to
10 minutes or until sauce is thickened
and bubbly. Remove from heat; stir in ¾
tsp. salt, ¼ tsp. pepper, and ⅛ tsp. nutmeg. Spoon ½ cup sauce into a lightly
greased 13- x 9-inch baking dish.
3. Drain spinach well, pressing
between paper towels.
4. Preheat oven to 425°. Stir together
spinach, cottage cheese, mozzarella
cheese, egg, reserved ¼ cup onion mixture, and remaining 1 tsp. salt and ¼
tsp. pepper.
5. Spread about 3 Tbsp. spinach mixture over 1 noodle; roll up firmly, and
place, seam side down, in prepared
baking dish. Repeat with remaining
noodles and spinach mixture. Spoon
remaining sauce over rollups, and
sprinkle with Parmesan cheese.
6. Bake at 425° for 20 to 25 minutes or
until golden and bubbly. Let stand 5
minutes before serving.

—**CAROLINE W. KENNEDY**, COVINGTON, GEORGIA

Three-Tomato Salad

fast fixin's • make ahead

MAKES 8 SERVINGS; **PREP:** 10 MIN.,
STAND: 3 HR.

You can use all red tomatoes, such as a combination of cherry, plum, and beefsteak. But add other varieties and colors, when available, for an even more beautiful presentation.

½ cup olive oil
3 Tbsp. red wine vinegar
2 tsp. dried Italian seasoning
1 tsp. sugar
1 tsp. salt
½ tsp. pepper
1 large yellow or red tomato, sliced
2 plum tomatoes, cut into wedges
1 pt. cherry tomatoes, cut in half
16 green leaf lettuce leaves
Salt and pepper to taste

1. Whisk together olive oil, red wine vinegar, and next 4 ingredients. Place tomatoes in a 2-qt. dish, and pour olive oil mixture over tomatoes. Cover and let stand 3 hours.
2. Place 2 lettuce leaves on each of 8 salad plates, and divide tomato mixture evenly among plates. Season with salt and pepper to taste.

—JACKIE GUARISCO, PORT ALLEN, LOUISIANA

Southern Sweet Tea

southernliving.com favorite

MAKES 2½ QT.; **PREP:** 5 MIN.,
COOK: 5 MIN., **STEEP:** 10 MIN.

We halved the original recipe for a smaller group, but it doubles easily. If you like tea that's really sweet, add the full cup of sugar.

2 family-size tea bags
½ to 1 cup sugar

1. Bring 3 cups water to a boil in a saucepan; add tea bags. Boil 1 minute; remove from heat. Cover and steep 10 minutes.
2. Remove and discard tea bags. Add desired amount of sugar, stirring until dissolved.
3. Pour into a 1-gal. container, and add 7 cups cold water. Serve tea over ice.

Peach Iced Tea: Combine 1½ qt. Southern Sweet Tea made with ½ cup sugar; 1 (33.8-oz.) bottle peach nectar; and ¼ cup lemon juice. Stir well. Serve over ice. **Makes** about 2½ qt.

Tea 'n' Lemonade: Combine 2 qt. Southern Sweet Tea made with ½ cup sugar; and 1 cup thawed lemonade concentrate, and stir well. Serve over ice. **Makes** 2¼ qt.

—VICKY SHERIDAN,
FOUNTAIN INN, SOUTH CAROLINA

QUICK & EASY

Fresh Tex-Mex

In 25 minutes or less, you can fill your table with the bold flavors of the Southwest.

Every now and then, we get the hunger for a mouthful of cheesy goodness and even a touch of spice. These delicious Tex-Mex dishes are full of flavor. Short ingredient lists and quick procedures make them easy to prepare.

Cheesy Black Bean Mash

fast fixin's

MAKES 4 TO 6 SERVINGS;
PREP: 15 MIN., **COOK:** 9 MIN.

This side dish can also be served as a dip with tortilla chips. Buy prechopped onion and minced garlic to make this even easier.

2 (15-oz.) cans black beans, rinsed and
    drained
¼ cup vegetable broth
1 small onion, chopped
1 jalapeño pepper, seeded and minced
1 Tbsp. olive oil
1 garlic clove, minced
½ tsp. salt
1 cup (4 oz.) shredded Mexican four-cheese
    blend

1. Process beans and broth in a food processor 10 to 15 seconds or until smooth.
2. Sauté onion and jalapeño pepper in hot oil in a large skillet 4 to 5 minutes or until tender. Add garlic, and sauté 1 minute. Add black bean puree and salt, stirring until blended. Cook, stirring frequently, 3 minutes or until bean mixture is thoroughly heated. Stir in cheese until melted. Serve immediately.

Quick Queso

fast fixin's

MAKES 6 TO 8 SERVINGS;
PREP: 10 MIN., COOK: 10 MIN.

Keep the queso warm by serving it in a small slow cooker or in a microwavable dish, so it can be easily reheated, if necessary.

2 Tbsp. butter
1 (4.5-oz.) can chopped green chiles
1 small onion, minced
2 Tbsp. all-purpose flour
1 cup milk
½ cup beer (not dark)
1 (8-oz.) block Monterey Jack cheese, shredded
1 tsp. ground cumin
¼ tsp. salt
Tortilla chips

1. Melt 2 Tbsp. butter in a large heavy saucepan over low heat; add chopped green chiles and minced onion, and cook 3 to 4 minutes or until softened. Whisk in 2 Tbsp. flour, and cook 1 minute. Whisk in milk and beer, and cook, whisking constantly, 3 to 4 minutes or until mixture is thickened. Add shredded cheese by ½ cupfuls, stirring until melted after each addition. Stir in ground cumin and salt. Serve warm with tortilla chips.

Lime Cream Sauce

fast fixin's • make ahead

MAKES ABOUT 1 CUP; PREP: 5 MIN.

Try this tangy sauce on beef, pork, or potatoes.

1 cup light sour cream
1 Tbsp. lime zest
2 Tbsp. fresh lime juice
½ tsp. salt
½ tsp. ground cumin
¼ tsp. ground pepper

1. Stir together 1 cup light sour cream and remaining ingredients in a small bowl. Serve immediately, or cover and chill up to 3 days.

Citrus-Avocado Salad With Tex-Mex Vinaigrette

southernliving.com favorite

MAKES 8 SERVINGS; PREP: 10 MIN.

Two bags of your favorite lettuce blend can be substituted for Bibb lettuce. Pomegranate seeds are a unique crunchy addition to this salad.

3 heads Bibb lettuce, torn
2 avocados, sliced
1 (24-oz.) jar refrigerated orange and grape-fruit sections, drained
Tex-Mex Vinaigrette
Garnishes: pomegranate seeds, fresh cilantro sprigs

1. Combine first 3 ingredients in a salad bowl. Toss with Tex-Mex Vinaigrette. Garnish, if desired. Serve immediately.
Note: For testing purposes only, we used Del Monte Sunfresh Citrus Salad for orange and grapefruit sections.

Tex-Mex Vinaigrette:

MAKES ⅔ CUP; PREP: 10 MIN.

½ cup fresh orange juice
¼ cup fresh lime juice
1 tsp. brown sugar
½ tsp. ground cumin
½ tsp. salt
½ tsp. pepper
⅓ cup olive oil

1. Combine first 6 ingredients in a small bowl. Whisk in oil in a slow, steady stream, whisking until smooth. Use immediately, or cover and chill up to 3 days. Whisk before serving.

Munch Madness

Tailgating around the TV has never tasted so good.

Forget being at the game—the fun is right here. Entertain your fellow fans with these mouthwatering recipes. They are based on game-day stadium favorites but have a little twist that will score winning points with any crowd.

Andouille Corn Poppers

MAKES 6 TO 8 SERVINGS; PREP: 15 MIN.,
FRY: 3 MIN. PER BATCH

These spicy, bite-size versions of corn dogs are irresistible. You'll need about 30 minutes and 1 qt. of oil for frying them.

1 (8½-oz.) package corn muffin mix
1 large egg
½ cup buttermilk
1 tsp. Creole seasoning
1 lb. andouille sausage, cut into 1-inch slices*
Peanut oil
Creole mustard

1. Whisk together corn muffin mix and next 3 ingredients. Dip sausages slices in batter, coating well.
2. Pour oil to depth of 1 inch into a Dutch oven; heat over medium-high heat to 375°. Fry sausages, in batches, 1½ minutes on each side or until golden brown. Drain on paper towels. Keep warm on a wire rack in an aluminum foil-lined jelly-roll pan in a 200° oven. Serve with mustard.

—LUCY FOLSOM, ATLANTA, GEORGIA

*1 (16-oz.) package cocktail-size smoked sausages, drained, may be substituted. For testing purposes only, we used Bryan Cocktail Smokies.

Playoff Chili

freezeable •make ahead

MAKES 14 SERVINGS (ABOUT 7 CUPS);
PREP: 25 MIN.; **COOK:** 2 HR., 15 MIN.

This chili is poured over a small, opened bag of corn chips for fun single servings.

1 lb. ground beef
1 lb. ground pork
1 large white onion, chopped
1 large green bell pepper, seeded and
    chopped
1 large red bell pepper, seeded and chopped
2 garlic cloves, minced
1 (14½-oz.) can diced tomatoes with green
    chiles
1 (12-oz.) bottle beer
1 (8-oz.) can tomato sauce
1 Tbsp. chili powder
1 tsp. ground cumin
1 tsp. sugar
1 tsp. salt
½ tsp. ground red pepper
½ tsp. black pepper
½ tsp. dried oregano
1 (16-oz.) can kidney beans, rinsed
    and drained
1 (16-oz.) can black beans, rinsed and
    drained
14 (1¼-oz.) bags corn chips
Garnishes: chopped onion, shredded
    Cheddar cheese, sour cream

1. Cook ground beef and next 5 ingredients in a Dutch oven over medium heat 10 minutes or until meat crumbles and is no longer pink. Stir in diced tomatoes with green chiles and next 9 ingredients, and bring to a boil. Cover, reduce heat to low, and simmer 1 hour and 45 minutes, stirring every 20 minutes. Add kidney beans and black beans; cover and cook 15 minutes.
2. Cut corn chip bags open at one long side. Spoon ½ cup chili on chips in each bag. Garnish, if desired.

—**DAN BUICE**, HOUSTON, TEXAS

Note: Chili may be frozen in a zip-top plastic freezer bag up to 3 months. For testing purposes only, we used Fritos Brand Original Corn Chips.

Parmesan-Black Pepper Popcorn

MAKES ABOUT 4 CUPS; **PREP:** 10 MIN.,
BAKE: 10 MIN.

1. Preheat oven to 325°. Drizzle contents of 1 (3.3-oz.) bag popped microwave popcorn (about 4 cups) with 2 Tbsp. melted butter, and sprinkle with ½ cup freshly grated Parmesan cheese and ¼ tsp. pepper. Toss gently to combine. Place in a lightly greased 15- x 10-inch jelly-roll pan, and bake at 325° for 10 minutes. Serve popcorn immediately.

Blue Cheese-Pecan Popcorn

MAKES ABOUT 4 CUPS; **PREP:** 10 MIN.,
FREEZE: 8 HR., **COOK:** 7 MIN., **BAKE:** 10 MIN.

1. Freeze 1 (4-oz.) block blue cheese for at least 8 hours or up to 24 hours. Preheat oven to 325°. Melt 2 Tbsp. butter in a small nonstick skillet over medium-low heat; add 1 cup chopped pecans, and cook, stirring often, 5 to 7 minutes or until lightly toasted and fragrant. Place contents of 1 (3.3-oz.) bag popped microwave popcorn (about 4 cups) in a 15- x 10-inch jelly-roll pan. Grate frozen cheese to equal 1 cup. Sprinkle 1 cup grated blue cheese over popcorn. Toss popcorn mixture with toasted pecans and ¼ tsp. pepper. Bake at 325° for 10 minutes. Serve popcorn immediately.

Gettin' Saucy

Sauces add a new dimension of flavor to everyday side dishes.

Pour a snappy sauce over simple vegetables, and suddenly you have something special. Traditionally used as a dip for grilled chicken and pork, Spicy Thai Peanut Sauce offers a quick way to add authentic Asian flavor to a bag of frozen stir-fry vegetables. Thinned with a little water, it even makes a terrific salad dressing.

Horseradish gives Colby-Jack Cheese Sauce an extra kick, but feel free to stir in different herbs and spices or substitute another type of cheese. For an encore presentation that will have everyone coming back for more, spoon it over a colorful medley of leftover vegetables. Sprinkle on a topping of buttered breadcrumbs or shredded cheese, and bake; or refrigerate it overnight for a great-tasting casserole that's ready to go in the oven when you get home from work.

Colby-Jack Cheese Sauce

MAKES 2 CUPS; **PREP:** 10 MIN.,
COOK: 6 MIN.

Versatile soup bases are seasoned pastes that add a big boost of concentrated flavor, similar to bouillon granules but much grander in taste.

¼ cup butter
¼ cup all-purpose flour
1 Tbsp. jarred chicken soup base
1½ cups milk
1 cup (4 oz.) shredded Colby-Jack
    cheese
1 Tbsp. horseradish
½ tsp. pepper

1. Melt ¼ cup butter in a heavy saucepan over low heat; whisk in flour and chicken soup base until smooth. Cook, whisking constantly, 1 minute. Gradually whisk in 1½ cups milk; cook over medium heat, whisking constantly, 3 to 5 minutes or until mixture is thickened and bubbly. Remove from heat, and whisk in Colby-Jack cheese, horseradish, and pepper, whisking until cheese is melted.

— **SHARON BUTERBAUGH**, AFTON, VIRGINIA

Reduced-fat Colby-Jack Cheese Sauce: Omit butter; substitute reduced-fat or fat-free milk and cheese for regular. Gradually whisk milk into flour in a heavy saucepan, whisking until smooth; cook over medium heat, whisking constantly, 3 to 5 minutes or until mixture is thickened and bubbly. Remove from heat, and whisk in chicken soup base, Colby-Jack cheese, horseradish, and pepper, whisking until cheese is melted.

Spicy Thai Peanut Sauce
MAKES 1 CUP; **PREP:** 10 MIN.

Traditionally used as a dip for grilled chicken and pork, this sauce offers a terrific way to add authentic Asian flavor to a bag of stir-fry veggies.

⅔ cup crunchy peanut butter
2 Tbsp. fresh lime juice
2 Tbsp. rice vinegar
2 Tbsp. soy sauce
2 Tbsp. dark sesame oil
2 tsp. sugar
½ tsp. ground ginger
½ tsp. garlic powder
¼ to ½ tsp. ground red pepper

1. Whisk together peanut butter, remaining ingredients, and 2 Tbsp. water until blended. Serve immediately, or cover and chill up to 7 days.

— **VANIA O'SHEA**, VIRGINIA BEACH, VIRGINIA

Sensational Breakfast

Offer a melt-in-your-mouth meal any morning of the week.

You'll jump out of bed for this amazing recipe. A down-home spin on the ever-popular eggs Benedict sandwiched between fluffy Southern-style biscuit halves, it is perfect for company or a casual, quiet morning. This dish will please anyone sitting at your table.

Spicy Ham-and-Eggs Benedict With Chive Biscuits
MAKES 4 SERVINGS; **PREP:** 15 MIN., **BAKE:** 25 MIN., **COOK:** 15 MIN.

We used frozen biscuits to save prep time on this dish.

4 frozen biscuits
2 Tbsp. butter, melted
3 Tbsp. chopped fresh chives, divided
1 (0.9-oz.) envelope hollandaise sauce mix
1 cup milk
1 Tbsp. lemon juice
¾ cup chopped lean ham
¼ to ½ tsp. ground red pepper
½ tsp. white vinegar
4 large eggs
2 cups loosely packed arugula
1 small avocado, sliced
Pepper to taste

1. Bake biscuits according to package directions. Combine melted butter and 1 Tbsp. chives; split biscuits, and brush with mixture. Place biscuits, buttered sides up, on a baking sheet, and bake at 375° for 5 minutes or until toasted.
2. Prepare hollandaise sauce mix according to package directions, using 1 cup milk and 1 Tbsp. lemon juice and omitting butter.

3. Cook ham, stirring occasionally, in a medium-size nonstick skillet over medium heat 3 to 4 minutes or until browned. Stir ham and ground red pepper into hollandaise sauce; keep warm.
4. Add water to a depth of 2 inches in a large saucepan. Bring to a boil; reduce heat, and maintain at a light simmer. Add ½ tsp. white vinegar. Break eggs, and slip into water, 1 at a time, as close as possible to surface of water. Simmer 3 to 5 minutes or to desired degree of doneness. Remove with a slotted spoon. Trim edges, if desired.
5. Place bottom biscuit halves, buttered sides up, on each of 4 individual serving plates. Top with arugula, avocado, and poached eggs. Spoon hollandaise sauce evenly on top of each egg. Sprinkle with remaining 2 Tbsp. chives and pepper to taste. Top with remaining biscuit halves, and serve immediately.

— **GLORIA BRADLEY**, NAPERVILLE, ILLINOIS

Note: For testing purposes only, we used frozen White Lily Southern Style Biscuits.

Honey-Ginger Fruit
southernliving.com favorite
MAKES 7 CUPS; **PREP:** 20 MIN.

Grape juice, honey, and ginger add punch to whatever fruit you have on hand. Serve this fruit combo alone or over yogurt or warm biscuits.

1 cup white grape juice
3 Tbsp. honey
1½ tsp. grated fresh ginger
1 pt. fresh strawberries, halved
3 oranges, sectioned
½ honeydew melon, chopped
1 cup seedless green grapes

1. Combine grape juice, honey, and ginger in a large bowl. Add remaining ingredients, tossing to coat. Serve immediately.

Spring for Flavor

Tips, tricks, and fresh ideas for foods you'll love.

Rich Rewards If you haven't tried Greek yogurt, you definitely should. You'll be hooked, as we were, with the first creamy spoonful. Topped with honey and granola, it turns fresh fruit into party fare. The only drawback is the price—but it's super-easy to make your own. Straining less expensive American yogurt removes the liquid and creates the same satiny-smooth texture and richness. Be sure to choose a brand that doesn't list gelatin as an ingredient; otherwise any type of yogurt will work, including fat-free.

Line a fine wire-mesh strainer with a paper coffee filter, and place over a deep bowl or measuring cup. Spoon yogurt into the filter; cover with plastic wrap, and chill 8 to 24 hours or until desired thickness. The longer the yogurt is strained, the thicker it becomes, eventually reaching the consistency of a soft cream cheese. After straining, it makes a terrific canvas for both sweet and savory ingredients and can be used in place of sour cream in many recipes.

Seasonal Eating There's no better time of year to enjoy fresh watercress than right now. The tender, spicy-sweet leaves add a peppery bite to salads and sandwiches. For a quick party pickup, spread garlic-and-herb cheese over toasted baguette slices; top with boiled shrimp, and tuck in a few sprigs of watercress. Try it warm as well—like spinach, it's best when barely wilted.

Shop for bright green bunches of watercress with small leaves and thin stems. Store watercress in the refrigerator with the stems in water and the leaves loosely covered with a plastic bag. When ready to serve, trim the stems, rinse with cold water, and dry with paper towels or in a salad spinner.

Posh Spice

Fresh ginger is a familiar ingredient in Asian-inspired dishes, but it also adds a spicy burst of flavor to many of our favorite Southern foods. You'll find dozens of top-rated recipes—from Fresh Ginger-and-Lemon Muffins to Bourbon-Marinated Pork Tenderloin—on myrecipes.com. Keep these tips in mind when using fresh ginger.

- **Look for fragrant, pale brown roots** with smooth skin—firm enough to make an audible snap when broken. To peel, scrape the skin gently with the side of a teaspoon, following the bumps and curves of the root. The flesh just below the skin is the most flavorful and often lost when using a vegetable peeler. A 1-inch piece yields about 1 Tbsp. minced or grated ginger.

- **Fresh ginger is added** to recipes in a number of different ways. Sliced ginger releases a subtle infusion of flavor when heated with oil or liquid. Chopped ginger delivers bold, sweet-hot bites of concentrated flavor. The juicy, paste-like consistency of finely grated ginger disperses flavor throughout the dish.

- **The flavor of dried ground ginger** can't replace that of fresh, but do try using a combination of both in baked goods.

- **Crystallized ginger,** available in the spice section, has been simmered in syrup and coated with granulated sugar. It's often used in sweet baked goods, but it's also delicious with many savory foods. Try sprinkling it over roasted root vegetables just before serving.

- **Fresh ginger contains an enzyme** that can curdle milk-based dishes and prevent gelatin from setting properly. Heat destroys the enzyme, so before using fresh ginger in recipes such as custards or congealed salads, blanch it in boiling water or microwave it at MEDIUM for just a few seconds or until hot.

Easy Springtime Party

Get a spectacular look and big flavors for less than $10 a person.

No-Fuss Entertaining

SERVES 6

Feta Cheese Truffles (see page 97)

Chicken Scaloppine With Spinach and Linguine

Easy Three-Seed Pan Rolls

Sweet Dip With Cookies and Fruit

Setting the table for a party is as easy as preparing these simple recipes. We covered a 6-foot table with two king-size sheets from the clearance aisle. A remnant of decorator fabric was used to make a colorful table runner and napkins.

Test Kitchens Notebook

To take the party outdoors, cut a mix of flowers from your garden or use single blooms from wholesale clubs or discount stores to arrange in jars. Cut stems, and remove any foliage that will fall below the water line. Place the flowers in a clean container with fresh water. Store in a cool place. If holding two or three days, recut stems, rinse container, and change water. Look for old canning jars and interesting containers at thrift stores and flea markets to creatively display beverages.

—VICKI A. POELLNITZ, ASSOCIATE FOOD EDITOR

Chicken Scaloppine With Spinach and Linguine

MAKES 6 SERVINGS; **PREP:** 25 MIN., **COOK:** 20 MIN.

This entrée comes together quickly as guests enjoy appetizers. For fast assembly, measure out and prep ingredients before anyone arrives.

1 lb. fresh asparagus
1 (16-oz.) package linguine
1 (9-oz.) package fresh spinach, thoroughly washed
¾ cup all-purpose flour
2 tsp. salt, divided
1½ tsp. pepper, divided
6 chicken cutlets (about 1½ lb.)
2 Tbsp. butter
2 Tbsp. olive oil
2 Tbsp. all-purpose flour
2½ cups chicken broth
1 Tbsp. lemon zest
3 Tbsp. fresh lemon juice
¼ cup capers, rinsed and drained
2 plum tomatoes, seeded and chopped
Grated Parmesan cheese

1. Snap off and discard tough ends of asparagus; cut asparagus spears in half crosswise.
2. Prepare linguine according to package directions, adding asparagus during last 2 minutes of cooking. Drain; return to pan. Stir in spinach; cover and keep warm over low heat.
3. Combine ¾ cup flour, 1½ tsp. salt, and 1 tsp. pepper in a large zip-top plastic bag. Add chicken cutlets; seal bag, and shake to lightly coat.
4. Melt 1 Tbsp. butter with 1 Tbsp. olive oil in a large nonstick skillet over medium-high heat. Cook 3 cutlets in skillet 2 to 3 minutes; turn and cook 2 to 3 minutes or until lightly browned and done. Remove cutlets from skillet.

Repeat procedure with remaining 1 Tbsp. butter, 1 Tbsp. oil, and 3 cutlets. (Chicken may be kept warm in a 250° oven on a wire rack.)
5. Whisk 2 Tbsp. flour into skillet, and cook 30 seconds. Whisk in chicken broth, next 3 ingredients, and remaining ½ tsp. salt and ½ tsp. pepper. Cook over medium-high heat 6 to 8 minutes or until slightly thickened, whisking to loosen particles from bottom of browned skillet. Pour over warm pasta mixture; toss to combine. Transfer to a serving dish, and sprinkle with tomatoes. Serve immediately with chicken and Parmesan cheese.

Worth the Splurge: Use Parmigiano-Reggiano cheese. Allow your guests to grate the cheese tableside right onto their plates.

Easy Three-Seed Pan Rolls

MAKES 9 ROLLS; **PREP:** 10 MIN., **RISE:** 4 HR., **BAKE:** 15 MIN.

These melt-in-your-mouth rolls start with frozen bread dough but taste as though they're made from scratch.

4 tsp. fennel seeds
4 tsp. poppy seeds
4 tsp. sesame seeds
9 frozen bread dough rolls
1 egg white, beaten
Melted butter

1. Combine first 3 ingredients in a small bowl. Dip dough rolls, 1 at a time, in egg white; roll in seed mixture. Arrange rolls, 1 inch apart, in a lightly greased 8-inch pan. Cover with lightly greased plastic wrap, and let rise in a warm place (85°), free from drafts, 3 to 4 hours or until doubled in bulk.
2. Preheat oven to 350°. Uncover rolls, and bake at 350° for 15 minutes or until golden. Brush with melted butter.
Note: For testing purposes only, we used Rhodes White Dinner Rolls for frozen rolls.

Party Cheat Sheet

1 week ahead:
- Gather items to set a pretty table. Have everything—glasses, dishes, serving pieces, flatware, napkins, table linens, and vases—clean, pressed, polished, and ready to go.
- Select music.
- Make shopping list.

Up to 3 days ahead:
- Shop for groceries (perishables and pantry items), wine, and flowers.
- Prepare Sweet Dip; cover and chill.
- Prepare Feta Cheese Truffles through Step 1.

1 day ahead:
- Measure wet and dry ingredients for Chicken Scaloppine. Place in small bowls or zip-top plastic bags; cover or seal. If necessary, refrigerate ingredients. (Don't cook pasta.)
- Snap off and discard tough ends of asparagus; cut in half crosswise. Cover and chill.
- Thoroughly wash and pat spinach dry, and place in a zip-top plastic bag. Seal and chill.
- Place flowers in selected vases.
- Set table.

3 to 4 hours before sitting down to eat:
- Prepare Easy Three-Seed Pan Rolls through Step 1.
- Shape Feta Cheese Truffles; roll in parsley. Cover and chill. Prepare accompaniments.
- Gather cookies, berries, and chocolate; arrange on serving tray.

30 minutes before guests arrive:
- Let truffles stand at room temperature. Arrange on tray with accompaniments.

30 minutes before sitting down to eat:
- Preheat oven to 350°.
- Start boiling water for pasta.

20 minutes before sitting down to eat:
- Bake rolls.
- Prepare Chicken Scaloppine. If you don't have enough oven space to keep batches of chicken warm, place on a wire rack in an aluminum foil-lined pan, and tent with foil.

Call guests to the table:
- Take Sweet Dip out of refrigerator.

After dinner:
- Arrange Sweet Dip on tray with goodies. Serve with coffee.

Worth the Splurge: The initial cost for these rolls is money well spent. You can make three scrumptious batches from the ingredients.

Three-Seed French Bread:
Substitute 1 (11-oz.) can refrigerated French bread dough for frozen bread dough rolls. Combine seeds in a shallow dish. Brush dough loaf with egg white. Roll top and sides of dough loaf in seeds. Place, seam side down, on a baking sheet. Cut and bake dough loaf according to package directions.

Sweet Dip With Cookies and Fruit
make ahead
MAKES 6 SERVINGS; **PREP:** 10 MIN.,
CHILL: 1 HR.

This creamy dessert dip is reminiscent of buttercream frosting swiped off a cake.

4 oz. cream cheese, softened
3 Tbsp. butter, softened
1 Tbsp. plain or vanilla yogurt
½ tsp. orange zest
2½ Tbsp. powdered sugar
Assorted cookies
Assorted berries
Dark chocolate squares

1. Beat first 4 ingredients at medium-high speed with an electric mixer until smooth. Gradually add sugar, beating until creamy. Cover and chill at least 1 hour or up to 3 days. Let dip stand at room temperature 30 minutes before serving. Serve with cookies, berries, and chocolate squares.

—DORI LANDRY, ALABASTER, ALABAMA

Worth the Splurge: Serve small, pretty imported cookies, one bar of the best dark chocolate, and a handful of fresh berries.

A New Side to Potatoes

Spuds take to a bevy of flavors and cooking methods, are good for you, and are priced right. Here we showcase the familiar reds as well as the hip-and-happening fingerlings and purple potatoes. We'll cook, roast, and even devil them in our attempt to satisfy your cravings. Let us know how you like 'em.

Roasted Fingerlings and Green Beans With Creamy Tarragon Dressing
family favorite
MAKES 4 TO 6 SERVINGS; PREP: 15 MIN., BAKE: 44 MIN.

We developed this potato-and-green bean dish to pair with the delicious dressing recipe from a reader. Fingerlings are not just available at gourmet stores. One editor purchases them at a wholesale club, while another buys them at a grocery store. Plan to make the dressing while the potatoes cook. (Pictured on page 164)

1½ lb. fingerling potatoes*
1½ Tbsp. olive oil, divided
1 tsp. salt, divided
¾ tsp. cracked pepper, divided
½ lb. tiny green beans (haricots verts)
Creamy Tarragon Dressing

1. Preheat oven to 425°. Cut fingerlings in half lengthwise, and place in a large bowl. Toss with 1 Tbsp. olive oil, ½ tsp. salt, and ½ tsp. pepper. Place potato halves, cut sides up, in a jelly-roll pan. Toss green beans with remaining ½ Tbsp. oil, ½ tsp. salt, and ¼ tsp. pepper, and place in another jelly-roll pan.

2. Bake potatoes at 425° for 30 to 32 minutes or until tender and browned. Remove from oven, and let potatoes stand in pan.

3. Bake green beans at 425° for 12 minutes.

4. Arrange green beans around roasted potatoes on a serving platter. Drizzle with Creamy Tarragon Dressing.
*1½ lb. small red potatoes, halved, may be substituted with a bake time of 35 minutes. 1½ lb. russet potatoes, quartered, may be substituted with a bake time of 40 minutes.

Creamy Tarragon Dressing:
MAKES ABOUT ¾ CUP; PREP: 10 MIN.

Our Food staff described the tarragon flavor as "just right." Chill remaining dressing, and use it the next day on a salad.

¼ cup buttermilk
2 Tbsp. fresh lemon juice
1 tsp. sugar
1 tsp. Dijon-style mustard
¾ tsp. salt
¼ tsp. coarsely ground pepper
½ cup olive oil
2 Tbsp. finely chopped green onion
1 Tbsp. chopped fresh tarragon

1. Whisk together first 6 ingredients in a small bowl until combined. Gradually whisk in oil in a slow, steady stream, whisking constantly until smooth. Whisk in green onion and tarragon. Use immediately, or store in an airtight container in refrigerator up to 2 days. Let chilled dressing stand 30 minutes before using.

—BARBARA HAHN, PARK HILLS, MISSOURI

Test Kitchens Advice

Our staff shares their top pointers for buying, storing, and prepping potatoes.

- **Good Looking = Great Quality:** Buy potatoes that are fairly clean and smooth; firm with no soft spots, nicks, or cracks; and sprout free. Make sure they are uniform in size. *Disclaimer:* A pretty potato on the outside can have a blackened space in the center called "hollow heart." It indicates a change in the growth rate. Discard.

- **The Green Issue:** If a potato is exposed to light, a component called solanine builds up and causes a green tinge on the skin. It will taste bitter. (It's possible, but not likely, to cause illness.) Don't buy a potato with green patches—it has been mishandled. At home, store potatoes in a dark, cool place, such as your pantry. Cut away small areas of green tinge at least ¼ inch below the peel.

- **Over time:** A potato stored at room temperature lasts one week. One kept in a 50° environment holds up for three weeks. Do not store in the refrigerator—the starches turn to sugar.

- **Go Easy When Cleaning:** A good rinse and rub with hands is all that's needed to prep thin-skinned potatoes. Use a soft vegetable brush on thicker skins, such as russets. Sprouts (nicknamed "eyes") are not poisonous and can often be rubbed off by hand.

- **Healthy Spin:** Save yourself a prep step whenever possible and skip peeling potatoes—just be sure to scrub them right before cooking. The peel is a good source of dietary fiber, and just under the peel you'll find the highest concentration of nutrients.

Deviled Potatoes

MAKES 12 SERVINGS; **PREP:** 30 MIN.,
BAKE: 55 MIN., **COOL:** 45 MIN., **CHILL:** 2 HR.

*These mini-stuffed potatoes are perfect
for appetizers and potluck. Choose potatoes that are more oval in shape to best
resemble deviled eggs. Baking the potato
shells before filling them sets the shape (so
they will not break when picked up) and
enhances the flavor. Don't overmix or the
texture will be gummy instead of creamy.
Petite indicates a potato about the size of
a plum tomato.*

14 petite red or yellow oval-shaped
    potatoes (about 1½ lb.)
1 Tbsp. olive oil
1 tsp. kosher salt
¼ cup mayonnaise
2 Tbsp. sweet-hot pickle relish
1 tsp. cider vinegar
1 tsp. spicy brown mustard
¼ tsp. pepper
¼ tsp. salt
⅛ tsp. hot sauce
⅛ tsp. ground celery seed (optional)
½ tsp. paprika (optional)
Garnishes: fresh dill sprigs, coarsely ground
    pepper

1. Preheat oven to 350°. Place potatoes
in a small bowl, and drizzle with oil.
Sprinkle with 1 tsp. kosher salt; toss to
coat. Place on a baking sheet.

To make the potato shells for
Deviled Potatoes, scoop out the
pulp from halved, roasted potatoes using a ¼-tsp. measuring
spoon.

2. Bake at 350° for 40 to 45 minutes or
until tender. Remove from oven, and let
cool 15 minutes.
3. Cut each potato in half lengthwise.
Carefully scoop out potato pulp into
a bowl, leaving shells intact. Discard
4 potato shells. Place remaining shells
on baking sheet, and bake 10 more
minutes. Let cool 30 minutes or until
completely cool.
4. Add mayonnaise, next 6 ingredients,
and, if desired, celery seed, to potato
pulp in bowl. Beat at medium speed
with an electric mixer until blended.
Spoon mixture generously into each
potato shell. Cover and chill 2 hours.
Sprinkle with paprika just before serving, if desired. Garnish, if desired.
Note: For testing purposes only, we
used Wickles Original Pickle Relish.

Cook Smart

Here's a quick primer on our favorite potatoes and the best method for cooking
each based on starch and moisture content. Our "aka" (also known as) listing
refers to the varieties commonly sold at the supermarket.

Russets: Starchy (or *floury*). Brown, netting-like appearance to the peel. Low
moisture content makes these great for baking, frying, or roasting. They make
fluffy, light-textured mashed potatoes but disintegrate when boiled for potato
salad. **AKA:** russets, Russet Burbank, Russet Norkotah, Idaho potatoes, baking
potatoes.

Golds: All-purpose (moisture and starch content is balanced). Yellow-gold interior color and buttery flavor is divine for mashed potatoes. Work well shredded
for potato pancakes such as latkes. **AKA:** Yukon gold, gold, Butter gold.

Reds: Waxy (high moisture content, low in starch). Perfect for potato
salads, parsleyed buttered potatoes, or roasted because they hold their shape.
Mashed potatoes will be thick and creamy. **AKA:** At our supercenter store, they
are labeled size A (small to medium-size) and B (petite to small). You may also
see them as Baby Red or Red Creamers.

Fingerlings: All-purpose. Best when roasted. Can be baked or steamed. Often
sold in a paper bag with mesh vents. **AKA:** French, Rose Finn Apple, and
Russian Banana. Ruby Crescent has a beautiful stripe of color in the center of
the potato when cut lengthwise.

Purple and Blue: All-purpose and versatile. Nutty flavor. Perfect boiled for potato
salad, yet often fried into chips. **AKA:** Purple Majesty, Purple Chief, or Delta Blues.

New potatoes are any potatoes
that have recently been harvested.
These are most often sold at roadside produce stands and farmers
markets. If the recipe calls for
peeling (especially for potatoes
being cooked in the microwave),
don't use a paring knife. Instead
use a vegetable peeler to remove
the thinnest amount of peel.

Warm Purple-and-Red Potato Toss
family favorite

MAKES 6 SERVINGS; **PREP:** 15 MIN.,
COOK: 20 MIN., **COOL:** 15 MIN.

With a hint of horseradish and a sprinkling of bacon, this delicious dish tastes great with a steak. Use purple and red potatoes about the size of an average tomato. To retain color, cook purples in their jackets. Our Test Kitchens prefers to cook potatoes for potato salad uncut and in their skins. Cut potatoes tend to break apart. (Pictured on page 165)

1¼ lb. small purple potatoes
1¼ lb. small red potatoes
½ cup mayonnaise
½ cup sour cream
2 Tbsp. horseradish
2 tsp. lemon juice
½ tsp. salt
½ tsp. pepper
3 green onions, sliced
5 cooked bacon slices,
    crumbled
Salt to taste
Garnish: fresh arugula

1. Bring potatoes and water to cover to a boil in a Dutch oven over medium-high heat. Cook 15 to 20 minutes or just until tender; drain well. Cool 15 minutes, and slice into wedges.
2. Whisk together mayonnaise and next 5 ingredients in a large bowl. Add potatoes, green onions, and 3 Tbsp. crumbled bacon; gently toss to coat. Season with salt to taste. Sprinkle with remaining bacon. Garnish, if desired.

—JANICE M. FRANCE, DEPAUW, INDIANA

Layered Green Bean-Red Potato Salad
southernliving.com favorite

MAKES 8 TO 10 SERVINGS; **PREP:** 20 MIN.,
COOK: 25 MIN., **STAND:** 25 MIN.,
CHILL: 4 HRS.

1½ cups mayonnaise
¼ cup white wine vinegar
3 Tbsp. sugar
1 Tbsp. finely chopped fresh or 1 tsp. dried
    tarragon
¼ tsp. salt
¼ tsp. freshly ground pepper
4 lb. small red potatoes
1½ lb. fresh green beans, trimmed and cut
    into 1½-inch pieces*
1 tsp. salt
2 large sweet onions, cut into ⅛-inch slices
    and quartered

1. Stir together mayonnaise and next 5 ingredients in a small bowl until blended; cover and chill.
2. Bring potatoes and water to cover to a boil over medium-high heat; cook 10 to 15 minutes or until potatoes are fork-tender. Drain potatoes, and let stand 25 minutes at room temperature or until cool. Cut into ¼-inch-thick slices.
3. Cook green beans in boiling water to cover 3 to 4 minutes or until crisp-tender; drain, and plunge into ice water to stop the cooking process. Drain and pat dry.
4. Layer half of potato slices in a large glass bowl; sprinkle evenly with ½ tsp. salt. Layer half each of green beans and onions over potatoes; spoon half of dressing evenly over top. Repeat layers, ending with dressing. Cover and chill 4 hours or up to 24 hours.
*2 (12-oz.) bags fresh ready-to-cook trimmed green beans may be substituted.

GET INSPIRED

Fresh Herb Flavor

We've concocted a simple, healthful recipe to start your season of outdoor cooking. Choose your favorite fresh herb to enhance the flavor of simple grilled chicken breasts. Remove the herb sprig before serving, if you'd like, or leave it as a garnish. The herbs will char a little because the sprigs will be next to the grate, but the result is a pretty and rustic look.

Herb-Grilled Chicken
MAKES 4 SERVINGS; **PREP:** 10 MIN.,
GRILL: 14 MIN.

Our top herb picks included fresh dill, basil, sage, rosemary, flat-leaf parsley, thyme, tarragon, and oregano.

1. Preheat grill to 350° to 400° (medium-high). Rub 4 (4- to 6-oz.) skinned and boned chicken breasts evenly with 2 Tbsp. olive oil; sprinkle with 1 tsp. salt and 1 tsp. pepper. Cut a small slit at 1 end of each chicken breast; tuck end of 1 fresh herb sprig into each slit, laying sprigs over top of chicken.
2. Grill chicken breasts, covered with grill lid, over 350° to 400° (medium-high) heat 6 to 7 minutes on each side or until done. If desired, remove and discard herb sprigs. Serve over fresh spinach.

Share the Joy

Fresh ideas for traditional Passover favorites highlight this inviting menu from Tamara and Eric Goldis of Birmingham, Alabama. Something wonderful is always cooking in their kitchen, and these delicious recipes are no exception. In fact, they're so good that you will want to enjoy them throughout the year.

Passover Menu

SERVES 4 TO 6

Garlic-Herb Roasted Chicken

Sweet Vegetable Kugel

Lemon Roasted Asparagus

Chocolate Fudge Cake or
Chunky Chocolate Brownies

Sweet Vegetable Kugel and Lemon Roasted Asparagus pair nicely with the main dish. End the meal with our rich Chocolate Fudge Cake or Chunky Chocolate Brownies that you can make ahead and freeze.

Garlic-Herb Roasted Chicken

MAKES 4 TO 6 SERVINGS; **PREP:** 10 MIN.;
BAKE: 1 HR., 15 MIN.; **STAND:** 10 MIN.

Add additional moistness and flavor by replacing the wire roasting rack with a colorful rack of carrots and celery ribs. Tuck in a few sprigs of fresh herbs, some unpeeled whole shallots, and apple slices. Aromatic apples and vegetables infuse the chicken with amazing flavor. After baking, the unpeeled shallots easily slip from their papery skins, adding a tasty side note to the sliced chicken.

3 garlic cloves, minced
2 tsp. chopped fresh thyme
2 tsp. chopped fresh rosemary
2 tsp. chopped fresh parsley
1 tsp. chopped fresh sage
1 tsp. salt
¾ tsp. freshly ground pepper
1 (4- to 5-lb.) whole chicken

1. Preheat oven to 450°. Stir together first 7 ingredients.
2. If applicable, remove giblets from chicken, and reserve for another use. Rinse chicken, and pat dry. Gently loosen and lift skin from breast and drumsticks with fingers. (Do not totally detach skin.) Rub herb mixture evenly underneath skin. Carefully replace skin. Place chicken, breast side up, on a lightly greased wire rack in a lightly greased shallow roasting pan.
3. Bake at 450° for 30 minutes. Reduce heat to 350°, and bake 45 minutes or until a meat thermometer inserted in thigh registers 180°, covering loosely with aluminum foil to prevent excessive browning, if necessary. Let chicken stand, covered, 10 minutes before slicing.

Sweet Vegetable Kugel

MAKES 8 SERVINGS; **PREP:** 25 MIN.;
BAKE: 1 HR., 7 MIN.; **COOL:** 15 MIN.

Yiddish for "pudding," a kugel may also be prepared with savory ingredients. This recipe, which includes grated carrots and apples, is a wonderful twist on sweet potato casserole.

¾ cup chopped pecans
4 cups peeled and grated sweet potato
    (about 1 extra large)
3 cups peeled and grated carrots
    (about 4 large)
2 cups peeled and grated Gala apples
    (about 2 large)
1 cup matzo meal
½ cup margarine, melted
½ cup sugar
1 large egg, beaten
1 tsp. salt
¾ tsp. ground cinnamon
¼ tsp. ground nutmeg

1. Preheat oven to 350°. Arrange pecans in a single layer on a baking sheet. Bake at 350° for 5 to 7 minutes or until lightly toasted and fragrant. Cool in pan on a wire rack 15 minutes or until completely cool. Reserve 3 Tbsp. pecans. Reduce oven temperature to 325°.
2. Stir together sweet potatoes, next 9 ingredients, and remaining pecans in a large bowl until blended; spoon mixture into 8 (8-oz.) lightly greased ramekins.
3. Bake, covered, at 325° for 45 minutes. Increase oven temperature to 350°; uncover and bake 15 minutes or until edges are golden brown. Top evenly with reserved toasted pecans.

TIP

Keeping Kosher

"Kosher for Passover" products, such as matzo (an unleavened, cracker-like bread) and cake mixes, are available seasonally in supermarkets. (1) Matzo meal, (2) finely ground matzo cake flour, and (3) small squares of matzo farfel are used in place of wheat flour and breadcrumbs, yielding delicious results in baked goods and casseroles.

Lemon Roasted Asparagus

fast fixin's

MAKES 8 SERVINGS; **PREP:** 10 MIN.,
BAKE: 15 MIN.

2 lb. fresh asparagus
3 garlic cloves, minced
¼ cup lemon juice
¼ cup olive oil
¾ tsp. salt
¼ tsp. pepper

1. Preheat oven to 400°. Snap off and discard tough ends of asparagus; place asparagus on a lightly greased baking sheet. Whisk together remaining ingredients; drizzle mixture over asparagus, tossing to coat.
2. Bake at 400° for 15 minutes or to desired degree of tenderness, turning once after 8 minutes.

Chocolate Fudge Cake

MAKES 8 SERVINGS; **PREP:** 15 MIN.,
COOK: 5 MIN., **BAKE:** 30 MIN.,
COOL: 30 MIN.

Baked in a pieplate, this don't-miss dessert boasts a super-rich chocolate flavor and moist texture.

Vegetable cooking spray
Unsweetened cocoa
8 oz. bittersweet chocolate, coarsely chopped
½ cup margarine
¾ cup granulated sugar
3 large eggs, beaten
1 tsp. vanilla extract
2 Tbsp. powdered sugar

1. Preheat oven to 350°. Lightly coat a 9-inch pieplate with cooking spray, and dust with cocoa.
2. Melt chopped chocolate and margarine in a heavy saucepan over low heat, stirring constantly, 3 to 5 minutes or until smooth; whisk in ¾ cup sugar, whisking until blended.
3. Whisk together eggs and vanilla in a large bowl. Gradually whisk in chocolate mixture, whisking until blended. Pour into prepared pieplate.
4. Bake at 350° for 30 minutes or until edges are dry and center is set. (Do not overbake.) Cool in pieplate on a wire rack 30 minutes or until completely cool. (Cake will fall slightly when removed from oven.) Dust with 2 Tbsp. powdered sugar just before serving.

Chunky Chocolate Brownies

southernliving.com favorite
MAKES 9 BROWNIES; **PREP:** 20 MIN.,
COOK: 5 MIN., **COOL:** 5 MIN., **BAKE:** 28 MIN.

Chocolate chunks make these brownies fudgy; decrease the baking time to 23 minutes to make them extra gooey.

¾ cup granulated sugar
⅓ cup butter
1 (11.5-oz.) package semisweet chocolate chunks, divided
2 large eggs
1 tsp. vanilla extract
¾ cup all-purpose flour
¼ tsp. salt
½ cup chopped hazelnuts or pecans, toasted
Powdered sugar

1. Preheat oven to 325°. Combine 2 Tbsp. water, granulated sugar, and butter in a 3 ½-qt. saucepan. Bring to a boil over medium heat, stirring constantly. Remove from heat, and stir in 1 cup chocolate chunks until smooth. Let cool 5 minutes. Add eggs, 1 at a time, stirring just until blended. Stir in vanilla.
2. Combine flour and salt; stir in remaining chocolate chunks and hazelnuts. Stir flour mixture into chocolate mixture in saucepan. Spread into a lightly greased 9-inch square pan.
3. Bake at 325° for 23 to 28 minutes. Cool in pan on a wire rack. Dust with powdered sugar. Cut into squares.

To freeze up to 3 months: Wrap baked brownies in aluminum foil, and place in a large zip-top plastic freezer bag. To thaw, remove brownies from plastic bag, and let stand at room temperature for 3 hours; unwrap and serve.

Healthy Living®

Spring is a great time to make some positive changes and healthful choices so that you'll feel your best.

Sneak in the Good Stuff

Please your toughest crowd with these healthful dishes

Getting your family to eat healthfully doesn't have to be a chore. We have the solution: Sneak some nutritious alternatives past them. Carefully hidden in these tasty recipes is a bounty of nutritious ingredients your picky eaters may even grow to love. They'll be eating better, and you'll feel good about it.

Tomato-Herb Pasta
family favorite • make ahead
MAKES 6 SERVINGS; **PREP:** 30 MIN.,
STAND: 30 MIN.

Turn this zesty side dish into a hearty entrée by adding cooked shrimp or chicken.

½ cup rice vinegar
1 Tbsp. sugar
½ medium-size red onion, thinly
    sliced
½ (12-oz.) package whole grain
    spaghetti
2 medium tomatoes, seeded and chopped
1 large cucumber, peeled and thinly sliced
    into half moons
4 green onions, thinly sliced
⅓ cup firmly packed fresh mint leaves,
    chopped
⅓ cup firmly packed fresh cilantro leaves,
    chopped
¼ cup fresh lime juice
2 Tbsp. canola oil
1 tsp. sugar
1 tsp. salt
½ tsp. dried crushed red pepper
¼ cup chopped peanuts

1. Whisk together vinegar and 1 Tbsp. sugar in a bowl. Add onion, and let stand 30 minutes; drain, reserving 2 Tbsp. vinegar mixture.

2. Prepare pasta according to package directions.
3. Place chopped tomatoes and next 9 ingredients in a serving bowl. Add hot cooked pasta, onion, and reserved vinegar mixture, gently tossing to combine. Sprinkle with peanuts. Serve immediately, or cover and chill up to 24 hours.

—**LISA CARR**, CEDAREDGE, COLORADO

Note: For testing purposes only, we used Mueller's Whole Grain Spaghetti.

Per serving: Calories 219; Fat 8g (sat 0.8g, mono 4.2g, poly 2.5g); Protein 6.7g; Carb 33.8g; Fiber 5.4g; Chol 0mg; Iron 1.8mg; Sodium 324mg; Calc 44mg

Healthy Benefits

- Flax seed is high in fiber, antioxidants (called lignans), and essential omega-3 fatty acids, which are known to decrease LDL (bad) cholesterol. One tablespoon will often meet the daily recommendation for omega-3 fatty acids.
- Cooking for your family can help them develop a taste for new ingredients and flavor profiles. Plus it allows more control over daily calories, protein, fat, and sodium than eating out.

Zucchini Soup

family favorite

MAKES 7 CUPS; **PREP:** 10 MIN.,
COOK: 25 MIN., **STAND:** 20 MIN.

*Your family won't notice the beans in
this pureed soup.*

1 cup chopped celery
1 cup chopped onion
1 Tbsp. olive oil
1½ lb. zucchini, cut into ¼-inch pieces
    (about 5 cups)
3 cups low-sodium chicken broth
1 (16-oz.) can cannellini beans, rinsed and
    drained
1 tsp. salt
¼ tsp. seasoned pepper

1. Sauté chopped celery and onion in
hot olive oil in a Dutch oven over
medium-high heat 8 minutes or until
tender.
2. Add zucchini and next 4 ingredients. Bring to a boil over medium heat;
reduce heat to low, and simmer 10 minutes or until zucchini is tender. Remove
from heat, and let stand 20 minutes.
3. Process soup, in batches, in a blender
or food processor 30 seconds or until
smooth. Return soup to Dutch oven,
and cook over medium heat 5 minutes
or until thoroughly heated.

—VICKY FUSTINE, DUNWOODY, GEORGIA

Note: You can also process soup with a
handheld immersion blender directly in
Dutch oven.

Per (1½-cup) serving (not including garnishes): Calories 129; Fat 3.6g
(sat 0.6g, mono 2.2g, poly 0.8g); Protein 7g; Carb 18.6g; Fiber 4.8g;
Chol 0mg; Iron 1.8mg; Sodium 534mg; Calc 58mg

• TIP •

Give Zucchini Soup an extra boost
of flavor and texture by topping
it with crumbled feta cheese and
radish slices. Add 1 cup chopped
cooked chicken or turkey to make
it a main dish

Baby Spinach Salad With Poppy Seed Dressing

family favorite

MAKES 6 SERVINGS; **PREP:** 10 MIN.,
BAKE: 8 MIN.

*Add a few ingredients to a bottled salad
dressing and you'll have a refreshing
topping for this salad.*

¼ cup sliced almonds
1 (6-oz.) package fresh baby spinach,
    thoroughly washed
¼ cup bottled poppy seed dressing
1 Tbsp. ground flax seed
1 Tbsp. sour cream
1 (11-oz.) can mandarin oranges, drained
½ small red onion, thinly sliced

1. Preheat oven to 350°. Place
almonds in a single layer in a shallow
pan, and bake at 350° for 8 minutes
or until toasted and fragrant, stirring
occasionally.
2. Place spinach in a large bowl. Stir
together poppy seed dressing, ground
flax seed, sour cream, and 2 Tbsp.
water in a small bowl; drizzle over
spinach, and toss to combine. Top with
oranges, onion, and almonds.
Note: For testing purposes only,
we used Kraft Creamy Poppy Seed
Dressing.

Per serving: Calories 96; Fat 6.4g (sat 1.1g, mono 1.6g, poly 0.7g);
Protein 1.9g; Carb 8.5g; Fiber 2.3g; Chol 1mg; Iron 1.1mg;
Sodium 131mg; Calc 39mg

Lemon-Blueberry Muffins

southernliving.com favorite

MAKES 1 DOZEN; **PREP:** 10 MIN,
COOK: 25 MIN,

*These tasty little muffins stir up quick
for a healthy, nutrient-packed treat
when you're on the go.*

1¾ cups all-purpose flour
2 tsp. baking powder
¼ tsp. salt
1 cup fresh or frozen blueberries, thawed
    and drained
¾ cup fat-free milk
½ cup sugar
¼ cup vegetable oil
2 tsp. grated lemon rind
1 tsp. vanilla extract
2 egg whites
Vegetable cooking spray

1. Preheat oven to 350°. Combine first
3 ingredients in a large mixing bowl;
add blueberries, and gently toss to coat.
Make a well in center of mixture.
2. Stir together milk, sugar, and next
3 ingredients; add to dry ingredients,
stirring just until moistened.
3. Beat egg whites at medium speed
with an electric mixer 1 minute or until
soft peaks form; fold into batter. Spoon
batter into muffin pans coated with
cooking spray, filling two-thirds full.
4. Bake at 350° for 20 to 25 minutes or
until done.

Per serving: Calories: 151; Fat: 5g (sat 0.4g, mono 2.7g, poly 1.4g);
Protein 3g; Fiber 1g; Chol. 0.3mg; Iron 0.8 mg; Sodium 133 mg;
Calc 50 mg

Grow Goodness

It's not as hard as it seems. Anyone can have a vegetable garden by following our tips.

A world full of rewards can be yours in a small-space vegetable garden. With a little planning, you can stretch your edible bounty from spring through fall.

Step 1: So Easy A small raised bed—we used a 4- x 4-foot kit—offers a plentiful yield without an overwhelming amount of effort. Put together your own planting box, or purchase a kit such as one from Gardener's Supply Company (www.gardeners.com, #36-487, $189). The assembly gives you a good workout and has you ready to grow in about an hour.

Location is key. Vegetables require at least four hours of direct sunlight, with summer veggies benefiting from more. For easy watering, place your bed where a hose can easily reach it. Remember, a garden close to the house gets tended more readily than one behind the garage.

Step 2: Adapt It If you have an odd-shaped area, build your own growing box to suit your space. Be aware, though, that a container wider than 4 feet makes harvesting the middle of the garden difficult. This is especially true for small children. **Tip:** Put landscape fabric—available at garden centers—under the bed prior to filling it with soil. This porous material prevents weeds and grass from pushing up through the garden but allows moisture to pass through.

Step 3: Great Growing
A garden is only as good as its soil, and a raised bed provides the chance to make the best dirt in town. Fill it with bagged topsoil, leaf compost (or purchased mushroom compost), and dehydrated cow manure. Mix it all together, filling the bed to 1 inch from the top. **Tip:** After seeds have sprouted, cover the soil with shredded-bark mulch to help retain valuable moisture.

Step 4: Moving On After a year, you will want more raised beds. An added benefit is that they're portable. If you like, move them around for variety, rebuild them, and add more to your garden. Transfer the soil, and you're ready to grow again. **Tip:** Next year, enrich the soil again with new leaf compost and dehydrated cow manure. Change the garden's plant placement annually to encourage optimum growing conditions.

Three Seasons of Goodness

Plan the garden carefully, and enjoy the benefits of fresh produce. Start some from seed and others from garden-center transplants.

Pick the Season	Seed	Transplant	Tip
Spring			
Snow peas or sugar snaps	x		Love cold weather; plant as soon as the soil can be worked.
Radishes	x		Plant additional seeds every two weeks for continuous supply.
Lettuce	x	x	Choose leaf selections for quickest harvest. Pick from the outside of the plant.
Spinach	x	x	A heat-tolerant selection such as 'Indian Summer' produces well into summer.
Summer			
Tomato		x	Kids love the cherry and grape tomatoes; consider one of the numerous small selections.
Eggplant		x	Soil must be warm prior to planting. Choose a petite selection such as 'Mini Fairy Tale.'
Bush beans	x		Plant a few seeds every two weeks to maintain a fresh supply. Try filet beans for the fastest reward; harvest them young while they're tender.
Peppers		x	Wait until soil warms to plant.
Summer squash	x	x	A small bed can handle only one plant. If first flowers fall off, don't panic. Later blooms produce fruit.
Fall/Winter			
Bok choy		x	Cut outer leaves for stir-fries; plant continues to grow for additional harvest.
Chard		x	Enjoy the leaves and stems of this sturdy green. Tolerates cold and warm weather.
Broccoli		x	Cut the main head, and watch for additional side shoots to appear.
Lettuce	x	x	Take advantage of the long, cool season; plant heading-type lettuce now.
Radicchio	x	x	Heads up in cold weather.
Snow peas or sugar snaps	x		Become more prolific as weather turns cold.

Refreshing Salads

Brighten your table with crisp, casual flair.

Impress your family and friends by serving fashionable salads. The classic mix of sugared almonds, mandarin oranges, and red onions gets a flavor face-lift in our Crispy Sesame Salad Stack. Strawberry-Pineapple Iceberg Wedges merges the elements of a fresh fruit cocktail with a typically savory salad. Both will liven up your taste buds with wonderful flavors and textures.

Crispy Sesame Salad Stack

fast fixin's

MAKES 6 SERVINGS; **PREP:** 15 MIN.

For a more casual presentation, toss together all the salad ingredients, and serve the Sesame Won Ton Crisps on the side. Make an extra batch of the won ton crisps to munch on or to top with your favorite cheese spread for a tasty snack. (Pictured on page 170)

1 (8-oz.) package mixed salad greens, thoroughly washed
Sesame Won Ton Crisps
1 (8.25-oz.) can mandarin orange segments, drained
2 green onions, sliced
6 Tbsp. chopped cashews
Fresh Orange-Soy Vinaigrette
Salt and pepper to taste

1. Layer ½ cup salad greens, 1 Sesame Won Ton Crisp, 3 Tbsp. salad greens, 1 Sesame Won Ton Crisp, and 1 Tbsp. salad greens on a serving plate. Carefully tuck 1 Tbsp. mandarin orange segments into salad greens. Repeat procedure with remaining salad greens, won ton crisps, and orange segments. Sprinkle with green onions and cashews. Drizzle with Fresh Orange-Soy Vinaigrette. Sprinkle with salt and pepper to taste. Serve immediately.

Sesame Won Ton Crisps:

MAKES 12 PIECES; **PREP:** 5 MIN.,
BAKE: 6 MIN.

Although we liked the color contrast of the white and black sesame seeds, feel free to omit one and double the other. Sesame seeds are best stored in the refrigerator for up to three months.

12 won ton wrappers
1 Tbsp. melted butter
½ tsp. white sesame seeds
½ tsp. black sesame seeds
¼ tsp. kosher salt

1. Preheat oven to 425°. Place won ton wrappers on an ungreased baking sheet. Brush 1 side of each wrapper with melted butter, and sprinkle with sesame seeds and salt.
2. Bake at 425° for 5 to 6 minutes or until golden brown.
Note: Won ton wrappers can be found in the refrigerated section of most supermarkets.

Fresh Orange-Soy Vinaigrette:

MAKES ABOUT ½ CUP; **PREP:** 10 MIN.

Orange juice replaces much of the oil you would typically find in most salad dressings for a lighter, tangier taste.

¼ cup rice vinegar
¼ cup orange juice
2 Tbsp. vegetable oil
1 Tbsp. soy sauce
2 Tbsp. dark brown sugar
1 tsp. freshly grated ginger
⅛ tsp. dry mustard
Salt to taste

1. Combine ¼ cup rice vinegar and next 6 ingredients in a food processor; pulse 3 to 4 times or until smooth. Season with salt to taste.

Strawberry-Pineapple Iceberg Wedges

family favorite • fast fixin's

MAKES 6 SERVINGS; **PREP:** 30 MIN.

A few additions, such as mint, salt, and pepper, pep up this simple iceberg-fruit salad. Look for seeded melon halves in the produce department to save a little time. (Pictured on page 170)

1 (16-oz.) package fresh strawberries, hulled
½ medium pineapple, peeled and cored
½ medium honeydew melon
¼ small cantaloupe
2 Tbsp. chopped fresh mint
1 head iceberg lettuce, cored and cut into 6 wedges
Kosher salt and freshly ground pepper to taste
Yogurt-Poppy Seed Dressing

1. Cut first 4 ingredients into ¼-inch pieces (about 2 cups each cubed strawberries, pineapple, and honeydew melon and 1 cup cubed cantaloupe). Toss with mint.
2. Arrange 1 lettuce wedge on each of 6 serving plates. Top evenly with fruit mixture. Sprinkle with salt and pepper to taste. Drizzle with Yogurt-Poppy Seed Dressing.

Yogurt-Poppy Seed Dressing:

MAKES 1 CUP; **PREP:** 10 MIN.

Yogurt and honey replace the oil and sugar typically found in this classic for a healthful, here-and-now dressing. We prefer Greek yogurt for its thick, rich flavor, but plain yogurt can be substituted for a thinner dressing.

1 cup plain Greek or plain yogurt
2 Tbsp. honey
2 Tbsp. fresh lemon juice
1 tsp. poppy seeds

1. Whisk together all ingredients in a small bowl. Store in an airtight container in refrigerator up to 5 days.

Fancy Ground Beef

It's a must-have in the Southern kitchen and is the base for a number of hearty dishes. These delectable offerings showcase ground beef in updated ways.

Dressed-up Hamburger Steak With Sweet Onion-Mushroom Gravy turns ground beef into something truly special. Serve it with crusty French bread and colorful steamed veggies. You can even prep the patties ahead and freeze them for up to 3 months. You can whip up the Greek Beef Wraps in less than 30 minutes and they pair nicely with French fries or pasta salad.

Cook's Notes

- These recipes were tested with ground round, which we think has the best lean-to-fat ratio and delivers the greatest value. Economical family-size packs of ground round are a smart way to trim your food budget. When these 3- to 4-lb. beauties are on sale, grab a pack or two, portion the meat into 1-lb. servings, and freeze for future use.
- Freeze recipe-size portions of uncooked ground beef in zip-top plastic freezer bags or plastic freezer containers for up to four months. Be sure to label, including the amount and date.

Greek Beef Wraps

family favorite • fast fixin's
MAKES 6 SERVINGS; PREP: 20 MIN.,
COOK: 9 MIN.

We call for flatbread wraps, but this delicious beef mixture would also be great in flour tortillas or pita pockets.

1 lb. ground round
1 small red onion, chopped
1 tsp. Greek seasoning
½ tsp. pepper
½ tsp. salt, divided
1 cucumber, peeled, seeded, and grated
1 (8-oz.) container sour cream
1 garlic clove, minced
1 Tbsp. chopped fresh dill weed
6 garden-spinach flatbread wraps
3 plum tomatoes, finely chopped
1 (4-oz.) package crumbled feta cheese

1. Cook first 4 ingredients and ¼ tsp. salt in a large skillet over medium-high heat, stirring often, 7 to 9 minutes or until beef crumbles and is no longer pink; drain well on paper towels.
2. Stir together cucumber, next 3 ingredients, and remaining ¼ tsp. salt. Spoon 2 Tbsp. cucumber mixture down center of each wrap; top with beef mixture, tomatoes, and feta. Roll up; serve with remaining cucumber mixture.
Note: For testing purposes only, we used Flatout Traditional Garden Spinach Wraps.

Hamburger Steak With Sweet Onion-Mushroom Gravy

freezeable • make ahead
MAKES 4 SERVINGS; PREP: 15 MIN.,
COOK: 20 MIN.

2 honey-wheat bread slices
1 lb. ground round
1 large egg, lightly beaten
2 garlic cloves, minced
½ tsp. salt
½ tsp. freshly ground pepper
1 (1.2-oz.) envelope brown gravy mix
1 Tbsp. vegetable oil
1 (8-oz.) package sliced fresh mushrooms
1 medium-size sweet onion, halved and thinly sliced

1. Process bread slices in a food processor 10 seconds or until finely chopped. Place breadcrumbs in a mixing bowl; add ground round and next 4 ingredients. Gently combine until blended, using your hands. Shape into 4 (4-inch) patties.
2. Whisk together brown gravy mix and 1½ cups water.
3. Cook patties in hot oil in a large skillet over medium-high heat 2 minutes on each side or just until browned. Remove patties from skillet. Add mushrooms and onion to skillet, and sauté 6 minutes or until tender. Stir in prepared gravy, and bring to a light boil. Return patties to skillet, and spoon gravy over each patty. Cover, reduce heat to low, and simmer 8 to 10 minutes.

—SHANNON WHITE, CUMMING, GEORGIA

Note: To make ahead, proceed with Step 1 as directed. Wrap each patty individually in plastic wrap, and place in a large zip-top plastic freezer bag. Freeze up to 3 months. Thaw frozen patties in refrigerator 8 hours; proceed with Steps 2 and 3.

Beef Lombardi
southernliving.com favorite
MAKES 6 SERVINGS; **PREP:** 10 MIN.,
COOK: 41 MIN., **BAKE:** 40 MIN.

1lb. ground round
1 (14 ½-oz.) can chopped tomatoes
1 (10-oz.) can diced tomatoes and green
    chiles
2 tsp. sugar
2 tsp. salt
¼ tsp. pepper
1 (6-oz.) can tomato paste
1 bay leaf
1 (6-oz.) package medium egg noodles
6 green onions, chopped (about ½ cup)
1 cup sour cream
1 cup (4 oz.) shredded sharp Cheddar
    cheese
1 cup shredded Parmesan cheese
1 cup (4 oz.) shredded mozzarella cheese
Garnish: fresh parsley sprigs

1. Preheat oven to 350°. Cook ground
round in a large skillet over medium
heat 5 to 6 minutes, stirring until it
crumbles and is no longer pink. Drain.
2. Stir in chopped tomatoes and next
4 ingredients; cook 5 minutes. Add
tomato paste and bay leaf, and simmer
30 minutes.
3. Cook egg noodles according to package directions; drain.
4. Stir together cooked egg noodles,
chopped green onions, and sour cream
until blended.
5. Place noodle mixture in bottom of
a lightly greased 13- x 9-inch baking
dish. Top with beef mixture; sprinkle
evenly with cheeses.
6. Bake, covered with aluminum foil, at
350° for 35 minutes. Uncover casserole,
and bake 5 more minutes. Garnish, if
desired.
Note: Freeze uncooked casserole up to
1 month, if desired. Thaw in refrigerator overnight. Bake as directed.
To lighten: Substitute low-fat or fat-
free sour cream and 2% reduced-fat
Cheddar cheese. Reduce amount of
cheeses on top to ½ cup each.

Try Calzones

Family-friendly Italian pies overflow with surprising flavor.

These mouthwatering recipes
are so simple to make and
perfect for satisfying weeknight dinners. Many grocery
store bakeries sell fresh
pizza dough (your favorite pizzeria may
sell dough too). Refrigerated pizza crust
dough is always a great alternative.

Muffuletta Calzones
MAKES 4 SERVINGS;
PREP: 20 MIN., **BAKE:** 24 MIN.

*These calzones have all the tasty traits of
the classic sandwich: crusty bread filled
with layers of provolone, ham, salami,
and the essential olive salad. For even
more flavor, add 1 tsp. dried Italian
seasoning and ½ tsp. dried crushed red
pepper to the cheese blend. Rinsing the
pickled vegetables removes some of the
brine, making them a little less salty.
Roll each piece of dough a little at a time
so it can rest and stretch more easily.*

2 Tbsp. olive oil, divided
1 cup jarred mixed pickled vegetables,
    rinsed and finely chopped
1 (7-oz.) package shredded provolone-
    Italian cheese blend
8 thin slices Genoa salami, chopped
    (about ⅛ lb.)
½ cup diced cooked ham
¼ cup sliced pimiento-stuffed Spanish
    olives
1 lb. bakery pizza dough
2 Tbsp. grated Parmesan cheese

1. Preheat oven to 425°. Stir together
1 Tbsp. olive oil, pickled vegetables,
and next 4 ingredients.
2. Place dough on a lightly floured
surface. Cut dough into 4 equal pieces.
Roll each piece into a 7-inch circle.

3. Place 2 dough circles on a lightly
greased baking sheet. Spoon vegetable mixture evenly on top of circles,
mounding mixture on dough and leaving a 1-inch border. Moisten edges
of dough with water, and top with
remaining 2 dough circles. Press and
crimp edges to seal. Cut small slits on
tops to allow steam to escape. Brush
with remaining 1 Tbsp. olive oil, and
sprinkle with Parmesan cheese.
4. Bake at 425° for 20 to 24 minutes or
until golden brown.

Sausage-and-Cheese Calzones
MAKES 6 SERVINGS; **PREP:** 10 MIN.,
COOK: 10 MIN., **BAKE:** 26 MIN.

*We also tested with frozen vegetables, but
we found better flavor and saved money
by using a fresh bell pepper and onion.*

1 lb. mild or spicy Italian sausage, casings
    removed
1 medium onion, halved and sliced
1 large yellow or red bell pepper, sliced
1 (15-oz.) container low-fat ricotta cheese
2 large eggs
1½ tsp. salt-free herb-and-spice
    seasoning
2 (13.8-oz.) cans refrigerated pizza crust
    dough
½ cup pizza sauce*
1 (8-oz.) package shredded Italian
    six-cheese blend, divided

1. Preheat oven to 425°. Sauté first 3
ingredients in a large nonstick skillet
over medium-high heat 10 minutes or
until meat crumbles and is no longer
pink and vegetables are lightly
browned. Remove from skillet, and
drain well.

2. Stir together ricotta cheese, eggs, and seasoning.

3. Unroll 1 can of dough on a lightly greased baking sheet. Stretch dough into a 10- x 13-inch rectangle. Spoon ¼ cup pizza sauce, 1 cup ricotta mixture, and half of sausage mixture on half of rectangle, leaving a 1-inch border. Sprinkle with 1 cup cheese. Moisten edges with water; fold dough over, pressing and crimping edges to seal. Cut 3 (1-inch) slits on top of dough to allow steam to escape. Repeat procedure with remaining dough, pizza sauce, ricotta mixture, sausage mixture, and cheese.

4. Bake at 425° for 24 to 26 minutes or until golden. Serve with additional warm pizza sauce, if desired.

— HEDY TARANTO, NEW ROCHELLE, NEW YORK

*Marinara sauce may be substituted.
Note: For testing purposes only, we used Mrs. Dash Original Herb Seasoning Blend.

Cheesy Mexican Calzones:

Prepare recipe as directed, substituting 1 lb. ground beef and ½ tsp. salt for sausage, 2 tsp. salt-free Southwest chipotle seasoning and ¾ tsp. salt for salt-free herb-and-spice seasoning, and shredded Mexican four-cheese blend for shredded Italian six-cheese blend.
Note: For testing purposes only, we used Mrs. Dash Southwest Chipotle Seasoning Blend.

Calzones With Pasta Sauce

MAKES 4 SERVINGS; **PREP:** 20 MIN,
BAKE: 25 MIN., **STAND:** 5 MIN.

1 cup small-curd cottage cheese
3 Tbsp. grated Parmesan cheese
1 large egg
1 Tbsp. chopped fresh or 1 tsp. dried parsley
½ tsp. garlic powder
1 (3.5-oz.) package pepperoni slices, chopped *
4 Monterey Jack cheese slices, chopped
2 (10-oz.) cans refrigerated pizza crusts
2 cups Pasta Sauce, thawed

1. Preheat oven to 375°. Stir together first 5 ingredients until blended. Stir in pepperoni and chopped cheese slices.
2. Divide each pizza dough into 4 portions. Roll each portion into a 7-inch circle. Spoon ½ cup cottage cheese mixture in center of each circle. Fold dough over filling, pressing edges to seal; place on a lightly greased aluminum foil-lined baking sheet. Prick dough several times with a fork.
3. Bake at 375° for 20 to 25 minutes or until golden. Let stand 5 minutes. Serve calzones with warm Pasta Sauce.
* Chopped cooked ham may be substituted.

Pasta Sauce:

MAKES 12 CUPS; **PREP:** 10 MIN.,
COOK: 2 HR., 10 MIN.

2 small onions, chopped
4 garlic cloves, chopped
¼ cup vegetable oil
2 (28-oz.) cans diced tomatoes, undrained
2 (12-oz.) cans tomato paste
8 cups water
¼ cup sugar
2 Tbsp. dried Italian seasoning
1 Tbsp. salt
1 Tbsp. dried basil
2 tsp. ground black pepper
1 tsp. dried crushed red pepper

1. Sauté onion and garlic in hot oil in a Dutch oven over medium heat 10 minutes or until onion is tender. Stir in diced tomatoes and remaining ingredients. Bring to a boil; reduce heat, and simmer, stirring often, 2 hours. Divide into portions. Freeze remaining sauce for other uses.

Wow Weeknight Meal

Pair impressive pork tenderloin with updated Southern classics for an unforgettable trio of dishes.

Dinner on the Double

SERVES 4

Bacon-Wrapped Pork Tenderloin

Creamy Cheese Grits and Spinach

Sautéed Brown Sugar Pears or Ginger-Pear Shortcakes

Here's a menu that you can put together on a hectic day, yet it is fancy enough for company. Prep, but don't bake, the tenderloin before work in the morning, giving the seasoning time to work its delicious magic. While the tenderloin bakes, whip up the grits, and prep the ingredients for the pears. As your family clears the table, cook the pears and gather the gingersnaps and ice cream to accompany the pears for dessert.

Bacon-Wrapped Pork Tenderloin

freezeable • make ahead

MAKES 4 SERVINGS; **PREP:** 10 MIN.,
BAKE: 25 MIN., **BROIL:** 5 MIN.,
STAND: 10 MIN.

Pork tenderloin usually comes packed in pairs. Go ahead and season the other tenderloin in the package with your favorite spice blend. Wrap and freeze to jump-start another meal.

1 (1-lb.) pork tenderloin
1 tsp. steak seasoning
3 bacon slices, cut in half crosswise

1. Preheat oven to 425°. Remove silver skin from pork tenderloin, leaving a thin layer of fat covering the pork. Sprinkle seasoning over pork. Wrap pork with bacon slices, and secure with wooden picks. Place pork on a lightly greased wire rack in an aluminum foil-lined roasting pan.
2. Bake at 425° for 25 minutes or until a meat thermometer inserted into thickest portion registers 155°. Increase oven temperature to broil. Broil 5 inches from heat 3 to 5 minutes or until bacon is crisp. Remove from oven; cover pork with foil, and let stand 10 minutes or until thermometer registers 160°.
Note: For testing purposes only, we used McCormick Grill Mates Montreal Steak Seasoning.

Creamy Cheese Grits and Spinach

family favorite • fast fixin's

MAKES 4 TO 6 SERVINGS; **PREP:** 10 MIN.,
COOK: 15 MIN.

1 (5-oz.) package fresh baby spinach, thoroughly washed
1 cup quick-cooking grits
1½ cups vegetable broth
1 cup 2% reduced-fat milk
½ tsp. salt
⅛ tsp. garlic powder
½ (8-oz.) package shredded mozzarella-provolone cheese blend

1. Coarsely chop spinach. Bring grits and next 4 ingredients to a boil in a medium saucepan over medium-high heat; reduce heat to low, and simmer, stirring occasionally, 10 to 12 minutes or until thickened. Stir in spinach and cheese until well blended and cheese is melted. Serve immediately.

Sautéed Brown Sugar Pears

family favorite • fast fixin's

MAKES 4 SERVINGS; **PREP:** 15 MIN.,
COOK: 11 MIN.

This recipe can be easily doubled.

1 Tbsp. lemon juice
2 Anjou pears, peeled and cut into eighths
¼ cup firmly packed brown sugar
2 Tbsp. butter
1 tsp. cornstarch
½ tsp. vanilla extract
Vanilla ice cream
Gingersnaps

1. Sprinkle lemon juice over pears. Melt sugar and butter in a large nonstick skillet over medium heat, stirring occasionally, 2 minutes or until melted and smooth. Reduce heat to low; add pears, and cook, stirring often, 6 to 8 minutes or until pears are tender.
2. Whisk together cornstarch and 1 tsp. water. Stir into pear mixture, and cook 1 minute or until thickened. Remove from heat, and stir in vanilla extract. Serve with vanilla ice cream and gingersnaps.

Ginger-Pear Shortcakes

southernliving.com favorite

MAKES 12 SERVINGS; **PREP:** 20 MIN.,
BAKE: 12 MIN.

2½ cups all-purpose baking mix
1 Tbsp. sugar
½ cup plus 2 Tbsp. milk
2 Tbsp. molasses
¼ cup chopped walnuts
3 Tbsp. chopped crystallized ginger
1 Tbsp. butter, melted
¼ tsp. ground cinnamon
¼ tsp. cloves
Sautéed Pears
Whipped cream

1. Preheat oven to 375°. Stir together baking mix, sugar, milk, and molasses until a soft dough forms; turn out onto a lightly floured surface, and knead 3 to 4 times.
2. Pat dough to ¼-inch thickness, and cut with a 2¾-inch round biscuit cutter. Place on a lightly greased baking sheet.
3. Combine walnuts and next 4 ingredients; pat onto biscuit tops.
4. Bake at 375° for 12 minutes or until lightly browned. Cool.
5. Split shortcakes in half. Layer half of biscuit halves with Sautéed Pears and whipped cream; top with remaining biscuit halves.

Sautéed Pears

MAKES ABOUT 2½ CUPS; **PREP:** 10 MIN.,
COOK: 7 MIN.

6 Bosc pears, peeled and sliced
2 Tbsp. lemon juice
3 Tbsp. butter
3 Tbsp. brown sugar
1 Tbsp. vanilla extract
⅛ tsp. salt

1. Toss together pears and lemon juice.
2. Melt butter in a large skillet over medium-high heat. Add pear mixture, tossing to coat, and cook about 2 minutes; add brown sugar. Bring to a boil; reduce heat to low, and simmer 5 minutes or until pears are soft and sauce thickens slightly. Stir in vanilla and salt.

One-Bite Appetizers

Entertaining just got tastier with a simple display of mini cheese nibbles.

These make-ahead cheese truffles are so much better than the cheese balls you might remember. They are just the right size and ready to pop into your mouth. We received these recipes from longtime reader Clairiece Gilbert Humphrey of Charlottesville, Virginia. Serve them with the menu on page 82 or at your next wine-and-cheese gathering. Mix and match the toppings and cheeses for endless combinations.

Feta Cheese Truffles
make ahead

MAKES 6 APPETIZER SERVINGS;
PREP: 20 MIN., CHILL: 1 HR.

4 oz. cream cheese, softened
1 (4-oz.) container crumbled feta cheese
½ tsp. Worcestershire sauce
2 tsp. finely chopped onion
¼ tsp. black pepper
½ cup chopped fresh parsley
Cucumber slices
Grape tomatoes
Kalamata olives
Whole almonds

1. Beat first 5 ingredients at medium speed with an electric mixer until well combined. Cover mixture tightly, and chill at least 1 hour or until firm (can chill up to 3 days).
2. Roll cheese mixture into ¾-inch-round balls. Roll each ball in parsley. Serve immediately, or cover and chill until ready to serve. If chilled, let stand 30 minutes before serving. Serve with cucumber slices, grape tomatoes, kalamata olives, and whole almonds.

Gorgonzola Truffles
make ahead

MAKES 6 APPETIZER SERVINGS;
PREP: 20 MIN., CHILL: 1 HR.

Crisp, crumbled bacon adds texture to these creamy truffles. Serve them with a hearty red wine. (Pictured on page 8)

4 oz. cream cheese, softened
1 (4-oz.) container crumbled Gorgonzola cheese
2 tsp. finely chopped onion
½ tsp. Worcestershire sauce
¼ tsp. black pepper
½ cup cooked and crumbled bacon
Apple and pear slices
Grapes

1. Beat first 5 ingredients at medium speed with an electric mixer until well combined. Cover tightly, and chill at least 1 hour or until firm (can chill up to 3 days).
2. Roll cheese mixture into ¾-inch-round balls. Roll each ball in bacon. Serve immediately, or cover and chill until ready to serve. If chilled, let stand 30 minutes before serving. Serve with apple and pear slices and grapes.

Goat Cheese Truffles
make ahead

MAKES 6 APPETIZER SERVINGS;
PREP: 20 MIN., CHILL: 1 HR.

4 oz. cream cheese, softened
1 (4-oz.) container crumbled goat cheese
½ tsp. Worcestershire sauce
2 tsp. finely chopped onion
¼ tsp. black pepper
½ cup toasted, chopped pecans
Dried figs
Dried apricots

1. Beat first 5 ingredients at medium speed with an electric mixer until well combined. Cover tightly, and chill at least 1 hour or until firm (can chill up to 3 days).
2. Roll cheese mixture into ¾-inch-round balls. Roll each ball in pecans. Serve immediately, or cover and chill until ready to serve. If chilled, let stand 30 minutes before serving. Serve with dried figs and apricots.

Sweet and Pretty

These special little cakes are almost effortless and too delicious to resist.

The rich, moist texture of this divine angel food cake is unlike any other. Made from scratch in minutes, it's baked in a 13- x 9-inch pan and spread with frosting that's a lemon lover's dream. The two-step method for mixing the cake batter is unique, calling for a blend of sugar and flour to be folded into a billowy mound of egg whites. The inspiration of a Texas chicken farmer's wife, the recipe was passed along to workers and on again to a *Southern Living* reader, who graciously shared it with us.

Heavenly Angel Food Cake

MAKES 15 SERVINGS; **PREP:** 15 MIN.,
BAKE: 35 MIN., **COOL:** 1 HR.

A luscious layer of cream cheese frosting spills over freshly cut slices of this cake. As a fun garnish, Gumdrop Rose Petals sparkle with homemade charm. You may also bake this batter in an ungreased angel food cake pan for 30 to 35 minutes or in 3 ungreased (9-inch) round pans for 15 to 18 minutes or until a wooden pick inserted in center comes out clean. (Pictured on page 6)

2½ cups sugar
1½ cups all-purpose flour
¼ tsp. salt
2½ cups egg whites
1 tsp. cream of tartar
1 tsp. vanilla extract
1 tsp. fresh lemon juice
Lemon-Cream Cheese Frosting
Garnishes: Gumdrop Rose Petals (see
   page 99), fresh mint leaves

1. Preheat oven to 375°. Line bottom and sides of a 13- x 9-inch pan with aluminum foil, allowing 2 to 3 inches to extend over sides of pan. (Do not grease pan or foil.) Sift together first 3 ingredients.

2. Beat egg whites and cream of tartar at high speed with a heavy-duty electric stand mixer until stiff peaks form. Gradually fold in sugar mixture, ⅓ cup at a time, folding just until blended after each addition. Fold in vanilla and lemon juice. Spoon batter into prepared pan. (Pan will be very full. The batter will reach almost to the top of the pan.)

3. Bake at 375° on an oven rack one-third up from bottom of oven 30 to 35 minutes or until a wooden pick inserted in center of cake comes out clean. Invert cake onto a lightly greased wire rack; let cool, with pan over cake, 1 hour or until completely cool. Remove pan; peel foil off cake. Transfer cake to a serving platter. Spread Lemon-Cream Cheese Frosting evenly over top of cake. Garnish, if desired.

Lemon-Cream Cheese Frosting:
MAKES ABOUT 3½ CUPS; **PREP:** 10 MIN.

This is a very soft frosting, perfect for spreading over a sheet cake. If you use it for a layer cake, reduce the lemon juice to 1 Tbsp.

1½ (8-oz.) packages cream cheese, softened
¼ cup butter, softened
¼ cup fresh lemon juice
1 (16-oz.) package powdered sugar
2 tsp. lemon zest

1. Beat cream cheese and butter at medium speed with an electric mixer until creamy; add lemon juice, beating just until blended. Gradually add powdered sugar, beating at low speed until blended; stir in lemon zest.

— **LINDA NESLONEY**, RHOME, TEXAS

Cook's Notes

- Cracking and separating fresh eggs doesn't take long, but you can make this recipe even faster using pasteurized egg whites—and there's no need to worry about leftover yolks! See page 99 to learn more.
- The slightest bit of grease can ruin beaten egg whites, so be sure the mixing bowl and whisk attachment are completely clean and dry and that no traces of yolk slip into the whites.
- It's important to beat the egg whites properly before adding the sugar mixture. Stiffly beaten egg whites will form a peak that holds its upright shape when the whisk is lifted; a soft peak will droop. If they are beaten too much, egg whites begin to curdle and can't be used.
- Use a large rubber spatula to fold in the sugar mixture, gently scooping down to the bottom of the center of the bowl and up to the edges in a circular motion.

Cakes in Bloom

Tips, tricks, and fun ideas for making gumdrop flowers.

Egg Express

Pasteurized egg whites not only offer a speedy shortcut when making cakes, but they're also safe to use in recipes calling for uncooked egg whites, such as a chilled mousse or soufflé. Don't be alarmed by their appearance—the consistency is much thinner than fresh egg whites, but the structure is the same. When testing recipes, we find they yield the same great results.

Crowning Glories

You don't need a green thumb to make the candy rose petals that garnish Heavenly Angel Food Cake (opposite page)—just a handful of gumdrops and a dish of granulated sugar. Pretty enough to turn any dessert into a special occasion, gumdrop flowers can be made weeks ahead and stored in an airtight container.

Gumdrops are super-inexpensive, so play around and have some fun—the less formal the shaping, the more natural the petals look. Like learning to crimp the edges of a piecrust, there's a rhythm that comes easily after making a few. Use these ideas as inspiration. Many of the tips and techniques for making rose petals can also be used to create other flowers.

- **Gumdrop Rose Petals:** Using your thumbs and forefingers, flatten one small gumdrop to ⅛-inch thickness, lengthening and widening to form a petal shape. Dredge lightly in granulated sugar to prevent sticking as you work. Repeat procedure for desired number of petals. Place petals on a wire rack, and let stand uncovered for 24 hours. Holding each petal between your thumbs and forefingers, use your thumb to press the lower center portion of the petal inward, cupping the petal. Gently curl the top outer edges of the petal backward.
- **Plan ahead when making rose petals:** They need to stand for about 24 hours to stiffen slightly before adding the finishing touches that make them look so realistic.
- **Use a single brightly colored gumdrop** to shape the petals, or knead two colors together—such as red and white to make pink. Add more white to soften the color and create a paler pink, or add a pinch of yellow to highlight a portion of the petal. Experiment with different color combinations to see which you like best. For the prettiest petals, don't over-blend the colors or be too exact with the shaping.
- **Dampen fingertips to prevent sticking** when kneading gumdrops together. (A folded paper towel moistened with water works great—it's like a stamp pad for your fingertips.) It's easier to work with just three or four gumdrops at a time when blending new colors. After kneading several together, dredge lightly in sugar, and divide the mixture into small gumdrop-size portions for shaping individual petals and flowers.

Party Pickups Gumdrop flowers really

dress up store-bought sweets for a spur-of-the-moment party. Plain lemon tarts, purchased from the bakery, glisten when topped with tiny bouquets of Gumdrop Honeysuckle blooms. They can even be used to add sparkle to place cards or brighten a napkin ring.

- **Gumdrop Honeysuckle:** Using your thumbs and forefingers, flatten one small yellow or white gumdrop to ⅛-inch thickness; dredge lightly in granulated sugar. Using a stephanotis cutter, cut shape; flatten slightly between fingertips, and dredge in granulated sugar. Roll shape to resemble a trumpet; gently press seam to seal. Fold petals down slightly to form a honeysuckle bloom. Repeat procedure for desired number of blooms.
- **To make peach-colored honeysuckle blooms,** knead 1 yellow and 2 white gumdrops together with about one-third of an orange gumdrop; dredge lightly in sugar, and divide into small gumdrop-size portions for shaping.
- **Try using the same cutter and rolling technique** with red gumdrops. Paired with fresh mint, the bright trumpet-shaped blooms make a spectacular garnish for a hummingbird cake.
- **After cutting the desired shapes** from flattened gumdrops, use the leftover scraps for rolling tiny buds and berries or other whimsical flowers.

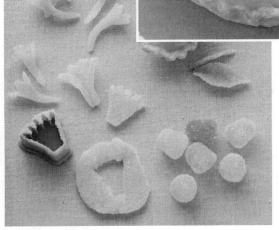

Fresh-Cut Flowers
Lavender and blue Gumdrop Violets, along with fresh mint leaves, make a magical border for a layer cake. **Tip:** Gumdrop colors can vary with packaging, so use the same brand of purple gumdrops for all your flowers.

While rose petals are shaped completely by hand, violets and honeysuckle blooms get a quick start with gumpaste cutters. Sold in small sets and flower-making kits, gumpaste cutters can be found in the cake-decorating section of crafts stores.

The same cutter and shaping technique can be used to create other flowers. For example, the blossom cutter used for violets also makes beautiful yellow forsythia and pink phlox.

- **Gumdrop Violets:** Using your thumbs and forefingers, flatten one small purple gumdrop to ⅛-inch thickness; dredge lightly in granulated sugar. Using a blossom cutter, cut shape; flatten slightly between fingertips, and dredge in granulated sugar. Pinch the center from behind, gently squeezing to form a bell-shaped blossom. Repeat procedure for desired number of violets.
- **You can use a small wooden dowel** to roll out the gumdrops before cutting and shaping, but we found it easier to simply flatten them between our thumbs and forefingers.
- **Lightly coating the cutter** with vegetable cooking spray minimizes sticking. The same trick works with scissors if you use them to cut leaf shapes or to snip and trim free-form flowers from flattened gumdrops.
- **When necessary, use the blunt tip** of a wooden pick or bamboo skewer to help release the shape from the cutter. After making several flowers, you may need to rinse and dry the cutter before reusing.

May

Grill It Your Way

When the weather warms up, invite friends over for a bring-your-own-meat party. Here we offer versatile and delicious side dishes for you to make, and then your guests can cook their meat the way they like it. It gets everybody outside and allows your guests to get involved with the cooking.

Bring-Your-Own-Meat Party

SERVES 8

Grilled Stuffed Peppers

Panzanella Salad

Grilled meat of choice or fish

Summer Vegetable Kabobs

Balsamic Strawberries or Chocolate Mint Sundaes

Grilled Stuffed Peppers
make ahead

MAKES ABOUT 24; **PREP:** 25 MIN., **GRILL:** 8 MIN.

Aluminum foil loaf pans hold peppers upright, which keeps the cheese inside. This method and cooking time works equally well with jalapeños, but we found the heat level of those peppers to be too unpredictable for everyone to enjoy.

2 pt. miniature sweet peppers

12 to 14 hickory-smoked bacon slices

1 (8-oz.) container garlic-and-herb spreadable cheese

8 (5- x 3-inch) disposable aluminum loaf pans

1. Preheat grill to 350° to 400° (medium-high). Cut ½ inch from stem end of each pepper. Remove and discard seeds and membranes.

2. Cut bacon slices in half crosswise. Microwave, in 2 batches, at HIGH 90 seconds or until bacon is partially cooked.

3. Spoon cheese into a 1-qt. zip-top plastic bag. (Do not seal.) Snip 1 corner of bag to make a small hole. Pipe cheese into cavity of each pepper, filling almost full.

4. Place 1 bacon half over cut side of each pepper, securing with a wooden pick.

5. Carefully cut 3 (1-inch) holes in bottom of each loaf pan. Turn pans upside down; place peppers, cut sides up, in holes in pans.

6. Grill peppers, in pans, covered with grill lid, over 350° to 400° (medium-high) heat 6 to 8 minutes or until bottoms of peppers are charred and bacon is crisp.

Note: To make ahead, prepare recipe as directed through Step 4. Cover and chill peppers 4 hours. Proceed with recipe as directed.

Panzanella Salad

MAKES 8 SERVINGS; **PREP:** 25 MIN., **GRILL:** 12 MIN.

This rustic and hearty Italian bread salad is an ideal accompaniment to any meal. The leftover tomato mixture is delicious tossed with fresh cooked pasta.

1 (12- to 16-oz.) ciabatta or Italian bread loaf

12 plum tomatoes, cut in half lengthwise

1 large red onion, cut into 8 wedges

5 Tbsp. olive oil, divided

½ seedless cucumber, halved and sliced

½ cup firmly packed chopped fresh basil

4 tsp. red wine vinegar

1½ tsp. minced garlic

Salt and pepper to taste

1. Preheat grill to 350° to 400° (medium-high). Cut bread loaf into 8 (1-inch-thick) slices; cut slices in half, if desired.

2. Drizzle tomatoes and onion with 2 Tbsp. oil, tossing to coat.

3. Grill tomatoes and onion, covered with grill lid, over 350° to 400° (medium-high) heat 3 to 4 minutes on each side or until lightly charred.

4. Coarsely chop grilled tomatoes and onion, and place in a medium bowl. Add 2 Tbsp. oil, cucumber, and next 3 ingredients. Season with salt and pepper to taste.

5. Brush bread slices with remaining 1 Tbsp. olive oil. Grill, without grill lid, over 350° to 400° (medium-high) heat 1 to 2 minutes on each side or until lightly browned and toasted.

6. Place grilled bread slices on individual serving plates; top with tomato mixture.

—**LORI WELANDER**, RICHMOND, VIRGINIA

TIP

Stylist Lisa Powell Bailey offers a few decorating tips to create a casual and festive setting for dinner with friends.

- Forget tablecloths; pick a color scheme for your party and paint an old picnic table to match.
- Fresh flowers on the table add a bright pop of color. Freesia is relatively inexpensive and has a pleasing aroma.
- For an evening party, lit trees and lots of candles keep the ambience festive.
- Dress up plain white plates by placing smaller colored or patterned plates on top.
- For an extra-special touch, buy cheap, colorful ribbons to tie in bows around rolled napkins for napkin rings.

Guidelines and Cook Times for Vegetable Kabobs

Cut vegetables thick so they will stay on skewers as they cook. Thread one type of vegetable onto each skewer, threading so the cut sides lie flat on the cooking grate to ensure even cooking. Grill skewers, covered with grill lid, over 350° to 400° (medium-high) heat according to the times below. Your goal is to achieve tender, slightly charred vegetables.

Bell peppers
- **PREP:** Cut into 1-inch-thick strips; thread skewers.
- **GRILL TIME:** 4 to 5 minutes on each side or until tender.

Cherry tomatoes
- **PREP:** Thread onto double skewers.
- **GRILL TIME:** 1 to 3 minutes on each side or just until skins begin to split.

Eggplant
- **PREP:** Cut Japanese eggplant into ¾-inch rounds. Cut Italian eggplant crosswise into quarters; cut into ¾-inch slices. Thread onto skewers.
- **GRILL TIME:** 5 to 6 minutes on each side or until tender.

Mushrooms
- **PREP:** Trim stems, and thread onto skewers.
- **GRILL TIME:** 3 to 5 minutes on each side or until tender.

Okra
- **PREP:** Remove stems, and thread onto double skewers.
- **GRILL TIME:** 6 to 8 minutes on each side or until tender.

Onions
- **PREP:** Cut into wedges, and thread onto skewers.
- **GRILL TIME:** 3 or 4 minutes on each side or until lightly charred.

Zucchini and squash
- **PREP:** Cut into ¾-inch rounds; thread onto skewers.
- **GRILL TIME:** 7 to 10 minutes on each side or until tender.

Summer Vegetable Kabobs

MAKES 8 SERVINGS; PREP: 25 MIN., SOAK: 1 HR., CHILL: 30 MIN., GRILL: VARIES

These kabobs marinate in a wine-and-honey vinaigrette. We suggest using a Chardonnay in the marinade.

12-inch-long wooden skewers
¼ cup dry white wine
¼ cup honey
3 garlic cloves, minced
2 Tbsp. balsamic vinegar
2 Tbsp. olive oil
1½ tsp. pepper
1 tsp. salt
16 cups assorted cut vegetables

1. Soak skewers in water 1 hour.
2. Whisk together wine and next 6 ingredients until well blended; reserve ¼ cup. Combine remaining white wine mixture and vegetables in a large bowl. Cover and chill at least 30 minutes or up to 2 hours. Remove vegetables from marinade, discarding marinade.
3. Preheat grill to 350° to 400° (medium-high). Thread vegetables onto skewers, and grill according to directions in "Guidelines and Cook Times for Vegetable Kabobs" box above.
4. Transfer skewers to a platter. Remove vegetables from skewers, if desired. Serve with reserved ¼ cup white wine mixture.

—LAURIE HAMAN, BOWDOINHAM, MAINE

Balsamic Strawberries

MAKES 8 SERVINGS ; PREP: 10 MIN., STAND: 2 HR.

Individual ice cream cups, short-bread cookies, and chocolate curls give Balsamic Strawberries an elegant presentation. Run a butter knife or offset spatula along sides of the ice-cream cups to easily remove the ice cream. Ice cream and cookies can be assembled a few hours ahead and placed in the freezer until ready to serve.

1 (16-oz.) container fresh strawberries, quartered
¼ cup sugar
4 tsp. balsamic vinegar
8 round shortbread cookies
8 (3-oz.) vanilla ice-cream cups
Garnishes: chocolate curls, fresh basil sprigs

1. Combine first 3 ingredients in a medium bowl; let stand 1 to 2 hours at room temperature, stirring occasionally.
2. Place shortbread cookies on individual servings plates. Remove ice cream from cups, and place on cookies. Spoon strawberry mixture over ice cream. Garnish, if desired. Serve immediately.
Note: For testing purposes only, we used Walkers Shortbread Rounds.

Chocolate Mint Sundaes

southernliving.com favorite
MAKES 8 SERVINGS; PREP: 5 MIN.

24 (0.25-oz.) chocolate-covered peppermint patties
½ cup. milk
Vanilla ice cream

1. Place peppermint patties and milk in a medium microwave-safe glass bowl. Cover and microwave at HIGH 1 minute or until patties melt, stirring every 15 seconds. Serve over ice cream.
NOTE: For testing purposes only, we used York Peppermint Patties.

—LIZ CHIZ, LOS ANGELES, CALIFORNIA

This month take your gatherings outdoors and enjoy the beautiful weather.

Fun on Cinco de Mayo

Celebrate May in a light way. Host your very own Mexican-style fiesta.

Cinco de Mayo Fiesta

SERVES 6

Fiesta Dip

Scarlet Margaritas

Tortilla-Crusted Pork

Avocado Fruit Salad

It's the perfect occasion to throw a party. To help you celebrate, we created a healthy Mexican-inspired Cinco de Mayo menu—complete with margaritas. The only additions you'll need are good company, decorations, and music. Dahlias will add true Mexican flair to your table and brighten your home throughout the spring and summer months. Spice up your decorations by using assorted fresh chiles and other peppers. Grab some maracas and dancing shoes, and bring your appetite for a fiesta to remember. Olé!

Fiesta Dip
make ahead

MAKES 1½ CUPS; **PREP:** 15 MIN., **CHILL:** 1 HR.

Make this dip a day ahead to get a jump-start on your party.

1 (8-oz.) package ⅓-less-fat cream cheese, softened
½ cup nonfat plain yogurt
¼ cup light mayonnaise
2 Tbsp. chopped fresh cilantro
1½ tsp. lime juice
½ tsp. hot sauce
¼ tsp. salt
⅓ cup chopped jarred roasted red bell peppers
2 Tbsp. finely chopped green onion
Fresh Squash Chips

1. Process first 7 ingredients in a food processor 30 to 45 seconds or until smooth, stopping to scrape down sides. Stir in red peppers and green onion. Cover and chill 1 hour. Serve with Fresh Squash Chips.

—MARIA ALDRIDGE, NEWLAND, NORTH CAROLINA

Per (¼-cup) serving (not including Fresh Squash Chips): Calories 132; Fat 10g (sat 4.9g, mono 1.9g, poly 0.2g); Protein 4.9g; Carb 5.7g; Fiber 0.1g; Chol 25mg; Iron 0.7mg; Sodium 325mg; Calc 69mg

Fresh Squash Chips:

MAKES 6 SERVINGS (ABOUT 4 CUPS); **PREP:** 10 MIN., **CHILL:** 30 MIN.

Soaking the veggies in cold water makes the chips perfectly crisp for dipping.

2 zucchini, cut into ¼-inch-thick rounds
2 yellow squash, cut into ¼-inch-thick rounds
¼ tsp. salt

1. Combine all ingredients and 4 cups cold water in a large bowl. Cover and chill 30 minutes; drain and pat dry with paper towels.

Per serving: Calories 21; Fat 0.2g (sat 0g, mono 0g, poly 0.1g); Protein 1.6g; Carb 4.4g; Fiber 1.4g; Chol 0mg; Iron 0.5mg; Sodium 86mg; Calc 19mg

Scarlet Margaritas
fast fixin's

MAKES 6 SERVINGS; **PREP:** 10 MIN.

Feel free to indulge in these sweet sippers. They have about half the calories of the traditional beverage. If pomegranates are not available, no problem. This drink is just as delicious without the fresh seeds.

4 cups crushed ice
1 cup pomegranate juice
½ cup orange liqueur
½ cup tequila
1 Tbsp. lime juice
¼ cup. pomegranate seeds (½ fresh pomegranate) (optional)
Lime wedges
Coarse salt
Garnish: lime slices

1. Process first 5 ingredients, and, if desired, pomegranate seeds in a blender 30 seconds or until frothy.
2. Rub rims of 6 glasses with lime wedges; dip in salt to coat. Pour margarita evenly into prepared glasses. Garnish, if desired. Serve immediately.

—GORDON BINGHAM, MOUNT PLEASANT, SOUTH CAROLINA

Note: For testing purposes only, we used Pom Wonderful 100% Pomegranate Juice.

Per (1-cup) serving: Calories 137; Fat 0g (sat 0g, mono 0g, poly 0g); Protein 0.2g; Carb 12.5g; Fiber 0g; Chol 0mg; Iron 0.1mg; Sodium 5mg; Calc 7mg

Healthy Living

Tortilla-Crusted Pork

MAKES 6 SERVINGS; **PREP:** 20 MIN.,
COOK: 12 MIN.

*These pork medallions are a Tex-Mex
lover's dream. Let the pork sear evenly
on each side to allow the coating to reach
maximum crispness.*

2 lb. pork tenderloin
½ cup finely crushed blue-corn tortilla chips
½ cup finely crushed tortilla chips
1 Tbsp. coarsely ground pepper
½ tsp. chili powder
½ tsp. salt
¼ tsp. ground cumin
3 Tbsp. extra virgin olive oil, divided
Pico de Gallo
Tomatillo Salsa
Garnish: fresh cilantro sprigs

1. Remove silver skin from tenderloin,
leaving a thin layer of fat covering tenderloin. Cut tenderloin into 1-inch-thick
medallions.
2. Combine blue-corn tortilla chips and
next 5 ingredients in a bowl. Brush pork
medallions with 1½ Tbsp. olive oil, and
dredge in tortilla chip mixture, pressing
mixture into medallions on all sides to
thoroughly coat.
3. Cook pork medallions in remaining
1½ Tbsp. hot oil in a large skillet over
medium heat 6 minutes on each side or
until done. Serve with salsas. Garnish,
if desired.

—KARIN JANE STERN, HUTTO, TEXAS

Per serving (not including salsas): Calories 262; Fat 12.5g (sat 2.8g,
mono 7.3g, poly 1.6g); Protein 32.4g; Carb 4.1g; Fiber 0.6g; Chol 98mg;
Iron 2mg; Sodium 262mg; Calc 21mg

Pico de Gallo:

make ahead

MAKES 3 CUPS; **PREP:** 15 MIN., **CHILL:** 1 HR.

*Pico de Gallo is best when made the day
you plan to serve it. Prepare it early the
morning of the party and spoon atop a
fried egg or in an omelet; just be sure to
save enough for the pork.*

2 medium tomatoes, seeded and diced
1 medium-size ripe avocado, diced
¼ cup diced white onion
1 serrano or jalapeño pepper, seeded and
    finely chopped
2 Tbsp. lime juice
1 Tbsp. extra virgin olive oil
Salt to taste

1. Toss together first 6 ingredients in a
medium bowl. Cover and chill 1 hour.
Season with salt to taste.

—KARIN JANE STERN, HUTTO, TEXAS

Per (½-cup) serving: Calories 83; Fat 6.9g (sat 0.9g, mono 4.5g,
poly 0.9g); Protein 1.2g; Carb 6g; Fiber 2.8g; Chol 0mg; Iron 0.4mg;
Sodium 5.7mg; Calc 12mg

Tomatillo Salsa:

make ahead

MAKES 3 CUPS; **PREP:** 15 MIN., **CHILL:** 1 HR.

*Serve this salsa with tortilla chips for a
quick snack.*

2 cups diced tomatillo
½ cup diced onion
2 Tbsp. chopped fresh cilantro
2 Tbsp. extra virgin olive oil
1 jalapeño pepper, seeded and finely
    chopped
1 Tbsp. lime juice
½ tsp. pepper
Salt to taste

1. Stir together first 7 ingredients in a
medium bowl. Cover and chill 1 hour.
Season with salt to taste.

Per (½-cup) serving: Calories 61; Fat 5g (sat 0.7g, mono 3.4g,
poly 0.9g); Protein 0.6g; Carb 4.2g; Fiber 1.2g; Chol 0mg; Iron 0.3mg;
Sodium 1.2mg; Calc 6.9mg

Healthy Benefits

- Avocados are an excellent
  source of folate and fiber. They're
  packed full of heart-healthy
  monounsaturated fats and have
  been found to lower LDL (bad)
  cholesterol and triglycerides.
- Cooking with chiles and other
  peppers not only enhances the
  flavor of your food but also adds
  nutrients such as vitamin A,
  vitamin C, and potassium.

Avocado Fruit Salad

make ahead

MAKES 6 CUPS; **PREP:** 15 MIN., **CHILL:** 1 HR.

*You can prepare this salad a day ahead,
but don't cut up the avocado or add garnishes until just before you serve it.*

1 (24-oz.) jar refrigerated orange and grape-
    fruit sections, rinsed, drained, and
    patted dry
1 (24-oz.) jar refrigerated tropical mixed fruit
    in light syrup, rinsed, drained, and
    patted dry
2 cups cubed fresh cantaloupe
1 medium-size ripe avocado, halved and cut
    into chunks
¼ cup chopped fresh mint
2 Tbsp. lime juice
Garnishes: light sour cream, crushed
    pistachios

1. Toss together first 6 ingredients.
Cover and chill 1 hour. Garnish, if
desired.

—CHRIS BRYANT, JOHNSON CITY, TENNESSEE

Note: For testing purposes only, we
used Del Monte SunFresh Citrus Salad
and Del Monte SunFresh Tropical
Mixed Fruit in Light Syrup With
Passion Fruit Juice.

Per (1-cup) serving (not including garnish): Calories 166; Fat 4.7g
(sat 0.7g, mono 2.8g, poly 0.6g); Protein 1.9g; Carb 32.8g; Fiber 3.5g;
Chol 0mg; Iron 1.3mg; Sodium 33mg; Calc 66mg

A Southern Secret

We're absolutely crazy about tart, creamy buttermilk. It's our Test Kitchens' favorite surprise ingredient.

It's probably the most misunderstood item in the dairy case. With flecks of butter punctuating its smooth texture, buttermilk as a beverage lacks a certain appeal. But as an ingredient, it's a Southern superstar. It enhances baked goods, adds richness to gravies, and offers a creamy base for salad dressings. Want light, tender biscuits or cake layers? Substitute buttermilk for some of the milk. Need a good soaking liquid for that chicken you're planning to fry or bake? Buttermilk not only boosts the flavor and tenderizes the meat, but it also helps the breading cling to the chicken.

Past generations crumbled cornbread into the tangy beverage as a light meal. While today we enjoy buttermilk in the cornbread, rather than the other way around, we still know a good thing when we taste it. Try these splendid recipes, and you'll want to adopt buttermilk as your own secret ingredient. But don't worry. We won't tell a soul.

A Not-so-Buttery Product

Though buttermilk seems richer and creamier than regular milk, it actually contains the same fat content as the whole, low-fat, and nonfat milks from which it is made. Originally, it was the liquid that remained after churning butter. Today's commercial buttermilk is made by adding lactic acid to pasteurized, homogenized milk, causing it to thicken and sour. (The process is similar to the one used to make sour cream and yogurt.) Some producers add a few flecks of butter for color and richness. The acid makes buttermilk a prized ingredient in baked goods—it tenderizes them and lends depth of flavor. It also makes this milk a long-lasting staple that will keep in the refrigerator for up to a week past its sell-by date.

Buttermilk-Garlic Mashed Potatoes
fast fixin's
MAKES 4 SERVINGS; PREP: 10 MIN., COOK: 6 MIN.

Buttermilk replaces some of the butter in these potatoes with outstanding results.

2 Tbsp. butter
3 garlic cloves, chopped
2 cups buttermilk
⅔ cup milk
½ tsp. salt
½ tsp. pepper
1 (22-oz.) package frozen mashed potatoes

1. Melt butter in a Dutch oven over medium heat; add garlic, and sauté 1 minute. Add buttermilk and next 3 ingredients. Cook, stirring constantly, 5 minutes or until thoroughly heated. Stir in potatoes until smooth.
Note: For testing purposes only, we used Ore-Ida Mashed Potatoes.

Cornbread Stew
MAKES 10 TO 12 SERVINGS; PREP: 15 MIN., BAKE: 15 MIN., COOK: 13 MIN.

Serve this stew as a side, or add leftover cooked ham or chicken for a casual main dish.

Basic Buttermilk Cornbread
1 shallot, minced
2 garlic cloves, minced
2 Tbsp. olive oil
6 cups vegetable broth
1½ cups (6 oz.) shredded Cheddar cheese
1 cup buttermilk
¼ tsp. salt
¼ tsp. pepper

1. Preheat oven to 400°. Crumble cornbread into bowl of a food processor. Pulse 6 to 8 times or until coarse crumbs form (about 5 cups coarse crumbs).
2. Spread crumbs on a 15- x 10-inch baking sheet. Bake at 400° for 15 minutes or until lightly toasted.
3. Sauté shallot and garlic in hot oil in a Dutch oven over medium heat 3 minutes or until tender. Stir in crumbs, broth, and next 4 ingredients; cook, stirring often, 10 minutes or until mixture thickens.

Basic Buttermilk Cornbread:
MAKES 8 SERVINGS; PREP: 10 MIN., BAKE: 38 MIN.

¼ cup butter
1½ cups buttermilk
1 large egg
2 cups self-rising cornmeal

1. Preheat oven to 425°. Melt ¼ cup butter in a 10-inch cast-iron skillet in oven 8 minutes.
2. Whisk together buttermilk and egg in a large bowl; add melted butter from skillet, whisking until blended. Whisk in cornmeal until smooth. Spoon into hot skillet.
3. Bake at 425° for 30 minutes or until golden.

—LEIGH WHATLEY, MARIETTA, GEORGIA

Herbed Beef Roast With Tomato Gravy
family favorite

MAKES 8 SERVINGS; **PREP:** 20 MIN.;
BAKE: 1 HR., 10 MIN.; **STAND:** 10 MIN.

Serve this traditional-style roast for company, or try our slow-cooked chuck roast variation for a delicious down-home dinner. Freeze any leftovers in the flavorful gravy to enjoy when there's no time to cook.

Vegetable cooking spray
2 tsp. minced garlic
2 tsp. chopped fresh rosemary
2 tsp. kosher salt
1 tsp. chopped fresh thyme
1 tsp. pepper
⅛ tsp. onion powder
1 (2-lb.) boneless beef rump roast
2 cups uncooked jasmine rice
Tomato Gravy

1. Preheat oven to 325°. Line a 13- x 9-inch pan with heavy-duty aluminum foil, and coat with cooking spray.
2. Combine minced garlic and next 5 ingredients in a small bowl. Rub garlic mixture over rump roast. Place roast in prepared pan.
3. Bake at 325° for 1 hour and 10 minutes or until a meat thermometer inserted in thickest portion registers 145° (medium rare). Let stand 10 minutes.
4. Meanwhile, prepare jasmine rice according to package directions. Cut roast into slices; serve with hot cooked rice and Tomato Gravy.

Herbed Chuck Roast: Prepare as directed in Step 1. Substitute 1 (2-lb.) boneless chuck roast, trimmed, for rump roast; combine rosemary and next 4 ingredients. Rub over roast. Cook roast in a large nonstick skillet over medium heat 5 minutes on each side or until browned. Place in prepared pan. Rub minced garlic over top of roast. Add ¾ cup beef broth to pan. Bake, covered, at 350° for 2 hours and 10 minutes or until fork-tender. Let stand 10 minutes. Proceed with recipe as directed in Step 4.

Tomato Gravy:
MAKES ABOUT 2 CUPS; **PREP:** 10 MIN.,
COOK: 10 MIN.

2 Tbsp. butter
2 Tbsp. all-purpose flour
1 (15-oz.) can beef broth
1½ Tbsp. tomato paste
¼ cup buttermilk
1 Tbsp. Worcestershire sauce
1 tsp. dark brown sugar

1. Melt butter in a small saucepan over medium heat; whisk in flour, and cook, whisking constantly, 1 minute. Slowly whisk in broth; bring to a boil. Whisk in tomato paste and next 3 ingredients; reduce heat, and simmer 5 minutes or until thoroughly heated.

—ANNA GINSBERG, AUSTIN, TEXAS

Buttermilk Drop Biscuits
MAKES 15 BISCUITS; **PREP:** 20 MIN.,
BAKE: 15 MIN.

Use a ¼-cup ice-cream scoop or lightly greased ¼-cup dry measuring cup to drop evenly sized biscuits.

3½ cups self-rising soft-wheat flour
2¼ tsp. baking powder
2¼ tsp. sugar
¼ cup shortening
¼ cup butter, chilled and cut into
    pieces
1½ cups buttermilk*
1 Tbsp. butter, melted

1. Preheat oven to 500°. Combine first 3 ingredients in a large bowl until well blended. Cut in shortening and butter with a pastry blender or a fork until crumbly. Add buttermilk, stirring just until dry ingredients are moistened.
2. Drop dough by ¼ cupfuls onto an ungreased baking sheet. Brush lightly with melted butter.
3. Bake at 500° for 12 to 15 minutes or until golden.
*Nonfat buttermilk may be substituted.
Note: For testing purposes only, we used White Lily Self-Rising Flour.

Cheese-Chive Drop Biscuits:
Stir ¾ cup (3 oz.) shredded Cheddar cheese and ¼ cup chopped fresh chives into crumbly flour mixture just before adding buttermilk. Increase buttermilk to 1¾ cups. Proceed with recipe as directed.

Fried Green Tomatoes
MAKES 6 TO 8 SERVINGS; **PREP:** 15 MIN.,
FRY: 6 MIN. PER BATCH

4 large green tomatoes
1½ cups buttermilk
1 Tbsp. salt
1 tsp. pepper
1 cup all-purpose flour
1 cup self-rising cornmeal
3 cups vegetable oil
Salt to taste

1. Cut tomatoes into ¼- to ⅓-inch-thick slices; place in a shallow dish. Pour buttermilk over tomatoes. Sprinkle with salt and pepper.
2. Combine flour and cornmeal in a shallow dish or pieplate. Dredge tomato slices in flour mixture.
3. Fry tomatoes, in batches, in hot oil in a large cast-iron skillet over medium heat 3 minutes on each side or until golden. Drain on paper towels. Sprinkle with salt to taste.

—CAROLYNE FISHER WILBANKS,
LAKE TOXAWAY, NORTH CAROLINA

Dipped first in buttermilk and then in a flour-and-cornmeal coating before frying, Fried Green Tomatoes come out hot, crisp, and juicy.

Strawberry-Buttermilk Sherbet

make ahead • freezeable

MAKES ABOUT 4½ CUPS; PREP: 15 MIN., CHILL: 1 HR., FREEZE: 2 HR.

The tang of buttermilk balances the sweetness of the berries in this top-rated dessert. (Pictured on page 7)

2 cups fresh strawberries*
2 cups buttermilk
1 cup sugar
1 tsp. vanilla extract
Garnish: fresh mint sprigs

1. Process strawberries in a food processor or blender 30 seconds or until smooth, stopping to scrape down sides. Pour strawberry puree through a fine wire-mesh strainer into a large bowl, pressing with back of a spoon. Discard solids. Add buttermilk, sugar, and vanilla to puree; stir until well blended. Cover and chill 1 hour.
2. Pour strawberry mixture into freezer container of a 1½-qt. electric ice-cream maker, and freeze according to manufacturer's instructions. (Instructions and times may vary.) Garnish, if desired.
*1 (16-oz.) package frozen strawberries, thawed, may be substituted.

Buttermilk Breakfast Cake

family favorite

MAKES 10 TO 12 SERVINGS; PREP: 20 MIN., BAKE: 45 MIN., COOL: 35 MIN.

Buttermilk replaces sour cream in our twist on Carol Ann Roberts Dumond's not-too-sweet Bundt cake.

1 (18.25-oz.) package white cake mix
1 cup buttermilk
½ cup melted butter
5 large eggs
3 Tbsp. light brown sugar
2 tsp. ground cinnamon
Shortening
1 Tbsp. granulated sugar
Buttermilk-Vanilla Glaze

GET INSPIRED

A Harvest by the Door

Imagine stepping out of your kitchen and picking your own fresh fruit. You can do just that by growing blueberries in a container—and it's not hard either. If you can grow an azalea, you can succeed with a blueberry bush. Just look at your local nursery for a rabbiteye blueberry that's already bearing fruit. (Our favorites are 'Delite' and 'Tifblue.') Plant it in a container filled with good soil and peat moss; then water it thoroughly. Be sure to place it in partial to full sun, and mulch well to help the plant retain moisture. Check daily during hot weather, because containers dry out quickly. Use an azalea fertilizer in the spring and fall. Not only will your blueberry bush look good year-round, providing bright fall color and great sculptural presence in winter, but you'll also be able to enjoy the sweet fruit for a month or so every summer.

Tip: Blueberries rank among the healthiest of foods. They are rich in antioxidants, such as vitamins C and E, and may reduce the risk of some kinds of cancer.

1. Preheat oven to 350°. Beat first 3 ingredients at medium speed with an electric mixer 1½ minutes or until thoroughly blended; add eggs, 1 at a time, beating well after each addition.
2. Stir together brown sugar and cinnamon in a small bowl.
3. Grease a 12-cup Bundt pan with shortening; sprinkle with 1 Tbsp. granulated sugar.
4. Spoon one-third of batter into prepared pan; sprinkle brown sugar mixture evenly over batter. Top with remaining batter.
5. Bake at 350° for 45 minutes or until a long wooden pick inserted in center of cake comes out clean. Cool cake in pan on a wire rack 15 minutes; remove from pan to wire rack, and cool 20 minutes. Drizzle Buttermilk-Vanilla Glaze over slightly warm cake.
Note: For testing purposes only, we used Pillsbury Moist Supreme Classic White cake mix.

Buttermilk-Vanilla Glaze:

MAKES ABOUT ⅓ CUP; PREP: 5 MIN.

1 cup powdered sugar
1 Tbsp. melted butter
1 tsp. vanilla extract
1 to 2 Tbsp. buttermilk

1. Stir together first 3 ingredients and 1 Tbsp. buttermilk until smooth, adding additional 1 Tbsp. buttermilk, if necessary, for desired consistency.

—CAROL ANN ROBERTS DUMOND,
PRIDES CROSSING, MASSACHUSETTS

Bowl of Goodness

Add comfort to your table with these sensational soups.

Roasted Red Pepper Soup With Pesto Croutons

MAKES 6 SERVINGS; **PREP:** 20 MIN.,
BAKE: 20 MIN., **COOK:** 15 MIN.,
COOL: 10 MIN.

This company-worthy starter delivers robust color and flavor. Serve it hot or cold. If you serve the soup cold, stir in an extra ¼ tsp. salt.

¼ cup refrigerated pesto, at room
    temperature
6 sourdough bread slices
1 Tbsp. butter
1 Tbsp. olive oil
1 garlic clove, minced
1 shallot, finely chopped
1 Tbsp. tomato paste
1 (15-oz.) jar roasted red bell peppers,
    rinsed and drained
4 cups low-sodium chicken broth
¼ cup half-and-half
1 Tbsp. chopped fresh parsley
Salt and pepper to taste
Garnishes: fresh flat-leaf parsley sprigs,
    shaved Parmesan cheese

1. Preheat oven to 350°. Spread pesto on 1 side of each bread slice. Cut each bread slice into ½- to 1-inch cubes. Place bread cubes in a single layer on a lightly greased aluminum foil-lined jelly-roll pan.
2. Bake at 350° for 16 to 20 minutes or until golden, turning once after 10 minutes. Remove from oven, and let cool.
3. Melt butter with oil in a large Dutch oven over medium-high heat. Add garlic and shallot, and cook, stirring constantly, 2 minutes or until vegetables are tender. Add tomato paste, and cook, stirring constantly, 1 minute. Stir in bell peppers and chicken broth; bring to a boil. Reduce heat to medium, and simmer, stirring occasionally, 5 minutes. Remove from heat; let cool 10 minutes.

4. Process red pepper mixture, in batches, in a blender or food processor 8 to 10 seconds until smooth, stopping to scrape down sides. Return red pepper mixture to Dutch oven; stir in half-and-half and parsley, and cook over medium heat 5 minutes or until thoroughly heated. Season with salt and pepper to taste.
5. Ladle soup into 6 bowls; top with croutons. Garnish, if desired.

— AMANDA FREMOUW, FRANKLIN, TENNESSEE

Asparagus Soup

MAKES 8 SERVINGS; **PREP:** 25 MIN.,
BAKE: 16 MIN., **COOK:** 25 MIN.,
COOL: 10 MIN.

1 lb. fresh asparagus
Olive oil cooking spray
½ tsp. kosher salt
½ tsp. pepper
4 Tbsp. butter
1 sweet onion, diced
2 medium-size red potatoes, peeled and diced
4 cups chicken broth
Salt and pepper to taste

1. Preheat oven to 400°. Snap off and discard tough ends of asparagus. Coat asparagus lightly with cooking spray, and arrange in an aluminum foil-lined jelly-roll pan. Sprinkle with ½ tsp. kosher salt and ½ tsp. pepper.
2. Bake at 400° for 16 minutes or until tender and slightly browned, turning after 8 minutes. Remove from oven; let cool.
3. Meanwhile, melt 2 Tbsp. butter in a large Dutch oven over medium-high heat; add onion, and cook, stirring frequently, 3 minutes or until tender. Add remaining butter, and stir until melted. Add potatoes, and cook, stirring occasionally, 3 minutes. Stir in chicken broth. Bring to boil; reduce heat to medium, and simmer 6 minutes or until potatoes are tender.

4. Chop asparagus into ¼-inch pieces. Add chopped asparagus to soup; cook, stirring occasionally, 4 minutes. Remove soup from heat, and let cool 10 minutes.
5. Process asparagus mixture, in batches, in a blender or food processor 8 to 10 seconds or until smooth, stopping to scrape down sides. Return asparagus mixture to Dutch oven. Cook over medium heat, stirring occasionally, 5 minutes or until thoroughly heated. Season with salt and pepper to taste. Serve immediately.

Corn-and-Crab Chowder
southernliving.com favorite
MAKES 10 CUPS; **PREP:** 20 MIN.,
COOK: 55 MIN.

6 bacon slices
2 celery ribs, diced
1 medium-size green bell pepper, diced
1 medium onion, diced
1 jalapeño pepper, seeded and diced
1 (32-oz.) container chicken broth
3 Tbsp. all-purpose flour
3 cups fresh corn kernels (6 ears)
1 lb. fresh lump crabmeat, drained and
    picked*
1 cup whipping cream
¼ cup chopped fresh cilantro
½ tsp. salt
¼ tsp. pepper
Oyster crackers

1. Cook bacon in a Dutch oven over medium heat 8 to 10 minutes or until crisp; remove bacon, and drain on paper towels, reserving 2 Tbsp. drippings in Dutch oven. Crumble bacon.
2. Sauté celery and next 3 ingredients in hot drippings 5 to 6 minutes or until tender.
3. Whisk together broth and flour until smooth. Add to celery mixture. Stir in corn. Bring to a boil; reduce heat, and simmer, stirring occasionally, 30 minutes. Gently stir in crabmeat and next 4 ingredients; cook 4 to 5 minutes or until thoroughly heated. Serve warm with crumbled bacon and oyster crackers.
*1 lb. peeled cooked shrimp or chopped cooked chicken may be substituted.

Fresh Catch

These bite-size fish nuggets are as easy to cook as chicken and just as versatile. When shopping for fish, see what looks the freshest. We chose catfish, salmon, and cod for these recipes, but any mild white fillets, such as tilapia or halibut, can be used with the same delicious results. You can also use a selection of frozen fish for these recipes. To preserve the fresh taste and texture, always thaw in the refrigerator, allowing about 24 hours for a 1-lb package.

Light Bites

Pan-Seared Salmon Nuggets

Here is a terrific low-fat technique for pan-frying almost any type of fish. You can cook a single serving or several batches—just be sure not to overcrowd the skillet, or the fish will steam rather than crisp and brown. These fall-apart tender salmon nuggets are great served over a medley of sautéed veggies, or toss them with a light and creamy pasta primavera.

1. Cut salmon fillets into 2-inch pieces. Sprinkle with desired amount of salt and pepper or your favorite seasoning blend. Coat lightly with vegetable cooking spray, and cook in a hot nonstick skillet over medium-high heat 1 minute on each side or until golden and fish begins to flake with a fork and is opaque throughout. Remove from heat, and add a generous splash of fresh lemon or lime juice just before serving.

Parmesan-Pecan-Crusted Fried Fish

MAKES 6 SERVINGS; **PREP:** 20 MIN., **COOK:** 4 MIN. PER BATCH

½ cup ground pecans
½ cup grated Parmesan cheese
½ cup fine, dry breadcrumbs
¼ cup finely chopped fresh parsley
¾ tsp. salt
½ tsp. pepper
2 lb. cod fillets
2 large eggs, beaten
½ cup olive oil

1. Stir together first 6 ingredients.
2. Cut fillets into 2-inch pieces; dip in eggs, and dredge in pecan mixture.
3. Cook fish, in batches, in hot oil in a large skillet over medium-high heat 1 minute on all sides or until golden; drain on paper towels. Place fish on a wire rack in a jelly-roll pan, and keep warm in a 200° oven.

— **ALTON F. FISCHER**, SAN ANTONIO, TEXAS

Buffalo Catfish

MAKES 6 SERVINGS; **PREP:** 15 MIN., **COOK:** 4 MIN. PER BATCH

1½ cups cracker meal
1 Tbsp. dried parsley flakes
1 tsp. salt
½ tsp. pepper
2 large eggs, beaten
¼ cup hot sauce
2 lb. catfish fillets
½ cup vegetable oil

1. Stir together first 4 ingredients. Whisk together eggs and hot sauce.
2. Cut fillets into 2-inch pieces; dip in egg mixture, and dredge in cracker meal mixture.
3. Cook fish, in batches, in hot oil in a large skillet over medium-high heat 1 minute on all sides or until golden; drain on paper towels. Place fish on a wire rack in a jelly-roll pan, and keep warm in a 200° oven.

— **CHARLOTTE KREMER**, VIRGINIA BEACH, VIRGINIA

Crispy Oven-Fried Catfish

southernliving.com favorite

MAKES 4 SERVINGS; **PREP:** 10 MIN., **CHILL:** 20 MIN., **BAKE:** 35 MIN.

Using a salt-free seasoning allows you to control the amount of salt in this dish while adding flavor at the same time.

1 cup low-fat buttermilk
4 (6-oz.) catfish fillets
2½ tsp. salt-free Creole seasoning
½ tsp. salt
3 cups cornflakes cereal, crushed
Vegetable cooking spray
Lemon wedges

1. Place 1 cup low-fat buttermilk in a large zip-top plastic freezer bag; add 4 (6-oz.) catfish fillets, turning to coat. Seal and chill 20 minutes, turning once.
2. Remove catfish fillets from buttermilk, discarding buttermilk. Sprinkle catfish fillets evenly with 2½ tsp. salt-free Creole seasoning and ½ tsp. salt.
3. Place 3 cups crushed cornflakes in a shallow dish. Dredge catfish fillets in cornflakes, pressing cornflakes gently onto each fillet. Place fillets on a rack coated with cooking spray in a roasting pan.
4. Bake catfish fillets at 425° for 30 to 35 minutes or until fish flakes with a fork. Serve catfish fillets immediately with lemon wedges.
Note: For testing purposes only, we used The Spice Hunter Cajun Creole Seasoning Salt Free.

Fast Flavor

Nothing beats the combination of fresh seafood and a spicy home-made sauce. This recipe is a snap to throw together, and it's economical too, because you can produce the exact amount of sauce you need. Try it once, and we guarantee you'll make it over and over.

Super-Quick Cocktail Sauce

MAKES ABOUT ½ CUP;
PREP: 5 MIN

1. Stir together ½ cup ketchup, 1 Tbsp. horseradish, 1 tsp. hot sauce, ¼ tsp. lemon zest, and ½ tsp. fresh lemon juice in a small bowl. Serve with cooked seafood.
Note: This sauce will keep in the refrigerator for up to five days.

Fast and Affordable

Thin cuts of meat that cook quickly are just right when you're in a rush. With a meat counter shortcut, you can assemble, prep, and cook a meal in less than an hour. Nutty Turkey Cutlets, for example, stay moist and juicy with a pecan-and-breadcrumb coating. Pair them with Sautéed Mushroom-and-Cheese Ravioli.

Nutty Turkey Cutlets
family favorite • fast fixin's
MAKES 4 SERVINGS; **PREP:** 10 MIN.,
COOK: 6 MIN.

You can substitute pork or chicken cutlets for turkey.

¾ cup fine, dry breadcrumbs
½ cup pecans
¾ tsp. salt
¾ tsp. pepper
1 (1-lb.) package boneless turkey cutlets
½ cup all-purpose flour
2 large eggs, lightly beaten
3 Tbsp. olive oil
Garnish: chopped fresh parsley

1. Process breadcrumbs and pecans in a food processor or blender 10 to 15 seconds or until finely ground.
2. Sprinkle ½ tsp. salt and ½ tsp. pepper over cutlets. Combine flour and remaining salt and pepper in a shallow dish or pieplate. Dredge turkey cutlets in flour mixture; dip in eggs, and dredge in breadcrumb mixture.

3. Sauté cutlets in hot oil in a large skillet over medium-high heat 3 minutes on each side or until golden. Remove from skillet, and serve immediately. Garnish, if desired.

> **•TIP•**
>
> Keep convenient products such as frozen vegetables or dried pasta in the freezer or pantry to accompany your main dish.

Sautéed Mushroom-and-Cheese Ravioli
family favorite
MAKES 4 TO 6 SERVINGS; **PREP:** 15 MIN.,
COOK: 22 MIN.

1 (25-oz.) package frozen cheese ravioli
3 Tbsp. butter
1 Tbsp. olive oil
1 (8-oz.) package sliced fresh mushrooms
¼ cup finely chopped sweet onion
½ tsp. kosher salt
½ tsp. pepper
2 Tbsp. chopped fresh parsley
2 Tbsp. grated Parmesan cheese

1. Cook ravioli according to package directions in a Dutch oven; drain and keep warm. Wipe Dutch oven clean.
2. Melt 2 Tbsp. butter with oil in Dutch oven over medium-high heat; add mushrooms and next 3 ingredients, and sauté 8 to 10 minutes or until vegetables are tender. Reduce heat to low, and stir in ravioli and remaining 1 Tbsp. butter, stirring until butter is melted. Add parsley, and toss gently to combine. Sprinkle with cheese, and serve immediately.
Note: For testing purposes only, we used Rosetto Cheese Ravioli.

The Perfect Bite

Host a no-fuss gathering with these updated, elegant recipes.

Marian Cooper Cairns is our resident party chow expert. She has created some irresistible flavor combos that are outrageously delicious *and* easy to make. From baby showers to cocktail parties, these little treats are perfect for springtime entertaining. Use the make-ahead Flaky Tartlet Shells to create the recipes on this page.

Flaky Tartlet Shells
make ahead

MAKES 24 TARTLET SHELLS; **PREP:** 15 MIN., **BAKE:** 8 MIN., **COOL:** 15 MIN.

If you are making several batches of shells, you can stack up to three unrolled piecrusts on top of each other and cut dough circles all at once. A tart tamper or drink muddler makes fast work of pressing dough into pans. (Both are available at kitchenware stores.)

½ (15-oz.) package refrigerated piecrust

1. Preheat oven to 425°. Unroll piecrust on a flat surface. Cut into 24 rounds using a 2-inch round cutter. Press rounds onto bottoms of ungreased miniature muffin cups. (Dough will come slightly up sides, forming a cup.) Prick bottom of each dough circle 4 times with a fork.
2. Bake at 425° for 6 to 8 minutes or until golden. Remove from pans to a wire rack, and let cool 15 minutes before filling.
Note: To make ahead, store baked tartlet shells in an airtight container in refrigerator for up to 2 days, or freeze up to 1 month. Thaw at room temperature 2 hours before filling.

Peach-and-Blue Cheese Bites
fast fixin's

MAKES 6 TO 8 APPETIZER SERVINGS; **PREP:** 10 MIN., **BAKE:** 6 MIN.
(Pictured on page 8)

1. Preheat oven to 350°. Arrange 24 Flaky Tartlet Shells (recipe at left) on a baking sheet. Cut 2 oz. Gorgonzola cheese into 24 very small pieces. Spoon ¼ rounded teaspoonful peach fruit spread into each shell; top with cheese. Sprinkle evenly with 3 Tbsp. chopped roasted salted almonds. Bake tartlets at 350° for 5 to 6 minutes or until cheese is melted.
Note: For testing purposes only, we used Smucker's Simply Fruit Peach Spreadable Fruit.

Ginger-Brie Bites: *(Pictured on page 8)* Prepare Peach-and-Blue Cheese Bites as directed, substituting ginger preserves for peach fruit spread and 3 oz. Brie, rind removed, for Gorgonzola cheese.

Pear-Havarti Bites: Prepare Peach-and-Blue Cheese Bites as directed, substituting pear preserves for peach fruit spread and 2 oz. Havarti cheese for Gorgonzola cheese.

Spicy-Sweet Goat Cheese Bites: Prepare Peach-and-Blue Cheese Bites as directed, substituting red pepper jelly for peach fruit spread and 2 oz. goat cheese for Gorgonzola cheese.

Chocolate-Hazelnut Tartlets
MAKES 6 TO 8 APPETIZER SERVINGS; **PREP:** 15 MIN.
(Pictured on page 8)

1. Spoon ½ cup jarred hazelnut spread into a 1-qt. heavy-duty zip-top plastic bag (do not seal). Snip 1 corner of bag to make a small hole. Pipe hazelnut spread evenly into 24 Flaky Tartlet Shells (recipe at left). Top each with sweetened whipped cream and a roasted salted hazelnut.
Note: For testing purposes only, we used Nutella for hazelnut spread.

Dulce de Leche Tartlets
fast fixin's

MAKES 6 TO 8 APPETIZER SERVINGS; **PREP:** 25 MIN.

Look for canned dulce de leche in the canned milk aisle. You can make these up to four hours ahead of time. Just chill until ready to serve. (Pictured on page 8)

1. Beat 4 oz. softened cream cheese, ¼ cup canned dulce de leche, 2 Tbsp. cream, and ⅛ tsp. ground cinnamon at medium speed with an electric mixer until combined. Beat at high speed 1 to 2 minutes or until creamy, stopping to scrape down sides. Spoon cream cheese mixture into a 1-qt. heavy-duty zip-top plastic bag (do not seal). Snip 1 corner of bag to make a small hole. Pipe cream cheese mixture evenly into 24 Flaky Tartlet Shells (recipe at left). Top each with sweetened whipped cream and a pinch of ground cinnamon.

Raspberry Cream Tartlets
MAKES 6 TO 8 APPETIZER SERVINGS; **PREP:** 25 MIN.
(Pictured on page 8)

1. Beat 4 oz. softened cream cheese at medium speed with an electric mixer until creamy. Stir in ¼ cup seedless raspberry preserves until combined. Beat at high speed 1 to 2 minutes or until mixture is creamy and smooth, stopping to scrape down sides. Spoon cream cheese mixture into a 1-qt. heavy-duty zip-top plastic bag (do not seal). Snip 1 corner of bag to make a small hole. Pipe cream cheese mixture evenly into 24 Flaky Tartlet Shells (recipe at left). Top each with sweetened whipped cream and a fresh raspberry.

Fresh basil and tangy balsamic vinaigrette awaken the simple flavors of Mini Caprese Bites.

Mini Caprese Bites
fast fixin's

MAKES 8 APPETIZER SERVINGS;
PREP: 20 MIN.

Grape tomatoes vary in size from week to week at the grocery store; some pints we found had only 24, while others had more than 40. Good news, you should still have enough mozzarella balls, because they are generally sold in 8-oz. containers with plenty for this recipe.

1 pt. grape tomatoes, halved
10 to 14 fresh small mozzarella cheese balls, cut into thirds*
32 (4-inch) wooden skewers**
¼ cup extra virgin olive oil
2 Tbsp. balsamic vinegar
¼ tsp. kosher salt
¼ tsp. pepper
6 thinly sliced fresh basil leaves
Kosher salt and pepper to taste

1. Thread 1 tomato half, 1 piece of cheese, and another tomato half onto each skewer. Place skewers in a shallow serving dish.

2. Whisk together oil and next 3 ingredients. Drizzle oil mixture over skewers; sprinkle with basil and salt and pepper to taste.

—MARCI PARHAM, BIRMINGHAM, ALABAMA

*1 (8-oz.) package fresh mozzarella, cut into ½-inch cubes, may be substituted.
**Wooden picks may be substituted.

Southern Sushi Bites
fast fixin's • make ahead

MAKES 10 APPETIZER SERVINGS;
PREP: 15 MIN.

Pick up tuna rolls at large supermarkets near the seafood department. Most varieties will come with wasabi, fresh pickled ginger, and soy sauce packets in the container, so there is no need to pick up any extra.

3 oz. cream cheese, softened
1 Tbsp. milk
1½ tsp. prepared wasabi
2 (8.25-oz.) packages prepared tuna sushi rolls
2 Tbsp. finely minced pickled vegetables
4 pickled okra, thinly sliced
Soy sauce
Pickled ginger

1. Beat first 3 ingredients at high speed with an electric mixer until creamy. Spoon cream cheese mixture into a 1-qt. heavy-duty zip-top plastic bag (do not seal). Snip 1 corner of bag to make a small hole. Pipe cream cheese mixture onto 1 cut side of each tuna roll. Top cream cheese mixture with pickled vegetables and okra. Serve immediately, or cover and chill up to 4 hours. Serve with soy sauce and pickled ginger.

Can't-Miss Casseroles

There's something about a really good vegetable casserole that's impossible to resist. Even picky eaters go back for second helpings. These deep-dish favorites are a great match for almost any entrée.

Fresh Corn Spoonbread
family favorite

MAKES 8 SERVINGS; **PREP:** 10 MIN.,
BAKE: 45 MIN.

1 cup white cornmeal mix
½ cup all-purpose flour
¼ cup sugar
1 tsp. salt
4 cups fresh corn kernels (about 5 to 6 ears)
2 cups plain yogurt
3 large eggs, lightly beaten
¼ cup butter, melted

1. Preheat oven to 350°. Stir together cornmeal mix and next 3 ingredients in a large bowl; make a well in center of mixture. Stir together corn and next 3 ingredients; add to cornmeal mixture, stirring just until dry ingredients are moistened. Spoon corn mixture into a lightly greased 2-qt. rectangular baking dish.

2. Bake at 350° for 40 to 45 minutes or until golden brown and set.

—BETH TRUEBLOOD, LANESVILLE, INDIANA

Easy Cheesy Potato Casserole

family favorite

MAKES 6 SERVINGS; **PREP:** 10 MIN.,
COOK: 12 MIN., **BAKE:** 45 MIN.,
STAND: 5 MIN.

1 (20-oz.) package refrigerated hash browns
1½ cups (6 oz.) 2% reduced-fat shredded Mexican four-cheese blend
1 (10¾-oz.) can reduced-fat cream of mushroom soup
1 (8-oz.) container reduced-fat sour cream
⅓ cup chopped fresh chives
1 garlic clove, pressed
½ tsp. salt
½ tsp. freshly ground pepper

1. Preheat oven to 350°. Cook hash browns in a lightly greased large non-stick skillet over medium heat, stirring occasionally, 12 minutes or until golden brown.
2. Stir together hashbrowns, 1 cup shredded cheese, and next 6 ingredients. Spoon mixture into a lightly greased 8-inch square baking dish, and sprinkle with remaining ½ cup cheese.
3. Bake at 350° for 40 to 45 minutes or until edges are lightly browned. Let stand 5 minutes before serving.

—**KIMBERLY SPIVEY**, CAMDEN, SOUTH CAROLINA

Summer Squash Casserole

family favorite

MAKES 8 SERVINGS; **PREP:** 25 MIN.,
COOK: 5 MIN., **BAKE:** 35 MIN.,
STAND: 10 MIN.

Layers of tender-crisp vegetables and golden crumb topping made this a hit at our tasting table.

1½ lb. yellow squash
1 lb. zucchini
1 small sweet onion, chopped
2½ tsp. salt, divided
1 cup grated carrots
1 (10¾-oz.) can cream of chicken soup
1 (8-oz.) container sour cream
1 (8-oz.) can water chestnuts, drained and chopped
1 (8-oz.) package herb-seasoned stuffing
½ cup butter, melted

1. Preheat oven to 350°. Cut squash and zucchini into ¼-inch-thick slices; place in a Dutch oven. Add chopped onion, 2 tsp. salt, and water to cover. Bring to a boil over medium-high heat, and cook 5 minutes; drain well.
2. Stir together 1 cup grated carrots, next 3 ingredients, and remaining ½ tsp. salt in a large bowl; fold in squash mixture. Stir together stuffing and ½ cup melted butter, and spoon half of stuffing mixture in bottom of a lightly greased 13- x 9-inch baking dish. Spoon squash mixture over stuffing mixture, and top with remaining stuffing mixture.
3. Bake at 350° for 30 to 35 minutes or until bubbly and golden brown, shielding with aluminum foil after 20 to 25 minutes to prevent excessive browning, if necessary. Let stand 10 minutes before serving.

—**MARIE T. SCOTT**, AUGUSTA, GEORGIA

Note: For testing purposes only, we used Pepperidge Farm Herb Seasoned Stuffing.

Two-Cheese Squash Casserole

southernliving.com favorite

MAKES 8 TO 10 SERVINGS; **PREP:** 30 MIN.,
COOK: 20 MIN., **BAKE:** 40 MIN.

The combination of Parmesan and Cheddar cheeses gives this casserole a delicious taste all its own.

4 lb. yellow squash, sliced
4 Tbsp. butter, divided
1 large sweet onion, finely chopped
2 garlic cloves, minced
2½ cups soft breadcrumbs, divided
1¼ cups shredded Parmesan cheese, divided
1 cup (4 oz.) shredded Cheddar cheese
½ cup chopped fresh chives
½ cup minced fresh parsley
1 (8-oz.) container sour cream
1 tsp. salt
1 tsp. freshly ground pepper
2 large eggs, lightly beaten
¼ tsp. garlic salt

1. Preheat oven to 350°. Cook squash in boiling water to cover in a large skillet 8 to 10 minutes or just until tender. Drain well; gently press between paper towels.
2. Melt 2 Tbsp. butter in skillet over medium-high heat; add onion and garlic, and sauté 5 to 6 minutes or until tender. Remove skillet from heat; stir in squash, 1 cup breadcrumbs, ¾ cup Parmesan cheese, and next 7 ingredients. Spoon mixture into a lightly greased 13- x 9-inch baking dish.
3. Melt remaining 2 Tbsp. butter. Stir together melted butter, remaining 1½ cups soft breadcrumbs, remaining ½ cup Parmesan cheese, and garlic salt. Sprinkle mixture evenly over top of casserole.
4. Bake at 350° for 35 to 40 minutes or until set.

Jazzed-Up Meatloaf

Make family meals special by trying these three tasty twists.

I t's always time for comfort food, and meatloaf is an ideal choice when you want to serve a feel-good supper. We've come up with some fresh, updated flavor profiles. All are soul-soothing, fairly simple to make, and anything but boring.

Tex-Mex Meatloaf
freezeable • make ahead
MAKES 6 SERVINGS; PREP: 20 MIN.;
BAKE: 1 HR., 10 MIN.; STAND: 10 MIN.

2 lb. ground round
1½ cups crushed tortilla chips, divided
1 (16-oz.) can chili beans in sauce, undrained
1 (10-oz.) can diced tomatoes with green chiles, drained
1½ tsp. chili powder
1 tsp. ground cumin
2 large eggs, lightly beaten
½ cup chopped onion
1 garlic clove, minced
1 tsp. salt
¼ tsp. pepper
½ cup salsa
Torn lettuce leaves
Tortilla chips
Toppings: sour cream, grated Cheddar cheese, chopped tomatoes, sliced olives, guacamole

1. Preheat oven to 350°. Stir together ground round, 1 cup crushed tortilla chips, beans, and next 8 ingredients in a large bowl just until combined.
2. Transfer mixture to a lightly greased 9-inch deep-dish pieplate. Place on a rimmed baking sheet. Bake at 350° for 45 minutes. Spoon ½ cup salsa evenly over meatloaf; sprinkle with remaining ½ cup tortilla chips. Bake 20 to 25 more minutes or until center is no longer pink. Let stand 10 minutes. Cut into

wedges. Serve over lettuce with tortilla chips and desired toppings.

Herbed Chicken Meatloaf
freezable • make ahead
MAKES 8 SERVINGS; PREP: 25 MIN.;
COOK: 7 MIN.; BAKE: 1 HR., 10 MIN.;
STAND: 10 MIN.

You can freeze slices of this meatloaf in a zip-top plastic freezer bag.

½ cup frozen diced onion, red and green bell pepper, and celery
1 tsp. olive oil
2 lb. ground chicken
½ cup fine, dry breadcrumbs
⅓ cup light mayonnaise
2 large eggs, lightly beaten
2 Tbsp. chopped fresh flat-leaf parsley
2 tsp. Greek seasoning
½ tsp. lemon zest
¼ tsp. salt
¼ tsp. freshly ground pepper
Pita rounds, split
Toppings: sliced cucumber, sliced tomatoes, crumbled feta cheese, plain yogurt, kalamata olives, lettuce leaves

1. Preheat oven to 350°. Sauté onion, red and green bell pepper, and celery in hot oil in a small skillet over medium-high heat 5 to 7 minutes or until vegetables are tender.
2. Stir together ground chicken, next 8 ingredients, and sautéed vegetables in a large bowl just until combined.
3. Place mixture in a lightly greased 9- x 5-inch baking dish. Bake at 350° for 1 hour to 1 hour and 10 minutes or until a meat thermometer registers 165°. Let stand 10 minutes before slicing. Serve meatloaf slices in pita rounds with desired toppings.
Note: For testing purposes only, we used Cavender's All Purpose Greek

Seasoning. You can freeze slices of Herbed Chicken Meatloaf in a heavy-duty zip-top freezer bag for up to three months. Thaw the frozen slices overnight in the refrigerator, and heat them in a microwave-safe container 1½ minutes on HIGH or until sizzling.

Tomato-Basil Meatloaf
freezeable • make ahead
MAKES 6 TO 8 SERVINGS; PREP: 10 MIN.;
BAKE: 1 HR., 15 MIN.; STAND: 5 MIN.

1 lb. ground chuck
1 lb. lean ground pork
1 (14.5-oz.) can diced tomatoes with basil, oregano, and garlic, drained
⅓ cup marinara sauce
⅓ cup Italian-seasoned breadcrumbs
1 large egg, lightly beaten
1 tsp. salt
1 tsp. pepper
½ cup (2 oz.) shredded mozzarella cheese

1. Preheat oven to 375°. Stir together ground chuck and pork in a large bowl.
2. Process diced tomatoes in a blender or food processor 5 seconds or until slightly chunky, stopping to scrape down sides as needed. Stir tomatoes, marinara sauce, and next 4 ingredients into ground beef mixture just until combined.
3. Shape into a 9- x 5-inch loaf; place meatloaf on a wire rack in an aluminum foil-lined jelly-roll pan.
4. Bake at 375° for 1 hour. Top with mozzarella cheese, and bake 15 more minutes or until center of loaf is no longer pink. Let stand 5 minutes before serving.
Note: To make ahead, prepare recipe as directed through Step 2. Shape into a 9- x 5-inch loaf, and cover with plastic wrap and aluminum foil. Freeze up to 2 months. Thaw in refrigerator 24 hours. Uncover and proceed with recipe as directed.

Ready for a Good Time

Tips, tricks, and fun ideas for party food.

Puttin' on the Ritz

A small dish lined with fresh herbs and fig leaves and a few flavorful toppings turn an inexpensive block of feta into something special. Sprinkle feta lightly with chopped fresh herbs and minced garlic, drizzle with olive oil, and tuck in a lemon slice for tang. You don't need a recipe—just use ingredients you have on hand. It's a great way to liven up the taste of milder cheeses such as fresh mozzarella or goat cheese. And don't throw away those leftover crumbles—they're delicious tossed with a salad.

Shelf Magic Pop open a jar of jelly or jam, and you have the start of something good. We found lots of quick and clever ways to use these fruity treats—including the savory cheese bites on page 112. The next time you need to set out something special on the spur of the moment, try one of these.

Blackberry-Basil Vinaigrette is a great basic that's just as delicious prepared with raspberry or blueberry preserves. Served over a salad of field greens and fresh fruit, it's a showstopper; it also makes the perfect partner for grilled chicken or pork. Pulse ½ (10-oz.) jar seedless blackberry preserves; ¼ cup red wine vinegar; 6 fresh basil leaves; 1 garlic clove, sliced; ½ tsp. salt; and ½ tsp. seasoned pepper in a blender 2 to 3 times or until blended. With blender running, add ¾ cup vegetable oil in a slow, steady stream, processing until smooth. **Makes** 1 cup. Prep: 5 min.

Fruit-flavored Butters are always a hit, and they're super easy to make—just stir together ½ cup softened butter and ¼ cup of your favorite jam or preserves. Spoon into a pretty dish, and serve immediately, or cover and chill up to a week. (If chilled, let stand at room temperature for about 30 minutes before serving.) Enjoy these spreads any time of day, with breakfast breads or dinner rolls. If you're feeling decadent, stir in a few tablespoons of finely chopped dark chocolate with the butter and jam, and spread on a hot biscuit or a slice of grilled pound cake. **Makes** ¾ cup. Prep: 5 min.

Spring Wraps Dress your favorite sandwich wraps in colorful sheets of scrapbooking paper, and they'll be ready for a party. Secure the paper around each wrap with matching stickers. You'll find a huge selection of patterns at any crafts store. Bright terra-cotta containers and saucers take the makings of a box lunch to a whole new level. Garden shops are a great source for fun twists on tableware. When using glazed terra-cotta as tableware, be sure the pieces are food safe and lead free.

June

Fresh from the Bayou

We spent the day hauling in the nets with shrimper Timmy Cheramie. Our biggest catch? His family recipes.

This is a perfect morning for a drag," says Timmy Cheramie, as he quickly unravels vibrant green nets into the water near Golden Meadow, Louisiana. A cool Gulf breeze and overcast skies create the ideal setting for capturing this region's prized commodity. About 45 minutes later, shrimp jump and pop as if in electrified water while Timmy hauls in the huge nets by hand. He brims with excitement the way most folks anticipate the opening kick-off of the Super Bowl. Surveying his impressive take (to be used later in the day for a down-home Cajun feast), he turns to Executive Editor Scott Jones with a huge smile and says, "It's in my blood, bro."

This third-generation shrimper handcrafts outrigging for his boat, sews his own trawling nets, and navigates this bayou's intricate estuaries from memory. But it is Timmy's knack for cooking that motivates his family to fire up the boats and head for their fish camp in the heart of Bayou Lafourche in anticipation of unbeatable food and fun.

"I learned how to cook as a kid on my stepfather's shrimp boat. It was a rite of passage," says Timmy. There were no recipes or cookbooks and, according to him, everything was done by eye. "My stepfather would be out on deck trawling and yelling down to the galley how things should be chopped and cooked. I took to it pretty fast, and it's something I've always enjoyed." Asked what attracts him most to cooking, Timmy responds without missing a beat, "I love to see people's faces light up. I know my food makes them feel good." We think you'll agree that his recipes are Cajun comfort food at its best.

Boiled Shrimp With Timmy's Shrimp Sauce

MAKES 8 TO 10 SERVINGS; **PREP:** 15 MIN., **COOK:** 55 MIN., **STAND:** 15 MIN.

The key to perfectly boiled shrimp is not to boil them at all. The shrimp are stirred into the pot once the vegetables are tender. The pot is then taken off the heat, and the shrimp soak in the seasoned water until done.

3 ears fresh corn, husks removed*
1 (3-oz.) package boil-in-bag
  shrimp-and-crab boil
¼ cup liquid shrimp-and-crab boil
  seasoning
2 large lemons, quartered
1 large onion, quartered
3 lb. small red potatoes
4 lb. unpeeled, large raw shrimp
8 cups ice cubes
3 Tbsp. salt
Timmy's Shrimp Sauce

1. Cut corn in half.
2. Bring boil-in-bag shrimp-and-crab boil, next 3 ingredients, and 3½ qt. water to a boil in a large stockpot over high heat. Add potatoes and corn. Cover and boil over medium-high heat 20 minutes or until potatoes and corn are tender.
3. Stir in shrimp; remove from heat. Cover and let stand 10 minutes. (Shrimp will turn pink, and shells will loosen slightly.) Stir in ice cubes and salt, and let stand 5 minutes. Drain, discarding boil bag. Serve with Timmy's Shrimp Sauce.
*6 (4-inch) ears frozen corn may be substituted. (Do not halve.)
Note: For testing purposes only, we used Zatarain's New Orleans Shrimp & Crab Boil and Zatarain's Concentrated Shrimp & Crab Boil seasoning.

Timmy's Shrimp Sauce:
fast fixin's • make ahead
MAKES ABOUT 1 CUP; **PREP:** 5 MIN.

1 cup mayonnaise
2 Tbsp. ketchup
1 Tbsp. dill pickle relish

1. Stir together mayonnaise and remaining ingredients. Store in an airtight container in refrigerator up to 7 days.

—TIMMY CHERAMIE, CUT OFF, LOUISIANA

White Beans and Rice

MAKES 6 TO 8 SERVINGS; **PREP:** 15 MIN.;
COOK: 1 HR., 5 MIN.

Timmy uses dried beans, but we streamlined the recipe by substituting canned beans.

6 (15.8-oz.) cans great Northern beans,
  divided
1 large onion, chopped
1 green bell pepper, chopped
4 garlic cloves, chopped
1 Tbsp. vegetable oil
¾ lb. smoked fully cooked ham, diced
1 cup chicken broth
¾ tsp. salt
¾ tsp. pepper
2 cups uncooked jasmine or long-grain rice

1. Rinse and drain 4 cans beans. (Do not drain remaining cans.)
2. Sauté onion, bell pepper, and garlic in hot oil in a Dutch oven over medium-high heat 7 to 8 minutes or until tender. Stir in undrained beans, 2 cans drained beans, ham, and next 3 ingredients. Bring to a boil; reduce heat, and simmer, stirring occasionally, 45 minutes.
3. Meanwhile, prepare rice according to package directions.
4. Stir in remaining 2 cans drained beans to mixture in Dutch oven. Cook 5 minutes or until thoroughly heated. Serve with hot cooked rice.

—DOREE CHERAMIE, CUT OFF, LOUISIANA
Note: For testing purposes only, we used Mahatma Jasmine Rice.

Bayou Fried Shrimp
family favorite

MAKES 6 TO 8 SERVINGS; **PREP:** 30 MIN., **STAND:** 15 MIN., **FRY:** 3 MIN. PER BATCH

In addition to fish fry mix, Timmy also uses self-rising flour to dredge shrimp. He says it gives the shrimp a "nice and puffy outside."

3 lb. unpeeled, large raw shrimp
2 cups milk
1 large egg
1 Tbsp. yellow mustard
1 tsp. Cajun seasoning
1 (12-oz.) package fish fry mix
1 Tbsp. Cajun seasoning
Vegetable oil

1. Peel shrimp, leaving tails on. Butterfly shrimp by making a deep slit down back of each from large end to tail, cutting to but not through inside curve of shrimp. Devein shrimp, and place in a large bowl.
2. Whisk together milk and next 3 ingredients. Pour mixture over shrimp. Let stand at least 15 minutes or up to 1 hour.
3. Combine fish fry mix and 1 Tbsp. Cajun seasoning. Dredge shrimp in fish fry mixture, and shake off excess. Arrange on baking sheets.
4. Pour oil to a depth of 3 inches into a Dutch oven; heat to 325°. Fry shrimp, in batches, 1½ minutes on each side or until golden brown; drain on wire racks over paper towels.

—TYLER CHERAMIE, CUT OFF, LOUISIANA

Note: For testing purposes only, we used Zatarain's Wonderful Fish-Fri and Walker & Sons "Slap Ya Mama" Cajun Seasoning.

Shrimp-and-Sausage Stew

MAKES 10 TO 12 SERVINGS; **PREP:** 30 MIN.; **COOK:** 3 HR., 5 MIN.

This stew is like gumbo without the roux. It gets its thick glossiness from a cornstarch-and-water slurry that's stirred in at the end.

4 lb. peeled, large raw shrimp
3 large onions, cut into 1-inch pieces
¼ cup vegetable oil
2 (15-oz.) cans tomato sauce
3 (14½-oz.) cans diced tomatoes with zesty green chiles
5 celery ribs, cut into 1-inch pieces
3 green bell peppers, seeded and cut into 1-inch strips
6 garlic cloves, chopped and divided
1 (1-lb.) package spicy smoked sausage, sliced
3 cups uncooked jasmine or long-grain rice
6 green onions, chopped
1 cup chopped fresh parsley
2 Tbsp. Cajun seasoning
¼ cup cornstarch

1. Butterfly shrimp by making a deep slit down back of each from large end to tail, cutting to but not through inside curve of shrimp. Devein shrimp.
2. Cook onions in hot oil in a large Dutch oven over medium heat, stirring often, 35 to 40 minutes or until golden brown. Add tomato sauce, and cook, stirring occasionally, 25 to 30 minutes or until thickened. Add diced tomatoes with green chiles, celery, bell peppers, and 2 cups water.
3. Bring to a boil over medium-high heat; reduce heat to medium, and simmer 30 minutes or until sauce thickens slightly. Add 3 garlic cloves, and simmer 30 minutes, stirring in 1 to 2 cups of water as needed to maintain a stew-like consistency. Stir in sausage, and simmer 30 minutes, stirring in 1 to 2 cups water as needed. Skim grease from surface as needed.
4. Meanwhile, prepare rice according to package directions.
5. Stir green onions, parsley, Cajun seasoning, and remaining 3 garlic cloves into sausage mixture. Simmer 10 minutes. Add shrimp, and bring to a boil over medium-high heat.
6. Stir together ¼ cup cornstarch and ½ cup water. Stir into shrimp-and-sausage mixture, stirring just until mixture is thick and glossy. Serve with hot cooked rice.

—TIMMY CHERAMIE, CUT OFF, LOUISIANA

Easy as Pie

Summer is all about simple, and these flavor-packed pies top our list of fun desserts. There's no need to wrangle with a rolling pin—just pat the crust in the pan. Fold together a creamy cheesecake filling, stir up a stovetop custard, or grab a muffin pan and bake up a batch of Chocolate-Key Lime Cupcake Pies. Then sit back and chill. Homemade has never been so easy.

Icebox Cheesecake

MAKES 8 SERVINGS; **PREP:** 15 MIN.,
CHILL: 8 HR.
(Pictured on page 169)

1 (8-oz.) package cream cheese, softened
1 cup powdered sugar
1 (8-oz.) container frozen whipped topping, thawed
1 tsp. vanilla extract
1 baked Butter Cookie or Pretzel Crust (see recipes on opposite page)
4 cups assorted fresh berries, pitted cherries, or sliced fruit
½ cup seedless blackberry jam
¼ cup orange liqueur

1. Beat cream cheese and powdered sugar at medium speed with an electric mixer until blended. Fold in whipped topping and vanilla; spoon into prepared crust. Cover and chill 8 hours.
2. Arrange fruit over cream cheese filling. Stir together jam and liqueur; drizzle over fruit.

—**SANDEE KAY DOWNHOUR**, COLUMBUS, OHIO

Mascarpone Pie: Substitute 1 (8-oz.) container mascarpone cheese for cream cheese, ¼ cup granulated sugar for powdered sugar, 2 cups whipped cream for whipped topping, and 1 baked Chocolate Butter Cookie Crust for Butter Cookie Crust. Prepare recipe as directed.

Cook's Notes

- Pulsing cookies in a food processor is a quick way to create crumbs. Some recipes call for finely ground crumbs, while others benefit from the texture of more coarsely crushed pieces. If you don't have a processor, place the cookies in a large zip-top plastic bag; partially close the bag, leaving a small opening in the top of the bag to allow air to escape. Gently crush cookies with a rolling pin or mallet.
- Spread the crumb mixture all the way up the sides and onto the lip of the pieplate. Pressing the crumb mixture partially up the sides of the pieplate creates a dense, uneven crust that is too shallow to hold the filling. To ensure the crust holds together and slices easily, firmly pat the cookie mixture in the pieplate so there are no loose crumbs.
- Be careful not to overbake the crust, or it may become too hard when cool—10 to 12 minutes is usually all that's needed to solidify the crumb mixture.
- Use a sharp, thin-bladed knife to cut through the filling and crust; then insert a pie server underneath each slice and lift it from the pan.
- A 9-inch glass pieplate works best for these recipes. Pottery pie dishes vary in size and shape, but most are large enough to hold a glass pieplate and make beautiful serving containers.

Pineapple Meringue Pie

MAKES 8 SERVINGS; **PREP:** 20 MIN.,
BAKE: 24 MIN., **COOL:** 2 HR.,
COOK: 10 MIN., **CHILL:** 4 HR.

Pineapple, like lemon juice, is acidic and will prevent the cornstarch from thickening properly if added before the custard is cooked. Chilling the pie after it cools at room temperature further sets the filling and makes for perfect slices.

2 cups pecan shortbread cookie crumbs
1⅓ cups sweetened flaked coconut, divided
¼ cup butter, melted
2 cups milk
¼ cup cornstarch
3 large eggs, separated
1 cup sugar, divided
1 (20-oz.) can crushed pineapple, drained
1 Tbsp. butter
1 tsp. vanilla extract

1. Preheat oven to 350°. Stir together cookie crumbs, 1 cup coconut, and ¼ cup melted butter; firmly press on bottom, up sides, and onto lip of a lightly greased 9-inch pieplate.
2. Bake at 350° for 10 to 12 minutes or until lightly browned. Remove to a wire rack, and let cool 1 hour or until completely cool.
3. Whisk together milk and cornstarch in a heavy saucepan, whisking until cornstarch is dissolved. Whisk in egg yolks and ¾ cup sugar, whisking until blended. Cook over medium-low heat, whisking constantly, 8 to 10 minutes or until a chilled pudding-like thickness. (Mixture will just begin to bubble and will be thick enough to hold soft peaks when whisk is lifted.) Remove from heat; stir in pineapple, 1 Tbsp. butter, and vanilla. Spoon immediately into cooled piecrust.
4. Beat egg whites at high speed with an electric mixer until foamy. Add remaining ¼ cup sugar, 1 Tbsp. at a time, beating until stiff peaks form and sugar is dissolved. Spread meringue over hot filling, sealing edges. Sprinkle remaining ⅓ cup coconut over meringue.

5. Bake at 350° for 10 to 12 minutes or until golden brown. Remove from oven to wire rack, and let cool 1 hour or until completely cool. Chill 4 hours.

— LILLIAN JULOW, GAINESVILLE, FLORIDA

Chocolate-Key Lime Cupcake Pies

family favorite • make ahead

MAKES 1 DOZEN; PREP: 30 MIN.,
BAKE: 20 MIN., COOL: 30 MIN., CHILL: 4 HR.
(Pictured on page 169)

12 jumbo-size aluminum foil baking cups
Vegetable cooking spray
1 (9-oz.) package chocolate wafer cookies
½ cup butter, melted
3 (8-oz.) packages cream cheese, softened
1½ cups sugar
2 tsp. key lime zest
⅓ cup fresh key lime juice
3 large eggs
Garnishes: sweetened whipped cream, fresh cherries and blackberries, fresh mint leaves

1. Preheat oven to 350°. Place 12 jumbo-size aluminum foil baking cups in lightly greased muffin pans, and coat with cooking spray.
2. Pulse chocolate wafer cookies in a food processor 8 to 10 times or until finely crushed. Stir together cookie crumbs and butter; firmly press on bottom and two-thirds up sides of each baking cup (about 3 Tbsp. crumbs per cup).
3. Beat cream cheese and sugar at medium speed with an electric mixer until blended. Add lime zest and lime juice, beating at low speed until well blended. Add eggs, 1 at a time, beating just until yellow disappears after each addition. Spoon mixture into prepared cups, filling completely full.
4. Bake at 350° for 20 minutes or until set. Cool in pans on wire racks 15 minutes. Remove from pans to wire racks, and let cool 15 minutes or until completely cool. Cover and chill 4 hours. Garnish, if desired.

— SUSAN SULIBURK, TULSA, OKLAHOMA

Crumb Crust Recipes

Crisp and cookie-thick, these over-the-rim crusts add a signature look to every pie. Unless otherwise noted, one standard-size (12- to 16-oz.) package of cookies or pretzel sticks will yield more than enough crumbs for each recipe. Different types of cookies require different amounts of butter and sugar, but the basic method for preparing and baking a crumb crust remains the same.

Crumb Crust Prep Steps: Stir together all ingredients; firmly press mixture on bottom, up sides, and onto lip of a lightly greased 9-inch pieplate. Bake at 350° for 10 to 12 minutes or until lightly browned. Remove to a wire rack, and cool 1 hour or until completely cool before filling.

- **Pretzel Crust:** 2 cups finely crushed pretzel sticks, ¼ cup firmly packed light brown sugar, ¾ cup melted butter
- **Chocolate Cookies-and-Cream Crust:** 2½ cups coarsely crushed cream-filled chocolate sandwich cookie crumbs, ⅓ cup melted butter
- **Vanilla Wafer Crust:** 2½ cups coarsely crushed vanilla wafer crumbs, ¼ cup powdered sugar, ½ cup melted butter
- **Butter Cookie Crust:** 2½ cups butter cookie crumbs (about 1½ [7.25-oz.] packages), ¼ cup powdered sugar, ⅓ cup melted butter
- **Chocolate Butter Cookie Crust:** 2½ cups chocolate-flavored butter cookie crumbs (about 1½ [7.25-oz.] packages), ¼ cup powdered sugar, ⅓ cup melted butter.

Note: For testing purposes, we used Pepperidge Farm Chessmen Cookies and Pepperidge Farm Chocolate Chessmen Cookies for regular and chocolate-flavored butter cookies.

Candy Bar Pie

MAKES 8 SERVINGS; PREP: 20 MIN.,
BAKE: 40 MIN., COOL: 1 HR., CHILL: 2 HR.
(Pictured on page 168)

3 (2.07-oz.) chocolate-coated caramel-peanut nougat bars
1 baked Pretzel Crust (see recipe above)
1½ (8-oz.) packages cream cheese, softened
½ cup sugar
⅓ cup sour cream
⅓ cup creamy peanut butter
2 large eggs
⅔ cup semisweet chocolate morsels
2 Tbsp. whipping cream
¼ cup coarsely chopped, lightly salted peanuts

1. Preheat oven to 325°. Cut candy bars into ¼-inch pieces; arrange over bottom of crust.
2. Beat cream cheese and sugar at medium speed with an electric mixer until blended. Add sour cream and peanut butter, beating at low speed until well blended. Add eggs, 1 at a time, beating just until yellow disappears after each addition. Spoon cream cheese mixture over candy on crust.
3. Bake at 325° for 35 to 40 minutes or until set. Remove to a wire rack, and let cool 1 hour or until completely cool. Cover and chill 2 hours.
4. Microwave chocolate and cream in a microwave-safe bowl at HIGH for 30 seconds or until melted and smooth, stirring at 15-second intervals. Drizzle over top of cooled pie, and sprinkle evenly with peanuts.

— KATHRYN T. HALL, BROOKHAVEN, MISSISSIPPI

Note: For testing purposes only, we used Snickers candy bars.

Peaches Are Here

This season's favorite fruit shines like never before with these creative updates.

A good peach tastes like summer. Imagine sinking your teeth into its succulent flesh, sweet juices running down the corners of your mouth, inhaling the incomparable aroma. When thinking of this Deep South delight, Assistant Food Editor Marian McGahey's mind always wanders to sweet pies cooling in her grandmother's kitchen and warm cobblers melting vanilla ice cream. But the versatile peach also lends its flavor to many other dishes, pairing well with a variety of cheeses for amazing salads and adding a twist to buttermilk pancakes. Experience this fruit in a whole new light with this delicious array of sweet *and* savory recipes.

Peach-Mango Daiquiris
fast fixin's
MAKES ABOUT 12 SERVINGS; **PREP:** 20 MIN.

Slushy cocktails don't get much better than this one that's loaded with fresh summer peaches. Cream of coconut can be found in the beverage aisle of your grocery store.

1 (24-oz.) jar mango slices
3 large ripe peaches (about 1¼ lb.), peeled and chopped*
1 (15-oz.) can cream of coconut
1 (6-oz.) can frozen lemonade concentrate, thawed
1½ cups dark rum

1. Drain mango slices, reserving ½ cup liquid. Process mango slices and peaches in a blender until smooth, stopping to scrape down sides. Pour peach mixture into a large container.
2. Process reserved mango liquid, cream of coconut, and lemonade concentrate in blender until smooth. Add coconut mixture and rum to peach mixture, stirring until combined. Use immediately.
3. Process 3 cups peach mixture with 2 cups ice in a blender until smooth. Repeat with remaining peach mixture and ice.
*1 (20-oz.) bag frozen sliced peaches, thawed, may be substituted.

Grilled Peach-and-Mozzarella Salad
family favorite
MAKES 4 SERVINGS; **PREP:** 25 MIN., **GRILL:** 10 MIN.

We found traditional peaches work better in this dish than white peaches, which have more sugar and water and don't hold up as well on the grill.

5 fresh peaches (not white)
3 green onions, sliced
¼ cup chopped fresh cilantro
3 Tbsp. honey
1 tsp. salt
1 tsp. lime zest
½ cup fresh lime juice
¾ tsp. ground cumin
¾ tsp. chili powder
1½ Tbsp. tequila (optional)
⅓ cup olive oil
Vegetable cooking spray
1 (6-oz.) package watercress or baby arugula, thoroughly washed
¾ lb. fresh mozzarella, cut into 16 (¼-inch) slices
Garnish: fresh cilantro sprigs

1. Peel and chop 1 peach. Cut remaining 4 peaches into 28 (¼-inch-thick) rounds, cutting through stem and bottom ends. (Cut peaches inward from sides, cutting each side just until you reach the pit. Discard pits.)
2. Process chopped peach, green onions, next 7 ingredients, and, if desired, tequila in a food processor 10 to 15 seconds or until smooth. Add oil, and pulse 3 to 4 times or until thoroughly combined.
3. Coat cold cooking grate of grill with cooking spray, and place on grill. Preheat grill to 350° to 400° (medium-high). Brush both sides of peach rounds with ⅓ cup peach dressing.
4. Grill peach rounds, covered with grill lid, over 350° to 400° (medium-high) heat 3 to 5 minutes on each side or until grill marks appear.
5. Arrange watercress evenly on 4 plates. Alternately layer 4 grilled peach rounds and 4 cheese slices over watercress on each plate. Top each with 3 more peach rounds. Drizzle with remaining peach dressing. Garnish, if desired.

Grilled Peach-and-Feta Salad: Preheat oven to 350°. Arrange ¼ cup pecans, chopped, in a single layer in a shallow pan. Bake 8 to 10 minutes or until toasted and fragrant, stirring after 5 minutes. Reduce peaches from 5 to 4, and reduce salt to ½ tsp. Substitute 8 cups loosely packed Bibb lettuce leaves (about 6 oz. or 1 to 2 heads of lettuce) for watercress and ¼ cup crumbled feta cheese for mozzarella cheese. Peel and chop 1 peach. Cut each of remaining 3 peaches into 8 wedges. Proceed with recipe as directed in Steps 2 through 4, decreasing grilling time for peach wedges to 2 to 3 minutes on each side or until grill marks appear. Divide Bibb lettuce and 4 cooked bacon slices, halved crosswise, among 4 plates or shallow bowls. Top with grilled peach wedges. Sprinkle with feta cheese and pecans. Serve with dressing. **Makes** 4 servings; Prep: 25 min., Bake: 10 min., Grill: 6 min.
Note: You can also use a grill pan to get those beautiful grill marks on the peaches.

Peach Buttermilk Pancakes

family favorite

MAKES 16 (4-INCH) PANCAKES;
PREP: 15 MIN., **COOK:** 8 MIN. PER BATCH

Serve these for breakfast or dessert with a sprinkle of ground cinnamon and chopped fresh mint.

2 cups all-purpose baking mix
2 Tbsp. sugar
2 tsp. baking powder
½ tsp. ground cinnamon
1½ cups buttermilk
1 large egg
1½ cups peeled, diced fresh peaches
Toppings: sweetened whipped cream, diced fresh peaches

1. Combine first 4 ingredients in a large bowl. Add buttermilk and egg, whisking until blended. Gently fold in peaches.
2. Pour batter by ¼ cupfuls onto a hot, lightly greased griddle. Cook pancakes 4 to 6 minutes or until tops are covered with bubbles and edges look dry and cooked; turn and cook other side until golden brown. Serve with desired toppings.

— ERIN ALLEN, LAKE WORTH, FLORIDA

GET INSPIRED

Cool Pops

As temperatures climb, everybody yearns for that perfect icy snack. Here it is: a good-for-you frozen concoction that will excite any taste bud.

Raspberry-Banana-Yogurt Freezer Pops

MAKES 10 POPS; **PREP:** 10 MIN.,
COOK: 5 MIN., **CHILL:** 30 MIN.,
FREEZE: 6 HR.

1. Process 1 cup low-fat vanilla yogurt and 1 banana in a blender 30 seconds or until smooth.
2. Bring 3 cups fresh or frozen raspberries and ½ cup honey to a boil in a medium saucepan over medium-high heat; reduce heat to low, and simmer 5 minutes. Pour mixture through a fine wire-mesh strainer into a bowl, using back of spoon to squeeze out juice and pulp. Discard skins and seeds. Cover and chill raspberry mixture 30 minutes.
3. Pour yogurt mixture evenly into 10 (2-oz.) pop molds. Top with raspberry mixture, and swirl, if desired. Top with lid of pop mold, and insert craft sticks, leaving 1½ to 2 inches sticking out of pop.
4. Freeze 6 hours or until sticks are solidly anchored and pops are completely frozen.

Tip: For a different taste, substitute 3 cups fresh or frozen blueberries or halved strawberries.

Pecan-Peach Cobbler

southernliving.com favorite

MAKES: 8 TO 10 SERVINGS; **PREP:** 35 MIN,
STAND: 10 MIN., **COOK:** 15 MIN.,
BAKE: 43 MIN.

12 to 15 fresh peaches, peeled and sliced (about 16 cups)*
3 cups sugar
⅓ cup all-purpose flour
½ tsp. ground nutmeg
1½ tsp. vanilla extract
⅔ cup butter
2 (15-oz.) packages refrigerated piecrusts
½ cup chopped pecans, toasted
¼ cup sugar
Vanilla ice cream

1. Preheat oven to 475°. Combine first 4 ingredients in a Dutch oven, and let stand 10 minutes or until sugar dissolves. Bring peach mixture to a boil; reduce heat to low, and simmer 10 minutes or until tender. Remove from heat; add vanilla and butter, stirring until butter is melted.
2. Unfold 2 piecrusts. Sprinkle ¼ cup pecans and 2 Tbsp. sugar evenly over 1 piecrust; top with other pie-crust. Roll to a 12-inch circle, gently pressing pecans into pastry. Cut into 1½-inch strips. Repeat with remaining piecrusts, pecans, and sugar.
3. Spoon half of peach mixture into a lightly greased 13- x 9-inch baking dish. Arrange half of pastry strips in a lattice design over top of peach mixture.

4. Bake at 475° for 20 to 25 minutes or until lightly browned. Spoon remaining peach mixture over baked pastry. Top with remaining pastry strips in a lattice design. Bake 15 to 18 more minutes. Serve warm or cold with vanilla ice cream.
*2 (20-oz.) bags frozen sliced peaches, thawed, may be substituted. Reduce sugar to 2 cups, flour to 3 Tbsp., and nutmeg to ¼ tsp.. Proceed as directed.
Note: To make ahead, let baked cobbler cool; cover and freeze up to 1 month. Thaw in refrigerator overnight. Uncover, and reheat in the oven at 250° for 45 minutes.

Rapid Risotto

A surprise shortcut turns this slow-cooking creamy rice into a great weeknight dish.

We never thought a hands-off approach to risotto would yield the same wonderful results as the traditional cooking method. But we were wrong. Risotto, a northern Italian rice dish, usually requires constant stirring from the cook. But a simple microwave technique makes multitasking in the kitchen possible. Use oven mitts to handle the bowl, as it might get hot during cooking. Also, the plastic wrap will form a steam-filled dome during cooking but will deflate when cooking stops. Be sure to angle the bowl away from your face when you remove the plastic wrap to avoid the hot steam.

Basic Microwave Risotto

MAKES 4 SERVINGS (ABOUT 3 CUPS);
PREP: 10 MIN., **COOK:** 22 MIN.

½ cup finely chopped sweet onion
2 Tbsp. butter
1 Tbsp. olive oil
1 garlic clove, minced
1 cup uncooked Arborio rice (short-grain)
2¾ cups low-sodium chicken broth
¼ cup dry white wine
¼ cup freshly grated Parmesan cheese
¼ to ½ cup low-sodium chicken broth
Salt and pepper to taste

1. Stir together first 4 ingredients in a medium-size microwave-safe bowl. Microwave at HIGH 3 minutes. Stir in Arborio rice, and microwave at HIGH 2 minutes.
2. Stir in 2¾ cups broth and ¼ cup wine. Cover tightly with plastic wrap. (Do not vent). Microwave at HIGH 9 minutes. Carefully swirl bowl without uncovering (to incorporate the mixture), and microwave at HIGH 8 minutes. Carefully remove and discard plastic wrap. Stir in cheese and ¼ cup chicken broth, stirring 30 seconds to 1 minute or until creamy. Add ¼ cup additional broth, 1 Tbsp. at a time, if necessary, for desired consistency. Season with salt and pepper to taste, and serve immediately.
Note: For testing purposes only, we used Rice Select Risotto Italian-Style Rice, an 1,100-watt microwave oven, and a 2½-liter glass bowl. We found that self-sealing plastic wraps, such as GLAD Press 'n Seal, do not work in these applications.

Cheese-and-Bacon Risotto:
Substitute 1 cup (4 oz.) freshly shredded extra-sharp Cheddar cheese for Parmesan cheese. Prepare Basic Microwave Risotto as directed (recipe at left), stirring in 3 Tbsp. jarred diced pimiento, drained, with cheese. Sprinkle with ¼ cup cooked and crumbled bacon and 2 thinly sliced green onions just before serving. **Makes** 4 servings; Prep: 10 min., Cook: 22 min.

Green Pea-and-Asparagus Risotto: Prepare Basic Microwave Risotto as directed (recipe at left). Meanwhile, snap off and discard tough ends of ½ lb. asparagus, and cut into 2-inch pieces. Sauté asparagus in a lightly greased nonstick skillet over medium heat 3 to 4 minutes or until crisp-tender; stir in ½ cup frozen sweet green peas, thawed. Stir asparagus mixture, 1 Tbsp. chopped fresh mint, 1 tsp. lemon zest, and 2 tsp. lemon juice into prepared risotto. Serve immediately. **Makes** 4 servings; Prep: 15 min., Cook: 26 min.

Portobello-Spinach Risotto:
Prepare Basic Microwave Risotto as directed (recipe at left). Meanwhile, sauté 1 (8-oz.) package sliced baby portobello mushrooms in 1 Tbsp. hot olive oil in a large nonstick skillet over medium-high heat 6 minutes or until tender. Stir in 3 cups firmly packed fresh spinach, and cook 1 minute or until wilted. Stir mushroom mixture into prepared risotto. Serve immediately. **Makes** 4 servings; Prep: 10 min., Cook: 29 min.

Parmesan-Squash Risotto:
Prepare Basic Microwave Risotto as directed (recipe at left), increasing Parmesan cheese to ½ cup. Stir 1 (12-oz.) package frozen cooked squash, thawed and drained, and 3 Tbsp. thinly sliced fresh basil into prepared risotto. Microwave at HIGH 1 minute. Serve immediately. **Makes** 4 servings; Prep: 10 min., Cook: 23 min.

Crispy Risotto Cakes

MAKES 4 SERVINGS; **PREP:** 10 MIN.,
COOK: 8 MIN.

*Need a plan for leftover risotto? Here's a
great idea.*

2 cups Basic Microwave Risotto, chilled
1 cup Japanese breadcrumbs (panko)
2 Tbsp. olive oil
Toppings: freshly grated Parmesan cheese,
    chopped fresh basil, marinara sauce

1. Shape risotto into 4 round patties
(about 3½ inches wide). Dredge in
breadcrumbs.
2. Cook patties in hot oil in a large nonstick skillet over medium-high heat 3 to
4 minutes on each side or until golden
brown. Serve cakes warm with desired
toppings.

The Rules of Risotto

Arborio rice is traditionally used
for risotto because of its high
starch content, which produces
the creamy texture of the dish.
Regular short-grain and medium-
grain rice may be substituted in a
pinch, but for best results always
look for imported Italian Arborio.
(Check the rice aisle in your local
supermarket; Arborio is often sold
with other specialty rices.) Do not
rinse risotto rice before cooking,
as you'll wash off the starch.

Cook, Toss, and Serve

Southerners love to savor fresh produce picked ripe from
the garden. Showcase summer's new crop: Pair veggies
with pasta and herbs for a delicious blend of flavors.

Lemon Veggies and Pasta
family favorite

MAKES 8 SERVINGS; **PREP:** 20 MIN.,
COOK: 10 MIN.

*We loved the combo of crunchy snow
peas, carrots, and fresh herbs in this
dish.*

½ (16-oz.) package rigatoni pasta
1 small onion, chopped
2 Tbsp. olive oil
¾ cup chicken broth
2 tsp. lemon zest
2 Tbsp. fresh lemon juice
1 cup fresh snow peas
1 cup matchstick carrots
2 Tbsp. chopped fresh basil
2 Tbsp. butter
½ tsp. chopped fresh thyme
¾ tsp. salt
¼ tsp. freshly ground pepper

1. Prepare pasta according to package
directions.
2. Meanwhile, sauté onion in hot oil in
a large skillet over medium-high heat 3
minutes. Reduce heat to medium. Stir
in chicken broth and next 4 ingredients;
bring to a boil. Cook 3 to 4 minutes or
until liquid is reduced by half.
3. Stir in hot cooked pasta, basil, butter, and thyme. Cook, stirring occasionally, 2 minutes or until thoroughly
heated. Season with salt and pepper.

—**NOEL KELSCH**, MOORPARK, CALIFORNIA

Mushroom-and-Spinach Toss
family favorite

MAKES 6 SERVINGS; **PREP:** 20 MIN.,
BAKE: 7 MIN., **COOK:** 12 MIN.

½ (16-oz.) package farfalle or bow-tie pasta
¼ cup pine nuts
2 Tbsp. butter
1 Tbsp. olive oil
1 (8-oz.) package sliced fresh mushrooms
¼ cup sun-dried tomatoes in oil, drained
    and coarsely chopped
2 garlic cloves, minced
¼ cup dry white wine
1 (6-oz.) package fresh baby spinach,
    thoroughly washed
¾ tsp. salt
½ tsp. pepper
½ cup freshly grated Parmesan cheese

1. Prepare pasta according to package
directions.
2. Preheat oven to 350°. Arrange ¼ cup
pine nuts in a single layer in a shallow
pan. Bake 5 to 7 minutes or until lightly
toasted and fragrant.
3. Melt butter with oil in a large skillet
over medium-high heat; add mushrooms,
and sauté 5 to 6 minutes or until golden
brown and most liquid has evaporated.
Reduce heat to medium, and add tomatoes and garlic; cook, stirring constantly,
1 to 2 minutes. Stir in wine, and cook 30
seconds, stirring to loosen particles from
bottom of skillet. Stir in hot cooked pasta
and spinach. Cook, stirring occasionally,
2 to 3 minutes or until spinach is wilted.
Stir in salt and pepper. Sprinkle with
Parmesan cheese and toasted pine nuts.
Serve immediately.

—**MAYDA MIRANDA**, TAMPA, FLORIDA

Green Bean-and-Tomato Pasta Salad

family favorite • make ahead

MAKES 6 SERVINGS; **PREP:** 20 MIN., **COOK:** 15 MIN.

½ (16-oz.) package rotini pasta
½ lb. fresh green beans, trimmed and cut into 1½-inch pieces
1 cup cherry tomatoes, halved
½ cup Basil-Honey-Garlic Vinaigrette
¼ cup chopped red onion

1. Bring a large Dutch oven of salted water to a boil over medium-high heat. Add pasta, and cook 5 minutes. Add green beans, and cook 5 to 6 minutes or until pasta is tender but still firm to the bite and green beans are tender. Drain and rinse with cold water; place in a large bowl.

2. Add tomatoes, vinaigrette, and onion, tossing to coat. Serve immediately, or cover and chill up to 2 hours.

Basil-Honey-Garlic Vinaigrette:

fast fixin's

MAKES 1 CUP; **PREP:** 10 MIN.

Try this simple dressing over your favorite tossed salad.

1 garlic clove
½ tsp. salt
½ cup extra virgin olive oil
⅓ cup balsamic vinegar
2 Tbsp. chopped fresh basil
2 Tbsp. honey
½ tsp. freshly ground pepper

1. Smash garlic and salt together using flat side of knife to make a paste.

2. Whisk together garlic paste, oil, and remaining ingredients until blended.

Kitchen Express: Whisk together ½ cup bottled balsamic vinaigrette, 1 Tbsp. chopped fresh basil, and 1 Tbsp. honey until blended. **Makes** about ½ cup; Prep: 5 min.

Note: For testing purposes only, we used Newman's Own Balsamic Vinaigrette.

Fresh Vegetable Penne

southernliving.com favorite

MAKES 6 SERVINGS; **PREP:** 25 MIN., **BAKE:** 30 MIN., **COOK:** 25 MIN.

1 (2-lb.) butternut squash, peeled and cut into 1½-inch cubes
1 Tbsp. olive oil, divided
¾ tsp. salt, divided
½ tsp. freshly ground black pepper, divided
1 cup chopped leek (about 1 medium)
½ tsp. minced fresh garlic
1 ½ cups vegetable or chicken broth
½ cup fat-free half-and-half
16 oz. uncooked penne pasta
½ cup frozen baby sweet peas
1 Tbsp. chopped fresh sage leaves
⅛ to ¼ tsp. dried crushed red pepper
¼ cup (1 oz.) shredded Italian three-cheese blend
Garnish: fresh sage leaves

1. Preheat oven to 425°. Place squash cubes on a large aluminum foil-lined jelly-roll pan coated with cooking spray. Drizzle squash with 1 tsp. oil, and sprinkle with ¼ tsp. salt and ¼ tsp. black pepper. Toss to coat.

2. Bake at 425° for 25 to 30 minutes or until squash is tender and golden, stirring occasionally.

3. Heat remaining 2 tsp. oil in a large nonstick skillet over medium-high heat; add leek, and sauté 5 minutes or until tender and lightly browned. Add garlic, and sauté 1 minute. Remove from heat, and set aside.

4. Process squash, vegetable broth, and half-and-half in a food processor until smooth.

5. Cook pasta according to package directions, omitting salt and oil. Add peas to boiling water during last 2 minutes of cooking time; drain. Return pasta and peas to pan. Stir in leek mixture, remaining ½ tsp. salt, remaining ¼ tsp. black pepper, 1 Tbsp. chopped sage, and crushed red pepper. Add processed squash mixture, tossing to coat. Sprinkle with Italian three-cheese blend. Garnish, if desired, and serve immediately.

Main-Dish Marinades

Turn ordinary cuts of pork, beef, and chicken into stellar entrées with flavorful soaking sauces. Nail the right combination of acidic, sweet, salty, and seasoning components—balanced with the perfect amount of marinating time—and you'll fall in love with the results. The food will be richly browned, with a tender (not mealy) texture and a hint of marinade flavor that doesn't overpower. Learn more by reading the "Marinade Mixology" tips below. Then tune up your skills with the "practice" recipes here, and before you know it you'll be mastering your own tasty concoctions.

Marinade Mixology

"Our recipes are a starting point to help you make your own easy marinades," says Test Kitchens food chemist Kristi Michele Crowe. Every marinade should have one or more ingredients from each of the four categories below. You also need a small amount of olive or vegetable oil to carry these flavors into the meat. "One suggestion," Kristi adds, "is to taste the marinade before adding the meat. Taste for a balance of flavors much as you would a salad dressing."

Acidic ingredients
Examples: buttermilk; lemon, lime, and orange juices; wine; beer; soft drinks; vinegar
Role: Breaks down proteins, allowing tenderization and penetration of flavors.

Sweet additions
Examples: sugar, honey, ketchup, molasses, maple syrup
Role: Promotes browning when searing meat in a skillet, cooking in the oven at a high temperature, or grilling.

Salty components
Examples: salt, soy sauce, chicken broth, teriyaki sauce, Worcestershire sauce
Role: Tenderizes meat by dissolving proteins. Keeps meat juicy during cooking by reducing amount of moisture lost during cooking; enhances flavor.

Spices and seasonings
Examples: fresh herbs, spices, garlic, mustard, shallots
Role: Pumps up the flavor.

Soda Pop-and-Soy Marinade
fast fixin's

MAKES ABOUT 1⅓ CUPS; **PREP:** 10 MIN.

Don't use diet soft drink—the pork won't brown, and the aftertaste will be unpleasant. Tie the roast with kitchen string to create a shape that will cook evenly, look great, and be easy to slice.

1 cup lemon-lime soft drink
1 Tbsp. light brown sugar
3 Tbsp. soy sauce
2 Tbsp. olive oil
1 Tbsp. Worcestershire sauce
2 garlic cloves, pressed
¾ tsp. ground ginger
⅛ tsp. ground cloves

1. Whisk together lemon-lime soft drink and remaining ingredients until thoroughly blended. Use immediately.

—TERI BRUSH, SANDY, UTAH

Grilled Pork Loin Roast: Place Soda Pop-and-Soy Marinade in a shallow dish or large zip-top plastic freezer bag. Pierce 1 (2½-lb.) pork loin roast several times with a knife; add roast to marinade, and turn to coat. Cover or seal, and chill 4 to 6 hours, turning occasionally. Light one side of grill, heating to 350° to 400° (medium-high) heat; leave other side unlit. Remove roast from marinade, discarding marinade. Pat roast dry, and sprinkle with 1 tsp. salt and ½ tsp. pepper. Tie with kitchen string, securing at 2-inch intervals. Place roast over lit side of grill, and grill, covered with grill lid, 5 minutes on each side or until browned. Transfer roast to unlit side, and grill, covered with grill lid, 1 hour or until a meat thermometer inserted into thickest portion registers 150°. Remove from grill, and let stand 10 minutes before slicing. Garnish with fresh flat-leaf parsley sprigs, if desired. **Makes** 6 to 8 servings; Prep: 20 min.; Chill: 6 hr.; Grill: 1 hr., 10 min.; Stand: 10 min.

Marinade Primer

Italian-Mustard Marinade

fast fixin's • make ahead

MAKES ABOUT 1¼ CUPS; **PREP:** 10 MIN.

1 cup buttermilk
2 Tbsp. red wine vinegar
2 tsp. Dijon mustard
1 small garlic clove, pressed
½ tsp. salt
½ tsp. pepper
1 Tbsp. drained capers, finely chopped
1 Tbsp. finely chopped fresh flat-leaf parsley

1. Whisk together first 6 ingredients until well combined; stir in capers and parsley. Use immediately, or cover and chill until ready to use. Store in an airtight container in refrigerator up to 3 days. If chilled, whisk before using.

—CHARLOTTE BRYANT, GREENSBURG, KENTUCKY

Italian Pan-Cooked Chicken Breasts: Pour Italian-Mustard Marinade into a shallow dish or large zip-top plastic freezer bag; add 4 (7- to 8-oz.) skinned and boned chicken breasts. Cover or seal, and chill at least 8 hours or up to 24 hours, turning occasionally. Remove chicken from marinade, discarding marinade. Pat chicken dry, and sprinkle with 1 tsp. salt and ½ tsp. pepper. Cook chicken in 1 to 2 Tbsp. hot olive oil in a large skillet over medium heat 6 to 8 minutes on each side or until done. **Makes** 4 servings; Prep: 10 min., Chill: 8 hr., Cook: 16 min.

Steak House-Style Marinade

fast fixin's • make ahead

MAKES ¾ CUP; **PREP:** 10 MIN.

Marinating time depends on the size and cut of the beef. This amount of marinade will flavor three (1½-inch-thick) beef tenderloin fillets. Let stand 30 minutes at room temperature to impart flavor, and then grill.

½ cup dark beer
2 Tbsp. olive oil
1 Tbsp. Worcestershire sauce
1 Tbsp. steak sauce
1 tsp. lemon zest
½ tsp. salt
¼ tsp. ground pepper

1. Whisk together beer and remaining ingredients until blended. Use immediately, or cover and chill until ready to use. Store in an airtight container in refrigerator up to 3 days. If chilled, let stand at room temperature 10 minutes before using. Whisk before using.
Note: For testing purposes only, we used A.1. Steak Sauce.

Steak House-Marinated Sirloin Steak: Pierce 1 (1-lb.) boneless sirloin steak several times with a fork. Place Steak House-Style Marinade in a shallow dish or large zip-top plastic freezer bag; add steak. Cover or seal; chill at least 4 hours or up to 6 hours, turning occasionally. Preheat grill to 350° to 400° (medium-high). Remove steak from marinade, discarding marinade. Pat steak dry, and sprinkle with ½ tsp. salt and ½ tsp. coarsely ground pepper. Grill steak, covered with grill lid, over 350° to 400° (medium-high) heat 4 minutes on each side or to desired degree of doneness. Let stand 10 minutes before slicing. **Makes** 4 servings; Prep: 10 min., Chill: 4 hr., Grill 8 min., Stand: 10 min.

Asian Marinade

MAKES ABOUT 1¼ CUPS; **PREP:** 10 MIN.

½ cup lite soy sauce
3 Tbsp. fresh lime juice (about 2 limes)
¼ cup olive oil
2 Tbsp. water
2 Tbsp. honey
1 garlic clove, pressed
2 tsp. minced fresh ginger
¼ tsp. crushed red pepper

1. Whisk together all ingredients. Use immediately, or cover and chill until ready to use. If chilled, whisk before using.

Zesty Pork Loin With Apricot-Pan Sauce: Place 1 (2-lb.) boneless pork loin roast in a shallow dish or large zip-top plastic freezer bag, and add Asian Marinade, turning to coat. Cover or seal, turning occasionally, and chill 6 hours or up to 24 hours. Preheat oven to 400°. Remove pork from marinade, discarding marinade. Sprinkle pork with pepper. Place on a lightly greased rack in an aluminum foil-lined roasting pan. Bake at 400° for 50 minutes to 1 hour or until meat thermometer inserted into thickest portion registers 155°. Remove pan from oven, and cover with foil; let stand 10 minutes or until thermometer registers 160°. Remove roast from pan, reserving drippings in pan; add water, if needed, to make drippings measure ¼ cup. Cut roast into slices; cover and keep warm. Combine ¼ cup pan drippings with ⅓ cup apricot preserves in a small microwave-safe bowl. Microwave at HIGH 1 minute or until melted, stirring once. Serve with sliced pork. **Makes** 6 servings; Prep: 10 min., Chill: 6 hr., Bake: 1 hr., Stand: 10 min.

Healthy Living.

Enjoy the fresh tastes of locally-grown produce all summer long.

Fuss-Free Menu

Your guests will love these simple, good-for-you recipes.

Laid-Back Summer Supper

SERVES 6

Open-faced Turkey Joes

Corn-and-Lima Bean Salad

Warm Blackberry Sauce Over Mango Sorbet

Some of the best parties are planned on the spur of the moment. No fancy linens, flatware, or china required. But even for these casual events, you need quick-fix, crowd-pleasing dishes. This simple, nutritious menu only takes about an hour and a half to make. Follow our cooking timeline for a path to low-stress culinary success.

Healthy Benefits

- Blackberries and other dark purple-colored fruits and vegetables are high in flavonoids, which help reduce inflammation in blood vessels and protect against chronic disease.
- Corn is an excellent source of folate, which is essential to red blood cell formation and nerve function.

Open-faced Turkey Joes

family favorite

MAKES 6 SERVINGS; **PREP:** 20 MIN.,
COOK: 35 MIN., **BAKE:** 13 MIN.

If you are watching your sodium intake, substitute ground turkey breast for Italian turkey sausage. Cut these sandwiches into waistline-friendly portions and let guests serve themselves.

1 (19½-oz.) package Italian turkey sausage, casings removed
1 (8-oz.) package fresh mushrooms, quartered
½ green bell pepper, finely chopped
1 (15½-oz.) jar spaghetti sauce
1 garlic clove, minced
2 Tbsp. tomato paste
1 tsp. dried onion flakes
¼ tsp. pepper
1 (12-oz.) French bread loaf
2 Tbsp. grated Parmesan cheese
¼ cup (1 oz.) shredded mozzarella cheese

1. Cook sausage in a Dutch oven over medium heat, stirring often, 10 minutes or until meat crumbles and is no longer pink; drain. Add mushrooms and bell pepper; cook over medium heat, stirring frequently, 5 minutes. Stir in next 5 ingredients; bring to a boil. Reduce heat to low, and simmer, stirring occasionally, 20 minutes.
2. Preheat oven to 400°. Cut bread in half lengthwise. Place bread, cut side up, on an aluminum foil-lined baking sheet. Bake 5 to 6 minutes or until toasted.
3. Spoon sausage mixture onto toasted bread, and sprinkle with cheeses.

Bake at 400° for 5 to 7 minutes or until cheese is melted and bubbly.

—**STEPHANIE NOLAN**, BRADENTON, FLORIDA

Note: For testing purposes only, we used Jennie-O Sweet Lean Italian Turkey Sausage.

Per serving: Calories 360; Fat 13.3g (sat 4.4g, mono 1.1g, poly 1g); Protein 23.1g; Carb 37.2g; Fiber 3g; Chol 60mg; Iron 3.9mg; Sodium 1269mg; Calc 148mg

Corn-and-Lima Bean Salad

family favorite • make ahead

MAKES 6 SERVINGS; **PREP:** 15 MIN.,
COOK: 5 MIN., **COOL:** 10 MIN., **CHILL:** 1 HR.

Our Test Kitchens Professionals found that the OXO Good Grips Corn Strippers are a great timesaver. They easily remove the kernels for both fresh and grilled corn. Be sure to wait until grilled corn is cool enough to handle. Save the cobs to make flavorful corn broth to use in another recipe (recipe on following page).

3 cups fresh corn kernels (6 ears)
1 Tbsp. olive oil
1 cup fresh baby lima beans*
¼ cup diced roasted red bell pepper
1 Tbsp. fresh basil leaves, cut into thin strips
1 Tbsp. lemon juice
¾ tsp. salt
¼ tsp. dried crushed red pepper

1. Sauté corn kernels in hot oil in a large skillet over medium-high heat 3 minutes or until tender; add lima beans, and cook 2 minutes. Remove from heat, and let cool 10 minutes.
2. Toss together lima bean mixture, bell pepper, and next 4 ingredients in a large bowl. Cover and chill 1 hour.
*1 cup frozen baby lima beans, thawed, may be substituted.

Per serving: Calories 130; Fat 3.5g (sat 0.5g, mono 2g, poly 0.9g); Protein 4.7g; Carb 23g; Fiber 4.1g; Chol 0mg; Iron 1mg; Sodium 310mg; Calc 10mg

Warm Blackberry Sauce Over Mango Sorbet

MAKES 6 SERVINGS; **PREP:** 10 MIN., **COOK:** 5 MIN.

A small cookie scoop, available at discount stores, will let you portion the sorbet accurately, giving your guests just a little something sweet after the meal.

2 pt. fresh blackberries, halved
¼ cup sugar
2½ tsp. orange zest
½ tsp. ground ginger
1 pt. mango sorbet
6 gingersnaps, crushed

1. Stir together first 4 ingredients in a saucepan over medium heat; cook, stirring constantly, 5 minutes or until thoroughly heated. Serve over sorbet; sprinkle with gingersnaps.
Note: For testing purposes only, we used Häagen-Dazs Mango Sorbet.

Per serving: Calories 184; Fat 1.2g (sat 0.2g, mono 0.4g, poly 0.4g); Protein 1.8g; Carb 44g; Fiber 5.9g; Chol 0mg; Iron 1.1mg; Sodium 47mg; Calc 35mg

Corn Broth

freezeable • make ahead

MAKES ABOUT 6 CUPS; **PREP:** 5 MIN., **COOK:** 35 MIN., **COOL:** 1 HR.

Don't throw away those cut-up corncobs; that's where serious flavor lies. Release their hidden potential by making this light and delicious Corn Broth. Use it in place of chicken or vegetable broth in your favorite recipes.

6 corncobs, kernels removed
½ tsp. salt

1. Bring corn cobs and 8 cups water to a light boil in a Dutch oven over medium-high heat. Reduce heat to low, and simmer 30 minutes.
2. Stir in salt. Pour broth through a fine wire-mesh strainer into a large glass bowl, discarding cobs and pulp.

Cover and let cool 1 hour or to room temperature. Store in an airtight container in refrigerator up to 1 week, or freeze up to 2 months.

Per 1-cup serving: Calories 15; Fat 0g (sat 0g, mono 0g, poly 0g); Protein 0g; Carb 3g; Fiber 0g; Chol 0mg; Iron 0mg; Sodium 168mg; Calc 0mg

Corn-and-Poblano Chowder

southernliving.com favorite

MAKES 4 (1-CUP) SERVINGS; **PREP:** 20 MIN., **BROIL:** 6 MIN., **STAND:** 10 MIN., **COOK:** 20 MIN.

Here's a great use for Corn Broth (recipe at left). Frozen creamed corn and fat-free cream cheese are the base for this spicy-sweet, creamy chowder.

1 large poblano pepper, cut in half lengthwise
1 (20-oz.) tube frozen creamed corn, thawed
1½ cups 1% low-fat or fat-free milk
¼ tsp. salt
⅛ to ¼ tsp. ground red pepper
¼ tsp. ground cumin
1½ to 2 cups Corn Broth or reduced-sodium, fat-free chicken broth
½ (8-oz.) package fat-free cream cheese, softened
Garnishes: thinly sliced jalapeño pepper strips, ground black pepper

1. Broil poblano pepper halves, skin side up, on an aluminum foil-lined baking sheet 6 inches from heat 5 to 6 minutes or until pepper looks blistered. Fold aluminum foil over pepper to seal, and let stand 10 minutes. Peel pepper; remove and discard seeds. Coarsely chop pepper; set aside.
2. Bring creamed corn and next 4 ingredients to a boil in a 3-quart saucepan over medium-high heat, stirring mixture constantly. Reduce heat to low, and simmer, stirring often, 10 minutes.
3. Stir 1½ cups Corn Broth into mixture. Whisk in softened cream cheese and chopped poblano pepper; cook, whisking often, 5 minutes or until cream cheese melts and mixture is thoroughly heated. Whisk in additional Corn Broth, if necessary, to reach desired consistency; garnish, if desired. Serve chowder immediately.

Per serving: Calories: 222; Fat 9.2g (sat 0.9g, mono 0.1g, poly 0.2g); Protein 12.5g; Carb:37.5g; Fiber 4.3g; Chol: 8mg; Iron 1.2mg; Sodium 803mg; Calc 244 mg

---

Time It Right

Perfect Prep

- Scoop sorbet into small bowls or sherbet glasses, and place in the freezer up to one day ahead.
- Make the Corn-and-Lima Bean Salad up to four hours ahead. Cover and chill until ready to serve.
- Prepare topping for Open-faced Turkey Joes through Step 1. When guests arrive, reheat the meat mixture over medium heat, stirring occasionally, 5 minutes or until thoroughly heated. Proceed as directed.

Fabulous Finale

- Invite your guests into the kitchen while preparing Warm Blackberry Sauce Over Mango Sorbet. Finish the dessert by spooning warm sauce atop the sorbet, ending with a light sprinkling of gingersnaps.
- Sit back and enjoy a job well done in the company of friends and family.

Eat Local

It's easy to find homegrown produce all over the South. Shop in season to get many benefits for you and your community.

Editor Sara Askew Jones plucks the yellow, pear-shaped tomato from the vine and pops it into her mouth. This tiny jewel yields a mega-ton of flavor, filling her taste buds with concentrated sweetness.

Edwin Marty, executive director at Jones Valley Urban Farm (JVUF) in Birmingham, watches her reaction, smiles, and says, "I don't think there is any way that anyone could dispute that a tomato grown locally is going to taste absolutely better than one shipped from across the country."

Edwin and others at JVUF—a community-based nonprofit organic farm—are part of a growing (pardon the pun) movement that promotes buying and eating area-grown produce.

Fresh and Fabulous for You

Eating local tastes and feels right for so many reasons. Just-picked seasonal produce yields off-the-chart flavor that's missing from globe-trotting fare. Produce grown in faraway states or other countries must be harvested long before its peak pick times so it can survive the journey and be market-ready.

Who can argue with better flavor when tempting those you love to eat their daily share of fruits and veggies? And with freshness comes a nutritional boost for most produce, a plus when every bite counts for eating healthfully.

"The food that you are going to buy from local farmers is going to have so many more nutrients because it is picked ripe," says Edwin. "It is picked when it's ready to be eaten, when the sun's energy has given it the maximum amount of flavor and sweetness."

Another benefit of buying local goods is saving energy—from reducing packaging expenses to cutting fossil fuel costs for long-distance hauling.

Plus, there's better variety. Local farmers (typically those you meet at your neighborhood or city markets) often grow unusual or heirloom selections not found at most commercial stores.

As if freshness, great flavor, seasonal variety, and environmental impact aren't enough to make you want to pull up a chair at the "eat local" table, then consider the economic impact. When you buy from area farmers, more of your food dollars stay in your community.

"People really can't imagine the implications of that," says Edwin. "When you buy something that wasn't produced in your area from a megamart, something like 10 cents stays in your community. If you go to the farmers market and pay a local farmer $1 for corn, 95% of that dollar stays in your area." *For more information about JVUF, visit www.jvuf.org.*

Natural Goodness

Make the choice to support your local farmers (and enjoy all the benefits of eating fresh fruits and vegetables) with these suggestions.

- **Farmers markets:** Most farmers markets take place on the weekends from May through October, making eating local an easy option during these months. Consider visiting a local market as part of your traveling experience. Most markets offer a heaping helping of fun, including music, good eats, and plenty of people watching.

  When shopping, ask questions. Not all markets are created equal. Some require that all products sold must be grown or made by the vendor. Others allow anyone to sell produce regardless of where it's grown. You might end up buying tomatoes shipped in from out of state, purchased in bulk, and repackaged by the seller. It's important to find out where produce was grown.

- **Farm or roadside stands:** Finding locally grown produce may be as easy as driving to and from work. Many farmers set up seasonal stands near busy intersections. However, as mentioned before, ask before you buy. What's offered may or may not come from your state, much less your immediate community. Venture to surrounding rural areas in search of just-picked offerings at farm stands.

- **Join a Community Supported Agriculture (CSA) program:** These programs connect farmers directly with the public. CSA members buy produce subscriptions and, in return, receive boxes of harvested goods on a weekly or monthly basis. This system works great for those who are willing to be flexible with weekly meal plans, because you get what the farmer picks.

- **U-Pick:** If you pick it yourself, then you know it's fresh. In addition, harvesting your own fruits or vegetables is a great way to incorporate a little fitness while enjoying the outdoors.

Easy Treats Anytime

Better make more than one batch—these dessert bites will disappear fast.

Luscious Lemon Bars
family favorite

MAKES 2 DOZEN; **PREP:** 20 MIN., **BAKE:** 1 HR., **COOL:** 1 HR.

2¼ cups all-purpose flour, divided
½ cup powdered sugar
1 cup cold butter, cut into pieces
4 large eggs
1½ cups granulated sugar
2 tsp. lemon zest
½ cup fresh lemon juice
1 tsp. baking powder
¼ tsp. salt
Powdered sugar
Garnish: lemon rind curls

1. Preheat oven to 350°. Line bottom and sides of a 13- x 9-inch pan with heavy-duty aluminum foil, allowing 2 to 3 inches to extend over sides; lightly grease foil.
2. Pulse 2 cups flour, ½ cup powdered sugar, and 1 cup butter in a food processor 5 to 6 times or until mixture is crumbly. Press mixture onto bottom of prepared pan.
3. Bake at 350° on an oven rack one-third up from bottom of oven 25 minutes or just until golden brown.
4. Whisk together eggs and next 3 ingredients in a large bowl until blended. Combine baking powder, salt, and remaining ¼ cup flour; whisk into egg mixture until blended. Pour lemon mixture into prepared crust.
5. Bake at 350° on middle oven rack 30 to 35 minutes or until filling is set. Let cool in pan on a wire rack 30 minutes. Lift from pan onto wire rack, using foil sides as handles, and let cool 30 minutes or until completely cool. Remove foil, and cut into 24 (2-inch) squares; sprinkle with powdered sugar. Garnish, if desired.

— **JAN KIMBELL**, VESTAVIA HILLS, ALABAMA

Coconut-Pecan-Lemon Bars: Preheat oven to 350°. Place 1 cup chopped pecans in a single layer on a baking sheet, and bake 8 to 10 minutes or until toasted and fragrant, stirring after 5 minutes. Proceed with recipe as directed through Step 2, adding toasted pecans to flour mixture before pressing mixture into pan. Bake crust as directed. Proceed with Step 4, decreasing granulated sugar to 1¼ cups and adding ½ cup sweetened flaked coconut and, if desired, 1 Tbsp. coconut rum to filling. Proceed with Step 5 as directed. Garnish with Toasted Coconut, if desired.

Toasted Coconut Garnish: Preheat oven to 350°. Place ½ cup sweetened flaked coconut in a single layer on a baking sheet. Bake 6 to 8 minutes or until lightly browned, stirring once after 4 minutes.

Blackberry-Lemon Bars: Prepare recipe as directed through Step 4. Pulse 2 cups fresh blackberries and ½ cup granulated sugar in a food processor 3 to 4 times or until blended. Transfer mixture to a small saucepan. Cook over medium-low heat, stirring often, 5 to 6 minutes or until thoroughly heated. Pour through a fine wire-mesh strainer into a bowl, gently pressing blackberry mixture with back of a spoon; discard solids. Drizzle over lemon mixture in pan. Proceed with Step 5. Garnish with fresh mint and blackberries, if desired.

Have a Sip

This refreshing beverage is just right for any summer event. Sparkling Punch is light, fresh, and easy on the eyes. Guests of all ages are sure to enjoy the alcohol-free version, but try our Champagne-enhanced variation for adults-only gatherings. And you can even make it ahead: Simply mix and chill the juices, but don't add the club soda until just before serving.

Sparkling Punch

MAKES ABOUT 9 CUPS; **PREP:** 5 MIN., **CHILL:** 1 HR.

Serve this pale pink punch in champagne flutes for an elegant touch. For a slightly sweeter finish, substitute ginger ale for club soda.

1 (12-oz.) can frozen pink lemonade concentrate, thawed
4 cups white cranberry juice cocktail
1 qt. club soda, chilled
Garnish: fresh mint sprigs

1. Stir together lemonade concentrate and cranberry juice cocktail in a large pitcher. Cover and chill at least 1 hour or up to 24 hours. Stir in club soda just before serving. Garnish, if desired.

— **INSPIRED BY DIANA COPPERNOLL**, LINDEN, NORTH CAROLINA

Champagne Punch: Substitute 1 (750-milliliter) bottle extra-dry Champagne or sparkling wine and ¼ cup orange liqueur for club soda; proceed with recipe as directed.

Note: For testing purposes only, we used Cointreau for orange liqueur.

Perfect for a Party

Everyone loves a potluck gathering for the fun, kinship, and really good food. For can't-resist dishes, we asked the Southern Foodways Alliance to share some of its members' tradition-steeped recipes (visit www.southernfoodways.com to learn more). They turned us on to a two-potato salad with tons of flavor, as well as a versatile pimiento cheese, which can be made up to a day in advance so that it's on hand and ready to turn into sandwiches.

Make this tangy New South Jalapeño Pimiento Cheese up to one day in advance. Jim Early notes that the jalapeño actually gets spicier overnight. "I pair the milder version with sweet iced tea and the spicier version with longnecks for getting friends together."

New South Jalapeño Pimiento Cheese

fast fixin's • make ahead

MAKES 6½ CUPS; PREP: 25 MIN.

Jim Early took first place out of 300 entries in the Southern Foodways Alliance Pimiento Cheese Invitational by creating this update of his mother's recipe. If you need a smaller amount, you can easily cut the recipe in half.

2 (8-oz.) blocks extra-sharp Cheddar
    cheese, shredded
1 (8-oz.) block mild Cheddar cheese,
    shredded
1 (8-oz.) package cream cheese, softened
2 (7-oz.) jars diced pimiento, drained
1 (12-oz.) jar roasted red bell peppers,
    drained
½ cup drained pickled jalapeño pepper
    slices
¼ cup mayonnaise
2 Tbsp. Worcestershire sauce
Assorted crackers or bread slices

1. Process first 3 ingredients, in batches, in a food processor 45 seconds or until well blended. Add pimiento and next 4 ingredients, and pulse 5 to 6 times or to desired consistency. Cover and chill up to 1 day. Serve with crackers or bread slices.

—JIM EARLY, WINSTON-SALEM, NORTH CAROLINA

Bacon-and-Sweet Potato Salad

chef recipe

MAKES 8 TO 10 SERVINGS; PREP: 30 MIN., COOK: 50 MIN., STAND: 15 MIN.

Kentucky native Stephen Barber was inspired by his Southern roots to create this flavor-packed salad.

3 large eggs
1 lb. sweet potatoes, peeled and cut into
    chunks
2 tsp. salt, divided
2 lb. red potatoes, quartered
6 bacon slices, diced
1 large red onion, chopped
¾ cup cider vinegar
1 Tbsp. mustard seeds
1 tsp. dried crushed red pepper
¼ cup canola oil
¼ tsp. pepper
1 bunch green onions, chopped
    (about 1 cup)
¼ cup chopped fresh parsley
Salt and pepper to taste (optional)

1. Place eggs in a single layer in a stainless steel saucepan. (Do not use non-stick.) Add water to a depth of 3 inches. Bring to a boil; cover, remove from heat, and let stand 15 minutes.
2. Drain immediately, and return eggs to pan. Fill pan with cold water and ice. Tap each egg firmly on the counter until cracks form all over the shell. Peel under cold running water. Chop eggs.
3. Bring sweet potatoes, ½ tsp. salt, and water to cover to a boil in a Dutch oven. Cook 10 minutes; add red potatoes, and cook 15 minutes or until tender. Drain.
4. Cook bacon in a large skillet over medium-high heat 8 to 10 minutes or until crisp; remove bacon, and drain on paper towels, reserving 1 Tbsp. drippings in skillet.
5. Sauté red onion in hot drippings 8 minutes or until tender. Reduce heat to low, and whisk in vinegar, mustard seeds, and red pepper; cook 2 minutes, whisking occasionally. Whisk in canola oil, pepper, and remaining 1½ tsp. salt.
6. Pour hot vinegar mixture over potatoes. Add eggs, bacon, green onions, and parsley, stirring gently to combine. Season with salt and pepper to taste, if desired.

—STEPHEN BARBER, BARBERSQ RESTAURANT, NAPA, CALIFORNIA

Southwestern Suppers

These wonderful dishes start with slow-cooked black beans.

Here's a different method for cooking dried black beans: hands-off in the slow cooker. You will have to soak them overnight before you begin, but the effort yields great results. Start the rehydrated beans in the morning to serve as a main dish for supper. This recipe yields 8 cups; plan to freeze in 2-cup portions to use in Creamy Black Bean Soup or Black Bean Chimichangas. With rice, beans, and their salad-like toppings, the chimichangas make a meal in themselves. Pair the soup with Mexican Cornbread or a quickly grilled quesadilla to make a meal.

Slow-cooker Black Beans
freezeable • make ahead

MAKES 8 CUPS; **PREP:** 15 MIN.;
SOAK: 8 HR.; **COOK:** 5 HR., 20 MIN.

1 (16-oz.) package dried black beans
2 bacon slices
1 large sweet onion, diced (about 2 cups)
2 celery ribs, diced (about ½ cup)
3 garlic cloves, chopped
2 cups diced cooked ham
½ tsp. ground cumin
¼ tsp. coarsely ground black pepper
¼ tsp. ground red pepper
1 (32-oz.) container low-sodium fat-free
  chicken broth

1. Rinse and sort beans according to package directions. Place beans in a 6-qt. slow cooker. Add water 2 inches above beans; let soak 8 hours. Drain and rinse. Return beans to slow cooker.
2. Cook bacon in a large skillet over medium-high heat 4 to 5 minutes or until crisp; remove bacon, and drain on paper towels, reserving 2 Tbsp. drippings in skillet. Crumble bacon; add to slow cooker.

3. Sauté onion, celery, and garlic in hot drippings 7 to 8 minutes or until tender. Reduce heat to medium, and stir in ham, cumin, and ground peppers. Sauté 5 minutes or until thoroughly heated. Stir in ½ cup chicken broth, and cook 2 minutes, stirring to loosen particles from bottom of skillet; add mixture to slow cooker. Stir in remaining chicken broth and 1 cup water.
4. Cover and cook on HIGH 5 hours or LOW 8 hours or until beans are tender.

Black Bean Chimichangas
family favorite • make ahead

MAKES 5 SERVINGS; **PREP:** 15 MIN.,
BAKE: 18 MIN.

These golden chimichangas are baked in the oven, not fried.

1 (8.8-oz.) pouch ready-to-serve Mexican-
  style rice and pasta mix
2 cups drained Slow-cooker Black
  Beans*
1 cup chunky medium salsa
1 cup (4 oz.) shredded Mexican four-cheese
  blend
2 cups shredded deli-roasted chicken
  (optional)
10 (8-inch) soft taco-size flour
  tortillas
¼ cup butter, melted
Toppings: shredded lettuce, diced tomatoes,
  sour cream, guacamole, olives

1. Prepare rice mix according to package directions.
2. Preheat oven to 400°. Stir together rice, next 3 ingredients, and, if desired, chicken. Spread ½ cup rice mixture just below center of each tortilla. Fold bottom third up and over filling of each tortilla, just until covered. Fold left and right sides of tortillas over, and roll up. Place,

seam sides down, on a lightly greased jelly-roll pan. Brush tops of tortillas with melted butter.
3. Bake at 400° for 15 to 18 minutes or until golden brown. Serve with desired toppings.
*1 (15-oz.) can black beans, rinsed and drained, may be substituted.
Note: For testing purposes only, we used Rice-A-Roni Express Mexican. To make ahead, prepare chimichangas as directed through Step 2; cover and chill 8 hours. Let stand at room temperature 30 minutes; bake as directed.

Creamy Black Bean Soup
family favorite

MAKES 16 CUPS; **PREP:** 15 MIN.,
COOK: 30 MIN.

1 medium onion, diced
  (about 1 cup)
1 tsp. minced garlic
1 Tbsp. olive oil
4 cups undrained Slow-cooker Black
  Beans*
1 (32-oz.) container chicken broth
2 (4.5-oz.) cans chopped green chiles,
  undrained
1 (14.5-oz.) can Mexican-style stewed
  tomatoes, undrained
1 (14.5-oz.) can diced tomatoes,
  undrained
1 (11-oz.) can whole kernel corn, rinsed and
  drained
2 Tbsp. chili powder
1 tsp. ground cumin
Toppings: sour cream, shredded Cheddar
  cheese, diced tomatoes, chopped
  fresh cilantro

1. Sauté onion and garlic in 1 Tbsp. hot oil in a Dutch oven over medium-high heat 6 minutes or until tender. Stir in Slow-cooker Black Beans and next 7 ingredients, stirring to loosen particles from bottom of Dutch oven; cover and bring to a boil. Uncover, reduce heat to medium-low, and simmer, stirring occasionally, 15 minutes.
2. Process 2 cups of soup in blender or food processor 30 seconds or until

smooth. Return to Dutch oven, and stir until blended. Serve with desired toppings.

*2 (15-oz.) cans black beans, rinsed and drained, may be substituted.

Mexican Cornbread
southernliving.com favorite

MAKES 8 SERVINGS; **PREP:** 15 MIN.,
BAKE: 40 MIN.

½ cup vegetable oil, divided
1 medium onion, chopped
1 garlic clove, minced
1 red bell pepper, finely chopped
1 jalapeño pepper, seeded and finely
  chopped
1 (15¼-oz.) can whole kernel corn,
  drained
1½ cups cornmeal mix
1 tsp. sugar
¼ tsp. ground cumin (optional)
¾ cup grated Monterey Jack cheese
2 large eggs
1 cup buttermilk

1. Preheat oven to 400°. Heat 2 Tbsp. oil in a nonstick skillet over medium heat; add onion and next 4 ingredients. Sauté 10 minutes or until tender. Remove from heat, and cool.
2. Stir together cornmeal mix, next 5 ingredients, and ¼ cup oil until blended. Stir in onion mixture.
3. Heat remaining 2 Tbsp. oil in a 9-inch cast-iron skillet in a 400° oven 10 minutes. Pour cornmeal mixture into skillet.
4. Bake at 400° for 30 minutes or until done.

Crispy and Oven-Fried

You don't need to fry chicken the traditional way to get that yummy golden crust and down-home taste. Try this simple method using crushed tortilla chips.

Tortilla Chip-Crusted Chicken

MAKES 4 SERVINGS; **PREP:** 15 MIN.,
BAKE: 20 MIN.

Use your favorite brand of chips in this dish that's ready in just 35 minutes. The Pineapple-Kiwi Salsa offers a fresh, slightly tart counterpart.

1 lb. chicken breast tenders
½ tsp. salt
¼ tsp. pepper
⅓ cup all-purpose flour
½ tsp. dried oregano
½ tsp. chili powder
¼ tsp. ground cumin
2 large eggs
2 garlic cloves, pressed
Vegetable cooking spray
2 cups crushed tortilla chips
Pineapple-Kiwi Salsa (optional)

1. Preheat oven to 425°. Sprinkle chicken with salt and pepper.
2. Stir together ⅓ cup flour and next 3 ingredients.
3. Whisk eggs just until foamy, and stir in pressed garlic.
4. Place a wire rack coated with cooking spray in a 15- x 10-inch jelly-roll pan.
5. Dredge chicken tenders in flour mixture, shaking off excess; dip in egg mixture, and dredge in crushed tortilla chips. Lightly coat chicken on each side with cooking spray; arrange chicken on wire rack.
6. Bake at 425° for 18 to 20 minutes or until golden brown and done, turning once after 12 minutes. Serve with Pineapple-Kiwi Salsa, if desired.

Pineapple-Kiwi Salsa:
fast fixin's • make ahead

MAKES 2 CUPS; **PREP:** 10 MIN.

Reader Catherine Bodi's fresh, colorful salsa originally included strawberries, but we loved the clean flavor of pineapple and kiwi. Make this up to two days ahead, and store in an airtight container in the refrigerator.

2 (8-oz.) cans pineapple tidbits, drained
2 kiwifruit, peeled and diced
2 Tbsp. fresh cilantro leaves, minced
2 Tbsp. fresh lime juice
1 tsp. minced jalapeño pepper
Salt to taste

1. Stir together first 5 ingredients; add salt to taste.

— **CATHERINE BODI**, WESTERVILLE, OHIO

Test Kitchens Notebook

- Dredging the chicken in the flour mixture first helps the coating stick.
- Crushed, naturally crunchy ingredients, such as tortilla or potato chips, corn flakes, and pita chips, make extra-crunchy coatings for oven-fried chicken.
- For easy cleanup, line the pan with aluminum foil.
- Baking on a rack allows the heat to get all the way around the chicken so that it crisps on both sides.

—**DONNA FLORIO**, SENIOR WRITER

Just-Right Shrimp

Tips, tricks, and secrets for perfectly cooked shrimp

Notes From the Bayou When Executive Editor Scott Jones and Test Kitchens Professional Pam Lolley traveled to Louisiana to cook with Timmy Cheramie (page 118), they brought home pages of handwritten notes filled with delicious details of the meals they shared. Pam re-created their culinary adventure for the Food staff to enjoy and passed along some of the things that make Timmy's recipes so special.

- Walker & Sons "Slap Ya Mama" Cajun Seasoning delivers a peppery punch without the double dose of salt found in some brands.
- When stirring up Shrimp-and-Sausage Stew, Timmy coaxes maximum flavor by layering his ingredients—first caramelizing the onions and then adding the tomato sauce and remaining veggies in stages.
- Timmy's recipe for Boiled Shrimp is easy and flawless. Immediately after stirring in the shrimp, he pulls the pot from the stove and leaves it to stand until the shrimp turn pink and the shells begin to loosen. Icing down the water and adding salt *after* the shrimp are cooked keeps them tender and easy to peel.

Stylish Cuts A simple technique known as butterflying gives Bayou Fried Shrimp a festive look. It's a quick step that's also used when preparing stuffed shrimp and other special dishes. Here's how we do it.

Peel shrimp, leaving the tails intact. Using a sharp paring knife, make a deep slit down the back of each shrimp, from the large end to the tail, cutting to but not through the inside curve of the shrimp. Open the shrimp to form a butterfly shape, and remove the dark vein.

Sizing Up the Selection Shrimp come in a wide range of sizes—from tiny cooked salad shrimp barely bigger than a BB pellet to the super-large variety. Although larger shrimp cost more and are a better choice for some recipes, they don't necessarily taste better.

When buying shrimp, look closely at the label and you'll see a set of numbers divided by a slash, such as 16/20 or 51/60. These numbers refer to the count (the number of shrimp per pound). While there are no regulations governing the use of such terms as "large" or "jumbo," stores *are* required to display the number of shrimp per pound.

Almost all shrimp are frozen at sea or soon thereafter—even if they are sold as "fresh" in stores. Select firm shrimp with a mild scent, or buy frozen ones with the shells on. Peeled and deveined shrimp are less protected against freezer burn. Bacteria can migrate, so avoid fresh-cooked shrimp that are displayed alongside raw fish or shellfish.

July

Savor the Outdoors With Friends

Spice up your next gathering with these irresistible recipes. The Cajun Burgers and Bacon-Wrapped Barbecue Burgers go beyond the expected; both are sure to be hits. And don't forget about the toppings, which dress up your favorite mayonnaise with a variety of bold flavors. (We also love dipping French fries and chips into these delectable mayos.) Round things out with two unique beverages and a batch of bake-ahead Frosted Sugar-'n'-Spice Cookies.

Backyard Burger Bar

SERVES 4

Ginger Beer

Cajun Burgers or Bacon-Wrapped Barbecue Burgers

Choice of flavored condiments

Steak Fries

Frosted Sugar-'n'-Spice Cookies

Pineapple Iced Tea Punch

Ginger Beer

MAKES 4 TO 6 SERVINGS; PREP: 5 MIN.

1 (4-inch) piece fresh ginger
4 cups ginger ale, chilled
2 (12-oz.) bottles amber beer, chilled
½ cup dark rum

1. Grate ginger using large holes of a box grater. Squeeze juice from grated ginger into a small bowl to equal 2 tsp.; discard solids.
2. Stir together juice from ginger, ginger ale, beer, and dark rum. Serve in chilled glasses.

Cajun Burgers

MAKES 4 SERVINGS; PREP: 20 MIN., GRILL: 12 MIN.

These bold-flavored burgers were inspired by a recipe from reader Rhonda Maiani of North Carolina.

¾ lb. ground chuck
¼ lb. ground pork sausage
¾ cup frozen diced onion, red and green bell pepper, and celery
1 Tbsp. paprika
1 tsp. salt
1 tsp. minced garlic
¼ tsp. ground red pepper
¼ tsp. ground black pepper
4 hamburger buns
Cajun Mustard
Toppings: lettuce, tomato slices, and onion

1. Preheat grill to 350° to 400° (medium-high). Gently combine ground chuck, sausage, and next 6 ingredients. Shape mixture into 4 (4-inch) patties.
2. Grill patties, covered with grill lid, over 350° to 400° (medium-high) heat 4 to 5 minutes on each side or until beef is no longer pink in center.
3. Grill hamburger buns, cut sides down, 1 to 2 minutes or until lightly toasted. Serve burgers on buns with Cajun Mustard and desired toppings.

Cajun Mustard:

MAKES ½ CUP; PREP: 10 MIN.

½ (8-oz.) jar spicy brown mustard
1 Tbsp. finely chopped green onions
1 tsp. minced garlic
1 tsp. hot sauce
1 tsp. honey

1. Stir together spicy brown mustard and remaining ingredients. Serve immediately, or cover and chill until ready to serve. Store in an airtight container in refrigerator up to 3 days.

Bacon-Wrapped Barbecue Burgers

MAKES 4 SERVINGS; PREP: 25 MIN., COOK: 5 MIN., CHILL: 10 MIN., GRILL: 12 MIN., STAND: 5 MIN.

These burgers are stuffed with a mushroom mixture. Serve extra mushrooms over the meat, with or without the bun. (Pictured on page 172)

8 bacon slices
1 (4.5-oz.) jar sliced mushrooms, drained and chopped
½ cup chopped Vidalia or sweet onion
2 tsp. olive oil
½ cup bottled honey barbecue sauce, divided
1½ lb. ground beef
Wooden picks
¼ tsp. salt
4 sesame seed hamburger buns, toasted

1. Arrange bacon on a paper towel-lined microwave-safe plate; cover with a paper towel. Microwave bacon at HIGH 2 minutes or until edges begin to crinkle and bacon is partially cooked.
2. Sauté mushrooms and onion in hot oil in a small nonstick skillet over medium heat 4 to 5 minutes or until tender and liquid is absorbed. Remove from heat; stir in 2 Tbsp. barbecue sauce.
3. Preheat grill to 350° to 400° (medium-high). Shape ground beef into 8 (5-inch) thin patties. Place 2 Tbsp. mushroom mixture in center of each of

4 patties. Top with remaining patties, pressing edges to seal. Shape into 4-inch patties. Wrap sides of each patty with 2 bacon slices, overlapping ends of each slice. Secure bacon using wooden picks. Sprinkle patties with salt. Cover and chill 10 minutes.

4. Grill patties, covered with grill lid, over 350° to 400° (medium-high) heat 5 to 6 minutes on 1 side. Turn and baste with half of remaining barbecue sauce. Grill 5 to 6 minutes or until beef is no longer pink in center. Turn and baste with remaining barbecue sauce. Remove from grill, and let stand 5 minutes. Remove wooden picks. Serve burgers on buns, and top with remaining mushroom mixture.

Note: For testing purposes only, we used Kraft Honey Barbecue Sauce.

Horseradish Mayonnaise:
MAKES ½ CUP; **PREP:** 10 MIN.
Stir together ½ cup mayonnaise, 1 Tbsp. horseradish, 2 tsp. chopped fresh chives, 2 tsp. fresh lemon juice, and ¼ tsp. pepper. Cover and chill until ready to serve. Store in an airtight container in refrigerator up to 1 week.

Fresh Herb Mayonnaise:
MAKES ½ CUP; **PREP:** 10 MIN.
Stir together ½ cup mayonnaise, 1 Tbsp. chopped fresh parsley, 1 Tbsp. chopped fresh basil, 1 Tbsp. chopped fresh chives, and 1 pressed garlic clove. Cover and chill until ready to serve. Store in an airtight container in refrigerator up to 1 week.

Spicy Chipotle Mayonnaise:
MAKES ½ CUP; **PREP:** 10 MIN.
Stir together ½ cup mayonnaise, 1 Tbsp. chopped chipotle peppers in adobo sauce, ¼ tsp. lime zest, and 1 tsp. fresh lime juice. Cover and chill until ready to serve. Store in an airtight container in refrigerator up to 1 week.

Citrus-Garlic Mayonnaise:
MAKES ¾ CUP; **PREP:** 10 MIN.
Stir together ¾ cup mayonnaise, 1 Tbsp. orange juice, 2 tsp. lemon juice, 1 pressed garlic clove, and ¼ tsp.

pepper. Cover and chill until ready to serve. Store in an airtight container in refrigerator up to 1 week.

Steak Fries
southernliving.com favorite
MAKES 4 SERVINGS; **PREP:** 5 MIN., **GRILL:** 12 MIN.

1 (28-oz.) bag frozen steak fries
Salt and pepper to taste

1. Grill steak fries, covered with grill lid, over medium-high heat (350° to 400°) 4 to 6 minutes on each side or until browned and crisp. Sprinkle grilled steak fries evenly with salt and pepper to taste.

Frosted Sugar-'n'-Spice Cookies
MAKES 2½ DOZEN; **PREP:** 1 HR., **CHILL:** 2 HR., **BAKE:** 10 MIN. PER BATCH, **COOL:** 33 MIN.

2 cups all-purpose flour
1 tsp. baking powder
½ tsp. baking soda
½ tsp. ground cinnamon
¼ tsp. salt
⅛ tsp. ground nutmeg
⅓ cup butter, softened
½ cup granulated sugar
½ cup firmly packed brown sugar
2 egg yolks
5 oz. cream cheese, softened
1 tsp. orange zest
1 tsp. vanilla extract
Simple White Frosting
Red and blue sprinkles

1. Stir together first 6 ingredients.
2. Beat butter and next 3 ingredients at medium speed with an electric mixer until creamy. Add cream cheese, orange zest, and vanilla; beat until well blended. Gradually add flour mixture, beating at low speed until blended.
3. Divide dough in half, shaping into 2 flattened disks. Cover with plastic wrap, and chill 2 to 24 hours.

4. Preheat oven to 350°. Place 1 dough disk on a floured surface. Roll to ¼-inch thickness; cut with a 4-inch star-shaped cutter. Place 1 inch apart on ungreased baking sheets. Repeat procedure with remaining dough disk.
5. Bake at 350° for 8 to 10 minutes or just until edges are lightly browned. Cool on baking sheets 3 minutes. Transfer to a wire rack, and let cool 30 minutes or until completely cool.
6. Spread with a thin layer of Simple White Frosting; top with sprinkles.
Note: To make ahead, prepare recipe as directed through Step 5. Freeze cookies in a heavy-duty zip-top plastic freezer bag up to 1 month. Thaw completely at room temperature before icing.

Simple White Frosting:
MAKES ABOUT 1½ CUPS; **PREP:** 10 MIN.

¼ cup butter, softened
⅛ tsp. salt
3 cups powdered sugar, divided
4 Tbsp. milk, divided

1. Beat butter, salt, 1½ cups powdered sugar, and 3 Tbsp. milk at medium speed with an electric mixer until blended. Gradually beat in remaining powdered sugar and milk.

Pineapple Iced Tea Punch
fast fixin's
MAKES ABOUT 3½ QT.; **PREP:** 5 MIN., **COOK:** 5 MIN., **STEEP:** 10 MIN.

2 family-size tea bags
1 cup sugar
1 (46-oz.) can unsweetened pineapple juice
1 cup lemon juice

1. Bring 3 cups water to a boil; add tea bags. Boil 1 minute, and remove from heat; cover and steep 10 minutes.
2. Remove and discard tea bags. Add sugar, stirring until dissolved.
3. Pour into a 1-gal. container. Stir in 2 cups water, pineapple juice, and lemon juice. Serve over ice.

Take Time for Breakfast

Enjoy a leisurely morning meal at home with a few friends. Make breakfast sandwiches while everyone sips coffee sweetened with one of our sugar blends. Let guests dollop, sprinkle, and drizzle cut-up fruit with yogurt, Quick Stovetop Granola, and Lemon-Ginger Honey. It's so good, you'll feel as if you're on vacation.

Open-Face Ham-and-Egg Sandwich

MAKES 4 SERVINGS; **PREP:** 20 MIN., **BAKE:** 14 MIN., **COOK:** 3 MIN., **STAND:** 2 MIN., **BROIL:** 2 MIN.

This recipe yields perfectly cooked fried eggs. It's easy to find the Italian bread in your grocer's fresh bakery area. Ciabatta is a wonderful toasting bread you may have to request.

½ (5-oz.) package arugula, thoroughly washed
1 Tbsp. chopped fresh basil
2 Tbsp. balsamic vinaigrette
1 Tbsp. butter, melted
4 (½-inch-thick) crusty Italian bread or ciabatta slices
1 Tbsp. butter
4 large eggs
¼ tsp. salt
¼ tsp. freshly cracked pepper
8 thin slices smoked ham (about ½ lb.)
4 thin slices sharp provolone cheese

Sweeten a Cup

Find turbinado sugar in the baking-products aisle. **Note:** For testing purposes only, we used Sugar in the Raw Turbinado Sugar.

Spicy Coffee Sugar: Whisk together ⅓ cup turbinado sugar, ½ tsp. ground cardamom, and ¼ tsp. ground ginger. **Makes** about ⅓ cup. Prep: 5 min.

Chocolate-Cinnamon Coffee Sugar: Whisk together ⅓ cup turbinado sugar, 6 Tbsp. sweetened ground chocolate, and ¼ tsp. ground cinnamon. **Makes** about ⅔ cup. Prep: 5 min. **Note:** For testing purposes only, we used Ghirardelli Sweet Ground Chocolate.

Spiced Chocolate Coffee Sugar: Whisk together ⅓ cup turbinado sugar, 6 Tbsp. sweetened ground chocolate, ¼ tsp. ground nutmeg, and ⅛ tsp. ground cardamom. **Makes** about ⅔ cup. Prep: 5 min. .

1. Preheat oven to 350°. Toss together first 3 ingredients in a medium bowl.
2. Brush melted butter on 1 side of each bread slice. Place bread slices, buttered sides down, on an aluminum foil-lined baking sheet.
3. Bake at 350° for 14 minutes, turning once after 8 minutes.
4. Meanwhile, melt 1 Tbsp. butter in a large nonstick skillet over medium heat. Gently break eggs into hot skillet, and sprinkle with salt and pepper. Cook 2 to 3 minutes or until whites are almost set. Cover, remove from heat, and let stand 1 to 2 minutes or until whites are set and yolks are cooked to desired degree of doneness.
5. Top each bread slice with 2 ham slices and 1 cheese slice. Broil 6 inches from heat 2 minutes or until cheese begins to melt.
6. Top each sandwich with ⅓ to ½ cup arugula mixture and 1 fried egg.
Note: For testing purposes only, we used Newman's Own Balsamic Vinaigrette and Boar's Head Black Forest Smoked Ham.

Lemon-Ginger Honey
make ahead

MAKES ⅔ CUPS; **PREP:** 5 MIN., **STAND:** 2 HR.

Drizzle over fruit, spread on hot biscuits, or stir into hot tea.

⅔ cup honey
2 tsp. lemon zest
½ tsp. fresh lemon juice
¼ tsp. ground ginger

1. Whisk together all ingredients in a small bowl. Cover and let stand 2 hours. Whisk before serving. Store in an airtight container at room temperature 3 to 5 days.

Quick Stovetop Granola
make ahead

MAKES 2 CUPS; **PREP:** 10 MIN.,
COOK: 5 MIN., **COOL:** 20 MIN.

3 Tbsp. light brown sugar
1½ Tbsp. butter
1 Tbsp. honey
2 cups cranberry-vanilla trail mix nutlike
   cereal nuggets

1. Cook sugar and butter in a large
skillet over medium-high heat, stirring
often, 2 minutes or until butter is melted and sugar is dissolved. Stir in honey
until blended. Stir in cereal; cook, stirring often, 2 to 3 minutes or until cereal
is lightly browned. Pour mixture onto
a wax paper-lined jelly-roll pan; spread
in an even layer. Let cool 20 minutes.
Store in an airtight container up to
1 week.

—**CYNTHIA GIVAN**, FORT WORTH, TEXAS

Note: For testing purposes only, we
used Post Trail Mix Crunch Cranberry
Vanilla Cereal.

Cooking Up Fun!

These Mississippi children
have a great time together in
the kitchen. Your family will
love their foolproof recipes.

Kids can be finicky eaters.
One sure way to open
their mouths to good food
and flavor is to get them
in the kitchen with chef
Art Smith, Oprah Winfrey's former
personal chef. Art created Common
Threads, a nonprofit program that
teaches children about healthy eating
and nourishes an appreciation of other
cultures through food and cooking.

Launched in Chicago in 2003, his pro-
gram now reaches kids in Kosciusko,
Mississippi, at the 32,000-square-foot
Oprah Winfrey Boys & Girls Club of
Kosciusko/Attala County.

Our visit with Florida native Chef
Art and his pint-size chefs in the club's
program was indeed a treat. Pizza was
the star attraction, and it was all kid
made. Art rolled up his sleeves in the
high-tech kitchen and began weaving
health facts into funny stories about
fresh veggies, pizza history, and cooking. With laser-beam focus on Chef
Art's directions, the junior cooks div-
vied up the pizza dough, rolling it into
near perfect rounds, ready to cover with
their favorite toppings.

"A circle of family and friends gathered around a table, sharing a meal, is
a terrific setting for teaching," Art says
passionately.

Easy Pizza Dough
chef recipe • make ahead

MAKES 6 (8-INCH) PIZZA DOUGH ROUNDS;
PREP: 10 MIN., **CHILL:** 2 HR.

*You can make the dough up to 24 hours
before you need it, or shape the dough
rounds and freeze for up to 3 months.*

1 cup warm water (100° to 110°)
¼ cup olive oil
1 (¼-oz.) envelope active dry yeast
2 tsp. honey
3½ cups all-purpose flour
1 tsp. kosher salt
Vegetable cooking spray

1. Process first 4 ingredients in a food
processor 20 seconds or until yeast is
dissolved and mixture is bubbly. Add
flour and salt; pulse 6 to 8 times or until
dough forms a ball and leaves sides of
bowl, adding more water if necessary.
2. Place dough in a large bowl coated
with cooking spray; lightly coat dough
with cooking spray. Cover and chill at
least 2 hours or up to 24 hours.
3. Place dough on a lightly floured surface. Divide dough into 6 equal

portions; roll each portion into an 8-
inch round. Use dough immediately,
or follow instructions below to make
ahead.

—**ART SMITH**, *BACK TO THE FAMILY COOKBOOK*,
CHICAGO, ILLINOIS

Note: Place Easy Pizza Dough rounds
on 2 lightly greased baking sheets.
Bake at 400° for 7 minutes. Let cool 20
minutes. Place in zip-top plastic freezer
bags; freeze up to 3 months. Let pizza
crusts stand at room temperature 20
minutes before adding toppings.

Basic Tomato Sauce
chef recipe • make ahead

MAKES ABOUT 2 CUPS; **PREP:** 20 MIN.,
COOK: 26 MIN., **COOL:** 15 MIN.

1 small sweet onion, chopped (about ¾ cup)
¼ cup olive oil
6 garlic cloves, minced
1 Tbsp. chopped fresh thyme
½ tsp. dried crushed red pepper
3 cups chopped tomatoes (about 6 medium)
1 Tbsp. light brown sugar
¼ cup chopped fresh basil
2 Tbsp. chopped fresh oregano
1 Tbsp. chopped fresh rosemary
1 tsp. salt
½ tsp. freshly ground pepper

1. Sauté onion in hot oil in a medium
saucepan over medium-high heat 3 to
4 minutes or until tender. Stir in garlic,
thyme, and red pepper, and sauté 2
minutes. Stir in tomatoes and brown
sugar. Reduce heat to medium-low, and
cook, stirring occasionally, 15 minutes.
2. Stir in basil and next 4 ingredients,
and cook 5 minutes. Remove from heat,
and let cool 15 minutes.
3. If desired, pulse tomato mixture, in
batches, in a food processor 3 to 4 times
or to desired consistency. Use immediately, or store in an airtight container in
refrigerator up to 3 days.

—**ART SMITH**, *BACK TO THE FAMILY COOKBOOK*,
CHICAGO, ILLINOIS

Note: To make ahead, prepare recipe as
directed. Place sauce in an airtight container. Freeze sauce up to 3 months.

Cheese-and-Sausage Mini Pizzas

family favorite

MAKES 6 (8-INCH) PIZZAS; **PREP:** 20 MIN.,
BAKE: 17 MIN., **COOK:** 11 MIN.

Easy Pizza Dough (recipe on page 141)
1 lb. turkey sausage, casings removed
Basic Tomato Sauce (recipe on page 141)
3 cups (12 oz.) shredded Italian three-
    cheese blend
Toppings: grated Parmesan cheese, sliced
    fresh mozzarella, turkey pepperoni,
    dried Italian seasoning

1. Preheat oven to 400°. Place Easy
Pizza Dough rounds on 2 lightly
greased baking sheets. Bake at 400° for
7 minutes.
2. Cook sausage in a large nonstick
skillet over medium-high heat 9 to 11
minutes or until meat is no longer pink,
breaking sausage into pieces while
cooking; drain.
3. Spread about ⅓ cup Basic Tomato
Sauce evenly over each pizza crust; top
each pizza with ½ cup cheese, ⅓ cup
cooked sausage, and desired toppings.
4. Bake at 400° for 8 to 10 minutes or
until crust is golden and cheese
is melted.

Summer Fresh Sides

Bring on the barbecue!
Familiar favorites take a
deliciously unexpected turn
in this updated collection of
cookout classics. The reci-
pes couldn't be simpler, and surprise
ingredients are the secret to their spectacular flavors.

Peanutty Coleslaw

make ahead

MAKES 6 SERVINGS; **PREP:** 15 MIN.,
CHILL: 1 HR.

*Crisp coleslaw is lightly dressed with the
salty snap of peanuts and wasabi. Wasabi
paste can be purchased in the Asian section of most supermarkets. If you prefer
a creamy coleslaw, double the amount of
dressing. (Pictured on page 173)*

½ cup chopped fresh cilantro
¼ cup chopped green onions
3 Tbsp. white vinegar
1 Tbsp. sesame oil
2 Tbsp. mayonnaise
1 tsp. sugar
1 tsp. grated fresh ginger
2 tsp. wasabi paste
½ tsp. salt
½ tsp. pepper
1 (16-oz.) package shredded coleslaw mix
¾ cup lightly salted peanuts

1. Whisk together first 10 ingredients
in a large bowl; add coleslaw mix, stirring to coat. Cover and chill 1 hour; stir
in peanuts just before serving.

— **DONNA SPEARS**, OXFORD, NORTH CAROLINA

Watermelon, Mâche, and Pecan Salad

MAKES 6 TO 8 SERVINGS; **PREP:** 20 MIN.,
BAKE: 7 MIN., **COOL:** 15 MIN.

*Spiked with the sweet-sharp heat of Pepper
Jelly Vinaigrette, cubes of watermelon
team up with crumbles of Gorgonzola
cheese. Mâche, a tender heirloom variety
of lamb's lettuce, has a slightly sweet, nutty
flavor, but is equally good when prepared
with baby lettuces. (Pictured on page 173)*

¾ cup chopped pecans
5 cups seeded and cubed watermelon
1 (6-oz.) package mâche, washed
Pepper Jelly Vinaigrette
1 cup crumbled Gorgonzola cheese

1. Preheat oven to 350°. Arrange
pecans in a single layer on a baking

sheet, and bake at 350° for 5 to 7 minutes or until lightly toasted and fragrant. Cool on a wire rack 15 minutes
or until completely cool.
2. Combine watermelon and mâche in a
large bowl; add vinaigrette, tossing gently to coat. Transfer watermelon mixture to a serving platter, and sprinkle
evenly with pecans and cheese.

Pepper Jelly Vinaigrette:
MAKES ¾ CUP; **PREP:** 10 MIN.

*This is also terrific drizzled over a trio of
sliced tomatoes, cucumbers, and onions.*

¼ cup rice wine vinegar
¼ cup pepper jelly
1 Tbsp. fresh lime juice
1 Tbsp. grated onion
1 tsp. salt
¼ tsp. pepper
¼ cup vegetable oil

1. Whisk together first 6 ingredients.
Gradually add oil in a slow, steady
stream, whisking until blended.

— **PAT PATERNOSTRO**, METARIE, LOUISIANA

Blue Cheese-and-Green Onion Potato Salad

fast fixin's • make ahead

MAKES 8 SERVINGS; **PREP:** 15 MIN.,
COOK: 15 MIN.

3 lb. new potatoes, quartered
2 tsp. salt, divided
⅓ cup sliced green onions
1 (8-oz.) container sour cream
½ cup refrigerated blue cheese dressing
½ tsp. freshly ground pepper
½ cup crumbled blue cheese

1. Bring potatoes, 1 tsp. salt, and water
to cover to a boil. Cook 10 to 15 minutes or just until tender; drain.
2. Stir together green onions, next 3
ingredients, and remaining salt in a large
bowl; add potatoes and blue cheese, stirring gently to coat. Serve immediately, or
cover and chill until ready to serve.

— **LORA K. BIERI**, ORLANDO, FLORIDA

Mango-Papaya Salsa

make ahead

MAKES ABOUT 8 CUPS; **PREP:** 20 MIN.,
CHILL: 3 HR.

*Wrapped in papery brown husks, toma-
tillos look like small green tomatoes, but
their pulp is firm rather than juicy and
peppered with tiny seeds. They bring a
refreshing citrus taste to recipes.*

6 fresh tomatillos, husks removed
3 mangoes, chopped
1 papaya, chopped
1 red bell pepper, chopped
1 small red onion, chopped
½ cup chopped fresh cilantro
1 jalapeño, seeded and finely chopped
2 Tbsp. fresh lemon juice
2 Tbsp. fresh lime juice
1 tsp. salt

1. Chop tomatillos. Stir together tomatillos, mangoes, and remaining ingredients. Cover and chill 3 hours.

— **KATHY CROWE**, MARIETTA, GEORGIA

Hot Mango Chutney Baked Beans

MAKES 10 SERVINGS; **PREP:** 20 MIN.,
COOK: 11 MIN., **BAKE:** 50 MIN.

*Molasses and brown sugar offset the heat
in this supercharged side.*

8 bacon slices
1 large sweet onion, chopped
1 (53-oz.) can pork and beans in tomato
    sauce, drained
1 (9-oz.) jar hot mango chutney
3 pickled jalapeño peppers, seeded and
    chopped
1 cup molasses
¼ cup firmly packed brown sugar
2 tsp. hot sauce

1. Preheat oven to 325°. Cook bacon in
a large skillet over medium-high heat
5 to 7 minutes or until crisp; remove
bacon, and drain on paper towels,
reserving 1 tsp. drippings in skillet.
Crumble bacon.

2. Sauté onion in hot drippings 3 to 4
minutes or until tender.
3. Stir together onion, pork and beans,
and next 5 ingredients; spoon into a
lightly greased 13- x 9-inch baking
dish. Top bean mixture with bacon.
4. Bake at 325° for 45 to 50 minutes
or until bubbly. Serve with a slotted
spoon.

— **SHARON J. THOMAS**, VIRGINIA BEACH, VIRGINIA

Fresh Corn Cakes

family favorite

MAKES ABOUT 3 DOZEN; **PREP:** 20 MIN.,
COOK: 7 MIN. PER BATCH

2½ cups fresh corn kernels (about 5 ears)
3 large eggs
¾ cup milk
3 Tbsp. butter, melted
¾ cup all-purpose flour
¾ cup yellow or white cornmeal
1 (8-oz.) package fresh mozzarella cheese,
    grated
2 Tbsp. chopped fresh chives
1 tsp. salt
1 tsp. freshly ground pepper

1. Pulse first 4 ingredients in a food
processor 3 to 4 times or just until corn
is coarsely chopped.
2. Stir together flour and next 5 ingredients in a large bowl; stir in corn
mixture just until dry ingredients are
moistened.
3. Spoon ⅛ cup batter for each cake
onto a hot, lightly greased griddle or
large nonstick skillet to form 2-inch
cakes (do not spread or flatten cakes).
Cook cakes 3 to 4 minutes or until tops
are covered with bubbles and edges
look cooked. Turn and cook other sides
2 to 3 minutes.

— **MAGDALENA DI ROCCO**,
BREVARD, NORTH CAROLINA

Green Bean, Grape, and Pasta Toss

family favorite • make ahead

MAKES 8 SERVINGS; **PREP:** 25 MIN.,
BAKE: 7 MIN., **COOK:** 12 MIN., **CHILL:** 3 HR.

*If you're a broccoli salad fan, you'll love
the combination of these colorful ingredients. Cook the pasta al dente, so it's firm
enough to hold its own when tossed with
the tangy-sweet salad dressing. (Pictured
on page 173)*

1 cup chopped pecans
8 bacon slices
1 lb. thin fresh green beans, trimmed and
    cut in half
1 (8-oz.) package penne pasta
1 cup mayonnaise
⅓ cup sugar
⅓ cup red wine vinegar
1 tsp. salt
2 cups seedless red grapes, cut in half
⅓ cup diced red onion
Salt to taste

1. Preheat oven to 350°. Arrange
pecans in a single layer on a baking
sheet, and bake at 350° for 5 to 7 minutes or until lightly toasted and
fragrant.
2. Cook bacon in a large skillet over
medium-high heat 5 to 7 minutes or
until crisp; remove bacon, and drain on
paper towels. Crumble bacon.
3. Cook beans in boiling salted water
to cover 5 minutes or until crisp-tender;
drain. Plunge beans into ice water to
stop the cooking process.
4. Meanwhile, prepare pasta according
to package directions; drain.
5. Whisk together mayonnaise and
next 3 ingredients in a large bowl; add
pecans, green beans, pasta, grapes, and
onion, stirring to coat. Season with salt
to taste. Cover and chill 3 hours; stir in
bacon just before serving.

— **SHERRI STRICKLAND**, CLINTON, NORTH CAROLINA

Fish Fry Done Right

Summer's the time for enjoying seafood. Try our twists on the classics.

T his weekend, invite friends over for a relaxing get-together. These delicious recipes offer a spin on standard fish fry fare. Serve Stuffed Sweet-and-Spicy Jalapeño Poppers as a tasty appetizer. Sweet-Hot Pecan Sauce, made from common pantry items, delivers a rich and nutty flavor and is a delicious alternative to ketchup or tartar sauce. Shrimp-and-Okra Hush Puppies combine Southern favorites with a delightful contrast of taste and texture. Get ready to fry up a scrumptious seafood jubilee.

Stuffed Sweet-and-Spicy Jalapeño Poppers

MAKES 4 TO 6 SERVINGS;
PREP: 15 MIN., **BAKE:** 10 MIN.,
COOL: 10 MIN., **FRY:** 2 MIN. PER BATCH
(Pictured on page 11)

1 cup pecans
1½ cups all-purpose baking mix
½ tsp. salt
½ tsp. pepper
1 (11.5-oz.) jar whole jalapeño peppers, drained
½ (8-oz.) container soft pineapple cream cheese
1 large egg, lightly beaten
Canola oil

1. Preheat oven to 350°. Place pecans in a single layer in a shallow pan. Bake at 350° for 10 minutes or until toasted and fragrant, stirring once after 5 minutes. Let cool 10 minutes.
2. Process pecans, baking mix, salt, and pepper in a food processor 8 to 10 seconds or until pecans are finely ground. Place pecan mixture in a large bowl.
3. Rinse peppers under cold running water; cut in half lengthwise. Remove and discard seeds and membranes. Pat peppers dry with paper towels.
4. Spoon 1 tsp. pineapple cream cheese into each pepper half. Dip in egg; dredge in pecan mixture.
5. Pour oil to depth of 2 inches into a Dutch oven; heat to 350°. Fry peppers, in batches, 30 seconds to 1 minute on each side or until golden brown. Drain peppers on a wire rack over paper towels; serve immediately.
Note: For testing purposes only, we used Bisquick All-Purpose Baking Mix.

Bayou Fish Fillets With Sweet-Hot Pecan Sauce

family favorite
MAKES 6 SERVINGS; **PREP:** 10 MIN.,
FRY: 3 MIN. PER BATCH
(Pictured on page 11)

1 (6-oz.) package cornbread mix
1½ tsp. Creole seasoning
½ tsp. salt
½ tsp. pepper
6 (6-oz.) cod or tilapia fillets
Canola oil
Sweet-Hot Pecan Sauce

1. Stir together cornbread mix and Creole seasoning until blended.
2. Sprinkle salt and pepper over fillets. Dredge fillets in cornbread mixture.
3. Pour oil to depth of 4 inches into a large Dutch oven; heat to 375°. Fry fillets, in batches, 1 to 1½ minutes on each side or until golden. Drain on a wire rack over paper towels. Serve with Sweet-Hot Pecan Sauce.
Note: For testing purposes only, we used Martha White Buttermilk Cornbread Mix.

Sweet-Hot Pecan Sauce:

fast fixin's • make ahead
MAKES 1 CUP; **PREP:** 15 MIN., **COOK:** 5 MIN.

This sensational sauce received our Food staff's highest rating. (Pictured on page 11)

¼ cup butter
¼ cup chopped red onion
1 tsp. minced garlic
½ cup pecan pieces, chopped
½ cup firmly packed light brown sugar
2 Tbsp. lemon juice
2 Tbsp. Worcestershire sauce
1 Tbsp. hot sauce

1. Melt butter in a medium saucepan over medium heat. Add onion, and sauté 3 minutes or until tender. Add garlic, and cook 1 minute. Stir in pecans and next 4 ingredients. Cook, stirring constantly, until sugar is dissolved. Store in an airtight container in refrigerator up to 1 week.

Shrimp-and-Okra Hush Puppies

family favorite

MAKES 8 SERVINGS (ABOUT 2½ DOZEN);
PREP: 10 MIN., **STAND:** 7 MIN.,
FRY: 5 MIN. PER BATCH
(Pictured on page 11)

1 cup self-rising yellow cornmeal mix
½ cup self-rising flour
1 cup medium-size raw shrimp, chopped
1 tsp. Creole seasoning
½ cup frozen diced onion, red and green bell pepper, and celery, thawed
½ cup frozen cut okra, thawed and chopped
1 large egg, lightly beaten
¾ cup beer
Canola oil

1. Stir together cornmeal mix and flour in large bowl until combined.
2. Sprinkle shrimp with Creole seasoning. Add shrimp, onion mixture, and okra to cornmeal mixture. Stir in egg and beer just until moistened. Let stand 5 to 7 minutes.
3. Pour oil to depth of 4 inches into a Dutch oven; heat to 350°. Drop batter by level tablespoonfuls into hot oil, and fry, in batches, 2 to 2½ minutes on each side or until golden brown. Drain on a wire rack over paper towels; serve immediately.
Note: Keep fried hush puppies warm in a 225° oven for up to 15 minutes. For testing purposes only, we used McKenzie's Seasoning Blend for diced onion, red and green bell pepper, and celery.

No-Cook Vanilla Ice Cream

southernliving.com favorite

MAKES 1 QT; **PREP:** 5 MIN., **CHILL:** 30 MIN.,
FREEZE: 2 HR., 5 MIN.

1 (14-oz.) can sweetened condensed milk
1 (5-oz.) can evaporated milk
2 Tbsp. sugar
2 tsp. vanilla extract
2 cups whole milk

1. Whisk all ingredients in a 2-quart pitcher or large bowl until blended. Cover and chill 30 minutes.

GET INSPIRED

Berry Yummy

In less than an hour you can serve up this simply divine dessert. Pop it in the oven just before you sit down to eat, and your family can enjoy it warm at meal's end.

Easy Blackberry Cobbler

MAKES 6 SERVINGS;
PREP: 10 MIN., **BAKE:** 35 MIN.,
STAND: 10 MIN. *(Pictured on page 174)*

1. Preheat oven to 375°. Place 4 cups fresh blackberries in a lightly greased 8-inch square baking dish; sprinkle with 1 Tbsp. lemon juice. Stir together 1 large egg, 1 cup sugar, and 1 cup all-purpose flour in a medium bowl until mixture resembles coarse meal. Sprinkle over fruit. Drizzle 6 Tbsp. melted butter over topping. Bake at 375° for 35 minutes or until lightly browned and bubbly. Let stand 10 minutes. Serve warm with ice cream or whipped cream, if desired. Garnish with fresh mint sprig, if desired.
Note: For a neat presentation, bake for the same amount of time in 6 (8-oz.) ramekins on an aluminum foil-lined baking sheet.

2. Pour milk mixture into freezer container of a 1-qt. electric ice-cream maker, and freeze according to manufacturer's instructions. (Instructions and times will vary.)
3. Remove container with ice cream from ice-cream maker, and place in freezer 15 minutes. Transfer to an airtight container; freeze until firm, about 1 to 1½ hours.
Note: For testing purposes only, we used a Rival 4-qt. Durable Plastic Bucket Ice Cream Maker and a Cuisinart Automatic Frozen Yogurt-Ice Cream & Sorbet Maker.

No-Cook Chocolate Ice Cream:
Omit sugar, vanilla, and whole milk. Add 2 cups whole chocolate milk and ⅔ cup chocolate syrup. Proceed as directed. **Makes** 1 quart.

No-Cook Chocolate-Almond Ice Cream: Prepare No-Cook Chocolate Ice Cream as directed. Remove container with ice cream from ice-cream maker, and place in freezer. Freeze 15 minutes. Stir ¾ cup toasted sliced almonds into prepared ice cream. Place in an airtight container; freeze until firm. **Makes** 1¼ qt.

—**LERA TOWNLEY**, ROANOKE, ALABAMA

Take advantage of the hot months to try some cool cocktails that will tone down the heat outdoors.

Toast Your Health

Enjoy happy hour in good conscience with these refreshing cocktails.

A drink just may do more good than you think. Research shows responsible and moderate alcohol consumption can be part of a healthful lifestyle. These beverages are full of wholesome ingredients, and they're portioned to give you a sensible amount of alcohol along with a bunch of goodness. So stir up a batch, and enjoy a guilt-free happy hour.

Healthy Benefits

- Balanced and moderate consumption of alcohol may reduce the risk of coronary heart disease among middle-aged and older adults.
- Honey contains many vitamins and essential minerals, such as vitamin B6, thiamin, niacin, calcium, copper, and iron.
- Mint helps prevent and treat nausea and stomach cramps and may reduce pain associated with headaches.
- Mangoes are high in soluble fiber and rich in vitamin C, betacarotene, and other essential antioxidants.

Fresh Peach Gelées

MAKES 16 (4-CUBE) SERVINGS;
PREP: 20 MIN., **STAND:** 1 MIN., **CHILL:** 8 HR.

1 cup sparkling white wine
½ cup vodka
¼ cup Peach Puree
1 (3-oz.) package peach-flavored gelatin*
1 (1-oz.) package unflavored gelatin
1 cup boiling water
Garnish: fresh peach slices

1. Stir together wine, vodka, and Peach Puree in an 11- x 7-inch baking dish; sprinkle gelatins over wine mixture. Let stand 1 minute.
2. Stir 1 cup boiling water into wine mixture, stirring until gelatin is dissolved. Cover and chill 8 hours or until set.
3. Cut gelatin into 64 (1-inch) cubes. Garnish, if desired.
* Sugar-free peach-flavored gelatin may be substituted.

Per serving (4 cubes): Calories 49; Fat 0g (sat 0g, mono 0g, poly 0g); Protein 0.9g; Carb 5.3g; Fiber 0g; Chol 0mg; Iron 0mg; Sodium 21mg; Calc 0mg

Peach Puree:

MAKES ABOUT 1 CUP; **PREP:** 10 MIN.

Use leftover puree as a spread for biscuits, a mix-in for warm oatmeal, or a topping for French toast or pancakes. It will keep for a few days in the refrigerator.

1 cup peeled and chopped fresh peaches
1 tsp. sugar

1. Process peaches, sugar, and 1 Tbsp. water in a blender 1 minute or until smooth. Transfer to a small bowl; cover and chill until ready to use.

Per (¼-cup) serving: Calories 20; Fat 0.1g (sat 0g, mono 0g, poly 0g); Protein 0.4g; Carb 5.1g; Fiber 0.6g; Chol 0mg; Iron 0.1mg; Sodium 0mg; Calc 3mg

Honey-Mint Spritzer

MAKES 1 SERVING; **PREP:** 5 MIN.

Three tablespoons of rum is a standard 1.5 fl. oz. serving of alcohol. You can measure all 80-proof (40% alcohol by volume) distilled spirits this way to track how many calories you've had.

3 Tbsp. light rum
2½ Tbsp. Honey Simple Syrup
2 Tbsp. fresh lime juice
Splash of club soda
Garnishes: fresh mint leaves and sprigs

1. Stir together first 3 ingredients in a glass filled with ice. Add a splash of soda. Garnish, if desired.

Per serving: Calories 185; Fat 0g (sat 0g, mono 0g, poly 0g); Protein 0.3g; Carb 24.4g; Fiber 0.3g; Chol 0mg; Iron 0.3mg; Sodium 7mg; Calc 12mg

Honey Simple Syrup:

MAKES ABOUT 2 CUPS; **PREP:** 5 MIN.,
COOK: 5 MIN., **STAND:** 30 MIN.,
CHILL: 4 HR.

Drizzle this syrup on top of vanilla ice cream or fruit sorbet, stir it into hot green tea, or use it to sweeten iced tea.

1 cup loosely packed fresh mint leaves
1 cup honey

1. Stir together mint, honey, and 1 cup water in a small saucepan over medium-high heat. Bring to a boil, stirring occasionally, and boil 1 minute or until honey is dissolved. Remove from heat, and let stand 30 minutes. Pour through a wire-mesh strainer into a cruet or airtight container, discarding mint leaves. Cover and chill 4 hours. Store in refrigerator up to 2 weeks.

Per (2½-Tbsp.) serving: Calories 80; Fat 0g (sat 0g, mono 0g, poly 0g); Protein 0.2g; Carb 21.8g; Fiber 0.2g; Chol 0mg; Iron 0.2mg; Sodium 2mg; Calc 7mg

Pimm's No. 1 Cup

MAKES 8 SERVINGS; **PREP:** 15 MIN.

There is no comparable substitute for the truly unique taste of Pimm's No. 1. This gin-based spirit should be available at your local liquor store.

1 cup Pimm's No. 1
1 cup thawed lemonade concentrate
1 cucumber, sliced
1 lemon, sliced
1 orange, sliced
4 cups club soda or seltzer water

1. Stir together first 5 ingredients in a large pitcher. Gently stir in soda. Serve immediately over ice.

Per (¾-cup) serving: Calories 147; Fat 0.2g (sat 0g, mono 0g, poly 0g); Protein 0.6g; Carb 21.2g; Fiber 1.1g; Chol 0mg; Iron 0.5mg; Sodium 27mg; Calc 24mg

Here's To Your Health

- We've known for some time that red wine contains compounds thought to fight certain types of cancer. Recently, USDA researchers discovered properties within wine that, in animal tests, have helped lower blood-sugar levels (good news for folks with diabetes). The compound, called pterostilbene, is most abundant in dark-skinned grapes.
- Research in Spain shows that folks who drink a couple of glasses of wine a day are almost 20 percent less likely to catch a cold than nondrinkers. Scientists say that compounds within the grapes are responsible—something other forms of alcohol, such as beer or spirits, can't deliver.

Proper Portions

Each of these drinks contains approximately 0.6 ounce of alcohol and represents a "moderate drink," according to the 2005 Dietary Guidelines for Americans. Due to differences in weight, women should consume no more than one drink per day, and men no more than two.

1 drink = 12 fl. oz. regular beer (about 150 calories), 1.5 fl. oz. 80-proof distilled spirits (about 100 calories), or 5 fl. oz. wine (about 100 calories)

Pomegranate Champagne Cocktail

southernliving.com favorite
MAKES 1 SERVING; **PREP:** 15 MIN.

Pomegranate juice is available in the refrigerated juice section or produce section of the grocery store. Turbinado is a raw, very coarse sugar with a mild brown sugar taste. Find it with other sugars. We found the rock candy stirrers at an imports store that carries wines and specialty food items.

1 turbinado sugar cube*
2 Tbsp. pomegranate juice**
½ cup Champagne or sparkling wine, chilled

1. Place sugar cube in a Champagne flute; add 2 Tbsp. pomegranate juice and ½ cup Champagne. Serve immediately.
*1 rock candy stirrer or granulated sugar cube may be substituted.
**2 Tbsp. cranberry juice cocktail may be substituted. Omit sugar cube.

Per serving: Calories 112; Fat 0g (Sat 0g, mono 0g, poly 0g); Protein 0.12g; Carb 8.87 g; Fiber 0g; Chol 0mg; Iron 0.05mg; Sodium 3.75mg; Calc5.02mg

Mango Bellinis

MAKES 6 SERVINGS; **PREP:** 15 MIN.

Threading a piece of thinly sliced mango on a cocktail skewer adds a touch of elegance to Mango Bellinis.

1 (16-oz.) bag frozen mango chunks, thawed
6 Tbsp. powdered sugar
1 (750-milliliter) bottle Champagne or sparkling wine, chilled
Garnish: thinly sliced mango

1. Process mango chunks, sugar, and ½ cup plus 2 Tbsp. water in a blender 30 seconds to 1 minute or until smooth, stopping to scrape down sides. Pour mixture through a wire-mesh strainer into a medium bowl; discard solids. Cover and chill until ready to serve (up to 4 hours).
2. Spoon 3 Tbsp. mango puree into each of 6 Champagne flutes. Fill with Champagne; gently stir. Garnish, if desired. Serve immediately.

Per serving: Calories 167; Fat 0g (sat 0g, mono 0g, poly 0g); Protein 0.5g; Carb 22.5g; Fiber 1.6g; Chol 0mg; Iron 0mg; Sodium 1mg; Calc 0.8mg

Help Yourself to a One-Dish Meal

Flavor-rich Shepherd's Pie is an easy choice for dinner on a busy weeknight. Our recipe includes traditional ground beef and potatoes jazzed up with a splash of red wine vinegar and mashed carrots. Serve it with your favorite summer vegetable salad.

Shepherd's Pie

freezeable • make ahead

MAKES 8 SERVINGS; **PREP:** 15 MIN.,
COOK: 25 MIN., **BAKE:** 15 MIN., **STAND:** 5 MIN.

1½ lb. ground round
1 cup chopped onion
½ (8-oz.) package fresh mushrooms, sliced
1 garlic clove, minced
1 cup frozen peas, thawed
4 tsp. beef bouillon granules
½ tsp. salt
½ tsp. dried thyme
¼ tsp. freshly ground pepper
1 Tbsp. all-purpose flour
1 (14½-oz.) can stewed tomatoes
1 bay leaf
2 Tbsp. red wine vinegar
Cheese-and-Carrot Mashed Potatoes

1. Brown beef in a large nonstick skillet over medium-high heat, stirring often, 10 minutes or until meat crumbles and is no longer pink. Remove ground beef from skillet using a slotted spoon; reserve 2 Tbsp. drippings in skillet. Reduce heat to medium.

2. Preheat oven to 400°. Sauté onion, mushrooms, and garlic in hot drippings over medium heat 10 to 11 minutes or until tender. Stir in ground beef, peas, and next 4 ingredients. Sprinkle flour over meat mixture. Increase heat to medium-high, and cook, stirring constantly, 1 minute. Stir in tomatoes, bay leaf, and vinegar, breaking up large tomato pieces with a spoon. Reduce heat to medium, and cook, stirring often, 3 minutes or until slightly thickened.

Remove bay leaf. Transfer mixture to a lightly greased 3-qt. baking dish or pan. Spoon Cheese-and-Carrot Mashed Potatoes evenly over meat mixture, smoothing with back of spoon.

3. Bake at 400° for 15 minutes or until thoroughly heated. Let stand 5 minutes before serving.

Note: To make ahead, prepare recipe as directed through Step 2. Cover tightly with aluminum foil. Freeze up to 1 month. Thaw in refrigerator 24 hours. Bake at 400° for 40 minutes or until thoroughly heated, shielding with aluminum foil after 25 minutes to prevent excessive browning.

Cheese-and-Carrot Mashed Potatoes:

MAKES 8 SERVINGS; **PREP:** 20 MIN.,
COOK: 10 MIN.

Use these colorful potatoes to top Shepherd's Pie or serve them as a side dish with meatloaf, pot roast, or your favorite steak.

1 (1-lb.) package baby carrots
1 Tbsp. butter
1 (22-oz.) package frozen mashed potatoes
2½ cups milk
1 cup (4 oz.) shredded Cheddar cheese
1 Tbsp. fresh thyme leaves
1 tsp. salt
¼ tsp. ground pepper

1. Place carrots and ¼ cup water in a large microwave-safe bowl. Cover tightly with plastic wrap; fold back a small edge to allow steam to escape. Microwave at HIGH 8 to 10 minutes or until carrots are tender. Drain.

2. Stir in butter. Coarsely mash carrots with a potato masher.

3. Prepare potatoes according to package directions, using 2½ cups milk. Stir in cheese, next 3 ingredients, and carrot mixture until well blended.

—ALBERTA WATSON, CHICAGO, ILLINOIS

Note: For testing purposes only, we used Ore-Ida Frozen Mashed Potatoes. Do not use refrigerated mashed potatoes.

Keep It Hot

One-dish meals are great to make ahead for supper or to take to a special gathering. Just remember, whether at home or away, it's important to keep hot foods hot (above 140°) and cold foods cold (below 40°). Remember the following food safety tips.

- Buy an instant-read thermometer—it's a great value and can easily go with the dish to check the temperature before serving.
- Always thaw food in the refrigerator.
- Thaw casseroles completely; then heat or cook them where they will be served. If preparing a casserole for a crowd, make it in several family-size baking dishes instead of one large food service pan.
- If heating or cooking a casserole before taking it out, transport it in an insulated chest or cardboard box lined with newspapers or clean towels to keep it hot.
- If there are leftovers, refrigerate them within two hours.

Grill Easy

Use this versatile vinaigrette as a marinade for grilled chicken and as a refreshing salad dressing.

Work smarter, not harder when feeding your family. Load up with enough marinated chicken to eat one night and save the tasty leftovers for later. Citrus Vinaigrette Grilled Chicken makes a lovely evening meal. Then use the extra cooked portions in Grilled Chicken Supper With Citrus Vinaigrette for a second extra-easy feast.

Citrus Vinaigrette Grilled Chicken

MAKES 4 SERVINGS; **PREP:** 15 MIN.,
CHILL: 2 HR., **GRILL:** 1 HR., **STAND:** 15 MIN.

The chicken cooks slowly over indirect heat for 1 hour, allowing you time to tackle other tasks before supper.

Citrus Vinaigrette, divided
8 bone-in chicken breasts

1. Reserve ½ cup Citrus Vinaigrette (cover and chill up to 5 days). Place 1 cup Citrus Vinaigrette in a large zip-top plastic freezer bag; add half of chicken, turning to coat. Repeat procedure with remaining vinaigrette and chicken. Seal bags, and chill at least 2 hours or up to 24 hours.
2. Light one side of grill, heating to 400° to 500° (high); leave other side unlit. Remove chicken from marinade, discarding marinade. Arrange chicken, skin sides up, over unlit side, and grill, covered with grill lid, 1 hour or until a meat thermometer inserted into thickest portion registers 170°. Let stand 15 minutes before serving. Serve half of

chicken immediately. Cover and chill remaining chicken 2 to 3 days.

Direct Heat Cooking Times: To cook chicken directly over heat, reduce heat to 350° to 400° (medium-high) heat, and grill, covered with grill lid, 28 minutes or until a meat thermometer inserted into thickest portion registers 170°, turning chicken every 7 minutes. Let chicken stand 15 minutes before serving.

Citrus Vinaigrette
make ahead
MAKES ABOUT 2½ CUPS; **PREP:** 10 MIN.,
COOK: 20 MIN., **CHILL:** 1 HR.

Use this vinaigrette on green salads with Asian flavors, or brush it on fish before grilling.

1½ cups orange juice
¾ cup fresh lemon juice
¾ cup white wine vinegar
⅓ cup orange marmalade
¼ cup soy sauce
2 Tbsp. honey
1 tsp. ground ginger
½ cup vegetable oil
2 Tbsp. sesame oil
1 tsp. salt
1 tsp. pepper

1. Whisk together first 7 ingredients in a saucepan over medium-high heat. Bring to a boil; reduce heat to medium-low, and simmer, whisking occasionally, 20 minutes or until reduced by half (about 2 cups). Transfer to a medium bowl; cover and chill 1 hour, whisking occasionally. Whisk in vegetable oil and remaining ingredients. Use immediately, or store in an airtight container in refrigerator up to 5 days.
Note: Keep an eye on this marinade when bringing to a boil—it can boil over quickly and easily.

Grilled Chicken Supper With Citrus Vinaigrette
MAKES 4 SERVINGS; **PREP:** 20 MIN.,
STAND: 30 MIN.

Leftover grilled chicken and a few extra ingrediens keep this salad simple to make.

3 cooked Citrus Vinaigrette Grilled Chicken breasts
2 (5-oz.) packages mixed salad greens, thoroughly washed
1 large red bell pepper, cut into thin strips
1 bunch green onions, chopped
½ cup Citrus Vinaigrette, divided
⅓ cup golden raisins
¼ cup chopped dry-roasted peanuts

1. Let chicken stand at room temperature 30 minutes.
2. Meanwhile, combine salad greens, bell pepper strips, green onions, and ⅓ cup Citrus Vinaigrette, tossing gently to coat. Place on a serving platter.
3. Skin and bone chicken; cut diagonally into ½-inch-thick slices. Arrange chicken strips on top of salad. Sprinkle with golden raisins and peanuts. Serve immediately with remaining Citrus Vinaigrette.

No-Fuss Tarts

The sun-warmed richness of summer stone fruit shines in these irresistible, free-form pies. All start with refrigerated piecrusts and couldn't be easier to make. Serve them plain or gussied up with two-ingredient Sweet Cream Topping or a scoop of ice cream. Either way, we're sure you'll be dazzled by their elegant simplicity.

What is Stone Fruit?

A stone fruit has a hard pit in the middle, surrounding a seed. Almonds, olives, mangoes, and even dates are all considered stone fruits (known as "drupes" in technical terms), but plums, peaches, nectarines, cherries, and apricots are the most well known.

Rustic Plum Tart
chef recipe

MAKES 8 SERVINGS; **PREP:** 20 MIN.,
STAND: 30 MIN., **BAKE:** 45 MIN.,
COOL: 20 MIN., **COOK:** 5 MIN.

If the plums are very ripe, their juices may ooze out of the tart and onto the parchment paper, but this adds to the dessert's charm. (Pictured on page 175)

Parchment paper
Vegetable cooking spray
1½ lb. plums, sliced
½ cup sugar
⅓ cup plum preserves
1 tsp. vanilla extract
¼ tsp. ground allspice
½ (15-oz.) package refrigerated piecrusts
1 Tbsp. all-purpose flour
1 large egg
1 Tbsp. sugar
Sweet Cream Topping (optional)

1. Line a baking sheet with parchment paper; coat parchment paper with cooking spray.
2. Preheat oven to 350°. Stir together plums and next 4 ingredients in a large bowl. Let stand 30 minutes, stirring occasionally.
3. Unroll piecrust on prepared baking sheet. Roll into a 12-inch circle.
4. Drain plum mixture, reserving the liquid. Toss plums in flour.
5. Mound plums in center of piecrust, leaving a 3-inch border. Fold piecrust border up and over plums, pleating as you go, leaving an opening about 5 inches wide in center.
6. Stir together egg and 1 Tbsp. water. Brush piecrust with egg mixture, and sprinkle with 1 Tbsp. sugar.
7. Bake at 350° for 45 minutes or until filling is bubbly and crust is golden. Carefully transfer tart on parchment paper to a wire rack; cool 20 minutes.
8. Meanwhile, bring reserved plum liquid to a boil in a small saucepan over medium heat. Boil 1 to 2 minutes or until slightly thickened. Let cool slightly. Brush or drizzle 1 to 2 Tbsp. hot plum liquid over exposed fruit in center of tart. Serve immediately with remaining plum syrup, and, if desired, Sweet Cream Topping.

— **BRUCE WIGHTMAN**, CEDAR CREST INN, ASHEVILLE, NORTH CAROLINA

Sweet Cream Topping: Stir together ½ cup sour cream and 2 tsp. brown sugar. Cover and chill 2 hours before serving. Stir just before serving.

Peach-Nectarine Tart: White peaches won't work as well in this tart because of their delicate texture. Prepare recipe as directed, substituting ¾ lb. peeled nectarines and ¾ lb. peeled peaches for plums and peach preserves for plum preserves.

Apricot Tart: Prepare recipe as directed, substituting fresh apricots for plums and apricot preserves for plum preserves. Omit allspice.

Fresh Cherry Tart: Prepare recipe as directed, substituting 1½ lb. fresh cherries, pitted, for plums and cherry preserves for plum preserves.

• TIP •

A Spoonful of Sugar You may need to adjust the amount of sugar, depending on the ripeness of your fruit. Taste the filling before baking, and increase the sugar as desired.

First-Rate Veggie Plate

These exceptional recipes dish up delicious flavor and some stylish twists.

Summer's the right time to enjoy a plateful of fresh produce. Load up with the best from your local farmers market, and then add a helping of mac 'n' cheese, which, of course, is considered a vegetable in the South. (And we're not about to argue with such a tasty tradition.) We turned to a few of our favorite chefs for recipes easy enough to make at home. These offer hip new takes on Southern classics. Crowder peas replace traditional butter beans in Crowder Pea Succotash, while cooking the squash in chicken broth gives Squash Casserole its depth of flavor. And we think this macaroni and cheese is to die for, so try it for yourself and let us know what you think.

Crowder Pea Succotash

chef recipe

MAKES 8 SERVINGS; **PREP:** 20 MIN., **COOK:** 11 MIN.

Move over butter beans. This succotash, based on crowder peas and jazzed up with fresh thyme and red bell pepper, is set to become a new classic.

½ large onion, finely diced
1 green bell pepper, finely diced
1 red bell pepper, finely diced
3 Tbsp. olive oil
2 cups fresh or frozen corn kernels
Crowder Peas
½ cup reserved Crowder Peas liquid
½ cup sliced green onions
1 Tbsp. fresh thyme leaves, finely
  chopped
½ tsp. salt
Garnish: fresh thyme sprig

1. Sauté onion and bell peppers in hot oil in a large skillet over medium heat 5 to 7 minutes or until tender. Stir in corn and Crowder Peas; cook 2 minutes or until thoroughly heated. Stir in ½ cup reserved Crowder Peas liquid, green onions, thyme, and salt; cook 1 to 2 minutes or until thoroughly heated. Garnish, if desired. Serve immediately.

—CHEF JASON SCHOLZ,
HIGH COTTON, GREENVILLE, SOUTH CAROLINA

Crowder Peas:

MAKES 4 SERVINGS; **PREP:** 15 MIN., **COOK:** 30 MIN., **COOL:** 30 MIN.

Freeze the flavorful leftover cooking liquid to use in soup or to cook rice.

½ large onion, cut in half
½ medium carrot, cut in half lengthwise
2 celery ribs, cut into 2-inch pieces
2 garlic cloves, peeled and cut in half
1 Tbsp. olive oil
2 Tbsp. jarred ham base
2 cups fresh or frozen crowder peas
2 fresh thyme sprigs
½ tsp. salt
½ tsp. pepper

1. Cook first 4 ingredients in hot oil in a Dutch oven over medium-high heat, stirring often, 5 minutes. Stir in ham base and 4 cups of water until well blended. Add peas, thyme, salt, and pepper, and bring mixture to a boil. Reduce heat to low, and simmer 20 minutes or until peas are done. Remove from heat; cool 30 minutes.
2. Drain peas, reserving cooking liquid for another use. Remove and discard onion, carrots, celery, and thyme sprigs.
Note: For testing purposes only, we used Superior Touch Better Than Bouillon ham base.

Condiments We Love

Sweet and spicy condiments are great complements to vegetable meals. Hot sauce, chowchow, pepper sauce, and relishes all add a tangy bite to squash, succotash, butter beans, and other mild flavors. Greens, especially, are enhanced by peppery sauces or sweet relishes. Supermarkets and specialty stores carry a wide variety of products, but pepper sauce, the simplest of the bunch, is the hands-down favorite of restaurants and home cooks across the South. It reigns supreme at our tasting table as well, but we also like homemade chowchow and Wickles Hoagie & Sub Sandwich Relish for topping peas and greens.

Gently cooking garlic in olive oil over medium heat yields two luscious results—mellow, golden garlic cloves and richly flavored oil that is tasty as a dip for bread, for sautéing chicken breasts, and stir-frying vegetables.

Squash Casserole

chef recipe • make ahead

MAKES 4 TO 6 SERVINGS; **PREP:** 15 MIN.,
COOK: 25 MIN., **BAKE:** 30 MIN.

You can cook the squash, carrot, and onion mixture up to a day ahead and store, tightly covered, in the refrigerator. Drain as directed, and proceed. You can substitute reduced-sodium chicken broth and cream of mushroom soup in this recipe with good results. (Pictured on page 10)

2 lb. yellow squash
1 cup grated carrot
½ cup diced onion
1 (14.5-oz.) can chicken broth
1 (10¾-oz.) can cream of mushroom soup
2 Tbsp. mayonnaise
¼ tsp. salt
¼ tsp. pepper
½ cup crushed cornflakes cereal

1. Preheat oven to 350°. Cut squash into ½-inch rounds. Cook squash and next 3 ingredients in a large skillet over medium heat, stirring often, 25 minutes or until tender. Drain well, reserving broth for another use; pat squash mixture dry with paper towels.
2. Stir together mushroom soup and next 3 ingredients in a large bowl; stir in squash mixture until blended. Spoon mixture into a lightly greased 11- x 7-inch baking dish; sprinkle with crushed cornflakes.
3. Bake at 350° for 25 to 30 minutes or until golden and bubbly.

—**MIKE ALTINE,** THE VARIETY STORE,
CHARLESTON, SOUTH CAROLINA

Green Beans With Caramelized Garlic

MAKES 6 TO 8 SERVINGS; **PREP:** 15 MIN.,
COOK: 24 MIN.

(Pictured on page 10)

1 garlic bulb
½ cup olive oil
2 lb. green beans, trimmed
1 red bell pepper, cut into thin strips
½ tsp. salt
½ tsp. pepper

1. Peel garlic cloves, and place in a small saucepan with olive oil. Cook over medium heat, stirring often, 6 to 7 minutes or until tender and golden. Remove garlic, using a slotted spoon. Reserve garlic and 2 Tbsp. garlic oil; store remaining oil in refrigerator.
2. Cook beans in boiling salted water to cover in a Dutch oven 8 to 9 minutes or until crisp-tender; drain. Plunge into salted ice water to stop the cooking process; drain.
3. Sauté bell pepper in 2 Tbsp. hot reserved garlic oil in Dutch oven over medium heat 3 minutes or until tender. Add beans and garlic cloves, tossing to coat; cook 4 to 5 minutes or until thoroughly heated. Toss beans with salt and pepper.

Grilled Sweet Onions

fast fixin's

MAKES 8 SERVINGS; **PREP:** 10 MIN.,
GRILL: 20 MIN.

1. Preheat grill to 350° to 400° (medium-high). Cut 4 large sweet onions into ½-inch-thick slices. Brush with 2 Tbsp. Fresh Herb Vinaigrette. Grill onions, covered with grill lid, 10 minutes on each side or until crisp-tender. Sprinkle with salt and pepper to taste. Serve with remaining Fresh Herb Vinaigrette, if desired.

Fresh Herb Vinaigrette:

make ahead

MAKES ABOUT ½ CUP; **PREP:** 10 MIN.

Make this vinaigrette up to two days ahead. Save any leftover vinaigrette for up to three days to use on a crisp garden salad.

1. Whisk together ¼ cup balsamic vinegar, 1 Tbsp. chopped fresh parsley, 1 Tbsp. chopped fresh basil, 1 Tbsp. chopped fresh thyme, ½ tsp. salt, and ¼ tsp. pepper. Gradually whisk in ¼ cup olive oil, whisking until vinaigrette is smooth.

Test Kitchens Notebook

Build a Better Veggie Plate

A veggie plate starts with mac 'n' cheese, and Not Yo' Mama's Mac 'n' Cheese (recipe on following page) is one of the best we've tasted. To round out a veggie plate, select one dish from several categories:
• something yellow
• something green
• something fried
• peas or beans
• something tomato
• cornbread

Not Yo' Mama's Mac 'n' Cheese

chef recipe • family favorite

MAKES 8 TO 10 SERVINGS; PREP: 30 MIN.,
BAKE: 22 MIN., COOK: 28 MIN.

"Decadent" is the only word to describe this top-rated specialty of John's City Diner in Birmingham. The smoked gouda adds marvelous flavor, but you can substitute regular gouda. Don't use preshredded cheese; it doesn't melt as smoothly. Shred the cheese and crisp the prosciutto up to one day ahead and chill. Toast the breadcrumbs ahead, and store them in a zip-top plastic bag. (Pictured on page 10)

1 cup Japanese breadcrumbs (panko)
1 (4-oz.) package thinly sliced
    prosciutto
1 (16-oz.) package penne pasta
½ cup butter
1 shallot, minced
¼ cup dry white wine
¼ cup all-purpose flour
2 cups milk
2 cups whipping cream
1 bay leaf
½ tsp. salt
¼ tsp. ground red pepper
2 (10-oz.) blocks sharp white Cheddar
    cheese, shredded
1 cup (4 oz.) shredded smoked Gouda
½ cup (2 oz.) shredded Parmesan cheese

1. Preheat oven to 400°. Bake breadcrumbs in a single layer on a baking sheet 5 to 7 minutes or until golden, stirring once after 2½ minutes.
2. Cook prosciutto, in batches, in a lightly greased large skillet over medium heat 3 to 4 minutes on each side or until crisp. Drain on paper towels; crumble.
3. Prepare pasta according to package directions.
4. Meanwhile, melt butter in a Dutch oven over medium heat; add shallot, and sauté 3 minutes or until tender. Add wine, stirring to loosen particles from bottom of Dutch oven, and cook mixture 1 minute.

5. Gradually whisk in flour until smooth; cook, whisking constantly, 2 minutes. Gradually whisk in milk and next 4 ingredients; cook, whisking constantly, 12 to 14 minutes or until mixture thickens and begins to bubble. Remove and discard bay leaf.
6. Place 4 cups (16 oz.) Cheddar cheese in a large heatproof bowl. Reserve remaining Cheddar cheese for another use. Add Gouda and Parmesan cheeses to bowl.
7. Gradually pour white sauce over cheeses, whisking until cheeses are melted and sauce is smooth.
8. Stir in pasta and prosciutto until blended. Pour into a lightly greased 13- x 9-inch baking dish; sprinkle with breadcrumbs.
9. Bake at 400° for 15 minutes or until bubbly. Serve immediately.

—SHANNON GOBER, JOHN'S CITY DINER, BIRMINGHAM, ALABAMA

Note: For testing purposes only, we used Fiorucci Riserva Prosciutto and Cracker Barrel Vermont White Sharp Cheddar.

No-Bake Not Yo' Mama's Mac 'n' Cheese: Omit breadcrumbs. Prepare recipe as directed in Steps 2 through 6. Stir pasta, prosciutto, and cheeses into white sauce. Serve immediately.

Pan-fried Okra, Onion, and Tomatoes

southernliving.com favorite

MAKES 8 SERVINGS; PREP: 15 MIN.,
FRY: 6 MIN. PER BATCH

2 lb. fresh okra
½ cup vegetable oil
1 medium-size red onion, thinly sliced
2 large tomatoes, seeded and thinly sliced
2 Tbsp. lime juice
1½ tsp. salt
1½ tsp. pepper
1 tsp. chicken bouillon granules

1. Cut okra in half lengthwise.
2. Pour ¼ cup oil into a large skillet over medium-high heat. Cook okra in

GET INSPIRED

Fig Tart

Premier Chef Chris Hastings boasts one of the summer's best desserts at his Hot and Hot Fish Club in Birmingham. Known for his passion and preference for local produce, Chris uses at least four different kinds of figs throughout the summer to produce his acclaimed Fig Tart. August is the peak time for this sweet treat, which he offers on the menu until about mid-September. Says one of the happy tasters from our staff: "It's like eating candy." If you want to savor Chris's Fig Tart for yourself, make a reservation at his Birmingham restaurant (2180 11th Court South) by calling (205) 933-5474. To try your own version at home, visit myrecipes.com and search "Black Mission Fig Tart."

hot oil, in batches, 6 minutes or until browned, turning occasionally. Remove from skillet, and drain well on paper towels. Add remaining ¼ cup oil as needed on second batch. Cool.
3. Stir together onion and next 5 ingredients in a large bowl. Add okra, tossing to coat. Serve at room temperature.

—ROMEY JOHNSON, WOODBRIDGE, VIRGINIA

Tasty Chicken Anytime

Bring good flavor to the table during the week with quick and affordable chicken thighs.

Dinner on a Dime

SERVES 4 TO 6

Chicken Thighs With
Chunky Tomato Sauce

Mixed Greens With Toasted Almonds
and Apple Cider Vinaigrette

Bakery rolls

Raisin-Oatmeal Cookies

Chicken is a mainstay of most family dinner menus, but it can be challenging to come up with new ideas. Thighs are economical and easily take on the flavor of seasoning blends or marinades. Purchase them with the bone in to save even more money at the checkout. If you have little ones, chop the zucchini and onion in Chicken Thighs With Chunky Tomato Sauce into smaller pieces; they will never know the difference. Serving the chicken over mashed potatoes makes this one-dish recipe hearty and filling. We've included a quick dessert recipe using a package of oatmeal cookie mix to conquer those sweet cravings. These simple and delicious dishes deliver comfort food fast.

Chicken Thighs With Chunky Tomato Sauce
family favorite
MAKES 4 TO 6 SERVINGS; **PREP:** 10 MIN.,
COOK: 29 MIN.
A splash of red wine vinegar and a can of fire-roasted tomatoes with garlic makes this dish a standout that's ready in less than an hour. (Pictured on page 171)

1 (22-oz.) package frozen mashed potatoes
2 lb. skinned and boned chicken thighs
1 Tbsp. Greek seasoning
2 Tbsp. olive oil
2 medium zucchini, chopped
½ cup diced onion
1 (14.5-oz.) can fire-roasted tomatoes with
   garlic, undrained
2 Tbsp. cold butter, cut up
1 Tbsp. red wine vinegar
¼ tsp. salt
¼ tsp. pepper

1. Prepare mashed potatoes according to package directions. Keep warm.
2. Meanwhile, sprinkle chicken with Greek seasoning. Cook chicken in hot oil in large skillet over medium-high heat 7 to 8 minutes on each side or until done. Remove from skillet, and keep warm.
3. Reduce heat to medium. Add zucchini and onion to skillet, and sauté 2 to 3 minutes or until tender. Add tomatoes, and cook, stirring often, 7 to 10 minutes or until slightly thickened. Remove from heat, and stir in butter and next 3 ingredients.
4. Serve chicken over potatoes. Spoon sauce over chicken and potatoes. Serve immediately.
Note: For testing purposes only, we used Ore-Ida Mashed Potatoes, Cavender's All Purpose Greek Seasoning, and Hunt's Fire Roasted Tomatoes Diced With Garlic.

Mixed Greens With Toasted Almonds and Apple Cider Vinaigrette
southernliving.com favorite
MAKES 8 SERVINGS; **PREP:** 10 MIN.,
CHILL: 2 HR.

1 large cucumber, thinly sliced
⅓ cup Apple Cider Vinaigrette
8 cups mixed salad greens
2 plum tomatoes, finely chopped
1 cup fresh blueberries
⅓ cup sliced almonds, toasted
½ cup (2 oz.) crumbled goat cheese

1. Combine cucumber and Apple Cider Vinaigrette; cover and chill 2 hours, stirring once. Remove and reserve cucumbers using a slotted spoon; reserve Apple Cider Vinaigrette.
2. Toss together salad greens, tomatoes, and blueberries. Sprinkle salad evenly with almonds and goat cheese before serving. Top with reserved marinated cucumber slices. Serve with reserved Apple Cider Vinaigrette.

Apple Cider Vinaigrette:
make ahead
MAKES 1 CUP; **PREP:** 10 MIN.

½ cup extra virgin olive oil
¼ cup apple cider vinegar
4 tsp. granulated sugar
1 Tbsp. brown sugar
1 Tbsp. balsamic vinegar
1 tsp. Worcestershire sauce
½ tsp. salt

1. Whisk together all ingredients until well combined.

—SUSAN AULER, AUSTIN, TEXAS

Raisin-Oatmeal Cookies

MAKES ABOUT 3 DOZEN; **PREP:** 10 MIN.,
STAND: 5 MIN., **BAKE:** 10 MIN. PER BATCH,
COOL: 1 MIN.

*A few on-hand ingredients jazz up a
store-bought mix for a quick treat.*

½ cup golden raisins*
⅓ cup hot water
1 (17.5-oz.) package oatmeal cookie mix
½ cup butter, softened
1 large egg
1 Tbsp. vanilla extract

1. Preheat oven to 375°. Combine raisins and ⅓ cup hot water. Let stand 5
minutes; drain.
2. Stir together cookie mix and next 3
ingredients. Add raisins, and stir until
blended. (Dough will be stiff.) Drop
dough by tablespoonfuls 2 inches apart
onto lightly greased baking sheets.
3. Bake, in batches, at 375° for 10 minutes or until golden brown. Cool on
baking sheets on wire rack 1 minute;
remove from pans to wire racks.
*Regular raisins may be substituted.
Note: For testing purposes only, we used
Betty Crocker Oatmeal Cookie Mix.

Test Kitchens Notebook

Cookie Baking Basics

For best results, bake only one pan
of cookies at a time, placing the
pan in the center of the oven. If you
have to bake two pans at a time,
position oven racks so they divide
the oven into thirds, and stagger
the pans on the racks. If cookies
begin to brown unevenly, switch
the pans halfway through the baking time. Don't bake cookies with
one pan directly over another pan.
One batch will invariably have tops
that are too dark, while the other
will have the opposite problem.

—**NATALIE KELLY BROWN**,
ASSISTANT FOOD EDITOR

Party With Punch

Cool off the South's hottest month with ice-cold sangría paired
with a delectable, no-fuss menu.

> ### Tex-Mex Menu
>
> #### SERVES 6 TO 8
>
> Sangria
>
> Citrus Shrimp Tacos
>
> Grilled Corn Salsa
>
> Tortilla chips
>
> Tres Leches Cake

Sangría

MAKES ABOUT 12 CUPS; **PREP:** 15 MIN.,
COOK: 3 MIN., **STAND:** 10 MIN.,
CHILL: 4 HR.

*Peach nectar is a sweet, intensely fla-
vored drink that's usually sold on the
international food aisle, with the fruit
juices, or with the cocktail mixes.*

¼ cup sugar
2 (750-milliliter) bottles dry red wine
½ cup orange juice
½ cup peach nectar*
¼ cup orange liqueur
2 to 3 cups club soda, chilled
1 lemon, thinly sliced
1 lime, thinly sliced
1 orange, thinly sliced
1 Granny Smith apple, thinly sliced

1. Bring sugar and 1¼ cups water to a
boil in a saucepan over medium-high
heat, stirring occasionally, until sugar
is dissolved. Remove from heat, and let
stand 10 minutes.
2. Combine sugar mixture, red wine,
and next 3 ingredients in a large container; cover and chill 4 hours. Stir
in club soda and next 4 ingredients

just before serving. Serve over ice, if
desired.
*½ cup orange juice may be substi-
tuted.
Note: For testing purposes only, we
used Columbia Crest Two Vines Merlot
for dry red wine and Grand Marnier for
orange liqueur.

Sangría Blanco: (*Pictured on page
176*) Omit orange juice and peach nectar.
Substitute dry white wine for red wine,
lemon-lime soft drink for club soda, and
1 pt. fresh strawberries for 1 Granny
Smith apple. Increase orange liqueur to
1 cup, 1 lemon to 2, 1 lime to 2, and 1
orange to 2. Prepare recipe as directed,
stirring in ¾ cup loosely packed fresh
mint leaves with wine in Step 2.

Citrus Shrimp Tacos

MAKES 6 TO 8 SERVINGS; **PREP:** 25 MIN.,
CHILL: 10 MIN., **GRILL:** 6 MIN.

*Soak wooden skewers in water at least 30
minutes before grilling to keep them from
burning. (Pictured on page 177)*

2 lb. unpeeled, large raw shrimp
20 (12-inch-long) skewers
2 Tbsp. Southwest seasoning
3 garlic cloves, minced
⅓ cup lime juice
3 Tbsp. lemon juice
16 (8-inch) soft taco-size flour tortillas,
    warmed
1 head iceberg lettuce, finely shredded
1 head radicchio, finely shredded
Southwest Cream Sauce
Grilled Corn Salsa
Garnish: fresh cilantro leaves

1. Peel shrimp; devein, if desired.
Thread shrimp onto skewers.

2. Preheat grill to 350° to 400° (medium-high). Combine Southwest seasoning and garlic in a long shallow dish; add lime juice, lemon juice, and shrimp, turning to coat. Cover and chill 10 minutes. Remove shrimp from marinade, discarding marinade.

3. Grill shrimp, without grill lid, 2 to 3 minutes on each side or just until shrimp turn pink. Remove shrimp from skewers. Serve in warm tortillas with next 4 ingredients. Garnish, if desired.

Note: For testing purposes only, we used Emeril's Southwest Seasoning.

Southwest Cream Sauce: Whisk together 1 (16-oz.) container sour cream; 1 garlic clove, minced; 2 Tbsp. finely chopped red onion; 1 tsp. chili powder; ½ tsp. ground cumin; ½ tsp. ground red pepper; and ¼ tsp. salt. Whisk in 2 Tbsp. chopped fresh cilantro and 2 Tbsp. fresh lime juice until smooth. Cover and chill until ready to serve. **Makes** about 2 cups; Prep: 10 min.

Grilled Corn Salsa

MAKES ABOUT 6 CUPS; **PREP:** 25 MIN., **GRILL:** 20 MIN., **COOL:** 15 MIN.
(*Pictured on page 177*)

3 ears fresh corn, husks removed
Vegetable cooking spray
1 tsp. salt
½ tsp. pepper
3 medium tomatoes, seeded and chopped
2 jalapeño peppers, seeded and minced
2 (15-oz.) cans black beans, rinsed and drained
¾ cup chopped fresh cilantro
⅓ cup fresh lime juice
2 Tbsp. chopped fresh mint
2 avocados
Tortilla chips (optional)

1. Preheat grill to 350° to 400° (medium-high). Lightly coat corn cobs with cooking spray. Sprinkle with salt and pepper.

2. Grill corn, covered with grill lid, 15 to 20 minutes or until golden brown, turning every 5 minutes. Remove from grill; cool 15 minutes.

3. Hold each grilled cob upright on a cutting board; cut downward, cutting kernels from cob. Discard cobs; place kernels in a large bowl. Gently stir in tomatoes and next 5 ingredients. Cover and chill until ready to serve, if desired.

4. If chilled, let corn mixture stand at room temperature 30 minutes. Peel and chop avocados; toss with corn mixture just before serving. Serve with tortilla chips, if desired.

Tres Leches Cake
southernliving.com favorite

MAKES 16 SERVINGS; **PREP:** 25 MIN.; **BAKE:** 25 MIN.; **STAND:** 2 HRS., 10 MIN.

This exceptional dessert takes a little extra effort, but it's worth it. The combination of textures—tender cake, fluffy frosting, and a pool of creamy sauce—will delight your family and friends. If you don't have a double boiler to make the frosting, place a metal mixing bowl over a saucepan instead.

7 large eggs, separated
½ cup butter, softened
1 cup sugar
2½ cups all-purpose flour
1 tsp. baking powder
½ tsp. salt
1 cup milk
1 tsp. vanilla extract
1 (14-oz.) can sweetened condensed milk
1 (12-oz.) can evaporated milk
¾ cup whipping cream
Fluffy Frosting
Garnish: lemon zest

1. Preheat oven to 350°. Beat egg yolks, butter, and sugar at medium speed with an electric mixer 2 minutes or until creamy.

2. Combine flour, baking powder, and salt. Add to egg yolk mixture alternately with milk, beginning and ending with flour mixture. Beat at low speed just until blended after each addition. Stir in vanilla.

3. Beat egg whites until stiff; fold gently into batter. Pour batter into a greased and floured 13- x 9-inch pan.

4. Bake at 350° for 25 minutes or until

Test Kitchens Notebook

Hot weather gatherings call for cool drinks, and refreshing Sangría is just right. This punch is a mixture of red and white wine, fruit juices, and club soda. Our recipes for Sangría and Sangría Blanco are some of the best we've ever tasted. This concoction is best served very cold, so be sure to chill the ingredients for several hours before stirring up a batch. Sangría pairs well with Tex-Mex food so invite a crowd over to enjoy it plus a casual and flavorful menu.

—KRISTI MICHELE CROW,
TEST KITCHENS PROFESSIONAL

a wooden pick inserted in center comes out clean. Let stand 10 minutes.

5. Pierce top of cake several times with a small wooden skewer. Stir together condensed milk, evaporated milk, and cream; gradually pour and spread over warm cake. (Pour about ¼ cup at a time, allowing mixture to soak into cake before pouring more.) Let stand 2 hours; cover and chill overnight, if desired. Spread top of cake with Fluffy Frosting before serving. Garnish, if desired.

Fluffy Frosting:

MAKES ABOUT 7½ CUPS; **PREP:** 10 MIN., **COOK:** 14 MIN.

6 egg whites
1 cup sugar
1 cup light corn syrup
1 Tbsp. fresh lemon juice (about ½ lemon)

1. Pour water to a depth of 1½ inches into bottom of double boiler over medium-high heat; bring to a boil. Reduce heat to a gentle boil. Place egg whites and sugar in top of double boiler. Beat at high speed with an electric mixer 5 to 7 minutes or until stiff peaks form. Gradually pour in corn syrup and lemon juice, beating 7 minutes or until spreading consistency.

—MELISSA GUERRA,
DISHES FROM THE WILD HORSE DESERT

Healthy Living.

Power Up Lunch

Maintain your energy throughout the afternoon by packing yourself a vibrant midday meal. These recipes will help you create healthy and tasty lunches that won't cause an afternoon meltdown. Prepare the dishes up to two days ahead and store in the refrigerator. If required, you can heat them up in a microwave, and they will be ready to eat in minutes. Add fresh fruits or veggies, nuts or cheese, and a sensible beverage, and you'll stay productive throughout the workday.

Healthy Benefits

- Nuts are rich in monounsaturated fats, polyunsaturated fats, and omega-3 fatty acids, helping to reduce LDL (bad) cholesterol and protect against heart disease.
- The calcium, vitamin D, and magnesium found in dairy products help develop and maintain bone density, reducing the risk of bone fractures and delaying the onset of osteoporosis.

Pork-and-Black Bean Power Lunch

fast fixin's • make ahead
MAKES 1 SERVING; **PREP:** 10 MIN.

You can make this recipe up to two days before serving. Prepare as directed through Step 2; cover and chill overnight. Then take it to work and store in a refrigerator until ready to heat as directed. It's loaded with whole grains, protein, and fiber and is sure to prevent any post-lunch crash.

1 (8.8-oz.) pouch ready-to-serve whole grain medley rice*
½ cup rinsed and drained canned black beans
¼ cup shredded fully cooked pork roast au jus
2 to 3 Tbsp. Cuban Salsa Verde

1. Remove ¾ cup rice from ready-to-serve pouch. Reserve remaining rice for another use.
2. Layer rice, beans, pork, and salsa, in this order, in a microwave-safe plastic container.
3. Cover with lid; lift 1 corner to allow steam to escape. Microwave at HIGH 1 to 2 minutes or until thoroughly heated. Stir before serving.
*1 (8.8-oz.) package ready-to-serve brown rice may be substituted.
Note: For testing purposes only, we used Uncle Ben's Ready Whole Grain Medley Brown & Wild Rice and Hormel Fully Cooked Pork Roast Au Jus.

Per serving (including 2 Tbsp. Cuban Salsa Verde): Calories 405; Fat 8.3g (sat 0.8g, mono 2.9g, poly 1.1g); Protein 23.4g; Carb 62.8g; Fiber 10.6g; Chol 35mg; Iron 2.8mg; Sodium 820mg; Calc 73mg

Cuban Salsa Verde:

fast fixin's
MAKES ⅓ CUP; **PREP:** 10 MIN.

1 cup loosely packed fresh cilantro leaves
4 green onions, chopped
1 Tbsp. lime juice
1 Tbsp. extra virgin olive oil
2 garlic cloves
1 tsp. honey
¼ tsp. salt
¼ tsp. dried crushed red pepper

1. Process all ingredients in a food processor 30 seconds or until smooth, stopping to scrape down sides.

Per (2-Tbsp.) serving: Calories 45; Fat 3.6g (sat 0.5g, mono 2.5g, poly 0.5g); Protein 0.5g; Carb 3.6g; Fiber 0.6g; Chol 0mg; Iron 0.3mg; Sodium 122mg; Calc 17mg

Potato, Bean, and Yogurt Soup

make ahead

MAKES 8½ CUPS; **PREP:** 20 MIN.,
COOK: 38 MIN., **STAND:** 10 MIN.

*Try packing this soup warm or cold in
an insulated container. The soup will
retain its temperature (up to 4 hours hot;
6 hours cold), making it easy to store at
your desk. The container's lid can double
as a serving dish.*

6 cups diced red potatoes (about 4 medium
    potatoes)
1 cup chopped celery
1 cup grated carrot
2 Tbsp. extra virgin olive oil
1 (16-oz.) can navy beans, rinsed and
    drained
1½ tsp. salt
1 tsp. dried dill weed
1 tsp. garlic powder
6 cups low-sodium chicken or vegetable
    broth
½ cup fat-free plain yogurt
Freshly ground pepper to taste

1. Sauté first 3 ingredients in hot oil in
a Dutch oven over medium heat 5 minutes. Add navy beans and next 3 ingredients, and cook, stirring often, 2 to 3
minutes. Add broth, and bring to a boil;
reduce heat to low, and simmer, stirring
occasionally, 20 to 30 minutes. Remove
from heat; let stand 10 minutes.
2. Transfer about 4 cups potato mixture to a food processor or blender
using a slotted spoon. Process 30 seconds or until smooth, stopping to scrape
down sides. Return pureed mixture to
Dutch oven, stirring until blended. Stir
in yogurt; season with pepper to taste.
Serve warm or cold. Store in refrigerator up to 1 week.
    —**CATHERINE S. VODREY,** EAST LIVERPOOL, OHIO

Per serving (about 1½ cups): Calories 305; Fat 6.7g (sat 1.2g,
mono 4.3g, poly 1g); Protein 14.9g; Carb 49.7g; Fiber 7.1g;
Chol 0.4mg; Iron 3.2mg; Sodium 773mg; Calc 98mg

Sweet Chili-Lime Noodles With Vegetables

fast fixin's • make ahead

MAKES 1 SERVING; **PREP:** 20 MIN.

*For easier prep, you can swap out the
fresh vegetables with 2 cups of a frozen
Asian-style vegetable blend.*

1 cup cooked whole grain spaghetti
    (2 oz. uncooked)
2 cups shredded bok choy*
¼ cup grated carrot
¼ cup fresh snow peas
Sweet Chili-Lime Sauce
¼ cup shredded cooked chicken (optional)

1. Place pasta, next 4 ingredients, and,
if desired, chicken in a medium-size
microwave-safe plastic container. Cover
with lid, and shake to combine.
2. Lift 1 corner of lid to allow steam to
escape. Microwave at HIGH 2 minutes
or until vegetables are tender.
*2 cups shredded coleslaw mix or shred-
ded cabbage may be substituted.
Note: For testing purposes only, we
used Mueller's Whole Grain Spaghetti.

Per serving (including Sweet Chili-Lime Sauce): Calories 344;
Fat 2.5g (sat 0.6g, mono 0.6g, poly 0.8g); Protein 21.2g;
Carb 61.3g; Fiber 8.9g; Chol 30mg; Iron 3.4mg; Sodium 641mg;
Calc 190mg

Sweet Chili-Lime Sauce:

fast fixin's

MAKES ABOUT 3 TBSP.; **PREP:** 5 MIN.

2 Tbsp. bottled sweet chili sauce
2 tsp. lime juice
½ tsp. fresh grated ginger
¼ tsp. minced garlic

1. Stir together all ingredients until
blended.

Per serving: Calories 77; Fat 0.1g (sat 0g, mono 0g, poly 0g);
Protein 0.1g; Carb 17.3g; Fiber 0.1g; Chol 0mg; Iron 0mg;
Sodium 500mg; Calc 2mg

A Taste of Summer

Juicy heirloom tomatoes are a
reason to celebrate with your
family and friends.

A simple get-together can
become a mini-vacation
for the mind and spirit. It
is a good break from your
daily routine. If you factor
a favorite food into the occasion, things
get even better.

That's what Cindy and George
Martin, owners of The Tasteful Garden
in Chulafinnee, Alabama, learned when
they hosted a tomato-tasting party with
friends Rod and Lori Palmer (Owl's
Hollow Farm, Gadsden, Alabama) and
Will and Laurie Moore (Moore Farms,
Woodland, Alabama). They sipped
wine, sampled their homegrown tomatoes, and compared notes on favorite
heirloom selections.

Tomatoes always spark lively conversation. "It's like people picking a dog,"
Cindy says. "They seem to choose a
tomato that reflects their personality."

Healthy Benefits

- Tomatoes are loaded with vitamin C and phytochemicals that
  promote good health.
- Growing your own tomatoes and
  other produce lowers the risk of
  food-borne illnesses occasionally found in mass-produced
  fruits and vegetables.

Old-Fashioned Flavor What does an heirloom tomato have that the new hybrids lack? "They offer more of everything," Cindy explains. "If a tomato is sweet, an heirloom is incredibly sweet. If a tomato is acidic, an heirloom selection is more so."

In the taste comparison, the men agree that 'Cherokee Purple' is number one. "This tomato has a rich, complex flavor," Will says.

"If I can get someone to taste a 'Cherokee Purple,' they're going to say 'That's the best tomato I've ever had,' " George claims.

Rod adds, "Sliced with a little salt, it doesn't get any better."

Each of the ladies, on the other hand, picked her own favorite. Cindy's choice is 'Rose de Berne.' "It's usually my first tomato of the year. I like a nice round tomato flavor," Cindy says.

Laurie Moore loves the yellow and green selections. "I enjoy 'Aunt Ruby's German Green' and 'Green Zebra,' " she states.

Lori Palmer prefers another old favorite. "When you eat a 'Brandywine' off the vine, you realize it's a different kind of tomato," she says.

The Facts of Flavor

George Martin demystifies the tomato's flavor traits.

- Dark-skinned tomatoes deliver the most acidic flavor.
- Yellow and orange selections are the sweetest.
- Red ones find balance between the two, with moderate acidity and sweetness.

Ripen Them Right

Will Moore suggests the best way to harvest your tomatoes for optimum flavor.

- Harvest a day or two before the tomato is fully ripe.
- Pick the fruit early in the morning before it heats up for the day.
- Let fruit sit on the kitchen counter until ready to eat. Do not refrigerate your tomatoes.

• TIP •

When you pick an heirloom tomato, cut it from the vine instead of pulling it loose. This prevents the fruit from bruising and makes each slice picture-perfect. If you're not sure which selection to fall in love with, purchase an assortment from a local farm stand and try them all.

Secrets to Success

Here are Rod Palmer's thoughts on growing the perfect heirloom tomato.

- Plant seedlings deep so the first set or two of branches is below the soil line.
- Put a handful of lime in the hole when planting. Heirlooms require a good dose of calcium to prevent blossom end rot. Pelletized lime converts to calcium as summer wears on.

Heirloom Selections

'Great White'
'Stump of the World'
'Mortgage Lifter'
'Roman Candle'
'Yellow Taxi'
'Costoluto Genovese'
'Cherokee Purple'
'Green Zebra'
'Rose de Berne'
'Big Zebra'
'Persimmon'
'Roma'
'Russian 117'

Look Sharp

We have plenty of professionals—and plenty of opinions—around our Test Kitchens. We asked them to name their favorite tomato knives; here's the short list.

The funky-looking one comes from Williams-Sonoma ($15 online). Its rounded tip lets you lift and carry the slices without spills. The green Color Coated Tomato Knife is sold by The Pampered Chef ($15 online). A serrated edge and nonstick coating make cutting tomatoes a breeze. We found the third pick, a 4½-inch serrated knife, for less than $10 at HomeGoods.

Quick and Tasty Banana Pudding, page 34

Shrimp and Grits, page 42

Bloody Mary
Punch, page 44

Baked Pears With
Oatmeal Streusel
Topping, page 43

Cream Cheese-Banana-Nut
Bread, page 43

Warm Purple-and-Red Potato Toss, page 86

Roasted Fingerlings and Green Beans With Creamy Tarragon Dressing, page 84

Creole Fried Rice, page 51

Pork Chops, Cabbage, and Apples, page 50

Lima Bean Cassoulet, page 50

Candy Bar
Pie, page 121

Icebox Cheese-
cake, page 120

Chocolate-Key Lime
Cupcake Pies, page 121

169

Crispy Sesame Salad
Stack, page 92

Strawberry-Pineapple
Iceberg Wedge, page 92

Chicken Thighs With Chunky
Tomato Sauce, page 155

Bacon-Wrapped Barbecue
Burgers, page 138

CLOCKWISE FROM TOP: **Watermelon, Mâche, and Pecan Salad, page 142; Peanutty Coleslaw, page 142; and Green Bean, Grape, and Pasta Toss, page 143**

Easy Blackberry Cobbler, page 145

Rustic Plum Tart, page 150

Sangría Blanco,
page 156

Citrus Shrimp Taco, page 156; Grilled Corn Salsa, page 157

Lean Green Lettuce Tacos, page 210

Prosciutto-Wrapped
Mango Bites, page 208

Party-Style
Pork Empanada,
page 209

Grilled Pork Roast
With Fruit Compote,
page 197

Grilled Pork Roast With Fruit Compote, page 197;
Caramelized Onion-Potato Gratin, page 198

Sweet Potato Squares With
Lemon-Garlic Mayonnaise,
page 196

Granola-Ginger
Baked Apples, page 198

Bananas Foster Ice-Cream
Pastry, page 199

JoAnn's Jambalaya,
page 199

Cranberry-Nectarine Salad,
page 213

Peppered Beef Soup served
in Toasted Bread Bowls,
page 211

Warm Ginger-Pear
Topping, page 203

Spiced Pomegranate
Sipper, page 203

Southern Soda Bread, page 232

Sunny Skillet Breakfast,
page 202

Molasses-Balsamic Pork
Kabobs With Green
Tomatoes and Plums,
page 239

Chicken-and-Corn Pies
With Cornbread Crust,
page 237

189

Roast Pork With Garlic-Onion Gravy, page 260

Oyster Dressing, page 261

Sweet Potato Cups, page 269

191

Coconut-Almond Cream
Cake, page 262

New Take on Lasagna

Try a time-saving spin on a much-loved classic.

Lasagna will always be one of those down-home favorites, perfect for family suppers or entertaining a crowd. These comforting recipes have all the same flavors of the traditional dish but are ready in just 45 minutes or less. We got creative and saved time by substituting refrigerated biscuit dough, egg noodles, and frozen ravioli for lasagna noodles, and the results were absolutely delicious.

Lasagna Pizza Cups

family favorite

MAKES 10 CUPS; PREP: 20 MIN.,
COOK: 5 MIN., BAKE: 20 MIN.

Luscious lasagna ingredients are layered inside these easy biscuit bites. Kids will love them. We don't recommend freezing these because it will alter the texture of the finished product.

½ lb. lean ground beef
1 small onion, chopped
2 garlic cloves, minced
1 (15-oz.) jar pizza sauce
1 (7.5-oz.) can refrigerated buttermilk
    biscuits
½ cup ricotta cheese
¾ cup (3 oz.) shredded mozzarella cheese

1. Preheat oven to 375°. Cook first 3 ingredients in a large skillet over medium heat, stirring occasionally, 5 minutes or until meat crumbles and is no longer pink. Drain well. Return meat mixture to skillet; stir in 1 cup pizza sauce. Remove from heat.
2. Press biscuits on bottom and up sides of lightly greased muffin cups. Spoon about 1 rounded tablespoonful meat mixture into each biscuit cup; top with ricotta cheese (about 1 heaping teaspoonful each). Sprinkle with shredded cheese.
3. Bake at 375° for 18 to 20 minutes or until golden. Remove from oven, and gently run a knife around outer edge of pizza cups to loosen from sides of pan. Remove cups from pan, using a spoon.
4. Place remaining pizza sauce in a small microwave-safe glass bowl; cover with plastic wrap. Microwave at HIGH 30 to 45 seconds or until thoroughly heated. Serve pizza cups with warm sauce.
Note: For testing purposes only, we used Pillsbury Buttermilk Biscuits and Ragú Homemade Style Pizza Sauce.

— **TRICIA GROVER**, JAMISON, PENNSYLVANIA

Skillet Lasagna

MAKES 6 SERVINGS;
PREP: 10 MIN., COOK: 20 MIN.,
STAND: 5 MIN.

1 small onion, chopped
1 tsp. minced garlic
1 Tbsp. olive oil
1 (26-oz.) jar tomato-and-basil pasta sauce
½ (12-oz.) package multigrain extra-wide
    egg noodles
¼ tsp. salt
¼ tsp. dried crushed red pepper
½ cup low-fat ricotta cheese
1 cup (4 oz.) shredded Italian six-cheese
    blend
2 Tbsp. chopped fresh basil (optional)

1. Sauté onion and garlic in hot oil in a 10-inch skillet over medium heat 5 minutes or until vegetables are tender. Stir in pasta sauce, egg noodles, and 1 cup water. Bring to a boil; reduce heat to medium to medium low, and simmer, stirring occasionally, 8 to 10 minutes or until pasta is just tender and liquid is almost absorbed. Stir in salt and crushed red pepper.
2. Stir together ricotta and ½ cup shredded cheese. Drop by heaping tablespoonfuls over pasta. Sprinkle with remaining ½ cup cheese.
3. Cook, covered, over low heat 5 minutes or until thoroughly heated and cheese is melted. Remove from heat, and let stand 5 minutes. Sprinkle with basil, if desired.
Note: For testing purposes only, we used Classico Tomato & Basil Pasta Sauce and Ronzoni Healthy Harvest Extra Wide Noodles.

Spinach-Ravioli Lasagna

MAKES 6 TO 8 SERVINGS;
PREP: 10 MIN., BAKE: 35 MIN.

Woodbridge Ghast Oak Chardonnay is the perfect match for the rich, baked goodness of this recipe.

1 (6-oz.) package fresh baby spinach,
    thoroughly washed
⅓ cup refrigerated pesto sauce
1 (15-oz.) jar Alfredo sauce
¼ cup vegetable broth*
1 (25-oz.) package frozen cheese-filled
    ravioli (do not thaw)
1 cup (4 oz.) shredded Italian six-cheese
    blend
Garnishes: chopped fresh basil, paprika

1. Preheat oven to 375°. Chop spinach, and toss with pesto in a medium bowl.
2. Combine Alfredo sauce and vegetable broth. Spoon one-third of alfredo sauce mixture (about ½ cup) into a lightly greased 2.2-qt. or 11- x 7-inch baking dish. Top with half of spinach mixture. Arrange half of ravioli in a single layer over spinach mixture. Repeat layers once. Top with remaining Alfredo sauce.
3. Bake at 375° for 30 minutes. Remove from oven, and sprinkle with shredded cheese. Bake 5 minutes or until hot and bubbly. Garnish, if desired.
*Chicken broth may be substituted.
Note: For testing purposes only, we used Santa Barbara Original Basil Pesto and Bertolli Alfredo Sauce.

Easiest Dessert

Spoon into one of these wonderful treats.

It's the season for cool comforts, and refrigerators will be humming with this dark chocolate twist on tiramisù. Brushed with coffee liqueur, buttery rich crumbles of homemade brownies are layered with creamy ribbons of mascarpone filling. Almost anything goes with this versatile treat. Feel free to serve smaller portions—espresso cups and shot glasses are especially fun for parties. Or simply spread the cheese mixture over the top of the completely cool, uncut brownies, and let guests help themselves after supper. Almost anything goes with this versatile treat.

Brownie Trifle is another easy and chocolaty summer refresher. Make it in a casserole dish for family-style serving or a trifle dish for company.

Brownie Tiramisù

MAKES 6 SERVINGS; **PREP:** 25 MIN.;
BAKE: 42 MIN.; **COOL:** 1 HR., 10 MIN.

Mascarpone gives the topping a special flavor, but an equal amount of softened cream cheese may be substituted. Almond-flavored liqueur makes a delicious substitute for coffee liqueur.

½ cup chopped pecans
⅓ cup coffee liqueur
⅓ cup strong brewed coffee
1½ (4-oz.) semisweet chocolate bars, divided
¾ cup butter
2¼ cups sugar, divided
3 large eggs
1 cup all-purpose flour
1 (8-oz.) container mascarpone cheese
1 tsp. vanilla extract
1 cup whipping cream

1. Preheat oven to 350°. Arrange pecans in a single layer on a baking sheet, and bake 5 to 7 minutes or until lightly toasted and fragrant.
2. Stir together coffee liqueur and brewed coffee.
3. Coarsely chop 1 chocolate bar. Microwave coarsely chopped chocolate and butter in a large microwave-safe bowl at MEDIUM (50% power) 1 to 1½ minutes or until melted and smooth, stirring at 30-second intervals. Whisk in 2 cups sugar and eggs, whisking until blended; stir in flour, stirring just until blended. Spoon batter into a lightly greased 11- x 7-inch pan.
4. Bake at 350° for 35 minutes or until center is set. Remove from oven, and cool in pan on a wire rack 10 minutes. Pierce brownie multiple times using the tines of a fork. Pour coffee mixture over brownie. Let cool on wire rack 1 hour or until completely cool.
5. Whisk together remaining ¼ cup sugar, mascarpone cheese, and vanilla in a large bowl. Beat whipping cream at medium speed with an electric mixer until stiff peaks form. Fold whipped cream into mascarpone mixture.
6. Crumble half of brownies, and divide evenly among 6 (8-oz.) glasses. Spoon half of mascarpone cheese mixture over brownies. Repeat procedure with remaining brownies and mascarpone cheese mixture.
7. Chop remaining half of chocolate bar into thin shreds. Sprinkle chocolate and pecans over mascarpone cheese mixture. Serve immediately, or cover and chill up to 24 hours.

—INSPIRED BY KAREN J. PALASZ,
FRANKLIN, WISCONSIN

Note: For testing purposes only, we used Kahlúa for coffee liqueur.

Brownie Trifle
MAKES 15 SERVINGS; **PREP:** 1 HR, 20 MIN;
CHILL: 2 HR.

For a change, assemble this trifle in a 3-qt. bowl. Measure the size of your bowl with water; it should hold at least 12 cups. Assemble the brownie pieces, marshmallow mixture, pudding, and caramel topping in several layers when using a deep bowl.

2 (21-oz.) packages chewy fudge brownie mix
1 (8-oz.) package cream cheese, softened
1 (7-oz.) jar marshmallow cream
2 (8-oz.) containers frozen whipped topping, thawed and divided
3 cups fat-free milk
2 (3.3-oz.) packages instant white chocolate pudding mix
1 (12¼-oz.) jar caramel topping

1. Prepare each brownie mix according to package directions for chewy brownies in a 13- x 9-inch pan. Cool; break into large pieces.
2. Beat cream cheese at medium speed with an electric mixer until creamy; beat in marshmallow cream. Stir in 1 container of whipped topping; set mixture aside.
3. Stir together milk and white chocolate pudding mix, stirring until thickened. Stir in remaining container of whipped topping.
4. Crumble half of brownie pieces in an even layer in bottom of a 13- x 9-inch baking dish. Pour cream cheese mixture evenly over brownies; drizzle evenly with caramel topping. Pour pudding evenly over caramel topping; crumble remaining brownie pieces over top. Cover and chill 2 hours.
Note: For testing purposes only, we used Duncan Hines Chewy Fudge Brownie Mix and Smuckers Caramel Topping.

September

Cozy Fireside Supper

Celebrate great food and friends with this surprisingly easy, laid-back menu.

Festive Fall Menu

SERVES 8

Guacamole-Goat Cheese Toasts

Sweet Potato Squares With
Lemon-Garlic Mayonnaise

Grilled Pork Roast With
Fruit Compote

Caramelized Onion-Potato Gratin

Mixed greens salad

Granola-Ginger Baked Apples

N ow's the time to take the party outside with temperatures cooling off and leaves making their showstopping color transition. That's exactly what Robert and Anne Trulock thought when they designed the outdoor living area of their Madison, Georgia home. "When the fireplace and grill are going at the same time, their wonderful aromas turn the backyard into my very own outdoor paradise. I can't think of a better way to relax in the fall," Robert says with a warm grin while turning the hearty Grilled Pork Roast.

Anne shares recipes for everything from flavor-packed appetizers to an updated classic fall dessert.

Guacamole-Goat Cheese Toasts

MAKES ABOUT 10 APPETIZER SERVINGS;
PREP: 15 MIN., **STAND:** 30 MIN.,
BAKE: 8 MIN.

PERFECT PARTNER: 2005 Villa Appalaccia, Pinot Grigio, Virginia; 2007 Flora Springs, Pinot Grigio, California

2 ripe avocados
3 Tbsp. finely chopped red onion, divided
½ medium-size jalapeño pepper, seeded and chopped
1 garlic clove, pressed
2½ tsp. fresh lime juice
¼ tsp. salt
¼ tsp. coarsely ground pepper
½ cup crumbled goat cheese
1 fresh tomatillo, husk removed
1 (7-oz.) package miniature white pita rounds*
2 Tbsp. olive oil
1 plum tomato, seeded and finely chopped
Coarsely ground pepper

1. Cut avocados in half. Scoop pulp into a bowl, and mash with a potato masher or fork until slightly chunky. Stir in 2 Tbsp. red onion and next 5 ingredients. Gently fold in cheese. Place plastic wrap directly on surface of mixture, and let stand at room temperature 30 minutes.
2. Meanwhile, preheat oven to 375°. Finely chop tomatillo.
3. Separate pita rounds lengthwise into two halves. Arrange in a single layer on a baking sheet; drizzle with olive oil.

4. Bake at 375° for 6 to 8 minutes or until toasted. Top each with 1 rounded teaspoonful avocado mixture. Stir together tomatillo, tomato, and remaining 1 Tbsp. red onion. Top avocado mixture with tomatillo mixture. Sprinkle with coarsely ground pepper to taste.

—ANNE TRULOCK, MADISON, GEORGIA

*1 (8.5-oz.) French bread baguette may be substituted for pita rounds. Cut bread diagonally into 42 (½-inch-thick) slices, discarding ends.
Note: For testing purposes only, we used Toufayan Bakeries Mini Pitettes.

Sweet Potato Squares With Lemon-Garlic Mayonnaise

MAKES 8 APPETIZER SERVINGS;
PREP: 30 MIN., **BAKE:** 20 MIN.,
COOK: 8 MIN.

The roasted goodness of the sweet potatoes and crispy smoked sausage deliver a pop of flavor in a small bite. Serve Sweet Potato Squares warm or at room temperature. Prepare the Lemon-Garlic Mayonnaise first if you choose to serve the Sweet Potato Squares warm. (Pictured on page 181)
PERFECT PARTNER: 2004 Linden, Claret, Virginia; 2005 Hogue, Cabernet-Merlot, Washington

2 lb. sweet potatoes, peeled and cut into 32 (1-inch) cubes
2 Tbsp. olive oil
½ tsp. pepper
¼ tsp. salt
½ lb. spicy smoked sausage, cut into 32 (½-inch) pieces
32 wooden picks
Lemon-Garlic Mayonnaise
Garnish: fresh thyme sprigs

1. Preheat oven to 450°. Place sweet potato cubes on a lightly greased 15- x 10-inch jelly-roll pan. Drizzle potatoes with 2 Tbsp. oil, and sprinkle with pepper and salt. Toss to coat.
2. Bake at 450° for 15 to 20 minutes, turning cubes twice.

3. Cook sausage in a large nonstick skillet over medium-high heat 3 to 4 minutes on each side or until browned. Drain on paper towels.

4. Place 1 sausage slice on top of 1 sweet potato cube; secure with a wooden pick. Repeat with remaining sausage slices and potato cubes. Serve with Lemon-Garlic Mayonnaise. Garnish, if desired.

—ANNE TRULOCK, MADISON, GEORGIA

Lemon-Garlic Mayonnaise:
MAKES ABOUT 1 CUP; **PREP:** 10 MIN.

1 cup mayonnaise
2 Tbsp. chopped fresh flat-leaf parsley
2 tsp. minced garlic
1 tsp. lemon zest
2 Tbsp. fresh lemon juice
½ tsp. pepper
¼ tsp. salt

1. Stir together all ingredients. Store in an airtight container in refrigerator up to 7 days.

Creamy Lemon-Garlic
Dressing: Stir together ⅓ cup Lemon-Garlic Mayonnaise, ¼ cup buttermilk, and a pinch of salt. **Makes** about ½ cup.

Grilled Pork Roast With Fruit Compote
MAKES 8 SERVINGS; **PREP:** 15 MIN.;
GRILL: 1 HR., 5 MIN.; **STAND:** 10 MIN.

You can ask the butcher to tie the roast. (Pictured on page 180)
PERFECT PARTNER: *2005 DelFosse, Cabernet Franc, Virginia; 2005 Columbia Crest, Two Vines Vineyard 10 Red, Washington*

1 (4-lb.) boneless pork loin roast, trimmed
Kitchen string
2 tsp. salt
1 tsp. pepper
2 Tbsp. chopped garlic
1 Tbsp. finely chopped fresh rosemary
1 Tbsp. chopped fresh thyme
2 Tbsp. olive oil
Fruit Compote

1. Tie pork with kitchen string, securing at 2-inch intervals. Sprinkle pork with salt and pepper. Stir together garlic and next 3 ingredients. Rub mixture over pork.

2. Light 1 side of a grill, heating to 350° to 400° (medium-high); leave other side unlit. Place pork over lit side, and grill, covered with grill lid, 8 to 10 minutes on each side or until browned. Move pork over unlit side, and grill, covered with grill lid, 45 minutes or until a meat thermometer inserted into thickest portion registers 145° to 150°. Let stand 10 minutes before slicing. Serve with Fruit Compote.

Fruit Compote:
make ahead
MAKES 2 CUPS; **PREP:** 15 MIN.,
COOK: 25 MIN.

16 dried Mission figlets, quartered*
1 Granny Smith apple, diced
12 dried apricots, thinly sliced
½ cup seedless red grapes, halved
½ cup chopped red onion
½ cup dry white wine
½ cup cider vinegar
1 cup sugar
½ tsp. salt
½ tsp. pepper

1. Combine all ingredients in a 3-qt. saucepan, and cook over medium heat,

stirring occasionally, 25 minutes or until thickened and liquid is reduced by three-fourths. (Mixture will continue to thicken as it cools.) Serve warm or at room temperature.

—ANNE TRULOCK, MADISON, GEORGIA

*12 dried Mission figs, coarsely chopped, may be substituted.
Note: For testing purposes only, we used Blue Ribbon Orchard Choice Mission Figlets.

Serving Suggestion

The robust fresh-herb crust of the Grilled Pork Roast pairs beautifully with the sweet and tart flavors of the Fruit Compote. Keep any leftover Fruit Compote in the refrigerator for up to two weeks, and serve it with creamy goat cheese or Brie and slices of fresh, crusty baguette for a wonderful snack or appetizer.

Caramelized Onion-Potato Gratin

MAKES 8 SERVINGS; **PREP:** 30 MIN.; **COOK:** 27 MIN.; **BAKE:** 1 HR., 10 MIN.; **STAND:** 10 MIN.

Cook's note: Stick a wooden pick into the middle of the gratin to test for doneness. The gratin is ready when the pick slides easily through the potatoes. (Pictured on page 181)

1¼ cups soft, fresh breadcrumbs

¼ cup chopped fresh parsley

3 Tbsp. grated Parmesan cheese

2 tsp. lemon zest

3 Tbsp. butter

2 large sweet onions, halved and thinly sliced

3 garlic cloves, minced

3 Tbsp. all-purpose flour

3½ cups milk

1¾ tsp. salt

1½ tsp. dried Italian seasoning

⅛ tsp. ground red pepper

1 (8-oz.) package shredded Italian six-cheese blend

3 lb. baking potatoes, peeled and thinly sliced

1. Preheat oven to 375°. Combine breadcrumbs, parsley, Parmesan cheese, and lemon zest in a small bowl.

2. Melt butter in a Dutch oven over medium-high heat; add onions, and cook, stirring often, 15 minutes or until onions are caramel colored; add garlic, and cook 1 minute.

3. Stir in flour, and cook, stirring constantly, 1 minute. Gradually whisk in milk and next 3 ingredients. Cook, whisking often, 8 to 9 minutes or until mixture thickens. Remove from heat; whisk in cheese until melted and smooth.

4. Layer half of potatoes in a lightly greased 13- x 9-inch baking dish; pour 2 cups sauce over potatoes in dish. Repeat layers once.

5. Bake, uncovered, at 375° for 1 hour and 10 minutes or until golden brown and potatoes are fork tender, topping with breadcrumb mixture during last 15 minutes of baking. Remove from oven, and let stand 10 minutes.

—ANNE TRULOCK, MADISON, GEORGIA

Lightened Caramelized Onion-Potato Gratin: Substitute 1% low-fat milk for whole milk, decrease butter to 1½ Tbsp., and increase flour to ¼ cup. Proceed with recipe as directed.

Granola-Ginger Baked Apples

MAKES 8 SERVINGS; **PREP:** 20 MIN., **BAKE:** 45 MIN., **COOK:** 6 MIN.

Finely crushed oat-and-honey granola bars, chopped crystallized ginger, and thick Greek yogurt are the secrets to this delectable and good-for-you dessert. Bosc pears also work well in place of apples. This recipe gets an extra level of flavor from the apple cider. Don't be tempted to use apple cider vinegar. (Pictured on page 182)

4 large Golden Delicious or Jonagold apples

3 (1.5-oz.) oat-and-honey granola bars, finely crushed

½ cup roasted salted almonds, chopped

¼ cup finely chopped crystallized ginger

¼ cup butter, softened

¾ tsp. ground cinnamon

1¾ cups apple cider

⅓ cup cherry preserves

1 (7-oz.) container Greek yogurt

1. Preheat oven to 375°. Cut apples in half, cutting through stem and bottom ends. Scoop out core and pulp, leaving a ¾-inch shell. Cut about ¼ inch from opposite side of apple, forming a flat base.

2. Stir together crushed granola bars and next 4 ingredients. Spoon mixture into apple shells, pressing to gently pack. Arrange apples in a 13- x 9-inch pan. Pour cider around apples in pan.

3. Bake at 375° for 25 to 45 minutes or until apples are tender, basting twice with pan juices.

4. Place apples on a serving plate. Add preserves to pan juices, and cook, over medium-high heat, stirring constantly, 5 to 6 minutes or until thickened. Serve apples with warm sauce and Greek yogurt.

Granola-Ginger Baked Pears: Substitute 4 Bosc pears for apples. Proceed with recipe as directed.

Note: Baking times will vary greatly due to the ripeness of your fruit. Begin testing for doneness by inserting a wooden pick directly into the fruit (not granola mixture) after 25 minutes of baking. A wooden pick should be able to pierce the fruit easily with just a little resistance. Overcooking will lead to the fruit losing its natural shape and becoming mushy. For testing purposes only, we used Nature Valley Oats 'N Honey Crunchy Granola Bars.

Jammin' Jambalaya

Awaken your taste buds with Creole-inspired recipes that are just right for a weeknight. Your family will love them too!

Creole Supper

SERVES 4

JoAnn's Jambalaya

Mixed greens salad

Garlic French Bread

Bananas Foster Ice-Cream Pastry

JoAnn's Jambalaya

MAKES 6 SERVINGS; **PREP:** 15 MIN.,
COOK: 35 MIN.

Andouille sausage adds bold flavor to JoAnn's Jambalaya. Reduce the heat by substituting your favorite smoked sausage for the andouille. (Pictured on page 184)

1 lb. andouille sausage, cut into
  ¼-inch-thick slices
1 (10-oz.) package frozen vegetable
  seasoning blend
1 (32-oz.) container low-sodium chicken
  broth
1 (14.5-oz.) can fire-roasted diced tomatoes
  with garlic
2 cups uncooked long-grain rice
2 Tbsp. chopped fresh parsley
1 tsp. Cajun seasoning
2 tsp. Worcestershire sauce
⅛ tsp. ground red pepper (optional)
2 Tbsp. thinly sliced green onions

1. Cook sausage in a large Dutch oven over medium-high heat, stirring frequently, 8 to 10 minutes or until browned. Remove sausage with a slotted spoon; drain on paper towels.
2. Add vegetable seasoning blend to hot drippings in Dutch oven, and sauté 3 to 5 minutes or until thoroughly heated. Add broth, next 5 ingredients, sausage, and if desired, ground red pepper. Bring to a boil; cover, reduce heat to low, and cook 18 to 20 minutes or until rice is tender and liquid is absorbed. Top with green onions, and serve immediately.
—INSPIRED BY JOANN LETO, TAMPA, FLORIDA
Note: For testing purposes only, we used McKenzie's Seasoning Blend frozen vegetables and Hunt's Fire Roasted Diced Tomatoes With Garlic.

Garlic French Bread

southernliving.com favorite
MAKES 8 TO 10 SERVINGS; **PREP:** 10 MIN.,
BAKE: 20 MIN.

½ cup butter, melted
6 garlic cloves, pressed
1 tsp. dried oregano
½ tsp. dried parsley flakes
1 (16-oz.) package French bread loaves

1. Preheat oven to 350°. Combine first 4 ingredients.
2. Cut bread loaves in half horizontally. Brush cut sides evenly with garlic mixture. Wrap loaves in aluminum foil, and place on a baking sheet.
3. Bake at 350° for 10 minutes. Remove foil, and bake 10 more minutes or until lightly browned and crisp. Serve immediately.
Note: For testing purposes only, we used Pepperidge Farm Twin French Bread Loaves. Freeze unbaked garlic bread, wrapped in aluminum foil and in a zip-top plastic freezer bag, up to 1 month, if desired. Remove bread from freezer bag, place on a baking sheet, and bake at 375° for 20 minutes. Unwrap foil, and bake 5 more minutes or until lightly browned.

Bananas Foster Ice-Cream Pastry

MAKES 4 SERVINGS; **PREP:** 10 MIN.,
BAKE: 25 MIN., **COOK:** 5 MIN.

Frozen puff pastry dough lends rich, buttery texture to this melt-in-your-mouth dessert. (Pictured on page 183)

½ cup chopped pecans
½ (17.3-oz.) package frozen puff pastry
  sheets, thawed*
Parchment paper
¼ cup butter
½ cup firmly packed brown sugar
1 Tbsp. orange juice
1 tsp. vanilla extract
½ tsp. ground cinnamon
Pinch of salt
4 bananas, cut into ⅓-inch-thick slices
Vanilla ice cream

1. Preheat oven to 350°. Bake pecans in a single layer in a shallow pan 8 to 10 minutes or until toasted and fragrant, stirring after 5 minutes. Remove from oven, and increase oven temperature to 400°.
2. Unfold 1 puff pastry sheet on a lightly floured surface. Roll into a 10-inch square, carefully smoothing creases. Cut into 4 (4- to 5-inch) circles using a cutter. Place on a parchment paper-lined baking sheet.
3. Bake at 400° for 10 to 15 minutes or until golden brown and puffed.
4. Heat butter and sugar in large non-stick skillet over low heat 2 minutes or until sugar is melted. Add orange juice, next 3 ingredients, and 1 Tbsp. water to skillet. Cook, whisking constantly, 2 minutes or until mixture is blended and smooth. Add bananas, and cook 1 minute.
5. Arrange pastry rounds on serving plates. Top each with about ½ cup banana mixture and ½ cup ice cream. Drizzle with any remaining sauce. Sprinkle with toasted pecans, and serve immediately.
—KATHRYN PULLIAM, MOBILE, ALABAMA
*Frozen puff pastry shells may be substituted for frozen puff pastry sheets.

A Week of Easy Meals

Any season can be hectic, so use our budget-friendly recipe plan to save time, money, and decision-making. Healthful, fresh ingredients transform simple recipes into down-home goodness. You'll grill one night for a trio of fast suppers and use the oven to round out the week.

Greek-Style Beef and Vegetables
family favorite

MAKES 4 SERVINGS; **PREP:** 20 MIN., **GRILL:** 14 MIN., **STAND:** 10 MIN.

Tender boneless top sirloin steak gives this dish maximum taste with minimal effort. This recipe calls for you to grill twice as much meat as you will need, so save half for Orange Beef Pasta to serve later in the week.

2 lb. (1-inch-thick) boneless top sirloin steak
3 Tbsp. olive oil, divided
2 tsp. kosher salt, divided
1 tsp. freshly ground pepper, divided
6 medium-size yellow squash, cut in half
1 red onion, cut into ½-inch-thick slices
1 lemon, cut in half
1 (10-oz.) box plain couscous
½ (4-oz.) package crumbled feta cheese
Chunky Cucumber-Mint Sauce

1. Preheat grill to 350° to 400° (medium-high). Rub steak with 1 Tbsp. oil, 1½ tsp. kosher salt, and ¾ tsp. pepper.
2. Brush squash and onion with remaining 2 Tbsp. oil; sprinkle with remaining ½ tsp. kosher salt and ¼ tsp. pepper.
3. Grill steak and vegetables, covered with grill lid, over 350° to 400° (medium-high) heat 5 to 7 minutes on each side or until steak reaches desired degree of doneness and vegetables are tender. Remove steak and vegetables from grill; squeeze juice from lemon over steak and vegetables. Cover steak and vegetables with aluminum foil, and let stand 10 minutes.
4. Meanwhile, prepare couscous according to package directions.
5. Cut steak across the grain into thin slices. Cover and chill half of sliced steak (about 1 lb.) up to 2 days. Top couscous with vegetables; sprinkle with feta cheese. Serve with remaining half of steak and Chunky Cucumber-Mint Sauce.

Chunky Cucumber-Mint Sauce: Stir together 1 cup plain yogurt; 3 Tbsp. sour cream; 1 small peeled, seeded, and chopped cucumber; 4 tsp. chopped fresh mint; and salt and pepper to taste. **Makes** about 1¾ cups; Prep: 10 min.

Rosemary Grilled Chicken Thighs

MAKES 4 TO 6 SERVINGS; **PREP:** 10 MIN., **CHILL:** 1 HR., **GRILL:** 14 MIN., **STAND:** 10 MIN.

The subtle flavor of these chicken thighs makes them the perfect partner for Sautéed Garlic Spinach and Southern-style Two-Cheese Grits. For a tasty alternative, try these with our quick Honey Mustard Sauce.

1 garlic clove, pressed
1 Tbsp. olive oil
2 Tbsp. Dijon mustard
2 Tbsp. honey
1 tsp. salt
1 tsp. chopped fresh rosemary*
½ tsp. pepper
1½ lb. skinned and boned chicken thighs**
½ lemon
Sautéed Garlic Spinach
Two-Cheese Grits

1. Combine garlic and next 6 ingredients in a large heavy-duty zip-top plastic bag, squeezing bag to combine ingredients. Add chicken, turning to coat, and seal bag. Chill 1 to 24 hours.
2. Preheat grill to 350° to 400° (medium-high). Remove chicken thighs from marinade, discarding marinade.
3. Grill chicken, covered with grill lid, over 350° to 400° (medium-high) heat 5 to 7 minutes on each side. Transfer chicken to a large piece of aluminum foil. Squeeze juice from lemon over chicken; fold foil around chicken, covering chicken completely. Let stand 10 minutes. Serve with Sautéed Garlic Spinach and Two-Cheese Grits.
*Fresh thyme, cilantro, or oregano may be substituted.
**1½ lb. skinned and boned chicken breasts may be substituted.

Rosemary Grilled Pork Tenderloin: Omit chicken thighs. Substitute 2 lb. pork tenderloin, and grill as directed 8 to 10 minutes on each side. Proceed with remainder of recipe as directed. **Makes** 4 to 6 servings; Prep: 10 min., Chill: 1 hr., Grill: 20 min., Stand: 10 min.

Sautéed Garlic Spinach: Heat 1 tsp. olive oil in a nonstick skillet over medium-high heat. Sauté 1 pressed garlic clove in hot oil 30 seconds. Add 1 (10-oz.) bag fresh spinach, thoroughly washed, to skillet, and cook 2 to 3 minutes or until spinach is wilted. Sprinkle with salt and pepper to taste. Serve spinach with slotted spoon or tongs. **Makes** 4 servings; Prep: 5 min., Cook: 4 min.

Two-Cheese Grits: Bring 4 cups water and 1 tsp. salt to a boil in a 3-qt. saucepan. Whisk in 1 cup uncooked quick-cooking grits; reduce heat to medium-low, and cook 5 to 6 minutes or until tender. Remove from heat, and stir in 1 cup (4 oz.) shredded Cheddar cheese, ½ cup (2 oz.) shredded

Parmesan cheese, and 2 Tbsp. butter. Sprinkle with pepper to taste. **Makes** 4 servings; Prep: 5 min., Cook: 10 min.

Honey Mustard Sauce: Stir together ½ cup mayonnaise, 2 Tbsp. Dijon mustard, and 2 Tbsp. honey. **Makes** about ¾ cup; Prep: 5 min.

Orange Beef Pasta
family favorite • fast fixin's

MAKES 4 TO 6 SERVINGS; **PREP:** 15 MIN., **COOK:** 5 MIN.

This tasty pasta delivers a salty-sweet zing from soy sauce and orange marmalade. It packs a nutritious punch with lightly sautéed carrots and snowpeas. Measure all ingredients before you begin cooking for the very best results.

½ (16-oz.) package vermicelli
1 Tbsp. vegetable oil
2 carrots, cut into ¼-inch slices
1½ cups snow peas, trimmed
1 (14-oz.) can beef broth
¼ cup soy sauce
¼ cup orange marmalade
¼ tsp. dried crushed red pepper
1 lb. cooked, sliced Greek-Style Beef
    (see opposite page)
Toppings: sliced green onions, toasted
    sesame seeds

1. Prepare pasta according to package directions.
2. Heat oil in a Dutch oven over medium-high heat. Add carrots and snow peas, and stir-fry 4 to 5 minutes or until crisp-tender. Stir in beef broth and next 3 ingredients.
3. Bring to a boil. Remove from heat; add Greek-Style Beef and hot cooked pasta; toss well to combine. Serve immediately with desired toppings.

Parmesan Chicken Thighs
family favorite

MAKES 4 TO 6 SERVINGS; **PREP:** 25 MIN., **COOK:** 12 MIN., **BAKE:** 20 MIN.

2 large eggs
1½ lb. skinned and boned chicken
    thighs
1½ tsp. kosher salt*
1 tsp. freshly ground pepper
1 cup Italian-seasoned breadcrumbs
½ cup vegetable oil
1 (24-oz.) jar marinara sauce
½ cup (2 oz.) shredded Parmesan
    cheese
½ (16-oz.) package vermicelli
3 Tbsp. butter
1 Tbsp. chopped fresh parsley
Tangy Feta Dressing Over Iceberg

1. Preheat oven to 375°. Whisk together eggs and 2 Tbsp. water.
2. Sprinkle chicken with salt and pepper. Dredge in breadcrumbs; dip in egg mixture, and dredge again in breadcrumbs.
3. Cook chicken, in batches, in hot oil in a 12-inch heavy skillet over medium heat 2 to 3 minutes on each side or until golden brown.
4. Arrange chicken in a lightly greased 13- x 9-inch baking dish.
5. Spoon marinara sauce over chicken, and sprinkle with Parmesan cheese.
6. Bake at 375° for 15 to 20 minutes or until cheese is melted and a meat thermometer inserted into thickest portion of chicken registers 170°.
7. Meanwhile, prepare pasta according to package directions. Toss hot cooked pasta with butter and parsley. Serve chicken over pasta with Tangy Feta Dressing Over Iceberg.
*1 tsp. table salt may be substituted.

Tangy Feta Dressing Over Iceberg: Stir together ½ cup mayonnaise, ½ (4-oz.) package crumbled feta cheese, 2 Tbsp. chopped fresh parsley, and 1 to 2 Tbsp. fresh lemon juice. Stir in pepper to taste. Spoon dressing over 5 cups shredded iceberg lettuce. **Makes** 4 servings; Prep: 10 min.

Chili-Cheeseburger Mac-and-Cheese
family favorite • fast fixin's

MAKES 4 SERVINGS; **PREP:** 10 MIN., **COOK:** 18 MIN.

At the tasting table, this delicious recipe was our hands-down favorite over a boxed hamburger meal.

1 (12-oz.) box shells and cheese
1 lb. ground beef
1 tsp. chili powder
¼ tsp. cumin
¼ tsp. salt
1 (15-oz.) can kidney beans, rinsed and
    drained
1 (14.5-oz.) can diced tomatoes with mild
    green chiles
2 Tbsp. chopped fresh parsley

1. Prepare shells and cheese according to package directions.
2. Meanwhile, brown beef in a 12-inch (2½-inch-deep) nonstick skillet or Dutch oven over medium-high heat, stirring often, 8 minutes or until no longer pink; drain and rinse under hot running water. Return beef to skillet; stir in chili powder, cumin, and salt. Cook 2 minutes. Add beans, tomatoes, and ¼ cup water. Cook 5 to 8 minutes or until most of liquid has evaporated.
3. Stir prepared pasta into beef mixture, and sprinkle with chopped fresh parsley. Serve immediately.
Note: For testing purposes only, we used Velveeta Shells & Cheese Original and Del Monte Diced Tomatoes with Zesty Mild Green Chilies.

Farmhouse Breakfast

Start with these classics for a relaxed weekend with company or a quiet morning with family.

You don't have to spend hours in the kitchen to make a great breakfast. Here are some easy-to-prepare dishes (mostly from scratch) that satisfy your craving for fresh ingredients and hearty flavor. Plus we've included a few shortcuts along the way. Our favorite find? Frozen biscuits. They taste nearly as good as grandma's, minus all the work. Just pop them in the oven, bake until fluffy and golden, and smother them with homemade Easy Redeye Gravy.

Sunny Skillet Breakfast

MAKES 6 SERVINGS; **PREP:** 15 MIN., **STAND:** 5 MIN., **COOK:** 16 MIN., **BAKE:** 14 MIN.

Shredded potatoes make this egg dish a complete meal. Soaking the potatoes in cold water keeps them from turning gray before cooking. It also rinses off some of the starch. Drain and pat them dry, so they won't stick to the cast-iron skillet. (Pictured on page 187)

3 (8-oz.) baking potatoes, peeled and shredded (about 3 cups firmly packed)*
1 Tbsp. butter
2 Tbsp. vegetable oil
1 small red bell pepper, diced
1 medium onion, diced
1 garlic clove, pressed
¾ tsp. salt, divided
6 large eggs
¼ tsp. pepper

1. Preheat oven to 350°. Place shredded potatoes in a large bowl; add cold water to cover. Let stand 5 minutes; drain and pat dry.

2. Melt butter with oil in a 10-inch cast-iron skillet over medium heat. Add bell pepper and onion, and sauté 3 to 5 minutes or until tender. Add garlic; sauté 1 minute. Stir in shredded potatoes and ½ tsp. salt; cook, stirring often, 10 minutes or until potatoes are golden and tender.

3. Remove from heat. Make 6 indentations in potato mixture, using back of a spoon. Break 1 egg into each indentation. Sprinkle eggs with pepper and remaining ¼ tsp salt.

4. Bake at 350° for 12 to 14 minutes or until eggs are set. Serve immediately.

*3 cups firmly packed frozen shredded potatoes may be substituted, omitting Step 1.

Veggie Confetti Frittata: Prepare recipe as directed through Step 2, sautéing ½ (8-oz.) package sliced fresh mushrooms with bell peppers and onion. Remove from heat, and stir in ¼ cup sliced ripe black olives, drained, and ¼ cup thinly sliced sun-dried tomatoes in oil, drained. Whisk together eggs, pepper, and remaining ¼ tsp. salt; whisk in ½ cup (2 oz.) shredded Swiss cheese. Pour egg mixture over potato mixture in skillet. Bake at 350° for 9 to 10 minutes or until set. Cut frittata into wedges, and serve immediately. **Makes** 6 servings; Prep: 20 min., Stand: 5 min., Cook: 16 min., Bake: 10 min.

Pecan Sugared Bacon

family favorite

MAKES 6 SERVINGS; **PREP:** 15 MIN., **BAKE:** 25 MIN., **STAND:** 5 MIN.

This recipe received our staff's highest rating. Freshly ground pepper gives it an extra bite.

2 Tbsp. coarsely chopped pecans
2 Tbsp. brown sugar
1½ tsp. freshly ground pepper
12 thick-cut bacon slices

1. Preheat oven to 400°. Process pecans in a food processor 20 seconds or until finely chopped. Stir together pecans, brown sugar, and pepper.

2. Place half of bacon in a single layer on a lightly greased wire rack in an aluminum foil-lined baking sheet. Repeat procedure with remaining bacon, placing on another lightly greased wire rack in a second foil-lined baking sheet. Press pecan mixture on top of bacon slices, coating well.

3. Bake at 400° for 22 to 25 minutes or until browned and crisp. Let stand 5 minutes.

Easy Redeye Gravy

fast fixin's

MAKES 6 SERVINGS; **PREP:** 10 MIN., **COOK:** 10 MIN.

This recipe was a special treat for reader Melody Lee during childhood visits to her grandmother's farm.

6 frozen biscuits
2 Tbsp. butter
6 biscuit-size country ham slices
1 Tbsp. all-purpose flour
1 cup strong brewed coffee
1½ Tbsp. brown sugar
⅛ to ¼ tsp. salt
⅛ tsp. freshly ground pepper
¼ tsp. hot sauce (optional)

1. Prepare frozen biscuits according to package directions.

2. Meanwhile, melt butter in large skillet over medium-high heat. Add ham, and cook 3 minutes on each side or until lightly browned; remove ham.

3. Add flour to skillet; cook, whisking constantly, 1 minute. Add brewed coffee, brown sugar, and ½ cup water. Cook, whisking constantly, 3 minutes or until thickened; return ham slices to skillet. Stir in salt, pepper, and, if desired, hot sauce.

4. Split warm biscuits in half. Top bottom halves with ham slices. Pour gravy over ham; cover with remaining biscuit halves. Serve immediately.

—MELODY LEE, DOTHAN, ALABAMA

Note: For testing purposes only, we used White Lily Southern Style and Buttermilk Frozen Biscuit Dough.

Warm Ginger-Pear Topping
fast fixin's

MAKES 4 TO 6 SERVINGS;
PREP: 15 MIN., **COOK:** 13 MIN.

Serve this warm spiced fruit over biscuits, waffles, pancakes, or ice cream. Your cook time may vary depending on the ripeness of the fruit—the riper the fruit, the shorter the cook time. (Pictured on page 186)

⅓ cup firmly packed brown sugar
1 tsp. cornstarch
4 Anjou pears, peeled and coarsely chopped
½ tsp. ground ginger
½ tsp. lemon juice
¼ tsp. almond extract
1 Tbsp. butter

1. Stir together sugar and cornstarch in a medium skillet. Add pears and next 3 ingredients, and bring to a boil over medium-high heat, stirring constantly. Boil 1 minute; reduce heat to medium-low, and simmer, stirring often, 8 to 12 minutes or until pears are tender. Stir in butter.

Warm Cinnamon-Apple Topping: Substitute 4 peeled and coarsely chopped Granny Smith apples for pears, ½ tsp. ground cinnamon and ¼ tsp. ground nutmeg for ground ginger, and ½ tsp. vanilla extract for ¼ tsp. almond extract. Proceed with recipe as directed.

Warm Two-Berry Topping: Substitute granulated sugar for brown sugar, 1½ cups each of frozen cranberries and frozen blueberries for pears, and ½ tsp. vanilla extract for ¼ tsp. almond extract. Omit ginger and cornstarch. Proceed with recipe as directed, simmering berries 7 minutes or until thickened. **Makes** 4 to 6 servings; Prep: 15 min., Cook: 8 min.

Fall Refresher

Here's a versatile beverage to serve regardless of the temperature. It's a cinnamon-, clove-, and ginger-spiced sipper. And you can drink it hot, iced, spiked, or fizzy. Stash this recipe in a safe place—it's ideal for the upcoming holidays.

Spiced Pomegranate Sipper
MAKES ABOUT 8 CUPS; **PREP:** 10 MIN.,
COOK: 18 MIN.

These juices are easy to find. (Pictured on page 186)

1 (2½-inch-long) cinnamon stick
5 whole cloves
5 thin fresh ginger slices
2 (16-oz.) bottles refrigerated 100% pomegranate juice
4 cups white grape juice
½ cup pineapple juice
Garnishes: pineapple chunks, orange rind curls

1. Cook cinnamon stick, cloves, and ginger in a Dutch oven over medium heat, stirring constantly, 2 to 3 minutes or until cinnamon is fragrant.

2. Gradually stir in juices. Bring to a boil over medium-high heat; reduce heat to medium-low, and simmer 15 minutes. Pour mixture through a wire-mesh strainer into a heat-proof pitcher; discard solids. Serve warm. Garnish, if desired.

Note: For testing purposes only, we used POM Wonderful 100% Pomegranate Juice and Welch's 100% White Grape Juice.

Tipsy Hot Spiced Pomegranate Sipper: Prepare recipe as directed. Stir in 1¼ cups almond liqueur just before serving. **Makes** 9¼ cups.

Cold Spiced Pomegranate Sipper: Prepare recipe as directed. Let stand 30 minutes. Cover and chill 2 hours. Store in refrigerator up to 2 days. Stir and serve over ice. **Makes** 8 cups; Prep: 10 min., Cook: 18 min., Stand: 30 min., Chill: 2 hr.

Fizzy Spiced Pomegranate Sipper: Prepare Cold Spiced Pomegranate Sipper as directed. Stir in 1 (33.8-oz.) bottle ginger ale just before serving. **Makes** 12 cups.

Ready Now: Eggplant

Produce stands are spilling over with this beautiful fruit, and it's so easy to prepare. Slice, brush with oil, sprinkle with s & p, and grill. Add our delicious sweet and tart topping, and you'll find it irresistible.

Bring Out the Best Flavor

We used globe eggplants for Grilled Eggplant With Sweet Pepper-Tomato Topping. Choose smaller ones for a delicate flavor and few seeds. A good rule of thumb: Buy those about the size of a 12-oz. water bottle. They should be glossy and free of dents, have a green cap, and spring back when gently pressed

Eggplants are very perishable, and there is a lot of discussion on whether or not to refrigerate them. We recommend storing in a cool, dry place such as on a countertop away from a range or window. Refrigeration often causes bitterness. Use within two days.

Grilled Eggplant With Sweet Pepper-Tomato Topping

MAKES 3 MAIN-DISH OR 5 SIDE-DISH SERVINGS; **PREP:** 10 MIN., **GRILL:** 6 MIN.

"Salting eggplant slices is a must," says Kristi Michele Crowe, PhD and our Test Kitchens food chemist. *"Salt fools the taste buds into overlooking the slight bitterness of this fruit. When grilling slices, no stand time is necessary."* (Eggplant casserole recipes usually call for slices to be placed on paper towels and salted to pull out moisture before baking.) Serve this dish with Italian bread for a meatless entrée or as a side to grilled chicken.

2 small eggplants (about 10 to 12 oz. each)*
2 Tbsp. olive oil
1 tsp. kosher salt
½ tsp. coarsely ground pepper
Sweet Pepper-Tomato Topping

1. Preheat grill to 400° to 450° (high).
2. Cut each eggplant lengthwise into 5 (½-inch-thick) slices. Brush both sides of eggplant with oil; sprinkle with salt and pepper.
3. Grill eggplant, covered with grill lid, over 400° to 450° (high) heat 2 to 3 minutes on each side or until lightly browned and slightly charred.
4. Serve immediately with Sweet Pepper-Tomato Topping.
*4 Chinese eggplants or 6 Japanese eggplants (about 1½ lb.), cut diagonally into ½-inch-thick slices, may be substituted for two small eggplants.

Sweet Pepper-Tomato Topping:

fast fixin's

MAKES ABOUT 3 CUPS; **PREP:** 15 MIN., **STAND:** 15 MIN.

This recipe is best when freshly made; however, you can cover and chill the mixture (without basil) up to two hours. Just know that the texture of the tomatoes will soften.

2 Tbsp. olive oil
1 Tbsp. white wine vinegar
1 tsp. salt
½ tsp. coarsely ground pepper
2 large tomatoes, seeded and chopped
1 yellow bell pepper, chopped
1 green bell pepper, chopped
4 green onions, sliced
½ cup pitted Spanish olives, quartered
½ cup golden raisins, coarsely chopped
¼ cup firmly packed fresh basil leaves, chopped

1. Stir together first 4 ingredients in a large bowl. Add tomatoes and next 5 ingredients, tossing gently to combine. Let stand 15 minutes. Gently stir in basil just before serving.

—INSPIRED BY LUCIANE GIAMPIETRO, KINGSPORT, TENNESSEE

Pork With Pizzazz

Why settle for a plain old chop or tenderloin when you can enjoy one of these creative choices? Slow-cooked Honey-Soy Appetizer Ribs take some effort, but the results are meltingly tender and rich. You'll find most of the ingredients in your pantry.

Honey-Soy Appetizer Ribs
family favorite • make ahead
MAKES 8 APPETIZER SERVINGS;
PREP: 15 MIN.; **COOK:** 30 MIN.;
GRILL: 1 HR., 45 MIN.; **STAND:** 10 MIN.

Have the butcher cut the ribs in half crosswise to make appetizer-size ribs. You can prepare the ribs through Step 2 the day before you plan to cook them. Cover and chill overnight. You may need to grill the ribs a little longer to compensate for the fact that they are cold.

2 slabs pork spareribs (about 4 lb.)
1 cup honey
⅓ cup soy sauce
3 Tbsp. sherry (optional)
2 tsp. garlic powder
½ tsp. dried crushed red pepper
Garnishes: sesame seeds, thinly sliced
   green onions
Quick Asian Barbecue Sauce (optional)

1. Rinse and pat ribs dry. If desired, remove thin membrane from back of ribs by slicing into it with a knife and then pulling it off. (This will make ribs more tender.)
2. Bring ribs and water to cover to a boil in a large Dutch oven over medium-high heat; reduce heat to medium, and simmer 30 minutes. Drain and pat dry. Place ribs in a 13- x 9-inch baking dish.
3. Stir together honey and next 4 ingredients; pour over ribs.
4. Light 1 side of grill, heating to 350° to 400° (medium-high) heat; leave other side unlit. Arrange ribs over unlit side of grill, reserving sauce in dish. Grill, covered with grill lid, 45 minutes.

Reposition rib slabs, placing slab closest to heat source away from heat and moving other slab closer to heat. Grill, covered with grill lid, 45 minutes to 1 hour or until tender, repositioning ribs and basting with reserved sauce every 20 minutes. Remove ribs from grill, and let stand 10 minutes. Cut ribs, slicing between bones. Garnish, if desired. Serve with Quick Asian Barbecue Sauce, if desired.

Quick Asian Barbecue Sauce:
MAKES ½ CUP; **PREP:** 5 MIN.

1. Stir together ½ cup barbecue sauce, 2 Tbsp. soy sauce, and 1 tsp. Asian sriracha hot chili sauce.

Pork Tenderloin-and-Tomato Salad
family favorite
MAKES 4 SERVINGS; **PREP:** 15 MIN.,
COOK: 20 MIN., **BAKE:** 15 MIN.,
STAND: 12 MIN.

Save the crumbled bacon from the dressing to scatter over the salad.

1 (1-lb.) pork tenderloin
1 Tbsp. coarsely ground pepper
¾ tsp. salt
2 Tbsp. olive oil
1 (5-oz.) package spring mix, thoroughly
   washed
3 large tomatoes, cut into ½-inch-thick
   slices
Warm Bacon Vinaigrette
Garnish: cooked and crumbled bacon

1. Remove silver skin from tenderloin, leaving a thin layer of fat.
2. Preheat oven to 400°. Rub pepper and salt over pork. Cook pork in hot oil in a large skillet over medium-high heat 5 minutes on all sides or until browned. Transfer pork to a 13- x 9-inch pan.
3. Bake at 400° for 15 minutes or until a meat thermometer inserted into thickest portion registers 155°. Let stand 10 to 12 minutes or until thermometer registers 160°.
4. Cut pork into ¼-inch-thick slices. Divide greens among 4 plates; arrange tomato slices and pork over greens. Serve immediately with Warm Bacon Vinaigrette. Garnish, if desired.

Warm Bacon Vinaigrette:
fast fixin's
MAKES ABOUT 1½ CUPS; **PREP:** 10 MIN.,
COOK: 14 MIN.

4 bacon slices
4 Tbsp. minced shallot
2 Tbsp. minced garlic
3 Tbsp. brown sugar
6 Tbsp. orange juice
5 Tbsp. balsamic vinegar
3 Tbsp. coarse grained mustard
⅓ cup olive oil
½ tsp. salt

1. Cook bacon in a large skillet over medium-high heat 8 to 10 minutes or until crisp; remove bacon, and drain on paper towels, reserving 2 Tbsp. drippings in skillet. Crumble bacon, and reserve for another use.
2. Cook shallots and garlic in hot drippings over medium heat, stirring occasionally, 3 minutes or until tender. Add brown sugar, and cook, stirring constantly, 1 minute or until sugar is dissolved.
3. Process garlic mixture, orange juice, and next 4 ingredients in a blender until combined.

— JANE ALVARADO, DALLAS, TEXAS

Pork-and-Pasta With Gorgonzola Cream

family favorite • fast fixin's

MAKES 4 SERVINGS; **PREP:** 20 MIN., **COOK:** 9 MIN.

1 (1-lb.) pork tenderloin
1 tsp. salt
½ tsp. dried oregano
½ tsp. dried basil
¼ tsp. pepper
¼ tsp. garlic powder
1 (12-oz.) package fettuccine
2 Tbsp. butter
2 Tbsp. balsamic vinegar
Gorgonzola Cream

1. Remove silver skin from tenderloin, leaving a thin layer of fat. Cut pork into 8 (¾-inch) medallions. Combine salt and next 4 ingredients. Sprinkle medallions with salt mixture.
2. Prepare pasta according to package directions.
3. Meanwhile, melt butter in a large nonstick skillet over medium-high heat; add medallions, and cook 2 to 3 minutes on each side or until lightly browned. Reduce heat to medium; stir in vinegar. Cook pork 1 to 1½ minutes on each side or until meat is done. Serve medallions over hot cooked pasta with Gorgonzola Cream.

Gorgonzola Cream:

MAKES ABOUT 1½ CUPS; **PREP:** 5 MIN., **COOK:** 5 MIN.

1. Melt 2 Tbsp. butter in a small skillet over low heat; stir in 1 cup half-and-half and ½ cup crumbled Gorgonzola cheese, stirring until cheese is melted.

—**MARLA CLARK**, MORIARTY, NEW MEXICO

Asian Pork Wraps

family favorite • fast fixin's

MAKES 8 SERVINGS; **PREP:** 15 MIN.

We streamlined these wraps by using bottled Asian dressing and pork from a local barbecue joint.

¾ cup low-fat sesame-ginger dressing
2 Tbsp. creamy peanut butter
1 tsp. dried crushed red pepper
1 lb. shredded barbecued pork without sauce
¾ cup dry roasted peanuts, coarsely chopped
8 (10-inch) burrito-size flour tortillas
1 head napa cabbage, shredded (about 8 cups)
1 (11-oz.) can mandarin oranges, drained
3 green onions, sliced
2 Tbsp. chopped fresh cilantro
2 Tbsp. chopped fresh mint

1. Whisk together sesame-ginger dressing and next 2 ingredients until smooth.
2. Drizzle half of dressing mixture over pork, tossing to combine. Stir in peanuts.
3. Place tortillas between damp paper towels. Microwave at HIGH 45 seconds; keep warm.
4. Place cabbage and next 4 ingredients in a large bowl; drizzle with remaining half of dressing mixture, tossing to coat.
5. Spoon about ½ cup pork mixture and ½ cup cabbage mixture just below center of each tortilla. Fold bottom third of tortillas up and over filling, just until covered. Fold left and right sides of tortillas over, and roll up.
Note: For testing purposes only, we used Newman's Own Lighten Up Low Fat Sesame Ginger Dressing.

Fast Sides

Stretch supper in a hurry with these tasty choices. Ten-minute Orange-Curry Carrots are ready by the time you set the table, while both Roasted Cauliflower and Lemon Slaw offer fast prep with hands-off time in the oven or fridge. Serve any of them with an entrée of your choosing for a satisfying meal.

Roasted Cauliflower

family favorite

MAKES 4 SERVINGS; **PREP:** 15 MIN., **BAKE:** 30 MIN.

Baking caramelizes the sugars, adding delicious flavor to this so-good-for-you vegetable. Even the choosiest children will have a hard time resisting the appeal of this easy-to-prepare side. Cut the head into "fans," drizzle with oil, season, and pop them into the oven.

2 Tbsp. olive oil
1 head cauliflower (about 1½ lb.)
½ tsp. salt
¼ tsp. pepper

1. Preheat oven to 425°. Drizzle a 15- x 10-inch jelly-roll pan with 1 Tbsp. olive oil. Cut cauliflower vertically into ¼-inch-thick slices. Arrange in a single layer on prepared pan. Drizzle cauliflower with remaining olive oil; sprinkle with salt and pepper.
2. Bake at 425° for 25 to 30 minutes or until golden brown. Sprinkle with salt to taste.

Spice up your food with this simple recipe. Black-eyed peas, collard greens, and just about anything fried (chicken, fish, or green tomatoes) will benefit from the easy, homemade heat.

Hot Pepper Sauce

make ahead

PREP: 10 MIN., **COOK:** 5 MIN., **STAND:** 5 MIN., **CHILL:** 3 WEEKS.

1. Fill 1 (14-oz.) glass jar with 1 cup red and green Thai chile peppers, stemmed, filling to about 1 inch from top of jar.
2. Bring 1 cup cider vinegar, 1 tsp. salt, and 1 tsp. sugar to a boil in a small saucepan over medium heat, stirring until salt and sugar are dissolved (about 2 to 3 minutes). Remove from heat, and let stand 5 minutes.
3. Pour hot mixture over peppers in jar. Cover and chill 3 weeks. Store in refrigerator up to 6 months.
Note: Chilling for 3 weeks allows the peppers to fire up the vinegar mixture. The longer it sits, the spicier it becomes. Remember to wear rubber gloves when filling the jars with peppers.

Easy Creamy Spinach

family favorite • fast fixin's

MAKES 6 SERVINGS; **PREP:** 10 MIN., **COOK:** 7 MIN.

We streamlined this rich dish inspired by reader Georgette Dugas by using frozen chopped onions and spinach.

2 (9-oz.) packages frozen chopped spinach, thawed
¼ cup frozen chopped onions, thawed
2 Tbsp. butter
1 garlic clove, minced
1 (6-oz.) package spreadable Swiss cheese
½ cup sour cream
½ tsp. salt
½ tsp. pepper

1. Drain thawed chopped spinach and thawed chopped onions well, pressing between paper towels.

2. Melt butter in a large skillet over medium heat; add spinach, onions, and minced garlic, and cook, stirring often, 3 minutes or until tender. Stir in Swiss cheese and next 3 ingredients until smooth (about 4 minutes). Serve immediately.

—**GEORGETTE DUGAS**, CROWLEY, LOUISIANA

Note: For testing purposes only, we used The Laughing Cow Original Creamy Swiss Flavor Spreadable Cheese Wedges.

Easy Creamy Collards: Substitute 1 (16-oz.) bag frozen chopped collard greens, thawed, for spinach and ½ cup milk for sour cream. Increase initial cook time to 8 minutes or until collards are cooked to desired tenderness. Prepare recipe as directed, stirring in 2 tsp. sugar with cheese.
Note: For testing purposes only, we used Pictsweet All Natural Chopped Collard Greens.

Lemon Slaw

make ahead

MAKES 6 SERVINGS; **PREP:** 10 MIN., **CHILL:** 2 HR.

The chilling time allows the flavors to develop and the cabbage to soften slightly.

1 cup mayonnaise
1 tsp. lemon zest
2 Tbsp. fresh lemon juice
2 Tbsp. rice wine vinegar
2 tsp. sugar
1 tsp. salt
1 tsp. paprika
½ tsp. coarsely ground pepper
½ tsp. Worcestershire sauce
2 (16-oz.) packages shredded coleslaw mix

1. Stir together first 9 ingredients in a large bowl until blended; add coleslaw mix, tossing to coat. Cover and chill 2 hours.

—**MARSHALL HALL**, KNOXVILLE, TENNESSEE

Orange-Curry Carrots

family favorite • fast fixin's

MAKES 4 SERVINGS; **PREP:** 10 MIN.

Place 1 (1-lb.) package crinkle-cut carrots and 3 Tbsp. water in a microwave-safe bowl. Cover bowl tightly with plastic wrap; fold back a small edge to allow steam to escape. Microwave at HIGH 5 minutes or until tender. Drain. Stir together ⅓ cup orange marmalade, 1 tsp. curry powder, and ½ tsp. salt. Toss gently with hot carrots.

Healthy Living.

Fall is a great time to entertain. Discover great recipes and healthy ideas for a tasting party and after-dinner drinks.

Party With Big Flavor

Excite your guests with this robust menu, using a new supermarket secret that makes entertaining easier than ever.

One bite of this menu made our Food staff fall instantly in love with a new kind of comfort food. You will too when you learn how easy it is to make these delicious dishes.

This crowd-pleasing party menu uses the newest line of nutritious Latin seasonings and rice and soup mixes created by Miami business partners Corina Mascaro and Celeste De Armas. "South American cuisine is where Italian food was 20 years ago," says Corina. "It's definitely becoming more familiar to the public—and it's healthy." For these reasons, the two women decided to bring the Nueva Cocina brand to supermarket shelves, hoping to inspire consumers. "We want to make everyday Latin food accessible to everyone," explains Corina.

Best of all, these products are all-natural and sport significantly lower sodium and fat than other seasoning mixes. Serve these easy dishes as smaller appetizer portions, or convert hearty Lean Green Lettuce Tacos and Party-Style Pork Empanada into supper servings—either way, they're delicious. Try them, and tell us what you think.

Prosciutto-Wrapped Mango Bites

fast fixin's • make ahead

MAKES 8 APPETIZER SERVINGS; **PREP:** 20 MIN.

You might want to double this recipe—these appetizers disappear fast. Ask for paper-thin slices of meat at the deli counter. To ease prep, look for a package of presliced mango in the produce section. We do not recommend jarred mango slices—they're too soft. (Pictued on page 179)

1 ripe mango, peeled
1½ cups loosely packed arugula
1 (1-oz.) package fresh basil
4 very thin prosciutto or country ham slices
¼ tsp. coarsely ground pepper

1. Cut mango into ¼- to ½-inch slices (about 16). Place 1 mango slice on top of 3 arugula leaves and 1 to 2 basil leaves.
2. Cut each prosciutto slice lengthwise into 4 strips. Wrap center of each mango bundle with 1 prosciutto strip.

Arrange on a serving platter, and sprinkle with pepper.
Note: To make ahead, prepare recipe as directed. Cover bites with damp paper towels, and chill 30 minutes.

Per serving (2 bites): Calories 29; Fat 0.6g (sat 0.2g, mono 0.04g, poly 0.1g); Protein 1.6g; Carb 5.2g; Fiber 0.8g; Chol 1.9mg; Iron 0.4mg; Sodium 68mg; Calc 30mg

Prosciutto-Wrapped Melon Bites: Substitute half of 1 small cantaloupe or honeydew for mango. Proceed with recipe as directed.

Proscuitto-Wrapped Pear Bites: Substitute 1 ripe pear, unpeeled, for mango. Cut pear as directed in Step 1. Toss together pear slices and ½ cup lemon-lime soft drink to prevent browning; drain. Proceed with recipe as directed.

Proscuitto-Wrapped Apple Bites: Substitute 1 Gala apple, unpeeled, for mango. Cut apple as directed in Step 1. Toss together apple slices and ½ cup lemon-lime soft drink to prevent browning; drain. Proceed with recipe as directed.
Note: To make ahead, prepare recipe as directed. Cover bites with damp paper towels, and chill 30 minutes.

Healthy Benefits

- Mangoes contain comforting enzymes that can help control stomach acid and sooth the painful symptoms of reflux.
- Cucumbers can help cool down high blood pressure, give your skin a radiant glow, and add more fiber to your day.

Healthy Living

Cuban Black Bean Dip
make ahead

MAKES ABOUT 2 CUPS; **PREP:** 15 MIN., **COOK:** 32 MIN., **COOL:** 30 MIN., **CHILL:** 2 HR.

We like Mexican sour cream for its rich texture. One tablespoon yields big flavor, so it's okay to indulge. Look for it in the dairy section of larger supermarkets.

1 (6-oz.) package Cuban-style black bean soup mix
1 Tbsp. olive oil
2 Tbsp. lime juice
½ tsp. cumin
¼ tsp. ground chipotle chile powder
2 Tbsp. Mexican crema or regular sour cream*
Garnishes: diced tomatoes, thinly sliced green onions
Fresh vegetable slices

1. Bring soup mix, olive oil, and 2½ cups water to a boil in a medium saucepan over high heat, stirring occasionally. Cover, reduce heat to low, and simmer, stirring occasionally, 25 minutes. Uncover and cook 5 to 7 minutes or until thick and beans are tender. Let cool 30 minutes.
2. Process soup mixture, lime juice, cumin, and chile powder in a food processor 20 seconds or until smooth. Spoon mixture into a serving bowl. Cover and chill 2 hours before serving. Store in refrigerator in an airtight container up to 2 days. Spread center of dip with Mexican crema, and garnish, if desired. Serve with fresh vegetable slices.

—ADAPTED FROM NUEVA COCINA WEB SITE

*Light sour cream may be substituted.
Note: For testing purposes only, we used Nueva Cocina Cuban Style Black Bean Soup Mix and Olé Crema Mexicana.

Per ¼-cup serving: Calories 94; Fat 2.5g (sat 0.7g, mono 1.3g, poly 0.3g); Protein 4.7g; Carb 14.2g; Fiber 4.6g; Chol 1.9mg; Iron 0.1mg; Sodium 352mg; Calc 7mg

Party-Style Pork Empanada
make ahead

MAKES 8 APPETIZER SERVINGS;
PREP: 25 MIN., **COOK:** 17 MIN., **BAKE:** 22 MIN.

(Pictured on page 179)

¼ cup slivered or sliced almonds
¾ lb. pork tenderloin (about 1 small tenderloin)
1 (1.25-oz.) envelope picadillo seasoning
½ medium-size sweet onion, chopped
1 small red bell pepper, chopped
1 Tbsp. olive oil
½ cup golden raisins
3 Tbsp. fresh lime juice
¼ cup chopped fresh cilantro
¼ cup light sour cream
½ tsp. pepper
1 (11-oz.) can refrigerated French bread dough
1 large egg, lightly beaten
Vegetable cooking spray
½ tsp. cumin seeds (optional)
Salsa
Garnish: lime wedges

1. Heat almonds in a large nonstick skillet over medium-low heat, stirring often, 4 to 6 minutes or until toasted and fragrant.
2. Preheat oven to 375°. Cut pork into ½-inch cubes. Toss together pork and picadillo seasoning.
3. Sauté onion and bell pepper in hot oil in skillet over medium-high heat 5 minutes or until tender. Add pork mixture, and sauté 6 minutes or until browned. Stir in raisins and lime juice, and cook 30 seconds. Remove from heat. Stir in almonds, cilantro, sour cream, and pepper.
4. Unroll dough on a lightly floured surface. Gently stretch dough into a 14- x 12-inch rectangle. Spoon pork mixture onto dough, leaving a 1½-inch border. Lightly brush edges of dough with egg, and roll up, starting at 1 long side and ending seam side down.
5. Carefully place dough, seam side down, on a baking sheet coated with cooking spray. Bring ends of roll together to form a ring, pinching edges together to seal. Lightly brush top and sides of dough with egg. Sprinkle with cumin seeds, if desired.
6. Bake at 375° for 18 to 22 minutes or until golden brown. Serve warm with salsa. Garnish, if desired.
Note: For testing purposes only, we used Nueva Cocina Picadillo Beef Seasoning and Pillsbury Refrigerated Crusty French Loaf. To make ahead, prepare recipe as directed through Step 5. Cover with lightly greased plastic wrap, and chill 2 hours. Proceed with recipe as directed.

Per serving: Calories 251; Fat 7.3g (sat 1.8g, mono 3.6g, poly 1.1g); Protein 14.4g; Carb 32.5g; Fiber 1.2g; Chol 52.6mg; Iron 2mg; Sodium 473mg; Calc 24mg

Lean Green Lettuce Tacos
fast fixin's

MAKES 8 APPETIZER SERVINGS;
PREP: 15 MIN., **COOK:** 11 MIN.

Queso fresco is Spanish for "fresh cheese." It has a soft and crumbly texture (similar to feta) with mild flavor. You can find it in the dairy section of larger supermarkets. (Pictured on page 178)

1 small zucchini, diced
1 small yellow squash, diced
½ lb. extra-lean ground beef
1 Tbsp. olive oil
1 (1.25-oz.) package taco fresco seasoning
1 (8-oz.) can no-salt-added tomato sauce
2 Tbsp. chopped fresh cilantro
1 Tbsp. lime juice
8 romaine lettuce leaves
Toppings: diced tomato, chopped fresh cilantro, chopped red onion, crumbled queso fresco*

1. Sauté first 3 ingredients in hot oil in a large nonstick skillet over medium-high heat 5 to 6 minutes or until meat crumbles and is no longer pink. Stir in seasoning until blended; cook 1 minute.
2. Reduce heat to low; stir in tomato sauce, and cook, stirring often, 3 to 4 minutes or until thoroughly heated. Remove from heat, and stir in cilantro and lime juice.
3. Serve meat mixture in romaine lettuce leaves with desired toppings.

—ADAPTED FROM NUEVA COCINA WEB SITE
*2% reduced-fat shredded Cheddar or Monterey Jack cheese may be substituted for queso fresco.
Note: For testing purposes only, we used Nueva Cocina Taco Fresco Ground Beef Seasoning.

Per serving: Calories 93; Fat 4.5g (sat 1.3g, mono 2.4g, poly 0.4g); Protein 6.7g; Carb 6.2g; Fiber 1g; Chol 10mg; Iron 1mg; Sodium 227mg; Calc 14mg

After-Dinner Delight

Coffee is making a comeback when it comes to our health. Find out what America's favorite morning drink has to offer. You'll want to serve these treats at your next get-together.

Creamy 100-Calorie Coffee
fast fixin's

MAKES ABOUT 4 (1-CUP) SERVINGS;
PREP: 15 MIN., **COOK:** 10 MIN.

2½ cups hot espresso or strong brewed coffee
2 cups 1% low-fat milk
3 Tbsp. sugar
1 tsp. vanilla extract

1. Whisk together all ingredients in a medium saucepan over medium heat, and cook, whisking occasionally, 10 minutes or until steamy.

—ADAPTED FROM AMERICAN DAIRY ASSOCIATION

⊂ TIP ⊃

Warm up with Creamy 100-Calorie Coffee. Froth up some hot, low-fat milk with a portable, handheld frother, available at most super-stores for about $10. Or have your coffee cold over ice.

Creamy 100-Calorie Iced
Coffee: Prepare recipe as directed. Let cool completely (about 20 minutes). Pour 1½ cups coffee mixture into compartments of 1 ice cube tray, and freeze 4 hours or until firm. Chill remaining coffee mixture until ready to serve. Place coffee ice cubes in a pitcher, and pour remaining coffee mixture over ice cubes. Serve immediately. Prep: 15 min., Cook: 10 min., Cool: 20 min., Freeze: 4 hr.

Per 9-oz. serving (about 1 cup): Calories 100; Fat 1.5g (sat 0.9g, mono 0.4g, poly 0.1g); Protein 5g; Carb 16.3g; Fiber 0g; Chol 5mg; Iron 0.1mg; Sodium 74mg; Calc 178mg

Café Con Leche Custard Cups
make ahead

MAKES 8 (½-CUP) SERVINGS;
PREP: 10 MIN., **COOK:** 12 MIN., **COOL:** 30 MIN.

These custard cups aren't heavy on the coffee, but they are luscious, low-fat treats for any occasion. Add chocolate espresso beans for an antioxidant-rich garnish.

⅓ cup all-purpose flour
⅛ tsp. salt
2½ cups 2% reduced-fat milk
1 (14-oz.) can fat-free sweetened condensed milk
2 egg yolks
2 Tbsp. instant coffee granules
2 tsp. vanilla extract
¾ cup thawed reduced-fat whipped topping
Garnishes: chopped and whole chocolate-covered espresso beans, 100-calorie shortbread cookies

1. Combine flour and salt in a 2-qt. heavy nonaluminum saucepan. Whisk in reduced-fat milk and next 3 ingredients, whisking until smooth. Cook over medium heat, whisking constantly, 10 to 12 minutes or until thickened. Remove from heat; stir in vanilla.
2. Fill a large bowl with ice; place saucepan in ice, and whisk custard occasionally until completely cool (about 30 minutes).
3. Spoon ½ cup custard into each of 8 (5-oz.) cups or glasses. Top each with 1 to 2 Tbsp. whipped topping, filling completely. Scrape top with a knife to level whipped topping. Garnish, if desired.

Note: To make ahead, pour cooled custard into a gallon-size zip-top plastic bag, gently pressing out excess air (to prevent a film from forming). Seal bag, and chill up to 24 hours. To serve, snip off 1 corner of bag, and pipe custard into serving cups.

Note: For testing purposes only, we used Nabisco 100 Calorie Packs Lorna Doone Shortbread Cookie Crisps.

Per ½-cup serving: Calories 233; Fat 3.5g (sat 2.1g, mono 1g, poly 0.3g); Protein 7.9g; Carb 41.1g; Fiber 0.2g; Chol 63.4mg; Iron 0.5mg; Sodium 136mg; Calc 233mg

Healthy Benefits

- Coffee is one of the best sources of disease-fighting antioxidants.
- Many studies reveal that drinking coffee on a regular basis reduces the risk of Parkinson's disease by 80%, colon cancer by 25%, and diabetes by up to 50%.

Simmer and Serve

Enjoy comfort in a bowl. These hearty, slow-cooked meals will remind you of favorite tastes from home.

Peppered Beef Soup
freezeable • make ahead
MAKES 12 CUPS; **PREP:** 20 MIN.;
COOK: 8 HR., 8 MIN.

This soup is reminiscent of a pot roast with all the fixings. The bread bowls are toasty on the outside and infused with broth on the inside. Freeze leftovers in an airtight container up to three months. Add a bit of canned broth when reheating to reach desired consistency. (Pictured on page 185)

1 (4-lb.) sirloin tip beef roast
½ cup all-purpose flour
2 Tbsp. canola oil
1 medium-size red onion, thinly sliced
6 garlic cloves, minced
2 large baking potatoes, peeled and diced
1 (16-oz.) package baby carrots
2 (12-oz.) bottles lager beer*
2 Tbsp. balsamic vinegar
2 Tbsp. Worcestershire sauce
2 Tbsp. dried parsley flakes
1 Tbsp. beef bouillon granules
1½ to 3 tsp. freshly ground pepper
4 bay leaves
Salt to taste
Toasted Bread Bowls (optional)

1. Rinse beef roast, and pat dry. Cut a 1-inch-deep cavity in the shape of an "X" on top of roast. (Do not cut all the way through roast.) Dredge roast in all-purpose flour; shake off excess.
2. Cook roast in hot oil in a Dutch oven over medium-high heat 1 to 2 minutes on each side or until lightly browned.
3. Place roast in a 6-qt. slow cooker. Stuff cavity with sliced red onion and

minced garlic; top roast with potatoes and baby carrots. Pour beer, balsamic vinegar, and Worcestershire sauce into slow cooker. Sprinkle with parsley, bouillon, and ground pepper. Add bay leaves to liquid in slow cooker.
4. Cover and cook on LOW 7 to 8 hours or until fork-tender. Remove bay leaves. Shred roast using two forks. Season with salt to taste. Serve in Toasted Bread Bowls, if desired.

—**LISA HURST**, BLACKSBURG, VIRGINIA

*3 cups low-sodium beef broth may be substituted.

Toasted Bread Bowls
fast fixin's • make ahead
MAKES 6 BOWLS; **PREP:** 10 MIN.,
BAKE: 10 MIN.

Make the easiest homemade croutons with the soft centers from these bread bowls. Preheat oven to 400°. Cut the reserved centers into 1-inch cubes; coat lightly with olive oil cooking spray. Place in a zip-top plastic bag; add 1 tsp. desired dried herbs or seasonings. Seal bag, and shake to coat. Spread bread cubes in a single layer on a baking sheet, and coat again with cooking spray. Bake at 400°, stirring occasionally, 7 to 9 minutes or until lightly toasted. Cool completely. Store in an airtight container for three days. (Pictured on page 185)

6 (5- to 6-inch) artisan bread rounds*
Vegetable cooking spray
2 Tbsp. grated Parmesan cheese

1. Preheat oven to 350°. Cut ½ to 1½ inches from top of each bread round; scoop out centers, leaving ½-inch-thick shells. Reserve soft centers for another use. Lightly coat bread shells and, if desired, cut sides of tops, with cooking spray. Place, cut sides up, on baking sheets. Sprinkle with cheese.
2. Bake at 350° for 8 to 10 minutes or until toasted.

*6 (4-inch) hoagie rolls may be substituted for bread rounds.

Mexican Pork Stew
make ahead

MAKES ABOUT 11 CUPS; **PREP:** 25 MIN.;
COOK: 1 HR., 31 MIN.

6 green onions, trimmed
1 bunch cilantro
Kitchen string
2½ lb. boneless pork shoulder
    roast
1 tsp. salt
1 tsp. pepper
3 garlic cloves
1 (10-oz.) can mild red enchilada
    sauce
2 medium-size baking potatoes,
    peeled and diced
10 (5½-inch) soft taco-size corn tortillas
2 (11-oz.) cans yellow corn with red
    and green bell peppers
Salt to taste
Toppings: lemon wedges, diced radishes,
    diced onion, shredded cabbage

1. Tie green onions and cilantro together with kitchen string. Trim and discard fat from pork, and cut pork into ¼-inch pieces. Season with salt and pepper.
2. Cook pork, in 3 batches, in a large Dutch oven over medium-high heat 5 to 7 minutes or until browned. Bring pork, garlic, and 6 cups water to a boil; skim fat, and discard. Cover, reduce heat to low, and simmer 30 minutes or until meat is tender. Stir in onion-and-cilantro bundle, enchilada sauce, and potatoes. Bring to a boil over medium-high heat; reduce heat to low, and simmer 20 minutes or just until potatoes are tender.
3. Meanwhile, heat tortillas, 1 at a time, in a hot nonstick skillet over medium-high heat 20 to 30 seconds on each side. Wrap tortillas in a towel to keep warm.
4. Remove and discard onion-and-cilantro bundle. Increase heat to medium. Stir in corn, and cook, uncovered, stirring occasionally, 8 to 10 minutes or until thoroughly heated. Season with salt to taste.

5. Serve soup with desired toppings and warm tortillas.

—GUADALUPE CORTES, ACWORTH, GEORGIA

Note: Store any leftovers in an airtight container in the refrigerator up to 2 days. When reheating, add enough water or canned broth to reach desired consistency.

Caribbean Black Bean Soup
freezeable • make ahead

MAKES 6 CUPS; **PREP:** 20 MIN.;
COOK: 2 HR., 14 MIN.

½ cup diced onion
2 Tbsp. brown sugar
1 Tbsp. chili powder
1 Tbsp. ground cumin
1 tsp. ground coriander
1 Tbsp. olive oil
1 tsp. minced garlic
1 (14-oz.) can fire-roasted diced tomatoes
1 (8-oz.) can tomato sauce
1½ cups chicken broth
½ cup orange juice
¼ cup tomato paste
1 lb. chicken breast tenders
2 (15-oz.) cans black beans, drained
½ tsp. salt
Toppings: diced avocado, chopped fresh
    cilantro

1. Sauté onion and next 4 ingredients in hot oil in a Dutch oven over medium heat 2 to 3 minutes or until onion is tender and fragrant. Add garlic, and cook 1 minute.
2. Stir in tomatoes and next 4 ingredients until well blended. Stir in chicken. Cover, reduce heat to low, and cook 2 hours. Shred chicken with two forks in Dutch oven. Add black beans, and cook 10 more minutes. Stir in salt. Serve with desired toppings.

—ANNA GINSBERG, AUSTIN, TEXAS

Note: Store any leftovers in an airtight container in the refrigerator up to 2 days, or freeze up to 3 months. Thaw in refrigerator. When reheating, add water or canned broth to reach desired consistency.

Corn-and-Bacon Soup
family favorite

MAKES ABOUT 8 CUPS; **PREP:** 15 MIN.,
COOK: 42 MIN.

We do not recommend freezing this recipe because it becomes too grainy.

4 bacon slices
1 medium onion, chopped (about 1 cup)
½ green bell pepper, chopped (about 1 cup)
1 garlic clove, minced
2 Tbsp. all-purpose flour
2 medium-size baking potatoes, peeled and
    cubed (about 3 cups)*
4 cups chicken broth
1 (16-oz.) package frozen whole kernel corn
½ tsp. salt
¼ tsp. pepper
1 (10-oz.) can diced tomatoes and green
    chiles
1 cup (4 oz.) shredded sharp Cheddar
    cheese
Salt to taste

1. Cook bacon in a Dutch oven over medium heat 5 minutes or until crisp. Remove bacon, and drain on paper towels, reserving drippings in Dutch oven. Crumble bacon.
2. Sauté onion, bell pepper, and garlic in hot drippings over medium-high heat 5 minutes or until tender. Add flour, and cook, stirring constantly, 1 minute.
3. Stir in potatoes and next 4 ingredients, and bring to a boil. Reduce heat to low, and simmer, stirring often, 30 minutes or until potatoes are tender.
4. Stir in tomatoes and green chiles and cheese; simmer 1 minute or until cheese is melted. Season with salt to taste. Serve with crumbled bacon.

—GEORGIE O'NEILL-MASSA,
GEORGETOWN, FLORIDA

*3 cups frozen country-style hash browns may be substituted.

Easy Brunswick Stew

southernliving.com favorite

MAKES 8 SERVINGS; **PREP:** 15 MIN.,
COOK: 12 HR.

*Cooking on LOW heat for a long time
makes the meat extremely tender, so it
shreds easily; HIGH heat yields a less
tender product.*

3 lb. boneless pork shoulder roast (Boston
    Butt)
3 medium-size new potatoes, peeled and
    chopped
1 large onion, chopped
1 (28-oz.) can crushed tomatoes
1 (18-oz.) bottle barbecue sauce
1 (14-oz.) can chicken broth
1 (9-oz.) package frozen baby lima beans,
    thawed
1 (9-oz.) package frozen corn, thawed
6 Tbsp. brown sugar
1 tsp. salt

1. Trim roast and cut into 2-inch
pieces. Stir together all ingredients in
a 6-qt. slow cooker.
2. Cover and cook on LOW 10 to 12
hours or until potatoes are fork-tender.
Remove pork with a slotted spoon, and
shred. Return shredded pork to slow
cooker, and stir well.

Harvest
Salads

September brings a bounty of
late-summer produce along
with the first crisp tastes of
fall. You'll enjoy them all in
this colorful collection of
easy-to-serve dishes.

Honey-Cinnamon
Vinaigrette

fast fixin's • make ahead

MAKES ABOUT 1 CUP; **PREP:** 10 MIN.

*Shelf magic at its best, this quick-and-
easy dressing adds a sweet note to some
of our favorite fall salads. It's especially
good with the peppery bite of fresh arugula topped with sliced apples and pears
or warm roasted root vegetables.*

1/3 cup cider vinegar
1/3 cup honey
1 tsp. ground cinnamon
1 tsp. dry mustard
1/2 tsp. salt
1/4 cup canola oil

1. Whisk together first 5 ingredients in
a small bowl. Add oil in a slow, steady
stream, whisking constantly until smooth.
Serve immediately, or cover and chill
until ready to serve. Store in an airtight
container in refrigerator up to 2 weeks.

—**INSPIRED BY CLAUDIA GOODWIN,**
DALEVILLE, VIRGINIA

Cranberry-Nectarine Salad

MAKES 4 SERVINGS; **PREP:** 10 MIN.,
BAKE: 6 MIN., **COOL:** 15 MIN., **STAND:** 5 MIN.

(Pictured on page 184)

1 (3-oz.) package Oriental-flavored ramen
    noodle soup mix
1/2 cup dried cranberries
1 cup hot water
1/3 cup canola oil
1 Tbsp. light brown sugar
2 Tbsp. balsamic vinegar
2 Tbsp. rice wine vinegar
1 Tbsp. soy sauce
1 (10-oz.) package gourmet mixed salad
    greens, thoroughly washed
3 large nectarines, peeled and cut in
    wedges
1/2 cup coarsely chopped walnuts
1 (4-oz.) package crumbled feta cheese

1. Preheat oven to 350°. Reserve flavor packet from soup mix. Crumble

noodles, and place in a single layer in a
shallow pan.
2. Bake at 350° for 5 to 6 minutes or
until toasted, stirring occasionally.
Cool completely in pan on a wire rack
(about 15 minutes).
3. Place cranberries in a small bowl;
add 1 cup hot water. Let stand 5 minutes; drain.
4. Whisk together reserved soup
flavor packet, canola oil, and next 4
ingredients in a large bowl. Add ramen
noodles, cranberries, gourmet greens,
and next 3 ingredients, tossing gently to
coat. Serve immediately.

—**DONNA TANNER,** ALEXANDER, ARKANSAS

Sugar Snap-Snow Pea
Salad

fast fixin's

MAKES 4 SERVINGS; **PREP:** 10 MIN.,
COOK: 7 MIN.

1 1/2 cups trimmed fresh sugar snap peas
    (about 5 oz.)
1 1/2 cups trimmed fresh snow peas
    (about 6 oz.)
1 Tbsp. soy sauce
1 Tbsp. pomegranate or cranberry juice
1 Tbsp. white vinegar
1 Tbsp. canola oil
2 tsp. minced fresh ginger
1 tsp. sugar
1 Tbsp. black or regular sesame seeds
1 cup frozen baby English peas, thawed

1. Arrange sugar snap peas and snow
peas in a steamer basket over boiling
water. Cover and steam 1 to 2 minutes or
until crisp-tender. Plunge peas into ice
water to stop the cooking process; drain.
2. Whisk together soy sauce and next 5
ingredients in a large bowl.
3. Heat sesame seeds in a small nonstick
skillet over medium-low heat, stirring
often, 4 to 5 minutes or until toasted and
fragrant. Add hot sesame seeds to soy
sauce mixture, stirring until blended.
Add sugar snap peas, snow peas, and
thawed English peas, tossing gently to
coat. Serve immediately.

—**JANINE WASHLE,** SONORA, KENTUCKY

- Pennies a serving, toasted ramen noodles add a nutty crunch to salads and slaws.
- When fresh field peas are unavailable, frozen peas are our first choice for salads. Their texture is firmer and less starchy than canned peas, which are usually reconstituted from dried peas.
- After testing several similar recipes for broccoli salad, we noticed a big difference in flavor when the florets were cut into smaller pieces, which allows the dressing to evenly coat the ingredients rather than pool at the bottom of the bowl.
- Naturally crisp and sweet, broccoli stems add a delicious counterpoint to the florets. When making salads, cut the florets from the stem, and separate the florets into small pieces using the tip of a paring knife. Peel away the tough outer layer of the stems, and finely chop, or cut into 1-inch pieces and pulse several times in food processor.

Broccoli Salad With Lemon Pepper–Blue Cheese Dressing

make ahead

MAKES 8 SERVINGS; **PREP:** 20 MIN.,
COOK: 5 MIN., **CHILL:** 2 HR.

A sprinkling of sugar creates the sweet-sharp taste of a traditional broccoli salad dressing, but you can reduce the amount if desired.

½ cup pine nuts
1 (4-oz.) package crumbled blue
   cheese
½ cup reduced-fat mayonnaise
½ cup reduced-fat sour cream
2 Tbsp. sugar
1 Tbsp. lemon zest
¼ cup fresh lemon juice
2 tsp. freshly ground pepper
¼ tsp. salt
⅛ tsp. ground red pepper
6 cups chopped fresh broccoli (about 1½ lb.)
1½ cups chopped Gala apple (1 large apple)
¾ cup dried cherries

1. Heat pine nuts in a small nonstick skillet over medium-low heat, stirring often, 4 to 5 minutes or until toasted and fragrant.
2. Whisk together blue cheese crumbles and next 8 ingredients in a large

bowl; add broccoli, apple, and cherries, gently tossing to coat. Cover and chill 2 to 8 hours; stir in toasted pine nuts just before serving.

—SUSAN ORECKLIN, AUSTIN, TEXAS

Ham-and-Field Pea Salad

MAKES 8 SERVINGS; **PREP:** 20 MIN.,
COOL: 1 HR., **CHILL:** 8 HR., **COOK:** 5 MIN.

Combining a variety of field peas, such as black-eyed peas, speckled butter beans, and lady peas, gives additional color and texture to this tasty salad. We stirred in bits of sautéed ham just before serving, but it's equally good without.

3 cups fresh or frozen assorted
   field peas
¼ cup sugar
¼ cup cider vinegar
2 garlic cloves, minced
1 tsp. hot sauce
¾ tsp. salt
¾ tsp. pepper
¼ cup vegetable oil
1 green bell pepper, diced
½ small red onion, diced
1 celery rib, diced
1 cup chopped ham
1 tsp. vegetable oil

1. Prepare peas according to package directions; drain and let cool 1 hour.
2. Whisk together sugar and next 5 ingredients in a large bowl. Add ¼ cup oil in a slow, steady stream, whisking constantly until smooth. Add cooked field peas, bell pepper, onion, and celery, tossing to coat; cover and chill 8 hours.
3. Sauté ham in 1 tsp. hot oil in a small skillet over medium-high heat 4 to 5 minutes or until lightly browned. Stir into pea mixture just before serving.

—INSPIRED BY HARWANDA ROWELL, SPRING, TEXAS

The Best of the 'Wursts

Try this fail-proof technique for juicy results every time.

There's no doubt, the best way to eat fresh sausage is right off the grill. But it takes finesse to get the sausage cooked through without burning or drying out the casing. Try our method: Boil raw sausage in beer for a few minutes before grilling to add rich flavor and partially cook the meat inside. This decreases your grilling time and chances of burning the sausage. The result is a perfectly grilled, juicy link. Be sure to sample these delicious accompaniments too.

Apple-Avocado Relish
fast fixin's
MAKES 2 CUPS; **PREP:** 10 MIN.

Try this as a dip with tortilla chips, or serve it with grilled shrimp, fish, or pork chops.

2 medium-size ripe avocados, diced
1 Golden Delicious apple, peeled and diced
2 green onions, thinly sliced
1 Tbsp. chopped fresh cilantro
1 Tbsp. olive oil
2 tsp. horseradish
¼ tsp. salt
¼ tsp. pepper

1. Stir together all ingredients. Serve immediately, or cover and let stand 30 minutes before serving.

Grilled Sausages
family favorite
MAKES 4 SERVINGS; **PREP:** 10 MIN., **COOK:** 10 MIN., **STAND:** 10 MIN., **GRILL:** 20 MIN.

4 fresh pork sausages*
2 (12-oz.) bottles lager beer**
2 (8-inch) hoagie rolls
Sweet Pepper-Onion Relish

1. Preheat grill to 350° to 400° (medium-high). Bring sausages and beer to a boil in a Dutch oven over medium-high heat. Cover, remove from heat, and let stand 10 minutes. Drain.
2. Cut a ½-inch-deep wedge from top of each roll. Reserve wedges for another use, if desired. Cut rolls in half crosswise.
3. Grill sausages, covered with grill lid, over 350° to 400° (medium-high) heat 8 to 10 minutes on each side or to desired degree of doneness.

4. Place 1 sausage in each roll half. Spoon desired amount of Sweet Pepper-Onion Relish over each sausage.
*Chicken sausages may be substituted.
**4½ cups water may be substituted.
Note: For testing purposes only, we used Johnsonville Stadium Style Brats and Yuengling Traditional Lager.

Sweet Pepper-Onion Relish:
MAKES 5 CUPS; **PREP:** 20 MIN., **BAKE:** 45 MIN., **COOL:** 30 MIN.

This relish also tastes great on grilled chicken or pork. For a tasty appetizer, serve with sliced rounds of French bread and a soft, creamy cheese.

2 red bell peppers, seeded and diced
2 yellow bell peppers, seeded and diced
1 large yellow onion, diced
3 garlic cloves, minced
2 Tbsp. olive oil
2 Tbsp. balsamic vinegar
1 tsp. salt
½ tsp. dried thyme
½ tsp. dried crushed red pepper

1. Preheat oven to 400°. Stir together all ingredients, and pour into an 11- x 7-inch baking dish. Bake 45 minutes or until soft, stirring every 5 minutes. Transfer pepper mixture and any liquid to a bowl. Let cool 30 minutes or to room temperature. Store in an airtight container in refrigerator up to 3 days.

—**KENT KAPLAN,** BIRMINGHAM, ALABAMA

Orange-Sauerkraut Salad
make ahead
MAKES 6 SERVINGS; **PREP:** 10 MIN., **CHILL:** 4 HR.

1 (16-oz.) jar sauerkraut, rinsed and drained
2 large carrots, grated
1 small sweet onion, chopped
½ cup raisins
2 tsp. orange zest
2 Tbsp. fresh orange juice
½ cup sugar
¼ cup vegetable oil
Garnish: fresh orange slices

1. Stir together sauerkraut and next 5 ingredients.
2. Whisk together sugar and vegetable oil. Pour over sauerkraut mixture; stir well to combine. Cover and chill at least 4 hours or up to 2 days. Drain just before serving. Garnish, if desired.

—**CLAIRIECE GILBERT HUMPHREY,** CHARLOTTESVILLE, VIRGINIA

Apricot Torte
southernliving.com favorite
MAKES 12 SERVINGS; **PREP:** 25 MIN., **BAKE:** 12 MIN. PER BATCH, **CHILL:** 8 HR.

3 cups all-purpose flour
1 cup butter, softened
¾ cup granulated sugar
⅛ tsp. salt
1 large egg
2 cups sour cream
1½ cups powdered sugar
1 cup chopped pecans, toasted
1 tsp. vanilla extract
1 (8-oz.) jar apricot preserves
Powdered sugar (optional)
Whipped cream (optional)

1. Preheat oven to 350°. Pulse flour and next 3 ingredients in a food processor 7 or 8 times or until mixture is crumbly. Add egg, and pulse 4 or 5 times until dough forms. Divide dough into 7 equal portions, shaping each portion into a ball.
2. Roll each ball to a 9-inch circle on inverted greased 9-inch cakepans covered with parchment paper.
3. Bake, in batches, at 350° for 10 to 12 minutes or until golden. Cool on pans.
4. Beat sour cream and next 3 ingredients at medium speed with an electric mixer until combined; chill.
5. Process preserves in a food processor until smooth.
6. Spread 6 cookie layers alternately with about 3 Tbsp. sour cream mixture and 3 Tbsp. apricot preserves; stack. Top with remaining cookie layer; chill 8 hours. Sprinkle top with powdered sugar, if desired; pipe whipped cream around outer edge, if desired.

Best-Ever Apple Pie

You have to try it, and we're revealing all our tricks to help you succeed. You'll make a tall tower of fall's favorite fruit—apples—in a crust we promise is great. Associate Food Editor Shirley Harrington is divulging her mom's closely guarded, secret piecrust-making method for the first time. Plan ahead to cozy up in your kitchen, bake, and anticipate. We think you'll adore each forkful of this top-rated apple pie.

TIPS

Yes, we did use 4½ pounds of apples! Use your fingers to position wedges tightly together as you form a tall stack of the fruit.

Instead of brushing the top crust with beaten egg white or yolk or dusting it with flour, we used 1 Tbsp. of the juices that remain in the bottom of the bowl the apple mixture was in. Not only does this carry the filling flavor to the top crust, but it also gives the pie a beautiful finish.

Double Apple Pie With Cornmeal Crust

MAKES 8 SERVINGS; **PREP:** 30 MIN.;
STAND: 30 MIN.; **BAKE:** 1 HR., 20 MIN.;
COOL: 1 HR., 30 MIN.

Don't skip the apple jelly—it makes the baked pie juices taste rich. It also decreases the cloudiness that sometimes occurs with a flour-thickened apple pie filling. (Pictured on page 12)

2¼ lb. Granny Smith apples
2¼ lb. Braeburn apples
¼ cup all-purpose flour
2 Tbsp. apple jelly
1 Tbsp. fresh lemon juice
½ tsp. ground cinnamon
¼ tsp. salt
¼ tsp. ground nutmeg
⅓ cup sugar
Cornmeal Crust Dough
Wax paper
3 Tbsp. sugar
1 Tbsp. butter, cut into pieces
1 tsp. sugar
Brandy-Caramel Sauce

1. Preheat oven to 425°. Peel and core apples; cut into ½-inch-thick wedges. Place apples in a large bowl. Stir in next 7 ingredients. Let stand 30 minutes, gently stirring occasionally.
2. Place 1 Cornmeal Crust Dough disk on a lightly floured piece of wax paper; sprinkle dough lightly with flour. Top with another sheet of wax paper. Roll dough to about ⅛-inch thickness (about 11 inches wide).

3. Remove and discard top sheet of wax paper. Starting at 1 edge of dough, wrap dough around rolling pin, separating dough from bottom sheet of wax paper as you roll. Discard bottom sheet of wax paper. Place rolling pin over a 9-inch glass pie plate, and unroll dough over pie plate. Gently press dough into pie plate.
4. Stir apple mixture; reserve 1 Tbsp. juices. Spoon apples into crust, packing tightly and mounding in center. Pour remaining juices in bowl over apples. Sprinkle apples with 3 Tbsp. sugar; dot with butter.
5. Roll remaining Cornmeal Crust Dough disk as directed in Step 2, rolling dough to about ⅛-inch thickness (13 inches wide). Remove and discard wax paper, and place dough over filling; fold edges under, sealing to bottom crust, and crimp. Brush top of pie, excluding fluted edges, lightly with reserved 1 Tbsp. juices from apples; sprinkle with 1 tsp. sugar. Place pie on a jelly-roll pan. Cut 4 to 5 slits in top of pie for steam to escape.
6. Bake at 425° on lower oven rack 15 minutes. Reduce oven temperature to 350°; transfer pie to middle oven rack, and bake 35 minutes. Cover loosely with aluminum foil to prevent excessive browning, and bake 30 more minutes or until juices are thick and bubbly, crust is golden brown, and apples are tender when pierced with a long wooden pick through slits in crust. Remove to a wire rack. Cool 1½ to 2 hours before serving. Serve with Brandy-Caramel Sauce.

Cornmeal Crust Dough:
make ahead

MAKES 2 DOUGH DISKS; **PREP:** 15 MIN.,
CHILL: 1 HR.

For a flaky crust, make sure the butter and shortening are cold. Our Food staff loved the flavor the apple cider brought to the crust. (Ice-cold water may be substituted for cider.)

2⅓ cups all-purpose flour
¼ cup plain yellow cornmeal
2 Tbsp. sugar
¾ tsp. salt
¾ cup cold butter, cut into ½-inch pieces
¼ cup chilled shortening, cut into ½-inch
    pieces
8 to 10 Tbsp. chilled apple cider

1. Stir together first 4 ingredients in a large bowl. Cut butter and shortening into flour mixture with a pastry blender until mixture resembles small peas. Mound mixture on 1 side of bowl.
2. Drizzle 1 Tbsp. apple cider along edge of mixture in bowl. Using a fork, gently toss a small amount of flour mixture into cider just until dry ingredients are moistened; move mixture to other side of bowl. Repeat procedure with remaining cider and flour mixture.
3. Gently gather dough into two flat disks. Wrap in plastic wrap, and chill 1 to 24 hours.

—CRUST INSPIRED BY SANDRA RUSSELL,
ORANGE PARK, FLORIDA

• TIP •

"I'm sold on the no-stir method for flaky piecrust that Shirley's mother uses," says Test Kitchens Professional Pam Lolley. (See Cornmeal Crust Dough recipe.) This "mound, moisten, move, and gather" technique prevents flattening the small pieces of butter and shortening that were cut into the flour. Instead the pieces remain plump and "fry" the flour surrounding them as the pie bakes. They disappear, leaving behind flaky layers.

Brandy-Caramel Sauce:
fast fixin's • make ahead

MAKES ABOUT 2 CUPS; **PREP:** 5 MIN.,
COOK: 5 MIN., **COOL:** 10 MIN.

We suggest using the full amount of butter in this sauce, although half of our tasting table thought it was fine with 2 Tbsp. Serve each slice with a small pitcher or shot glass of this rich sauce.

1 cup whipping cream
1½ cups firmly packed brown sugar
2 Tbsp. to ¼ cup butter
2 Tbsp. brandy*
1 tsp. vanilla extract

1. Bring whipping cream to a light boil in a large saucepan over medium heat, stirring occasionally. Add sugar, and cook, stirring occasionally, 4 to 5 minutes or until sugar is dissolved and mixture is smooth. Remove from heat, and stir in butter, brandy, and vanilla. Let cool 10 minutes.
*Apple cider may be substituted.
Note: To make ahead, prepare recipe as directed. Store in an airtight container in refrigerator up to 1 week. To reheat, let stand at room temperature 30 minutes. Place mixture in a microwave-safe bowl, and microwave at HIGH 1 minute, stirring after 30 seconds.

Need a Shortcut?

Quick Cornmeal Crusts:
Unroll 1 (15-oz.) package refrigerated piecrusts as directed; place each piecrust on a surface lightly sprinkled with plain yellow cornmeal. Sprinkle top of crusts with additional cornmeal. Using a rolling pin, press cornmeal into crusts. Use immediately. **Makes** 2 crusts; Prep: 10 min.

Fast Caramel Sauce:
Stir together 1 (19-oz.) jar butterscotch-caramel topping, 2 Tbsp. brandy, and ⅛ tsp. salt in a microwave-safe bowl. Microwave at HIGH 1½ minutes or until warm, stirring at 30-second intervals. Serve immediately. **Makes** about 2¼ cups; Prep: 5 min.
Note: For testing purposes only, we used Smucker's Special Recipe Butterscotch Caramel Flavor Topping.

Fresh Ideas for Shrimp

Make a quick stop by the seafood counter, and pick up a pound of shrimp. We'll show you seven fast and flavorful ways to make it special.

Carolina Grilled Shrimp

MAKES 4 APPETIZER SERVINGS;
PREP: 20 MIN., **SOAK:** 30 MIN.,
CHILL: 20 MIN., **GRILL:** 6 MIN.

4 (12-inch) wooden skewers
1 lb. unpeeled, jumbo raw shrimp
    (16/20 count)
2 Tbsp. olive oil
¼ cup chili sauce
2 Tbsp. fresh lemon juice
2 Tbsp. Worcestershire sauce
2 garlic cloves, minced
¼ tsp. ground red pepper

1. Soak wooden skewers in water
30 minutes.
2. Peel shrimp; devein, if desired.
Thread shrimp onto skewers. Place in a
13- x 9-inch baking dish.
3. Whisk together olive oil and next
5 ingredients in a bowl; pour over
shrimp. Cover and chill 20 minutes.
Remove shrimp from marinade, discarding marinade.
4. Preheat grill to 350° to 400° (medium-
high). Grill shrimp, covered with grill
lid, 2 to 3 minutes on each side or just
until shrimp turn pink.

— **CAROL S. NOBLE**, BURGAW, NORTH CAROLINA

Marinated Lemon Shrimp and Artichokes

make ahead

MAKES 4 SERVINGS; **PREP:** 25 MIN.,
COOK: 5 MIN., **CHILL:** 4 HR.

1 lb. unpeeled, large raw shrimp
    (31/40 count)
1 (14-oz.) can whole artichoke hearts,
    drained
¾ cup white vinegar
½ cup fresh lemon juice
½ cup olive oil
¼ cup honey
1 tsp. hot sauce
½ tsp. salt
½ tsp. freshly ground pepper
1 small red onion, cut in half and sliced
1 lemon, sliced
Garnish: chopped fresh basil

1. Bring 2 qt. water to a boil in a
Dutch oven; add shrimp, and cook 3
to 5 minutes or just until shrimp turn
pink. Drain and rinse with cold water.
Peel shrimp, leaving tails on; devein, if
desired. Cut artichoke hearts in half.
2. Whisk together vinegar and next
6 ingredients in a large bowl. Pour mixture into a large zip-top plastic freezer
bag; add shrimp, artichoke hearts,
onion, and lemon, turning to coat. Seal
and chill 4 hours, turning occasionally.
Drain mixture, discarding marinade.
Place in serving bowls. Garnish, if
desired.

**Marinated Lemon Shrimp With
Olives:** Prepare recipe as directed,
substituting 1 (5¾-oz.) jar pimiento-
stuffed Spanish olives, drained, for
1 (14-oz.) can artichoke hearts. Omit
garnish.

— **KAY HOWE**, PAIGE, TEXAS

Spicy Shrimp Spoon Bread

MAKES 8 SERVINGS; **PREP:** 25 MIN.,
COOK: 6 MIN., **BAKE:** 45 MIN.,
STAND: 10 MIN.

1 lb. unpeeled, medium-size raw shrimp
    (41/50 count)
¼ cup butter
1 small sweet onion, diced
1 (4.5-oz.) can chopped green chiles,
    undrained
1 (20-oz.) package frozen cream-style corn,
    thawed
1 (16-oz.) container sour cream
2 large eggs
1 (6-oz.) package buttermilk cornbread mix
2 cups (8 oz.) shredded Cheddar-Jack
    cheese with peppers

1. Peel shrimp; devein, if desired.
Coarsely chop shrimp. Preheat oven
to 375°.
2. Melt butter in a large skillet over
medium-high heat; add onion, and
sauté 2 to 3 minutes or until tender. Stir
in shrimp, and sauté 2 to 3 minutes or
just until shrimp turn pink. Remove
from heat, and stir in green chiles.
3. Whisk together corn, sour cream,
and eggs in a large bowl until blended;
whisk in cornbread mix just until
blended. Stir shrimp mixture and
1½ cups shredded Cheddar-Jack
cheese into corn mixture just until
blended; pour into a lightly greased
13- x 9-inch baking dish, and sprinkle
with remaining ½ cup shredded cheese.
4. Bake at 375° for 45 minutes or until
a wooden pick inserted in center comes
out clean. Let stand 10 minutes before
serving.

— **INSPIRED BY ZAN BROCK**, JASPER, ALABAMA

Note: For testing purposes only, we
used Martha White Cotton Country
Buttermilk Cornbread Mix.

Sizing Up Shrimp

When buying shrimp, check the label and you'll see a set of numbers divided by a slash, such as 16/20 or 51/60. These numbers refer to the count or number of shrimp per pound. While there are no regulations governing the use of such terms as "large" or "jumbo," stores are required to display the number of shrimp per pound, so we'll begin including the count with our recipes to use as a guideline. One location may label a 41/50 count shrimp as medium size, while another may label it as large and charge a premium price.

Shrimp and Collards
fast fixin's

MAKES 4 SERVINGS; **PREP:** 30 MIN.,
COOK: 18 MIN., **STAND:** 4 MIN.

1 lb. unpeeled, medium-size raw shrimp
    (41/50 count)
8 bacon slices
1 (14-oz.) can chicken broth
3 Tbsp. olive oil, divided
1⅓ cups uncooked couscous
¼ tsp. freshly ground pepper
1 (16-oz.) package frozen chopped collard
    greens, thawed
1 tsp. jarred ham-flavored soup base

1. Peel shrimp; devein, if desired.
2. Cook bacon in a large skillet over medium-high heat 8 to 10 minutes or until crisp; remove bacon, and drain on paper towels, reserving 1 Tbsp. drippings in skillet. Crumble bacon.
3. Bring chicken broth and 1 Tbsp. olive oil to a boil in a large saucepan over medium-high heat. Remove from heat, and stir in couscous; cover and let stand 4 minutes.
4. Meanwhile, sprinkle shrimp with pepper. Heat remaining 2 Tbsp. olive oil and reserved drippings over medium-high heat; add shrimp, collards, and soup base, and cook, stirring occasionally, 5 to 8 minutes or just until shrimp turn pink.
5. Fluff couscous with a fork. Stir couscous and crumbled bacon into shrimp mixture in skillet. Serve immediately.

—**SUSAN SCARBOROUGH**,
FERNANDINA BEACH, FLORIDA

Fig-and-Horseradish-Glazed Shrimp
fast fixin's

MAKES 4 APPETIZER SERVINGS;
PREP: 15 MIN., **COOK:** 4 MIN.

If you're a fan of sweet-and-sour shrimp, you'll love this recipe. Serve with softened cream cheese and a crusty loaf of warm French bread for a short-order appetizer. Or stir in strips of sautéed bell pepper and onion, and spoon over rice for a one-dish meal.

1 lb. unpeeled, large raw shrimp
    (31/40 count)
3 Tbsp. butter
1 Tbsp. olive oil
2 garlic cloves, minced
½ cup fig or apricot preserves
2 Tbsp. refrigerated horseradish
2 tsp. Dijon mustard

1. Peel shrimp; devein, if desired.
2. Melt butter with oil in a large skillet over medium-high heat; add shrimp and garlic, and sauté 2 minutes. Increase heat to high; stir in fig preserves, horseradish, and mustard, and sauté 1 to 2 minutes or just until shrimp turn pink. Remove from heat, and serve immediately.

—**BEVERLEY SIBERTSON**, KINGSPORT, TENNESSEE

Shrimp With Feta Cheese
southernliving.com favorite
MAKES 4 SERVINGS; **PREP:** 20 MIN.,
COOK: 30 MIN.

This shrimp recipe blends a trio of herbs for a great entrée.

1 lb. unpeeled, large raw shrimp
    (31/40 count)
1 Tbsp. butter
1 tsp. lemon juice
1 medium onion, halved and thinly
    sliced
2 Tbsp. olive oil
½ cup dry white wine
½ cup clam juice
1 garlic clove, minced
3 to 4 plum tomatoes, coarsely
    chopped
2 tsp. chopped fresh oregano
1 tsp. chopped fresh basil
1 tsp. chopped fresh parsley
1 cup crumbled feta cheese
Garnish: fresh oregano sprig

1. Peel shrimp; devein, if desired.
2. Melt butter in a large skillet over medium heat; add shrimp and lemon juice, and sauté 2 to 3 minutes or just until shrimp turn pink. Remove shrimp from skillet.
3. Sauté onion in hot oil until tender. Add wine, clam juice, and garlic. Reduce heat, and simmer 10 minutes. Add tomato, and simmer 5 more minutes. Stir in shrimp, oregano, basil, and parsley. Sprinkle with feta. Serve over hot cooked pasta or with crusty bread. Garnish, if desired.

It's Cookie-Baking Time!

Sweet Inspirations When Assistant Test Kitchens Director Rebecca Kracke Gordon stirs up one of her special creations, we come running. Crisp and buttery, rich and gooey, big batch or small—one versatile recipe for All-Time Favorite Chocolate Chip Cookies delivers them all. Store cookie dough in an airtight container or zip-top plastic freezer bag, and chill up to three days or freeze up to six months. For slice-and-bake cookies, shape dough into logs, wrap in parchment paper, and place in zip-top plastic freezer bags. Allow frozen dough to thaw overnight in the refrigerator. Another option is to use a small ice-cream scoop to shape dough into balls; place on a baking sheet, and freeze until firm. Transfer frozen balls to a zip-top plastic freezer bag. Remove as needed, and bake right from the freezer, allowing two to three minutes extra baking time.

Flavor Cravings All sorts

of goodies can be added to Rebecca's recipe to create other signature cookies. Here are a few of our staff favorites.

- **Chocolate Chip-Pretzel Cookies:** Prepare recipe as directed, beating in 2 cups coarsely crushed pretzel sticks with morsels.
- **Cranberry-White Chocolate Cookies:** Substitute 1 (12-oz.) package white chocolate morsels, 1 (6-oz.) package sweetened dried cranberries, and 1 cup pistachios for chocolate morsels. Proceed as directed.
- **White Chocolate-Covered Pretzel Cookies:** Prepare recipe as directed, beating in 1 (7-oz.) bag white chocolate-covered mini pretzel twists, coarsely crushed, with morsels.
- **Almond-Toffee Cookies:** Substitute 6 (1.4-oz.) chopped chocolate-covered toffee candy bars and 1½ cups toasted slivered almonds for chocolate morsels. Proceed as directed.
- **Turtle Cookies:** Substitute 1 (7-oz.) package milk chocolate-caramel-pecan clusters, coarsely chopped, and 1 (12-oz.) package dark chocolate morsels for semisweet chocolate morsels. Proceed as directed. **Note:** For testing purposes only, we used Nestlé Turtles.
- **Nutty Peanut Butter-Chocolate Chip Cookies:** Decrease salt to ½ tsp. Decrease morsels to 1 (12-oz.) package. Add 1 cup creamy peanut butter with butter and sugars, and add 1 cup lightly salted peanuts with morsels. Increase flour to 2½ cups plus 2 Tbsp. Proceed as directed. (Dough will look a little moist.)

All-Time Favorite Chocolate Chip Cookies

MAKES ABOUT 5 DOZEN; **PREP:** 30 MIN., **BAKE:** 14 MIN. PER BATCH, **COOL:** 15 MIN.

Bake 10 minutes for a soft and chewy cookie or up to 14 minutes for a crisp cookie. (Pictured on page 13)

¾ cup butter, softened
¾ cup granulated sugar
¾ cup firmly packed dark brown sugar
2 large eggs
1½ tsp. vanilla extract
2¼ cups plus 2 Tbsp. all-purpose flour
1 tsp. baking soda
¾ tsp. salt
1½ (12-oz.) packages semisweet chocolate morsels
Parchment paper

1. Preheat oven to 350°. Beat butter and sugars at medium speed with a heavy-duty electric stand mixer until creamy. Add eggs and 1½ tsp. vanilla, beating until blended.
2. Combine flour, baking soda, and salt in a small bowl; gradually add to butter mixture, beating just until blended. Beat in morsels just until combined. Drop by tablespoonfuls onto parchment paper-lined baking sheets.
3. Bake at 350° for 10 to 14 minutes or until desired degree of doneness. Remove to wire racks, and cool completely (about 15 minutes).

October

Boo, Y'all!

Follow our tips to throw an easygoing get-together for your favorite goblins, pretty princesses, superheroes, *and* their parents on October's spookiest night. Our make-ahead menu and scary-but-stylish decorations will wow your guests and be the talk of the neighborhood.

Haunting (But Not Daunting) Menu

SERVES 8 TO 10

(These recipes easily double to serve more.)

Onion-Bacon Dip

Assorted multigrain and vegetable chips

Monster Meatball Sandwiches

Barbecue Stew

Mummy Dogs

Cereal-and-Granola "Apples"

Chocolate Ghost Cakes

Onion-Bacon Dip

MAKES 2½ CUPS; **PREP:** 10 MIN., **COOK:** 28 MIN., **CHILL:** 1 HR.

1 large leek
6 bacon slices
1 large sweet onion, minced
1 (8-oz.) package cream cheese, softened
1 cup sour cream
½ tsp. salt
1 (2-lb.) acorn squash
Assorted multigrain and vegetable chips
Garnish: chopped fresh chives

1. Remove and discard root end and dark green top of leek. Cut in half lengthwise, and rinse thoroughly under cold running water to remove grit and sand; thinly slice leek.
2. Cook bacon in a large skillet over medium-high heat 6 to 8 minutes or until crisp; remove bacon, and drain on paper towels, reserving 1 Tbsp. drippings in skillet. Crumble bacon.
3. Sauté onion and leek in hot drippings 15 minutes or until tender and golden.
4. Stir together onion mixture, bacon, cream cheese, sour cream, and salt. Cover and chill 1 hour.
5. Cut about ½ to 1 inch from top of squash; remove and discard seeds.
6. Heat a small skillet over medium-high heat. Place squash, cut side down, in skillet, and cook 3 to 5 minutes or until cut side is golden brown and caramelized. Serve dip in squash with assorted chips. Garnish, if desired.

Monster Meatball Sandwiches

family favorite • make ahead
MAKES 16 SERVINGS; **PREP:** 10 MIN., **COOK:** 30 MIN.

32 bite-size frozen meatballs
1 (9-oz.) jar mango chutney
1 cup chicken broth
16 fresh dinner rolls
1 (16-oz.) jar sweet-hot pickle sandwich relish

1. Stir together first 3 ingredients in a medium saucepan. Bring to a boil over medium-high heat; reduce heat to low, and simmer, stirring occasionally, 25 to 30 minutes.
2. Cut rolls vertically through top, cutting to but not through bottom. Place 2 meatballs in each roll. Top with desired amount of relish.
Note: For testing purposes only, we used Wickles Hoagie & Sub Sandwich Relish.

To make ahead: Prepare meatballs as directed through Step 1. Store in an airtight container in refrigerator 3 to 4 days.

Barbecue Stew

family favorite • make ahead
MAKES 8 SERVINGS; **PREP:** 15 MIN.; **BAKE:** 1 HR., 30 MIN.; **COOK:** 30 MIN.

1 (3-lb.) boneless pork loin roast
1 Tbsp. barbecue seasoning
1 (18-oz.) bottle smoky mesquite barbecue sauce
1 (14-oz.) can chicken broth
1 (32-oz.) container chicken broth
2 (16-oz.) bags frozen vegetable soup mix
2 (14.5-oz.) cans fire-roasted diced tomatoes*
1 cup frozen whole kernel corn
½ tsp. salt
1 (24-oz.) package frozen olive oil, rosemary, and garlic oven fries
1 (22-oz.) package frozen sweet potato fries

1. Preheat oven to 350°. Rinse and pat roast dry. Rub barbecue seasoning over roast. Place in an aluminum foil-lined 13- x 9-inch pan. Pour barbecue sauce and 1 (14-oz.) can chicken broth over roast. Cover tightly with aluminum foil.
2. Bake at 350° for 1½ hours or until fork tender. Remove roast from pan, reserving drippings in pan. Shred roast with 2 forks.
3. Carefully pour drippings into a Dutch oven. Add shredded pork, 1 (32-oz.) container chicken broth, and next 4 ingredients. Bring mixture to a boil over medium-high heat; reduce heat to medium-low, and simmer, stirring occasionally, 30 minutes.
4. Meanwhile, prepare oven fries and sweet potato fries according to package directions; serve with stew.
*2 (14.5-oz.) cans diced tomatoes may be substituted.
Note: For testing purposes only, we used McCormick Grill Mates Barbecue Seasoning; Alexia Olive Oil, Rosemary, & Garlic Oven Fries; and Alexia Sweet Potato Julienne Fries.

To make ahead: Prepare recipe through Step 3. Store in an airtight container in refrigerator up to 4 days. Reheat in a large Dutch oven while the oven preheats to cook fries.

Mummy Dogs
MAKES 12 SERVINGS; PREP: 15 MIN.,
BAKE: 15 MIN., STAND: 5 MIN.

1 (11-oz.) can refrigerated breadstick dough
12 bun-length hot dogs
Wooden picks (optional)
Vegetable cooking spray

1. Preheat oven to 400°. Unroll breadstick dough, and separate into 12 strips at perforations. Gently stretch each strip to a length of 8 inches.
2. Wrap 1 dough strip lengthwise around each hot dog. Secure with wooden picks, if necessary. Coat lightly with cooking spray. Place on a lightly greased baking sheet.

3. Bake at 400° for 15 minutes or until golden brown. Let stand 5 minutes. (If using wooden picks, remove before serving.)

Garlic Mummy Dogs: Substitute 1 (11-oz.) can refrigerated garlic breadstick dough. Proceed with recipe as directed.

Parmesan-Garlic Mummy Dogs: Substitute 1 (11-oz.) can refrigerated Parmesan-garlic breadstick dough. Proceed with recipe as directed.

Garlic-Herb Mummy Dogs: Substitute 1 (11-oz.) can refrigerated garlic-herb breadstick dough. Proceed with recipe as directed.

Cereal-and-Granola "Apples"
family favorite • make ahead
MAKES 8 SERVINGS; PREP: 25 MIN.,
COOL: 30 MIN., STAND: 5 MIN.

Hang these "apples" from the trees so kids can stay dry while "bobbing" for them.

¼ cup butter
1 (10-oz.) package regular marshmallows
3 cups crisp rice cereal
4 cups granola
Vegetable cooking spray
Wax paper
4 (8-inch) pretzel rods, broken in half
1 (12-oz.) package semisweet chocolate morsels
Orange decorator sugar crystals

1. Microwave butter and marshmallows in a lightly greased large microwave-safe bowl at HIGH 3 minutes, stirring after 2 minutes. Stir until smooth.
2. Stir in cereal and granola, in batches, until well coated.
3. Coat hands with cooking spray. Shape warm mixture into 8 (4-inch) balls (about 1 cup each), lightly greasing hands as needed. Place balls on wax paper. Press 1 pretzel rod half, broken

end down, into top of each ball. Let cool completely (about 30 minutes).
4. Microwave chocolate morsels in a microwave-safe bowl at HIGH 2 minutes, stirring after 1 minute. Stir until smooth. Let stand, stirring occasionally, 5 minutes. Drizzle chocolate over balls; sprinkle with sugar.

To make ahead: Wrap in plastic wrap, and store at room temperature for up to 2 days.

Crisp Rice Cereal "Apples": Omit granola, and increase crisp rice cereal to 7 cups. Proceed with recipe as directed.

Chocolate Ghost Cakes
fast fixin's
MAKES 10 SERVINGS; PREP: 20 MIN.,
STAND: 2 MIN.

Serve these festive little treats alongside bags of candy corn.

½ (12-oz.) container ready-to-spread white frosting
1 (11-oz.) package cream-filled chocolate cake squares
1 (0.68-oz.) tube black decorating gel

1. Microwave frosting in a microwave-safe bowl at HIGH 30 seconds to 1 minute or until melted; stir until smooth. Let stand 2 minutes.
2. Place 1 cup melted frosting in a gallon-size zip-top plastic bag. (Do not seal.) Snip 1 corner of bag to make a small hole. Pipe frosting onto each cake square in the shape of a ghost, adding remaining frosting to bag as needed. Pipe 2 dots on each cake using black gel to form eyes.
Note: For testing purposes only, we used Little Debbie Devil Squares and Betty Crocker Decorating Gel.

Healthy Living.

Take control of your health by eating well with
these nutrient-packed favorites.

Cooking Up Good Health

Let these easy recipes be the inspiration for delicious meals at
your supper table.

Simple changes in your diet could mean the difference between illness and well-being. "Eating well is the only way," insists Janet Gaffney on the topic of staying healthy. This devoted cooking teacher in Mount Pleasant, South Carolina, is also a six-year survivor of breast cancer. "When tragedy strikes, you really start to evaluate your health and what you can do to change it," says Janet.

One of her secrets to conquering cancer: Eat fresh, local, and organic—including lots of colorful, antioxidant-rich produce. "As I was going through treatment, I couldn't think of eating another vegetable that might possibly be polluted with pesticides," Janet says.

Healthy Benefits

- Deep, rich color in produce is a key indicator of vital, cell-protecting nutrients. Eating at least five servings of various fruits and veggies a day can greatly reduce the risks of developing cancer and other diseases.
- Eating foods low in saturated fat—such as lean meats, olive and nut oils, legumes, and whole grains—can help keep estrogen levels down, inhibiting the growth of cancer cells.

Red Pepper-and-Pear Soup
MAKES 7 CUPS; **PREP:** 15 MIN.,
COOK: 40 MIN., **COOL:** 20 MIN.

2 Tbsp. butter
2 tsp. olive oil
3 large red bell peppers, sliced
2 carrots, sliced
2 shallots, sliced
2 Anjou pears, peeled and sliced
1 (32-oz.) container fat-free chicken broth
1/2 tsp. dried crushed red pepper
1/2 tsp. ground black pepper
1/4 tsp. salt
Dash of ground red pepper
Garnishes: thinly sliced fresh pears, plain
    yogurt, chopped fresh chives

1. Melt butter with oil in a Dutch oven over medium heat; add bell peppers and next 3 ingredients, and sauté 8 to 10 minutes or until tender.
2. Stir in chicken broth and next 4 ingredients. Bring to a boil; cover, reduce heat to low, and simmer 25 to 30 minutes. Let cool 20 minutes.
3. Process soup, in batches, in a food processor until smooth, stopping to scrape down sides. Return to Dutch oven, and keep warm until ready to serve. Garnish, if desired.
Note: To make ahead, let soup cool, and store in an airtight container in refrigerator up to 2 days. Reheat in a saucepan over medium-low heat, stirring often.

Per cup (not including garnishes): Calories 103; Fat 5.2g (sat 2.3g, mono 1.9g, poly 0.4g); Protein 1.9g; Carb 14.4g; Fiber 3.6g; Chol 9mg; Iron 0.7mg; Sodium 654mg; Calc 24mg

Red Lentils
MAKES 5 CUPS; **PREP:** 15 MIN.,
COOK: 36 MIN.

"This recipe is always a hit with my health-conscious family and guests," says Nancy Santiago, Janet's assistant. Find lentils at almost any supermarket in the dried legume section.

2 Tbsp. butter
1/2 sweet onion, diced
4 garlic cloves, minced
2 (14-oz.) cans reduced-sodium fat-free
    chicken broth*
1 (14.5-oz.) can diced tomatoes with garlic
    and onion
1 1/4 cups red or brown lentils, rinsed
1/2 tsp. ground turmeric
1/2 tsp. ground cumin
1/4 tsp. pepper
1/4 cup chopped fresh basil
Salt to taste

1. Melt butter in a large skillet over medium heat. Add onion and garlic, and sauté 6 minutes or until onion is tender. Add broth and next 5 ingredients. Bring to a boil; reduce heat to low, and simmer, uncovered, stirring occasionally, 30 minutes or until lentils are tender. Stir in basil and salt to taste. *2 (14-oz.) cans vegetable broth may be substituted.

Per ½-cup serving (not including salt to taste): Calories 138; Fat 3.8g (sat 1.6g, mono 0.6g, poly 0.1g); Protein 6g; Carb 20.8g; Fiber 4.9g; Chol 7.6mg; Iron 2mg; Sodium 407mg; Calc 54mg

Food for Thought

- **Go local**. Visit farm stands and outdoor markets for an abundance of inexpensive produce. You can also subscribe to local produce deliveries. To learn more visit southernliving.com/localmarkets.

- **Eat in season**. "If it's not available to you now, then maybe you shouldn't be eating it," says Janet. Enjoy seasonal fruits and vegetables while they're at their nutritional peak. "I always stock up and freeze some for later," she adds.

- **Grow your own**. What your body needs might be in your own backyard. Homegrown veggies and herbs offer the same amount of cancer-fighting antioxidants as store-bought produce but without the pesticides and high prices.

- **Shop smart**. Nowadays, most major grocery stores and superstores offer organic products. Though some items tend to be more expensive, not all are. Shop around—you just might be pleasantly surprised.

Roasted Vegetables

MAKES 8 SERVINGS; **PREP:** 30 MIN., **STAND:** 30 MIN., **BAKE:** 30 MIN.

1 medium eggplant, peeled and cubed
¼ tsp. salt
2 zucchini, sliced
1 large sweet potato, peeled and sliced
1 onion, peeled and cut into eighths
1 red bell pepper, cut into 1-inch pieces
¼ cup olive oil
1 Tbsp. chopped fresh rosemary
¼ tsp. pepper
Salt to taste

1. Sprinkle eggplant with salt, and let stand 30 minutes. Pat dry.
2. Preheat oven to 400°. Toss together eggplant and remaining ingredients, and arrange in a single layer in 2 aluminum foil-lined jelly-roll pans.
3. Bake at 400° for 30 minutes or until vegetables are tender and golden brown. Season with salt to taste.

Per serving (not including salt to taste): Calories 109; Fat 7.2g (sat 1g, mono 5.4g, poly 0.7g); Protein 1.4g; Carb 10.7g; Fiber 3.4g; Chol 0mg; Iron 0.4mg; Sodium 83mg; Calc 20mg

Poached Salmon

MAKES 6 SERVINGS; **PREP:** 10 MIN., **COOK:** 10 MIN.

8 garlic cloves, divided
½ cup loosely packed fresh parsley leaves
¼ cup loosely packed fresh mint leaves
½ tsp. salt
3 Tbsp. extra virgin olive oil
½ bunch fresh parsley
3 lemons, sliced
6 (6-oz.) 1-inch-thick salmon fillets
Garnish: lemon slices

1. Process 2 garlic cloves, ½ cup parsley leaves, ¼ cup mint leaves, and ½ tsp. salt in a food processor until smooth, stopping to scrape down sides as needed. With processor running, pour oil through food chute in a slow, steady stream, processing until smooth.

TIP

If you can boil water, then you can poach salmon. First, create a flavorful poaching liquid by adding garlic, herbs, and lemon to water in a large skillet. Then simply bring the water to a slight boil, add the salmon fillets, and reduce heat to a simmer. You'll have a heart-healthy main dish in minutes.

2. Smash remaining 6 garlic cloves, using flat side of a knife.
3. Pour water to a depth of 2½ inches into a large skillet over medium-high heat. Add smashed garlic, ½ bunch fresh parsley, and lemon slices; bring to a boil. Add salmon fillets; return liquid to a boil, reduce heat to low, and simmer 7 to 10 minutes or until fish flakes with a fork. Remove salmon from skillet; discard liquid in skillet. Serve salmon with garlic-parsley mixture. Garnish, if desired.

Per serving: Calories 282; Fat 13.4g (sat 2g, mono 7.1g, poly 3.2g); Protein 37.1g; Carb 0.7g; Fiber 0.2g; Chol 97mg; Iron 1.7mg; Sodium 320mg; Calc 33mg

Whip Up a Side

These hearty, mouthwatering veggie dishes are just the thing for cool autumn nights and a tasty way to stretch meals.

Forget about regular old mashed potatoes. Update your dinner plate with these tasty sides using cauliflower, turnips, and butternut squash to create rich flavors that pair well with roasted meats and poultry. Be sure to try Chipotle Butternut Mash, which offers a taste of the Southwest with spicy chipotle peppers, lime juice, and cilantro.

Apple-Turnip Mashed Potatoes

family favorite

MAKES ABOUT 8 SERVINGS (4 CUPS);
PREP: 20 MIN., **COOK:** 32 MIN.

This rustic and delicious recipe has a chunky consistency.

1 lb. turnips, peeled and cut into 1-inch
   pieces
1 lb. Yukon gold potatoes, peeled and cut
   into 1-inch pieces
3 bacon slices, cut into ¼-inch pieces
2 medium-size Golden Delicious apples,
   peeled and chopped
¼ cup Roasted Garlic
1 tsp. chopped fresh thyme
¾ cup buttermilk
2 Tbsp. melted butter
Salt and pepper to taste

1. Bring turnips, potatoes, and salted water to cover to a boil in a Dutch oven; cook 15 to 20 minutes or until tender. Drain.
2. Cook bacon in a medium nonstick skillet over medium-high heat 5 to 6 minutes or until crisp; remove bacon, reserving 2 Tbsp. drippings in skillet. Crumble bacon. Sauté apples in hot drippings in skillet 6 minutes or until tender and lightly browned.

3. Combine apples, turnips, potatoes, Roasted Garlic, and thyme in a bowl; mash with a potato masher until blended. (Mixture will be chunky.) Stir in buttermilk and butter. Season with salt and pepper to taste. Transfer to a bowl.
4. Serve immediately, or, if desired, microwave mixture at HIGH 1 to 2 minutes or until thoroughly heated, stirring at 1-minute intervals. Sprinkle with bacon just before serving.

Kitchen Express: Substitute 2 tsp. jarred roasted minced garlic for ¼ cup Roasted Garlic. Proceed with recipe as directed, sautéing garlic with apples in Step 2.

Roasted Garlic:

make ahead

MAKES ½ CUP; **PREP:** 10 MIN.,
COOK: 35 MIN., **COOL:** 15 MIN.

Perfectly roasted garlic also tastes great spread on toasted French bread or a grilled steak.

4 garlic bulbs
2 Tbsp. olive oil
¼ tsp. kosher salt

1. Preheat oven to 425°. Cut off pointed end of each garlic bulb; place bulbs on a piece of aluminum foil. Drizzle with oil, and sprinkle with salt. Fold foil to seal.
2. Bake at 425° for 30 to 35 minutes; let cool 15 minutes. Squeeze pulp from garlic cloves into a small bowl. Store in an airtight container in the refrigerator up to 3 days.

Roasted Winter Squash

southernliving.com favorite
MAKES 6 SERVINGS; **PREP:** 10 MIN.,
BAKE: 35 MIN.

It takes just 10 minutes to prepare this quick, seasonal vegetable dish that boasts the sweet flavor combination of honey and butter.

3 lb. butternut squash, acorn squash, or
   spaghetti squash
1 Tbsp. butter, melted
½ Tbsp. honey
¼ tsp. salt
¼ tsp. pepper

1. Preheat oven to 450°.
2. Remove stem from squash. Cut squash in half lengthwise; remove and discard seeds. Cut each half into 4 wedges, and place on an aluminum foil-lined jelly-roll pan. (If using spaghetti squash, cut each half into 2 wedges.)
3. Stir together butter and honey until blended. Brush squash evenly with butter mixture; sprinkle evenly with salt and pepper.
4. Bake at 450° for 30 to 35 minutes or until tender, turning once. Cut skins from squash wedges, and discard.

Brown Butter Cauliflower Mash

MAKES ABOUT 6 SERVINGS (3½ CUPS);
PREP: 15 MIN., **COOK:** 15 MIN.

1 medium head cauliflower (about 2 lb.),
   chopped*
½ cup sour cream
¾ tsp. salt
½ tsp. pepper
¼ cup grated Parmesan cheese
1 Tbsp. chopped fresh chives
2 Tbsp. butter
Garnish: fresh chives

1. Fill a large Dutch oven with water to depth of ¼ inch. Arrange cauliflower in Dutch oven. Cook, covered, over medium-high heat 7 to 10 minutes or until tender. Drain.

2. Process cauliflower, sour cream, salt, and pepper in a food processor 30 seconds to 1 minute or until smooth, stopping to scrape down sides as needed. Stir in Parmesan cheese and chives. Place in a bowl.

3. If desired, microwave mixture at HIGH 1 to 2 minutes or until thoroughly heated, stirring at 1-minute intervals.

4. Cook butter in a small heavy saucepan over medium heat, stirring constantly, 4 to 5 minutes or until butter begins to turn golden brown. Remove from heat, and immediately drizzle butter over cauliflower mixture. Garnish, if desired. Serve immediately.

— JENNIFER PINNA, RALEIGH, NORTH CAROLINA

*2 (16-oz.) bags frozen cauliflower may be substituted. Cook cauliflower according to package directions. Proceed with recipe as directed, beginning with Step 2.

Chipotle Butternut Mash
family favorite

MAKES ABOUT 8 SERVINGS (4½ CUPS);
PREP: 20 MIN., **COOK:** 18 MIN.,
COOL: 15 MIN.

We love frozen, already pureed butternut squash, but we don't recommend it for this recipe because it gives the mash a soupy consistency.

2 medium butternut squash
    (about 3½ lb.)
½ (8-oz.) package cream cheese,
    softened
1 canned chipotle pepper in adobo
    sauce
1 Tbsp. fresh lime juice
1¼ tsp. salt
¼ cup firmly packed fresh cilantro
    leaves

1. Cut each squash lengthwise into 4 pieces; remove and discard seeds. Bring squash and salted water to cover to a boil in a Dutch oven; cook 15 to 18 minutes or until fork-tender. Drain and let cool 15 minutes. Peel squash, and cut into large pieces.

GET INSPIRED

Satisfying Snack
Every busy mom needs a tasty and easy way to satisfy her family's between-meal cravings. Here's our latest take on a popular favorite.

On-the-Go Munchies
MAKES 15 SERVINGS; **PREP:** 10 MIN.

1. Combine 5 cups rice cereal squares, 1 (2-lb.) bag candy-coated chocolate pieces, 1 (16-oz.) bag mini-pretzel twists, 1 (14-oz.) package bite-size parmesan-and-garlic cheese crackers, and 1 (12-oz.) container honey-roasted peanuts in a large bowl. Store in an airtight container.

Note: For testing purposes only, we used Rice Chex for rice cereal squares and Sunshine Cheez-It Parmesan & Garlic for bite-size parmesan-and-garlic cheese crackers.

2. Process squash, cream cheese, and next 3 ingredients in a food processor 30 seconds to 1 minute or until smooth, stopping to scrape down sides as needed. Add cilantro, and pulse 5 to 6 times or until cilantro is chopped.

3. Transfer mixture to a microwave-safe bowl. Microwave at HIGH 1 to 2 minutes or until thoroughly heated, stirring at 1-minute intervals.

— SARAH DEHAY, NASHVILLE, TENNESSEE

More Meal Ideas

Turn leftovers into a delicious soup for lunch the next day. Thin leftover veggie mash (even if it's only ½ cup) with equal parts milk and chicken broth to reach desired consistency.

Brown Butter Cauliflower Soup: Stir together 1 cup Brown Butter Cauliflower Mash, ⅓ to ½ cup chicken broth, and ⅓ to ½ cup milk.

Chipotle Butternut Soup: Stir together 1 cup Chipotle Butternut Mash, ⅓ to ½ cup chicken broth, and ⅓ to ½ cup milk.

Slow-cooked Comfort

Nine surefire recipes your family will love and that will fit your budget to a tee.

Slow cookers are countertop appliances with plenty of bonuses. Their moist, gentle cooking helps turn money-saving value meat cuts into fork-tender bites of flavor, leaving you with plenty of hands-off time too.

You don't have to head outside to cook mouthwatering ribs. Sweet-and-Spicy Baby Back Ribs will satisfy your cravings. Slow-simmered Harvest Lamb Stew and Braised Oxtails and Vegetables finish with tender meat and rich gravies that are just right for sopping. Turkey Breast and Herb-Cornbread Stuffing, along with an irresistible Southern side such as Candied Yams, makes an easy Sunday dinner. Don't forget dessert: Warm, gooey Rocky Road Chocolate Cake is studded with toasted pecans, marshmallows, and chocolate morsels. It's almost a s'more in a bowl.

The creativity of Test Kitchens professional Angela Sellers inspired these recipes that turn simple ingredients into full-flavored dishes. They'll surely bring the family back for seconds.

Sweet-and-Spicy Baby Back Ribs

MAKES 8 SERVINGS; **PREP:** 20 MIN.; **COOK:** 4 HR., 10 MIN.

For small appetizer portions, ask the butcher to cut the ribs in half crosswise.

3 green onions, chopped
1 Tbsp. minced fresh ginger
1½ tsp. minced garlic
1 Tbsp. vegetable oil
1 (12-oz.) bottle chili sauce
1 (8-oz.) bottle hoisin sauce
½ cup applesauce
½ cup beer
2 Tbsp. Worcestershire sauce
1 Tbsp. country-style Dijon mustard
1 to 3 tsp. hot sauce
2 slabs baby back ribs (about 5 lb.)

1. Sauté first 3 ingredients in hot oil in a small saucepan over medium heat 3 to 5 minutes or until tender. Stir in next 7 ingredients. Bring to a boil; reduce heat to medium-low, and simmer 5 minutes.
2. Place half of ribs in a single layer in a lightly greased 6-qt. slow cooker. Pour half of sauce mixture over ribs. Top with remaining ribs in a single layer. Pour remaining sauce mixture over ribs. Cover and cook on LOW 4 hours or until tender. Transfer to a serving platter.

Spiced Spareribs: Substitute 5 lb. pork spareribs for baby back ribs. Proceed with recipe as directed, cooking on HIGH 4 hours or until tender.

Turkey Breast and Herb-Cornbread Stuffing
family favorite

MAKES 8 SERVINGS; **PREP:** 20 MIN.; **COOL:** 30 MIN.; **COOK:** 4 HR., 9 MIN.; **STAND:** 15 MIN.

1 (6-oz.) package buttermilk
    cornbread mix
1 (2½-lb.) bone-in, skin-on turkey
    breast
1 tsp. salt
¼ tsp. pepper
¼ cup butter
½ cup chopped onion
½ cup chopped celery
¼ cup chopped fresh parsley
1½ tsp. poultry seasoning
1½ cups herb-seasoned stuffing mix
2 large eggs, lightly beaten
1 (14-oz.) can low-sodium chicken broth

1. Prepare cornbread mix according to package directions; let cool completely (about 30 minutes). Coarsely crumble cornbread (about 3 cups).
2. Rinse turkey, and pat dry. Sprinkle with salt and pepper.
3. Melt butter in a large skillet over medium heat; add turkey to skillet, skin side down, and cook 3 to 4 minutes or until browned. Remove from skillet. Add onion and next 3 ingredients to skillet, and sauté 3 to 5 minutes or until tender.
4. Stir together onion mixture, stuffing mix, eggs, low-sodium chicken broth, and crumbled cornbread in a large bowl.
5. Place stuffing mixture in a lightly greased 6-qt. slow cooker. Top with turkey, skin side up. Cover and cook on LOW 4 hours or until a meat thermometer inserted into thickest portion registers 170° and stuffing registers 165°. Remove turkey from slow cooker, and let stand 15 minutes before serving.
Note: For testing purposes only, we used Martha White Buttermilk Cornbread Mix and Pepperidge Farm Herb Seasoned Stuffing.

Candied Yams
family favorite

MAKES 6 TO 8 SERVINGS; **PREP:** 15 MIN.;
COOK: 4 HR., 2 MIN.

We updated this reader recipe so that it can be cooked in a slow cooker. It's an extra-easy choice to heat and take to your next family gathering or potluck dinner.

¼ cup butter
2 tsp. vanilla extract
¼ tsp. salt
1 cup granulated sugar
1 cup firmly packed brown sugar
4 lb. sweet potatoes, peeled and cut into
    ½-inch-thick slices
2 Tbsp. cornstarch

1. Microwave butter in a microwave-safe bowl at HIGH 30 seconds to 1 minute or until melted; stir in vanilla and salt.
2. Stir together granulated sugar and brown sugar in a medium bowl.
3. Layer potatoes and sugar mixture in a lightly greased 6-qt. slow cooker, beginning with potatoes and ending with sugar mixture. Pour butter mixture over top. Cover and cook on LOW 4 hours or until potatoes are tender.
4. Transfer potatoes to a serving dish using a slotted spoon, reserving liquid in slow cooker. Keep potatoes warm.
5. Remove ⅓ cup liquid from slow cooker; whisk cornstarch into ⅓ cup liquid until smooth. Carefully pour remaining liquid from slow cooker into a medium saucepan. Whisk in cornstarch mixture. Bring to a boil over medium heat; cook 1 to 2 minutes or until thickened. Pour over potatoes. Serve immediately.

—RUBY CAMPBELL,
SANFORD, NORTH CAROLINA

Braised Oxtails and Vegetables

MAKES 8 SERVINGS; **PREP:** 15 MIN.;
COOK: 6 HR., 20 MIN.

Our Food staff loved this recipe, and several folks had not tried oxtails before. The slow cooker is perfect for cooking value meats such as oxtails, which are extra flavorful.

4 lb. oxtails, cut at joints
1½ tsp. salt
½ tsp. pepper
1 Tbsp. vegetable oil
1 (14-oz.) can fat-free beef broth
1 (15-oz.) can diced tomatoes,
    drained
½ cup dry red wine
4 carrots, peeled and coarsely
    chopped
1 medium-size sweet onion, cut into
    8 wedges
1 tsp. dried thyme
Hot cooked grits
Chopped fresh thyme (optional)

1. Rinse oxtails, and pat dry. Remove and discard silver skin, if necessary. Sprinkle oxtails with salt and pepper.
2. Cook oxtails in hot oil in a Dutch oven over medium heat 10 minutes on each side or until browned. Transfer oxtails to a 6-qt. slow cooker.
3. Add broth and next 5 ingredients to slow cooker. Cover and cook on HIGH 6 hours or until meat is tender. Serve over hot cooked grits. Sprinkle with chopped fresh thyme, if desired.

Braised Short Ribs and Vegetables: Substitute 4 lb. beef short ribs, trimmed and cut in half, for oxtails. Proceed with recipe as directed.

Harvest Lamb Stew
freezeable • make ahead

MAKES 8 SERVINGS; **PREP:** 20 MIN.;
COOK: 4 HR., 51 MIN.

A hearty lamb stew over mashed potatoes is a great seasonal supper. This recipe also works using beef. You can make it up to 24 hours in advance and freeze any leftovers in zip-top plastic freezer bags for up to two months.

2½ lb. lean lamb stew meat (about 1-inch
    pieces)
1½ tsp. salt
¼ tsp. freshly ground pepper
¼ cup all-purpose flour
4 Tbsp. olive oil
1 (6-oz.) can tomato paste
1 (14.5-oz.) can beef broth
1 cup chopped celery
1 cup chopped sweet onion
3 garlic cloves, crushed
1 small butternut squash (about 1 lb.),
    peeled, seeded, and chopped
Hot cooked mashed potatoes (optional)
Garnish: fresh parsley sprigs

1. Rinse lamb stew meat, and pat dry. Sprinkle with salt and pepper; toss in flour, shaking off excess.
2. Cook half of lamb in 2 Tbsp. hot oil in a Dutch oven over medium-high heat, stirring occasionally, 10 minutes or until browned. Repeat procedure with remaining lamb and oil. Stir in tomato paste; cook 1 minute. Add broth, and stir to loosen particles from bottom of Dutch oven. Transfer mixture to a 6-qt. slow cooker.
3. Stir in celery, onion, and garlic. Top with butternut squash. (Do not stir to incorporate.) Cover and cook on LOW 4½ hours or until meat is tender. Serve over hot cooked mashed potatoes, if desired. Garnish, if desired.

Harvest Beef Stew: Substitute 2½ lb. beef stew meat for lamb. Proceed with recipe as directed.

Rocky Road Chocolate Cake

family favorite

MAKES 8 TO 10 SERVINGS; **PREP:** 15 MIN.;
COOK: 3 HR., 40 MIN.; **STAND:** 15 MIN.

This cake will look like it needs to cook just a little longer, but by the time the topping is set, it's ready to serve. When it's done and still warm, top with marshmallows, chocolate morsels, and pecans just before serving.

1 (18.25-oz.) package German chocolate
    cake mix
1 (3.9-oz.) package chocolate instant
    pudding mix
3 large eggs, lightly beaten
1 cup sour cream
⅓ cup butter, melted
1 tsp. vanilla extract
3¼ cups milk, divided
1 (3.4-oz.) package chocolate cook-and-
    serve pudding mix
½ cup chopped pecans
1½ cups miniature marshmallows
1 cup semisweet chocolate morsels
Vanilla ice cream (optional)

1. Beat cake mix, next 5 ingredients, and 1¼ cups milk at medium speed with an electric mixer 2 minutes, stopping to scrape down sides as needed. Pour batter into a lightly greased 4-qt. slow cooker.
2. Cook remaining 2 cups milk in a heavy nonaluminum saucepan over medium heat, stirring often, 3 to 5 minutes or just until bubbles appear (do not boil); remove from heat.
3. Sprinkle cook-and-serve pudding mix over batter. Slowly pour hot milk over pudding. Cover and cook on LOW 3½ hours.
4. Meanwhile, heat pecans in a small nonstick skillet over medium-low heat, stirring often, 3 to 5 minutes or until lightly toasted and fragrant.
5. Turn off slow cooker. Sprinkle cake with pecans, marshmallows, and chocolate morsels. Let stand 15 minutes or until marshmallows are slightly melted. Spoon into dessert dishes, and serve with ice cream, if desired.

Sensational Sheet Cakes

These sweet treats earned our highest rating. They're easy to bake and even easier to take to any gathering.

Chocolate Marble Sheet Cake

family favorite

MAKES 12 SERVINGS; **PREP:** 20 MIN.,
BAKE: 28 MIN., **COOL:** 1 HR.

This sheet cake is a real treat for chocoholics. The rich, creamy frosting blends coffee with cocoa for delightful mocha flavor. (Pictured on page 13)

1 cup butter, softened
1¾ cups sugar, divided
2 large eggs
2 tsp. vanilla extract
2½ cups all-purpose flour
1 Tbsp. baking powder
½ tsp. salt
1 cup half-and-half
¼ cup unsweetened cocoa
3 Tbsp. hot water
Mocha Frosting

1. Preheat oven to 325°. Beat butter and 1½ cups sugar at medium speed with a heavy-duty electric stand mixer 4 to 5 minutes or until creamy. Add eggs, 1 at a time, beating just until blended after each addition. Beat in vanilla extract.
2. Sift together flour, baking powder, and salt. Add to butter mixture alternately with half-and-half, beginning and ending with flour mixture. Beat at low speed just until blended after each addition, stopping to scrape bowl as needed.
3. Spoon 1¼ cups batter into a 2-qt. bowl, and stir in cocoa, 3 Tbsp. hot water, and remaining ¼ cup sugar until well blended.
4. Spread remaining vanilla batter into a greased and floured 15- x 10-inch jelly-roll pan. Spoon chocolate batter onto vanilla batter in pan; gently swirl with a knife or small spatula.
5. Bake at 325° for 23 to 28 minutes or until a wooden pick inserted in center of cake comes out clean. Cool cake completely in pan on a wire rack (about 1 hour). Spread top of cake with Mocha Frosting.

Mocha Frosting:

fast fixin's

MAKES 2⅓ CUPS; **PREP:** 10 MIN.

3 cups powdered sugar
⅔ cup unsweetened cocoa
3 Tbsp. hot brewed coffee
2 tsp. vanilla extract
½ cup butter, softened
3 to 4 Tbsp. half-and-half

1. Whisk together sugar and cocoa in a medium bowl. Combine coffee and vanilla.
2. Beat butter at medium speed with a heavy-duty electric stand mixer until creamy; gradually add sugar mixture alternately with coffee mixture, beating at low speed until blended. Beat in half-and-half, 1 Tbsp. at a time, until smooth and mixture has reached desired consistency.

—**CHERYL DRAPER,** CHICAGO, ILLINOIS

Mocha-Almond Frosting:

Decrease vanilla extract to 1 tsp. Proceed with recipe as directed, adding ½ tsp. almond extract to coffee mixture in Step 1.

Apple-Ginger Spice Cake
family favorite

MAKES 12 SERVINGS; **PREP:** 15 MIN., **BAKE:** 20 MIN., **COOL:** 10 MIN.

Inspired by the super-fast So-Easy Cherry-Fudge Cake (recipe below), we came up with this fall twist using gingerbread cake mix and apple filling.

1 (14.5-oz.) package gingerbread cake mix
1 (21-oz.) can apple pie filling
2 large eggs
¼ cup all-purpose flour
1 tsp. almond extract
1 cup powdered sugar
¼ cup sour cream

1. Preheat oven to 350°. Beat first 5 ingredients at low speed with a heavy-duty electric stand mixer 20 seconds; increase speed to medium, and beat 1 minute. Pour batter into a greased and floured 15- x 10-inch jelly-roll pan.
2. Bake at 350° for 20 minutes or until a wooden pick inserted in center comes out clean. Cool cake in pan on a wire rack 10 minutes.
3. Whisk together powdered sugar and sour cream until smooth. Drizzle over cake. Serve cake warm or at room temperature.
Note: For testing purposes only, we used Betty Crocker Gingerbread Cake & Cookie Mix and Comstock More Fruit Apple Pie Filling or Topping.

So-Easy Cherry-Fudge Cake
family favorite

MAKES 12 TO 15 SERVINGS; **PREP:** 15 MIN.; **BAKE:** 30 MIN.; **COOL:** 1 HR., 10 MIN.; **COOK:** 1 MIN.

1 (18.25-oz.) package devil's food cake mix
1 (21-oz.) can cherry pie filling
2 large eggs
1 tsp. almond extract
1 cup sugar
⅓ cup milk
5 Tbsp. butter
1 cup semisweet chocolate morsels

1. Preheat oven to 350°. Beat first 4 ingredients at low speed with a heavy-duty electric stand mixer 20 seconds; increase speed to medium, and beat 1 minute. Pour batter into a greased and floured 13- x 9-inch pan.
2. Bake at 350° for 27 to 30 minutes or until a wooden pick inserted in center comes out clean. Cool cake in pan on a wire rack 10 minutes.
3. Bring sugar, milk, and butter to a boil in a heavy 2-qt. saucepan over medium-high heat, stirring occasionally; boil 1 minute. Remove from heat; stir in chocolate morsels until melted and smooth. Quickly spread frosting over warm cake. Cool completely (about 1 hour). —ROSELLEN T. KINSINGER, HOLIDAY ISLAND, ARKANSAS

Note: For testing purposes only, we used Duncan Hines Moist Deluxe Devil's Food Cake Mix and Comstock Original Country Cherry Pie Filling or Topping.

Coconut Sheet Cake
southernliving.com favorite

MAKES 12 SERVINGS; **PREP:** 15 MIN., **BAKE:** 45 MIN., **FREEZE:** 30 MIN.

3 large eggs
1 (8-oz.) container sour cream
1 (8.5-oz.) can cream of coconut
½ tsp. vanilla extract
1 (18.25-oz.) package white cake mix
Coconut-Cream Cheese Frosting

1. Preheat oven to 350°. Beat eggs at high speed with an electric mixer 2 minutes. Add sour cream, ⅓ cup water, and next 2 ingredients, beating well after each addition. Add cake mix, beating at low speed just until blended. Beat at high speed 2 minutes. Pour batter into a greased and floured 13- x 9-inch pan.
2. Bake at 325° for 40 to 45 minutes or until a wooden pick inserted in center comes out clean. Cool cake in pan on wire rack. Cover pan with plastic wrap, and freeze cake 30 minutes. Remove from freezer.

3. Spread Coconut-Cream Cheese Frosting on top of chilled cake. Cover and store in refrigerator.
Note: If desired, cake can be baked in 1 greased and floured 15- x 10-inch jelly-roll pan for 30 to 32 minutes or until a wooden pick inserted in center comes out clean. **MAKES** 15 servings.

Coconut-Cream Cheese Frosting:
MAKES 4 CUPS; **PREP:** 10 MIN.

1 (8-oz.) package cream cheese, softened
½ cup butter, softened
3 Tbsp. milk
1 tsp. vanilla extract
1 (16-oz.) package powdered sugar, sifted
1 (7-oz.) package sweetened flaked coconut

1. Beat cream cheese and butter at medium speed with an electric mixer until creamy; add milk and vanilla, beating well. Gradually add sugar, beating until smooth. Stir in coconut.

—JULIE STEIN, BIRMINGHAM, ALABAMA

Old-Fashioned Oatmeal Cake

family favorite

MAKES 12 TO 15 SERVINGS; **PREP:** 20 MIN., **STAND:** 20 MIN., **BAKE:** 30 MIN., **BROIL:** 5 MIN., **COOL:** 4 HR.

Don't be tempted by the aroma of the warm cake; let it cool completely after broiling so the topping has time to melt and stick to the tender cake layer.

1 cup uncooked regular oats
½ cup butter, cut into pieces
1¼ cups boiling water
1⅓ cups all-purpose flour
1 tsp. baking soda
1 tsp. ground cinnamon
½ tsp. ground nutmeg
2 large eggs
1 cup firmly packed brown sugar
¾ cup granulated sugar
Brown Sugar-Pecan Topping or
    Brown Sugar-Walnut Topping

1. Preheat oven to 350°. Place oats and butter in bowl of an electric mixer. Pour 1¼ cups boiling water over oat mixture; cover and let stand 20 minutes.
2. Stir together flour, baking soda, cinnamon, and nutmeg.
3. Add eggs, 1 at a time, to oat mixture, beating at medium speed just until blended after each addition. Gradually add sugars, beating just until blended. Gradually add flour mixture, beating just until blended after each addition. Pour batter into a greased and floured 13- x 9-inch pan.
4. Bake at 350° for 26 to 30 minutes or until a wooden pick inserted in center of cake comes out clean. (Cake will begin to pull away from sides of pan.) Remove cake from oven; increase oven temperature to broil.
5. Spoon Brown Sugar-Pecan or Brown Sugar-Walnut Topping onto warm cake. Gently spread topping over cake using back of a spoon.
6. Broil cake 3 inches from heat 3 to 5 minutes or until sugar is bubbly and lightly browned. Let cake cool completely (about 3 to 4 hours).

Brown Sugar-Pecan Topping:

fast fixin's

MAKES ABOUT 3 CUPS; **PREP:** 10 MIN.

1 cup firmly packed brown sugar
1 cup chopped pecans
1 cup sweetened flaked coconut
½ cup butter, softened
⅓ cup milk

1. Beat together all ingredients at medium speed with an electric mixer until well combined.

— ROSEMARY COLE,
GULF SHORES, ALABAMA

Brown Sugar-Walnut Topping:

Substitute chopped walnuts for chopped pecans, if desired. Proceed with recipe as directed.

Stir Up a Batter

These luscious loaves are slightly sweet—similar in taste and texture to muffins. They don't require yeast, so they are fast and easy to do.

Southern Soda Bread

MAKES 2 LOAVES; **PREP:** 15 MIN.; **BAKE:** 1 HR., 20 MIN.; **COOL:** 1 HR., 10 MIN.

Serve this Southern take on the Irish classic warm from the oven with a cup of tea or to accompany a meal. We especially loved it toasted and served with jam or honey butter. (Pictured on page 186)

4½ cups all-purpose flour
⅔ cup sugar
4½ tsp. baking powder
1½ tsp. baking soda
1½ tsp. salt
3 cups buttermilk
3 large eggs, lightly beaten
4½ Tbsp. butter, melted

1. Preheat oven to 350°. Whisk together first 5 ingredients in a large bowl. Make a well in center of mixture. Add buttermilk, eggs, and butter, whisking just until thoroughly blended. (Batter should be almost smooth.) Pour batter into 2 lightly greased 8½- x 4½-inch loaf pans.
2. Bake at 350° for 45 minutes. Rotate pans in oven, and shield with aluminum foil. Bake 30 to 35 minutes or until a long wooden pick inserted in center comes out clean. Cool in pans on a wire rack 10 minutes. Carefully run a knife along edges of bread to loosen from pans. Remove from pans to wire rack, and cool completely (about 1 hour).

— MRS. RICHARD D. CONN, KANSAS CITY, MISSOURI

Bake and Freeze

Quick bread makes a lovely gift to share with neighbors and friends. Keep a loaf (or several) on hand in the freezer. Place whole or partial loaves in heavy-duty freezer bags, and freeze up to two months. For faster thawing, cut the loaves into halves or thirds. Thaw at room temperature one hour or until completely thawed. To recapture the lusciousness of warm bread from the oven, cut bread into ½-inch-thick slices, and bake on an aluminum foil-lined baking sheet at 350° for 10 to 12 minutes, turning at 8 minutes.

Peanut Streusel Bread

MAKES 1 LOAF; **PREP:** 15 MIN.;
BAKE: 1 HR., 5 MIN.; **COOL:** 1 HR., 10 MIN.

If you turn this bread out of the pan to cool, some of the streusel topping will fall off. Instead, line the pan with heavy-duty aluminum foil, and you'll be able to easily lift out the bread.

Vegetable cooking spray
1 large egg
1 cup firmly packed light brown sugar
2 Tbsp. creamy peanut butter
2 Tbsp. butter, melted
2 cups all-purpose flour
1 tsp. baking powder
½ tsp. baking soda
½ tsp. salt
1 cup buttermilk
Peanut Streusel Topping

1. Preheat oven to 350°. Line bottom and sides of a 9- x 5-inch loaf pan with heavy-duty aluminum foil, allowing 2 to 3 inches to extend over sides. Lightly grease foil with cooking spray.
2. Beat egg and sugar at medium speed with an electric mixer 2 minutes or until creamy; add peanut butter and butter, beating until blended.
3. Stir together flour and next 3 ingredients in a medium bowl; whisk in egg mixture and buttermilk just until blended. (Batter will be slightly lumpy.)
4. Spoon about ⅔ cup Peanut Streusel Topping on bottom of prepared pan. Spoon half of batter over streusel, gently spreading batter to sides of pan to cover streusel. Repeat procedure once. Sprinkle remaining ⅔ cup Peanut Streusel Topping over batter, gently pressing topping into batter.
5. Bake at 350° for 1 hour and 5 minutes or until a long wooden pick inserted in center comes out clean, shielding with foil after 45 minutes, if necessary. Cool in pan on a wire rack 10 minutes. Lift loaf from pan, using foil sides as handles. Place loaf on a wire rack. Carefully pull down sides of foil. Cool loaf completely (about 1 hour).

Peanut Streusel Topping: Stir together 1 cup chopped dry-roasted, salted peanuts; ½ cup all-purpose flour; ¼ cup butter, melted; 3 Tbsp. firmly packed light brown sugar; 2 Tbsp. granulated sugar; and ⅛ tsp. salt in a medium bowl. Let stand 15 minutes or until mixture is firm. Crumble into small pieces. **Makes** about 2 cups; Prep: 10 min., Stand: 15 min.

Chocolate Chip-Peanut Streusel Bread: Prepare recipe as directed through Step 3; stir ¾ cup semisweet chocolate mini-morsels into batter. Proceed with recipe as directed.

— INSPIRED BY DOLORES VACCARO,
PUEBLO, COLORADO

Blueberry Bread

MAKES 1 LOAF; **PREP:** 10 MIN.; **BAKE:** 1 HR.;
COOL: 1 HR., 10 MIN.

1½ cups all-purpose flour
1 tsp. salt
1 tsp. baking powder
⅛ tsp. ground cinnamon
1 cup fresh or frozen blueberries
1 cup sugar
½ cup milk
⅓ cup butter, melted
2 large eggs
1 tsp. lemon zest
2 Tbsp. lemon juice

1. Preheat oven to 350°. Stir together flour and next 3 ingredients in a medium bowl; stir in blueberries.
2. Whisk together sugar and next 5 ingredients in a medium bowl until thoroughly blended. Add to flour mixture, stirring just until blended. Pour batter into a lightly greased 8½- x 4½-inch loaf pan.
3. Bake at 350° for 1 hour or until a long wooden pick inserted in center comes out clean. Cool in pan on a wire rack 10 minutes. Remove from pan to wire rack, and cool completely (about 1 hour).

Blackberry Bread: Prepare recipe as directed in Step 1, substituting 1½ cups fresh or frozen blackberries for blueberries. Proceed with recipe as directed, increasing bake time to 1 hour and 15 minutes or until a long wooden pick inserted in center comes out clean.

Better-for-You Breakfast

No doubt about it, our breakfast recipes are some of the most popular and most requested. Considering our readers' fondness for Southwestern flavors and their nutrition savvy, we found it a no-brainer to select this great wrap. And it will be just as welcome at lunch or dinner.

Healthy Morning

SERVES 6

Over-the-Border Breakfast
Sausage Wraps

Mixed Fruit With Vanilla-Apple Syrup

Orange juice

Iced Coffee

Over-the-Border Breakfast Sausage Wraps

family favorite

MAKES 6 SERVINGS; **PREP:** 15 MIN.,
COOK: 28 MIN.

Reduced-fat cheese and egg substitute make these wraps as healthful as they are hearty.

1 (12-oz.) package 50%-less-fat ground
   pork sausage
Vegetable cooking spray
1 to 2 tsp. hot sauce
1 (16-oz.) carton Southwestern-flavored egg
   substitute
6 (8-inch) soft taco-size whole wheat or
   white flour tortillas
1½ cups (6 oz.) shredded reduced-fat
   Mexican cheese blend
Toppings: salsa, nonfat sour cream,
   chopped green onions

1. Cook sausage in a large nonstick skillet coated with cooking spray over medium-high heat 10 minutes or until sausage crumbles and is no longer pink. Tilt pan to drain well; pat sausage dry with paper towels. Stir in hot sauce.
2. Cook egg substitute in a large skillet coated with cooking spray over medium-high heat, without stirring, 1 to 2 minutes or until mixture begins to set on bottom.
3. Gently stir to slightly break up eggs. Cook, stirring occasionally, 3 to 4 minutes or until eggs are thickened and moist. (Do not overstir.) Remove skillet from heat.
4. Lightly coat both sides of tortillas with cooking spray. Spoon sausage, eggs, and cheese down center of each tortilla. Fold sides over, enclosing filling completely, and gently press to seal.
5. Cook wraps, in 2 batches, folded sides down, in a large skillet coated with cooking spray over medium-high heat 3 minutes or until lightly browned. Carefully turn, and cook 2 to 3 more minutes or until lightly browned and cheese is melted. Cut each wrap in half, and serve immediately with desired toppings.
Note: For testing purposes only, we used Jimmy Dean 50% Less Fat Than Regular Pork Sausage and Egg Beaters With Yolk Southwestern egg substitute.

Mixed Fruit With Vanilla-Apple Syrup

family favorite • make ahead

MAKES 6 SERVINGS; **PREP:** 15 MIN.,
COOK: 12 MIN., **COOL:** 30 MIN.,
CHILL: 2 HR.

For the best texture, choose crisp apples. Instead of Granny Smith, you can also use Fuji or McIntosh. Bartlett or Bosc pears would also make great choices.

⅓ cup sugar
¼ cup apple juice
1 tsp. vanilla extract
2 Granny Smith apples, chopped
2 oranges, peeled, sectioned, and
   halved
1 cup red seedless grapes
2 tsp. fresh lemon juice

1. Stir together sugar, apple juice, and ¼ cup water in a small saucepan. Bring to a boil; reduce heat, and simmer, stirring occasionally, 10 to 12 minutes or until mixture is reduced by about one-third. Remove pan from heat; stir in vanilla, and cool 30 minutes. Chill 2 hours.
2. Combine apples and next 3 ingredients in a large bowl. Drizzle chilled

syrup over fruit, gently tossing to coat. Serve immediately, or cover and chill fruit mixture up to 24 hours.

Note: Syrup may be stored in an airtight container up to 1 week in the refrigerator.

Iced Coffee

southernliving.com favorite

MAKES ½ CUP; **PREP:** 15 MIN.

This traditional Louisiana recipe came to us from the chefs at Commander's Palace and was adapted from their cookbook, Commander's Kitchen. *Make a batch of concentrate to keep in the refrigerator for hot or cold coffee. If you purchase coffee beans, grind them to percolator coarseness.*

¼ cup Coffee Concentrate
Milk (optional)
Sugar (optional)

1. Stir together ¼ cup each of Coffee Concentrate and water, and, if desired, stir in desired amounts of milk and sugar. Serve over ice.

Coffee Concentrate:

MAKES 1¾ QT; **PREP:** 30 MIN.,
STAND: 12 HR.

½ lb. ground coffee with chicory or dark roast ground coffee
7 cups cold water
1½ tsp. vanilla extract

1. Stir together ground coffee and 7 cups cold water in a pitcher until all ground coffee is wet; let coffee mixture stand 12 hours at room temperature.

2. Pour coffee mixture through a large, fine wire-mesh strainer, discarding grounds. Clean strainer; place a coffee filter or double layer of cheesecloth in strainer, and pour coffee mixture through lined strainer. Add vanilla; cover and chill up to 1 month.

GET INSPIRED

An Apple a Day

There's more than one way to serve this perennial favorite. Use the season's fresh harvest to create an appetizer that will have your family and friends clamoring for more.

Applelicious Sandwiches

MAKES 14 APPETIZER SANDWICHES;
PREP: 20 MIN., **COOK:** 21 MIN.

1. Thinly slice 2 Gala apples. Heat ¼ cup chopped walnuts in a small non-stick skillet over medium heat, stirring often, 3 to 5 minutes or until toasted and fragrant. Combine 1 (8-oz.) package of softened cream cheese, 1 (4.4-oz.) container blue cheese crumbles, 1 Tbsp. honey, and toasted walnuts until blended. Add freshly ground pepper to taste. Spread 1 side of each of 28 thin bread slices (1 [16-oz.] package) with 1 Tbsp. cream cheese mixture. Divide ½ (5-oz.) package arugula, thoroughly washed, among 14 bread slices. Top with apple slices and remaining 14 bread slices, cream cheese mixture sides down. Melt 1 Tbsp. butter on a griddle over medium heat. Cook 7 sandwiches 3 to 4 minutes on each side until golden and cheese is melted. Repeat procedure with 1 Tbsp. butter and remaining sandwiches.

Tip: If you don't have a griddle, omit butter, and cook sandwiches, in batches, in a lightly greased large nonstick skillet 3 to 4 minutes on each side or until golden and cheese is melted.

Note: For testing purposes only, we used Pepperidge Farm Very Thin White Bread.

Triple-Duty Spreads

Talk about bang for the buck. These recipes are delicious as spreads, dips, or sauces. We raved over hamburgers dressed with Ranch-Rémoulade Spread. Creamy Sun-dried Tomato-Tapenade Spread cozies up to grilled vegetables, pork, or chicken and makes a terrific dip for breadsticks. Our favorite use was serving chilled dollops of the spread over grilled steak.

Southwest White Bean Spread

make ahead

MAKES ABOUT 1¼ CUPS; **PREP:** 10 MIN., **CHILL:** 2 HR., **STAND:** 30 MIN.

This recipe stands out when paired with sun-dried tomato pita chips. It's also the perfect condiment for cold roast beef sandwiches or as a tasty (and good-for-you) sauce drizzled over grilled chicken or pork.

1 garlic clove
1 (15.5-oz.) can cannellini or great Northern beans, rinsed and drained
⅓ cup loosely packed fresh cilantro leaves
3 Tbsp. fresh lime juice
2 Tbsp. olive oil
½ tsp. ground cumin
Salt to taste
Pita chips, sliced cucumbers, and olives

1. Pulse garlic, next 5 ingredients, and 2 Tbsp. water in a food processor 3 or 4 times or until combined; process 1 to 2 minutes or until smooth, stopping to scrape down sides. Add salt to taste. Cover and chill at least 2 hours or up to 3 days. Let stand at room temperature 30 minutes before serving. Drizzle with additional olive oil, if desired. Serve with pita chips, sliced cucumbers, and olives.

— RAE-RAE MILLER, MOBILE, ALABAMA

Smoky Southwestern Spread: Prepare recipe as directed, adding 1½ Tbsp. chopped chipotle peppers in adobo sauce to mixture in food processor before pulsing. Chill as directed.

Green Chile Spread: Prepare recipe as directed, omitting water and adding 1 (4-oz.) can chopped green chiles to mixture in food processor before pulsing. Chill as directed.

Pickled Jalapeño Spread: Prepare recipe as directed, adding 1 Tbsp. chopped pickled jalapeño pepper slices to mixture in food processor before pulsing. Chill as directed.

Creamy Sun-dried Tomato-Tapenade Spread

fast fixin's make ahead

MAKES ABOUT 2 CUPS; **PREP:** 10 MIN.

1 (8-oz.) container refrigerated olive bruschetta topping, drained
1 (8-oz.) package cream cheese, softened
¼ cup extra-moist sun-dried tomato halves, chopped
1 Tbsp. chopped fresh basil

1. Beat together all ingredients with an electric mixer at medium speed until thoroughly combined. Cover and chill until ready to serve. Store in refrigerator in an airtight container up to 1 week.
Note: For testing purposes only, we used Gia Russa Olive Bruschetta Topping and California Sun-Dry Sun Dried Tomatoes, Halves.

Creamy Sun-dried Tomato-Tapenade Crostini: Preheat oven to 350°. Thinly slice 1 (16-oz.) French bread baguette. Spread about 1 Tbsp. Creamy Sun-dried Tomato-Tapenade Spread on each baguette slice. Arrange on a baking sheet. Bake 10 minutes. **Makes** 6 appetizer servings; Prep: 10 min., Bake: 10 min.

Canadian Bacon-Tomato-Tapenade Pizza: Preheat oven to 375°. Spread 1 cup Creamy Sun-dried Tomato-Tapenade Spread over 1 (14-oz.) prebaked Italian pizza crust. Place crust on a baking sheet. Sprinkle with 5 Canadian bacon slices, cut into thin strips (about 1 cup); 1 cup chopped artichoke hearts; ¾ cup grape tomato halves; and 2 Tbsp. grated Parmesan cheese. Bake 30 minutes or until lightly brown. **Makes** 4 to 6 servings; Prep: 15 min., Bake: 30 min.

Ranch-Rémoulade Spread

fast fixin's make ahead

MAKES ABOUT 1½ CUPS; **PREP:** 10 MIN.

1 cup mayonnaise
¼ cup Ranch dressing
1 large dill pickle, diced (about ½ cup)
1 Tbsp. country-style Dijon mustard
1 Tbsp. dill pickle juice
Assorted fresh vegetables

1. Stir together first 5 ingredients until blended. Cover and chill until ready to serve. Serve with assorted fresh vegetables. Store in refrigerator in an airtight container up to 1 week.
Note: For testing purposes only, we used Grey Poupon Country Dijon Mustard.

Easy Chicken Pies

When the weather starts to turn cool, we automatically crave comfort food. All the hearty foods sometimes avoided in the dense heat of summertime now become top priority. These chicken pies are good examples. They are simple, filling, and only need a salad or green vegetable to make a well-rounded meal. You can substitute canned chicken in both recipes, making them even faster and more affordable.

Chicken-and-Corn Pies With Cornbread Crust
family favorite

MAKES 5 SERVINGS; **PREP:** 25 MIN.,
COOK: 10 MIN., **BAKE:** 30 MIN.

You can keep most of the ingredients for this pot pie in the pantry for a filling, last-minute supper. (Pictured on page 189)

1 (10-oz.) can enchilada sauce
1 (10-oz.) can Mexican diced tomatoes
   with lime juice and cilantro, drained
2 cups frozen whole kernel corn
1 tsp. chili powder
3 cups chopped cooked chicken*
1 (6-oz.) package Mexican-style
   cornbread mix
²⁄₃ cup milk
1 large egg
2 Tbsp. vegetable oil
1 cup (4 oz.) shredded Mexican four-cheese
   blend, divided
Toppings: sliced pickled jalapeño peppers,
   sour cream

1. Preheat oven to 375°. Stir together enchilada sauce and next 3 ingredients in a 3½-qt. saucepan over medium heat until combined; cook, stirring occasionally, 10 minutes. Stir in chicken.
2. Whisk together cornbread mix, next 3 ingredients, and ¾ cup cheese in a small bowl just until blended.
3. Pour chicken mixture into 5 lightly greased (10-oz.) ramekins. Spoon cornbread mixture over hot chicken mixture. Sprinkle with remaining ¼ cup cheese. Divide ramekins onto 2 jelly-roll pans.

4. Bake at 375° for 30 minutes or until golden and bubbly. Serve with desired toppings.
*2 (12.5-oz.) cans chicken, drained, may be substituted.
Note: Mixture may be prepared in a lightly greased 11- x 7-inch baking dish. Bake as directed, omitting jelly-roll pans.

Easy Chicken Pie
family favorite • make ahead
MAKES 6 SERVINGS; **PREP:** 25 MIN.,
BAKE: 45 MIN., **STAND:** 10 MIN.

½ (15-oz.) package refrigerated
   piecrusts
1 (10¾-oz.) can cream of chicken
   soup with herbs
3 cups chopped cooked
   chicken*
3 cups frozen peas and carrots
1 cup low-sodium chicken broth
¾ cup buttermilk
¼ cup dry white wine
1½ Tbsp. cornstarch

1. Preheat oven to 400°. Unroll piecrust on a lightly floured surface; roll into a 14- x 12-inch rectangle.
2. Stir together soup and next 6 ingredients in a medium bowl. Pour into a lightly greased 11- x 7-inch baking dish. Top with piecrust; fold edges under, and crimp. Cut slits in top for steam to escape.

3. Bake at 400° for 45 minutes or until golden and bubbly. Let stand 10 minutes before serving.
*2 (12.5-oz.) cans chicken, drained, may be substituted.
Note: To make ahead, prepare recipe as directed through Step 2. Cover tightly with aluminum foil, and freeze up to 1 month. Preheat oven to 400°. Remove pie from freezer, and let stand at room temperature 30 minutes. Loosen foil, and place pie on a foil-lined baking sheet. Bake, covered, for 1 hour and 30 minutes. Uncover and bake 15 to 20 minutes or until golden and bubbly.

Mushroom-Bacon Chicken Pie:
Cook 5 bacon slices in a large skillet over medium heat 5 minutes on each side or until crisp. Remove bacon slices, reserving drippings in skillet. Crumble bacon. Sauté 1 (8-oz.) package sliced fresh mushrooms in hot drippings 10 minutes or until tender. Add 2 minced garlic cloves, and sauté 1 minute. Prepare recipe as directed, stirring mushroom mixture and crumbled bacon into chicken mixture.

Unbeatable Combos

Tender, juicy, and sizzling with flavor, kabobs are so simple to fix, you can enjoy them any night of the week. As for ingredients, almost anything goes with these versatile recipes. Pork can easily stand in for chicken, or try using boneless chicken thighs instead of breasts. Swap apples and partially cooked sweet potatoes for green tomatoes and plums, or amp up the heat by substituting poblano chiles for bell peppers. The possibilities are endless!

Spicy Thai Chicken Kabobs
family favorite

MAKES 4 TO 6 SERVINGS; **PREP:** 20 MIN.,
CHILL: 8 HR., **SOAK:** 30 MIN.,
GRILL: 16 MIN.

Stir up a superfast peanut sauce, and marinate the chicken before you head out for the day. The remaining ingredients can be quickly put together when you get home from work.

½ cup creamy peanut butter
½ cup lite soy sauce
¼ cup firmly packed light brown sugar
1 Tbsp. lime zest
1 tsp. dried crushed red pepper
1½ lb. skinned and boned chicken breasts, cut into 1-inch pieces
8 (12-inch) wooden or metal skewers
1 bunch green onions, cut into 2-inch pieces
1 large red bell pepper, cut into 1-inch pieces
1 large yellow bell pepper, cut into 1-inch pieces
32 fresh snow peas
16 basil leaves

1. Whisk together first 5 ingredients and ½ cup water in a large shallow dish or zip-top plastic freezer bag; reserve ¾ cup. Add chicken to dish, turning to coat. Cover or seal, and chill 8 hours, turning occasionally.
2. Soak wooden skewers in water 30 minutes.
3. Preheat the grill to 350° to 400° (medium-high). Remove chicken from marinade, discarding marinade. Thread chicken, onions, and next 4 ingredients alternately onto wooden skewers, leaving ¼ inch between pieces.
4. Grill kabobs, covered with grill lid, over 350° to 400° (medium-high) heat 6 to 8 minutes on each side or until done. Remove from grill, and baste with reserved ¾ cup marinade.

— **NANCY HAJECK**, FAIRVIEW, TENNESSEE

Spicy Thai Pork Kabobs:
Substitute 1 (1.5-lb.) package pork tenderloin, trimmed, for chicken. Proceed with recipe as directed.

Bacon-Wrapped Barbecue Chicken Kabobs

MAKES 4 TO 6 SERVINGS; **PREP:** 15 MIN.,
CHILL: 1 HR., **SOAK:** 30 MIN., **COOL:** 5 MIN.,
GRILL: 12 MIN.

Chicken and bacon are threaded ribbon-style on these fun skewers. Serve them with extra barbecue sauce for dipping.

⅔ cup barbecue sauce
⅓ cup chili sauce
1½ Tbsp. Worcestershire sauce
12 chicken tenders (about 1½ lb.)
12 (6-inch) wooden or metal skewers
6 bacon slices, cut in half crosswise

1. Whisk together first 3 ingredients in a large shallow dish or zip-top plastic freezer bag; add chicken, turning to coat. Cover or seal, and chill 1 hour, turning once.
2. Meanwhile, soak wooden skewers in water 30 minutes.
3. Preheat grill to 350° to 400° (medium-high). Microwave bacon, in 2 batches, on a microwave-safe plate at HIGH 1 minute. Let cool 5 minutes.
4. Remove chicken from marinade, discarding marinade. Place 1 bacon piece on top of each chicken tender; thread 1 bacon-topped chicken tender onto each skewer.

Made To Order

- Inspired by a favorite gumbo recipe, Creole Turkey-and-Sausage Kabobs team with rice for a hearty meal the whole family will love. Always in season, frozen okra threads easily onto skewers for a time-saving shortcut.
- Premarinated meats and poultry always offer a speedy solution for last-minute suppers. Low in fat, rubs and seasoning blends also add fast flavor and help seal in juices.
- Pair vegetables and fruit with similar cook times, such as bell pepper and summer squash, and keep the pieces uniform in size. If you'd like to add potatoes or carrots, parboil them first until almost done but still firm.
- When cutting an onion into wedges, leave the root end intact so the layers hold together for easy handling. For extra-tender grilled onions, microwave the wedges at HIGH for 1 to 2 minutes before threading onto skewers.
- Tightly packed skewers take longer to grill, so leave a small amount of space between each piece to ensure quick, even cooking.

5. Grill kabobs, covered with grill lid, over 350° to 400° (medium-high) heat 5 to 6 minutes on each side or until done.

— KARL MYNYK, OREFIELD, PENNSYLVANIA

Molasses-Balsamic Pork Kabobs With Green Tomatoes and Plums

family favorite

MAKES 4 TO 6 SERVINGS; **PREP:** 20 MIN., **SOAK:** 30 MIN., **GRILL:** 18 MIN.

An unbeatable combo, these kabobs caramelize to a smoky sweetness when grilled. (Pictured on page 188)

8 (12-inch) wooden or metal skewers
1 (1.5-lb.) package pork tenderloin, trimmed and cut into 1½-inch pieces
4 large plums, quartered
2 medium-size green tomatoes, cut into eighths
2 medium-size red onions, cut into eighths
2 tsp. seasoned salt
2 tsp. pepper
½ cup molasses
¼ cup balsamic vinegar

1. Soak wooden skewers in water 30 minutes.
2. Preheat grill to 350° to 400° (medium-high). Thread pork and next 3 ingredients alternately onto skewers, leaving ¼ inch between pieces. Sprinkle kabobs with seasoned salt and pepper. Stir together molasses and vinegar.
3. Grill kabobs, covered with grill lid, over 350° to 400° (medium-high) heat 12 minutes, turning after 6 minutes. Baste kabobs with half of molasses mixture, and grill 3 minutes. Turn kabobs, baste with remaining half of molasses mixture, and grill 3 more minutes or until done.

Molasses-Balsamic Chicken Kabobs With Green Tomatoes and Plums: Substitute 1½ lb. skinned and boned chicken breasts for pork. Proceed with recipe as directed.

Molasses-Balsamic Turkey Kabobs With Green Tomatoes and Plums: Substitute 2 (¾-lb.) turkey tenderloins for pork. Proceed with recipe as directed.

Molasses-Balsamic Pork Kabobs With Green Apples and Peppers: Substitute 1 Granny Smith apple, cut into eighths, and 1 large red bell pepper, cut into 1-inch pieces, for plums and green tomatoes. Proceed with recipe as directed.

— KURT GODSHALL, SHELBYVILLE, KENTUCKY

Creole Turkey-and-Sausage Kabobs

MAKES 4 TO 6 SERVINGS; **PREP:** 20 MIN., **SOAK:** 30 MIN., **GRILL:** 18 MIN.

8 (12-inch) wooden or metal skewers
2 (¾-lb.) turkey tenderloins, cut into 1½-inch chunks
¾ lb. smoked sausage, cut into 1-inch slices
½ (16-oz.) package frozen whole okra, thawed
1 large red bell pepper, cut in 1-inch pieces
1½ tsp. Creole seasoning

1. Soak wooden skewers in water 30 minutes.
2. Preheat grill to 350° to 400° (medium-high). Thread turkey, smoked sausage, okra, and bell pepper alternately onto skewers, leaving ¼ inch between pieces; sprinkle with Creole seasoning.
3. Grill kabobs, covered with grill lid, over 350° to 400° (medium-high) heat 18 minutes or until done, turning every 6 minutes.

Creole Chicken-and-Sausage Kabobs: Substitute 1½ lb. skinned and boned chicken breasts for turkey. Proceed with recipe as directed.

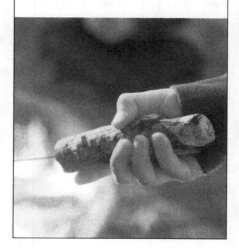

Meatloaf Makeover

Simple recipe updates take this comfort classic from bland and boring to something special.

Here's our secret for moist, tender meatloaf: Use a light touch when combining the ingredients. Overmixing compacts the meat, leading to dry, tough results. Let the meatloaf stand after baking, which helps retain moisture, the same way you allow a steak or roast to rest before carving.

Beef-and-Sausage Meatloaf With Chunky Red Sauce

MAKES 12 SERVINGS (2 MEATLOAVES); **PREP:** 15 MIN., **BAKE:** 50 MIN., **STAND:** 10 MIN.

Cook once for two meals. Serve one meatloaf for supper, and chill the other for at least eight hours. Slice the chilled meatloaf, and reheat to create open-face sandwiches. Or freeze the second loaf for a meal later in the month.

1 lb. ground sirloin*
1 lb. ground pork sausage
1 sleeve multigrain saltine crackers, crushed
1 (15-oz.) can tomato sauce
1 green bell pepper, diced
½ cup diced red onion
2 large eggs, lightly beaten
Chunky Red Sauce

1. Preheat oven to 425°. Line bottom and sides of 2 (8- x 4-inch) loaf pans with aluminum foil, allowing 2 to 3 inches to extend over sides; fold foil down around sides of pan. Lightly grease foil.
2. Gently combine first 7 ingredients in a medium bowl. Shape mixture into 2 loaves. Place meatloaves in prepared pans.
3. Bake at 425° for 50 minutes or until a meat thermometer inserted into thickest portion registers 160°. Let stand 10 minutes. Remove meatloaves from pans, using foil sides as handles. Serve with Chunky Red Sauce.
*Ground chuck or lean ground beef may be substituted.
Note: If serving 1 meatloaf, let remaining cooked meatloaf stand until completely cool (about 30 minutes). Wrap tightly in plastic wrap and aluminum foil, and place in a large zip-top plastic bag. Store in refrigerator 2 to 3 days, or freeze up to 1 month.

Chunky Red Sauce:

MAKES ABOUT 3 CUPS; **PREP:** 5 MIN., **COOK:** 15 MIN.

1 (26-oz.) jar vegetable spaghetti sauce
1 (14.5-oz.) can fire-roasted diced tomatoes*
2 tsp. dried Italian seasoning
¼ tsp. pepper

1. Stir together all ingredients in a large saucepan over medium heat. Cook, stirring frequently, 15 minutes or until thoroughly heated.
—**VICKI CHILDERS**, HUNTINGTON, WEST VIRGINIA

*1 (14.5-oz.) can diced tomatoes may be substituted.
Note: For testing purposes only, we used Ragu Garden Combination Pasta Sauce and Hunt's Fire Roasted Diced Tomatoes.

Beef-and-Sausage Meatloaf With Chunky Red Sauce on Cheese Toast

family favorite
MAKES 6 SERVINGS; **PREP:** 15 MIN., **BAKE:** 37 MIN.

1 cooked Beef-and-Sausage Meatloaf, chilled
1 (12-oz.) French bread loaf
1 (8-oz.) block mozzarella cheese, grated and divided
Chunky Red Sauce (recipe at left)
2 Tbsp. chopped fresh parsley

1. Preheat oven to 325°. Cut chilled meatloaf into 6 (1-inch-thick) slices. Place on an aluminum foil-lined baking sheet.
2. Bake for 30 minutes. Remove to a wire rack. Increase oven temperature to 400°.
3. Cut bread diagonally into 6 (1-inch-thick) slices. Place on an aluminum foil-lined baking sheet. Sprinkle evenly with 1 cup (4 oz.) mozzarella cheese.
4. Bake at 400° for 5 to 7 minutes or until cheese is melted and bubbly. Place 1 meatloaf slice on each piece of cheese toast. Top with desired amount of Chunky Red Sauce. Sprinkle with parsley and remaining cheese.

One Great Meatloaf, Three Practical Choices

We tested Beef-and-Sausage Meatloaf With Chunky Red Sauce comparing three types of ground beef (ground chuck, sirloin, and 92% lean ground beef) with pleasing results—not a dry slice in the bunch. The only tip you might need is to blot any excess oil from the higher-fat-content chuck version after baking. It's a personal preference. Watch for sales, and select the version that best suits your budget.

Tex-Mex Mini Meatloaves
family favorite

MAKES 8 SERVINGS; **PREP:** 20 MIN.,
BAKE: 47 MIN.

*These mini loaves taste like enchiladas.
You need to purchase fresh sausage in
casings like Italian links, not the dried
variety that's similar to pepperoni.
Freeze leftovers up to a month.*

1 lb. fresh chorizo sausage, casings
     removed
1 lb. ground pork
1 (15-oz.) can black beans, rinsed and
     drained
1 (15-oz.) can whole kernel corn, rinsed and
     drained
1 cup finely crushed nacho cheese-flavored
     tortilla chips
1 cup frozen diced onion, red and green bell
     pepper, and celery
2 large eggs, lightly beaten
2 Tbsp. chopped fresh cilantro
1 tsp. fajita seasoning
1 cup (4 oz.) shredded Mexican four-cheese
     blend
Toppings: guacamole, sour cream, salsa

1. Preheat oven to 375°. Gently combine first 9 ingredients in a medium
bowl. Press mixture into 16 lightly
greased muffin pan cups. Place on an
aluminum foil-lined baking sheet.
2. Bake at 375° for 45 minutes.
Sprinkle with cheese. Bake 2 more minutes or until cheese is melted and bubbly. Serve with desired toppings.

— ZAN BROCK, JASPER, ALABAMA

Note: For testing purposes only, we
used Doritos Nacho Cheese Flavored
Tortilla Chips and McCormick Fajitas
Seasoning Mix.

Delicious and Golden

Roast golden beets, and you're in for a sweet surprise. Lightly
dressed with a brown sugar-and-vanilla vinaigrette, this party-
worthy salad is the perfect choice for easy entertaining.

> **•TIP•**
>
> For this delectable salad, you can
> roast and peel the beets up to two
> days ahead, and chill them in a
> zip-top bag. When prepping, don't
> peel them or trim the little tails on
> the bottom. Do remove the greens,
> but leave an inch of the stems to
> ensure the pigment remains inside
> the beets during roasting. Similar
> in flavor to Swiss chard, beet
> greens can be prepared in the
> same way as turnips or collards.

Pecan-Beet Salad
make ahead

MAKES 4 TO 6 SERVINGS; **PREP:** 20 MIN.;
BAKE: 1 HR., 7 MIN.; **COOL:** 30 MIN.

*Toasted pecans and creamy Gorgonzola
cheese add the finishing touch to this
gourmet greens salad.*

6 medium-size golden beets
     (about 6 oz. each)
1 cup pecan halves
¼ cup rice wine vinegar
1 large shallot, minced
2 Tbsp. light brown sugar
½ tsp. salt
½ tsp. freshly ground pepper
½ tsp. vanilla extract
¼ cup canola oil
1 (5-oz.) package gourmet mixed salad
     greens, thoroughly washed
1 cup crumbled Gorgonzola
     cheese

1. Preheat oven to 400°. Trim beet
stems to 1 inch; gently wash beets.

Wrap individually in aluminum foil,
and place on a jelly-roll pan.
2. Bake at 400° for 1 hour or until
tender. Transfer to a wire rack, and let
cool, wrapped in foil, 30 minutes.
3. Meanwhile, decrease oven temperature to 350°. Bake pecan halves
in a single layer in a jelly-roll pan 5 to
7 minutes or until lightly toasted and
fragrant. Cool completely on wire rack
(about 15 minutes).
4. Whisk together vinegar and next 5
ingredients in a small bowl. Add oil in
a slow, steady stream, whisking constantly until smooth.
5. Peel beets, and remove stem ends.
Cut beets into ½-inch wedges; gently
toss with ⅓ cup vinegar mixture.
6. Arrange greens on a serving platter.
Top with beet mixture, Gorgonzola
cheese, and pecans; serve with remaining vinaigrette.

— INSPIRED BY PAT PATERNOSTRO,
METAIRIE, LOUISIANA

No-Fuss Ravioli

Won ton wrappers make a convenient stand-in for fresh pasta dough. Found in the refrigerated produce section of your grocery store, these versatile wrappers can be filled and folded in half to create tender and tasty pockets of flavor.

Cheese Ravioli With Spicy Tomato Sauce

family favorite

MAKES 4 SERVINGS;
PREP: 30 MIN., **COOK:** 11 MIN.

This dish hits the table in less than 45 minutes. Change the level of spiciness by adjusting the amount of dried crushed red pepper.

1 cup ricotta cheese
½ cup freshly shredded Parmesan cheese
¾ tsp. black pepper
⅓ cup chopped fresh basil, divided
½ (16-oz.) package won ton wrappers
1 pt. cherry tomatoes, halved
2 Tbsp. olive oil
½ cup chicken broth
1 tsp. white wine vinegar
¼ to ½ tsp. dried crushed red pepper
¼ tsp. salt
Garnishes: fresh basil leaves, freshly shaved Parmesan cheese

1. Stir together first 3 ingredients and 3 Tbsp. chopped fresh basil in a small bowl.

2. Arrange 1 won ton wrapper on a clean, flat surface. (Cover remaining wrappers with plastic wrap or a damp towel to prevent drying out.) Lightly moisten edges of wrapper with water. Place about 1½ tsp. cheese mixture in center of wrapper; fold 2 opposite corners together over cheese mixture, forming a triangle. Press edges together to seal, removing any air pockets. Cover with plastic wrap or a damp cloth. Repeat procedure with remaining wrappers and cheese mixture.

3. Cook ravioli, in 2 batches, in boiling salted water to cover in a Dutch oven over medium-high heat 3 minutes. Remove with a slotted spoon, and drain well on a lightly greased wire rack. Divide cooked ravioli among 4 individual serving bowls.

4. Sauté tomatoes in hot oil in a large skillet over medium-high heat 2 minutes or just until soft. Add broth and white wine vinegar; cook 2 to 3 minutes or until tomatoes begin to wilt. Stir in dried crushed red pepper, salt, and remaining basil. Pour sauce over ravioli. Garnish, if desired. Serve immediately.

Working With Won Ton Wrappers

Making your own ravioli at home has never been easier. Keep filled ravioli from drying out by placing it on a lightly greased, parchment paper-lined jelly-roll pan and covering it with a damp towel. If you want to get a head start on dinner, assemble these delectable little dumplings a day ahead, cover, and refrigerate until ready to cook.

Crispy 'n' Sweet Pumpkin Dumplings

MAKES 30 DUMPLINGS (ABOUT 10 SERVINGS); **PREP:** 30 MIN., **FRY:** 40 SEC. PER BATCH

These sweet little treats are great for entertaining a crowd and are a fun alternative to pumpkin pie.

1 (15-oz.) can pumpkin
¼ cup granulated sugar
2 Tbsp. light brown sugar
2 Tbsp. honey
¾ tsp. pumpkin pie spice
½ (16-oz.) package won ton wrappers
Vegetable oil
Powdered sugar

1. Stir together first 5 ingredients in a medium bowl.

2. Arrange 1 won ton wrapper on a clean, flat surface. (Cover remaining wrappers with plastic wrap or a damp towel to prevent drying out.) Lightly moisten edges of wrapper with water. Place about 2 tsp. pumpkin mixture in center of wrapper; fold 2 opposite corners together over pumpkin mixture, forming a triangle. Press edges together to seal, removing any air pockets. Cover with plastic wrap or a damp cloth. Repeat procedure with remaining wrappers and pumpkin mixture.

3. Pour oil to depth of 3 inches in a Dutch oven; heat to 375°. Fry dumplings, 3 at a time, about 20 seconds on each side or until golden brown and edges are crisp. Drain on paper towels. Sprinkle with powdered sugar, and serve immediately.

Crispy 'n' Sweet Chocolate-Hazelnut Dumplings: Omit first 5 ingredients. Whisk together ½ (8-oz.) package softened cream cheese, 1 cup hazelnut spread, and 3 Tbsp. all-purpose flour until blended and smooth. Proceed with recipe as directed, beginning with Step 2.

Note: For testing purposes only, we used Nutella for hazelnut spread.

Grilled Cheese and Chili

These recipes create a hearty, soul-soothing supper to fit your fast-paced lifestyle.

Grilled Cheese Supper

SERVES 4

Extra Cheesy Grilled Cheese

Quick Turkey Chili

Tortilla chips

Iced tea

Busy moms need an easy dinner option now that after-school activities are in full swing. Quick Turkey Chili is a snap to assemble. Including prep and cook time, you'll have it ready in an hour. If you have time, make a double batch and store some in the freezer for a jump-start on a future meal. Your family won't be able to resist the buttery aroma of Extra Cheesy Grilled Cheese sandwiches sizzling on the griddle. Get ready for simple and delicious weeknight fare.

Extra Cheesy Grilled Cheese

family favorite

MAKES 4 SANDWICHES; **PREP:** 10 MIN., **COOK:** 8 MIN. PER BATCH

¼ cup butter, softened
1 Tbsp. grated Parmesan cheese
8 Italian bread slices
4 (¾-oz.) provolone cheese slices
4 (¾-oz.) mozzarella cheese slices

1. Stir together butter and Parmesan cheese in a small bowl.
2. Spread 1½ tsp. butter mixture on 1 side of each bread slice. Place 4 bread slices, buttered sides down, on wax paper. Top with provolone and mozzarella cheeses; top with remaining bread slices, buttered sides up.
3. Cook sandwiches, in batches, on a hot griddle or in a nonstick skillet over medium heat, gently pressing with a spatula, 4 minutes on each side or until golden brown and cheese is melted.

Quick Turkey Chili

family favorite

MAKES 6 TO 8 SERVINGS; **PREP:** 15 MIN., **COOK:** 46 MIN.

Don't let the long list of ingredients deter you; chances are you'll have most of them on hand.

1 medium onion, chopped
1 Tbsp. vegetable oil
2 garlic cloves, chopped
1 lb. ground turkey
2 Tbsp. chili powder
2 tsp. ground cumin
3 Tbsp. tomato paste
1 (28-oz.) can diced tomatoes
1 (16-oz.) can red kidney beans, rinsed and drained
1 cup chicken broth
1 cup beer*
1 tsp. salt
½ tsp. pepper
¼ cup chopped fresh cilantro
Garnish: sour cream

1. Sauté chopped onion in hot oil in a large Dutch oven over medium-high heat 5 minutes or until tender; add garlic, and sauté 1 minute.
2. Add turkey, chili powder, and cumin, and cook, stirring often, 8 minutes or until meat crumbles and is no longer pink. Stir in tomato paste, and cook 2 minutes. Add tomatoes and next 5 ingredients. Bring mixture to a boil; cover, reduce heat to low, and simmer, stirring occasionally, 30 minutes. Stir in cilantro. Garnish, if desired.
***Chicken broth may be substituted.

Eco-Friendly Kitchen

Transform your space with these easy, practical ideas and see how small changes add up to big benefits for our planet.

Trash Matters—Recycle In many

neighborhoods, Green living begins just outside the front door with curb-side recycling. Paper, plastic, and aluminum account for 85% of packaging materials, and each is recyclable. Aside from produce, most grocery items are packaged in containers made to be recycled. If your family plows through a pantry full of groceries every week like we do here, start recycling. You'll be amazed at how much trash and precious resources you'll save from going into landfills. When we began a voluntary recycling program, the news spread quickly, and from the inspiration of one kitchen, we're now kicking off a pilot recycling program for our entire company!

Crack the code by checking with local recycling centers for a listing of what can and cannot be recycled in your neighborhood. Before you begin, simplify sorting by designating colored containers or bags for easy separation and collection.

Going Green One Kitchen at a Time

Everywhere you turn, Green is the word. Grasping the basics begins by cutting our daily production of household waste. An average kitchen contributes more than 200 pounds of waste each year. Take the challenge, and go Green with the *Southern Living* Test Kitchens as we reduce, reuse, and recycle our way into an eco-friendly kitchen.

3 Simple Steps:
1. Compost fruit and vegetable peels and pulp.
2. Buy local produce to cut down on the amount of oil consumed in transport.
3. Choose vegetable-based dishwashing detergents over petroleum-based products.

Shopper Chic The checkout line dilemma—paper or plastic?

Neither is acceptable for environmentally savvy shoppers. Paper bags generate an extreme amount of air and water pollution during production, and plastic bags pose serious threats to wildlife because they do not decompose. The solution is simple: Choose reusable cloth bags made from lightweight canvas, nylon, or recycled cotton. Eco-bags, as they are often called, are durable, budget-friendly alternatives for transporting groceries. Bags can be purchased in most supermarkets, online, and at local farmer's markets. Select those that compress easily for storage, and stash several in your car.

Choosing to reuse helps decrease our consumption of precious natural resources and minimizes the volume of nonbiodegradable materials in our landfills. By making the switch, our Test Kitchens Professionals prevent an estimated 312 bags each per year from ending up in public landfills.

Bring on the Green Visit southernliving.

com/greenkitchen for more ideas, tips, and resources for transforming your kitchen. Considering a home composting program? You can also download a *Southern Living* design for building a compost bin made completely of recycled materials.

Cooking School

Promise Buttery Spread

Discover the great buttery taste this heart-healthy spread provides.

Toasted Walnut and Pesto Pasta

MAKES 4 SERVINGS; **PREP:** 20 MIN., **COOK:** 23 MIN., **COOL:** 5 MIN.

2 Tbsp. chopped walnuts
½ (16-oz.) package whole wheat penne pasta
1 garlic clove
½ cup loosely packed fresh basil leaves
¼ cup loosely packed fresh parsley leaves
3 Tbsp. PROMISE Buttery Spread, divided
½ lb. skinned and boned chicken breasts, thinly sliced
1 cup diced zucchini
1 small red bell pepper, cut into thin strips
Garnish: fresh parsley sprig

1. Heat nuts in a 10-inch nonstick skillet over medium-low heat, stirring often, 3 minutes or until toasted and fragrant. Remove nuts from heat, and let cool 5 minutes.
2. Cook pasta according to package directions; drain, reserving ¼ cup pasta water.
3. Meanwhile, process walnuts and garlic in a blender or food processor 10 seconds or until finely chopped. Add basil, parsley, and 2 Tbsp. buttery spread; process 30 seconds or until blended.
4. Melt remaining 1 Tbsp. buttery spread in skillet over medium heat; add chicken, and cook, stirring occasionally, 6 to 7 minutes or until lightly browned. Remove chicken from skillet.

5. Add zucchini and bell pepper to skillet, and cook over medium heat, stirring occasionally, 4 minutes or until tender. Return chicken and any accumulated juices to skillet, and cook 1 minute or until chicken is done. Toss hot penne with chicken mixture, pesto, and reserved pasta water. Garnish, if desired.

Italian-Style Chicken Tostadas

MAKES 16 SERVINGS; **PREP:** 10 MIN., **BAKE:** 6 MIN., **COOK:** 7 MIN., **BROIL:** 3 MIN.

2 whole wheat pita rounds
2 Tbsp. PROMISE Buttery Spread
1 cup thinly sliced onion
1 (7-oz.) jar roasted red bell peppers, drained and thinly sliced
1 cup shredded cooked chicken
2 Tbsp. shredded Parmesan cheese
¼ tsp. salt
2 Tbsp. loosely packed fresh basil leaves , thinly sliced (optional)
¼ cup (1 oz.) shredded part-skim mozzarella cheese
Garnish: fresh basil sprig

1. Preheat oven to 375°. Split pitas in half horizontally to make 4 rounds. Arrange pitas on a baking sheet, cut side up. Bake 6 minutes or until lightly toasted. Increase oven temperature to broil.
2. Meanwhile, melt buttery spread in a 10-inch nonstick skillet over medium-high heat; add onion, and cook, stirring occasionally, 5 minutes or until onions begin to brown. Add roasted peppers and chicken, and cook, stirring constantly, 2 minutes or until thoroughly heated. Stir in Parmesan cheese, salt, and, if desired, basil.
3. Top pitas with chicken mixture; sprinkle with mozzarella cheese.
4. Broil 5 inches from heat 2 to 3 minutes or just until cheese is melted. Cut into quarters. Garnish, if desired.

Ginger-Glazed Carrot Cake

MAKES 12 SERVINGS; **PREP:** 20 MIN.; **BAKE:** 35 MIN.; **COOL:** 1 HR., 10 MIN.

A sweet, buttery glaze drizzled atop this cinnamon and ginger-flavored cake makes it extra-rich.

Vegetable cooking spray
1 cup all-purpose flour
1 tsp. baking powder
¾ tsp. ground cinnamon
¼ tsp. baking soda
¼ tsp. ground ginger
¼ tsp. salt
⅓ cup PROMISE Buttery Spread
½ cup granulated sugar
⅓ cup firmly packed dark brown sugar
½ tsp. vanilla extract
2 large eggs
⅓ cup low-fat plain yogurt
1½ cups grated carrots (about 3 large carrots)
½ cup powdered sugar
1 Tbsp. fat-free milk
2 tsp. PROMISE Buttery Spread
¼ tsp. ground ginger
Garnish: slivered almonds

1. Preheat oven to 350°. Place a large piece of aluminum foil over bottom of a 9-inch springform pan. Attach sides of pan; fold excess foil around outside of pan. Coat bottom of springform pan with cooking spray.
2. Stir together flour and next 5 ingredients.
3. Beat ⅓ cup buttery spread, granulated sugar, and brown sugar at medium speed with an electric mixer until light and fluffy (about 5 minutes). Beat in vanilla; add eggs, 1 at a time, beating 1 minute after each addition.
4. Beat in yogurt. Gradually beat in flour mixture; add carrots, and beat until blended. Spoon into prepared pan.
5. Bake at 350° for 35 minutes or until a wooden pick inserted in center comes out clean. Remove from oven, and gently

run a knife around outer edge of cake to loosen. Cool on a wire rack 10 minutes; remove sides of pan, and let cake cool 1 hour or until completely cool.

6. Stir together powdered sugar and next 3 ingredients. Drizzle glaze over cooled cake. Garnish, if desired.

General Tso's Chicken and Broccoli

MAKES 4 SERVINGS; **PREP:** 15 MIN., **COOK:** 6 MIN.

¾ lb. skinned and boned chicken breasts
1 (14½-oz.) can low-sodium fat-free
  chicken broth
4 Tbsp. cornstarch, divided
2 Tbsp. brown sugar
1 to 2 Tbsp. hot chili sauce
1½ Tbsp. rice wine or white vinegar
2 cups broccoli florets
2 tsp. lite sodium soy sauce
3 Tbsp. PROMISE Buttery Spread

1. Place chicken breasts between 2 sheets of plastic wrap, and flatten to ¼-inch thickness, using a rolling pin or flat side of a meat mallet. Thinly slice chicken.
2. Whisk together broth, 2 Tbsp. cornstarch, hot chili sauce, sugar, and vinegar.
3. Place broccoli and 2 Tbsp. water in a microwave-save bowl. Cover with plastic wrap; fold back a small edge to allow steam to escape. Microwave at HIGH 1 minute. Combine chicken and soy sauce in a medium bowl; toss with remaining 2 Tbsp. cornstarch to coat.
4. Melt buttery spread in a 12-inch nonstick skillet over medium-high heat; add chicken, and cook, stirring occasionally, 3 minutes or until done. Transfer chicken to a serving platter; keep warm.
5. Bring broth mixture to a boil in skillet over high heat, stirring frequently. Reduce heat to low, and simmer, stirring occasionally, 1 minute or until thickened. Add broccoli, and toss to coat. Cook 1 minute or until thoroughly heated. Pour sauce over chicken. Serve immediately.

Black Forest Ginger Cookies

MAKES 32 COOKIES; **PREP:** 25 MIN.,
BAKE: 10 MIN., **COOL:** 22 MIN.

2 cups plus 2 Tbsp. all-purpose flour
¼ cup unsweetened cocoa
1 tsp. ground ginger
¾ tsp. baking powder
¾ tsp. baking soda
¼ tsp. salt
6 Tbsp. PROMISE Buttery Spread
1 cup firmly packed light brown sugar
1 (6-oz.) container fat-free chocolate yogurt
1 large egg
1 cup chopped dried cherries or cranberries
¼ cup finely chopped pecans

1. Preheat oven to 375°. Stir together first 6 ingredients in a medium bowl.
2. Beat buttery spread and brown sugar with an electric mixer at medium speed 3 minutes or until creamy. Beat in yogurt and egg until blended. Gradually beat in flour mixture just until blended. Stir in cherries and pecans. Drop dough by 2 tablespoonfuls, 4 inches apart, onto lightly greased baking sheets.
3. Bake at 375° for 10 minutes or until edges are crisp and centers are set. Cool on baking sheets on wire racks 2 minutes; remove to wire racks, and cool 20 minutes or until completely cool.

Kitchen-Aid

Use your KitchenAid Stand Mixer and handy attachments to make a large assortment of dishes.

Black-eyed Pea Falafel With Sun-dried Tomato Hummus

MAKES 6 SERVINGS; **PREP:** 30 MIN.,
CHILL: 30 MIN., **COOK:** 6 MIN. PER BATCH

KITCHENAID Electric Stand Mixer
KITCHENAID Food Grinder Attachment
2 (15-oz.) cans black-eyed peas, rinsed and drained
1 garlic clove, minced
½ cup minced onion
3 Tbsp. chopped fresh cilantro
2 Tbsp. chopped fresh parsley
½ tsp. salt
½ tsp. ground cumin
¼ tsp. ground red pepper
20 saltine crackers, finely crushed
2 Tbsp. all-purpose flour
1 large egg, lightly beaten
Wax paper
1 (10-oz.) container plain hummus
⅓ cup drained sun-dried tomatoes in oil
½ cup canola oil
Pita bread, grape tomatoes, cucumbers,
  arugula (optional)

1. Attach food grinder attachment to electric stand mixer according to manufacturer's instructions. Grind peas and next 7 ingredients according to manufacturer's instructions using the coarse grinding plate.
2. Stir together crackers and flour in a bowl. Stir ½ cup cracker mixture and egg into ground pea mixture until well blended. Reserve remaining cracker mixture.
3. Shape pea mixture into 18 (2-inch) cakes (about 1½ Tbsp. each), and place on a wax paper-lined jelly-roll pan. Cover and chill 30 minutes to 24 hours.
4. Pulse together hummus and sun-dried tomatoes in a food processor 5 to 6 times or until tomatoes are pureed.
5. Dredge cakes in reserved cracker mixture. Fry cakes, in batches, in hot oil in a large nonstick skillet 2 to 3 minutes on each side or until crisp and golden brown, adding more oil as needed. Drain on paper towels. Serve with hummus mixture and, if desired, pita bread, grape tomatoes, cucumbers, and arugula.

Sweet Potatoes and Shrimp

MAKES 4 SERVINGS; PREP: 35 MIN.,
COOK: 36 MIN., STAND: 5 MIN.

KITCHENAID Electric Stand Mixer
KITCHENAID Fruit and Vegetable Strainer
    Attachment
1¼ lb. unpeeled, medium-size raw shrimp
3½ lb. sweet potatoes, peeled
¼ cup milk
3 Tbsp. butter
¾ tsp. salt
½ tsp. freshly ground pepper
6 bacon slices
1 (8-oz.) package sliced fresh mushrooms
2 Tbsp. cornstarch
3 garlic cloves, minced
3 Tbsp. apple juice
2 Tbsp. dry white wine
1 tsp. fresh lemon juice
Garnish: fresh flat-leaf parsley sprigs

1. Peel shrimp; devein, if desired.
2. Pierce potatoes several times with
tines of a fork. Place on a microwave-safe
plate; cover with damp paper towels.
3. Microwave potatoes at HIGH 10 to
12 minutes or until tender. Let stand
5 minutes. Cut into 1-inch cubes.
4. Attach fruit and vegetable strainer
attachment to electric stand mixer
according to manufacturer's instructions. Strain potatoes into a bowl
according to manufacturer's instructions. Scrape any remaining potato
puree from strainer tray into bowl. Stir
together potato puree, milk, and next 3
ingredients. Cover and keep warm.
5. Cook bacon in a large skillet over
medium heat 8 to 10 minutes or until
crisp. Remove bacon, and drain on
paper towels, reserving 2 Tbsp. drippings in skillet. Crumble bacon.
6. Sauté mushrooms in hot drippings 8 minutes or until tender. Remove from skillet.
7. Toss shrimp in cornstarch. Add
shrimp to skillet, and sauté over
medium heat 3 to 5 minutes. Add garlic
and next 3 ingredients. Increase heat

to medium-high, and cook 1 minute or
just until shrimp turn pink.
8. Spoon sweet potato mixture onto a
serving platter. Top with shrimp mixture and mushrooms. Sprinkle with
bacon. Garnish, if desired.

Ground Chicken Lettuce Wraps

MAKES 4 SERVINGS; PREP: 30 MIN.,
COOK: 11 MIN.

KITCHENAID Electric Stand Mixer
KITCHENAID Food Grinder Attachment
1 lb. skinned and boned chicken breasts, cut
    into long, narrow strips
2 garlic cloves
1 Tbsp. canola oil
2 tsp. sesame oil
3 green onions, chopped
2 Tbsp. hoisin sauce
4 tsp. lite soy sauce
1 tsp. lime zest
4 tsp. fresh lime juice, divided
1 (1-inch) piece fresh ginger, peeled
⅓ cup sweet chili sauce*
8 large iceberg lettuce leaves
Garnishes: chopped green onions, chopped
    peanuts, soy sauce

1. Attach food grinder attachment to
electric stand mixer according to manufacturer's instructions. Grind chicken
with garlic according to manufacturer's
instructions using the fine grinding plate.
2. Cook chicken mixture in hot oils in a
large nonstick skillet over medium heat
8 to 10 minutes or until chicken is done.
Stir in green onions, next 3 ingredients,
and 1 Tbsp. lime juice. Cook 1 minute.
3. Grate ginger using the large holes of a
box grater. Squeeze juice from grated ginger
into a bowl to equal ½ tsp.; discard solids.
4. Stir together ginger juice, chili sauce, 1
tsp. water, and remaining 1 tsp. lime juice
until blended. Serve chicken on lettuce leaves
with ginger-chili sauce. Garnish, if desired.
*Hot chili sauce may be substituted.

Sweet Potato Ravioli With Collard Greens

MAKES 9 SERVINGS; PREP: 1 HR., 15 MIN.;
STAND: 1 HR., 5 MIN.; COOK: 1 HR., 5 MIN.

KITCHENAID Electric Stand Mixer
KITCHENAID Pasta Sheet Roller/Cutter
    Attachment
1¼ cups all-purpose flour
½ tsp. salt
1 large egg
2 Tbsp. olive oil
1 large sweet potato (about 22 oz.)
4 Tbsp. butter, divided
Salt and pepper to taste
1 small onion, diced
¾ cup (3 oz.) diced cooked country ham
2 garlic cloves, minced
1 (1-lb.) package fresh collard greens,
    washed and trimmed
1 Tbsp. molasses
1½ tsp. chicken bouillon granules
¼ tsp. dried crushed red pepper
1 egg white, lightly beaten

1. Combine flour and salt on a flat surface, using fingers. Make a well in center
of mixture, and add egg, oil, and
3 Tbsp. water. Using fingers, incorporate flour gradually until a soft dough
forms. Knead dough on a lightly floured
surface 3 to 4 minutes or until smooth
and elastic. Cover with plastic wrap, and
let stand at room temperature 1 hour.
2. Meanwhile, pierce potato several times
with tines of a fork. Place on a microwave-
safe plate; cover with damp paper towels.
3. Microwave at HIGH 10 minutes or
until tender. Let stand 5 minutes; peel
potato, and mash with a fork or potato
masher. Stir in 2 Tbsp. butter. Season
with salt and pepper to taste.
4. Sauté onion in remaining 2 Tbsp.
butter in a medium Dutch oven over
medium heat 7 minutes or until tender.
Add ham and garlic; sauté 1 minute.
Stir in collard greens and next 3 ingredients, tossing to coat; stir in 11 cups
water. Bring to a boil over medium-high

heat. Reduce heat to medium-low, and simmer 45 minutes or until greens are tender.

5. Meanwhile, attach pasta maker attachment to electric stand mixer according to manufacturer's instructions. Divide dough into 2 equal portions. Flatten into disks. Feed dough disks into pasta maker, 1 at a time, adjusting pasta sheet roller and mixer speed as you work according to manufacturer's instructions. Lay pasta sheets on a lightly floured surface.

6. Dollop level tablespoonfuls of potato mixture 1½ inches apart on 1 pasta sheet. Brush egg white around filling on pasta sheet; top with remaining pasta sheet. Gently press pasta sheets together around filling to seal, removing any air pockets. Using a ravioli cutter or a knife, cut pasta sheets into 3- x 2-inch ravioli. Place ravioli on a lightly greased jelly-roll pan. Sprinkle with flour to prevent sticking, if desired. Cover with a damp cloth. Repeat procedure with remaining potato mixture and pasta sheet scraps, rerolling scraps as directed in Step 5.

7. Cook ravioli, in batches, in boiling salted water to cover 2 minutes or until ravioli float to top; drain. Place 2 ravioli in each of 9 shallow serving bowls. Top with collard greens mixture. Serve immediately.

Brown Butter-Pecan-Bourbon Ice Cream

MAKES ABOUT 1 QT.; **PREP:** 25 MIN., **COOK:** 10 MIN., **CHILL:** 1 HR.

KITCHENAID Electric Stand Mixer
KITCHENAID Ice Cream Maker Attachment
½ cup butter
1 cup chopped pecans
1½ cups milk
1½ cups heavy cream
¾ cup sugar
8 egg yolks
2 to 4 Tbsp. bourbon
1 tsp. vanilla extract
Garnish: chocolate-dipped pecan halves

1. Melt butter in a medium skillet over medium heat. Cook, stirring frequently, 2 to 3 minutes or until butter turns light brown and golden. Add pecans, and sauté 1 to 2 minutes or until lightly browned and toasted. Remove pecans with a slotted spoon, reserving browned butter and pecans separately.

2. Bring milk, cream, and sugar to a boil in a medium saucepan over medium heat, stirring occasionally. Remove from heat, and stir in browned butter.

3. Beat egg yolks at medium-high speed with electric stand mixer until thick and pale (about 2 to 3 minutes). Gradually stir one-fourth of hot cream mixture into eggs. Add yolk mixture to remaining hot cream mixture, stirring constantly. Cook over medium-low heat, stirring constantly, 5 minutes or until a candy thermometer registers 170° and mixture lightly coats back of a spoon.

4. Pour mixture through a fine wire-mesh strainer into a bowl. Stir in bourbon, vanilla, and pecans. Cover and chill 1 hour.

5. Attach ice cream maker attachment to mixer according to manufacturer's instructions. Prepare ice cream according to manufacturer's instructions, using stir speed 1, for 15 to 20 minutes or until mixture reaches desired consistency. Serve immediately, or transfer to an airtight container and freeze to desired texture. Garnish, if desired.

National Peanut Board

USA-GROWN PEANUTS add a crunchy texture and nutty flavor to these favorites.

Sweet Potato-Peanut Soup

MAKES 8 CUPS; **PREP:** 15 MIN., **COOK:** 31 MIN., **COOL:** 10 MIN.

2 Tbsp. butter
1 medium onion, chopped
¾ cup chopped celery
2 garlic cloves, chopped
6 cups fat-free chicken broth
3 large sweet potatoes, peeled and cut
    into 1-inch cubes (about 2¼ lb.)
2 tsp. chopped fresh sage
¼ cup creamy peanut butter made with
    USA-GROWN PEANUTS
2 tsp. cider vinegar
¾ tsp. salt
¼ tsp. freshly ground pepper
Garnishes: finely chopped
    USA-GROWN PEANUTS, sour cream or
    crème fraîche

1. Melt butter in a Dutch oven over medium heat; add onion and celery, and sauté 6 minutes or until tender. Add garlic, and sauté 1 minute.

2. Add broth, potatoes, and sage. Bring to a boil; cover, reduce heat to low, and simmer 20 minutes or until potatoes are very tender. Remove from heat. Uncover and let cool 10 minutes.

3. Process potato mixture, in batches, in a food processor or blender until smooth. Return mixture to Dutch oven; whisk in peanut butter and next 3 ingredients.

4. Cook soup over medium-low heat, stirring often, 3 to 4 minutes or until thoroughly heated. Garnish, if desired.

Per cup (not including garnish): Calories 176; Fat 7.1g (sat 2.7g, mono 2.7g, poly 1.3g); Protein 8.2g; Carb 21.2g; Fiber 3.4g; Chol 7.5mg; Iron 0.9mg; Sodium 605mg; Calc 41mg

Peanut-Dusted Pork Medallions With Citrus Pan Sauce

fast fixin's

MAKES 4 SERVINGS; **PREP:** 15 MIN.,
COOK: 10 MIN.

1 (1- to 1.25-lb.) pork tenderloin
4 Tbsp. light roast peanut flour made
    with USA-GROWN PEANUTS
1 tsp. ground cumin
½ tsp. ground red pepper
1¼ tsp. salt, divided
⅓ cup fat-free chicken broth
¼ cup fresh orange juice
2 Tbsp. fresh lemon juice
2½ Tbsp. honey
1 tsp. all-purpose flour
3 Tbsp. aromatic peanut oil made with
    USA-GROWN PEANUTS,
    divided
1 garlic clove, minced
Garnishes: fresh flat-leaf parsley
    sprigs, orange rind curls

1. Remove silver skin from tenderloin, leaving a thin layer of fat. Cut pork diagonally into 1-inch-thick slices.
2. Stir together peanut flour, cumin, red pepper, and 1 tsp. salt in a shallow bowl or pie plate. Reserve 2 tsp. peanut flour mixture. Dredge pork in remaining peanut flour mixture, shaking off excess.
3. Whisk together broth, next 4 ingredients, and reserved 2 tsp. peanut flour mixture in a small bowl.
4. Heat 2 Tbsp. peanut oil in a large skillet over medium-high heat. Add pork, and cook 3 minutes on each side or until done. Transfer to a serving platter. Keep warm.
5. Heat remaining 1 Tbsp. peanut oil in skillet over medium heat. Add garlic, and sauté about 30 seconds. Add broth mixture to skillet, stirring to loosen particles from bottom of skillet. Bring to a boil, whisking constantly; cook 2 minutes or until slightly thickened. Stir

in remaining ¼ tsp. salt. Pour sauce over pork. Garnish, if desired.
Note: For testing purposes only, we used 12% fat light roast peanut flour.

Per serving (not including garnish): Calories 326; Fat 16.3g (sat 3.6g, mono 7.4g, poly 4.3g); Protein 30g; Carb 15.4g; Fiber 1g; Chol 79mg; Iron 2mg; Sodium 825mg; Calc 21mg

Chili-Peanut Spring Greens

fast fixin's

MAKES 4 SERVINGS; **PREP:** 15 MIN.,
COOK: 7 MIN., **STAND:** 4 MIN.

1 lb. fresh spinach, stems removed
4 Tbsp. dry roasted, salted
    USA-GROWN PEANUTS
2 Tbsp. aromatic peanut oil made with
    USA-GROWN PEANUTS, divided
1 medium onion, finely chopped
1 medium tomato, seeded and finely
    chopped
1 jalapeño pepper, seeded and finely
    chopped
⅓ cup vegetable broth
½ tsp. salt
1 tsp. fresh lemon juice

1. Coarsely chop spinach.
2. Process peanuts in a blender or food processor 10 to 15 seconds or until finely ground.
3. Heat ground peanuts in a large skillet over medium heat, stirring constantly, 1 to 2 minutes or until lightly toasted and fragrant. Remove from skillet.
4. Heat 1 Tbsp. peanut oil in skillet over medium heat. Add onion, tomato, and pepper, and sauté 3 to 4 minutes or until onion is tender. Transfer mixture to a small bowl; keep warm.
5. Add broth and salt to skillet. Bring to a boil over medium heat. Add spinach, in batches, stirring just until spinach begins to wilt.
6. Remove from heat. Top spinach with onion mixture; sprinkle with 2 Tbsp. toasted ground peanuts. Cover and let stand 3 to 4 minutes or until spinach is tender.

7. Transfer to a serving platter. Drizzle with lemon juice and remaining 1 Tbsp. peanut oil. Sprinkle with remaining 2 Tbsp. toasted ground peanuts. Serve immediately.

Per serving: Calories 139; Fat 11g (sat 1.8g, mono 5.2g, poly 3.7g); Protein 4.6g; Carb 8.8g; Fiber 3.3g; Chol 0mg; Iron 2.5mg; Sodium 493mg; Calc 95mg

Chili-Peanut Greens: Substitute 1 lb. kale for spinach. Prepare recipe as directed through Step 5. Reduce heat to medium-low; cover and cook 4 minutes. Remove from heat, and proceed with recipe as directed in Step 6, letting kale stand, covered, 5 minutes or until tender. Proceed with Step 7 as directed. Prep: 15 min., Cook: 10 min, Stand: 5 min.

Per serving: Calories 154; Fat 11g (sat 1.8g, mono 5.2g, poly 3.8g); Protein 4.6g; Carb 12.6g; Fiber 3.9g; Chol 0mg; Iron 1.4mg; Sodium 456mg; Calc 100mg

Chocolate-Peanut Ice Cream Squares With Peanut Butter Sauce

family favorite • make ahead

MAKES 16 SQUARES; **PREP:** 30 MIN.;
BAKE: 18 MIN.; **COOL:** 15 MIN.;
FREEZE: 8 HR., 30 MIN.; **STAND:** 10 MIN.

A peanut crust and warm Peanut Butter Sauce envelope these ice cream squares.

1½ cups coarsely chopped dry roasted,
    salted USA-GROWN PEANUTS
¼ cup light roast peanut flour made with
    USA-GROWN PEANUTS
¼ cup all-purpose flour
¼ cup butter, melted
3 Tbsp. sugar
Vegetable cooking spray
2 qt. chocolate ice cream, softened
1 cup peanut protein powder made with
    USA-GROWN PEANUTS
Peanut Butter Sauce
Garnish: coarsely chopped USA-GROWN
    PEANUTS

1. Preheat oven to 350°. Stir together first 5 ingredients in a medium bowl until well blended.

2. Line outside bottom and sides of an 8-inch square pan with heavy-duty aluminum foil, allowing 2 to 3 inches to extend over sides. Carefully lift foil off of pan, and place inside the pan. Lightly coat foil with cooking spray. Press peanut mixture on bottom of pan.

3. Bake at 350° for 15 to 18 minutes or until lightly browned. Cool completely on a wire rack (about 15 minutes).

4. Beat ice cream and peanut protein powder at medium speed with an electric mixer until well blended. Pour mixture over prepared crust, spreading to edges of pan. Smooth top of mixture using a spatula. (Pan will be almost completely full.) Cover and freeze 8 hours or up to 1 month.

5. Let ice cream stand at room temperature 10 minutes. Lift ice cream from pan, using foil sides as handles. Place on a cutting board.

6. Peel foil back from edges of ice cream. Run a knife under hot water, and pat dry. Cut ice cream into 16 equal squares. Place on a serving platter or individual plates, and freeze 30 minutes. Serve with Peanut Butter Sauce. Garnish, if desired.

Note: For testing purposes only, we used 12% fat light roast peanut flour.

Per square and 1 Tbsp. Peanut Butter Sauce (not including garnish): Calories 469; Fat 30.7g (sat 13.4g, *mono 4.85g, *poly 2.6g); Protein 11.8g; Carb 38.8g; Fiber 2.5g; Chol 123.6mg; Iron 1.6mg; Sodium 276mg; Calc 168mg

*Mono and poly amounts for peanut protein powder not available.

Peanut Butter Sauce:

MAKES ABOUT 1 CUP; **PREP:** 5 MIN., **COOK:** 7 MIN.

½ cup granulated sugar
½ cup milk
2 tsp. all-purpose flour
2 tsp. light corn syrup
⅛ tsp. salt
⅓ cup creamy peanut butter made with
 USA-GROWN PEANUTS
½ tsp. vanilla extract

1. Whisk together first 5 ingredients in a small saucepan. Cook over medium heat, whisking constantly, 3 minutes or until sugar is dissolved. Bring to a boil. Reduce heat to low, and cook, whisking constantly, 3 to 4 minutes or until mixture is thickened. Remove from heat, and whisk in peanut butter and vanilla. Serve immediately.

Note: To make ahead, prepare recipe as directed. Cover and chill up to 24 hours. Warm sauce in a small saucepan over low heat, stirring in 1 to 2 tsp. milk as needed to thin sauce.

Per serving: Calories 64; Fat 3g (sat 0.7g, mono 1.4g, poly 0.7g); Protein 1.6g; Carb 8.6g; Fiber 0.3g; Chol 1.1mg; Iron 0.1mg; Sodium 47mg; Calc 10mg

Peanut Streusel Mango Muffins

freezeable • make ahead

MAKES 1 DOZEN; **PREP:** 15 MIN., **BAKE:** 24 MIN., **COOL:** 30 MIN.

Remove muffins from pan after baking using a knife or metal spatula instead of inverting and losing streusel.

½ cup coarsely chopped dry roasted, salted
 USA-GROWN PEANUTS
¼ cup light roast peanut flour made with
 USA-GROWN PEANUTS
2 cups all-purpose flour, divided
½ cup firmly packed light brown sugar, divided
5½ Tbsp. butter, melted and divided
1 tsp. baking soda
½ tsp. baking powder
½ tsp. ground cinnamon
¼ tsp. salt
2 medium mangoes (about 2 lb.), peeled and
 chopped*
½ cup granulated sugar
½ cup low-fat buttermilk
1 large egg
12 aluminum foil baking cups

1. Preheat oven to 375°. Stir together chopped peanuts, peanut flour, ½ cup all-purpose flour, ¼ cup light brown sugar, and 3½ Tbsp. melted butter until mixture is crumbly.

2. Stir together baking soda, next 3 ingredients, and remaining 1½ cups all-purpose flour in a bowl.

3. Process mango in a blender or food processor 15 to 20 seconds or until pureed. Pour puree into a measuring cup to equal 1 cup. (If necessary, discard any remaining puree, or reserve for another use.)

4. Whisk together 1 cup mango puree, granulated sugar, buttermilk, egg, remaining ¼ cup brown sugar, and remaining 2 Tbsp. melted butter in a medium bowl until well blended. Gradually whisk in flour mixture just until combined.

5. Place baking cups in a muffin pan. Spoon batter into cups, filling two-thirds full. Sprinkle peanut streusel mixture over batter.

6. Bake at 375° for 22 to 24 minutes or until a wooden pick inserted in center comes out clean. Cool in pan on a wire rack 10 minutes. Gently transfer muffins from pan to a wire rack using a knife or metal spatula, and cool completely (about 20 minutes).

*2 cups frozen cubed mango, thawed, may be substituted.

Note: To make ahead, freeze baked, cooled muffins in a heavy-duty zip-top plastic freezer bag up to 1 month. To reheat, remove muffins from baking cups, wrap in a paper towel, and microwave at HIGH 20 seconds or until thoroughly heated. For testing purposes only, we used 12% fat light roast peanut flour.

Per muffin: Calories 256; Fat 8.7g (sat 3.9g, mono 2.9g, poly 1.2g); Protein 4.6g; Carb 41g; Fiber 1.5g; Chol 32mg; Iron 1.5mg; Sodium 270mg; Calc 43mg

Mahatma Rice and Success Rice

These versatile rice dishes fit any occasion and any time schedule.

Lemony Chicken and Jasmine Rice With Spinach and Artichokes

MAKES 4 TO 6 SERVINGS; **PREP:** 25 MIN., **COOK:** 20 MIN.

1 lb. skinned and boned chicken breasts, cut into thin strips
1 cup chopped onion
1 cup chopped red bell pepper
1 Tbsp. vegetable oil
1 cup MAHATMA Jasmine Rice, uncooked
1 (14-oz.) can chicken broth
1 (14-oz.) can artichoke hearts, drained and quartered
2 Tbsp. fresh lemon juice
1 tsp. salt (optional)
1 cup firmly packed fresh baby spinach
¼ cup (1 oz.) shredded Parmesan cheese

1. Sauté chicken, onion, and bell pepper in hot oil in a large skillet over medium-high heat 5 minutes. Stir in rice, next 3 ingredients, and, if desired, salt. Bring mixture to a boil; cover, reduce heat to low, and simmer 15 minutes or liquid is absorbed and rice is tender. Remove from heat, and stir in spinach. Transfer to a serving platter, and sprinkle with cheese.

Sage Butternut Squash Soup With Brown Rice

MAKES 8 SERVINGS; **PREP:** 45 MIN., **COOK:** 30 MIN., **COOL:** 10 MIN.

1 (3.5-oz.) bag SUCCESS Brown Rice, uncooked
1½ cups chopped onion
½ cup chopped carrot
¼ cup chopped celery
1 Tbsp. minced garlic
1 Tbsp. vegetable oil
2 lb. butternut squash, peeled, seeded, and cut into 1-inch cubes
3 cups low-sodium chicken broth
2 Tbsp. chopped fresh sage
½ cup fat-free evaporated milk
Salt and pepper to taste
1 Tbsp. chopped fresh sage (optional)

1. Prepare rice according to package directions.
2. Sauté onion and next 3 ingredients in hot oil in a large Dutch oven over medium heat 5 minutes. Add squash, broth, and 2 Tbsp. chopped fresh sage. Bring to a boil, reduce heat to medium-low, and cook 25 minutes or until squash is tender. Let cool 10 minutes.
3. Process squash mixture, in batches, in a blender until smooth, stopping to scrape down sides as needed. Return mixture to Dutch oven, and stir in evaporated milk, salt and pepper to taste, and, if desired, 1 Tbsp. chopped fresh sage. Serve soup in individual bowls with a scoop of brown rice.

Bombay Dream Rice Pudding

MAKES 4 SERVINGS (ABOUT 5 CUPS); **PREP:** 10 MIN.; **COOK:** 1 HR., 5 MIN.; **CHILL:** 1 HR.

1 cup MAHATMA Basmati Rice, uncooked
3 cups milk
½ cup sugar
½ cup evaporated milk
½ tsp. ground cardamom
½ cup roasted, salted pistachios, finely chopped
Garnish: fresh mint sprigs

1. Bring rice and 4 cups water to a boil in a saucepan over medium-high heat; reduce heat to low, and simmer, uncovered, 20 minutes. Drain rice; return to saucepan.
2. Stir milk and sugar into rice. Cook, uncovered, over low heat 40 minutes. Stir in evaporated milk and cardamom. Cook 5 minutes. Remove from heat. Stir in pistachios.
3. Spread pudding into a 13- x 9-inch baking dish. Cover and chill 1 to 24 hours. Serve in dessert bowls. Garnish, if desired.

Honey-Ginger Baked Salmon With Jasmine Rice

MAKES 4 SERVINGS; **PREP:** 20 MIN., **COOK:** 6 MIN., **CHILL:** 15 MIN., **BAKE:** 20 MIN.

2 (3.5-oz.) bags SUCCESS Jasmine Rice, uncooked
⅓ cup orange juice
⅓ cup honey
¼ cup lite soy sauce
1 Tbsp. minced garlic
1 Tbsp. minced fresh ginger
4 (4-oz.) salmon fillets
¼ cup sliced green onions

1. Prepare rice according to package directions.
2. Preheat oven to 375°. Cook orange juice and next 4 ingredients in a small saucepan over medium heat, stirring occasionally, 1 minute; let cool slightly.
3. Reserve ⅔ cup marinade; transfer remaining marinade to a large shallow dish or zip-top plastic freezer bag; add salmon. Cover or seal, and chill 15 minutes. Remove salmon from marinade, discarding marinade. Place salmon in an aluminum foil-lined pan.
4. Bake at 375° for 20 minutes or to desired degree of doneness.
5. Meanwhile, cook reserved marinade in a small saucepan over medium heat 5 minutes or until sauce is thick and syrupy.
6. Transfer rice to a serving platter, and top with salmon. Drizzle with sauce, and sprinkle with green onions.

Creamy Shrimp and Rice

MAKES 4 SERVINGS; **PREP:** 15 MIN.,
COOK: 9 MIN.

1 lb. unpeeled, medium-size, cooked shrimp
1 (3.5-oz.) bag SUCCESS White, Brown, or
    Jasmine Rice, uncooked
1 (12-oz.) package sliced fresh mushrooms
½ tsp. minced garlic
1 Tbsp. olive oil
1 (8-oz.) container chive-and-onion cream
    cheese, softened
2 cups firmly packed fresh baby spinach
1 to 2 Tbsp. lemon juice
½ cup grated Parmesan cheese

1. Peel shrimp; devein, if desired.
2. Prepare rice according to package
directions.
3. Sauté mushrooms and garlic in hot oil
in a large nonstick skillet over medium-
high heat 6 minutes or until mushrooms
are golden. Stir in cream cheese, and
cook, stirring constantly, 30 seconds or
until melted. Stir in shrimp, spinach,
and ¼ cup water; cook 2 minutes or
until thoroughly heated and shrimp turn
pink. Fold in rice, lemon juice, and up
to ¼ cup additional water, if necessary,
for desired consistency. (Mixture should
be creamy.) Sprinkle with Parmesan
cheese, and serve immediately.

Barilla Pasta

Jazz up meals for family and
friends with these crowd-
pleasing recipes.

Piccolini Mini Farfalle With Zucchini, Chicken, and Tomato

MAKES 4 TO 6 SERVINGS; **PREP:** 15 MIN.,
COOK: 20 MIN.

1 (16-oz.) box BARILLA Piccolini Mini
    Farfalle
½ cup diced onion
2 Tbsp. extra virgin olive oil
2 medium zucchini, diced (about 2 cups)
8 oz. skinned and boned chicken
    breast, diced
1 cup diced fresh tomatoes
¼ cup whipping cream
Salt and pepper to taste

1. Sauté onion in hot olive oil in a
medium skillet over medium-high heat
7 minutes or until tender. Add zucchini,
and sauté 4 minutes or until tender.
Add chicken, and sauté 5 minutes or
until done. Reduce heat to medium; stir
in tomatoes, cream, and salt and pepper
to taste. Cook, stirring occasionally,
4 minutes or until slightly thickened.
2. Cook pasta according to package
directions; drain. Toss hot cooked
pasta with sauce. Serve immediately.

Penne With Chicken, Spinach, and Tomatoes With Balsamic Vinaigrette

MAKES 6 SERVINGS; **PREP:** 10 MIN.,
COOK: 20 MIN., **COOL:** 10 MIN.

1 (14.5-oz.) box BARILLA PLUS Penne
1 lb. skinned and boned chicken breasts,
    diced
½ cup extra virgin olive oil, divided
¼ cup balsamic vinegar
2 tsp. Dijon mustard
Salt and freshly ground pepper to taste
2½ cups (3 oz.) firmly packed fresh
    spinach, chopped
2½ cups seeded and chopped fresh tomatoes
½ cup thinly sliced red onion
½ cup diced yellow bell pepper

1. Sauté chicken in 1 Tbsp. hot olive oil in a
medium skillet 5 to 6 minutes or until done.
2. Whisk together vinegar and mustard
in a small bowl. Gradually whisk in 6
Tbsp. olive oil until smooth. Season
with salt and pepper to taste.
3. Cook pasta according to package directions; drain. Spread pasta in a single layer
on a baking sheet. Drizzle with remaining
1 Tbsp. olive oil. Let cool 10 minutes.
4. Toss together pasta, chicken, vinegar mixture, spinach, and remaining ingredients in
a large bowl. Season with salt and pepper to
taste. Serve immediately, or, if desired, cover
and chill 1 hour before serving.

Farfalle With Prosciutto and Green Peas

MAKES 6 TO 8 SERVINGS; **PREP:** 10 MIN.,
COOK: 25 MIN.

1 (16-oz.) box BARILLA Farfalle
1 small onion, chopped
2 Tbsp. extra virgin olive oil
2 (3.5-oz.) packages prosciutto, cut
    into thin strips
1½ cups frozen green peas, thawed
½ cup dry white wine
2 cups half-and-half
½ cup heavy cream
Salt and freshly ground pepper to taste
½ cup freshly grated Parmesan cheese

1. Cook onion in hot olive oil in a large
(3-inch-deep) skillet or Dutch oven over
medium heat, stirring occasionally, 5
minutes. Add prosciutto and peas, and
cook, stirring occasionally, 3 minutes.
Stir in wine, and cook 3 to 4 minutes or
until mixture is reduced by half. Stir in
half-and-half and cream. Season with
salt and pepper to taste. Cook 1 to 2
minutes or until slightly thickened.
2. Cook pasta according to package
directions; drain. Toss hot cooked
pasta with cream mixture. Stir in
cheese.

Three Cheese Tortellini-and-Vegetable Primavera

MAKES 6 TO 8 SERVINGS; **PREP:** 15 MIN., **COOK:** 20 MIN.

1 (13-oz.) package BARILLA Three
    Cheese Tortellini
½ bunch (8 oz.) asparagus
½ cup thinly sliced green onions,
    white part only (1 bunch)
1 small zucchini, seeded and diced
3 Tbsp. extra virgin olive oil
2 plum tomatoes, peeled and diced
Salt and freshly ground pepper to taste
½ cup freshly grated Parmigiano-
    Reggiano cheese

1. Snap off and discard tough ends of asparagus. Cut tips from asparagus, and place in a bowl. Cut remaining asparagus into ¼-inch pieces; add to bowl.
2. Sauté asparagus, green onions, and zucchini in hot olive oil in a large skillet over medium heat 8 minutes. Add tomatoes, and cook 2 minutes. Season with salt and pepper to taste.
3. Cook pasta according to package directions; drain. Stir into asparagus mixture; sprinkle with cheese. Serve immediately.

Whole Grain Thin Spaghetti With Pesto

MAKES 4 TO 6 SERVINGS; **PREP:** 20 MIN., **COOK:** 15 MIN.

1 (13.25-oz.) box BARILLA Whole Grain Thin
    Spaghetti
½ garlic clove
2 Tbsp. pine nuts
2 Tbsp. grated Parmesan cheese
1 Tbsp. grated Romano cheese
1 (1-oz.) package fresh basil, stems removed
    (about 1 cup firmly packed fresh basil leaves)
⅓ cup extra virgin olive oil
Salt and pepper to taste
2 oz. fresh green beans, trimmed and cut
    into ½-inch pieces (about ½ cup)
½ cup cubed potatoes (¼-inch cubes)

1. Process garlic and next 3 ingredients in a blender 15 seconds. Add basil and olive oil. Process 2 minutes or until smooth, stopping to scrape down sides as needed. Season with salt and pepper to taste.
2. Cook green beans in boiling water to cover in a small saucepan 3 minutes; drain. Cook pasta according to package directions, adding potatoes during last 5 minutes of cooking; drain.
3. Toss together pasta and potato mixture, green beans, and pesto sauce in a large bowl. Serve immediately.

Pilgrim's Pride

You can count on chicken for healthy and hearty recipes.

Easy Mediterranean Appetizer Platter With Yogurt Dip

MAKES 12 SERVINGS; **PREP:** 15 MIN., **CHILL:** 4 HR.

1 (32-oz.) container plain low-fat
    yogurt
2 green onions, minced
3 Tbsp. chopped fresh dill
1 Tbsp. chopped fresh mint
1 Tbsp. fresh lemon juice
1 tsp. minced garlic
½ tsp. salt
½ tsp. pepper
1 (32-oz.) package PILGRIM'S PRIDE
    Breaded Chicken Breast Nuggets
Pita chips
Assorted vegetables

1. Line a wire-mesh strainer with 3 layers of cheesecloth or 1 coffee filter. Place strainer over a bowl. Spoon yogurt into strainer. Cover and chill 4 hours or up to 12 hours. Remove yogurt, discarding strained liquid.
2. Combine strained yogurt, green onions, and next 6 ingredients.
3. Prepare chicken according to package directions. Serve with yogurt dip, pita chips, and assorted vegetables.

Lemon-Spinach Chicken

MAKES 4 SERVINGS; **PREP:** 15 MIN., **COOK:** 15 MIN.

1 (10-oz.) package fresh spinach
½ cup all-purpose flour
¾ tsp. salt
½ tsp. freshly ground pepper
4 (6-oz.) PILGRIM'S PRIDE
    EatWellStayHealthy Boneless,
    Skinless Chicken Breasts
2 Tbsp. butter
½ cup chicken broth
¼ cup dry white wine
1 tsp. lemon zest
2 Tbsp. fresh lemon juice
2 garlic cloves, minced
Garnish: grape tomato halves

1. Cook spinach in a lightly greased large nonstick skillet over medium-high heat, stirring often, 2 minutes or until wilted. Transfer spinach to a bowl.
2. Combine flour, salt, and pepper in a shallow dish; dredge chicken in flour mixture.
3. Melt butter in skillet; add chicken, and cook 4 to 5 minutes on each side or until golden and done. Remove chicken from skillet, reserving drippings in skillet.
4. Add chicken broth and next 4 ingredients to skillet, and bring to a boil, stirring to loosen particles from bottom of skillet. Cook, stirring occasionally, 2 minutes or until reduced by half. Stir in spinach, and cook 1 minute or until thoroughly heated. Serve chicken over spinach mixture. Garnish, if desired.

Chicken-on-a-Stick With Italian Dipping Sauces

family favorite • fast fixin's
MAKES 8 SERVINGS; **PREP:** 10 MIN.

Serve this dish for an easy and fun weeknight meal or as an appetizer at your next get-together.

1 (28-oz.) package PILGRIM'S PRIDE
    Breaded Chicken Breast Strips
14 to 18 (6-inch) wooden
    skewers
Fresh Herb Sauce
Sun-dried Tomato Aïoli
Alfredo-Artichoke Dip
Garnish: fresh parsley sprigs

1. Prepare chicken according to package directions. Carefully thread 1 tender onto each skewer. Serve with dipping sauces. Garnish, if desired.

Fresh Herb Sauce:

fast fixin's • make ahead
MAKES ABOUT 1½ CUPS; **PREP:** 10 MIN.

When storing, cover the surface of the sauce with plastic wrap to prevent discoloration. It should keep for 1 week in the refrigerator. The longer the yogurt is strained the thicker and creamier it will become.

2 garlic cloves
1 (1-oz.) package fresh basil leaves, stems
    removed
4 mint sprigs, stems removed
1 cup firmly packed fresh flat-leaf parsley
    leaves (about 1 bunch)
½ cup grated Parmesan cheese
½ tsp. salt
½ tsp. freshly ground pepper
½ cup warm water
½ cup olive oil
2 Tbsp. red wine vinegar

1. Process garlic in a food processor 20 seconds or until minced. Add basil

leaves and next 5 ingredients; process 10 seconds.
2. Whisk together water, oil, and vinegar. With processor running, pour oil mixture through food chute in a slow, steady stream, processing just until blended.

Sun-dried Tomato Aïoli:

fast fixin's • make ahead
MAKES 2 CUPS; **PREP:** 10 MIN.

1½ cups light mayonnaise
⅓ cup firmly packed sun-dried tomatoes in
    oil, drained
¼ cup milk
1 garlic clove
2 tsp. chopped fresh rosemary
1 tsp. lemon zest
½ tsp. salt
½ tsp. freshly ground pepper

1. Process all ingredients in a food processor 15 seconds or until smooth, stopping to scrape down sides as needed. Cover and chill until ready to serve. Store in an airtight container in refrigerator up to 1 week.

Alfredo-Artichoke Dip:

MAKES 2 CUPS; **PREP:** 10 MIN.,
COOK: 5 MIN.

1 (14-oz.) can extra-small artichoke hearts,
    drained and finely chopped
1 (10-oz.) container refrigerated light
    Alfredo sauce
½ cup milk
¼ cup grated Parmesan cheese
1 Tbsp. chopped fresh oregano
1 tsp. minced garlic
½ tsp. pepper

1. Stir together all ingredients in a medium saucepan; cook over medium heat, stirring often, 5 minutes or until mixture is thoroughly heated and cheese is melted.

Chicken Portobello Lasagna

make ahead
MAKES 6 SERVINGS; **PREP:** 20 MIN.,
COOK: 10 MIN., **BAKE:** 1 HR.,
STAND: 10 MIN.

1 (10-oz.) package frozen chopped spinach,
    thawed
1 Tbsp. butter
3 (6-oz.) PILGRIM'S PRIDE
    EatWellStayHealthy Boneless, Skinless
    Chicken Breasts, diced
1 (8-oz.) package sliced fresh baby porto-
    bello mushrooms
1 (10¾-oz.) can reduced-fat cream of mush-
    room soup
1 (8-oz.) container reduced-fat sour cream
½ tsp. pepper
¼ tsp. salt
1 (8-oz.) block 2% reduced-fat sharp
    Cheddar cheese, shredded
6 no-boil lasagna noodles
3 Tbsp. grated Parmesan cheese

1. Preheat oven to 350°. Drain spinach well, pressing between paper towels.
2. Melt butter in a large Dutch oven over medium-high heat; add chicken and mushrooms, and sauté 10 minutes or until chicken is done and mushrooms are tender. Remove from heat. Stir in spinach, soup, and next 3 ingredients; fold in cheese.
3. Spoon one-fourth of chicken mixture in a lightly greased 8- x 8-inch square baking dish. Arrange 2 noodles on top of mixture. Repeat layers twice; top with remaining chicken mixture. Sprinkle with Parmesan cheese.
4. Bake, covered, at 350° for 45 minutes; uncover and bake 15 minutes or until bubbly. Let stand 10 minutes before serving.
Note: To make ahead, prepare recipe as directed through Step 2. Cover and chill at least 8 hours or up to 24 hours. Let stand at room temperature 30 minutes; proceed with recipe as directed.

Honey-Pecan Chicken Thighs

MAKES 4 TO 6 SERVINGS; **PREP**: 15 MIN., **CHILL**: 2 HR., **BAKE**: 40 MIN.

½ tsp. salt
½ tsp. ground black pepper
½ tsp. dried thyme
¼ tsp. ground red pepper
8 PILGRIM'S PRIDE Boneless Skinless Chicken Thighs
¾ cup honey, divided
¾ cup Dijon mustard, divided
2 garlic cloves, minced
1 cup finely chopped pecans
½ tsp. curry powder

1. Combine first 4 ingredients; sprinkle over chicken in a shallow dish. Stir together ½ cup honey, ½ cup mustard, and garlic; pour over chicken, turning chicken to coat. Cover and chill 2 hours. Remove chicken from marinade, discarding marinade.
2. Preheat oven to 375°. Place chicken on a lightly greased wire rack in an aluminum foil-lined broiler pan. Sprinkle with pecans, pressing lightly to secure.
3. Bake at 375° for 35 to 40 minutes or until chicken is done and pecans are lightly browned.
4. Stir together remaining ¼ cup honey, ¼ cup mustard, and curry powder; serve sauce with chicken.

Hellmann's

This creamy pantry staple adds moistness and flavor in many ways.

Spinach-Artichoke Gratin

MAKES 6 TO 8 SERVINGS; **PREP**: 15 MIN., **COOK**: 10 MIN., **BAKE**: 15 MIN., **STAND**: 5 MIN.

2 cups chopped yellow onions
2 Tbsp. all-purpose flour
1¼ cups milk
¾ cup (3 oz.) freshly shredded Parmesan cheese
¼ cup HELLMANN'S or Best Foods Real Mayonnaise
½ (14-oz.) can artichoke hearts, drained and quartered
1 tsp. salt
¼ tsp. freshly ground pepper
2 (10-oz.) packages frozen spinach, thawed and well drained

1. Preheat oven to 425°. Sauté onions in a lightly greased large nonstick skillet over medium heat 6 minutes or until tender. Add flour, and cook, stirring constantly, 30 seconds to 1 minute. Add milk; cook, stirring frequently, 2 to 3 minutes or until thickened. Remove from heat.
2. Stir in ¼ cup Parmesan cheese and next 4 ingredients. Add spinach, and stir until thoroughly combined. Transfer spinach mixture to a lightly greased 8-inch square baking dish. Sprinkle with remaining ½ cup Parmesan cheese.
3. Bake at 425° for 15 minutes or until cheese is melted and mixture is bubbly. Let stand 5 minutes before serving.

Twice-Baked Potatoes

MAKES 8 SERVINGS; **PREP**: 25 MIN.; **BAKE**: 1 HR., 20 MIN.; **COOL**: 10 MIN.

4 (9-oz.) medium-size baking potatoes
½ cup HELLMANN'S or Best Foods Real Mayonnaise
2 Tbsp. chopped fresh chives
1 garlic clove, pressed
Salt and pepper to taste
1½ cups (6 oz.) shredded colby-Jack cheese blend
Garnish: chopped fresh chives

1. Preheat oven to 425°. Bake potatoes on a lightly greased baking sheet 1 hour or until tender. Remove from oven, and let cool 10 minutes. Reduce oven temperature to 350°.
2. Cut potatoes in half lengthwise; carefully scoop out pulp into a large bowl, leaving shells intact. Mash together pulp, mayonnaise, next 3 ingredients, and ½ cup cheese. Spoon potato mixture into shells; sprinkle with remaining 1 cup cheese. Return potatoes to baking sheet.
3. Bake potatoes at 350° for 20 minutes or until thoroughly heated and cheese is melted. Garnish, if desired.
Note: To make ahead, prepare recipe as directed through Step 2. Cover and chill up to 24 hours. Let potato halves come to room temperature (about 30 minutes), and bake them as directed in Step 3.

Delta-Style Catfish

MAKES 6 SERVINGS; **PREP**: 10 MIN., **BROIL**: 12 MIN.

3 cups cornflakes cereal, finely crushed
⅔ cup grated Parmesan cheese
1 tsp. paprika
½ tsp. salt
½ cup HELLMANN'S or Best Foods Real Mayonnaise*
1 tsp. Worcestershire sauce
6 (4- to 6-oz.) catfish or tilapia fillets
1½ tsp. Cajun seasoning
Vegetable cooking spray
3 Tbsp. chopped fresh parsley
Garnish: lemon wedges

1. Preheat oven to broil. Stir together first 4 ingredients in a large shallow bowl or pie plate. Whisk together mayonnaise and Worcestershire sauce in a small bowl.
2. Brush mayonnaise mixture onto both sides of catfish fillets. Sprinkle

¼ tsp. Cajun seasoning onto 1 side of each fillet.

3. Dredge fillets in cornflake mixture; transfer to a wire rack coated with cooking spray. Place wire rack in an aluminum foil-lined pan.

4. Broil 6 inches from heat 6 minutes on each side or until golden brown and fish flakes with a fork. Sprinkle with parsley. Serve immediately. Garnish, if desired.

*½ cup HELLMANN'S or Best Foods Light Mayonnaise may be substituted.

Winter Fruit Salad

MAKES 8 SERVINGS; **PREP:** 30 MIN., **CHILL:** 1 HR.

½ cup HELLMANN'S or Best Foods Real Mayonnaise*
2 Tbsp. honey
1 tsp. lemon zest
1½ Tbsp. fresh lemon juice
¼ tsp. ground ginger
Pinch of salt
1 large Braeburn apple, chopped
1 large Granny Smith apple, chopped
1 large pear, chopped
1½ (6-oz.) packages fresh baby spinach, thoroughly washed
4 thick-cut bacon slices, cooked and crumbled
⅓ cup honey-roasted flavored sliced almonds
⅓ cup sweetened dried cranberries

1. Whisk together first 6 ingredients in a medium bowl; reserve ¼ cup. Stir apples and pear into remaining mayonnaise mixture. Cover and chill 1 hour.
2. Place spinach on a serving platter or 8 individual serving plates. Spoon apple mixture over spinach; sprinkle with bacon, almonds, and cranberries. Serve with reserved dressing. Serve immediately.

*HELLMANN'S Light or Best Foods Light Mayonnaise may be substituted.

Squash Casserole

MAKES 8 SERVINGS; **PREP:** 15 MIN., **COOK:** 25 MIN., **BAKE:** 30 MIN.

3 lb. yellow squash, cut into ¼-inch-thick rounds
1 small onion, chopped
4½ tsp. salt
16 saltine crackers, divided
1½ cups (6 oz.) shredded sharp Cheddar cheese, divided
½ cup HELLMANN'S or Best Foods Real Mayonnaise*
1 large egg, lightly beaten
2 Tbsp. butter, melted
¼ tsp. pepper
⅛ tsp. salt

1. Cook first 3 ingredients in boiling water to cover in a Dutch oven 25 minutes or until squash is very tender. Drain well; mash mixture with a fork.
2. Preheat oven to 350°. Crush 10 crackers, and stir into squash mixture; stir in ½ cup cheese and next 5 ingredients. Spoon mixture into a lightly greased 11- x 7-inch baking dish.
3. Crush remaining 6 crackers, and sprinkle over squash mixture; top with remaining 1 cup cheese.
4. Bake, uncovered, at 350° for 30 minutes or until cheese is melted and mixture is bubbly.

*½ cup HELLMANN'S or Best Foods Light Mayonnaise may be substituted.
Note: To make ahead, prepare recipe as directed through Step 2. Cover and chill 8 to 24 hours. Let stand at room temperature 30 minutes. Uncover and proceed with recipe as directed.

Oscar Mayer

Lunch meats are the key ingredient in these quick recipes.

Curried Tea Sandwiches
fast fixin's • make ahead
MAKES 5 SERVINGS (20 APPETIZER SANDWICHES); **PREP:** 20 MIN.

To make these ahead, cover sandwiches with a damp paper towel, place in a heavy-duty zip-top plastic freezer bag, and chill up to 2 hours.

½ (8-oz.) package cream cheese, softened
2 Tbsp. mango chutney
¼ tsp. curry powder
1 (9-oz.) package OSCAR MAYER Deli Fresh Shaved Honey Smoked Turkey
10 pumpernickel party bread slices
10 rye party bread slices
10 shaved Parmesan cheese slices (optional)
2 cups loosely packed arugula

1. Stir together first 3 ingredients. Spread mixture on 1 side of each bread slice. Divide turkey slices among 5 pumpernickel bread slices and 5 rye bread slices. If desired, top with Parmesan cheese. Top with arugula and remaining bread slices. Cut sandwiches in half, and secure with wooden picks, if desired.

Southwest Turkey Benedict

fast fixin's

MAKES 5 SERVINGS; **PREP:** 15 MIN.,
COOK: 5 MIN.

5 (5-inch) fajita-size corn tortillas
½ tsp. white vinegar
5 large eggs
1 (0.9-oz.) envelope hollandaise sauce
    mix
1 Tbsp. chopped fresh cilantro
1 Tbsp. pureed chipotle peppers in
    adobo sauce
1 (9-oz.) package OSCAR MAYER Deli
    Fresh Shaved Mesquite Turkey
Garnish: chopped fresh cilantro

1. Heat tortillas according to package directions. Keep warm.
2. Add water to depth of 3 inches in a large shallow saucepan. Bring to a boil; reduce heat, and maintain at a light simmer. Add vinegar. Break eggs, and slip into water, 1 at a time, as close as possible to surface. Simmer 3 to 5 minutes or to desired degree of doneness. Remove with a slotted spoon. Trim edges, if desired.
3. Meanwhile, prepare hollandaise according to package directions, stirring in cilantro and chipotle peppers.
4. Divide turkey slices among tortillas (about 6 slices each). Top each with 1 poached egg and chipotle hollandaise sauce. Serve immediately. Garnish, if desired.

Muffaletta Pasta Salad

fast fixin's • make ahead
MAKES 5 SERVINGS; **PREP:** 15 MIN.

Serve this quick pasta salad with French bread.

1 (19-oz.) package frozen cheese tortellini
½ (9-oz.) package OSCAR MAYER Deli
    Fresh Shaved Virginia Brand Ham, cut
    into bite-size pieces
½ (7-oz.) package OSCAR MAYER Deli Fresh
    Shaved Beef Salami, cut into bite-size
    pieces
1 cup olive salad, drained
½ cup olive oil vinaigrette
2 Tbsp. chopped fresh parsley
½ tsp. freshly ground pepper
Garnish: fresh parsley sprigs

1. Prepare tortellini according to package directions.
2. Toss together tortellini, ham, and next 5 ingredients. Serve immediately, or cover and chill 2 to 8 hours. Garnish, if desired.

Ham-Apple-Cheddar Quesadillas

family favorite

MAKES 5 SERVINGS; **PREP:** 10 MIN.,
    COOK: 4 MIN. PER BATCH

5 (10-inch) burrito-size flour
    tortillas
1 Tbsp. Dijon mustard
2½ cups (10 oz.) shredded sharp Cheddar
    cheese
1 (9-oz.) package OSCAR MAYER Deli Fresh
    Shaved Brown Sugar Ham
1 Granny Smith apple, thinly sliced
Fig preserves

1. Spread half of each tortilla with mustard. Sprinkle ½ cup cheese over mustard on each tortilla. Top with ham and apple slices. Fold tortillas in half over filling.

2. Heat a lightly greased griddle or large nonstick skillet over medium-high heat just until hot. Cook quesadillas, in batches, 2 minutes on each side or until cheese melts and outside browns. Remove from heat, and cut into wedges. Serve with fig preserves.

Philly Beef Panini

fast fixin's

MAKES 4 SERVINGS; **PREP:** 10 MIN.,
COOK: 7 MIN.

½ onion, sliced
½ green bell pepper, sliced
½ red bell pepper, sliced
2 tsp. olive oil, divided
Salt and pepper to taste
1 (10-oz.) package prebaked thin Italian
    pizza crust
1 (7-oz.) package OSCAR MAYER Deli Fresh
    Shaved Roast Beef
3 (1-oz.) provolone cheese slices

1. Cook first 3 ingredients in 1 tsp. hot oil in a medium skillet over medium-high heat, stirring occasionally, 5 minutes or until crisp-tender. Sprinkle with salt and pepper to taste.
2. Top half of pizza crust with roast beef. Spoon onion mixture over roast beef; top with cheese slices. Fold crust over filling, and brush both sides of crust with remaining 1 tsp. olive oil.
3. Cook in a preheated panini press 2 minutes or until golden brown. Cut into 4 wedges, and serve immediately.
Note: If you don't have a panini press, heat a large nonstick skillet over medium-high heat 1 minute. Reduce heat to medium, and place sandwich in hot skillet. Place a heavy skillet on top of sandwich, and cook 2 minutes on each side or until golden brown.

November

Break Bread Together

With their city slowly on the mend, these New Orleans friends gather to give heartfelt thanks.

A great meal with friends can help heal most anything, which is well understood by the folks gathered around Richard and Mathilde Currence's Uptown New Orleans dining table. Their smiles shine as warmly as the silverware, and the conversation swings from pure fun to deep reflection. Hurricane Katrina is never far from anyone's mind in this place. Life is marginally back to normal, but the enormity of what was lost puts lots of things in perspective.

"Part of what the storm did was make us realize how precious these times are and that there are no guarantees for tomorrow," says Lolis Eric Elie. "The friends you've been meaning to call may no longer be there. So we're much more cognizant of taking advantage of the 'now.' " For all at this table, that means sharing favorite recipes with one another as well as with all of you.

Pableaux Johnson, who recently relocated to Louisville, Kentucky, figures his Cajun cooking will help endear him to a fresh circle of companions there. His Roast Pork With Garlic-Onion Gravy (which he admits to shamelessly stealing from Lolis) will be a powerful inducement for dinner guests. "That roast is literally irresistible," he says. "People are drawn to it."

We were drawn to the entire luscious menu and think you'll want to try these dishes for your own Thanksgiving celebration. From Lolis's mom's Stuffed Mirlitons to John Currence's amazing Oyster Dressing to Brooks Hamaker's lavish Coconut-Almond Cream Cake, the meal is full-bodied and richly flavored. The recipes are just what you'd expect from some of New Orleans's finest home cooks. They'll enliven your table and offer a nod to the enduring strength of this unique city and its food.

Roast Pork With Garlic-Onion Gravy

MAKES 8 SERVINGS; **PREP:** 25 MIN., **COOK:** 23 MIN., **BAKE:** 4 HR., **STAND:** 20 MIN.

It's worth purchasing a meat thermometer for this recipe. We used an instant-read version, but a standard one would work equally well. Cook the roast to 180° to 185° for incredibly tender but sliceable meat. Pableaux likes to cook the roast an hour or so longer (to about 190°) for meat that falls apart. (Pictured on page 190)

1 (5- to 6-lb.) bone-in pork shoulder roast

10 garlic cloves, halved

Kitchen string

5 tsp. Cajun seasoning

2 Tbsp. vegetable oil

3 medium onions, halved and sliced

3 celery ribs, chopped

1 (14.5-oz.) can low-sodium chicken broth

3 Tbsp. all-purpose flour

5 Tbsp. cold water

Garnishes: red grapes, sliced pears, collard green leaves, persimmons

1. Preheat oven to 325°. Make 20 small, deep cuts in roast, and insert garlic pieces. Tie roast with kitchen string, securing at 2-inch intervals. Rub Cajun seasoning onto roast.

2. Cook roast in hot oil in a large heavy skillet over high heat 2 minutes on all sides or until browned. Remove from skillet. Reduce heat to medium. Add onions and celery to skillet; cook, stirring frequently, 5 to 8 minutes or until tender. Place onion mixture in a roasting pan; top with roast. Add broth to pan. Cover loosely with heavy-duty aluminum foil.

3. Bake at 325° for 3½ to 4 hours or until a meat thermometer inserted into thickest portion registers 180° to 185°. Remove roast from pan; cover with foil, and let stand 20 minutes before slicing.

4. Pour pan drippings through a wire-mesh strainer into a measuring cup to equal 2 cups, adding additional broth or water, if necessary. Discard solids.

5. Whisk together 3 Tbsp. flour and 5 Tbsp. cold water in a medium saucepan. Whisk in pan drippings. Cook over medium-high heat, whisking often, 6 to 7 minutes or until thickened. Serve with pork. Garnish, if desired.

—**PABLEAUX JOHNSON**, LOUISVILLE, KENTUCKY

Serving Suggestion

Roast Pork With Garlic-Onion Gravy is an elegant treatment for a pork shoulder or Boston butt roast. These affordable cuts are full of flavor. Thinly slice any leftovers, and serve on your favorite roll for a delicious lunch or a quick supper. This will taste great paired with coleslaw or melted cheese.

Oyster Dressing

chef recipe • make ahead

MAKES 8 SERVINGS; **PREP:** 30 MIN., **COOK:** 24 MIN., **STAND:** 10 MIN., **BAKE:** 45 MIN.
(Pictured on page 191)

2 medium onions, diced
4 celery ribs, diced
2 red bell peppers, diced
2 green bell peppers, diced
4 garlic cloves, minced
¼ cup olive oil
2 (8-oz.) containers fresh oysters, drained and coarsely chopped
⅔ cup dry white wine
½ cup chicken broth
¼ cup butter
3 bay leaves
2 Tbsp. fresh thyme leaves
2 tsp. black pepper
1 tsp. salt
1 tsp. crushed dried red pepper
1 tsp. hot pepper sauce
2 large eggs
½ cup grated Parmesan cheese
Sizzlin' Skillet Cornbread, crumbled
Garnishes: fresh parsley sprig, grated Parmesan cheese

1. Preheat oven to 375°. Sauté first 5 ingredients in hot oil in a large skillet over medium heat 15 to 20 minutes or until tender and lightly browned. Stir in oysters and next 9 ingredients; cook 3 to 4 minutes or until edges of oysters begin to curl. Remove from heat; let stand 10 minutes. Remove bay leaves.
2. Place mixture in a large bowl; stir in eggs and cheese. Fold in cornbread. Place mixture in a lightly greased 3-qt. or 13- x 9-inch baking dish.
3. Bake at 375° for 40 to 45 minutes or until lightly browned. Garnish, if desired.

—CHEF JOHN CURRENCE, CITY GROCERY, OXFORD, MISSISSIPPI

Note: To make ahead, prepare as directed through Step 2. Cover tightly, and freeze up to 1 month. Thaw in refrigerator 24 hours. Let stand at room temperature 30 minutes. Proceed as directed.

Sizzlin' Skillet Cornbread:

MAKES 6 SERVINGS; **PREP:** 15 MIN., **BAKE:** 15 MIN., **COOL:** 30 MIN.

2 Tbsp. bacon drippings
2 cups buttermilk
1 large egg
1¾ cups self-rising cornmeal mix

1. Preheat oven to 450°. Coat bottom and sides of a 10-inch cast-iron skillet with bacon drippings; heat in oven 10 minutes.
2. Whisk together remaining ingredients; pour batter into hot skillet.
3. Bake at 450° for 15 minutes or until lightly browned. Invert cornbread onto a wire rack. Cool completely (about 30 minutes).

Creamed Collards

chef recipe

MAKES 8 TO 10 SERVINGS; **PREP:** 20 MIN., **COOK:** 40 MIN.

Try this easy method for cutting up the bacon: Remove wrapping from bacon. Place the entire pound of cold bacon on a cutting board, and slice into ½-inch cubes.

4½ lb. fresh collard greens*
1 lb. bacon, chopped
¼ cup butter
2 large onions, diced
3 cups chicken broth
½ cup apple cider vinegar
1 tsp. salt
½ tsp. pepper
Béchamel Sauce

1. Rinse collard greens. Trim and discard thick stems from bottom of collard green leaves (about 2 inches); coarsely chop collards.
2. Cook bacon, in batches, in an 8-qt. stock pot over medium heat 10 to 12 minutes or until crisp. Remove bacon with a slotted spoon, and drain on paper towels, reserving drippings in Dutch oven. Reserve ¼ cup bacon.
3. Add butter and onions to hot drippings in skillet. Sauté onions 8 minutes or until tender. Add collards, in batches, and cook, stirring occasionally, 5 minutes or until wilted. Stir in chicken broth, next 3 ingredients, and remaining bacon.
4. Bring to a boil. Reduce heat to low, and cook, stirring occasionally, 15 minutes or to desired degree of tenderness. Drain collards, reserving 1 cup liquid.
5. Stir in Béchamel Sauce. Stir in reserved cooking liquid, ¼ cup at a time, to desired consistency. Transfer to a serving dish, and sprinkle with reserved ¼ cup bacon.
*2 (1-lb.) packages fresh collard greens, thoroughly washed, trimmed, and chopped, may be substituted.

Béchamel Sauce:

chef recipe • make ahead

MAKES ABOUT 4½ CUPS; **PREP:** 10 MIN., **COOK:** 9 MIN.

Béchamel (bay-shah-MEHL) is the French term for white sauce.

½ cup butter
2 medium shallots, minced
2 garlic cloves, pressed
¾ cup all-purpose flour
4 cups milk
½ tsp. salt
½ tsp. pepper
¼ tsp. ground nutmeg

1. Melt butter in a heavy saucepan over low heat; add shallots and garlic, and sauté 1 minute. Whisk in flour until smooth. Cook 1 minute, whisking mixture constantly.
2. Increase heat to medium. Gradually whisk in milk; cook over medium heat, whisking constantly, 5 to 7 minutes or until mixture is thickened and bubbly. Stir in salt, pepper, and nutmeg.

—CHEF JOHN CURRENCE, CITY GROCERY, OXFORD, MISSISSIPPI

Note: Mixture can be made ahead and stored in an airtight container in the refrigerator up to 2 days. Warm sauce over low heat before using.

Stuffed Mirlitons

MAKES 8 SERVINGS; **PREP:** 30 MIN.;
COOK: 1 HR., 12 MIN.; **COOL:** 30 MIN.;
BAKE: 30 MIN.

Toss baby greens with a splash of tangy vinaigrette to pair with the rich mirlitons as a first course.

4 medium mirlitons (chayote squash)
    (about ¾ lb. each)
1¼ lb. peeled, medium-size raw shrimp
    (31/35 count)
½ cup butter
1 medium onion, finely chopped
½ medium-size green bell pepper,
    chopped
2 celery ribs, finely chopped
3 green onions, chopped
3 garlic cloves, minced
¼ cup chopped fresh parsley
1¼ cups fine, dry breadcrumbs, divided
¾ tsp. salt
½ tsp. black pepper
¼ tsp. ground red pepper
1 large egg, lightly beaten
2 Tbsp. butter

1. Place mirlitons in salted water to cover in a large Dutch oven; bring to a boil over medium-high heat. Cook 45 to 50 minutes or until very tender when pierced with a fork. Drain mirlitons, and cool 30 minutes.
2. Meanwhile, devein shrimp, if desired. Coarsely chop shrimp.

Taste of the South

Mirlitons, or chayote (chi-OH-tay) squash, are common in South Louisiana cooking. Their flavor is very mild, rather like a cross between zucchini and cucumber, so they make a great foil for rich stuffings.

You can substitute zucchini or even yellow squash for most recipes that call for mirlitons.

3. Preheat oven to 350°. Cut mirlitons in half lengthwise; remove and discard seeds. Carefully scoop out pulp into a bowl, leaving a ¼-inch-thick shell. Finely chop pulp.
4. Melt ½ cup butter in a large, deep skillet or Dutch oven over medium heat; add onion, and cook, stirring occasionally, 5 minutes or until tender. Reduce heat to low; add bell pepper and next 4 ingredients, and sauté 12 minutes or until tender. Stir in mirliton pulp; cook, stirring often, 5 minutes. Stir in 1 cup breadcrumbs until combined. Remove from heat; stir in shrimp. Stir in salt and next 3 ingredients.
5. Microwave 2 Tbsp. butter at HIGH 10 to 15 seconds or until melted. Spoon mirliton mixture into shells, pressing down lightly. Sprinkle with remaining ¼ cup breadcrumbs. Place mirlitons in 2 (11- x 7-inch) baking dishes. Drizzle with melted butter.
6. Bake at 350° for 30 minutes or until lightly browned.

—GERRI M. ELIE, NEW ORLEANS, LOUISIANA

Stuffed Squash: Substitute 7 medium zucchini or yellow squash for mirlitons. Omit Steps 1 through 3. Microwave squash at HIGH 3 minutes. Cut each in half lengthwise. Carefully scoop out pulp into a bowl, leaving a ¼-inch-thick shell. Finely chop pulp. Devein shrimp, if desired; coarsely chop shrimp. Proceed with recipe as directed, beginning with Step 4.
Note: For testing purposes only, we used an 1,100-watt microwave.

Coconut-Almond Cream Cake

MAKES 12 SERVINGS; **PREP:** 30 MIN.;
BAKE: 47 MIN.; **COOL:** 1 HR., 10 MIN.

Brooks makes this cake with the precision of a skilled baker who has made his masterpiece many times. If the tops of the layers are a little rounded, he recommends leveling them with a serrated knife. "This is a tall cake," he says, "and it needs to be level if you want your friends to admire your work before they devour the cake—as they absolutely will." (Pictured on page 192)

2 cups sweetened flaked coconut
½ cup sliced almonds
Parchment paper
3½ cups all-purpose flour
1 Tbsp. baking powder
½ tsp. salt
1½ cups unsalted butter, at room
    temperature
1¼ cups granulated sugar
1 cup firmly packed light brown sugar
5 large eggs
1 cup whipping cream
⅓ cup coconut milk
1 Tbsp. vanilla extract
1 Tbsp. almond extract
Coconut-Almond Filling
Coconut-Cream Cheese Frosting
Garnishes: kumquats, currants, fresh mint
    sprigs

1. Preheat oven to 325°. Bake coconut in a single layer in a shallow pan 6 minutes. Place almonds in a single layer in another shallow pan; bake, with coconut, 7 to 9 minutes or until almonds are fragrant and coconut is lightly browned, stirring occasionally.
2. Line 3 (9-inch) round cake pans with parchment paper. Grease and flour paper.
3. Sift together flour, baking powder, and salt in a very large bowl.
4. Beat butter at medium speed with a heavy-duty electric stand mixer until creamy; gradually add sugars, beating until blended. Beat 8 minutes or until very fluffy, scraping bottom and sides of

Grandma Erma's Spirited Cranberry Sauce

make ahead

MAKES ABOUT 3½ CUPS; **PREP:** 5 MIN., **COOK:** 10 MIN., **COOL:** 15 MIN., **CHILL:** 8 HR.

bowl as needed. Add eggs, 1 at a time, beating well after each addition (about 30 seconds per egg). Stir in whipping cream and next 3 ingredients.

5. Gently fold butter mixture into flour mixture, in batches, just until combined. Pour batter into prepared pans.

6. Bake at 325° for 30 to 32 minutes or until a wooden pick inserted in center comes out clean. Cool in pans on wire racks 10 minutes; remove from pans to wire racks, and cool completely (about 1 hour).

7. Place 1 cake layer on a serving plate. Spread half of chilled Coconut-Almond Filling over cake layer. Top with 1 layer, pressing down gently. Repeat procedure with remaining half of Coconut-Almond Filling and remaining cake layer.

8. Gently spread Coconut-Cream Cheese Frosting on top and sides of cake. Press toasted coconut onto sides of cake; sprinkle toasted almonds on top. Garnish, if desired.

—BROOKS HAMAKER, NEW ORLEANS, LOUISIANA

Coconut-Almond Filling:

make ahead

MAKES 3 CUPS; **PREP:** 10 MIN., **COOK:** 5 MIN., **CHILL:** 8 HR.

This filling acts as a glue to hold the layers together and works best when chilled, so don't skip that step.

2 Tbsp. cornstarch
1 tsp. almond extract
1¼ cups whipping cream
½ cup firmly packed light brown sugar
½ cup unsalted butter
2¼ cups loosely packed sweetened flaked coconut
¼ cup sour cream

1. Stir together cornstarch, almond extract, and 2 Tbsp. water in a bowl.

2. Bring whipping cream, brown sugar, and butter to a boil in a saucepan over medium heat. Remove from heat, and immediately whisk in cornstarch mixture. Stir in coconut and sour cream. Cover and chill 8 hours.

Coconut-Cream Cheese Frosting:

fast fixin's

MAKES ABOUT 3 CUPS; **PREP:** 10 MIN.

1. Beat 2 (8-oz.) packages cream cheese, softened, and ½ cup unsalted butter, softened, at medium speed with an electric mixer until creamy. Gradually add 2 cups powdered sugar, beating at low speed until blended. Increase speed to medium, and beat in 1 Tbsp. cream of coconut and 1 tsp. vanilla extract until smooth.

Taste a New Tradition

A sparkling bowl of jewel-colored cranberry sauce is an absolute must for the holiday table. Simple to make, this sophisticated twist tops our list of gourmet gift ideas. Fill a jar, tie on a ribbon, and add a decorative label with storage instructions.

Port wine and orange liqueur are the secret ingredients in this dish. You'll need about 1 lb. of cranberries. Most are sold in 12-oz. bags, so pick up two and freeze the extra. And don't limit it to turkey—try the sauce on sandwiches, or spread over a warm round of brie.

2 cups sugar
½ cup port
4 cups fresh cranberries
¼ cup orange liqueur

1. Stir together sugar, port, and ¾ cup water in a heavy 3-qt. saucepan until blended. Add cranberries; bring to a boil, and cook over medium-high heat, stirring often, 8 to 10 minutes or until cranberry skins begin to split. Remove from heat, and let cool 15 minutes.

2. Pulse cranberry mixture in a food processor 3 to 4 times or until the berries are almost pureed; stir in orange liqueur. Cover and chill 8 hours before serving. Store in refrigerator in an airtight container up to 2 weeks. Serve chilled or at room temperature.

—LESLIE SUTHERLAND, FORT WORTH, TEXAS

Note: For testing purposes only, we used Grand Marnier for orange liqueur.

Turkey Tenderloins With Cranberry Sauce: *(Pictured on page 1)* Preheat oven to 400°. Sprinkle 1½ lb. turkey tenderloins with 1 tsp. each salt and freshly ground pepper. Place tenderloins in a lightly greased 15- x 10-inch jelly-roll pan. Bake 20 to 25 minutes or until a meat thermometer inserted into thickest portion registers 170°. Brush tenderloins with Grandma Erma's Spirited Cranberry Sauce. Garnish with fresh sage or rosemary, if desired. **Makes** 4 servings; Prep: 10 min., Bake: 25 min.

Discover some delicious ways to eat healthfully.
Plus, celebrate the season with good-for-you gifts.

Extraordinary Oats

Rediscover a healthy favorite with these new twists.

Even grandma knew a good ol' bowl of oatmeal is an energy powerhouse. High in protein and fiber, it's ideal for maintaining heart health while keeping you satisfied. Using oats as an ingredient in tasty recipes reaps maximum benefits.

Creamy Oatmeal

MAKES 4 SERVINGS; **PREP:** 10 MIN.,
STAND: 5 MIN., **COOK:** 36 MIN.

¼ cup chopped dried apricots
2 cups 1% low-fat milk
¼ cup firmly packed brown sugar
½ cinnamon stick
3 whole cloves
¼ tsp. kosher salt
1 cup steel-cut Irish oats

1. Place apricots in a small bowl with hot water to cover, and let stand 5 minutes or until plump. Drain.
2. Cook milk, next 4 ingredients, and 2 cups water in a heavy nonaluminum saucepan over medium heat, stirring often, 5 to 6 minutes or just until bubbles appear (do not boil). Remove from heat; remove cinnamon stick and cloves with a slotted spoon, and discard.
3. Stir in oats. Cook over low heat, stirring often, 30 minutes or until done. Top with apricots, and serve immediately.
Note: For testing purposes only, we used McCann's Steel-Cut Irish Oatmeal.

Per serving: Calories 279; Fat 4.1g (sat 1.2g, mono 1.2g, poly 1g); Protein 9.9g; Carb 53.1g; Fiber 4.5g; Chol 5mg; Iron 2.7mg; Sodium 191mg; Calc 194mg

Creamy Wheat Cereal: Substitute ¾ cup uncooked quick-cooking (2½-minute) creamy wheat cereal for 1 cup Irish oats. Proceed with recipe as directed, reducing cook time in Step 3 to 3 to 5 minutes or until done.
Note: For testing purposes only, we used Original (2½-minute) Cream of Wheat.

Per serving: Calories 253; Fat 1.5g (sat 0.8g, mono 0.4g, poly 0.1g); Protein 7.9g; Carb 51.6g; Fiber 1.4g; Chol 5mg; Iron 2.1mg; Sodium 191mg; Calc 179mg

Mixed Berry Cobbler

MAKES 6 SERVINGS; **PREP:** 10 MIN.,
STAND: 5 MIN., **BAKE:** 1 HR.

2 cups granola
½ cup 1% low-fat milk
2 (12-oz.) packages frozen mixed berries
¼ cup firmly packed brown sugar
2 tsp. cornstarch
1 tsp. ground cinnamon
½ tsp. orange zest
¼ tsp. ground nutmeg
Vegetable cooking spray
Plain fat-free yogurt

1. Preheat oven to 350°. Stir together granola and milk in a small bowl. Let stand 5 minutes.
2. Toss together berries and next 5 ingredients in a large bowl. Spoon berry mixture into an 8-inch square baking dish.
3. Stir granola mixture, and spoon over berry mixture. Lightly coat with cooking spray.

4. Bake at 350° for 1 hour or until bubbly. Serve with yogurt.
Note: For testing purposes only, we used Quaker 100% Natural Granola, Oats & Honey at one tasting and Heartland Original Granola Cereal at another.

Per serving: Calories 328; Fat 8.1g (sat 1.2g, mono 0.1g, poly 0.3g); Protein 8.8g; Carb 57.3g; Fiber 8.6g; Chol 1.1mg; Iron 3.1mg; Sodium 133mg; Calc 126mg

Anytime Peach Cobbler:

Substitute 1 (20-oz.) package frozen sliced peaches for frozen mixed berries. Proceed with recipe as directed.

Per serving: Calories 296; Fat 7.6g (sat 1.2g, mono 0.1g, poly 0g); Protein 8.1mg; Carb 49g; Fiber 3.6g; Chol 1mg; Iron 2.4mg; Sodium 132mg; Calc 93mg

Oatmeal-Honey Waffles

MAKES 8 WAFFLES; **PREP:** 20 MIN.,
BAKE: 10 MIN., **COOL:** 10 MIN., **COOK:** 15 MIN.

1 cup uncooked regular oats
1½ cups all-purpose flour
1 tsp. baking powder
½ tsp. salt
2 large eggs, separated
1½ cups 1% low-fat milk
4 Tbsp. melted butter
2 Tbsp. honey
Toppings: butter, maple syrup

1. Preheat oven to 350°. Bake oats in a single layer in a shallow pan 10 minutes or until lightly toasted, stirring after 5 minutes. Let cool on a wire rack 10 minutes. Process oats in a blender or food processor 30 seconds or until finely ground.
2. Sift together flour, baking powder, and salt in a large bowl; stir in toasted ground oats.
3. Beat egg whites at high speed with an electric mixer until soft peaks form.

4. Whisk together egg yolks, milk, butter, and honey in a medium bowl; gently stir into oat mixture. Gently fold in egg whites just until blended.
5. Cook batter in a preheated, oiled waffle iron until golden. Serve each waffle with 1 tsp. butter and 1 Tbsp. maple syrup, if desired.

Per 1-waffle serving (including 1 tsp. butter and 1 Tbsp. maple syrup): Calories 312; Fat 12g (sat 6.8g, mono 3.3g, poly 0.9g); Protein 7.1g; Carb 45g; Fiber 1.6g; Chol 72mg; Iron 2.1mg; Sodium 253mg; Calc 122mg

Nutritious Gift Ideas

- A share of a local CSA (Community Supported Agriculture), **www.localharvest.org.** "As a foodie I think this is just about the coolest gift I could ever receive.
- Category 5 (red) RayLen Winery, **www.raylenvineyards.com.** Grand Cuvée Blanc de Blanc (Champagne), Beachaven Vineyards & Winery, **www.beachavenwinery.com.**
- Viognier (white) Chester Gap Cellars, **www.chestergapcellars.com.** Wine is full of antioxidants, so in moderation it's a healthy way to enjoy a drink during the holidays.

—**Scott Jones,** Executive Editor

Good-for-You Gifts

Discover our favorite presents, including some healthy bars.

Whole Grain Marshmallow Crispy Bars
MAKES 24 BARS; **PREP:** 15 MIN., **COOK:** 5 MIN., **STAND:** 15 MIN.

3 Tbsp. butter
1 (10.5-oz.) bag miniature marshmallows
1 (15-oz.) box multi-grain cluster cereal
1¼ cups dried cranberries, divided
Vegetable cooking spray

1. Melt butter in a large saucepan over low heat. Add marshmallows, and cook, stirring constantly, 4 to 5 minutes or until melted and smooth. Remove from heat.
2. Stir in cereal and 1 cup dried cranberries until well coated.
3. Press mixture into a 13- x 9-inch baking dish coated with cooking spray. Chop remaining ¼ cup dried cranberries, and sprinkle on top. Let stand 10 to 15 minutes or until firm. Cut into 24 bars.
Note: For testing purposes only, we used Kashi GOLEAN Crunch! cereal.

Per bar: Calories 132; Fat 1.9g (sat 0.9g, mono 0.4g, poly 0.1g); Protein 2.6g; Carb 27.6g; Fiber 1.7g; Chol 4mg; Iron 0.6mg; Sodium 22mg; Calc 8mg.

Salads To Rave About

A few touches bring these salads to the table in style.

Grilled Pork Tenderloin Salad With Roasted Sweet Potatoes
MAKES 6 SERVINGS; **PREP:** 30 MIN., **BAKE:** 25 MIN., **GRILL:** 24 MIN., **STAND:** 10 MIN.

3 small sweet potatoes (about 1½ lb.)
2 tsp. olive oil
½ tsp. ground allspice
¼ tsp. ground red pepper
1½ tsp. salt, divided
1 (2-lb.) package pork tenderloin
½ tsp. freshly ground black pepper
8 cups gourmet mixed salad greens
1 (4-oz.) package crumbled feta cheese
½ small red onion, halved and sliced
¾ cup sweetened dried cranberries
½ cup sliced honey-roasted almonds
Raspberry Salad Dressing

1. Preheat oven to 450°. Peel sweet potatoes, and cut into ½-inch-thick wedges; toss with oil, allspice, red pepper, and ½ tsp. salt. Arrange potato wedges in a single layer on a lightly greased jelly-roll pan.
2. Bake at 450° on an oven rack one-third up from bottom of oven 10 minutes; turn potatoes, and bake 10 to 15 minutes or until crisp-tender. Remove from oven, and let cool.
3. Preheat grill to 350° to 400° (medium-high). Sprinkle pork with ½ tsp. black pepper and remaining 1 tsp. salt. Grill pork, covered with grill lid, 6 to 8 minutes on all sides or until a meat thermometer inserted into thickest portion registers 150° to 155°. Remove from grill; let stand 10 minutes. Cut diagonally into ½-inch-thick slices.
4. Toss together greens and next 4 ingredients in a large bowl; transfer to a serving platter, and top with sliced pork and sweet potatoes. Serve with Raspberry Salad Dressing.

—**KATHY HUDSON,** JONESTOWN, TEXAS
Note: For testing purposes only, we used Sunkist Almond Accents Honey Roasted Flavored Sliced Almonds.

Raspberry Salad Dressing:
MAKES ABOUT ¾ CUP; **PREP:** 5 MIN.

¼ cup white wine vinegar
2 Tbsp. raspberry preserves
1 Tbsp. honey
½ cup olive oil

1. Whisk together first 3 ingredients in a bowl until blended. Add olive oil in a slow, steady stream, whisking constantly until blended

Savory Blue Cheesecakes With Waldorf Salad

fast fixin's

MAKES 12 SERVINGS; **PREP:** 20 MIN.,
BAKE: 7 MIN.

(Pictured on page 15)

½ cup chopped walnuts
1 large Gala apple, diced
1 large Granny Smith apple, diced
2 Tbsp. fresh lemon juice
2 celery ribs, finely chopped
½ cup golden raisins
1 (11.5-oz.) bottle refrigerated blue cheese
     vinaigrette, divided
2 (5-oz.) packages spring mix, thoroughly
     washed
Savory Blue Cheesecakes

1. Preheat oven to 350°. Bake walnuts
in a single layer in a shallow pan 5 to
7 minutes or until lightly toasted and
fragrant.
2. Toss diced apples with lemon juice
in a medium bowl; add walnuts, celery,
raisins, and ½ cup vinaigrette, stirring
to coat.
3. Divide greens among 12 salad plates;
place 1 Savory Blue Cheesecake over
greens on each plate. Spoon about
½ cup apple mixture over each cheesecake. Serve with remaining vinaigrette.
Note: For testing purposes only, we
used Marie's Blue Cheese Vinaigrette.

Savory Blue Cheesecakes:

MAKES 12 SERVINGS; **PREP:** 10 MIN.,
BAKE: 40 MIN., **COOL:** 30 MIN.,
CHILL: 4 HR., **FREEZE:** 30 MIN.

12 paper baking cups
Vegetable cooking spray
2 (8-oz.) packages cream cheese,
     softened
½ cup sour cream
1 (4-oz.) package crumbled blue
     cheese
1 Tbsp. all-purpose flour
½ tsp. dried parsley flakes
½ tsp. dried marjoram
¼ tsp. granulated garlic
2 large eggs

1. Preheat oven to 325°. Place 12 paper
baking cups in a muffin pan, and coat
with cooking spray.
2. Beat cream cheese and next 6 ingredients at medium speed with an electric
mixer until blended. Add eggs, 1 at a
time, beating just until yellow disappears after each addition. Spoon cream
cheese mixture into prepared baking
cups, filling completely full.
3. Bake at 325° for 40 minutes or until
set. Let cool in pan on a wire rack 15
minutes. Remove from pan to wire rack,
and let cool completely (about 15 minutes). Cover and chill 4 hours. Freeze
15 to 30 minutes or until cheesecakes
can be easily removed from baking
cups. Remove and discard baking cups.

—TRACIE NEWLIN, TUCKER, GEORGIA

WHAT'S FOR SUPPER?

Shrimp Scampi

Capture the essence of a
classic Italian-style dish in
30 minutes.

30-Minute Shrimp Supper

SERVES 4

Shrimp Scampi

Mixed greens salad

Cheesy Garlic Bread

Ice cream

Shrimp Scampi

MAKES 4 SERVINGS; **PREP:** 20 MIN.,
COOK: 10 MIN.

(Pictured on page 14)

1 lb. peeled, large raw shrimp (31/35 count)
1 (12-oz.) package angel hair pasta
½ cup butter
¼ cup finely chopped onion
3 garlic cloves, finely chopped
1 tsp. salt-free Italian-herb
     seasoning
1 tsp. Worcestershire sauce
1 Tbsp. fresh lemon juice
¼ cup freshly grated Romano or
     Parmesan cheese
1 Tbsp. chopped fresh parsley

1. Devein shrimp, if desired.
2. Prepare pasta according to package
directions.
3. Meanwhile, melt butter in a large
skillet over medium-high heat; add
onion and garlic, and sauté 3 to 5 minutes or until tender. Stir in Italian-herb
seasoning and Worcestershire sauce.
4. Reduce heat to medium. Add
shrimp, and cook, stirring occasionally, 3 to 5 minutes or just until
shrimp turn pink. Stir in lemon juice.
Toss shrimp mixture with pasta, and
sprinkle with cheese and parsley. Serve
immediately.

—INSPIRED BY DOREEN SIDOR, ROANOKE, VIRGINIA

Note: For testing purposes only,
we used Mrs. Dash Italian Medley
Seasoning Blend. We prefer Wild
American Shrimp for better flavor in
the Test Kitchens.

Cheesy Garlic Bread

MAKES 6 SERVINGS; **PREP:** 10 MIN.,
BAKE: 7 MIN.

1 (12-oz.) French bread loaf
3 garlic cloves, peeled*
Pinch of salt
1 cup (4 oz.) shredded Italian six-cheese
     blend
¼ cup butter, softened
1 tsp. salt-free Italian-herb seasoning

1. Preheat oven to 350°. Cut bread diagonally into slices.
2. Place peeled garlic cloves on a cutting board with salt. Smash garlic and salt together using flat side of a knife to make a paste.
3. Stir together garlic paste, cheese, butter, and seasoning. Spread butter mixture on 1 side of each bread slice. Place bread on a baking sheet.
4. Bake at 350° for 5 to 7 minutes or until golden and cheese is melted.

*1½ tsp. jarred minced garlic may be substituted. Omit salt, and stir minced garlic together with cheese, butter, and seasoning in Step 3.

Note: For testing purposes only, we used Mrs. Dash Italian Medley Seasoning Blend.

QUICK & EASY

Show-off Desserts

Serve up sweet satisfaction in 45 minutes or less.

Mocha Java Cakes

MAKES 6 SERVINGS; **PREP:** 15 MIN.,
BAKE: 16 MIN., **STAND:** 10 MIN.

1 Tbsp. butter
1 cup butter
8 oz. bittersweet chocolate morsels
4 egg yolks
4 large eggs
2 cups powdered sugar
¾ cup all-purpose flour
1 tsp. instant espresso or instant coffee
 granules
Pinch of salt
Garnish: powdered sugar

1. Preheat oven to 425°. Grease 6 (6-oz.) ramekins or individual soufflé dishes with 1 Tbsp. butter.
2. Microwave 1 cup butter and chocolate morsels in a microwave-safe bowl at HIGH 2 minutes or until chocolate is melted and mixture is smooth, whisking at 1-minute intervals.
3. Beat egg yolks and eggs at medium speed with an electric mixer 1 minute. Gradually add chocolate mixture, beating at low speed until well blended.
4. Sift together sugar and next 3 ingredients. Gradually whisk sugar mixture into chocolate mixture until well blended. Divide batter among prepared ramekins. Place ramekins in a 15- x 10-inch jelly-roll pan.
5. Bake at 425° for 16 minutes or until a thermometer inserted into cakes registers 165°. Remove from oven, and let stand 10 minutes. Run a knife around outer edge of each cake to loosen. Carefully invert cakes onto dessert plates. Garnish, if desired.

Note: For testing purposes only, we used Ghirardelli 60% Cacao Bittersweet Chocolate Chips.

Coffee Liqueur Java Cakes: Omit instant espresso. Prepare recipe as directed through Step 3. Sift together sugar, flour, and salt. Gradually whisk sugar mixture into chocolate mixture until well blended. Whisk in ⅓ cup coffee liqueur. Proceed with recipe as directed, baking cakes 14 to 16 minutes or until a thermometer inserted into cakes registers 165°.

Note: For testing purposes only, we used Kahlúa for coffee liqueur.

Orange Java Cakes: Prepare recipe as directed through Step 3. Sift together sugar, flour, and salt. Gradually whisk sugar mixture into chocolate mixture until well blended. Whisk in ¼ cup orange liqueur and 1 tsp. orange zest.

Fresh Fruit Tart With Mascarpone Cheese

MAKES 6 TO 8 SERVINGS; **PREP:** 15 MIN.,
BAKE: 12 MIN., **COOL:** 15 MIN.

2 (8-oz.) packages mascarpone cheese, softened
½ cup powdered sugar
1 tsp. lemon zest
1 tsp. lemon juice
½ (15-oz.) package refrigerated piecrusts
5 kiwifruit, peeled and sliced
1 cup fresh raspberries
¼ cup apricot jam*

1. Preheat oven to 450°. Whisk together mascarpone cheese and next 3 ingredients in a medium bowl. Cover and chill.
2. Meanwhile, fit piecrust into a 9-inch tart pan with removable bottom; press into fluted edges. Fold any excess dough over outside of pan, and pinch to secure to pan. (This will keep piecrust from sliding down pan as it bakes.) Line crust with aluminum foil, and fill with pie weights or dried beans.
3. Bake at 450° for 8 minutes. Remove weights and foil, and bake 3 to 4 more minutes or until golden brown. Remove from oven to a wire rack, and cool completely (about 15 minutes). Gently tap excess crust from sides of pan, using a rolling pin.
4. Spoon mascarpone mixture into cooled tart shell, spreading to edges. Arrange kiwifruit around outer edge of tart; place raspberries in center.
5. Combine apricot jam and 1 Tbsp. water in a small microwave-safe glass dish. Microwave at HIGH 25 seconds. Stir until well blended. Pour apricot mixture through a fine wire-mesh strainer into a bowl; discard solids. Brush fruit in tart with apricot mixture. Serve immediately.

—INSPIRED BY AMY ELIZABETH REX,
ALPHARETTA, GEORGIA

*Apple jelly may be substituted. Decrease water to 2 tsp. in Step 5 and do not strain jelly mixture after heating.

Cheesecake-Filled Fresh Fruit Tart: Substitute 2 cups ready-to-eat cheesecake filling for mascarpone cheese. Increase lemon juice to 2 tsp. Proceed with recipe as directed.

Holiday Dinners®

Get ready to celebrate, Southern style! Our annual special section offers fantastic recipes that will make your parties the talk of the town.

Ultimate Holidays

The cornerstone dish for the holiday meal is turkey, and we've found a real winner in Delta Roasted Turkey. Its unusual cooking method, which comes to us from reader Elizabeth Heiskell, produces a crisp exterior with incredibly juicy meat. Pair this scrumptious entrée with the updated Sweet Potato Cups and a few of our other favorite recipes.

THANKSGIVING DINNER

SERVES 8

Delta Roasted Turkey With Million-Dollar Gravy

Cornbread 'n' Squash Dressing (page 285)

Sweet Potato Cups

Basic Green Bean Casserole (page 288)

Fresh Fruit Tart With Mascarpone Cheese (page 267)

Grand Mimosas

Delta Roasted Turkey With Million-Dollar Gravy

family favorite

MAKES 8 TO 10 SERVINGS; **PREP:** 30 MIN.;
SOAK: 15 MIN.; **BAKE:** 3 HR., 30 MIN.;
STAND: 20 MIN.

"My grandmother served this turkey every Thanksgiving and Christmas, so I continue the tradition with my family. I haven't changed a thing," says Elizabeth Heiskell.

Cheesecloth
3½ cups low-sodium chicken broth, divided
5 thick hickory-smoked bacon slices
½ cup butter, softened
2 tsp. salt
2 tsp. pepper
1 (14-lb.) whole fresh or frozen turkey, thawed
Kitchen string
2 cups dry white wine
2 bay leaves
6 black peppercorns
4 fresh thyme sprigs
4 fresh parsley sprigs
1 cup butter
3 Tbsp. all-purpose flour
2 Tbsp. butter, softened

1. Cut cheesecloth into a 3-ft. square. (Cheesecloth should be large enough to wrap around entire turkey.) Soak cheesecloth in 1 cup broth 15 minutes. Wring out cheesecloth, discarding excess broth. Lay cheesecloth on top of a roasting rack in a roasting pan. Place bacon slices in center of cheesecloth.

2. Preheat oven to 500°. Combine ½ cup softened butter, salt, and pepper. Remove giblets and neck from turkey, and pat turkey dry with paper towels. Loosen and lift skin from turkey breast with fingers, without totally detaching skin; rub about one-third of butter mixture underneath skin. Carefully replace skin, and rub remaining butter mixture over outside of turkey. Tie ends of legs together with kitchen string; tuck wingtips under. Place turkey, breast side down, on top of bacon in roasting pan. Lift sides of cheesecloth up and over turkey. Twist ends of cheesecloth together, and secure them tightly with string. Trim excess cheesecloth and string.

3. Stir together wine, next 4 ingredients, and 1 cup broth. Pour into roasting pan.

4. Bake turkey at 500° for 30 minutes.

5. Meanwhile, heat 1 cup butter and ½ cup broth in a saucepan over low heat just until butter is melted. Pour mixture over turkey. Reduce oven temperature to 300°, and bake 2½ hours, basting with pan drippings every 30 minutes.

6. Remove turkey from oven, and increase oven temperature to 400°. Carefully transfer turkey to a cutting board, using clean dish towels. Remove and discard cheesecloth and bacon. Carefully return turkey, breast side up, to roasting pan.

Expert Know-how

Test Kitchens Professional Marian Cooper Cairns shares her tips and secrets for success when making Delta Roasted Turkey.

- Carefully read the recipe before beginning, and allow plenty of time to cover all the steps. It's involved but definitely worth it.
- The cheesecloth needs to cover the entire bird, so make sure you have a large enough piece.
- A V-shaped roasting rack works best, but your favorite roasting rack will work just fine.
- Flipping the turkey may seem daunting, but using two clean dish towels or oven mitts makes the job much easier. Don't be afraid to make it a two-person task, if needed.
- Before completely removing the wrapped turkey from the oven, baste the cheesecloth; this will keep it from sticking to the skin.
- Use a small ladle or large spoon to skim the fat from the gravy before bringing it to a boil.

7. Bake turkey at 400° for 30 minutes or until skin is golden brown and a meat thermometer inserted into thickest portion of thigh registers 170° to 175°. Transfer turkey to a serving platter, reserving pan drippings in roasting pan. Let turkey stand 20 minutes before carving.

8. Pour pan drippings through a fine wire-mesh strainer into a 4-cup glass measuring cup. Let stand 10 minutes. Remove excess fat from surface of drippings.

9. Pour 2 cups drippings into a medium saucepan; stir in remaining 1 cup broth. Bring to a boil over medium-high heat. Combine flour and 2 Tbsp. butter to form a smooth paste. Whisk butter mixture into broth mixture, and cook, whisking constantly, 2 minutes or until thickened. Serve with turkey.

—ELIZABETH HEISKELL,
CLEVELAND, MISSISSIPPI

Sweet Potato Cups
family favorite • make ahead
MAKES 8 SERVINGS; PREP: 30 MIN.;
BAKE: 1 HR., 25 MIN.; STAND: 20 MIN.

Elizabeth uses a zester or channel knife to make designs on the outsides of oranges. Save the orange pulp to make delicious Grand Mimosas to enjoy while you are preparing this special dish.
(Pictured on page 191)

6 small sweet potatoes (about 2¾ lb.)
4 large navel oranges
1 (14-oz.) can sweetened condensed milk
3 Tbsp. melted butter
2 tsp. vanilla extract
2 tsp. orange zest
¼ tsp. salt
⅛ tsp. ground nutmeg
⅛ tsp. ground allspice
⅛ tsp. ground cinnamon
1 cup miniature marshmallows

1. Preheat oven to 425°. Place sweet potatoes on an aluminum foil-lined baking sheet. Bake at 425° for 45 minutes or until tender. Let stand 20 minutes. Reduce oven temperature to 350°.

2. Meanwhile, cut oranges in half crosswise. Scoop out pulp using a spoon, leaving peel intact. Reserve orange pulp for another use.

3. Peel sweet potatoes, and place potato pulp in a large bowl. Add sweetened condensed milk and next 7 ingredients. Beat at medium speed with an electric mixer until smooth, stopping occasionally to remove any tough fibers, if necessary. Spoon about ½ cup mixture into each orange cup. Place orange cups in a 13- x 9-inch baking dish.

4. Bake at 350° for 20 minutes. Remove from oven, and top with marshmallows, pressing lightly to adhere. Bake 15 to 20 minutes or until marshmallows are melted and golden brown.

—ELIZABETH HEISKELL, CLEVELAND, MISSISSIPPI

Note: Orange cups and sweet potatoes can be made 1 day ahead. Chill scooped orange cups and baked sweet potatoes in separate zip-top plastic bags until ready to assemble.

Pecan-Ginger-Sweet Potato
Cups: Prepare recipe as directed through Step 3, adding ¾ tsp. ground ginger with sweetened condensed milk. Bake cups at 350° for 20 minutes. Top with ½ cup chopped pecans; top with marshmallows as directed. Proceed with recipe as directed.

Grand Mimosas
fast fixin's
MAKES 6 TO 8 SERVINGS; PREP: 10 MIN.

1. Stir together 1 (750-ml.) bottle chilled Champagne or sparkling wine, 2 cups chilled fresh orange juice, and ¼ to ⅓ cup orange liqueur. Serve immediately. **Makes** 6 to 8 servings.

Note: For testing purposes only, we used Grand Marnier for orange liqueur.

A Hip Way To Celebrate

Take a cue from this couple to freshen up your Hanukkah menu.

This couple puts a fun-loving spin on the usual holiday fare. "Our best parties are grab-a-plate style," says Mindi Shapiro Levine, as she and husband Brett prepare for visitors. "We like it when guests settle on barstools and hang out," Brett chimes in.

Their Hanukkah celebration is smartly streamlined. "We opted to skip the appetizer and a brisket dish," says Mindi, "so everyone has plenty of appetite for latkes."

Golden Potato Latkes
make ahead

MAKES: ABOUT 2 DOZEN; **PREP:** 30 MIN., **COOK:** 10 MIN. PER BATCH

Combining butter and oil for frying yields great flavor and browning. We love the large size and consistent heat of an electric skillet, but a nonstick skillet will work. (Use two skillets to cook more at one time.)

3 lb. Yukon gold potatoes, unpeeled
1 medium onion
2 Tbsp. lemon juice
2 large eggs, lightly beaten
½ cup unsalted matzo meal
1 tsp. kosher salt
¾ tsp. pepper
6 Tbsp. butter
6 Tbsp. peanut oil
Kosher salt
Garnishes: small Yukon gold potatoes, fresh green onions

1. Grate potatoes and onion through large holes of a box grater; toss with lemon juice. Spread mixture onto 2 clean, dry kitchen towels. Roll up each towel, starting with 1 long side. Wring towels to squeeze out the excess liquid. Place potato mixture in a large bowl.

2. Stir in eggs, matzo meal, salt, and pepper. (Mixture will be dry but will hold its shape when pressed together.)

3. Melt 2 Tbsp. butter with 2 Tbsp. oil in a deep electric skillet heated to 375° or a large nonstick skillet over medium to medium-high heat. Drop 6 to 8 loosely packed ¼ cupfuls potato mixture into hot butter mixture; press lightly to flatten into 3-inch rounds. Cook 3 to 5 minutes on each side or until golden brown. Drain on paper towels. Sprinkle with additional salt. Repeat procedure with remaining butter, oil, and potato mixture. Serve latkes immediately, or keep warm on a wire rack on a baking sheet in a 250° oven up to 30 minutes. Garnish, if desired.

Note: For testing purposes only, we used Manischewitz Unsalted Matzo Meal.

Golden Potato-Parsnip Latkes:
Prepare recipe as directed, reducing potatoes to 2 lb. and grating 1 lb. peeled parsnips with potatoes and onion. Garnish with fresh parsnip slices and fresh parsley sprigs, if desired.

Golden Carrot-Zucchini Latkes:
Prepare recipe as directed, reducing potatoes to 1 lb. and grating 1 lb. peeled carrots and 1 lb. zucchini with potatoes and onion. Garnish with shaved carrots and zucchini, if desired.

Note: To make the garnish, use a vegetable peeler to shave thin, lengthwise strips of carrot and zucchini. To make garnish ahead, wrap strips in damp paper towels, place in zip-top plastic bags, and chill up to 24 hours.

Cook's Notes

We liked Mindi's use of Yukon gold potatoes over baking potatoes for three reasons: The thin peel allows you to shred them unpeeled, which saves time. The flavor is rich and buttery, and the latkes fry up very crispy.

Horseradish-Sour Cream Sauce

make ahead

MAKES: 1 CUP; **PREP:** 10 MIN.,
CHILL: 30 MIN.

1 (8-oz.) container sour cream
2 Tbsp. thinly sliced fresh chives
4 tsp. horseradish
1 tsp. lemon zest
½ tsp. coarsely ground pepper
¼ tsp. salt
Garnish: sliced fresh chives

1. Stir together the first 6 ingredients. Cover and chill 30 minutes before serving. Garnish, if desired. Store in an airtight container in refrigerator up to 2 days.

Spiced-Thyme Applesauce

fast fixin's • make ahead

MAKES: 1¾ CUPS; **PREP:** 10 MIN.,
COOK: 7 MIN.

Mindi gave us a heads-up that the ginger, thyme, and cloves combo was different but delicious. We agreed. Butter adds a richness and creaminess to the texture that's worth the calories.

1 cup chunky applesauce
1 large ripe pear, peeled and finely chopped
1 Tbsp. butter
1 tsp. fresh lemon juice
1 tsp. finely grated fresh ginger
¾ tsp. finely chopped fresh thyme
⅛ tsp. ground cloves
⅛ tsp. kosher salt

1. Stir together all ingredients in a medium saucepan. Bring to a boil over medium-high heat, stirring often; reduce heat to low, and simmer, stirring occasionally, 5 to 7 minutes or until pear is tender.
Note: For testing purposes only, we used Musselman's Chunky Apple

Sauce. To make ahead, prepare recipe as directed. Store in an airtight container in refrigerator up to 2 days. Microwave in a microwave-safe glass bowl at HIGH 1 to 2 minutes or until sauce is thoroughly heated, stirring at 30-second intervals.

Smoked Salmon-Avocado Salad

fast fixin's

MAKES: 6 TO 8 SERVINGS; **PREP:** 15 MIN.

The Levines make the dressing tart to balance the richness of the pan-fried latkes. For a weekday supper, they suggest whisking in a little extra olive oil and serving with French bread. Roll the salmon into spirals if you have extra time when making this salad.

¼ cup olive oil
3 Tbsp. fresh lemon juice
1 tsp. Dijon mustard
¾ tsp. sugar
½ tsp. kosher salt
¼ tsp. pepper
1 (5-oz.) package arugula, thoroughly washed*
6 radishes, thinly sliced
2 (4-oz.) packages thinly sliced smoked salmon
1 avocado, sliced

1. Whisk together first 6 ingredients. Gently toss together arugula, radishes, and half of olive oil mixture in a large bowl. Arrange on a serving platter with salmon and avocado. Serve immediately with remaining olive oil mixture.
*1 (5-oz.) package spring mix, thoroughly washed, may be substituted.
Note: For testing purposes only, we used Echo Falls Smoked Salmon at one tasting, and Woodsmoke Provisions at another.

Mindi's Doughnuts and Easy Raspberry Sauce

fast fixin's

MAKES: 8 SERVINGS; **PREP:** 10 MIN.,
STAND: 10 MIN.

Doughnuts are a true passion for Mindi—she even asks for them instead of birthday cake. "This recipe is an awesome sweet to add to your brunch menus, too," says Mindi.

1 (10-oz.) jar seedless raspberry fruit spread
2 Tbsp. orange liqueur*
½ tsp. vanilla extract
1 cup whipping cream
1 Tbsp. powdered sugar
4 dozen glazed yeast doughnut holes

1. Microwave fruit spread in a microwave-safe glass bowl at HIGH 45 seconds or until warm and easy to stir. Stir in liqueur and vanilla. Let stand 10 minutes or until slightly thickened but still smooth.
2. Beat whipping cream at medium speed with an electric mixer until foamy; gradually add powdered sugar, beating until soft peaks form.
3. Serve doughnut holes with fruit spread mixture and whipped cream.
*2 Tbsp. orange juice may be substituted for liqueur.
Note: For testing purposes only, we used Smucker's Simply Fruit Seedless Red Raspberry for fruit spread.

Let's Do Lunch

Join these *Southern Living* fans as they gather for a splendid holiday meal.

Lunch Bunch

SERVES 6

Brandy Slush

Bacon-Wrapped Water Chestnuts

Ragoût of Mushrooms
With Creamy Polenta

Citrus Salad

Quick Yeast Rolls

Cheesecake Squares

On the third Monday of each month, a congenial group of friends gathers for lunch in Alexandria, Virginia. Ginger Arnold, Anita Guthrie, Betty Heilig, Gayle Shaw, Amy Southard, and Ann Vernon—The *Southern Living* Lunch Bunch as they call themselves—choose their recipes from the pages of our magazine.

We joined them for a holiday celebration where they shared some of their own dishes combined with favorites from past issues. Citrus Salad is a bright complement to creamy Ragoût of Mushrooms With Creamy Polenta, while Bacon-Wrapped Water Chestnuts provides a sweet-and-salty before-lunch nibble. Let these outstanding recipes along with the warmth and laughter of these friends resonate with you and your family this holiday season.

Brandy Slush
freezeable • make ahead
MAKES: 19 CUPS; **PREP:** 15 MIN.,
STEEP: 5 MIN., **COOL:** 30 MIN.,
FREEZE: 4 HR.

This recipe makes a big batch, so keep one bag in the freezer up to three months.

9 cups boiling water, divided
4 regular-size tea bags
2 cups sugar
1 (12-oz.) can frozen orange juice
   concentrate, thawed
1 (12-oz.) can frozen lemonade concentrate,
   thawed
1²⁄₃ cups brandy
¼ cup lime juice
4 (10-oz.) bottles club soda, chilled
Garnish: lime slices

1. Pour 2 cups boiling water over tea bags; cover and let steep 5 minutes. Remove and discard tea bags, squeezing gently.
2. Stir together remaining 7 cups boiling water and 2 cups sugar in a Dutch oven, stirring until sugar is dissolved. Stir in tea mixture, orange juice concentrate, and next 3 ingredients. Let cool to room temperature (about 30 minutes). Divide mixture between 2 (1-gal.) zip-top plastic freezer bags; freeze 4 hours.
3. Remove bags from freezer 30 minutes before serving. Squeeze 1 bag with hands to break mixture into chunks; pour into a pitcher, and stir in 2 bottles club soda until slushy. Repeat procedure with remaining bag, if desired. Garnish each serving, if desired.

Bacon-Wrapped Water Chestnuts
MAKES 10 TO 12 APPETIZER SERVINGS;
PREP: 20 MIN., **BAKE:** 45 MIN.

1 (8-oz.) can sliced water chestnuts
12 oz. fresh pineapple chunks, cut into
   1-inch pieces
15 bacon slices, halved
¼ cup teriyaki sauce

1. Preheat oven to 400°. Place 1 water chestnut slice on top of 1 pineapple chunk; wrap with 1 bacon piece. Repeat procedure with remaining water chestnuts, pineapple, and bacon. Place, seam sides down, in a lightly greased broiler pan.
2. Bake at 400° for 20 to 25 minutes; baste both sides with teriyaki sauce. Turn and bake 20 more minutes or until bacon is crisp. Serve immediately.

Ragoût of Mushrooms With Creamy Polenta
MAKES: 6 SERVINGS; **PREP:** 15 MIN.,
COOK: 14 MIN.

Don't let polenta scare you—it's just the Italian version of grits. Substitute your favorite red wine here if you don't have port.

1 cup halved and thinly sliced shallots
3 garlic cloves, minced
4 Tbsp. olive oil
2 (8-oz.) packages sliced baby portobello
   mushrooms*
2 (3.5-oz.) packages fresh shiitake
   mushrooms, stemmed and sliced
½ cup port wine
1 cup chicken broth
4 Tbsp. fresh flat-leaf parsley, chopped
4 Tbsp. butter
1½ Tbsp. fresh thyme leaves
¾ tsp. salt
½ tsp. pepper
Creamy Polenta
Freshly shaved Parmesan cheese
Garnish: fresh thyme sprigs

1. Sauté shallots and garlic in olive oil in a large skillet over medium heat 2 minutes. Increase heat to medium-high, add mushrooms, and cook, stirring constantly, 4 to 5 minutes. Stir in port; cook 2 minutes. Stir in broth and next 5 ingredients. Reduce heat to low, and simmer 5 minutes or until slightly thickened.

2. Serve over Creamy Polenta with shaved Parmesan cheese. Garnish, if desired.

*2 (8-oz.) packages sliced fresh button mushrooms may be substituted.

Creamy Polenta:
fast fixin's
MAKES: 6 SERVINGS; **PREP:** 5 MIN.,
COOK: 8 MIN

Polenta can be found in the gourmet or international section of the grocery store. Don't let the polenta boil, or it will spatter.

7 cups chicken broth
2 cups instant polenta
1 (8-oz.) package 1/3-less-fat cream cheese

1. Bring 6 cups chicken broth to a light boil in a Dutch oven over medium-high heat; slowly stir in polenta. Reduce heat to low, and cook, stirring constantly, 2 to 3 minutes or until polenta thickens. (Do not boil.) Stir in cream cheese until blended. Stir in remaining chicken broth. Cover and keep warm.

—**ANITA GUTHRIE**, ALEXANDRIA, VIRGINIA

Citrus Salad
MAKES: 6 SERVINGS; **PREP:** 30 MIN.,
BAKE: 8 MIN.

This salad is also delicious without nuts.

2 Tbsp. chopped walnuts or pecans (optional)
1 (5-oz.) bag mixed baby greens, thoroughly washed
2 navel oranges, peeled and sectioned
1 large grapefruit, peeled and sectioned
1 pear, peeled and thinly sliced
1 cup seedless red grapes
Orange Vinaigrette

1. Preheat oven to 350°. Bake nuts in a single layer in a shallow pan for 6 to 8 minutes or until toasted and fragrant.

2. Place greens in a large bowl. Add orange sections and next 3 ingredients. Drizzle with 1/4 cup Orange Vinaigrette, tossing gently to coat. Sprinkle toasted nuts over salad, and serve immediately with remaining vinaigrette.

Orange Vinaigrette:
fast fixin's
MAKES: ABOUT 1 1/4 CUPS; **PREP:** 10 MIN.

1/4 cup white wine vinegar
2 tsp. orange zest
3 Tbsp. fresh orange juice
1 Tbsp. sugar
1/2 tsp. salt
1/2 tsp. pepper
3/4 cup olive oil

1. Whisk together first 6 ingredients in a small bowl; add oil in a slow, steady stream, whisking until blended.

—**BETTY HEILIG**, ALEXANDRIA, VIRGINIA

Quick Yeast Rolls
freezeable • make ahead
MAKES: 2 DOZEN; **PREP:** 20 MIN.,
STAND: 5 MIN., **RISE:** 45 MIN.,
BAKE: 15 MIN.

Make these rolls up to one month ahead. Wrap cooled rolls loosely in foil, place in a zip-top plastic freezer bag, and freeze. Heat foil-wrapped rolls in a 325° oven for 30 minutes or until warm.

1 (1/4-oz.) envelope active dry yeast
1/4 cup warm water (105° to 115°)
1 tsp. sugar
2 Tbsp. sugar
2 Tbsp. butter, softened
1 1/4 tsp. salt
1 large egg
1 1/4 cups milk
4 cups all-purpose flour
2 Tbsp. melted butter

1. Stir together yeast, 1/4 cup warm water, and 1 tsp. sugar in a 2-cup glass measuring cup; let stand 5 minutes.

2. Beat 2 Tbsp. sugar, softened butter, and salt at medium speed with a heavy-duty electric stand mixer until creamy. Add egg, milk, and yeast mixture, beating until blended. Gradually add flour, beating at low speed until smooth. Turn dough out onto a well-floured surface, and knead until smooth and elastic (2 to 3 minutes). Place in a well-greased bowl, turning to grease top.

3. Cover and let rise in a warm place (85°), free from drafts, 30 minutes or until doubled in bulk.

4. Preheat oven to 400°. Punch dough down; turn dough out onto a floured surface. Divide dough into 24 pieces; shape into balls. Place in 2 greased 9-inch square pans. Cover and let rise in a warm place (85°), free from drafts, 15 minutes.

5. Bake at 400° for 15 minutes or until golden. Brush tops with melted butter, and serve immediately.

Cheesecake Squares
make ahead
MAKES 9 SERVINGS; **PREP:** 30 MIN.,
BAKE: 30 MIN., **COOL:** 1 HR., **CHILL:** 8 HR.

This dessert delivers rich, chocolate-coffee flavor and a truffle-like texture.

Chocolate Crust
1 (8-oz.) package cream cheese, softened
1 (3-oz.) package cream cheese, softened
2/3 cup sugar
6 large eggs
1/3 cup whipping cream
2 tsp. instant coffee granules
9 (1-oz.) semisweet chocolate baking
    squares
1 Tbsp. plus 1 tsp. vanilla extract
Garnishes: powdered sugar, shaved
    chocolate, thawed whipped topping

1. Prepare Chocolate Crust as directed.
Increase oven temperature to 375°.
2. Beat cream cheeses and sugar at
medium speed with an electric mixer
2 to 3 minutes or until light and fluffy.
Add eggs, 1 at a time, beating just until
blended after each addition.
3. Microwave whipping cream in a 1-
cup microwave-safe measuring cup at
HIGH 30 seconds or until very hot. Stir
in coffee granules until completely dissolved. Cool coffee mixture slightly.
4. Microwave chocolate in a
microwave-safe bowl at HIGH 1 minute. Microwave 1 more minute, stirring
at 15-second intervals. Add melted
chocolate, vanilla, and coffee mixture
to cream cheese mixture. Beat at low
speed just until blended. Pour mixture
into prepared Chocolate Crust.
5. Bake at 375° for 30 minutes or until
edges are firm and center is still soft.
Let cool to room temperature (about 1
hour); cover and chill 8 hours. Garnish,
if desired.

Chocolate Crust:
MAKES 1 (9-INCH) CRUST; **PREP:** 15 MIN.,
COOK: 5 MIN., **BAKE:** 8 MIN.,
COOL: 15 MIN., **CHILL:** 30 MIN.

1/3 cup butter
2 (1-oz.) semisweet chocolate baking
    squares
1 1/3 cups fine, dry breadcrumbs
1/3 cup sugar

1. Preheat oven to 350°. Stir together
butter and chocolate in a medium-size
heavy saucepan over low heat, stirring
often, 3 to 5 minutes or until chocolate
is melted. Remove from heat, and stir
in breadcrumbs and sugar until well
blended. Press mixture onto bottom of
a lightly greased 9-inch square pan.
2. Bake at 350° for 8 minutes. Cool on a
wire rack 15 minutes. Chill 30 minutes.

— AMY SOUTHARD, ARLINGTON, VIRGINIA

Sweet on Tamales

Don't miss this twist on an authentic Mexican treat that's as much fun to make as to eat.

Families all over the South
have special holiday tradi-
tions. Within the Hispanic
community, making tamales
tops the list. Most folks
think of these steamed bundles of
goodness as strictly savory, usually
filled with pork or chicken. But Sylvia
Calvano of Hoover, Alabama, recalls
her mother's dessert tamales. "My mom
was born and raised in Mexico, so
tamales were always an important part
of our Christmas celebration," she says.

Sugar-and-Spice Fruit Tamales
MAKES ABOUT 14 TAMALES; **PREP:** 45 MIN.,
SOAK: 1 HR., **COOK:** 35 MIN., **STAND:** 5 MIN.

These sweet tamales, served with cinnamon-infused vanilla sauce, are a festive surprise that's tough to beat.

18 dried corn husks
2/3 cup shortening
1 1/2 cups corn masa mix
3 Tbsp. light brown sugar
1 tsp. baking powder
1 tsp. ground cinnamon
1/2 tsp. salt
1/2 cup warm milk
1/2 cup canned pumpkin
1 (20-oz.) can crushed pineapple in heavy
    syrup, drained
1/2 cup raisins, chopped
Kitchen string
Vanilla Sauce
Mexican Chocolate Sauce

1. Soak corn husks in hot water to
cover 30 minutes. Separate husks, and
continue soaking 30 more minutes.
Drain husks, and pat dry. Tear 4 small-
est husks into 14 strips.
2. Beat shortening at medium speed
with a heavy-duty electric stand mixer
2 minutes. Combine masa and next 4
ingredients. Gradually beat masa mixture into shortening. Beat shortening
mixture 2 minutes, scraping down sides
of bowl as needed.
3. Gradually add warm milk to shortening mixture, beating at medium
speed just until blended and scraping
down sides as needed. Add pumpkin,
and beat at medium speed 3 minutes.
Cover dough with plastic wrap.
4. Using hands lightly coated with
masa mix, spread about 2 Tbsp. dough
into a 3- x 4-inch rectangle on right side
of 1 husk, leaving a 1/2-inch border on
right side and a 2-inch border from
narrow bottom end of husk.

Test Kitchens Know-how

- With hands lightly coated in corn masa mix, spread about 2 Tbsp. dough into a 3- x 4-inch rectangle on the right side of 1 husk, leaving a ½-inch border on the right side and a 2-inch border from the narrow bottom end of the husk (photo 1).
- Spoon about 1 Tbsp. pineapple down center of dough (photo 2), and then sprinkle with about 1½ tsp. chopped raisins (photo 3).
- Roll up husk, rolling left side over right, enclosing fruit filling completely in dough. Fold the bottom narrow end up and over (photo 4), and secure with husk strip or kitchen string (photo 5).

5. Spoon about 1 Tbsp. pineapple down center of dough. Sprinkle with about 1½ tsp. raisins. Roll up husk, rolling left side over right, enclosing pineapple mixture and raisins completely in dough. Fold bottom narrow end up and over, and secure with husk strips or kitchen string. Repeat procedure with remaining corn husks, dough, pineapple, and raisins.

6. Place 2 tamales side by side, seam sides inward and open ends facing same direction. Tie tamales together with kitchen string, securing bundles at top above dough. Repeat with remaining tamales.

7. Arrange tamale bundles, open ends up, in a steamer basket over boiling water in a large Dutch oven. Cover and steam 35 minutes, adding more boiling water as needed. Remove tamales from Dutch oven, and let stand 5 minutes. Serve with Vanilla Sauce and Mexican Chocolate Sauce.

— SYLVIA CALVANO, HOOVER, ALABAMA

Note: For testing purposes only, we used Masa Brosa Harina de Maiz Instant Corn Masa.

Vanilla Sauce:

fast fixin's • make ahead

MAKES ABOUT 1 CUP; PREP: 10 MIN.,
COOK: 5 MIN.

¾ cup whipping cream
½ cup firmly packed light brown sugar
½ tsp. ground cinnamon
⅛ tsp. ground nutmeg
Pinch of salt
1 vanilla bean, split lengthwise
1 Tbsp. butter

1. Combine first 5 ingredients in a small saucepan. Carefully scrape seeds from vanilla bean into saucepan. Add bean to saucepan, and cook mixture over medium heat, whisking constantly, until smooth (about 2 minutes). Reduce heat to medium-low. Cook, whisking constantly, 2 to 3 minutes or until thickened.

2. Remove saucepan from heat. Carefully remove vanilla bean. Stir in butter until melted. Serve immediately. Store sauce in an airtight container in refrigerator up to 5 days.

Note: To reheat, warm sauce in a small saucepan over low heat, stirring in 1 to 2 tsp. whipping cream as needed to thin sauce.

Mexican Chocolate Sauce:

fast fixin's

MAKES ABOUT 1½ CUPS; PREP: 5 MIN.,
COOK: 3 MIN.

2 (4.4-oz.) packages Mexican chocolate, broken into pieces
¾ cup whipping cream
2 tsp. light brown sugar
Pinch of salt
1 Tbsp. butter

1. Combine first 4 ingredients in a small saucepan. Cook, whisking occasionally, over low heat until mixture is smooth and chocolate is melted (about 3 minutes). Remove from heat. Whisk in butter until melted. Serve sauce immediately.

Note: For testing purposes only, we used Nestlé Abuelita Marqueta Mexican Chocolate.

Party in Style With Light Fare

Eat, drink, and enjoy a buffet of good-for-you foods. After sampling these great-tasting recipes, your family and friends will be ready to dish up a second helping.

Treat your guests to a selection of delectable dishes, from appetizer to dessert, that are so full of flavor, you'd never guess that they are wholesome, too. That's the goal of Hebni (pronounced ebony) Nutrition Consultants. This non-profit group of Florida-based dietitians works together throughout the year teaching nutrition and healthy lifestyle tips to culturally diverse communities.

During the Christmas season, they gather for a year-end meeting around a festive table filled with an abundance of familiar foods made from recipes adapted from *The Family Style Soul Food Diabetes Cookbook*. The menu includes Dan the Man's Pork Loin Roast, marinated for deep flavor, and Power Salad—sweet potatoes and apples tossed with toasted walnuts—and more. Creamy Hebni Banana Pudding brings the meal and the year to a sweet ending.

Good-for-You Buffet

SERVES 8

Shrimp on Flats

Dan the Man's Pork Loin Roast

Sautéed Spinach

Power Salad

Hebni Banana Pudding

Shrimp on Flats

make ahead

MAKES: 10 TO 12 APPETIZER SERVINGS;
PREP: 20 MIN., **COOK:** 4 MIN.,
COOL: 30 MIN., **BROIL:** 5 MIN.

You can make the salad for this appetizer up to 24 hours in advance.

12 oz. unpeeled, large raw shrimp
1 Tbsp. extra virgin olive oil
1 tsp. freshly ground pepper
¼ tsp. salt
1 Tbsp. fresh lime juice, divided
¼ cup loosely packed fresh flat-leaf parsley
¼ cup fat-free sour cream
¼ cup plain low-fat yogurt
¼ cup finely chopped fresh tarragon*
3 Tbsp. chopped fresh chives
2 Tbsp. capers, drained
2 tsp. extra virgin olive oil
1 (8.5-oz.) French bread baguette, cut into
   ¼-inch-thick slices

1. Peel shrimp; devein, if desired. Stir together shrimp and 1 Tbsp. olive oil in large nonstick skillet; sprinkle with pepper and salt.

2. Cook shrimp over medium-high heat 1½ to 2 minutes on each side or just until shrimp turn pink. Remove shrimp to a large bowl, and toss with 1 tsp. lime juice. Cool completely (about 30 minutes). Finely chop shrimp.

3. Preheat oven to broil. Process parsley, sour cream, yogurt, and remaining 2 tsp. lime juice in a food processor or blender until parsley is finely chopped. Season parsley sauce with salt and pepper to taste.

4. Stir together shrimp, tarragon, and next 3 ingredients in large bowl. Place 1 Tbsp. shrimp mixture on top of each slice of French bread, and place on a baking sheet.

5. Broil 5 inches from heat 4 to 5 minutes or until shrimp mixture is lightly browned. Remove from oven, and drizzle with parsley sauce. Serve immediately.

*1 Tbsp. finely chopped fresh thyme may be substituted.

Dan the Man's Pork Loin Roast

MAKES: 8 SERVINGS; **PREP:** 15 MIN.,
CHILL: 2 HR., **STAND:** 40 MIN.,
GRILL: 45 MIN.

This spice-flavored pork roast pairs nicely with Sautéed Spinach.

½ cup lite soy sauce
1 Tbsp. Caribbean jerk seasoning
1 (3-lb.) boneless pork loin roast, trimmed
¼ cup brown sugar blend sweetener
¼ cup bourbon

1. Stir together lite soy sauce and jerk seasoning. Place roast in a 2-gal. zip-top plastic freezer bag. Pour soy sauce mixture over roast. Seal bag, and chill 2 to 12 hours, turning occasionally.

2. Preheat grill to 350° to 400° (medium-high). Remove roast from marinade, discarding marinade. Pat roast dry with paper towels. Let stand at room temperature 30 minutes.

3. Stir together brown sugar blend sweetener and bourbon in a microwave-safe glass measuring cup. Microwave at HIGH 1 minute or until sugar blend is dissolved, stirring after 30 seconds.

4. Grill roast, covered with grill lid, over 350° to 400° (medium-high) heat 25 minutes. Baste with brown sugar blend mixture; turn and baste other side. Grill, covered with grill lid, 20 minutes or until a meat thermometer inserted into thickest portion registers 145°, basting after 10 minutes. Remove from heat, and let stand 10 minutes before slicing.

Note: For testing purposes only, we used Splenda Brown Sugar Blend Sweetener.

Sautéed Spinach
fast fixin's

MAKES: 8 TO 10 SERVINGS; **PREP:** 5 MIN., **COOK:** 4 MIN.

This vegetable side was inspired by a recipe in the The New Soul Food Cookbook for People With Diabetes *by Fabiola D. Gaines and Roniece A. Weaver.*

2 (10-oz.) bags fresh spinach, thoroughly washed
2 garlic cloves, minced
½ tsp. salt
½ tsp. pepper
2 tsp. olive oil

1. Sauté spinach and next 3 ingredients in hot oil in a large nonstick Dutch oven over medium-high heat 3 to 4 minutes or until slightly wilted.

Power Salad
make ahead

MAKES: 8 TO 10 SERVINGS; **PREP:** 25 MIN., **COOK:** 27 MIN., **CHILL:** 2 HR.

Make this salad up to 12 hours ahead.

¼ cup chopped walnuts
2¼ lb. sweet potatoes (about 4 medium), peeled and cut into ½-inch cubes
2 lb. Granny Smith apples (about 4 medium), cut into ½-inch cubes
2 Tbsp. fresh lime juice
2 Tbsp. no-calorie sweetener
3 Tbsp. raisins
¼ tsp. salt
½ cup plain fat-free yogurt
3 Tbsp. reduced-fat mayonnaise

1. Heat nuts in a small nonstick skillet over medium-low heat, stirring often, 8 to 10 minutes or until lightly toasted and fragrant.

2. Arrange potatoes in a steamer basket or stainless-steel colander in a 4- to 6-qt. Dutch oven over boiling water. Cover and steam 16 to 17 minutes or until potatoes are fork-tender. Plunge potatoes into ice water to stop the cooking process; drain.

3. Place apples in large bowl. Sprinkle with lime juice and no-calorie sweetener; toss gently to coat. Stir in sweet potatoes, raisins, salt, and 3 Tbsp. walnuts.

4. Stir together yogurt and mayonnaise. Add yogurt mixture to sweet potato mixture, tossing gently to coat. Sprinkle with remaining 1 Tbsp. walnuts. Cover and chill 2 to 12 hours.

Note: For testing purposes only, we used Splenda No-Calorie Sweetener.

Hebni Banana Pudding
make ahead

MAKES: 10 (½-CUP) SERVINGS; **PREP:** 30 MIN.; **CHILL:** 2 HR., 5 MIN.

This banana dessert is the signature recipe for the Hebni dietitians. We made chic individual servings, but you can serve it family style too.

4 medium bananas, cut into ¼-inch slices
½ cup orange juice
1 (1-oz.) package fat-free, sugar-free vanilla instant pudding mix
2 cups 1% low-fat milk
1 (8-oz.) container fat-free frozen whipped topping, thawed
50 reduced-fat vanilla wafers

1. Place bananas in a medium bowl. Pour orange juice over bananas, and stir gently.

2. Prepare vanilla pudding according to package directions in a large bowl using low-fat milk. Cover and chill 5 minutes. Stir in whipped topping.

3. Drain bananas, discarding juice. Layer pudding, vanilla wafers, and banana slices in 10 (6-oz.) glasses. Chill 2 hours.

Note: To serve family style, layer one-fourth each of vanilla wafers, bananas, and pudding mixture in a 3-qt. glass bowl. Repeat layers 3 times, ending with pudding mixture. Cover and chill 2 hours to 24 hours.

Recipes courtesy of *The Family Style Soul Food Diabetes Cookbook* by Fabiola D. Gaines, RD, LD; Roniece A. Weaver, MS, RD, LD; Rojean L. Williams, MS, RD, LD; and Chef Shawn Fralin. The book is available at www.diabetes.org ($16.95 plus shipping) or in bookstores.

Warm Cheese Appetizers

Simple enough to put together on short notice, these quick crowd-pleasers can also be prepared well before guests arrive. Reheat Feta Cheese Squares straight from the freezer, and then pass them around on a pretty tray. A fondue pot or mini slow cooker keeps Colby-Pepper Jack Cheese Dip warm until the party winds down.

Spinach-and-Parmesan Crostini

fast fixin's • make ahead

MAKES 1 DOZEN; **PREP:** 10 MIN., **BAKE:** 10 MIN.

Prepare the spinach-and-cheese mixture up to a day ahead; cover and chill in an airtight container.

1 (10-oz.) package frozen spinach, thawed
1 (8-oz.) package cream cheese, softened
1 cup freshly grated Parmesan cheese
¼ cup mayonnaise
1 large garlic clove, minced
¼ tsp. freshly ground pepper
½ (16-oz.) French bread loaf, cut diagonally into ½-inch slices
⅓ cup pine nuts

1. Preheat oven to 325°. Drain spinach well, pressing between paper towels.
2. Stir together spinach and next 5 ingredients in a medium bowl. Top each bread slice with 2 Tbsp. cheese mixture. Sprinkle with pine nuts. Place bread slices on a baking sheet.
3. Bake at 325° for 10 minutes or until thoroughly heated and nuts are toasted.

Colby-Pepper Jack Cheese Dip

make ahead

MAKES 10 SERVINGS; **PREP:** 15 MIN., **BAKE:** 30 MIN.

Spice things up with this scoopable twist on creamy chicken enchiladas. Prepare up to a day ahead; cover and chill in an airtight container, and bake just before serving.

1 (8-oz.) package cream cheese, softened
⅔ cup sour cream
⅓ cup mayonnaise
1 Tbsp. finely chopped canned chipotle pepper in adobo sauce
2 tsp. chili powder
2 cups chopped cooked chicken
2 cups (8 oz.) shredded colby-Jack cheese blend
1 (4-oz.) can chopped green chiles
4 green onions, finely chopped
2 jalapeño peppers, seeded and minced
¼ cup chopped fresh cilantro
Garnish: fresh cilantro sprig
Tortilla and sweet potato chips

1. Preheat oven to 350°. Stir together first 5 ingredients in a large bowl until smooth. Stir in chicken and next 5 ingredients until blended. Spoon mixture into a lightly greased 8-inch square baking dish.
2. Bake at 350° for 30 minutes or until bubbly. Garnish, if desired. Serve with tortilla and sweet potato chips.

—VICKI ROSS, AUSTIN, TEXAS

Feta Cheese Squares

freezeable • make ahead

MAKES 5 DOZEN; **PREP:** 10 MIN., **BAKE:** 30 MIN., **COOL:** 10 MIN.

Bake up to 1 month ahead, and freeze in an airtight container or zip-top plastic freezer bag. Preheat oven to 350°, and bake frozen squares on a baking sheet for 10 to 15 minutes or until thoroughly heated.

2 cups all-purpose baking mix
1½ tsp. baking powder
¼ tsp. salt
1 cup milk
½ cup butter, melted
4 (4-oz.) packages feta cheese with garlic and herbs, crumbled
1 (8-oz.) container small-curd cottage cheese
3 large eggs, lightly beaten

1. Preheat oven to 350°. Stir together first 3 ingredients in a large bowl. Stir in milk and remaining ingredients, stirring just until dry ingredients are moistened. Spoon cheese mixture into a lightly greased 15- x 10-inch jelly-roll pan.
2. Bake at 350° for 30 minutes or until golden brown and set. Remove from oven, and let cool on a wire rack 10 minutes. Cut into 1½-inch squares, and serve immediately.

—APHRODITE HERO, RESTON, VIRGINIA

Note: For testing purposes only, we used Bisquick All-Purpose Baking Mix.

Irresistible Pecan Goodies

The South's favorite nut shines in these oh-so-easy treats.

These tasty, holiday-ready treats deliver big value: They're simple to make but taste like you spent all day in the kitchen. For Crunchy Pecan Pie Bites, simply stir together the ingredients in one bowl, spoon the mixture into mini pastry shells, and bake. Velvety Pecan Candy requires that you melt, stir, and spread the mixture in a jelly-roll pan to harden.

Paradise Pecan Cookies

MAKES 1 DOZEN; PREP: 15 MIN., BAKE: 27 MIN., COOL: 20 MIN.

1 cup chopped pecans
Parchment paper
3 egg whites
1 cup sugar
20 saltine crackers, crushed

1. Preheat oven to 350°. Bake pecans in a single layer in a shallow pan 8 to 10 minutes or until toasted and fragrant.
2. Line a baking sheet with parchment paper; lightly grease parchment paper.
3. Beat egg whites at high speed with an electric mixer until soft peaks form. Gradually add sugar, and beat until stiff peaks form. Fold pecans and crackers into egg whites. Drop by rounded tablespoonfuls onto prepared baking sheet.

4. Bake at 350° for 17 minutes or until lightly browned. Cool on baking sheet 1 minute. Remove to wire racks, and cool completely (about 20 minutes).

Crunchy Pecan Pie Bites

MAKES ABOUT 6 DOZEN; PREP: 15 MIN., BAKE: 10 MIN. PLUS 22 MIN. PER BATCH, COOL: 30 MIN.

3 cups chopped pecans
¾ cup sugar
¾ cup dark corn syrup
3 large eggs, lightly beaten
2 Tbsp. melted butter
1 tsp. vanilla extract
⅛ tsp. salt
5 (2.1-oz.) packages frozen mini-phyllo pastry shells

1. Preheat oven to 350°. Bake pecans in a single layer in a shallow pan 8 to 10 minutes or until toasted and fragrant.
2. Stir together sugar and corn syrup in a medium bowl. Stir in pecans, eggs, and next 3 ingredients.
3. Spoon about 1 heaping teaspoonful pecan mixture into each pastry shell, and place on 2 large baking sheets.
4. Bake at 350° for 20 to 22 minutes or until set. Remove to wire racks, and let cool completely (about 30 minutes). Store in an airtight container up to 3 days.

Mini Pecan Pies: (*Pictured on page 1*) Substitute 1½ (8-oz.) packages frozen tart shells for frozen mini-phyllo pastry shells. Prepare recipe as directed through Step 2. Spoon about ¼ cup pecan mixture into each tart shell. Place tart shells on a large baking sheet. Proceed with recipe as directed in Step 4, increasing bake time to 25 to 30 minutes or until set. Garnish with currants, if desired. **Makes** 1 dozen; Prep: 15 min., Bake: 30 min.

—ROSE M. CLINTON, ALEXANDRIA, LOUISIANA

Velvety Pecan Candy

MAKES ABOUT 3 DOZEN (ABOUT 3 LB.); PREP: 10 MIN., BAKE: 10 MIN., CHILL: 2 HR.

To serve a crowd, make two recipes of this candy, one each of vanilla and chocolate. Also, cut candy into smaller 1-inch squares so it will go further.

3 cups coarsely chopped pecans
Wax paper
1½ lb. vanilla or chocolate candy coating, coarsely chopped
1 (14-oz.) can sweetened condensed milk
¼ tsp. salt
1 tsp. vanilla extract

1. Preheat oven to 350°. Bake pecans in a single layer in a shallow pan 8 to 10 minutes or until toasted and fragrant.
2. Line a 15- x 10-inch jelly-roll pan with wax paper. Lightly grease wax paper.
3. Microwave candy coating, sweetened condensed milk, and salt in a 2-qt. microwave-safe bowl at HIGH 3 to 5 minutes, stirring at 1-minute intervals. Stir until smooth. Stir in vanilla extract and pecans. Spread in an even layer in prepared pan. Cover and chill 2 hours or until set.
4. Turn candy out onto cutting board, and cut into 2-inch squares. Store, covered, at room temperature.

—CAROL S. NOBLE, BURGAW, NORTH CAROLINA

Going Nutty

We recommend toasting pecans to enhance their nutty flavor and add crunchiness. With their high oil content, nuts can burn quickly, so stay close. Watch the time, but if you notice a nutty fragrance in the air, go ahead and take them out of the oven.

Christmas Eve Fun

You won't be left out of any of the festivities with our Test Kitchens Director's make-ahead brunch.

Christmas Eve Brunch

SERVES 2

Gentlemen's Casserole

Winter Fruit Compote

Cranberry-Orange Tea Bread Muffins

Kane's Peppery Bloody Mary

Since courtship, Test Kitchens Director Lyda Jones Burnette and her husband, Kane, have enjoyed a fireside brunch on Christmas Eve morning while listening to A Festival of Nine Lessons and Carols on National Public Radio. This menu is mostly make-ahead—so like the Burnettes, you can relax and enjoy the beginning of the Christmas festivities.

Gentlemen's Casserole

make ahead

MAKES 2 SERVINGS; **PREP:** 25 MIN., **BAKE:** 20 MIN., **COOK:** 6 MIN.

This recipe easily doubles to serve four. Bake pastry shells the day before to make Christmas Eve morning even more relaxing. Remove pastry tops, and reheat shells on a baking sheet at 350° for five minutes.

1 (10-oz.) package frozen puff pastry shells
1 Tbsp. butter
⅓ cup chopped cooked ham
1 Tbsp. chopped green onions
4 large eggs, lightly beaten
Gruyère Cheese Sauce
¼ cup grated Gruyère cheese
Dash of paprika
Garnish: chopped green onions

1. Bake 4 pastry shells according to package directions. Reserve remaining shells for another use.
2. Melt butter in a medium-size non-stick skillet over medium heat; add ham and green onions. Sauté 2 minutes or until green onions are tender. Add eggs, and cook, without stirring, 1 to 2 minutes or until eggs begin to set on bottom. Gently draw cooked edges away from sides of pan to form large pieces. Cook, stirring occasionally, 1 to 2 minutes or until eggs are thickened and moist. (Do not overstir.) Gently fold in Gruyère Cheese Sauce.
3. Spoon egg mixture into prepared pastry shells. Sprinkle with cheese and paprika. Garnish, if desired. Serve immediately.

Chicken-and-White Cheddar Casserole: Substitute extra-sharp white Cheddar cheese for Gruyère, Cheddar Cheese Sauce for Gruyère Cheese Sauce, and chopped cooked chicken for ham. Proceed with recipe as directed.

Gruyère Cheese Sauce:

fast fixin's • make ahead

MAKES ABOUT ¾ CUP; **PREP:** 10 MIN., **COOK:** 6 MIN.

You can make this sauce up to two days ahead and store in the refrigerator. Reheat in a microwave-safe bowl at HIGH 1½ minutes, stirring halfway through.

¾ cup milk
1 Tbsp. butter
1 Tbsp. all-purpose flour
½ cup grated Gruyère cheese
¼ tsp. salt
⅛ tsp. pepper

1. Microwave milk in a 2-cup microwave-safe glass measuring cup at HIGH 1 minute.
2. Melt butter in a small heavy saucepan over medium heat; gradually whisk in flour. Cook 1 minute, whisking constantly. Gradually whisk in warm milk; cook over medium heat, whisking constantly, 3 to 5 minutes or until thickened and bubbly. Remove from heat; whisk in cheese, salt, and pepper.

Cheddar Cheese Sauce: Substitute extra-sharp white Cheddar cheese for Gruyère. Proceed with recipe as directed.

Winter Fruit Compote

make ahead

MAKES 4 SERVINGS; **PREP:** 15 MIN., **COOK:** 25 MIN., **STAND:** 5 MIN., **COOL:** 30 MIN., **CHILL:** 2 HR.

To avoid any leftover Champagne, buy a split (187 ml.) of Champagne for this recipe.

½ cup sugar
1 cup Champagne or sparkling wine
2 Ruby Red grapefruits, peeled and sectioned
2 oranges, peeled and sectioned
Garnish: maraschino cherries with stems

1. Cook sugar in a small saucepan over medium heat, tilting pan occasionally, 10 minutes or until caramel colored. Remove from heat, and gradually pour Champagne over sugar (mixture will bubble and seize). Let stand 5 minutes.

2. Cook mixture over medium-low heat, stirring occasionally, 15 minutes or until sugar is dissolved (mixture will be syrupy). Remove from heat, and let cool 30 minutes.

3. Combine grapefruit and orange sections in a bowl. Pour Champagne mixture over fruit. Cover and chill 2 to 24 hours. Garnish, if desired.

White Grape Winter Fruit Compote: Substitute white grape juice for Champagne. Proceed with recipe as directed.

Cranberry-Orange Tea Bread Muffins

freezeable • make ahead

MAKES 2 DOZEN; **PREP:** 25 MIN.,
BAKE: 35 MIN.

½ cup chopped pecans
2 cups all-purpose flour
1½ tsp. baking powder
1 tsp. salt
½ (12-oz.) package fresh cranberries
    (about 2 cups)
1 cup sugar
¼ cup butter, softened
1 large egg, lightly beaten
¾ cup orange juice
24 aluminum foil miniature baking cups
Vegetable cooking spray
Orange-Cream Cheese Glaze
Garnish: Candied Kumquat Slices

1. Preheat oven to 350°. Bake pecans in a single layer in a shallow pan 8 to 10 minutes or until toasted and fragrant, stirring occasionally.

2. Whisk together flour, baking powder, and salt.

3. Pulse cranberries and sugar in a food processor 3 to 4 times or just until chopped.

4. Beat butter at medium speed with an electric mixer until creamy. Add egg, beating until well blended. Gradually add flour mixture alternately with orange juice, beginning and ending with flour mixture. Beat at low speed until blended after each addition. Stir in cranberry mixture and pecans.

5. Place baking cups in miniature muffin pans; coat with cooking spray. Spoon batter into baking cups, filling completely.

6. Bake at 350° for 25 minutes or until a wooden pick inserted in center comes out clean. Remove from pans to a wire rack; spoon Orange-Cream Cheese Glaze over warm muffins. Garnish with Candied Kumquat Slices, if desired.
Note: To make ahead, place unglazed muffins in a heavy-duty zip-top plastic freezer bag; freeze up to 2 months. Let thaw at room temperature before icing.

Orange-Cream Cheese Glaze:

MAKES ABOUT 1 CUP; **PREP:** 10 MIN.

1 (3-oz.) package cream cheese, softened
1 Tbsp. orange juice
¼ tsp. vanilla extract
1½ cups sifted powdered sugar

1. Beat cream cheese at medium speed with an electric mixer until creamy. Add orange juice and vanilla; beat until smooth. Gradually add powdered sugar, beating until smooth.

Candied Kumquat Slices:

MAKES 3½ DOZEN; **PREP:** 15 MIN.,
COOK: 10 MIN., **STAND:** 24 HR.

You can strain the syrup left after making kumquat slices to flavor iced tea or lemonade.

Cut 8 kumquats into ⅛-inch-thick slices. Stir together ½ cup sugar and ½ cup water in a small heavy saucepan. Bring

Make-Ahead Timeline

Up to two months ahead:
● Bake Cranberry-Orange Tea Bread Muffins, but leave them unglazed. Freeze in a zip-top plastic freezer bag.

Day Before:
● Make Candied Kumquat Slices for muffins. Cover loosely with plastic wrap, and let stand at room temperature.
● Make Gruyère Cheese Sauce for Gentlemen's Casserole. Cover and chill.
● Make Winter Fruit Compote, and chill.
● Bake puff pastry shells for Gentlemen's Casserole. Store at room temperature in a zip-top plastic freezer bag.

Day of:
● Make Kane's Peppery Bloody Mary. (recipe on page 282)
● Make Orange-Cream Cheese Glaze.
● Thaw muffins at room temperature. Top with glaze and kumquat slices.
● Reheat pastry shells on a baking sheet at 350° for 5 minutes.
● Microwave Gruyère Cheese Sauce.
● Scramble eggs for Gentlemen's Casserole, fold in cheese sauce, and spoon into pastry shells..

to a boil over medium heat. Reduce heat to medium-low, and stir in kumquat slices; simmer 10 minutes. Remove from heat; remove kumquat slices, 1 at a time, shaking off excess sugar-water mixture. Place kumquats in a bowl with ¼ cup sugar; toss to coat. Transfer kumquats to wax paper. Cover loosely with plastic wrap, and let stand 24 hours.

—**CINDY LUCY**, TUSCALOOSA, ALABAMA

Kane's Peppery Bloody Mary

fast fixin's

MAKES 2 SERVINGS; **PREP:** 10 MIN.

Pickled okra, rather than celery, makes a tangy stir for this cocktail. This delicious recipe received our Test Kitchens' highest rating.

1 tsp. chopped fresh basil
1 tsp. chopped fresh cilantro
1 tsp. chopped fresh chives
1⅓ cups tomato juice
½ cup pepper vodka
6 Tbsp. fresh lemon juice
1½ to 3 tsp. green hot sauce
1 tsp. Worcestershire sauce
Large pinch of celery salt
Pinch of sea salt
Freshly ground pepper to taste
Garnishes: pickled okra, lemon wedges

1. Combine first 3 ingredients in a cocktail shaker. Press leaves against bottom of cup using a wooden spoon to release flavors; stir in tomato juice and next 7 ingredients. Transfer half of mixture to a 2-cup glass measuring cup.
2. Place ice in cocktail shaker, filling halfway full. Cover with lid, and shake vigorously until thoroughly chilled. Strain into a glass over ice. Repeat procedure with remaining tomato mixture. Garnish, if desired.
Note: For testing purposes only, we used Absolut Peppar Vodka and Tabasco Green Pepper Sauce.

Kane's Bloody Mary: Substitute regular vodka for pepper vodka. Proceed with recipe as directed.

5 Easy Sauces for Steak

Splurge on a mouthwatering and memorable holiday entrée.

It's hard to beat a perfectly cooked beef tenderloin fillet crusted with kosher salt and crushed black pepper. Whether cooked on the grill or in the pan, the meat will melt in your mouth when you follow our tips. Top your entrée with a complementary sauce for an impressive holiday supper. These wonderful ones pair well with other cuts of steak, such as flank, rib-eye, or flat-iron, and are also great with roast beef.

Look for whole beef tenderloins on sale during the holidays at grocery stores and wholesale clubs.

Grilled Filet Mignon

fast fixin's

MAKES 4 SERVINGS; **PREP:** 5 MIN.,
COOK: 12 MIN., **STAND:** 5 MIN.

We cook our tenderloin fillets to medium-rare. If you like your meat cooked medium or well done, increase the grilling or pan-searing time per side. (Cook approximately 1 minute more on each side for medium, 2 minutes more on each side for medium-well, and 3 minutes more on each side for well done.)

4 (6-oz.) beef tenderloin fillets
1 tsp. freshly cracked pepper
½ tsp. kosher salt

1. Preheat grill to 350° to 400° (medium-high). Sprinkle fillets with pepper and salt.
2. Grill, covered with grill lid, over 350° to 400° (medium-high) heat 4 to 6 minutes on each side or to desired degree of doneness. Let fillets stand 5 minutes.

Pan-Seared Filet Mignon

fast fixin's

MAKES 4 SERVINGS; **PREP:** 10 MIN.,
COOK: 14 MIN., **STAND:** 5 MIN.

Prepare Pan-Seared Filet Mignon in a cast-iron or heavy-duty skillet to create a crisp, flavorful exterior and juicy interior. We don't recommend a nonstick skillet for this recipe, because the steak will not brown properly.

4 (6-oz.) beef tenderloin fillets
1 tsp. freshly cracked pepper
½ tsp. kosher salt
2 Tbsp. butter
2 Tbsp. olive oil

1. Sprinkle fillets with pepper and salt.
2. Melt butter with olive oil in a large stainless steel or cast-iron skillet over medium heat. Add fillets, and cook 5 to 7 minutes on each side or to desired degree of doneness. Let fillets stand 5 minutes.

Creamy Horseradish Sauce

fast fixin's • make ahead

MAKES ABOUT ¼ CUP; **PREP:** 10 MIN.

¼ cup reduced-fat sour cream
1½ tsp. horseradish
1 tsp. Dijon mustard

1. Stir together all ingredients. Serve immediately, or cover and chill up to 3 hours.

—**NORA HENSHAW**, OKEMAH, OKLAHOMA

Balsamic-Fig Sauce

MAKES 1 CUP; **PREP:** 10 MIN., **COOK:** 7 MIN.

We tried substituting regular balsamic vinegar for aged balsamic vinegar but found the taste too sharp and pungent.

1 cup aged balsamic vinegar
⅓ cup fig preserves
⅓ cup port wine
½ tsp. kosher salt
½ tsp. freshly ground pepper
1 Tbsp. cognac (optional)

1. Bring first 5 ingredients to a boil in a saucepan over medium-high heat; reduce heat to medium, and simmer 6 to 7 minutes or until mixture is reduced by half. Remove from heat; stir in cognac, if desired. Serve warm.

— LILLIAN JULOW, GAINESVILLE, FLORIDA

Note: For testing purposes only, we used Alessi 20-Year Balsamic Vinegar aged in wood.

Béarnaise Sauce

MAKES ABOUT ¾ CUP; **PREP:** 15 MIN., **COOK:** 25 MIN.

Try our express version using a mix if you're short on time or not comfortable making it from scratch.

4 shallots, finely chopped
    (about ½ cup)
¾ cup dry white wine
2 Tbsp. chopped fresh tarragon
3 Tbsp. white wine vinegar
¼ tsp. ground black pepper
3 egg yolks
⅛ tsp. salt
⅛ tsp. ground red pepper
2 Tbsp. lemon juice
½ cup butter, cut into pieces and at room
    temperature

GET INSPIRED

Delicious Bread

Who says you can't enjoy fresh-tasting bread in 20 minutes flat? Wow the whole family with "Mom's secret recipe" tonight.

Easy Garlic Bread

MAKES 4 TO 6 SERVINGS; **PREP:** 10 MIN., **COOK:** 2 MIN., **BAKE:** 8 MIN.

1. Preheat oven to 400°. Cut 4 artisan rolls in half horizontally. Melt ½ cup butter in a small saucepan over medium-low heat. Add 2 minced garlic cloves and ¼ tsp. dried Italian seasoning, and cook, stirring constantly, 1 to 2 minutes or until fragrant. Brush butter mixture on cut sides of bread. Place bread, cut sides up, on a lightly greased baking sheet. Bake 7 to 8 minutes or until lightly toasted.

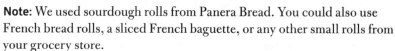

Note: We used sourdough rolls from Panera Bread. You could also use French bread rolls, a sliced French baguette, or any other small rolls from your grocery store.

---

1. Cook first 5 ingredients in a small saucepan over medium heat, stirring occasionally, 8 to 10 minutes or until liquid has evaporated.
2. Pour water to depth of 1½ inches into a 3½-qt. saucepan over medium-high heat; bring to a boil. Reduce heat to medium, and simmer.
3. Whisk together egg yolks, salt, and red pepper in a 3-qt. heatproof bowl; gradually add lemon juice, whisking constantly. Place bowl over simmering water, and cook, whisking constantly, 3 minutes or until mixture thickens.
4. Whisk butter pieces, in 3 batches, into egg mixture, whisking constantly until butter is melted and mixture is smooth and thickened. Remove from heat. Stir in shallot mixture. Serve immediately.

Speedy Béarnaise Sauce: Prepare 1 (0.9-oz.) envelope béarnaise sauce mix according to package directions, stirring in 1 Tbsp. lemon juice and 1 Tbsp. chopped fresh tarragon during last minute of cook time.
Note: For testing purposes only, we used McCormick Béarnaise Sauce Mix. The classic Béarnaise Sauce cannot be made ahead. However, Speedy Béarnaise Sauce can be made 1 day ahead and stored in the refrigerator. To reheat, place bowl over simmering water, and cook, whisking constantly, until mixture is warm.

Green Peppercorn Sauce

MAKES 2 CUPS; **PREP:** 15 MIN., **COOK:** 16 MIN.

2 Tbsp. butter
3 shallots, chopped (about ⅓ cup)
2 garlic cloves, minced
2 Tbsp. green peppercorns in brine, drained
1 (14-oz.) can fat-free beef broth
⅓ cup brandy*
2 Tbsp. Dijon mustard
⅓ cup heavy cream
2 tsp. cornstarch

1. Melt butter in a large skillet over medium-high heat; add shallots, garlic, and peppercorns, and sauté 2 minutes or just until tender. Stir in beef broth, brandy, and mustard. Bring to a boil, and cook, stirring occasionally, 12 minutes or until mixture is reduced by half.
2. Stir together cream and cornstarch until smooth. Add cornstarch mixture to sauce, and cook, stirring constantly, 2 minutes or until thickened.
*Apple juice may be substituted.

— **DOREEN SIDOR**, ROANOKE, VIRGINIA

Macadamia Pesto

MAKES 1½ CUPS; **PREP:** 10 MIN.

This hearty recipe can be covered with plastic wrap and kept chilled in the refrigerator for up to 10 days. Be sure to press plastic wrap directly on top of pesto to keep the green color. It can also be frozen for up to two months.

1½ cups loosely packed fresh basil leaves
½ cup salted macadamia nuts
4 large garlic cloves, minced
¾ cup extra virgin olive oil
¾ cup freshly grated Parmesan cheese
½ tsp. salt
¼ tsp. pepper

1. Process first 3 ingredients in a food processor 3 minutes until smooth, stopping to scrape down sides as needed. With processor running, pour oil through food chute in a slow, steady stream. Add cheese, salt, and pepper, and process 2 seconds or until smooth.

— **HANNAH L. LOWTHER**, BEVERLY HILLS, FLORIDA

Creative Sides

If you're looking for recipes that go from ordinary to extraordinary, you've come to the right place.

Cindy Crosby of Plano, Texas, knows no fear when it comes to cooking. She loves to create her own concoctions, and if she does consult a recipe, she's sure to add her own personal touch. "I like the excitement of taking a risk or two, maybe adding the unexpected to a classic dish," says Cindy. For instance, in Tropical Sweet Potato Casserole she includes pineapple and coconut, giving the beloved Southern dish a bit of island flair.

Creamy Baked Sweet Onions

family favorite

MAKES: 4 SERVINGS; **PREP:** 30 MIN., **COOK:** 10 MIN., **BAKE:** 30 MIN.

2 (10-oz.) packages cipolline or boiler onions, unpeeled*
2 Tbsp. butter
2 Tbsp. all-purpose flour
1½ cups milk
1½ cups (6 oz.) shredded sharp white Cheddar cheese
1 tsp. hot sauce
¼ tsp. salt
⅛ tsp. ground white pepper
¼ cup crushed round buttery crackers
1 Tbsp. melted butter

1. Preheat oven to 350°. Cook onions in a large saucepan in boiling water to cover 5 to 7 minutes. Drain onions, cool slightly, and peel. Place in a lightly greased 8-inch square baking dish.
2. Melt 2 Tbsp. butter in a heavy saucepan over medium heat; whisk in flour until smooth, and cook, whisking constantly, 1 minute. Gradually whisk in milk, and cook, whisking constantly, 1 minute or until thickened and bubbly. Add cheese and next 3 ingredients; whisk 2 minutes or until cheese is melted. Pour mixture over onions in dish.
3. Stir together crushed crackers and 1 Tbsp. melted butter; sprinkle over top of casserole.

Delightful Cipolline Onions

These small Italian onions have a sweet, delicate flavor and hold their flat shape well, making them a perfect choice for roasting whole. Cipolline onions have thin, less papery skins than larger varieties and should be stored in a cool, dry place. Expect to pay a bit more for them, but they're definitely worth it. These are usually sold prepackaged in the produce section (near other onions).

Holiday Dinners

4. Bake at 350° for 25 to 30 minutes or until bubbly.

*20 oz. sweet onions, peeled and cut into wedges, may be substituted. Omit boiling onions in Step 1; peel and place in baking dish as directed.

Cornbread 'n' Squash Dressing

MAKES: 8 SERVINGS; **PREP:** 15 MIN., **COOK:** 20 MIN., **BAKE:** 45 MIN.

An 8-inch skillet or pan of baked corn-bread will yield about 5 cups crumbled.

1 lb. yellow squash, coarsely chopped
¼ cup butter
1 large sweet onion, chopped
1 medium-size red bell pepper, chopped
2 celery ribs, chopped
1 (10¾-oz.) can cream of chicken soup
1 (14-oz.) can chicken broth
¾ tsp. freshly ground black pepper
¼ to ½ tsp. ground red pepper
½ tsp. poultry seasoning
5 cups cooked, crumbled cornbread

1. Preheat oven to 350°. Cook squash in boiling water to cover in a large skillet 8 to 10 minutes or just until tender. Drain well on paper towels.
2. Melt butter in skillet over medium-high heat; add onion, bell pepper, and celery, and sauté 8 to 10 minutes or until vegetables are tender. Remove skillet from heat. Stir in soup and next 4 ingredients. Gently stir in corn-bread and squash. Spoon into a lightly greased 13- x 9-inch baking dish.
3. Bake at 350° for 40 to 45 minutes or until golden.
Note: To make ahead, prepare recipe as directed through Step 2. Cover unbaked casserole, and chill up to 24 hours. Let stand 30 minutes or to room temperature. Bake as directed.

GET INSPIRED

Roasted Winter Squash
MAKES 6 TO 8 SERVINGS; **PREP:** 15 MIN. **BAKE:** 1 HR., **STAND:** 10 MIN.
(Pictured on page 1)

1. Preheat oven to 400°. Cut 1 (2- to 3-lb.) butternut squash, 1 (2- to 3-lb.) spaghetti squash, and 1 (1- to 2-lb.) acorn squash in half lengthwise, and remove seeds. Place squash, cut sides up, on an aluminum foil-lined baking sheet. Microwave ¼ cup butter and 2 Tbsp. honey at HIGH 1 minute or until melted; stir until blended. Brush cut sides of squash with butter mixture. Sprinkle with 1 tsp. salt and ¼ tsp. pepper. Bake, uncovered, 1 hour or until tender; let stand 10 minutes. Cut into large pieces, and serve.

Tip: Instead of discarding the fresh squash seeds, rinse 1 cup seeds under running water; pat dry with paper towels. Toss seeds with 1 Tbsp. olive oil, 1 Tbsp. ground thyme, and 1½ tsp. kosher salt; place in a single layer on a lightly greased baking sheet. Bake at 350° for 20 to 25 minutes or until toasted. Serve over a salad or just enjoy them as a snack. **Makes** 1 cup; Prep: 10 min., Bake: 25 min.

Tropical Sweet Potato Casserole

MAKES: 8 SERVINGS; **PREP:** 15 MIN.; **BAKE:** 1 HR., 45 MIN.; **COOL:** 10 MIN.

6 lb. sweet potatoes
1 (8-oz.) can crushed pineapple, drained
¾ cup firmly packed dark brown sugar
¼ cup butter, softened
¼ cup dark rum
½ tsp. ground cinnamon
1 cup miniature marshmallows
½ cup sweetened flaked coconut

1. Preheat oven to 400°. Bake potatoes 1 hour and 15 minutes or until tender. Let cool 10 minutes, and peel. Reduce oven temperature to 350°.
2. Mash potatoes with a potato masher or fork until smooth, or press through a ricer. Stir in crushed pineapple and next 4 ingredients. Spoon mixture into a lightly greased 13- x 9-inch baking dish.
3. Bake at 350° for 20 minutes. Sprinkle marshmallows and coconut over top, and bake 8 to 10 more minutes or until golden.

Fix-and-Freeze Favorites

Home-cooked goodness is as close as your freezer with these easy, make-ahead meals. Timesaving shortcuts and simple-to-follow recipes deliver long-simmered flavor with little effort.

Let the whole family in on the fun. Start with a hands-off slow-cooker recipe, and then roast a double batch of vegetables. Or bake a casserole while you stir up a stove-top stew. Be sure to read "From Our Kitchen" on page 289 for helpful packaging and freezing tips.

Roasted Vegetables and Rice

freezeable • make ahead

MAKES 6 SERVINGS; **PREP:** 20 MIN., **BAKE:** 40 MIN.

Frozen separately, roasted vegetables also make a colorful addition to soups, stews, and pasta dishes.

1 lb. zucchini, diced
1 lb. yellow squash, diced
1 large sweet onion, diced
1 large red bell pepper, diced
2 Tbsp. olive oil
1 tsp. seasoned salt
½ tsp. freshly ground pepper
2 (8.5-oz.) packages ready-to-serve brown and wild rice mix
½ cup chopped roasted salted almonds

1. Preheat oven to 450°. Toss together first 7 ingredients until vegetables are well coated. Place vegetables in a single layer in a jelly-roll pan.
2. Bake at 450° for 20 minutes. Stir vegetables, and bake 20 more minutes or until slightly crisp and golden.
3. Prepare rice according to package directions. Stir together rice, almonds, and hot vegetables.

Note: For testing purposes only, we used Uncle Ben's Ready Whole Grain Medley Brown & Wild Rice.

To make ahead: Prepare vegetables as directed through Step 2. Let cool completely. Transfer to airtight containers or heavy-duty zip-top plastic freezer bags, and freeze up to one month. Thaw in refrigerator 8 to 24 hours. Reheat in a large skillet over medium-high heat, stirring often, 5 to 6 minutes or until thoroughly heated and any extra liquid is reduced. Proceed with recipe as directed, or use vegetables as desired.

Creamy Slow-cooker Chicken

freezeable • make ahead

MAKES 6 SERVINGS, **PREP:** 10 MIN.; **COOK:** 4 HR., 15 MIN.

Pair this versatile, low-fat recipe with Roasted Vegetables and Rice, or use in other innovative ways. Shred the cooked chicken, and toss with hot cooked pasta. Create a casserole or jump-start a filling for easy enchiladas or a fast pot pie. Or splurge and spoon this dish over freshly baked biscuits.

6 skinned and boned chicken breasts (about 2½ lb.)
2 tsp. seasoned salt
2 Tbsp. canola oil
1 (10¾-oz.) can reduced-fat cream of mushroom soup
1 (8-oz.) package ⅓-less-fat cream cheese
½ cup dry white wine
1 (0.7-oz.) envelope Italian dressing mix
1 (8-oz.) package sliced fresh mushrooms

1. Sprinkle chicken with seasoned salt. Cook chicken, in batches, in hot oil in a large skillet over medium-high heat 2 to 3 minutes on each side or just until browned. Transfer chicken to a 5-qt. slow cooker, reserving drippings in skillet.
2. Add soup, cream cheese, white wine, and Italian dressing mix to hot drippings in skillet. Cook over medium heat, stirring constantly, 2 to 3 minutes or until cheese is melted and mixture is smooth.
3. Arrange mushrooms over chicken in slow cooker. Spoon soup mixture over mushrooms. Cover and cook on LOW 4 hours. Stir well before serving.

—NATALIE PRITCHARD, COLUMBIA, SOUTH CAROLINA

Note: For testing purposes only, we used Good Seasons Italian All Natural Salad Dressing & Recipe Mix.

To make ahead: Prepare recipe as directed. Transfer to a 13- x 9-inch baking dish, and let cool completely. Freeze up to one month. Thaw in refrigerator 8 to 24 hours. To reheat, cover tightly with aluminum foil, and bake at 325° for 45 minutes. Uncover and bake 15 minutes or until thoroughly heated.

Ham-and-Bean Soup

MAKES 8 SERVINGS; **PREP:** 15 MIN., **COOK:** 58 MIN.

This is a great way to use leftover holiday ham. You'll need about 2 cups to replace the ham steak.

1 (16-oz.) lean ham steak
2 Tbsp. olive oil
1 large onion, diced
1 bunch green onions, chopped
2 large carrots, diced
2 celery ribs, diced
1 Tbsp. jarred ham-flavored soup base
½ tsp. pepper
2 (15-oz.) cans navy beans, drained
2 (15-oz.) cans cannellini beans, drained
1 (15½-oz.) can black-eyed peas, drained
4 large Yukon gold potatoes, peeled and diced (about 2 lb.)
Garnish: Fall Potato Leaves (page 290)

1. Trim fat from ham steak; coarsely chop ham. Reserve bone.

2. Cook ham in hot oil in a Dutch oven over medium-high heat, stirring often, 6 to 8 minutes or until browned. Add diced onion and next 5 ingredients, and sauté 5 minutes or until onion is tender.

3. Stir in reserved ham bone, navy beans, and next 3 ingredients; add water to cover. Bring to a boil; cover, reduce heat to low, and cook, stirring occasionally, 45 minutes. Remove and discard bone before serving. Garnish, if desired.

—ANDREA BOLEY, PALM BAY, FLORIDA

Ham-and-Bean Soup With Fresh Spinach: Prepare recipe as directed, stirring in 1 (5-oz.) package fresh baby spinach, thoroughly washed, just before serving.

Pork Chili Stew

MAKES 6 SERVINGS; PREP: 10 MIN.,
COOK: 45 MIN.

½ cup all-purpose flour
3 Tbsp. chili powder
2 tsp. salt
1½ tsp. ground cumin
2 lb. boneless pork loin, cut into 1-inch
    cubes
2 Tbsp. canola oil
1 large onion, diced
4 garlic cloves, minced
2 (16-oz.) cans kidney beans,
    undrained
2 (16-oz.) cans whole kernel white corn,
    drained
2 (10-oz.) cans diced tomatoes and green
    chiles with lime juice and cilantro,
    undrained
2 (4.5-oz.) cans chopped green chiles,
    undrained

1. Stir together first 4 ingredients. Reserve 2 Tbsp. flour mixture. Dredge pork in remaining flour mixture.

2. Cook pork in hot oil in a Dutch oven over medium-high heat, stirring often, 8 to 10 minutes or until browned. Add

onion and garlic, and sauté 5 minutes.

3. Stir in kidney beans and next 3 ingredients, and bring to a boil. Sprinkle with reserved 2 Tbsp. flour mixture, and stir until blended. Cover, reduce heat to low, and cook, stirring occasionally, 30 minutes.

—TONYA LLOYD, BASTROP, TEXAS

Italian Jambalaya

MAKES 6 TO 8 SERVINGS; PREP: 20 MIN.,
COOK: 35 MIN.

Orzo pasta replaces rice in this clever twist on a Creole favorite. The sauce is also delicious spooned over hot cooked spaghetti. Depending on the level of heat you prefer, use mild or regular tomatoes with green chiles or a can of each.

1 lb. Italian sausage, casings removed
2 skinned and boned chicken breasts,
    coarsely chopped (about 1 lb.)
2 boneless center-cut pork chops, chopped
    (about 1 lb.)
1 (10-oz.) package frozen diced onion, red
    and green bell peppers, and celery
3 garlic cloves, minced
1 Tbsp. dried Italian seasoning
1 tsp. salt
½ tsp. pepper
2 (10-oz.) cans diced tomatoes and green
    chiles
1 (6-oz.) can tomato paste
Hot cooked orzo or other pasta (about 8 oz.,
    uncooked)
Garnishes: thinly sliced green onions,
    shredded Parmesan cheese

1. Brown Italian sausage in a Dutch oven over medium-high heat, stirring often, 5 minutes or until sausage crumbles and is no longer pink. Remove sausage from Dutch oven using a slotted spoon, reserving drippings in Dutch oven.

2. Cook chicken and pork in hot drippings in Dutch oven over medium-high heat, stirring often, 4 to 5 minutes or until browned on all sides. Add frozen onion mixture and next 4 ingredients, and sauté 5 minutes. Stir in diced tomatoes and green chiles, tomato paste, ¼ cup water, and Italian sausage; cover, reduce heat to low, and cook, stirring often, 20 minutes.

3. Stir hot cooked orzo into jambalaya just before serving, or serve over hot cooked pasta. Garnish, if desired.

—JAMES D. WHITE, GULFPORT, MISSISSIPPI

Freezing Soups, Stews, and Sauces

Prepare recipe as directed. Let cool completely, using one of the two methods below. Cooling times will vary, but package and freeze food promptly—as soon as it reaches room temperature. Transfer to airtight containers or zip-top plastic freezer bags, and freeze up to one month. Thaw in the refrigerator 8 to 24 hours.

● Place the stockpot or Dutch oven in a sink with ice water. (To ensure rapid cooling, fill the sink with ice water to the same level as the food in your stockpot, and add more ice as needed.) Let stand, uncovered, stirring often, until completely cool.

● Transfer hot food to large, shallow containers (such as 13- x 9-inch baking dishes). Let stand, uncovered, stirring occasionally, until completely cool.

Green Bean Casserole: Three Ways

We have turned this holiday standard into something new and special. These recipes are quick and tasty. You can make the white sauce and blanch the fresh beans up to two days ahead.

Buttermilk White Sauce

fast fixin's • make ahead

MAKES ABOUT 2 CUPS; **PREP:** 10 MIN., **COOK:** 5 MIN.

Measure the flour as you would for baking by lightly spooning it into a measuring cup and leveling with the back of a knife. This will help you avoid a thick, pastelike sauce. Don't try to add both milk and buttermilk at one time—the sauce will curdle.

2 Tbsp. butter
¼ cup all-purpose flour
1½ cups milk
½ cup buttermilk
1 Tbsp. Ranch dressing mix
¼ tsp. salt
¼ tsp. pepper

1. Melt butter in a medium-size heavy saucepan over medium heat; whisk in flour until smooth. Cook 1 minute, whisking constantly. Gradually whisk in 1½ cups milk; cook over medium heat, whisking constantly, 3 to 4 minutes or until mixture is thickened and bubbly. Remove from heat, and whisk in buttermilk and remaining ingredients until smooth.

— **INSPIRED BY HAZEL KING,** LUFKIN, TEXAS

Note: Sauce can be made up to two days ahead. Prepare recipe as directed; cover and chill in an airtight container. Whisk in 2 Tbsp. milk, and microwave at HIGH 1 minute, stirring at 30-second intervals.

Simple Blanched Green Beans

MAKES 6 TO 8 SERVINGS; **PREP:** 10 MIN., **COOK:** 6 MIN.

(Pictured on page 1)

1. Cook 1½ lb. fresh green beans, trimmed, in boiling salted water to cover 4 to 6 minutes or to desired degree of doneness; drain. Use immediately, or plunge into ice water to stop the cooking process; drain and pat dry. Store in a zip-top plastic bag in refrigerator up to 2 days.

Basic Green Bean Casserole

MAKES 6 TO 8 SERVINGS; **PREP:** 10 MIN., **BAKE:** 30 MIN.

We found mixing Japanese breadcrumbs (panko) and French fried onions made for a crisp, less greasy topping. You can find panko with other breadcrumbs on the baking aisle or on the ethnic foods aisle. This dish is delightful with any simple grilled or roasted meat, poultry, or pork.

Buttermilk White Sauce
Simple Blanched Green Beans
1 cup French fried onions, crushed
½ cup Japanese breadcrumbs (panko)

1. Preheat oven to 350°. Stir together white sauce and green beans. Place mixture in a lightly greased 13- x 9-inch or 3-qt. baking dish.
2. Combine French fried onions and breadcrumbs. Sprinkle over green bean mixture.

3. Bake at 350° for 25 to 30 minutes or until golden brown and bubbly. Serve immediately.
Note: For testing purposes only, we used French's French Fried Onions.

Cheddar-Pecan Green Bean Casserole

MAKES 6 TO 8 SERVINGS; **PREP:** 10 MIN., **BAKE:** 30 MIN.

We suggest you shred the Cheddar cheese yourself for smooth and even melting.

Buttermilk White Sauce
1 cup finely chopped jarred roasted red bell peppers
1 cup (4 oz.) freshly shredded sharp Cheddar cheese, divided
Simple Blanched Green Beans
1 cup French fried onions, crushed
½ cup Japanese breadcrumbs (panko)
½ cup chopped pecans

1. Preheat oven to 350°. Combine Buttermilk White Sauce, peppers, and ½ cup cheese; add green beans, tossing gently to combine. Place in a lightly greased 13- x 9-inch or 3-qt. baking dish.
2. Combine French fried onions, breadcrumbs, pecans, and remaining ½ cup cheese; sprinkle over mixture.
3. Bake at 350° for 25 to 30 minutes or until golden and bubbly. Serve dish immediately.

Simple Pecan-Green Bean Casserole: Omit shredded sharp Cheddar cheese. Preheat oven to 350°. Place French fried onions, Japanese breadcrumbs, and chopped pecans in an even layer in a 15- x 10-inch jelly-roll pan. Bake 8 to 10 minutes or until toasted, stirring after 5 minutes. Prepare Buttermilk White Sauce and Simple Blanched Green Beans as directed. (Do not plunge beans into ice water.) Gently toss together green beans and roasted red bell peppers, and spoon onto a serving platter. Top with Buttermilk White Sauce, and sprinkle with toasted pecan mixture. **Makes** 6 to 8 servings; Prep: 10 min., Bake: 10 min.

Frozen Assets

Tips, tricks, and cool ideas for easy freezing.

Freezer FYI

- Keep your freezer at 0°. Use a freezer thermometer, and adjust the temperature dial if needed. Always cool food to room temp before freezing. When freezing several items at a time, place in a single layer in the coldest part of the freezer, leaving plenty of space for air circulation.
- Label and date containers, and include baking or reheating instructions. (It's easier to write on freezer bags before you fill them.) Keep a list of what's on hand.
- Use airtight, moisture-proof containers and wrapping materials that are specifically designed for freezer use. Choose a container that fits the amount of food you're freezing. Soups and other liquids expand when frozen, so leave a ¼- to ½-inch headspace below the rim of the container.
- Vacuum-packing foods is the best way to prevent freezer burn. To shrink-wrap foods in freezer bags without a vacuum sealer, press out as much air as possible. Close the bag, leaving a ½-inch opening. Insert a drinking straw through the opening and suck out any remaining air until the bag shrinks around the food. Quickly slip out straw and seal the bag completely.
- Check the directions on zip-top plastic freezer bags and wrapping materials for guidelines on microwave use. They may be recommended for defrosting foods but not for reheating at a higher level of power.
- Some frozen foods can be heated without thawing, but make sure the container is rated freezer-to-oven-safe by the manufacturer.

Home-Cooked Convenience

Freeze family-size portions of soups, stews, and sauces in empty cereal boxes for space-saving stackable storage. Line a box with a large zip-top plastic freezer bag, folding the edges of the bag over the edges of the box (the way you would place a liner in a trash can), so that the box supports the bag. Fill the bag, seal it, and freeze vertically while still inside the box. Once frozen, remove the filled bag from the box and stack horizontally. Downsize to smaller freezer bags and boxes for fewer servings.

The Dish on Casseroles

Everyone loves a good casserole, and this little trick lets you stock the freezer without tying up your dishes. Line the bottom and sides of a casserole dish with heavy-duty aluminum foil, allowing 2 to 3 inches to extend over sides; fill with prepared recipe. Cover and freeze two to three hours or until firm. Lift the frozen casserole from the dish, using the foil sides as handles, and freeze in a zip-top plastic freezer bag. You'll need an extra-large 2-gallon bag for 13- x 9-inch baking dishes, and a 1-gallon bag for 9-inch square baking dishes.

To serve, remove the foil from frozen casserole, and return casserole to original baking dish; cover and let thaw in the refrigerator (allow 24 to 48 hours). Let stand 30 minutes at room temperature, and bake as directed.

Ready, Set, Freeze To quick-freeze individual cupcakes, tarts, and other baked goods, arrange in a single layer in a jelly-roll pan, and freeze one to two hours or until firm. Transfer to an airtight container or zip-top plastic freezer bag, and remove desired portions as needed. Many savory items, such as meatballs or twice-baked potatoes, can be frozen in the same way.

To prevent wrapping from sticking to frosting, quick-freeze cakes, uncovered, until firm, and then package. To serve, remove wrapping and thaw overnight in the refrigerator in a protective container or cake keeper.

Cashing In on Flavor

Cutting the cost of groceries is easier than you think, even if you don't have time to clip coupons. Supermarkets offer sales on a revolving basis throughout the year. The best bargains are always on the front page of their weekly circulars, and the savings can be greater than those at discount stores and shopping clubs. Known as loss leaders, these are the specials stores advertise at rock-bottom prices to attract customers. You might catch a sale on chicken breasts or pork loin one week and ground beef the next. Buy in bulk, and prepare several recipes to freeze.

It only takes a few minutes to marinate and freeze chicken breasts for grilling, cubed pork loin for kabobs, or strips of beef for a stir-fry. Place in zip-top plastic freezer bags. Remove as much air as possible; seal the bag, and knead several times to circulate the marinade. Lay sealed bags flat in a jelly-roll pan, and freeze. Once solidly frozen, the bags are easily stacked. Freezing food flat not only saves space, but it also allows the food to freeze and thaw more rapidly. The faster food freezes, the better. Slow freezing allows large ice crystals to form and damages the cell structure when thawed.

Make the most of every purchase. Limp vegetables that are past their prime can still add terrific flavor to homemade soups and stews. Cube and freeze extra bread and rolls for croutons, or give them a whirl in the food processor and make your own breadcrumbs. Freeze crushed crackers and potato chips to top a casserole. You can even freeze wine in ice cube trays to use when cooking. Like loose change, those bits and pieces really add up.

Festive Trimmings

The decorative leaves that top our Ham-and-Bean Soup on page 286 are cut from thinly sliced Yukon gold and sweet potatoes. We also use them as a garnish for seasonal casseroles and side dishes. Sprinkled with sugar instead of salt, sweet potato leaves make a colorful addition to holiday cakes and pies.

Fall Potato Leaves
make ahead

MAKES ABOUT 20 LEAVES; **PREP:** 15 MIN., **COOK:** 2 MIN. PER BATCH

1 large sweet potato (about 12 oz.)
1 large Yukon gold potato (about 8 oz.)
½ cup canola oil
Kosher salt to taste

1. Cut potatoes into ⅛-inch-thick slices, placing slices in a large bowl of ice water as you work to prevent discoloration.
2. Cut potato slices into leaves, using assorted 2- to 3-inch leaf-shaped cutters. Return leaves to ice water until ready to use.
3. Drain potato leaves, and dry well with paper towels. Cook potato leaves, in batches, in hot oil in a large skillet over medium-high heat 1 minute on each side or until golden brown. Season with salt to taste.
Note: To make ahead, prepare recipe as directed; place cooked leaves in a single layer in a jelly-roll pan. Freeze on pan until firm, and transfer to a zip-top plastic freezer bag. To reheat, place leaves in a single layer on a lightly greased baking sheet. Preheat oven to 350°, and bake 8 to 10 minutes or until thoroughly heated.

December

Sweet New Holiday Favorites

Use our clever shortcuts for great taste and simplicity.

Borrow our smart tips for baking with ease and confidence. Sweet bites such as Peppermint Pinwheel Cookies and Easy Swirled Fudge make great treats for holiday gift-giving. And there's no need to be intimidated, because our festive cakes start with a mix. One of our favorite secret ingredients, sour cream adds a rich, moist texture that is sure to please. So go ahead, and take our shortcuts without compromising style and taste.

Peppermint Pinwheel Cookies

freezeable • make ahead

MAKES 4 DOZEN; **PREP:** 35 MIN.,
FREEZE: 4 HR., **BAKE:** 7 MIN. PER BATCH,
COOL: 35 MIN.

These cookies are delicious eaten at room temperature, or chill them 30 minutes for a firm, cool filling. (Pictured on cover)

½ cup butter, softened
1 cup sugar
1 large egg
½ tsp. vanilla extract
1¾ cups all-purpose flour
½ tsp. baking soda
¼ tsp. salt
¾ tsp. red food coloring paste
Parchment paper
Peppermint Frosting

1. Beat butter at medium speed with a heavy-duty electric stand mixer until creamy; gradually add sugar, beating until light and fluffy. Add egg and vanilla, beating until blended, scraping bowl as needed.

2. Combine flour, baking soda, and salt; gradually add flour mixture to butter mixture, beating at low speed until blended.

3. Divide dough into 2 equal portions. Roll 1 portion of dough into a 12- x 8-inch rectangle on a piece of lightly floured plastic wrap.

4. Knead food coloring paste into remaining portion of dough while wearing rubber gloves. Roll tinted dough into a rectangle as directed in Step 3. Invert untinted dough onto tinted dough; peel off plastic wrap. Cut dough in half lengthwise, forming 2 (12- x 4-inch) rectangles. Roll up each rectangle, jelly-roll fashion, starting at 1 long side, using bottom piece of plastic wrap as a guide. Wrap in plastic wrap, and freeze 4 hours or up to 1 month.

5. Preheat oven to 350°. Cut ends off each dough log, and discard. Cut dough into ¼-inch-thick pieces, and place on parchment paper-lined baking sheets.

6. Bake at 350° for 6 to 7 minutes or until puffed and set; cool cookies on baking sheets 5 minutes. Remove to wire racks, and cool completely (about 30 minutes).

7. Place Peppermint Frosting in a heavy-duty zip-top plastic freezer bag. Snip 1 corner of bag to make a small hole. Pipe about 2 tsp. frosting onto half of cookies; top with remaining cookies, gently pressing to form a sandwich.

Peppermint Frosting:

MAKES 1¾ CUPS; **PREP:** 10 MIN.

¼ cup butter, softened
1 (3-oz.) package cream cheese, softened
2 cups powdered sugar
1 Tbsp. milk
⅛ tsp. peppermint extract

1. Beat butter and cream cheese at medium speed with an electric mixer until creamy. Gradually add powdered sugar, beating at low speed until blended. Increase speed to medium, and gradually add milk and peppermint extract, beating until smooth.

Snowy Chocolate Baby Cakes

MAKES 24 SERVINGS; **PREP:** 45 MIN.,
BAKE: 22 MIN., **COOL:** 35 MIN.

During testing, we found that muffin cups ranged from 2½ to 3 oz. each. The size you have will determine your yield.

1 (18.25-oz.) package devil's food cake mix
1 (16-oz.) container sour cream
½ cup milk
¼ cup butter, melted
2 large eggs
1 tsp. vanilla extract
24 paper muffin cups
Winter White Glaze
Garnishes: red cinnamon candies, fresh bay leaves*

1. Preheat oven to 350°. Beat first 6 ingredients at low speed with an electric mixer just until dry ingredients are moistened. Increase speed to medium, and beat 1 to 2 minutes or until smooth, stopping to scrape bowl as needed. Spoon batter into 24 greased and floured muffin cups.

2. Bake at 350° for 20 to 22 minutes or until a wooden pick inserted in center comes out clean. Cool in pans 5 minutes. Remove from pans to wire racks, and cool completely (about 30 minutes).

3. Arrange cakes upside down on a serving platter. Drizzle Winter White Glaze over cakes (about 1 Tbsp. per cake), spreading with a spatula to thoroughly cover cakes. Garnish, if desired.
*Fresh mint leaves may be substituted.
Note: For testing purposes only, we used Duncan Hines Moist Deluxe Devil's Food Premium Cake Mix.

Winter White Glaze:

MAKES ABOUT 2 CUPS; **PREP:** 5 MIN.

4 cups powdered sugar
1 Tbsp. meringue powder
¼ cup hot water

1. Beat together all ingredients with an electric mixer until smooth. Use glaze immediately.

Sugar-and-Spice Cake

MAKES 12 SERVINGS; **PREP:** 1 HR.;
BAKE: 22 MIN.; **COOL:** 1 HR., 5 MIN.;
FREEZE: 1 HR.

(Pictured on cover)

1 (18.25-oz.) package white cake mix
1 (16-oz.) container sour cream
¼ cup butter, melted
2 large eggs
2 tsp. apple pie spice
1 tsp. vanilla extract
½ tsp. almond extract (optional)
Vanilla Buttercream
Garnishes: sparkling sugar, clear edible
    glitter, rosemary sprigs, pecan halves,
    cranberries

1. Preheat oven to 350°. Beat together first 6 ingredients and, if desired, almond extract at low speed with an electric mixer just until dry ingredients are moistened. Increase speed to medium, and beat 2 minutes or until batter is smooth, stopping to scrape down bottom and sides of bowl as needed. Pour batter into 3 greased and floured 8-inch round cake pans.
2. Bake at 350° for 20 to 22 minutes or until a wooden pick inserted in center comes out clean. Cool in pans on wire racks 5 minutes; remove from pans to wire racks, and cool completely (about 1 hour). Wrap in plastic wrap, and freeze 1 hour or up to 1 month.
3. Spread Vanilla Buttercream between layers and on top and sides of cake. Garnish, if desired.
Note: For testing purposes only, we used Duncan Hines Moist Deluxe Classic White Cake Mix.

Vanilla Buttercream:

MAKES ABOUT 6 CUPS; **PREP:** 10 MIN.

1 (8-oz.) package cream cheese, softened
1 cup butter, softened
2 (16-oz.) packages powdered sugar
1 Tbsp. milk
1 tsp. vanilla extract
¼ tsp. salt

1. Beat cream cheese and butter at medium speed with an electric mixer until creamy. Gradually add powdered sugar and next 3 ingredients, beating at low speed just until blended. Increase speed to medium, and beat until well blended and smooth.

Easy Swirled Fudge

MAKES ABOUT 1¾ LB.; **PREP:** 15 MIN.,
STAND: 3 MIN., **CHILL:** 2 HR.

A very thin crust forms over the surface of the fudge while you microwave the white chocolate mixture. Don't be alarmed—once you swirl the two together, it will become smooth again.

Parchment paper
½ cup butter
1 (16-oz.) package powdered sugar,
    sifted
½ cup unsweetened cocoa
¼ cup milk
¼ tsp. salt
1 Tbsp. vanilla extract
1 (4-oz.) white chocolate baking bar, chopped
2 Tbsp. whipping cream

1. Line bottom and sides of an 8-inch square pan with parchment paper, allowing 2 to 3 inches to extend over sides.
2. Microwave butter in a large microwave-safe glass bowl at HIGH for 30-second intervals until melted. Gently stir in powdered sugar and next 3 ingredients. (Mixture will be lumpy.) Microwave 30 seconds; add vanilla.
3. Beat mixture at medium-low speed with an electric mixer until well blended and smooth. Pour into prepared pan, spreading to edges of pan.

4. Microwave white chocolate and whipping cream in a small microwave-safe glass bowl at HIGH until white chocolate is melted (about 30 seconds to 1 minute), stirring at 30-second intervals. Stir until mixture is smooth. Let stand 1 to 3 minutes or until slightly thickened. Spoon mixture over fudge in pan, swirling with a paring knife. Cover and chill until firm (about 2 hours).
Note: We tested in an 1,100-watt and a 1,250-watt microwave oven. Cook times will vary depending on your microwave wattage; be sure to follow the descriptions in the recipe for best results.

Come for Dinner

Treat your guests to a plate of holiday magic with this impressive and doable menu.

The soothing aroma of a wood-burning fireplace fills the crisp mountain air. It's one of those amazing winter days when it looks and feels like it could snow any minute. "I love this weather," says Scott Counce as he takes a break from decorating his front door to sip a mug of warm apple cider. "It's just so much fun to get the house all festive. I love it. My wife loves it. It really gets us in the spirit."

Scott and his wife, Katherine, like to entertain year-round, but for their annual Christmas dinner, the couple, who own The Merry Wine Market in Black Mountain, North Carolina, take it up a notch. "When it comes to decorating, it's all about what my wife and I call natural and casual elegance," Scott says with a big smile.

As hosts, though, the Counces' main goal is to make everyone comfortable and the occasion fuss-free. This sensibility carries over to the kitchen where Katherine, a trained chef, creates dishes with unexpected twists without being too fancy.

Goat Cheese-Pesto Crostini

chef recipe • fast fixin's

MAKES ABOUT 8 APPETIZER SERVINGS; PREP: 20 MIN., BAKE: 10 MIN.

1 (8.5-oz.) French bread baguette
½ cup refrigerated pesto
½ (10.5-oz.) package fresh goat cheese
⅓ cup sun-dried tomatoes, drained and cut into thin strips
7 pitted whole green olives, sliced

1. Preheat oven to 375°. Cut baguette into 28 (½-inch-thick) slices, and place on a lightly greased baking sheet. Bake at 375° for 5 minutes.
2. Spread 1 side of each bread slice with a layer of pesto and goat cheese. Top half of bread slices with sun-dried tomato strips and remaining half with sliced olives. Bake at 375° for 5 minutes.

—KATHERINE COUNCE,
BLACK MOUNTAIN, NORTH CAROLINA

Pork Loin Roast With Carolina Apple Compote

chef recipe

MAKES 8 TO 10 SERVINGS; PREP: 20 MIN., CHILL: 2 HR., COOK: 46 MIN., BAKE: 1 HR., STAND: 15 MIN.

Trussing the roast holds its shape and promotes even cooking.

3 garlic cloves, minced
3 tsp. dried Italian seasoning
2 tsp. salt
½ tsp. pepper
1 (3-lb.) boneless pork loin roast
Kitchen string
2 tsp. canola oil
2 lb. Gala apples, unpeeled
1 Tbsp. lemon juice
1 cup apple cider
5 Tbsp. sugar
2½ tsp. orange zest
½ tsp. ground cinnamon
Pinch of ground cloves
1 Tbsp. butter

1. Combine first 4 ingredients. Rub mixture on all sides of pork roast. Tie pork with kitchen string, securing at 1-inch intervals. Cover and chill 2 hours.
2. Preheat oven to 375°. Brown roast in hot oil in a large skillet over medium-high heat 2 to 4 minutes on all sides. Place pork on a lightly greased rack in an aluminum foil-lined roasting pan.
3. Bake at 375° for 1 hour or until a meat thermometer inserted into thickest portion registers 150°. Cover roast with foil, and let stand 15 minutes before slicing.
4. Meanwhile, cut apples into bite-size pieces; sprinkle with lemon juice.
5. Add cider and next 4 ingredients to skillet. Cook over medium heat, stirring occasionally, 10 minutes or until slightly thickened. Add apples, and cook, stirring occasionally, 20 minutes or just until apples are tender and liquid is absorbed. Stir in butter until melted, and remove skillet from heat. Stir any accumulated pan juices from roast into compote. Serve compote immediately with pork.

—KATHERINE COUNCE,
BLACK MOUNTAIN, NORTH CAROLINA

Home-style Butterbeans

MAKES 6 TO 8 SERVINGS; **PREP:** 10 MIN.;
COOK: 2 HR., 10 MIN.

5 bacon slices, diced
1 small onion, minced
½ cup firmly packed brown sugar
1 (16-oz.) package frozen butterbeans
¼ cup butter
2 tsp. salt
1 tsp. cracked pepper

1. Cook bacon and onion in a large Dutch oven over medium heat 5 to 7 minutes. Add brown sugar, and cook, stirring occasionally, 1 to 2 minutes or until sugar is dissolved. Stir in butterbeans and butter until butter is melted and beans are thoroughly coated. Stir in 12 cups water.
2. Bring to a boil over medium-high heat; reduce heat to low, and simmer, stirring occasionally, 2 hours or until beans are very tender and liquid is thickened and just below top of beans. Stir in salt and pepper.

—SCOTT COUNCE,
BLACK MOUNTAIN, NORTH CAROLINA

Home-style Lima Beans:

Substitute 1 (16-oz.) package frozen baby lima beans for butterbeans. Proceed with recipe as directed.

Butternut Squash Risotto
chef recipe

MAKES 6 TO 8 SERVINGS; **PREP:** 15 MIN.,
COOK: 35 MIN.

Top with freshly grated Parmesan cheese, if desired.

1 large butternut squash (about 1 lb.), peeled and seeded
8 cups vegetable broth*
3 Tbsp. butter
1¼ cups finely chopped onion
2 cups Arborio rice (short-grain)
½ cup dry white wine
½ cup freshly grated Parmesan cheese
¼ cup whipping cream
Salt and pepper to taste

1. Cut squash into ½- to ¾-inch cubes.
2. Bring broth to a boil in a large saucepan over medium heat; cover and reduce heat to low. Keep warm.
3. Meanwhile, melt butter in a large Dutch oven over medium heat. Add onion, and sauté 5 minutes or until tender. Add squash, and cook, stirring occasionally, 4 minutes. Add rice, and cook 2 minutes. Stir in wine; cook 1 minute.
4. Bring to a boil over medium-high heat. Reduce heat to low; add ½ cup hot broth, stirring constantly, until liquid is absorbed. Repeat procedure with remaining broth, ½ cup at a time. (Total cooking time is about 20 minutes.) Stir in Parmesan cheese and cream. Season with salt and pepper to taste. Transfer to a large serving bowl. Serve immediately.

—KATHERINE COUNCE,
BLACK MOUNTAIN, NORTH CAROLINA

*8 cups chicken broth may be substituted.

Bacon-Brown Sugar Brussels Sprouts
chef recipe • fast fixin's

MAKES 6 TO 8 SERVINGS; **PREP:** 10 MIN.,
COOK: 18 MIN.

4 bacon slices
1 (14-oz.) can chicken broth
1 Tbsp. brown sugar
1 tsp. salt
1½ lb. Brussels sprouts, trimmed and halved

1. Cook bacon in a Dutch oven over medium heat 10 minutes or until crisp. Remove bacon, and drain on paper towels, reserving drippings in Dutch oven. Crumble bacon.
2. Add broth, brown sugar, and salt to drippings in Dutch oven, and bring to a boil. Stir in Brussels sprouts. Cover and cook 6 to 8 minutes or until tender. Transfer Brussels sprouts to a serving bowl using a slotted spoon, and sprinkle with crumbled bacon. Serve immediately.

—KATHERINE COUNCE,
BLACK MOUNTAIN, NORTH CAROLINA

Christmas Shortbread Cookies
chef recipe

MAKES 16 (4¾-INCH) COOKIES;
PREP: 20 MIN., **BAKE:** 15 MIN. PER BATCH,
COOL: 6 MIN.

2 cups unsalted butter, softened
4½ cups all-purpose flour
1¼ cups lightly packed light brown sugar
Pinch of salt

1. Preheat oven to 275°. Beat all ingredients at medium speed with a heavy-duty electric stand mixer just until combined.
2. Place dough on a lightly floured surface, and roll to ⅛-inch thickness. Cut with a 4¾-inch Christmas tree-shape cookie cutter. Place 1 inch apart on ungreased baking sheets.
3. Bake at 275° for 15 minutes or until golden brown. Let cool on baking sheet 1 minute. Remove to wire racks, and cool completely (about 5 minutes).

—KATHERINE COUNCE,
BLACK MOUNTAIN, NORTH CAROLINA

All-New Classic

Great gift ideas don't come much better than the new *Southern Living® Cookbook* in ring-binder format.

Enjoy a few weeknight-worthy dishes—or elegant entertaining menus—from this handsome new ring-bound volume. The pages lie flat, allowing you to cook your favorite recipes and follow the picture-perfect step-by-step instructions with ease. In true *Southern Living* style, the recipes are as simple to follow as they are delicious. For example, pop Five-Bean Bake in the oven, and then head out for your evening walk. You'll come home to a fragrant, full-bodied side dish. The *Southern Living® Cookbook* is sure to become one of your favorites and will be a much-appreciated gift. Find it in your favorite bookstore, or visit www.oxmoorhouse.com. To order by phone, call 1-888-859-8056.

Tuscan Pork Chops

fast fixin's

MAKES 4 SERVINGS; **PREP:** 10 MIN., **COOK:** 10 MIN.

¼ cup all-purpose flour
1 tsp. salt
¾ tsp. seasoned pepper
4 (1-inch-thick) boneless pork chops
1 Tbsp. olive oil
3 to 4 garlic cloves, minced*
⅓ cup balsamic vinegar
⅓ cup chicken broth
3 plum tomatoes, seeded and diced
2 Tbsp. drained capers
Garnish: fresh parsley sprigs

1. Combine first 3 ingredients in a shallow dish; dredge pork chops in flour mixture.
2. Cook pork in hot oil in a large nonstick skillet over medium-high heat 1 to 2 minutes on each side or until golden brown. Remove pork from skillet.
3. Add garlic to skillet, and sauté 1 minute. Add vinegar and broth, stirring to loosen particles from bottom of skillet; stir in tomatoes and capers.
4. Return pork to skillet; bring sauce to a boil. Cover, reduce heat, and simmer 4 to 5 minutes or until pork is done. Serve pork with tomato mixture. Garnish, if desired.
*1 Tbsp. jarred minced garlic may be substituted.

Fresh Spinach Sauté

fast fixin's

MAKES 6 SERVINGS; **PREP:** 10 MIN., **COOK:** 6 MIN.

2 garlic cloves, minced
2 tsp. olive oil
3 (10-oz.) packages fresh spinach, thoroughly washed and torn
½ tsp. salt
½ tsp. dried crushed red pepper
1 Tbsp. fresh lemon juice
¼ cup (1 oz.) freshly shredded Parmesan cheese

1. Sauté garlic in hot oil in a large Dutch oven over medium-high heat 1 minute. Reduce heat to medium; add spinach, salt, and red pepper. Cook, stirring occasionally, 5 minutes or until spinach wilts. Add lemon juice. Sprinkle with Parmesan cheese. Serve immediately.

Five-Bean Bake

MAKES 8 SERVINGS; **PREP:** 10 MIN.; **COOK:** 13 MIN.; **BAKE:** 1 HR., 30 MIN.

8 bacon slices
1 large onion, diced
1 (31-oz.) can pork and beans
1 (16-oz.) can chickpeas, rinsed and drained
1 (16-oz.) can kidney beans, rinsed and drained
1 (15.25-oz.) can lima beans, rinsed and drained
1 (15-oz.) can black beans, rinsed and drained
1 cup ketchup
½ cup firmly packed brown sugar
¼ cup cider vinegar

1. Preheat oven to 350°. Cook bacon in a large skillet over medium-high heat 8 minutes or until crisp; remove bacon, and drain on paper towels, reserving 2 Tbsp. drippings in skillet. Sauté onion in hot drippings 5 minutes or until tender.
2. Combine bacon, onion, ½ cup water, pork and beans, and remaining ingredients in a lightly greased 13- x 9-inch baking dish.
3. Bake, covered, at 350° for 1 hour; uncover and bake 30 more minutes.

10-Minute Elegant Appetizers

Bring on the holidays with fresh style and big flavor.

Delicious food + great friends = good times. But let's face it, this time of year is crazy-busy. You can impress, even if time is short, with these super-fast, eye-catching starters that won't break the bank. Have Andouille With Smoked Paprika and Red Wine ready in a snap for last-minute company. Or, for an almost-spontaneous party, make our entire selection of recipes in less than two hours. It's really easy. Start with quality ingredients, and add pizzazz with a few flavor stir-ins and great presentation ideas. Keep this section handy—it's your secret plan to wow your guests this season.

Mini Caviar Parfaits
fast fixin's

MAKES 6 SERVINGS; **PREP:** 10 MIN.

A tiny scoop of caviar adds bling to layers of sour cream, lemon-freshened guacamole, and tomato. To pull this together fast, purchase peeled, boiled eggs in the deli or dairy section of your local supermarket. Use leftover caviar to add a special touch to deviled eggs.

½ cup sour cream
1 medium avocado, diced
2 Tbsp. minced red onion
2½ tsp. lemon juice
¾ tsp. chopped fresh dill
Salt and pepper to taste
1 small plum tomato, seeded and finely chopped
1 large hard-cooked egg, peeled and finely chopped
1 (2-oz.) jar black caviar, chilled and drained
Thin breadsticks, assorted crackers

·TIP·

Caviar-buying tips: We used less expensive, shelf-stable lumpfish caviar found near the canned tuna. It costs around $5 for a small jar. Another affordable choice is salmon caviar. Its bright orange color would look stunning atop each parfait. Try fresh caviar if your seafood department stocks it. It may cost a tad more, but you only need a few teaspoons.

1. Spoon sour cream into a 1-qt. zip-top plastic freezer bag. Snip 1 corner of bag to make a small hole; pipe sour cream into 6 (2-oz.) shot glasses.
2. Combine avocado and next 3 ingredients in a bowl. Mash with a fork, and season with salt and pepper to taste.
3. Spoon avocado mixture over sour cream in shot glasses. Top each with tomato, egg, and ½ to 1 tsp. caviar. Reserve remaining caviar for another use. Serve parfaits with breadsticks and assorted crackers.

Andouille With Smoked Paprika and Red Wine
fast fixin's

MAKES 8 SERVINGS; **PREP:** 10 MIN., **COOK:** 10 MIN.

Norman King, the newest member of our Test Kitchens, shared this recipe. He serves the sausage with warm bread to sop up the leftover garlicky sauce.

1 lb. andouille sausage, cut into ½-inch rounds*
2 Tbsp. olive oil
1 Tbsp. chopped fresh oregano
2 tsp. minced garlic
¾ tsp. smoked paprika**
½ cup dry red wine
Garnish: fresh oregano sprigs

1. Cook sausage in hot oil in a large skillet over medium-high heat 3 minutes on each side or until browned.
2. Stir in oregano, garlic, and paprika, and cook 1 minute or until fragrant. Add red wine, and cook, stirring often, 2 to 3 minutes or until wine is reduced and thickened. Transfer to a shallow bowl, and garnish, if desired. Serve with wooden picks.
*Spicy smoked sausage may be substituted for andouille.
**¼ tsp. ground cumin and ½ tsp. regular paprika may be substituted.

Don't fuss with setting up a full bar. Pick your favorite brands of wine and beer, and serve one signature cocktail for the evening. Try one of these three quick drinks using liquor cabinet staples gin, vodka, and bourbon.

Bourbon Smash: Place 6 fresh or frozen raspberries, 1 Tbsp. sugar, 1 small lime wedge, and 3 to 4 mint or basil leaves in a chilled 10-oz. tumbler. Gently press raspberry mixture against sides of cup with a cocktail muddler or back of a spoon to release flavors. Fill glass with crushed ice and ¼ cup bourbon; stir well. Serve immediately with a cocktail straw. **Makes** 1 serving; Prep: 5 min.

Orange Lady: Combine 6 Tbsp. gin, ¼ cup orange juice, 2 Tbsp. powdered sugar, 3 Tbsp. lemon juice, and 2 Tbsp. orange liqueur in a cocktail shaker; fill with crushed ice. Cover with lid, and shake until thoroughly chilled. Remove lid, and strain into 2 chilled glasses. Serve immediately. **Makes** 2 servings; Prep: 5 min.

Vicki's Dirty Martini: The secret is to chill everything except the vermouth in the freezer before you start. To make a "filthy" martini, increase the olive juice by a few tablespoons. Fill a cocktail shaker with crushed ice. Add 3 Tbsp. vermouth; cover with lid, and shake until thoroughly chilled. Discard vermouth, reserving ice in shaker. Add ½ cup vodka and 3 Tbsp. Spanish olive brine to ice in shaker; cover with lid, and shake until thoroughly chilled (about 30 seconds). Pour into a chilled martini glass. Serve immediately with a large pimiento-stuffed Spanish olive. **Makes** 1 serving; Prep: 5 min.

Warm Brie With Ginger-Citrus Glaze
fast fixin's
MAKES 6 TO 8 SERVINGS; **PREP:** 10 MIN., **BAKE:** 9 MIN.

This appetizer comes together quickly. Pop the cheese in the oven, make your glaze in the microwave, and gather fresh fruit. You're done in about 10 minutes. Place the Brie directly on an oven-safe serving plate, and bake as directed. The hot plate will keep the cheese warm and gooey longer. If you are serving bread with this warm cheese, place slices on the same baking sheet with the Brie. They will toast while the cheese cooks.

1 (8-oz.) Brie round
¼ cup ginger preserves*
1 Tbsp. honey
2 tsp. apple cider vinegar
1½ tsp. orange zest
½ tsp. chopped fresh rosemary
¼ tsp. salt
¼ tsp. freshly ground pepper
Assorted crackers, fresh fruit
Garnish: fresh rosemary sprig

1. Preheat oven to 400°. Trim and discard rind from top of Brie. Place Brie on a lightly greased baking sheet. Bake 7 to 9 minutes or until cheese is just melted.
2. Meanwhile, microwave preserves and next 6 ingredients in a small microwave-safe glass bowl at HIGH 30 seconds; stir until blended and smooth. Microwave at HIGH 1 minute. Let stand while cheese bakes.
3. Transfer Brie to a serving dish; drizzle warm glaze immediately over Brie. Serve with assorted crackers and fresh fruit. Garnish, if desired.
*¼ cup fig preserves may be substituted for ginger preserves.
Note: For testing purposes only, we used Dundee Ginger Preserves.

Instant Italian Cheese Tray
MAKES 8 SERVINGS; **PREP:** 10 MIN.

Make a ho-hum cheese tray spectacular with a few unexpected additions. One large wedge of cheese looks like you splurged, but it's actually less expensive than offering several smaller choices.

Warm Fennel-Olive Sauté (recipe below)
1 (8-oz.) wedge fontina cheese
2 Fuyu persimmons, sliced
¼ lb. thinly sliced prosciutto
Sliced ciabatta bread

1. Arrange all ingredients on a large serving platter or cutting board.

Warm Fennel-Olive Sauté
fast fixin's
MAKES 12 SERVINGS; **PREP:** 10 MIN., **COOK:** 8 MIN.

A dish of olives is always at home on any cocktail party menu. When it's cold out, warm up the olives and add a little spice with dried crushed red pepper and fennel seeds. You'll have a crowd favorite in no time. Save your leftovers; they can be kept up to five days and reheated, if desired.

1 lemon
1 tsp. minced garlic
¾ tsp. fennel seeds
½ tsp. dried crushed red pepper
⅓ cup extra virgin olive oil
1½ cups mixed olives
8 pickled okra, cut in half lengthwise
1 fennel bulb, cored and sliced
½ cup lightly salted roasted almonds

1. Remove lemon peel in strips using a vegetable peeler, reserving lemon for another use.
2. Sauté lemon peel, garlic, fennel seeds, and red pepper in hot oil in a large skillet over medium heat 1 minute. Add olives and next 3 ingredients, and cook, stirring occasionally, 5 to 7 minutes or until fennel is crisp-tender. Transfer to a shallow serving dish.

Smoked Trout-and-Horseradish Spread

fast fixin's

MAKES 2 CUPS; **PREP:** 10 MIN.

Transform leftovers into crostini by topping toasted French bread rounds with this creamy spread and a sprinkle of finely diced apples and toasted pecans.

8 oz. smoked trout
1 (8-oz.) package cream cheese, softened
2 green onions, sliced
¼ cup loosely packed fresh parsley leaves
5 tsp. horseradish
1 Tbsp. chopped fresh dill
1 tsp. lemon zest
2 tsp. lemon juice
½ tsp. freshly ground pepper
¼ tsp. salt
Granny Smith apple slices, celery sticks, flatbread crackers
Garnish: lemon slices

1. Remove and discard skin and bones from trout, if necessary. Flake trout into small pieces.
2. Pulse cream cheese and next 8 ingredients in a food processor 7 to 8 times or until combined, stopping to scrape down sides as needed. Stir in trout. Transfer to a serving dish. Serve immediately, or cover and chill up to 2 days. If chilled, let stand 30 minutes at room temperature before serving. Serve with apples, celery, and flatbread crackers. Garnish, if desired.

Smoked Salmon-and-Horseradish Spread: Substitute 2 (4-oz.) packages smoked salmon, finely chopped, for trout. Omit Step 1. Proceed with recipe as directed.

• TIP •

Keep sliced apples or pears from browning by tossing them with lemon-lime soda. It works just like lemon juice but without the sour taste. The citric acid in the soda will keep the fruit looking fresh.

Spread a Little Cheer

Making eco-friendly Magic Reindeer Food is fun for the whole family. What the reindeer don't eat, the birds are certain to enjoy later.

One of Executive Editor Scott Jones' great stress busters during the busy holidays is to get in the kitchen with his girls. There's just something therapeutic about the experience that brings him down to reality and gets him in the true spirit of the season. He highly recommends making time for it. He and his girls celebrate Christmas Eve by preparing goodies for Santa and his reindeer. (Yes, Santa still exists.) Both recipes are super-easy for kids of any age to make, and preparing them is a terrific way to teach little ones a few kitchen skills such as measuring and mixing.

Magic Reindeer Food

fast fixin's

MAKES 4 CUPS; **PREP:** 10 MIN.

As you're mixing together the ingredients, make sure little hands don't reach in for a taste—this snack is definitely for reindeer only.

2 cups regular oats
2 cups sunflower tropical birdseed mix
2 Tbsp. red decorator sugar crystals
2 Tbsp. green decorator sugar crystals

1. Combine all ingredients in a 2-qt. zip-top plastic bag.
Note: For testing purposes only, we used Hartz Bonanza Parrot & Other Large Hookbill Gourmet Diet birdseed.

Santa Snack Mix

make ahead

MAKES 8 CUPS; **PREP:** 10 MIN., **COOK:** 5 MIN., **BAKE:** 1 HR., **COOL:** 20 MIN.

4 cups toasted oat bran cereal
1 cup multigrain cluster cereal
1 cup chopped pecans
1 tsp. ground allspice
¼ tsp. salt
¾ cup honey
½ cup butter
1 cup jumbo red raisins
Wax paper

1. Preheat oven to 250°. Combine first 5 ingredients in a large bowl.
2. Cook honey and butter together in a small saucepan over low heat, stirring occasionally, until butter is melted and mixture is blended and smooth (about 5 minutes).
3. Pour honey mixture over cereal mixture, stirring to coat. Spread in a single layer on a lightly greased aluminum foil-lined 15- x 10-inch jelly-roll pan.
4. Bake at 250° for 55 minutes, stirring once every 10 to 15 minutes. Stir in raisins, and bake 5 more minutes. Spread immediately on wax paper; cool 20 minutes. Store in an airtight container up to 1 week.
Note: For testing purposes only, we used Quaker Oat Bran for toasted oat bran cereal and Kashi GOLEAN Crunch for multigrain cluster cereal.

Pizza in a Pie

Serve great carryout taste the whole family will enjoy.

Pizzeria Night

SERVES 4

Italian-Style Pizza Pot Pie

Iceberg Lettuce Wedges With Zesty
Buttermilk Ranch Dressing

Cinnamon Nuggets

We've come up with an unexpected twist on this Southern favorite. Italian-Style Pizza Pot Pie is topped with a package of refrigerated piecrust dough to seal in the enticing flavor of meat-filled herbed tomato sauce. Cinnamon Nuggets make use of leftover dough to satisfy those sweet cravings. We're all trying to save a little money, so an at-home pizzeria night should get rave reviews.

Italian-Style Pizza Pot Pie

MAKES 4 TO 6 SERVINGS; **PREP:** 15 MIN.,
COOK: 30 MIN., **BAKE:** 20 MIN.,
STAND: 10 MIN.

This main dish combines a winning trio of meats, cheeses, and vegetables. Reserve excess dough for the Cinnamon Nuggets.

¾ lb. ground round
¼ lb. mild Italian sausage, casings removed
1 small onion, chopped
2 garlic cloves, minced
1 (8-oz.) package sliced fresh mushrooms
1 (26-oz.) jar tomato-and-basil pasta sauce
½ tsp. dried Italian seasoning
¼ tsp. salt
1 (13.8-oz.) package refrigerated pizza crust dough
Parchment paper
1 cup (4 oz.) shredded Italian five-cheese blend
Cinnamon Nuggets

1. Preheat oven to 450°. Cook ground round and sausage in a large skillet over medium-high heat, stirring often, 8 to 10 minutes or until meat crumbles and is no longer pink. Drain beef mixture, reserving 1 tsp. drippings in skillet. Reduce heat to medium.
2. Sauté onion in hot drippings 2 minutes. Add garlic, and cook 1 minute or until tender. Add mushrooms, and sauté 8 to 10 minutes or until most of liquid has evaporated. Stir in beef mixture, pasta sauce, Italian seasoning, and salt. Bring to a light boil, and simmer 5 minutes.
3. Meanwhile, unroll dough on a lightly floured piece of parchment paper. Invert 1 (9-inch) round baking dish or pie plate onto center of dough. Cut dough around edge of baking dish,

making a 9-inch circle. Remove excess dough around baking dish; cover and chill, reserving for Cinnamon Nuggets. Remove baking dish.
4. Pour beef mixture into baking dish, and sprinkle with cheese. Immediately top with dough circle. Cut an "X" in top of dough for steam to escape. Place baking dish on an aluminum foil-lined baking sheet.
5. Bake at 450° for 16 to 20 minutes or until crust is golden brown. Let stand 10 minutes before serving. Serve with Cinnamon Nuggets.
Note: For testing purposes only, we used Classico Tomato & Basil sauce and Pillsbury Classic Pizza Crust.

Piecrust-Topped Pizza Pot Pie:

Substitute ½ (15-oz.) package refrigerated piecrusts for pizza dough. Proceed with recipe as directed, omitting Step 3. (Place entire piecrust over filling in baking dish in Step 4. Edges of piecrust will hang over side of baking dish.)

Cinnamon Nuggets:

fast fixin's

MAKES 16 NUGGETS; **PREP:** 10 MIN.,
BAKE: 10 MIN.

Pop these in the oven while the pot pie rests for a simple after-dinner treat.

Reserved refrigerated pizza dough from Italian-Style Pizza Pot Pie
1 Tbsp. melted butter
2 tsp. sugar
1 tsp. ground cinnamon

1. Preheat oven to 400°. Cut reserved dough into 1½- x 2-inch pieces. Place dough pieces on a lightly greased baking sheet. Brush tops of pieces with butter.
2. Combine sugar and cinnamon in a small bowl. Sprinkle dough pieces with cinnamon-sugar mixture.
3. Bake at 400° for 10 minutes or until golden brown.

Iceberg Lettuce Wedges With Zesty Buttermilk Ranch Dressing

MAKES 4 SERVINGS; PREP: 15 MIN.,
STAND: 30 MIN.

A touch of horseradish adds a little kick to this dressing. Leftover dressing can be stored in refrigerator up to seven days.

1 cup mayonnaise
1 cup buttermilk
1 (1-oz.) envelope buttermilk Ranch
    dressing mix*
2 Tbsp. chopped fresh parsley
1 to 2 Tbsp. horseradish
1 tsp. lemon zest
¼ tsp. pepper
1 large head iceberg lettuce, cored and
    quartered
1 small cucumber, halved and sliced
½ cup thinly sliced red onion
¼ cup grated Parmesan cheese

1. Whisk together first 7 ingredients in a medium bowl. Let stand 30 minutes.
2. Arrange lettuce on a serving platter or individual plates. Top with cucumber and onion; sprinkle with Parmesan cheese. Serve with dressing.
*1 (0.4-oz.) envelope buttermilk Ranch dressing mix may be substituted.

One-Dish Breakfasts

Start with prepared breads from the freezer case to make these recipes ultra-easy.

Italian Bread Pudding

MAKES 6 SERVINGS; PREP: 15 MIN.,
CHILL: 4 HR., BAKE: 55 MIN., STAND: 5 MIN.

Italian Bread Pudding is a fine morning entrée, or serve it as a side with an evening meal.

5 large eggs*
1 cup milk
1½ tsp. Dijon mustard
1 tsp. dried basil
¾ tsp. salt
⅛ to ¼ tsp. ground red pepper
1 (9.5-oz.) package frozen mozzarella-
    and-Monterey Jack cheese Texas toast,
    chopped
3 plum tomatoes, seeded and chopped
    (about 1¼ cups)
8 fully cooked bacon slices, chopped
1 cup grated Cheddar cheese
Garnish: fresh basil leaves

1. Whisk together first 6 ingredients until blended.
2. Layer half of Texas toast in a lightly greased 11- x 7-inch baking dish; sprinkle with half each of tomatoes, bacon, and cheese. Repeat layers once. Pour egg mixture over toast and cheese. Cover and chill 4 to 24 hours.
3. Preheat oven to 325°. Bake casserole 50 to 55 minutes or until center is set. Let stand 5 minutes before serving. Garnish, if desired
*1¼ cups egg substitute may be substituted for whole eggs.
Note: For testing purposes only, we used Pepperidge Farm Mozzarella and Monterey Jack Texas Toast.

—INSPIRED BY CINDY SNOWDEN,
BYFIELD, MASSACHUSETTS

Texas Toast Bread Pudding:
Omit dried basil, tomatoes, and bacon. Proceed with recipe as directed.
Note: For testing purposes only, we used Pepperidge Farm Mozzarella and Monterey Jack Texas Toast.

Sausage Roll Casserole: Omit dried basil, tomatoes, and bacon. Increase cheese to 1½ cups. Substitute 1 (18-oz.) package frozen sausage wrap rolls for Texas toast. Break apart sausage rolls; cut each roll crosswise into thirds, cutting across sausage. Proceed with recipe as directed.
Note: For testing purposes only, we used Sister Schubert's Sausage Wrap Rolls.

Cinnamon Roll Breakfast Bake

MAKES 6 TO 8 SERVINGS; PREP: 15 MIN.,
CHILL: 4 HR., BAKE: 60 MIN.,
STAND: 5 MIN.

3 egg yolks*
2 large eggs*
2 cups milk
2 Tbsp. sugar
1 tsp. ground cinnamon
1 tsp. vanilla extract
¼ tsp. salt
1 (16-oz.) package frozen cinnamon rolls
½ cup golden raisins
2 Tbsp. butter, cut into ¼-inch cubes

1. Whisk together first 7 ingredients until blended.
2. Break apart cinnamon rolls, and chop. Place in a lightly greased 11- x 7-inch baking dish. Toss raisins with rolls in dish. Pour egg mixture over top; dot with butter. Cover and chill 4 to 24 hours.
3. Preheat oven to 325°. Bake casserole 55 to 60 minutes or until set and golden. Let stand 5 minutes before serving.
*1 cup egg substitute may be substituted for egg yolks and whole eggs.
Note: For testing purposes only, we used Sister Schubert's Cinnamon Yeast Rolls.

Orange-Apricot Breakfast Bake: Substitute ⅛ tsp. ground nutmeg for 1 tsp. cinnamon, 1 (16-oz.) package orange yeast rolls for cinnamon rolls, and ½ cup chopped dried apricots for raisins. Proceed with recipe as directed.

Celebrate the Season

Here's a heartfelt gift from the *Southern Living* family that you can unwrap page by page.
We offer five stellar menus selected by you, our readers.

Party Starters

Test Kitchen Secrets

- Make a pitcher or two of Pomegranate Margaritas and refrigerate them for quick drinks. This way, you can spend your time mingling with guests rather than refilling drinks.
- Serve the marinated shrimp over ice to keep them chilled. Fill a large bowl with ice, making a well in the center of the ice. Place a second bowl with Marinated Shrimp on top.
- Most of these recipes are a snap to double, so you can prepare as much as you need to feed a crowd. Keep extra food in the refrigerator and set it out as you need it. (Exception: We don't recommend doubling Southwest Fondue.)

Here's our easiest get-together for the holidays. You'll find we skipped fussy hors d'oeuvres and went with pickup appetizers, including Spicy Southwestern Deviled Eggs, top vote receiver Marinated Shrimp, and cocktail-size Chipotle-Barbecue Meatballs. Each dish for this low-maintenance party has a short ingredient list, easy prep, and get-ahead ideas. Stress-free, you'll have time to make your place look terrific, put on your party clothes, and treat yourself to a Pomegranate Margarita. The food needs little tending during the party, allowing you to have a great time.

Marinated Shrimp
winning recipe
MAKES 8 TO 10 APPETIZER SERVINGS;
PREP: 20 MIN., COOK: 3 MIN., CHILL: 6 HR.

2 lb. unpeeled, large raw shrimp
    (21/25 count)
1½ cups white vinegar
1 cup vegetable oil
½ cup sugar
¼ cup capers, undrained
1½ tsp. celery salt
½ to 1 tsp. salt
1 medium-size red or white onion, sliced
    and separated into rings

1. Bring 6 cups salted water to a boil; add shrimp, and cook 3 minutes or just until shrimp turn pink. Drain and rinse with cold water. Peel shrimp, leaving tails on. Devein, if desired.
2. Combine vinegar and next 5 ingredients in a shallow dish; add shrimp alternately with onion. Cover and chill 6 to 24 hours, turning often. Drain shrimp, discarding marinade, before serving.

Marinated Shrimp With Rosemary: Prepare recipe as directed, adding 2 Tbsp. chopped fresh rosemary to vinegar mixture in Step 2.

Marinated Shrimp With Olives: Prepare recipe as directed, adding ½ cup pitted kalamata olives, rinsed and drained, with onion, and using ½ tsp. salt.

Winning Recipe: Marinated Shrimp

Why we love it:

- "Nothing says 'easy' like fast-cooking shrimp. The recipe itself is not only short and sweet from an ingredient and method standpoint, but it's also make ahead. Combine that with its terrific flavor, and you have a bona fide hit." —**ASHLEY LEATH**, ASSISTANT RECIPE EDITOR
- "I think anytime you serve shrimp you make your guests feel special. Best of all, Marinated Shrimp is as pretty as it is delicious."
  —**DONNA FLORIO**, FOOD SENIOR WRITER

Why you love it:

- "My husband always makes an ice bowl inlayed with cranberries. We place the bowl on a holiday metal tray and serve the marinated shrimp in it."
  —**JUDITH FUSELIER-PHILLIPS**, WILLS POINT, TEXAS
- "It is so easy and so good! If you're in a time crunch, you can purchase frozen cooked and peeled shrimp, let them thaw in the fridge overnight, and then assemble everything the next day." —**RENE COLLINS**, RIDGELAND, MISSISSIPPI
- "I always serve this recipe with herbed crackers. I brush saltines with melted butter, sprinkle them with a dried herb mix, and then bake them in the oven for a few minutes. It takes everything up a notch."
  —**CAROLAN KVIKLYS**, MARLTON, NEW JERSEY

Black Bean-and-Mango Salsa

MAKES 8 APPETIZER SERVINGS;
PREP: 15 MIN., **CHILL:** 1 HR.

1 (15-oz.) can black beans, rinsed and drained
1 mango, peeled and chopped
1 small green bell pepper, chopped
2 plum tomatoes, seeded and chopped
4 green onions, chopped
¼ cup Italian vinaigrette dressing
1 Tbsp. fresh lime juice
2 tsp. chopped fresh cilantro
½ tsp. garlic salt
½ tsp. seasoned pepper
½ tsp. chili powder
½ tsp. hot sauce
Assorted tortilla chips

1. Stir together first 12 ingredients in a medium bowl; cover and chill 1 to 24 hours. Serve with assorted tortilla chips.

Black Bean-and-Corn Salsa:

Substitute 1 (11-oz.) can shoepeg corn, rinsed and drained, for mango. Proceed with recipe as directed.

◖ T I P ◗

Make Black Bean-and-Mango Salsa a day ahead to save on time. This recipe can be halved if needed.

Spicy Southwestern Deviled Eggs

make ahead

MAKES 2 DOZEN; **PREP:** 15 MIN.,
COOK: 12 MIN., **STAND:** 10 MIN.

The fresher the eggs, the more difficult they can be to peel. For ease of peeling, buy and refrigerate your eggs 7 to 10 days before cooking them.

1 dozen large eggs
6 Tbsp. mayonnaise
2 to 4 Tbsp. pickled sliced jalapeño peppers, minced
1 Tbsp. yellow mustard
½ tsp. ground cumin
⅛ tsp. salt
Garnish: sliced pickled jalapeño peppers

1. Place eggs in a single layer in a stainless-steel saucepan. (Do not use nonstick.) Add water to a depth of 3 inches. Bring to a boil; cook 1 minute. Cover, remove from heat, and let stand 10 minutes. Drain.
2. Tap each egg firmly on the counter until cracks form all over the shell. Peel under cold running water.
3. Cut eggs in half crosswise, and carefully remove yolks. Mash yolks in a bowl; stir in mayonnaise and next 4 ingredients. Spoon or pipe egg yolk mixture into egg white halves. Serve immediately, or cover and chill 1 hour before serving. Garnish, if desired.
　　　　　—**EDIE BULLARD**, DETROIT, MICHIGAN

Lemon-Parsley Deviled Eggs:

Substitute 1 Tbsp. chopped fresh parsley for jalapeño peppers, 1 Tbsp. Dijon mustard for yellow mustard, and ½ tsp. lemon zest for ground cumin. Proceed with recipe as directed.

Chipotle-Barbecue Meatballs
make ahead
MAKES 12 TO 14 APPETIZER SERVINGS;
PREP: 10 MIN., **COOK:** 50 MIN.

1 (28-oz.) bottle barbecue sauce
1 (18-oz.) jar cherry preserves
3 canned chipotle peppers in adobo sauce, undrained
1 Tbsp. adobo sauce from can
1 (32-oz.) package frozen meatballs

1. Whisk together first 4 ingredients and 1½ cups water in a Dutch oven. Bring to a boil over medium-high heat. Add meatballs, and return to a boil. Reduce heat to medium, and simmer, stirring occasionally, 40 to 45 minutes. (Sauce will thicken.) Keep warm in a slow cooker on WARM or LOW, if desired.
Note: For testing purposes only, we used Rosina Italian Style Meatballs.

Chipotle-Barbecue Sausage Bites: Substitute 2 (16-oz.) packages cocktail-size smoked sausages for meatballs. Proceed with recipe as directed, decreasing water to ½ cup and simmering mixture 15 minutes. **Makes** 12 to 14 appetizer servings; Prep: 10 min., Cook: 20 min.

Southwest Fondue
fast fixin's
MAKES 6 CUPS; **PREP:** 20 MIN.

Serve this dip in a fondue pot to keep it warm.

1 (16-oz.) package pepper-Jack pasteurized prepared cheese product, cubed
1 lb. processed or deli white American cheese slices, torn
1¼ cups milk
2 to 3 plum tomatoes, seeded and diced
¼ cup chopped fresh cilantro
Garnish: chopped fresh cilantro
Assorted dippers: toasted bread cubes, corn chips, pretzels, thin breadsticks, pita chips

1. Combine first 3 ingredients in a large microwave-safe bowl. Microwave at HIGH 8 minutes or until cheese is melted, stirring every 2 minutes. Stir in tomatoes and cilantro. Garnish, if desired. Serve with desired dippers.
Note: For testing purposes only, we used Velveeta Pepper Jack for pasteurized prepared cheese product.

Southwest Fondue With Chorizo: Prepare recipe as directed. Stir in 9 oz. finely chopped, fully cooked chorizo. **Makes** 7 cups; Prep: 20 min.

Southwest Fondue With Beef: Brown 1 lb. lean ground beef in a large skillet over medium-high heat, stirring often, 8 to 10 minutes or until meat crumbles and is no longer pink; drain. Proceed with recipe as directed. Stir in cooked ground beef. **Makes** about 7 cups; Prep: 15 min., Cook: 10 min.

Pomegranate Margaritas
chef recipe • make ahead
MAKES 4 SERVINGS; **PREP:** 10 MIN.

Mix up batches of the margarita mixture ahead of time, and chill. Shake to order when friends arrive. We suggest using a tequila labeled plata *or silver. For a festive touch, dip rims of glasses in lime juice and then in sanding sugar.*

¼ cup sugar
¼ cup hot water
1½ cups pomegranate juice
¾ cup tequila
½ cup fresh lime juice (about 6 limes)
¼ cup orange liqueur

1. Stir together ¼ cup sugar and ¼ cup hot water until sugar is dissolved. Stir in pomegranate juice and next 3 ingredients.
2. Pour desired amount of pomegranate juice mixture into a cocktail shaker filled with ice cubes. Cover with lid, and shake 30 seconds or until thoroughly chilled. Remove lid, and strain into chilled cocktail glasses. Repeat procedure with remaining pomegranate mixture. Serve immediately.
—LANNY LANCARTE II,
LANNY'S ALTA COCINA MEXICANA,
FORT WORTH, TEXAS

Note: For testing purposes only, we used Triple Sec orange liqueur.

Cranberry Margaritas: Substitute cranberry juice for pomegranate juice. Proceed with recipe as directed.

Merry Morning

Deck the halls with ease and elegance for a casual Christmas Day gathering.

Christmas Brunch

SERVES 6 TO 8

Breakfast Enchiladas

Hot Tomato Grits

Skewered Fruit With Rum Drizzle

Pepper Jelly Danish

Hot Chocolate With Almond Liqueur

Rudolph's Spritzer

Brunch Punch

Christmas brunch is a favorite in households across the South. Start the most anticipated day of the year with a menu that's festive enough to celebrate the spirit of the season and diverse enough to satisfy everyone at the table. Breakfast Enchiladas and Hot Tomato Grits will keep you going until supper time, set off by the bright flavors of Skewered Fruit With Rum Drizzle. Rudolph's Spritzer complements them all with its fruity, fizzy charm, just right for children and adults. Finish with a sweet touch—serve Pepper Jelly Danish, or offer a smorgasbord of leftover cookies and cakes.

Breakfast Enchiladas
winning recipe
MAKES 8 SERVINGS; **PREP:** 20 MIN., **COOK:** 16 MIN., **BAKE:** 30 MIN.

1 (1-lb.) package hot ground pork sausage
2 Tbsp. butter
4 green onions, thinly sliced
2 Tbsp. chopped fresh cilantro
14 large eggs, beaten
¾ tsp. salt
½ tsp. pepper
Cheese Sauce
8 (8-inch) soft taco-size flour tortillas
1 cup (4 oz.) shredded Monterey Jack cheese with peppers
Toppings: grape tomato halves, sliced green onions, chopped fresh cilantro

1. Preheat oven to 350°. Cook sausage in a large nonstick skillet over medium-high heat, stirring frequently, 6 to 8 minutes or until sausage crumbles and is no longer pink. Remove from skillet; drain well, pressing between paper towels. Wipe skillet clean.
2. Melt butter in skillet over medium heat. Add green onions and cilantro, and sauté 1 minute. Add eggs, salt, and pepper, and cook, without stirring, 2 minutes or until eggs begin to set on bottom. Gently draw cooked edges away from sides of pan to form large pieces. Cook, stirring occasionally, 4 to 5 minutes or until eggs are thickened but still moist. (Do not overstir.) Remove from heat, and gently fold in 1½ cups Cheese Sauce and sausage.
3. Spoon about ¾ cup egg mixture down center of each flour tortilla; roll up. Place, seam side down, in a lightly greased 13- x 9-inch baking dish. Pour remaining Cheese Sauce over tortillas; sprinkle with Monterey Jack cheese.
4. Bake at 350° for 30 minutes or until sauce is bubbly. Serve enchiladas with desired toppings.

Cheese Sauce:
MAKES ABOUT 4 CUPS; **PREP:** 10 MIN., **COOK:** 8 MIN.

⅓ cup butter
⅓ cup all-purpose flour
3 cups milk
1 (8-oz.) block Cheddar cheese, shredded (about 2 cups)
1 (4-oz.) can chopped green chiles
¾ tsp. salt

1. Melt butter in a heavy saucepan over medium-low heat; whisk in flour until smooth. Cook, whisking constantly, 1 minute. Gradually whisk in milk; cook over medium heat, whisking constantly, 7 minutes or until thickened. Remove from heat, and whisk in remaining ingredients until cheese is melted.

Enchilada Advice

- Associate Food Editor Mary Allen Perry likes the make-ahead ease of this enchilada casserole. Let it stand at room temperature for 30 minutes, and bake as directed. Make the Cheese Sauce before scrambling the eggs so the sauce will be ready to add at the proper time.
- Create an enchilada condiment bar stocked with sour cream, sliced pickled jalapeño peppers, traditional salsa, and salsa verde made from chopped green chiles.
- Freeze leftover enchiladas in pairs in airtight containers for four to six weeks.

Celebrate the Season

Winning Recipe: Breakfast Enchiladas (recipe on previous page)

Why we love it:

- "Hello? Mexican + Breakfast = Yum!"
  —**MARIAN COOPER CAIRNS**, TEST KITCHENS PROFESSIONAL
- "Brunch on Christmas Day has to be two things: make ahead and casual. Breakfast Enchiladas perfectly fill the bill. This casserole is family friendly. You just can't fail with Tex-Mex." —**ASHLEY LEATH**, ASSISTANT RECIPE EDITOR
- "The combination of cheesy goodness and Southwestern flavors makes it a crowd-pleaser. The fact that it can be made ahead is just salsa on the enchilada." —**MARY ALLEN PERRY**, ASSOCIATE FOOD EDITOR

Why you love it:

- "We have friends who make us Breakfast Enchiladas for Christmas every year. They deliver it in a 'breakfast basket,' which includes orange juice, coffees, and directions on how to bake the casserole. When we get up on Christmas morning, we pop it in the oven, and it bakes while we open presents. One Christmas they were out of town, and we didn't get one. We were sooooo disappointed." —**LINDA HAMRICK**, MARION, IOWA
- "I voted for Breakfast Enchiladas because my family and I love Mexican food anytime, especially for brunch. I make this recipe a little more healthful by using ground turkey sausage, egg substitute, and 2% shredded Mexican cheese blend." —**MARTHA HOWARD**, DAHLONEGA, GEORGIA

Hot Tomato Grits

MAKES 6 SERVINGS; **PREP:** 10 MIN.,
COOK: 30 MIN., **STAND:** 5 MIN.

This oh-so-Southern dish is perfect for breakfast but is fine for other meals too. Pair it with roast beef and green beans for a delicious Sunday supper. Warm your serving dish in a 100° oven or warming drawer for about 10 minutes before spooning in grits. Cook the bacon in advance to help trim last-minute hands-on preparation time.

2 bacon slices, chopped
2 (14½-oz.) cans chicken broth
½ tsp. salt
1 cup uncooked quick-cooking grits
2 large tomatoes, peeled and chopped
2 Tbsp. canned chopped green chiles
1 cup (4 oz.) shredded Cheddar cheese

1. Cook bacon in a heavy saucepan over medium-high heat 8 to 10 minutes or until crisp. Remove bacon, reserving drippings in pan. Drain bacon on paper towels.
2. Gradually add broth and salt to hot drippings in pan; bring to a boil. Stir in grits, tomatoes, and chiles; return to a boil, stirring often. Reduce heat, and simmer, stirring often, 15 to 20 minutes.
3. Stir in cheese; cover and let stand 5 minutes or until cheese is melted. Top with bacon. Serve immediately.

Skewered Fruit With Rum Drizzle

MAKES 8 SERVINGS; **PREP:** 25 MIN.,
SOAK: 30 MIN., **BROIL:** 10 MIN.

These kabobs are also great for dessert with vanilla ice cream and a sprinkle of toasted coconut. Involve budding chefs by having them help thread the fruit onto skewers.

8 to 10 (6-inch) wooden or metal skewers
2 bananas, cut into ½-inch slices
1 Tbsp. lemon juice
½ pineapple, peeled and cut into 1-inch pieces
2 star fruit, cut into ½-inch pieces*
2 Tbsp. sugar
¼ tsp. ground cinnamon
2 Tbsp. dark rum

1. Soak wooden skewers in hot water 30 minutes. Toss banana slices with lemon juice.
2. Thread banana slices, pineapple, and star fruit alternately onto skewers. Place on a wire rack in an aluminum foil-lined broiler pan. Cover and chill up to 8 hours, if desired.
3. Preheat oven to broil. Combine sugar and cinnamon; sprinkle over fruit.
4. Broil 4 inches from heat 5 minutes on each side or until lightly browned. Drizzle with rum.
*One peeled papaya, cut into ½-inch pieces, makes a tasty substitute if star fruit (carambola) is hard to find.

Pepper Jelly Danish

MAKES 8 SERVINGS; **PREP:** 25 MIN.,
BAKE: 18 MIN. PER BATCH

The versatile combination of cream cheese and pepper jelly travels from the cocktail party to the breakfast table in this super-simple Danish. We love this recipe prepared with jalapeño pepper jelly too. This combo is just as delicious in a pastry as it is spread on a cracker. Reader Martha Foose uses a locally produced honey-infused pepper jelly; we added 1 Tbsp. of honey to regular pepper jelly for a similar taste.

4 (8-oz.) cans refrigerated crescent rolls
1 (8-oz.) package cream cheese, softened
1 large egg, lightly beaten
⅓ cup red pepper jelly
1 Tbsp. honey

1. Preheat oven to 375°. Unroll 1 can crescent roll dough on a lightly floured surface; divide into 2 pieces, separating at center perforation. Press each piece into a 7-inch square, pressing perforations to seal.
2. Bring corners of each dough square to center, partially overlapping each; gently press corners into centers using thumb, making a small indentation. Repeat procedure with remaining cans of crescent rolls. Transfer to lightly greased baking sheets.
3. Stir together cream cheese and egg; stir together pepper jelly and honey. Spoon 2 Tbsp. cream cheese mixture into center of each dough circle, and top with 2 tsp. pepper jelly mixture.
4. Bake, in batches, at 375° for 15 to 18 minutes or until golden brown.

—**MARTHA FOOSE**, MOCKINGBIRD BAKERY,
GREENWOOD, MISSISSIPPI

Hot Chocolate With Almond Liqueur

fast fixin's

MAKES ABOUT 5 CUPS; **PREP:** 10 MIN.,
COOK: 8 MIN.

Test Kitchens Professional Marian Cooper Cairns recommends heating your serving container with warm water so that it won't cool down the hot chocolate mixture when you add it.

¼ cup boiling water
⅓ cup chocolate syrup
4 cups milk
⅓ cup almond liqueur

1. Stir together boiling water and chocolate syrup in a medium saucepan; add milk, stirring until blended. Cook over medium heat 6 to 8 minutes or until thoroughly heated. Remove from heat, and stir in liqueur.
Note: For testing purposes only, we used Amaretto for almond liqueur.

Hot Chocolate With Hazelnut Liqueur: Substitute hazelnut liqueur for almond liqueur. Proceed with recipe as directed.
Note: For testing purposes only, we used Frangelico for hazelnut liqueur.

Rudolph's Spritzer

make ahead

MAKES 2 ABOUT QT.; **PREP:** 10 MIN.

This light and sparkly citrus thirst-quencher is a tasty choice for children and adults. Serve it with maraschino cherries with stems to add pizzazz to each serving. For extra chill, freeze cherries in ice trays (do not add water).

5 cups orange juice
2 cups chilled lemon-lime soft drink
½ cup maraschino cherry juice
¼ cup fresh lemon juice

1. Stir together all ingredients; serve over ice.

Rudolph's Tipsy Spritzer:
Prepare recipe as directed. Stir in 1½ cups vodka. **Makes** about 9½ cups; Prep: 10 min.

Brunch Punch

fast fixin's • make ahead

MAKES ABOUT 3 QT.; **PREP:** 10 MIN.

1 (46-oz.) can pineapple juice, chilled
3 cups orange juice, chilled
2 cups cranberry juice, chilled
¾ cup powdered sugar
¼ cup lime juice

1. Stir together all ingredients. Serve immediately, or cover and chill 2 to 24 hours. Stir before serving.

Countdown to a Cocktail Supper

Pull out all the stops for a make-ahead crowd-pleasing meal.

Make-Ahead Magic

1 week ahead:
- Make and freeze cupcakes.

2 days ahead:
- Prepare Frozen Sangría, Mock Tea Sangría, and Caribbean Cashews.
- Prepare all dips, and place in serving dishes. (All the dips will easily double if you only want to make a few but still serve a crowd.)

1 day ahead:
- Prepare soup, and chill.
- Mix and form crab cakes; chill.
- Prep and chill vegetables for dip station.
- Label and arrange serving pieces.

4 hours ahead:
- Ice down beer and wine.
- Thaw cupcakes, and prepare frosting.
- Set out cupcake decorations.

2 hours ahead
- Place soup in slow cooker set on LOW to reheat.

1 hour ahead:
- Thaw Frozen Sangría.

30 minutes ahead
- Set out dips and vegetables.

Company's Coming

SERVES 8 TO 12

Maryland Crab Cakes With Creamy Caper-Dill Sauce

Caribbean Cashews

Bacon-Cheese Dip

Smoky Ranch Dip

Fresh Lemon-Basil Dip With Blanched Green Beans

Fresh Herb Sauce

Sun-dried Tomato Aïoli

Butternut Squash-Parsnip Soup

Mock Tea Sangría

Frozen Sangría

Create-your-own cupcake station

Hosting a cocktail party doesn't have to be a fancy affair. See how easy it is to feed a festive crowd with our delicious make-ahead recipes and drinks. Keep the party flowing by offering a different dish in rooms throughout the house, allowing guests to roam and mingle while they enjoy good food. For extra fun, offer a create-your-own cupcake station, where folks choose their favorite frosting and toppings.

Maryland Crab Cakes With Creamy Caper-Dill Sauce

winning recipe

MAKES 3 DOZEN; **PREP:** 30 MIN., **COOK:** 24 MIN., **CHILL:** 2 HR.

We recommend serving these crab cakes from a location near the kitchen so replenishing them is simpler. The large surface area of an electric skillet makes cooking the cakes easier.

2 lb. fresh lump crabmeat*
½ cup minced green onion
½ cup minced red bell pepper
1 Tbsp. olive oil
½ cup Italian-seasoned breadcrumbs
1 large egg, lightly beaten
½ cup mayonnaise
1 Tbsp. fresh lemon juice
1 tsp. Old Bay seasoning
½ tsp. pepper
Dash of Worcestershire sauce
2 Tbsp. butter
Garnish: fresh dill
Creamy Caper-Dill Sauce

1. Rinse, drain, and flake crabmeat, being careful not to break up lumps; remove any bits of shell.
2. Sauté green onion and bell pepper in hot oil in a large nonstick skillet 8 minutes or until tender. Stir together green onion mixture, breadcrumbs, and next 6 ingredients. Gently fold in crabmeat. Shape into 36 (1½-inch) patties (about 1 heaping tablespoonful each). Place on an aluminum foil-lined baking sheet; cover and chill 2 to 8 hours.
3. Melt butter in a large nonstick skillet over medium heat. Add patties, and cook, in batches, 3 to 4 minutes on each side or until golden. Drain on paper towels. Keep warm on a wire rack in a 200° oven. Garnish, if desired. Serve with Creamy Caper-Dill Sauce.
*Regular crabmeat may be substituted.
Note: You can make these up to 1 week ahead. Form the patties and freeze on

Celebrate the Season

a parchment paper-lined cookie sheet. Thaw overnight. Cook as directed.

Shrimp Cakes With Creamy Caper-Dill Sauce: Substitute 1 lb. peeled, medium-size cooked shrimp (36/40 count), deveined, for crabmeat. Pulse shrimp in a food processor 8 times or until finely chopped. Proceed with recipe as directed, beginning with Step 2 and shaping mixture into 28 (1-inch) patties (about 1 Tbsp. each). **Makes** 28 cakes; Prep: 30 min., Cook: 24 min., Chill: 2 hr.

Creamy Caper-Dill Sauce:
MAKES 1¼ CUPS; PREP: 10 MIN.

¾ cup mayonnaise
½ cup sour cream
¼ tsp. lemon zest
2 Tbsp. fresh lemon juice
1 Tbsp. drained capers
2 tsp. chopped fresh dill
1 tsp. Dijon mustard
¼ tsp. salt
¼ tsp. pepper

1. Stir together all ingredients. Store in an airtight container in refrigerator up to 3 days.

—ANN MCINERNEY, BETHESDA, MARYLAND

Caribbean Cashews
MAKES 2 CUPS; **PREP:** 5 MIN.,
BAKE: 24 MIN., **COOL:** 40 MIN.

You will want to make extra of this addictive snack to have on hand throughout the holidays. Store cashews in the freezer for up to a month.

1 Tbsp. butter
1 (9.75-oz.) container lightly salted whole cashews (about 2 cups)
2 tsp. orange zest
2 tsp. Caribbean jerk seasoning
Wax paper

Winning Recipe: Maryland Crab Cakes With Creamy Caper-Dill Sauce

Why we love it:
- "When people serve crab cakes, they always get praise. It is something that you don't have all the time, and this is a special Christmas occasion."
  —VANESSA MCNEIL ROCCHIO, TEST KITCHENS SPECIALIST
- "These are meaty, not full of filler like so many cakes. You can really taste the crab. It's nice to be able to cook them on the griddle—that allows you to serve up a lot of them at one time." —DONNA FLORIO, FOOD SENIOR WRITER

Why you love it:
- "My family loves this recipe. I'm from Maryland, and this recipe, with the Creamy Caper-Dill Sauce, is a new twist from the traditional way Maryland crab cakes are served. Wow, wow, wow!"
  —BEVERLY O'FERRALL, LINKWOOD, MARYLAND
- "Nothing beats this recipe. In fact, it's so good I suggest doubling the recipe, as people tend to eat twice what you expect."
  —WYVETA KIRK, BENTON, ARKANSAS

1. Preheat oven to 350°. Heat butter in an 8-inch cake pan in oven 3 to 4 minutes or until melted; stir in nuts, orange zest, and seasoning.
2. Bake at 350° for 20 minutes, stirring occasionally. Arrange cashews in a single layer on wax paper, and let cool completely (about 40 minutes). Store in an airtight container.

Caribbean Almonds: Substitute whole natural almonds (with skin) for cashews. Proceed with recipe as directed, stirring ½ tsp. salt in with jerk seasoning.

Caribbean Pecans: Substitute pecan halves for cashews. Proceed with recipe as directed, stirring ½ tsp. salt in with jerk seasoning.

Bacon-Cheese Dip
make ahead
MAKES 1½ CUPS; PREP: 20 MIN.,
CHILL: 2 HR., STAND: 15 MIN.

½ cup sour cream
1 (4-oz.) package crumbled blue cheese
1 (3-oz.) package cream cheese, softened
2 Tbsp. diced onion
⅛ tsp. hot sauce
4 bacon slices, cooked and crumbled
Garnishes: chopped fresh parsley, crumbled blue cheese
Assorted crackers

1. Process first 5 ingredients in a blender or food processor until smooth, stopping to scrape down sides. Stir in half of bacon. Cover and chill 2 hours. Let stand at room temperature 15 minutes before serving. Sprinkle with remaining bacon. Garnish, if desired. Serve with assorted crackers.

Celebrate the Season

Smoky Ranch Dip

make ahead

MAKES ABOUT 1½ CUPS; **PREP:** 5 MIN.,
CHILL: 30 MIN.

*We love this dip so much that we created
four variations that are sure to please a
crowd.*

1 (1-oz.) envelope Ranch dressing mix
1½ cups light sour cream
2 tsp. finely chopped canned chipotle
    peppers in adobo sauce
1 tsp. adobo sauce from can
Potato chips, assorted vegetables

1. Whisk together first 4 ingredients.
Cover and chill 30 minutes. Serve with
chips or assorted vegetables.

       —**MATT CAINE**, HELENA, ALABAMA

Barbecue Ranch Dip: Omit chipotle peppers and adobo sauce. Stir in
2 Tbsp. barbecue sauce. Serve with
roasted red new potatoes.

Lime-Cilantro Ranch Dip: Omit
chipotle peppers and adobo sauce. Stir
in 1 Tbsp. chopped fresh cilantro and
1 Tbsp. fresh lime juice. Serve with
quesadillas, tacos, or chili.

Lemon-Parsley Ranch Dip: Omit
chipotle peppers and adobo sauce. Stir
in 1 Tbsp. chopped fresh parsley and
1 Tbsp. fresh lemon juice. Serve with
steamed asparagus.

Horseradish Ranch Spread:
Omit chipotle peppers and adobo
sauce. Stir in 2 tsp. horseradish. Spread
on dinner rolls, and top with thinly
sliced deli roast beef.

Green Bean Blanching How-To

- Be sure to trim green beans before blanching.
- Cook beans, in batches, in boiling water to cover 3 to 5 minutes or until crisp-
tender. Plunge into ice water to stop the cooking process; drain. Cover and
chill beans until ready to serve with dip.

Fresh Lemon-Basil Dip With Blanched Green Beans

MAKES ABOUT 25 SERVINGS; **PREP:** 20 MIN.

2 cups mayonnaise
1 cup chopped fresh basil
1 (8-oz.) container sour cream
2 Tbsp. lemon zest
¼ tsp. salt
Garnishes: lemon zest, lemon slices
6 lb. fresh green beans, blanched
    (see How-To box above)

1. Whisk together first 5 ingredients until blended. Cover and chill.
Garnish, if desired. Serve with
blanched green beans.

Fresh Herb Sauce

MAKES ABOUT 1½ CUPS; **PREP:** 10 MIN.

*When storing, cover the surface of the
sauce with plastic wrap to prevent discoloration. It should keep for 1 week in
the refrigerator.*

2 garlic cloves
1 (1-oz.) package fresh basil leaves, stems
    removed
4 mint sprigs, stems removed
1 cup firmly packed fresh flat-leaf parsley
    leaves (about 1 bunch)
½ cup grated Parmesan cheese
½ tsp. salt
½ tsp. freshly ground pepper
½ cup warm water
½ cup olive oil
2 Tbsp. red wine vinegar
Assorted vegetables

1. Process garlic in a food processor 20
seconds or until minced. Add basil and
next 5 ingredients; process 10 seconds.
2. Whisk together ½ cup warm water,
oil, and vinegar. With processor running, pour oil mixture through food
chute in a slow, steady stream, processing just until blended. Serve with
assorted vegetables.

Sun-dried Tomato Aïoli

make ahead • fast fixin's

MAKES 2 CUPS; **PREP:** 10 MIN.

*Jazz up a turkey sandwich with some
leftover äioli.*

1½ cups light mayonnaise
⅓ cup firmly packed sun-dried tomatoes in
    oil, drained
¼ cup milk
1 garlic clove
1 tsp. chopped fresh rosemary
1 tsp. lemon zest
½ tsp. salt
½ tsp. freshly ground pepper
Garnish: rosemary sprig
Potato chips, assorted vegetables

1. Process all ingredients in a food
processor 15 seconds or until smooth,
stopping to scrape down sides as
needed. Cover and chill until ready to
serve. Garnish, if desired. Serve with
assorted chips and vegetables. Store in
an airtight container in refrigerator up
to 1 week.

Butternut Squash-Parsnip Soup

make ahead

MAKES ABOUT 6 CUPS; **PREP:** 15 MIN.;
STAND: 1 HR.; **COOK:** 2 HR., 30 MIN.

Reduce the heat on the slow cooker to WARM once guests arrive.

2 Tbsp. butter
2 Tbsp. olive oil
1 large sweet onion, chopped
3 parsnips, peeled and chopped*
1 Granny Smith apple, peeled, cored, and chopped
1½ tsp. salt
1 tsp. pepper
3 (12-oz.) packages frozen butternut squash, thawed**
5 cups low-sodium fat-free chicken broth
¼ cup whipping cream
⅛ tsp. paprika
⅛ tsp. ground cumin
Garnishes: chopped fresh chives, sour cream

1. Melt butter with olive oil in a large Dutch oven over medium heat; add onion and next 4 ingredients, and sauté 20 minutes or until onion is caramel colored. Add squash and chicken broth. Bring to a boil over medium-high heat. Reduce heat to medium, and simmer, stirring often, 10 minutes. Remove from heat; let stand 1 hour. If desired, cover and chill up to 2 days.
2. Process squash mixture, in batches, in a blender or food processor until smooth, stopping to scrape down sides. Pour mixture into a 6-qt. slow cooker. Stir in whipping cream, paprika, and cumin. Cover and cook on LOW 2 hours, stirring occasionally. Garnish, if desired.
*3 carrots, peeled and chopped, may be substituted.
1 (3- to 4-lb.) butternut squash may be substituted. Preheat oven to 400°. Cut squash in half; remove seeds. Place squash, cut sides down, on a lightly greased aluminum foil-lined baking sheet. Bake at 400° for 45 minutes or until squash pulp is tender. Remove from oven. Let cool 20 minutes. Scoop out squash pulp, discarding shells. **Note: For testing purposes only, we used McKenzie's Southland Microwaveable Butternut Squash.

Mock Tea Sangría

make ahead

MAKES 9 CUPS; **PREP:** 25 MIN.,
STEEP: 5 MIN. **CHILL:** 2 HR.

You can substitute 1 cup orange juice and 1 cup lemon-lime soft drink for orange soft drink.

1 (10-oz.) package frozen raspberries, thawed
⅓ cup sugar
1 family-size tea bag
2 cups red grape juice
1 lemon, sliced
1 lime, sliced
1 (16-oz.) bottle orange soft drink, chilled

1. Process raspberries in a blender or food processor until smooth, stopping to scrape down sides. Pour puree through a fine wire-mesh strainer into a large container, discarding raspberry seeds.
2. Bring sugar and 3 cups water to a boil in a saucepan, stirring often. Remove from heat; add tea bag. Cover and steep 5 minutes.
3. Remove tea bag with a slotted spoon, squeezing gently; cool tea mixture slightly. Stir together raspberry puree, tea mixture, grape juice, and lemon and lime slices. Cover and chill 2 to 48 hours. Stir in orange soft drink, and serve immediately over ice.

Frozen Sangría

freezeable • make ahead

MAKES ABOUT 1½ GAL.; **PREP:** 10 MIN.,
FREEZE: 24 HR.

This makes about 24 servings without breaking the bank. Total cost is about $13.

1 gal. sangría
1 (12-oz.) can frozen limeade concentrate, thawed
1 (2-liter) bottle lemon-lime soft drink
2 cups sliced oranges, lemons, and limes

1. Place 1 (2-gal.) zip-top plastic freezer bag inside another 2-gal. zip-top plastic freezer bag. Place bags in a large bowl. Combine first 3 ingredients in the inside bag. Seal both bags, and freeze 24 hours. (Double bagging is a precaution to avoid spills.)
2. Remove mixture from freezer 1 hour before serving, squeezing occasionally until slushy. Transfer mixture to a 2-gal. container. Stir in fruit.

—PATRICIA LETTUNICH AND VALERIE DAVIS,
FABENS, TEXAS

Kid-Friendly Frozen Sangría:
Substitute cranberry juice for sangría. Proceed with recipe as directed.

Create a Cupcake Station

As a fun finale, set up a decorate-and serve-yourself cupcake station.

- **The cupcakes:** Bake both types of cupcakes if you'd like to offer flavor options. If you're short on time, bake them up to a week ahead and freeze them, or pick up unfrosted cupcakes at your local bakery.
- **The frostings:** Spoon each flavor of buttercream frosting into a clear plastic piping bag, twisting the top of the bag closed and tying it off with a tartan plaid holiday ribbon. Label the frosting flavors. Set the piping bags next to the cupcakes.
- **The decorations:** Set out bowls of colorful toppings. Options include assorted red and green holiday candies, colored sugar sprinkles, chopped créme de menthe chocolate mints, and flaked coconut.

Basic White Cupcakes

MAKES 2 DOZEN; **PREP:** 10 MIN.;
BAKE: 25 MIN.; **COOL:** 1 HR., 10 MIN.

You can also stir these together by hand with great results. Because the mixer adds more air to the batter, you'll end up with 17 cupcakes rather than 24 when you stir them by hand.

1 (18.25-oz.) package white cake mix with pudding
1¼ cups buttermilk
¼ cup butter, melted
2 large eggs
2 tsp. vanilla extract
½ tsp. almond extract
Paper baking cups
Vegetable cooking spray
Desired buttercream

1. Preheat oven to 350°. Beat first 6 ingredients at low speed with an electric mixer just until dry ingredients are moistened. Increase speed to medium, and beat

2 minutes or until batter is smooth, stopping to scrape bowl as needed.
2. Place paper baking cups in muffin pans, and coat with cooking spray; spoon batter into baking cups, filling two-thirds full
3. Bake at 350° for 20 to 25 minutes or until a wooden pick inserted in center comes out clean. Cool in pans on wire racks 10 minutes; remove from pans to wire racks, and let cool completely (about 1 hour). Spread cupcakes with desired buttercream.
Note: For testing purposes only, we used Pillsbury Moist Supreme Classic White Cake Mix.

Coconut Cupcakes: Prepare Basic White Cupcakes as directed. Spread with Coconut Buttercream (recipe at right), and sprinkle with sweetened flaked coconut.

Moist Chocolate Cupcakes

MAKES 2 DOZEN; **PREP:** 10 MIN.;
BAKE: 25 MIN.; **COOL:** 1 HR., 10 MIN.

1 (18.25-oz.) package German chocolate cake mix
1 (16-oz.) container sour cream
¼ cup butter, melted
2 large eggs
1 tsp. vanilla extract
Paper baking cups
Vegetable cooking spray
Desired buttercream

1. Preheat oven to 350°. Beat first 5 ingredients at low speed with an electric mixer just until dry ingredients are moistened. Increase speed to medium, and beat 1 to 2 minutes or until smooth, stopping to scrape bowl as needed.
2. Place paper baking cups in muffin pans, and coat with cooking spray; spoon batter into baking cups, filling two-thirds full.
3. Bake at 350° for 20 to 25 minutes or until a wooden pick inserted in center comes out clean. Cool in pans on wire racks 10 minutes; remove cupcakes

from pans to wire racks, and let cool completely (about 1 hour). Spread with desired buttercream.

Chocolate-Mint Cupcakes: Prepare cupcakes as directed. Prepare Chocolate Buttercream as directed, stirring in ¼ cup finely chopped thin crème de menthe chocolate mints. Frost cupcakes. Garnish with shaved or chopped thin crème de menthe chocolate mints, if desired.
Note: For testing purposes only, we used Andes Thins: Creme de Menthe.

Vanilla Buttercream

MAKES 3 CUPS; **PREP:** 10 MIN.

½ cup butter, softened
1 (3-oz.) package cream cheese, softened
1 (16-oz.) package powdered sugar
¼ cup milk
1 tsp. vanilla extract
Garnishes: green candy-coated chocolate pieces, green candy sprinkles

1. Beat butter and cream cheese at medium speed with an electric mixer until creamy. Gradually add powdered sugar, beating at low speed until mixture is blended. Slowly beat in milk and vanilla. Increase speed to medium, and beat until smooth. Garnish, if desired.

Chocolate Buttercream: Prepare Vanilla Buttercream as directed. Microwave 1 cup (6 oz.) dark chocolate morsels in a microwave-safe bowl at MEDIUM (50% power) 1½ to 2 minutes or until melted and smooth, stirring at 30-second intervals. Gradually add melted chocolate to Vanilla Buttercream; beat until blended.
Note: For testing purposes only, we used Hershey's Special Dark Chocolate Chips.

Coconut Buttercream: Prepare Vanilla Buttercream as directed, substituting cream of coconut for milk.

New Year's Day Party

Launch the year with a luxe gathering that extends the glimmer of the holidays one more day.

January 1 Get-together

SERVES ABOUT 12

11 a.m. Come On In

Hot Roast Beef Party Sandwiches

Red Roosters

Fruity Salad With Sugared Almonds and Sweet-Hot Vinaigrette

2 p.m. Halftime Sampler

Warm Turnip Green Dip

Grilled Herbed Chicken Drumettes With White Barbecue Sauce

Dixie Caviar Cups

Peel-and-Eat Shrimp With Dipping Sauces

4 p.m. Sweet Wrap-Up

Dressed Up Cheesecake Bars

Make a New Year's resolution to host this casual party. Welcome friends with a Red Rooster—the toasting beverage of the day. Steer them toward the awesome Hot Roast Beef Party Sandwiches, our Fruity Salad With Sugared Almonds and Sweet-Hot Vinaigrette, and a comfy seat to catch glimpses of the bowl games on your big screen. Near party's end indulge in Dressed Up Cheesecake Bars.

Hot Roast Beef Party Sandwiches

winning recipe

MAKES 12 TO 16 SERVINGS; **PREP:** 20 MIN., **COOK:** 6 MIN., **BAKE:** 30 MIN.

Get ahead of holiday parties. Plan to stash a few batches of these casual, three-bite sandwiches in your freezer. Read more about our winning recipe on the following page

½ cup finely chopped walnuts
2 (9.25-oz.) packages dinner rolls
⅔ cup peach preserves
½ cup mustard-mayonnaise blend
¾ lb. thinly sliced deli roast beef, chopped
½ lb. thinly sliced Havarti cheese
Salt and pepper (optional)

1. Preheat oven to 325°.
2. Heat walnuts in a small nonstick skillet over medium-low heat, stirring often, 5 to 6 minutes or until lightly toasted and fragrant.
3. Remove rolls from packages. (Do not separate rolls.) Cut rolls in half horizontally, creating 1 top and 1 bottom per package. Spread preserves on cut sides of top of rolls; sprinkle with walnuts. Spread mustard-mayonnaise blend on cut sides of bottom of rolls; top with roast beef and cheese. Sprinkle with salt and pepper, if desired. Cover with top halves of rolls, preserves sides down, and wrap in aluminum foil.
4. Bake at 325° for 30 minutes or until cheese is melted. Slice into individual sandwiches. Serve immediately.
Note: To make ahead, prepare recipe as directed through Step 3, and freeze up to 1 month. Thaw overnight in refrigerator, and bake as directed in Step 4. For testing purposes only, we used Rainbo Dinner Time Rolls, Hellmann's Dijonnaise Creamy Dijon Mustard, and Boar's Head Londonport Roast Beef.

Red Roosters

fast fixin's

MAKES 9 CUPS; **PREP:** 5 MIN.

Make up several pitchers of this not-too-sweet beverage, cover them, and chill before the party starts. Or try our freeze-ahead Slushy Red Roosters, and ask a guest to tend the blender.

4 cups cranberry juice cocktail
3 cups orange juice
2 cups vodka
Garnishes: fresh cranberries, lemon slices

1. Stir together first 3 ingredients in a large pitcher. Serve over ice. Garnish, if desired.

Slushy Red Roosters: Substitute 1 (12-oz.) can frozen orange juice concentrate, thawed, for 3 cups orange juice. Stir together cranberry juice cocktail, orange juice concentrate, vodka, and 4½ cups water. Place 1 (1-gal.) zip-top plastic freezer bag inside another 1-gal. zip-top plastic freezer bag. Pour about 4 cups cranberry mixture into inside bag. Seal both bags. Repeat procedure with remaining cranberry mixture. (Double bagging is a precaution to avoid spills.) Freeze bags 24 hours. Remove bags from freezer; let stand 5 minutes. Process cranberry mixture, 1 bag at a time, in a blender or food processor until desired consistency. Pour into glasses. Serve immediately. **Makes** 3 qt.; Prep: 10 min., Freeze: 24 hr., Stand: 5 min.

—JUDI BURNS, MONROEVILLE, ALABAMA

Winning Recipe: Hot Roast Beef Party Sandwiches (recipe on previous page)

Why we love it:

- "This is such a great, updated twist on the classic ham-on-poppy seed rolls recipe. It's so simple to make and can be prepared ahead and frozen. It's perfect for this busy time of year." —**LYDA JONES BURNETTE**, TEST KITCHENS DIRECTOR
- "The recipe's petite size and easy use for a variety of parties make it incredibly versatile. New Year's Day celebrations are usually more laid-back and informal, and these sandwiches are the perfect snack."
  —**NORMAN KING**, TEST KITCHENS PROFESSIONAL

Why you love it:

- "Easy on the budget and huge on the taste buds." —**KIM CLAY**, LAWRENCEVILLE, GEORGIA
- "I love these sandwiches because they can be prepared way ahead, giving you more time to enjoy the party. Plus, using peach preserves is so Southern." —**MITZI POOLE**, MOBILE, ALABAMA
- "My hands-down favorite. To save time, I prepare several batches ahead of time by spreading the ingredients on the entire loaf at once instead of making individual sandwiches. I wrap them in foil packets and stash in a warm oven. This way I can replenish trays of hot sandwiches throughout the party."
  —**CATHERINE MCCOY**, FREDERICK, MARYLAND

Fruity Salad With Sugared Almonds and Sweet-Hot Vinaigrette

MAKES 12 SERVINGS; **PREP:** 15 MIN.

Salads can get messy-looking when you're serving buffet style. So make the salad on two platters: One to put out when guests arrive, and a second (covered with plastic wrap and kept in the fridge) to bring out when the first is almost gone.

1 head Bibb lettuce, torn
2 (5-oz.) packages gourmet mixed salad greens, thoroughly washed*
1 fresh peeled and cored pineapple, cut into ½-inch cubes (about 3 cups)
4 kiwifruit, peeled and sliced
2 (11-oz.) cans mandarin oranges, drained and chilled
1 cup green or red seedless grapes, cut in half
Sugared Almonds
Sweet-Hot Vinaigrette

1. Toss lettuce and salad greens together in a large bowl. Place lettuce mixture on 2 large serving platters. Top with pineapple and next 3 ingredients. Sprinkle with Sugared Almonds, and serve with Sweet-Hot Vinaigrette.
*10 cups loosely packed, torn salad greens may be substituted.

Sugared Almonds:
make ahead
MAKES 1 CUP; **PREP:** 5 MIN., **COOK:** 8 MIN., **COOL:** 20 MIN.

These are so good, you might have to make an extra batch to snack on.

1 cup slivered almonds
½ cup sugar
Wax paper

1. Stir together almonds and sugar in a large 3½-qt. saucepan over medium heat, and cook, stirring constantly, 8 minutes or until golden and fragrant. (Sugar will clump initially; continue stirring until melted and golden.) Spread mixture in an even layer on lightly greased wax paper on a baking sheet, and let cool 20 minutes. Break into pieces, and store in an airtight container up to 1 week.

Sweet-Hot Vinaigrette:
make ahead
MAKES 1 CUP; **PREP:** 5 MIN., **CHILL:** 30 MIN.

Whisk the dressing right before serving. Or prep in a container with a lid, make sure it seals tightly, and shake to remix.

½ cup vegetable oil
½ cup balsamic vinegar
¼ cup sugar
½ tsp. salt
½ tsp. pepper
½ tsp. hot sauce

1. Whisk together all ingredients. Cover and chill 30 minutes. Store in an airtight container in refrigerator for up to 3 days.
—**ANDREA DUCHARME**, LAFAYETTE, LOUISIANA

● **TIP** ●

The salad dressing and sugared almonds can be made several days ahead. Pineapple, oranges, and grapes can be prepped a day ahead.

Warm Turnip Green Dip
make ahead

MAKES 4 CUPS; **PREP:** 15 MIN.,
COOK: 20 MIN., **BROIL:** 5 MIN.

To make the dish spicier, offer guests several brands of hot sauce on the side.

5 bacon slices, chopped
½ medium-size sweet onion, chopped
2 garlic cloves, chopped
¼ cup dry white wine
1 (16-oz.) package frozen chopped turnip
   greens, thawed
12 oz. cream cheese, cut into pieces
1 (8-oz.) container sour cream
½ tsp. dried crushed red pepper
¼ tsp. salt
¾ cup freshly grated Parmesan cheese
Garnish: dried crushed red pepper
Assorted crackers, flatbread, and gourmet
   wafers

1. Preheat oven to broil. Cook chopped bacon in a Dutch oven over medium-high heat 5 to 6 minutes or until crisp; remove bacon, and drain on paper towels, reserving 1 Tbsp. drippings in Dutch oven.
2. Sauté onion and garlic in hot drippings 3 to 4 minutes. Add wine, and cook 1 to 2 minutes, stirring to loosen particles from bottom of Dutch oven. Stir in turnip greens, next 4 ingredients, and ½ cup Parmesan cheese. Cook, stirring often, 6 to 8 minutes or until cream cheese is melted and mixture is thoroughly heated. Transfer to a lightly greased 1½-qt. baking dish. (Make certain that you use a broiler-safe baking dish.) Sprinkle with remaining ¼ cup Parmesan cheese.
3. Broil 6 inches from heat 4 to 5 minutes or until cheese is lightly browned. Sprinkle with bacon. Garnish, if desired. Serve with assorted crackers, flatbread, and wafers.
Note: To make ahead, prepare recipe as directed through Step 2. Cover

and chill 8 hours. Bake, covered with aluminum foil, at 350° for 30 minutes. Uncover and bake 30 minutes. Sprinkle with bacon. Serve with assorted crackers and chips.

Warm Spinach-Artichoke Dip: Substitute 2 (10-oz.) packages frozen spinach, thawed and drained, and 1 (14-oz.) can quartered artichoke hearts, drained and coarsely chopped, for turnip greens. Proceed with recipe as directed.

Grilled Herbed Chicken Drumettes With White Barbecue Sauce
family favorite

MAKES 12 SERVINGS; **PREP:** 15 MIN.,
CHILL: 4 HR., **GRILL:** 25 MIN.

Depending on where you live in the South, it may be 85° on January 1 or chilly. If it's the latter, our team says to "bundle up, and do it." The grilled herb flavors and juicy results are worth a brief shiver. After you place the chicken on the grill, don't move it until time to turn or the chicken will stick to the cooking grate.

1 Tbsp. dried thyme
1 Tbsp. dried oregano
1 Tbsp. ground cumin
1 Tbsp. paprika
1 tsp. onion powder
1 tsp. salt
½ tsp. pepper
5 lb. chicken drumettes
White Barbecue Sauce
Garnish: green onion curls

1. Combine first 7 ingredients. Rinse chicken, and pat dry; rub mixture over chicken. Place chicken in a zip-top plastic freezer bag. Seal bag, and chill 4 to 24 hours. Remove chicken from bag, discarding bag.

2. Preheat grill to 350° to 400° (medium-high) heat. Grill chicken, covered with grill lid, over medium-high heat 20 to 25 minutes or until done, turning once. Serve with White Barbecue Sauce. Garnish, if desired.

Grilled Herbed Chicken Drumsticks: Substitute 10 to 12 drumsticks for drumettes. Proceed with recipe as directed, increasing grilling time to 25 to 30 minutes or until done, turning once. **Makes** 12 drumsticks; Prep: 15 min., Chill: 4 hr., Grill: 30 min.

White Barbecue Sauce:
make ahead

MAKES 1¾ CUPS; **PREP:** 10 MIN.

1½ cups mayonnaise
¼ cup white wine vinegar
1 garlic clove, minced
1 Tbsp. coarsely ground pepper
1 Tbsp. spicy brown mustard
2 tsp. horseradish
1 tsp. sugar
1 tsp. salt

1. Stir together all ingredients until well blended. Cover and chill until ready to serve. Store in an airtight container in refrigerator up to 1 week.

Dixie Caviar Cups

MAKES 15 APPETIZER SERVINGS;
PREP: 15 MIN., **CHILL:** 24 HR.

Here's to good luck for the year! Show off a few Dixie Cups assembled, and then let guests make their own cups. Or, for a more casual presentation, serve black-eyed pea mixture in a bowl, garnish with sour cream, and serve with scoop-style tortilla chips.

1 (15.8-oz.) can black-eyed peas, rinsed and drained
1 cup frozen whole kernel corn
1 medium-size plum tomato, seeded and finely chopped
½ medium-size green bell pepper, finely chopped
½ small sweet onion, finely chopped
2 green onions, sliced
1 jalapeño pepper, seeded and minced*
1 garlic clove, minced
½ cup Italian dressing
2 Tbsp. chopped fresh cilantro
30 Belgian endive leaves (about 3 bunches)
½ cup sour cream

1. Combine first 9 ingredients in a large zip-top plastic freezer bag. Seal bag, and chill 24 hours; drain.
2. Spoon mixture into a bowl; stir in cilantro. Spoon about 1 rounded Tbsp. mixture into each endive leaf. Dollop with sour cream.

—INSPIRED BY CAMILLE WARLICK,
MERIGOLD, MISSISSIPPI

*2¼ tsp. finely chopped pickled jalapeño peppers may be substituted.
Note: For testing purposes only, we used Bush's Best Blackeye Peas.

Peel-and-Eat Shrimp With Dipping Sauces

MAKES 12 SERVINGS; **PREP:** 10 MIN.,
COOK: 5 MIN., **STAND:** 20 MIN.

Set up a serving area for the shrimp and sauces, and let everyone help themselves. To shortcut prep, ask your seafood monger to steam the shrimp for you.

¼ cup Old Bay seasoning
3 lb. unpeeled, large raw shrimp (26/30 count)
Garnishes: lemon slices and wedges, fresh parsley sprigs
Tangy Garlic Tartar Sauce
Smoky Rémoulade Sauce
Spicy Cocktail Sauce

1. Combine 9 cups water and Old Bay seasoning in a Dutch oven. Bring to a boil; add shrimp. Cover, remove from heat, and let stand 15 to 20 minutes or just until shrimp turn pink. Drain well; garnish, if desired. Serve immediately with sauces.

Chilled Peel-and-Eat Shrimp With Dipping Sauces: Prepare recipe as directed. Place cooked shrimp in a glass bowl. Cover and chill 2 to 24 hours. Serve with sauces. Prep: 10 min., Cook: 5 min., Chill: 2 hr.

Tangy Garlic Tartar Sauce:

MAKES ABOUT 2¼ CUPS; **PREP:** 10 MIN.,
CHILL: 2 HR.

2 cups mayonnaise*
1 (3.5-oz.) jar capers, drained
3 garlic cloves, pressed
¼ cup Dijon mustard

1. Combine all ingredients in a blender; process until smooth, stopping once to scrape down sides. Cover and chill 2 hours before serving. Store in an airtight container in refrigerator up to 3 days.
*Light mayonnaise may be substituted.

Smoky Rémoulade Sauce:

make ahead

MAKES ABOUT 2 CUPS; **PREP:** 10 MIN.,
CHILL: 2 HR.

2 cups mayonnaise
¼ cup Creole mustard
2 large garlic cloves, pressed
2 Tbsp. chopped fresh parsley
1 Tbsp. fresh lemon juice
2¼ tsp. smoked paprika*
¾ tsp. ground red pepper

1. Whisk together all ingredients until blended. Cover and chill 2 hours before serving. Store in an airtight container in refrigerator up to 3 days.
*Regular paprika may be substituted.

Spicy Cocktail Sauce:

make ahead

MAKES ABOUT 2 CUPS; **PREP:** 10 MIN.,
CHILL: 30 MIN.

¾ cup bottled chili sauce
½ cup ketchup
6 Tbsp. horseradish
2 Tbsp. plus 2 tsp. fresh lemon juice
2¼ tsp. Worcestershire sauce
1 to 1½ tsp. hot sauce
¼ tsp. salt
¼ tsp. pepper

1. Stir together all ingredients until blended. Cover and chill 30 minutes before serving. Store in an airtight container in refrigerator up to 5 days.
Note: For testing purposes only, we used Heinz Chili Sauce.

Dressed Up Cheesecake Bars

MAKES 2 DOZEN; **PREP:** 15 MIN.;
BAKE: 48 MIN.; **COOL:** 2 HR., 20 MIN.;
CHILL: 8 HR.

We did not call for sugar in the crust—it's tasty without it, and the sauces add sweetness. Arrange a mini buffet so guests may customize their cheesecake bars with sauces and sprinkles.

2 cups graham cracker crumbs
½ cup butter, melted
4 (8-oz.) packages cream cheese, softened
¾ cup sugar
¼ cup all-purpose flour
3 large eggs
1 Tbsp. vanilla extract
Cherries Jubilee Sauce
Dark Chocolate Sauce
Hot Caramel Sauce
Cashew-and-Gingered-Apricot Sprinkles
Whipped Cream (optional)

1. Preheat oven to 350°. Stir together graham cracker crumbs and butter; press into bottom of a lightly greased 13- x 9-inch pan.
2. Bake at 350° for 8 minutes. Remove from oven, and cool completely on a wire rack (about 20 minutes).
3. Beat cream cheese at medium speed with an electric mixer until smooth. Combine sugar and flour; gradually add to cream cheese, beating just until blended. Add eggs, 1 at a time, beating until blended after each addition. Stir in vanilla. Pour mixture over prepared crust, spreading to edges of pan.
4. Bake at 350° for 35 to 40 minutes or until set. Remove from oven, and cool on a wire rack (about 2 hours). Cover and chill 8 hours. Cut into bars. Serve with Cherries Jubilee Sauce, Dark Chocolate Sauce, Hot Caramel Sauce, and Cashew-and-Gingered-Apricot Sprinkles. Dollop with whipped cream, if desired.

Cherries Jubilee Sauce:

MAKES 3 CUPS; **PREP:** 10 MIN.,
COOK: 8 MIN.

The cherries for this recipe come in a bag and do not have syrup, liquid, or sweetening. Any time you add alcohol to a pan of ingredients, remove the pan from the heat first.

½ cup sugar
1 Tbsp. cornstarch
½ cup orange juice
2 (12-oz.) packages frozen dark sweet cherries (do not thaw)
½ tsp. orange zest (optional)
¼ cup brandy
Garnish: orange zest

1. Whisk sugar and cornstarch in a medium skillet; whisk in orange juice. Cook over medium heat, whisking constantly, 2 minutes or until thickened. Stir in cherries, and, if desired, orange zest. Bring to a boil over medium heat; reduce heat, and simmer, stirring often, 5 minutes. Remove from heat.
2. Stir in brandy, and return to heat. Cook, stirring constantly, 30 seconds. Cool slightly. Garnish, if desired.
Note: Try this sauce on pancakes or waffles for an indulgent breakfast.

Dark Chocolate Sauce:

fast fixin's

MAKES ABOUT 1 CUP; **PREP:** 5 MIN.

1 (4-oz.) bittersweet chocolate baking bar, chopped
¾ cup heavy cream

1. Microwave chocolate and cream in a small microwave-safe bowl at HIGH 1½ minutes or until melted and smooth, stirring at 30-second intervals.
Note: For testing purposes only, we used Ghirardelli 60% Cocoa Bittersweet Chocolate Baking Bar.

Hot Caramel Sauce:

make ahead

MAKES 2 CUPS; **PREP:** 5 MIN.,
COOK: 7 MIN., **COOL:** 10 MIN.

1½ cups firmly packed light brown sugar
¾ cup butter
¾ cup whipping cream
2 tsp. vanilla extract
Garnish: chopped pecans

1. Cook brown sugar and butter in a heavy 2-qt. saucepan over medium heat, stirring constantly, 3 to 4 minutes or until butter is melted and mixture is smooth.
2. Gradually stir in whipping cream. Bring mixture to a boil over medium heat, stirring constantly; boil, stirring constantly, 3 minutes. Remove from heat; stir in vanilla. Cool 10 minutes before serving. Garnish, if desired.
Note: To make ahead, prepare recipe as directed. Cover and chill up to 1 week. Reheat in a microwave-safe bowl at MEDIUM-HIGH (70% power) 3 to 4 minutes or until bubbly, stirring at 1-minute intervals. Cool slightly.

Cashew-and-Gingered-Apricot Sprinkles:

fast fixin's

MAKES ABOUT 1 CUP; **PREP:** 10 MIN.

Crystallized ginger is usually packaged in a glass jar and sold along with other spices, but we've found it, for a lower price, in the ethnic food and dried fruit aisles. The pieces are larger and will take longer to mince. Stir these ingredients together just before serving to keep the nuts crunchy.

½ cup chopped salted cashews
⅓ cup finely chopped dried apricots
2 Tbsp. minced crystallized ginger

1. Stir together all ingredients.

Grand & Gracious

Festive decorations and fabulous food set the perfect tone for a spirited feast.

Such a Delectable Dinner

SERVES 8

Beef Tenderloin With Henry Bain Sauce

Sweet Onion Pudding

Simple Roasted Asparagus

Baby Blue Salad

Creamy Bell Pepper 'n' Tomato Soup

Refrigerator Yeast Rolls

Cream Cheese-Coconut-Pecan Pound Cake

Once they're seated in the fabulous setting you've created, your guests will be thrilled with the menu you've chosen. It's a beautiful balance of delicacies—some to make ahead and others that you can prepare immediately before the meal.

Many of these are recipes that the *Southern Living* Food staff turns to time and again for our own celebrations, as so many readers do. Entrées don't come any grander than beef tenderloin, and the Henry Bain Sauce served with this one is a Kentucky classic. Surround it with top-rated sides, and you have a meal guaranteed to make memories. But the final bite is often the one you remember most, and you chose Cream Cheese-Coconut-Pecan Pound Cake to finish off this fabulous meal.

Beef Tenderloin With Henry Bain Sauce

MAKES 8 SERVINGS; **PREP:** 5 MIN., **BAKE:** 35 MIN., **STAND:** 15 MIN.

Henry Bain was the head waiter at Louisville's Pendennis Club. He created this sauce, which became a Derby and year-round Louisville favorite with beef. Freeze any leftover sauce for later use.

¼ cup butter, softened
2 tsp. salt
1 tsp. freshly ground pepper
1 (4½- to 5-lb.) beef tenderloin, trimmed
Henry Bain Sauce*
Garnish: fresh thyme sprigs

1. Preheat oven to 500°. Stir together butter, salt, and pepper; rub over tenderloin. Place tenderloin on a lightly greased wire rack in a 15- x 10-inch jelly-roll pan. (Fold under narrow end of tenderloin to fit on rack.)
2. Bake at 500° for 30 to 35 minutes or until a meat thermometer inserted into thickest portion registers 145° (medium-rare). Cover tenderloin loosely with aluminum foil, and let stand 15 minutes before serving. Serve tenderloin with Henry Bain Sauce. Garnish, if desired.
*Spicy Horseradish Sauce may be substituted for Henry Bain Sauce.

Pork Tenderloin With Carolina Apple Compote: Omit ¼ cup butter. Substitute 3 (1-lb.) pork tenderloins for beef tenderloin and Carolina Apple Compote (page 294) for Henry Bain Sauce. Reduce salt to 1½ tsp. and pepper to ¾ tsp. Melt 3 Tbsp. butter in large skillet over medium-high heat; add pork, and cook 3 minutes on each side or until browned. Proceed with recipe as directed in Step 2, sprinkling salt and pepper over pork, and reducing bake time to 18 minutes or until a meat thermometer inserted into thickest portion registers 150°. Serve with Carolina Apple Compote.

Henry Bain Sauce:

make ahead

MAKES 6 CUPS; **PREP:** 10 MIN., **CHILL:** 2 HR.

To serve warm, microwave 2 cups of sauce at HIGH 2 minutes, stirring after 1 minute.

1 (9-oz.) bottle chutney
1 (14-oz.) bottle ketchup
1 (12-oz.) bottle chili sauce
1 (10-oz.) bottle steak sauce
1 (10-oz.) bottle Worcestershire sauce
1 tsp. hot sauce

1. Process chutney in a food processor until smooth. Add ketchup and remaining ingredients, and process until blended. Cover and chill 2 hours or up to 1 week.
Note: For testing purposes only, we used Major Grey's Chutney and A1 Steak Sauce.

Spicy Horseradish Sauce:

make ahead

MAKES 1 CUP; **PREP:** 5 MIN., **CHILL:** 1 HR.

⅔ cup reduced-fat sour cream
3 Tbsp. horseradish
2 Tbsp. light mayonnaise
1 Tbsp. white wine vinegar
1 tsp. dry mustard
¼ tsp. salt
¼ tsp. ground red pepper

1. Stir together all ingredients in a small bowl. Cover and chill 1 hour or up to 3 days.

Celebrate the Season

Single-Oven Strategy

For those who don't have double ovens, follow our plan for a low-stress kitchen-to-table meal.

- Heat soup on the cooktop.
- Bake the tenderloin (30 to 35 minutes at 500°). It needs to stand at least 15 minutes, but longer is fine; it's what we do for this menu. The tenderloin will stand about 45 minutes before it's sliced. Slice while the onion pudding stands and the asparagus are broiling.
- Reduce oven temp to 350°, and bake the Sweet Onion Pudding. Remove from oven, and let stand while the asparagus broil.
- Set the oven to broil. Broil the asparagus on the upper rack while the rolls warm on the bottom rack.

Sweet Onion Pudding

MAKES 8 SERVINGS; **PREP:** 20 MIN., **COOK:** 40 MIN., **BAKE:** 40 MIN.

½ cup butter
6 medium-size sweet onions, thinly sliced
6 large eggs, lightly beaten
2 cups whipping cream
1 (3-oz.) package shredded Parmesan cheese
3 Tbsp. all-purpose flour
2 Tbsp. sugar
2 tsp. baking powder
1 tsp. salt
Garnish: fresh thyme sprigs

1. Melt butter in a large skillet over medium heat; add onions. Cook, stirring often, 30 to 40 minutes or until caramel colored; remove from heat.
2. Preheat oven to 350°. Whisk together eggs, cream, and Parmesan cheese in a large bowl. Combine flour and next 3 ingredients in a separate bowl; gradually whisk into egg mixture until blended. Stir onions into egg mixture; spoon into a lightly greased 13- x 9-inch baking dish.
3. Bake at 350° for 35 to 40 minutes or until set. Garnish, if desired.

Simple Roasted Asparagus

MAKES 8 SERVINGS; **PREP:** 5 MIN., **BROIL:** 4 MIN. PER BATCH

You may need to increase the broil time, depending on the size of your asparagus.

2 lb. fresh asparagus
¼ cup olive oil
1 tsp. sugar
½ tsp. salt
½ tsp. freshly ground pepper

1. Preheat oven to broil. Snap off and discard tough ends of asparagus. Arrange in 2 (15- x 10-inch) jelly-roll pans. Drizzle with olive oil.
2. Broil, in 2 batches, 5½ inches from heat 4 minutes or until tender. Sprinkle with sugar, salt, and pepper.
—**SHIRLEY CORRIHER**, ATLANTA, GEORGIA

Simple Roasted Green Beans:

Substitute 2 lb. small, thin, fresh green beans, trimmed, for asparagus. Proceed with recipe as directed, broiling, in 2 batches, 7 to 8 minutes or until crisp-tender. **Makes** 8 servings; Prep: 10 min., Broil: 8 min. per batch

Timeline for Success

Make and freeze up to one month ahead:
- Cream Cheese-Coconut-Pecan Pound Cake (add glaze the morning of the party). Place baked and completely cooled pound cake or cake layers in large zip-top plastic freezer bags, and freeze.
- Sweet-and-Spicy Pecans
- Refrigerator Yeast Rolls
- Creamy Bell Pepper 'n' Tomato Soup (Prepare through Step 2, and freeze up to one month. Thaw in refrigerator overnight. Proceed with recipe as directed.)
- Christmas Croutons (Or make these a day ahead, cool completely, and store in an airtight container or zip-top plastic bag.)

Up to 1 week ahead:
- Make and chill Henry Bain Sauce
- Gather serving platters, dishes, and utensils. Label serving pieces with corresponding recipes. Lay out place settings, and press tablecloth and linens.

Up to 1 day ahead:
- Make and chill Balsamic Vinaigrette for Baby Blue Salad.
- Trim and prep asparagus or green beans. Chill in zip-top plastic bag. Measure out seasonings.
- Caramelize onions for Sweet Onion Pudding. Chill in zip-top plastic bag. (Bring to room temp before assembling recipe.)
- Prep salad greens, and peel and slice oranges for Baby Blue Salad. (Strawberries are best prepped the same day.)

Baby Blue Salad

chef recipe • fast fixin's
MAKES 8 SERVINGS; **PREP:** 25 MIN.

This is one of our all-time favorite recipes developed by chef Franklin Biggs and served at his restaurant in Homewood, Alabama. It's equally delicious served as a main dish topped with sliced beef or pork tenderloin or strips of hot, grilled chicken.

2 (5-oz.) packages gourmet mixed salad greens
3 large oranges, peeled and cut into thin slices
1 qt. strawberries, quartered
4 oz. blue cheese, crumbled
Sweet-and-Spicy Pecans
Balsamic Vinaigrette

1. Place greens on 8 individual serving plates. Top with oranges and strawberries. Sprinkle with cheese and pecans. Serve with Balsamic Vinaigrette.

Baby Blue Salad With Fresh Pears: Substitute 2 large Bartlett pears, cut into thin slices, for oranges. Proceed with recipe as directed.

Baby Blue Salad With Grapefruit and Avocado: Substitute feta cheese for blue cheese, and 2 grapefruit, peeled and cut into thin slices, for oranges. Add 2 avocados, thinly sliced, with cheese. Proceed with recipe as directed.

Party Decorating Ideas

1. Purchase a wide-nib calligraphy pen for printing guests' names on place cards. Or print them from your computer using a fancy font.
2. Instead of using a tablecloth, arrange sheer runners across the width of the table.
3. Use florist picks in the flower arrangement for holding stems that are too pliable to insert into florist foam.
4. Fill out your mantel arrangement using ornaments that complement the colors of your flowers.
5. Make fresh blooms the main element of a wreath, or cover a wreath form with seasonal greenery and add a few flowers as accents.
6. Cut pieces of sheer fabric (approximately 18 x 60 inches) to tie into graceful loops on chair backs.
7. Purchase inexpensive gold glass chargers from an imports store. Change your tableware with the season but use the chargers throughout the year.
8. Choose satin ribbon for making quick decorations. Twist a length around the foot of a compote or onto the handle of a cake server.
9. Purchase inexpensive votives by the dozen, and space them around the room, mixed among ornaments and pieces of greenery.
10. Use inverted terra-cotta saucers to add height to pillar candles; a spritz of spray paint will make them the perfect color.

Sweet-and-Spicy Pecans:

fast fixin's • freezeable
MAKES 1 CUP; **PREP:** 5 MIN., **SOAK:** 10 MIN.,
BAKE: 10 MIN.

¼ cup sugar
1 cup warm water
1 cup pecan halves
2 Tbsp. sugar
1 Tbsp. chili powder
⅛ tsp. ground red pepper

1. Preheat oven to 350°. Stir together ¼ cup sugar and 1 cup warm water until sugar dissolves. Add pecans, and soak 10 minutes. Drain, discarding syrup.
2. Combine 2 Tbsp. sugar, chili powder, and red pepper. Add pecans, tossing to coat. Place pecans on a lightly greased baking sheet.
3. Bake at 350° for 10 minutes or until golden brown, stirring once after 5 minutes.

Balsamic Vinaigrette:

fast fixin's
MAKES 1⅔ CUPS; **PREP:** 5 MIN.

You can make this dressing ahead; just be sure to let it stand at room temperature for about an hour before serving.

½ cup balsamic vinegar
3 Tbsp. Dijon mustard
3 Tbsp. honey
2 large garlic cloves, minced
2 small shallots, minced
¼ tsp. salt
¼ tsp. pepper
1 cup olive oil

1. Whisk together first 7 ingredients until blended. Gradually add olive oil in a slow, steady stream, whisking constantly until blended.

—**CHEF FRANKLIN BIGGS**, HOMEWOOD GOURMET,
HOMEWOOD, ALABAMA

Creamy Bell Pepper 'n' Tomato Soup

MAKES ABOUT 10 CUPS; **PREP:** 10 MIN., **COOK:** 40 MIN., **COOL:** 10 MIN.

2 Tbsp. butter
3 garlic cloves, finely chopped
2 (28-oz.) cans crushed tomatoes
1 (14-oz.) can low-sodium chicken broth
2 (12-oz.) jars roasted red bell peppers, drained
1 Tbsp. sugar
1 (0.6-oz.) envelope zesty Italian dressing mix
2 cups half-and-half
¼ tsp. ground red pepper
¼ tsp. freshly ground black pepper
Christmas Croutons
Garnish: freshly ground black pepper

1. Melt butter in a large Dutch oven over medium heat; add garlic, and sauté 1 minute or until slightly golden. Stir in tomatoes and next 4 ingredients; cook, stirring occasionally, over medium heat 30 minutes. Remove from heat, and let cool 10 minutes.
2. Process mixture, in small batches, in a blender or food processor until smooth, stopping to scrape down sides. Return mixture to Dutch oven.
3. Stir in half-and-half, and cook, stirring occasionally, over low heat 8 to 9 minutes or until thoroughly heated; stir in red and black peppers. Serve with Christmas Croutons. Garnish, if desired.

Christmas Croutons:

MAKES 20 (3-INCH) TREES; **PREP:** 10 MIN., **BAKE:** 12 MIN.

Save the scraps of bread you'll have from making the croutons for fresh breadcrumbs. Freeze scraps up to three months, and then pulse in a food processor until crumbled.

10 white bread slices
3 Tbsp. butter, melted
1 tsp. dried Italian seasoning
¼ tsp. cracked pepper

1. Preheat oven to 350°. Cut each bread slice into 2 trees, using a 3-inch tree-shape cutter. Stir together butter, Italian seasoning, and pepper. Brush onto 1 side of each bread slice. Transfer trees to a baking sheet.
2. Bake at 350° for 12 minutes or until golden.

Refrigerator Yeast Rolls

freezeable • make ahead

MAKES ABOUT 7 DOZEN; **PREP:** 45 MIN., **STAND:** 5 MIN., **CHILL:** 8 HR., **RISE:** 45 MIN., **BAKE:** 10 MIN.

1 (¼-oz.) envelope active dry yeast
2 cups warm water (105° to 115°)
6 cups bread flour
½ cup sugar
½ tsp. salt
½ cup shortening
2 large eggs
½ cup butter, melted
Orange Butter

1. Stir together yeast and 2 cups warm water in a medium bowl; let mixture stand 5 minutes.
2. Stir together flour, sugar, and salt in a large bowl. Cut shortening into flour mixture with a pastry blender until crumbly; stir in yeast mixture and eggs just until blended. (Do not overmix.)

Cover dough, and chill 8 hours.
3. Roll dough to ¼-inch thickness on a well-floured surface (dough will be soft); cut with a 1½-inch round cutter, rerolling dough scraps as needed.
4. Brush rounds with melted butter. Make a crease across each round with a knife, and fold rounds in half, gently pressing edges together to seal. Place in a 15- x 10-inch jelly-roll pan and a 9-inch round cake pan. (Edges of dough should touch.) Cover and let rise in a warm place (85°), free from drafts, 45 minutes or until doubled in bulk.
5. Preheat oven to 400°. Bake rolls 8 to 10 minutes or until golden. Serve with Orange Butter.

—ETHELWYN LANGSTON, ALBERTVILLE, ALABAMA

Orange Butter:

fast fixin's

MAKES ¾ CUP; **PREP:** 5 MIN.

Feel free to shape your butter using butter molds. We used 3½-inch Christmas tree-shape molds. One recipe will make four molds.

½ cup butter, softened
¼ cup orange marmalade

1. Stir together butter and marmalade until blended. Serve immediately, or cover and chill until ready to serve. Store in an airtight container in refrigerator up to 1 week.

Blackberry Butter: Substitute blackberry preserves for orange marmalade. Proceed with recipe as directed.

Fig Butter: Substitute fig preserves for orange marmalade. Proceed with recipe as directed.

Strawberry Butter: Substitute strawberry preserves for orange marmalade. Proceed with recipe as directed.

—HELEN H. MAURER, CHRISTMAS, FLORIDA

Winning Recipe: Cream Cheese-Coconut-Pecan Pound Cake

Why we love it:

- "I love this cake! It's chock-full of so many wonderful things it's almost like a main course. It's just sweet enough, and the chewy coconut and crunchy pecans give it a nice texture. And it's so very Southern. "

  —DONNA FLORIO, FOOD SENIOR WRITER

- "This recipe is nice because the pound cake is so easy to make, and the whole package has such a 'wow' factor without having to frost the entire cake. You can even use your favorite pound cake recipe and then try our frosting and decorating ideas to put the 'wow' on it."

  —VANESSA MCNEIL ROCCHIO, TEST KITCHENS SPECIALIST/FOOD STYLIST

Why you love it:

- "This is my definition of decadent. Pecans and bourbon with cream cheese and coconut bring a smile to this Southern girl's heart and stomach."

  —KAY HORTON, TOWNSEND, TENNESSEE

- "This cake is amazing. It transports with no problem and still has that great impact and presentation of a decadent dessert."

  —KRISTEN CAMERON, ARIPEKA, FLORIDA

- "This has to be one of the best-tasting cakes I have ever made. My daughter usually ends up taking what's left back to college, and now all of her roommates look forward to her coming home as much as we do."

  —JENEAN GRAY, PARROTTSVILLE, TENNESSEE

Cream Cheese-Coconut-Pecan Pound Cake

winning recipe

MAKES 10 TO 12 SERVINGS; **PREP:** 20 MIN.; **BAKE:** 1 HR., 42 MIN.; **COOL:** 1 HR., 30 MIN.

The bourbon gives this pound cake a wonderful aroma and flavor, but you may substitute an equal amount of milk, if desired.

1 cup chopped pecans
1½ cups butter, softened
1 (8-oz.) package cream cheese, softened
3 cups sugar
6 large eggs
3 cups all-purpose flour
½ tsp. salt
¼ cup bourbon
½ cup sweetened shredded coconut
1½ tsp. vanilla extract

1. Preheat oven to 350°. Bake pecans in a single layer on a baking sheet 5 to 7 minutes or until lightly toasted and fragrant. Cool completely on a wire rack (about 15 minutes). Reduce oven temperature to 325°.
2. Beat butter and cream cheese at medium speed with an electric mixer until creamy. Gradually add sugar, beating at medium speed until light and fluffy. Add eggs, 1 at a time, beating just until yellow disappears after each addition.
3. Sift together flour and salt; add to butter mixture alternately with bourbon, beginning and ending with flour mixture. Beat at low speed just until blended after each addition. Stir in coconut, vanilla, and pecans. Pour batter into a greased and floured 10-inch (12-cup) tube pan.
4. Bake at 325° for 1 hour and 30 minutes to 1 hour and 35 minutes or until

a long wooden pick inserted in center of cake comes out clean. Cool in pan on a wire rack 10 to 15 minutes. Remove from pan to wire rack; cool completely (about 1 hour).

Cream Cheese-Bourbon-Pecan Pound Cake: Increase pecans to 1½ cups. Omit coconut. Proceed with recipe as directed.

—DAPHNE HARRELL, BROWNWOOD, TEXAS

Brown Sugar-Praline Glaze

MAKES 1 CUP; **PREP:** 5 MIN., **COOK:** 6 MIN.

For best results, use a serrated knife and a gentle sawing motion to cut through the glaze.

¼ cup butter
½ cup firmly packed brown sugar
1 tsp. light corn syrup
1½ cups powdered sugar
2 Tbsp. milk
½ tsp. vanilla extract

1. Melt butter in a 1-qt. saucepan over medium heat. Whisk in brown sugar and corn syrup; cook 1 minute. Add powdered sugar, milk, and vanilla; whisk until creamy (about 2 minutes). Remove from heat, and use glaze immediately.
Note: Pour all of Brown Sugar Praline Glaze immediately over cooled cake in a circular motion.

Versatile Fruit Sides

Make-ahead Sherry-Baked Winter Fruit is our go-to recipe when planning holiday menus. It's lovely for dinner with roasted turkey, pork loin, or ham, but also great for a breakfast, as a dessert, or served as an appetizer.

Sherry-Baked Winter Fruit

MAKES 6 TO 8 SERVINGS; **PREP:** 15 MIN.,
CHILL: 12 HR., **BAKE:** 50 MIN., **STAND:** 15 MIN.

You'll find apple cider either with shelf-stable or refrigerated juices. Either can be used, so choose the best value. Use dry sherry, not the much sweeter cream sherry.

1 (10-oz.) package dried Mission figlets, trimmed and halved
1 (7-oz.) package dried apricots
1 (5-oz.) package dried apples
2 cups apple cider
⅔ cup dry sherry
½ cup golden raisins
2 navel oranges, peeled and sectioned
1 (3-inch) cinnamon stick
Brown Sugar-Lemon Sour Cream (optional)
Garnish: orange slices

1. Place first 8 ingredients in an 11- x 7-inch baking dish; gently toss to combine. Cover with aluminum foil, and chill 12 to 24 hours.
2. Preheat oven to 350°. Bake fruit, covered, 45 to 50 minutes or until thoroughly heated and fruit is soft.
3. Let stand, covered, 15 minutes. Remove and discard cinnamon stick. Serve with a slotted spoon and, if desired, Brown Sugar-Lemon Sour Cream. Garnish, if desired.

—SHIRLEY A. GLAAB, HATTIESBURG, MISSISSIPPI

Port-Baked Winter Fruit: Substitute port for sherry. Proceed with recipe as directed.
Simple Baked Winter Fruit: Substitute 1 (12-oz.) can thawed apple juice concentrate and 1 cup water for apple cider and sherry. Proceed with recipe as directed.
Tropical Plum Sherry-Baked Winter Fruit: Substitute 1 (10-oz.) package dried pitted plums, 1 (6-oz.) package dried pineapple, and 1 (5-oz.) package dried mango, chopped, for figs, apricots, and apples. Proceed with recipe as directed.

Brown Sugar-Lemon Sour Cream

MAKES ABOUT 1 CUP; **PREP:** 5 MIN.,
CHILL: 30 MIN.

This quick sauce would be delicious served over fresh berries or granola, or dolloped on pound cake.

1 (8-oz.) carton sour cream
2 Tbsp. brown sugar
1 tsp. lemon zest
1 tsp. vanilla extract

1. Stir together all ingredients. Cover and chill 30 minutes or up to 48 hours.

Lightened Brown Sugar-Lemon Sour Cream: Substitute 1 (8-oz.) container light sour cream for regular. Proceed with recipe as directed.

Healthy Living.

Down-Home Delicious

Have your comfort and eat it too with these updated and budget-friendly recipes.

Food is a temptation this time of year, but you can feel good about these down-home dishes. We put a better-for-you spin on a few Southern classics. Plus it pays to cook at home. Check out the cost per serving for each dish; all ring up at less than $2.50.

Chicken-and-White Bean Chili pairs perfectly with mouthwatering Sour Cream Cornbread. Need a quick and scrumptious side? Easy Skillet Pimiento Mac 'n' Cheese is ready in about 20 minutes, start to finish. Later, curl up in a cozy chair with Spiced Caramel-Apple Bread Pudding—it tastes better that way.

Healthy Benefits

- Rinsing and draining canned veggies and beans can reduce the sodium content by about 40%.
- Fiber-rich recipes, such as Chicken-and-White Bean Chili, help to increase satiety and prevent overeating.

Chicken-and-White Bean Chili

MAKES 11 CUPS; **PREP:** 10 MIN.,
COOK: 15 MIN., **COST PER SERVING:** $2.42

We used a rotisserie chicken from the supermarket deli. One chicken generally yields 3 to 4 cups chopped meat.

3 to 4 cups chopped cooked chicken
4 (16-oz.) cans navy beans, rinsed and drained
4 (4-oz.) cans chopped green chiles
1 (14-oz.) can low-sodium fat-free chicken broth
2 Tbsp. Chili Seasoning Mix
Garnishes: sour cream, fresh cilantro sprig

1. Stir together first 5 ingredients in a Dutch oven; bring to a boil over medium-high heat, stirring occasionally. Cover, reduce heat to low, and simmer, stirring occasionally, 15 minutes. Garnish, if desired.

Per cup (not including garnishes): Calories 295; Fat 4.1g (sat 1.1g, mono 1.3g, poly 1.1g); Protein 26.7g; Carb 38.3g; Fiber 9.9g; Chol 38.2mg; Iron 4.3mg; Sodium 700mg; Calc 86mg

Chili Seasoning Mix:

MAKES ABOUT 1⅓ CUPS; **PREP:** 5 MIN.

This versatile seasoning mix yields big dividends in timesaving suppers. Keep a jar on hand all winter, and you'll be ready to stir up a delicious batch of tasty chili any time.

¾ cup chili powder
2 Tbsp. ground cumin
2 Tbsp. dried oregano
2 Tbsp. dried minced onion
2 Tbsp. seasoned salt
2 Tbsp. sugar
2 tsp. dried minced garlic

1. Stir together all ingredients. Store seasoning mix in an airtight container at room temperature up to 4 months. Shake or stir well before using.

Per Tbsp.: Calories 15; Fat 0g (sat 0g, mono 0g, poly 0g); Protein 0.2g; Carb 2.9g; Fiber 0.7g; Chol 0mg; Iron 0.5mg; Sodium 541mg; Calc 12mg

Easy Skillet Pimiento Mac 'n' Cheese

MAKES 6 SERVINGS; **PREP:** 10 MIN.,
COOK: 10 MIN., **COST PER SERVING:** $1.13

For quick prep, shred the cheese and measure the ingredients while the pasta cooks.

½ (16-oz.) package penne pasta, uncooked
2 Tbsp. all-purpose flour
1½ cups 1% low-fat milk
1 cup (4 oz.) shredded sharp Cheddar cheese
1 (4-oz.) jar diced pimiento, drained
¾ tsp. salt
¼ tsp. pepper
Pinch of paprika

1. Prepare pasta according to package directions.

2. Whisk together flour and ¼ cup milk. Add flour mixture to remaining milk, whisking until smooth.

3. Bring milk mixture to a boil in a large skillet over medium heat; reduce heat to medium-low, and simmer, whisking constantly, 3 to 5 minutes or until smooth. Stir in cheese and next 4 ingredients until smooth. Stir in pasta, and cook 1 minute or until thoroughly heated. Serve immediately.

—MELISSA QUINONES, EUSTIS, FLORIDA

Per serving: Calories 250; Fat 7.3g (sat 4.6g, mono 0.2g, poly 0.1g); Protein 12.3g; Carb 34.7g; Fiber 1.6g; Chol 22mg; Iron 1.7mg; Sodium 446mg; Calc 217mg

Easy Skillet Green Chile Mac 'n' Cheese: Substitute 1 cup (4 oz.) shredded Monterey Jack cheese for Cheddar cheese and 1 (4-oz.) can chopped green chiles, undrained, for diced pimiento. Proceed with recipe as directed.

Per serving: Calories 251; Fat 7.3g (sat 4.6g, mono 0.2g, poly 0.1g); Protein 11.6g; Carb 34.1g; Fiber 1.5g; Chol 22mg; Iron 1.7mg; Sodium 491mg; Calc 229mg

Easy Skillet Whole Grain Mac 'n' Cheese: Substitute ½ (13.5-oz.) package whole grain penne pasta for regular. Proceed with recipe as directed.

Per serving: Calories 215; Fat 7.9g (sat 4.4g, mono 0.2g, poly 0.9g); Protein 11.1g; Carb 29.8g; Fiber 3.8g; Chol 22.4mg; Iron 1.5mg; Sodium 444mg; Calc 222mg

Sour Cream Cornbread

MAKES 8 SERVINGS; **PREP:** 10 MIN.,
BAKE: 24 MIN., **COST PER SERVING:** 55 CENTS

1½ cups self-rising cornmeal mix
½ cup all-purpose flour
1 (15-oz.) can low-sodium cream-style corn
1 (8-oz.) container light sour cream
3 large eggs, lightly beaten
2 Tbsp. chopped fresh cilantro
½ cup (2 oz.) 2% reduced-fat shredded Cheddar cheese (optional)

1. Preheat oven to 450°. Heat a 10-inch cast-iron skillet in oven 5 minutes.

2. Stir together cornmeal mix and flour in a large bowl; add corn and next 3 ingredients, stirring just until blended. Lightly grease skillet, and pour batter into skillet.

3. Bake at 450° for 22 to 24 minutes or until golden brown and cornbread pulls away from sides of skillet. If desired, top with cheese, and bake 1 minute or until cheese is melted and bubbly.

Per serving (including cheese topping): Calories 254; Fat 6g (sat 2.9g, mono 1g, poly .8g); Protein 9.7g; Carb 43.1g; Fiber 2.9g; Chol 92mg; Iron 2.5mg; Sodium 518mg; Calc 158mg

Spiced Caramel-Apple Bread Pudding

MAKES 8 SERVINGS; **PREP:** 20 MIN.,
COOK: 2 MIN., **CHILL:** 1 HR., **BAKE:** 50 MIN.,
COST PER SERVING: $1.18

1 Granny Smith apple, peeled and chopped
½ tsp. ground cinnamon, divided
½ (16-oz.) Italian bread loaf, cut into bite-size pieces
Vegetable cooking spray
3 large eggs
1½ cups 2% reduced-fat milk
1 cup apple cider
¼ cup firmly packed brown sugar
1 tsp. vanilla extract
¼ tsp. ground nutmeg
Toasted Pecan-Caramel Sauce

1. Sauté apple and ¼ tsp. cinnamon in a lightly greased skillet over medium-high heat 2 minutes or until tender. Stir together bread and apple in an 11- x 7-inch baking dish coated with cooking spray.

2. Whisk together eggs, next 5 ingredients, and remaining ¼ tsp. cinnamon; pour over bread mixture in baking dish. Cover and chill 1 hour.

3. Preheat oven to 350°. Bake bread mixture 45 to 50 minutes or until top is crisp and golden brown. Serve warm with Toasted Pecan-Caramel Sauce.

Per serving: Calories 299; Fat 7.2g (sat 2.1g, mono 2.9g, poly 1.5g); Protein 8.1g; Carb 51.6g; Fiber 1.4g; Chol 85mg; Iron 1.5mg; Sodium 241mg; Calc 146mg

Toasted Pecan-Caramel Sauce:
MAKES ABOUT ¾ CUP; **PREP:** 10 MIN.,
BAKE: 10 MIN., **COOK:** 14 MIN.

This sauce also makes a great topping for low-fat ice cream.

¼ cup chopped pecans
¾ cup sugar
1 tsp. light corn syrup
½ cup evaporated milk
1½ tsp. butter

1. Preheat oven to 350°. Bake pecans in a single layer in a shallow pan 8 to 10 minutes or until toasted and fragrant.

2. Sprinkle sugar in an even layer in a small saucepan. Stir together syrup and ⅓ cup water, and pour over sugar in saucepan. Cook, without stirring, over medium-high heat 12 to 14 minutes or until sugar is dissolved and mixture is golden.

3. Remove from heat. Gradually whisk in evaporated milk. (Mixture will bubble.) Stir in butter and toasted pecans.

Per 4½ tsp.: Calories 119; Fat 3.4g (sat 0.7g, mono 1.7g, poly 0.8g); Protein 1.6g; Carb 21.7g; Fiber 0.4g; Chol 3mg; Iron 0.1mg; Sodium 24mg; Calc 50mg

Party Tips in a Pinch

Entertaining tricks and fresh ideas for food you'll love

Host a Beer Swap It's no secret around the Test Kitchens that Test Kitchens Professional Marian McGahey and her husband, Lee, prefer a good beer to a glass of wine. This time of year is Lee's absolute favorite because of the huge variety of limited edition batches that debut. Brewers pull out secret special recipes with tons of flavor and complexity in the fall and winter. To make the most of this short and busy time, this couple hosts a tasting party. With little investment, they get to sample more brews than they otherwise could in one season. Invite a few close friends with instructions to bring one or two six-packs. Set out small glasses and a few snacks. Open a few bottles to sample, and swap the rest to enjoy throughout the holidays. (Choices will vary from state to state. Marian and Lee are always on the lookout for small microbrews. This lets them support local and regional breweries as they share something new with their friends.) Their personal picks from across the South include Terrapin Beer Company in Georgia, The Duck-Trap Craft Brewery in North Carolina, Dogfish Head Craft Brewery in Delaware, and Real Ale Brewing Company in Texas.

Pantry Surprise

Turn canned chickpeas or black-eyed peas into a unique and affordable party snack. Simply toss them in olive oil with a few seasonings and roast until crisp. The key is to bake the beans as long as possible without letting them burn. This will dry them out, making them extra-crunchy like nuts. Enjoy by the handful or sprinkle over a salad. We found a few chickpeas popped like popcorn while being roasted, so use a long handled spoon or spatula while stirring the pan. These are best the day they are made, but you can store in an airtight container up to one day.

Chili-Roasted Chickpeas: Preheat oven to 425°. Combine 2 (16-oz.) cans chickpeas, rinsed and drained; 3 Tbsp. olive oil; 1½ tsp. chili powder; 1 tsp. pepper; ¾ tsp. ground cumin; and ½ tsp. salt in a medium bowl. Transfer to a lightly greased 17- x 12-inch jelly-roll pan. Bake 45 to 50 minutes or until crispy and dry, stirring every 10 minutes. Let cool 20 minutes. **Makes** about 2½ cups; Prep: 10 min., Bake: 50 min., Cool: 20 min.

Chili-Roasted Black-Eyed Peas: Substitute 2 (15.8-oz.) cans black-eyed peas, rinsed and drained, for chickpeas. Proceed with recipe as directed.

No-Fuss Chocolate Bar Entertaining friends with a homemade meal makes a great hobby. But if you run out of time to make dessert, no worries. Just set up a chocolate station. Pick your favorite chocolate candies at the grocery, and pour into small glasses. Break a candy bar into pieces. Cut up a bakery brownie into bite-size squares and unwrap a few truffles. Add a few shot glasses with ice cream or chocolate milk.

Collect everything on a pretty tray, and watch your guests' eyes open wide with delight. It brings out the kid in everyone. This super-simple display is a fanciful and clever end to an intimate dinner party or is a pretty and edible centerpiece at a cocktail party. The best part: no baking or mixing required!

5-Ingredient Entertaining

Quick Party Starters

Ease into entertaining with these worry-free appetizers and beverages.

Warm Brie With Pear Preserves

MAKES: 12 SERVINGS; **PREP:** 10 MIN., **BAKE:** 4 MIN.

Leaving the edible white rind on the Brie and cutting the cheese into wedges are two steps toward a quick finish. Serve Brie with thin gingersnaps, fruit, or crackers.

½ cup pear preserves
2 Tbsp. sweet white wine
1½ tsp. chopped fresh thyme or
    ½ tsp. dried thyme
2 (8-oz.) rounds Brie
¼ cup chopped walnuts
Garnishes: fresh thyme sprigs, walnut
    halves

1. Preheat oven to 450°. Combine first 3 ingredients in a small glass bowl; set bowl aside.
2. Cut each round of Brie into 6 wedges. Place wedges close together on a lightly greased baking sheet; sprinkle each round with 2 Tbsp. chopped walnuts.
3. Bake at 450° for 4 minutes or just until cheese begins to soften in the center. Meanwhile, microwave preserves mixture on HIGH 20 seconds or just until thoroughly heated. Using 2 spatulas, carefully remove each Brie round intact from baking sheet, and immediately place on a serving platter. Spoon melted preserves over Brie. Garnish, if desired. Serve hot.
Note: For testing purposes only, we used Riesling Wine.

Fix It Faster: Heat Brie with toppings, 1 round at a time, in the microwave on HIGH 1½ minutes on a microwave-safe plate. You don't even have to cut Brie into wedges.

Brie Cheese Wafers

MAKES: 5 DOZEN WAFERS OR 7 DOZEN STRAWS; **PREP:** 17 MIN., **BAKE:** 8 MIN. PER BATCH, **CHILL:** 8 HR.

½ lb. Brie, softened
½ cup butter, softened
2 cups all-purpose flour
¼ tsp. salt
¼ tsp. ground red pepper
¼ tsp. Worcestershire sauce

1. Position knife blade in food processor bowl; add Brie (with rind) and butter. Process until blended, stopping often to scrape down sides. Add flour and remaining ingredients, pulsing until a soft dough forms.
2. Divide dough in half, and shape each portion into an 8-inch log; wrap in plastic wrap, and chill 8 hours.
3. Preheat oven to 375°. Cut dough into ¼-inch slices; or use a cookie press fitted with a star-shaped disk to shape dough into straws, following manufacturer's instructions. Place slices or straws on ungreased baking sheets.
4. Bake at 375° for 8 minutes or until lightly browned. Transfer to wire racks to cool.

Garlic-Pepper-Parmesan Crisps

MAKES: 8 DOZEN; **PREP:** 24 MIN., **BAKE:** 10 MIN. PER BATCH

12 oz. freshly grated Parmigiano-Reggiano
    cheese
2 tsp. minced fresh garlic
1 tsp. freshly ground pepper

1. Preheat oven to 350°. Combine all ingredients in a small bowl, stirring well. Sprinkle cheese mixture into a 1½-inch round cutter on a nonstick

baking sheet. Repeat procedure with cheese mixture, placing 16 circles on each sheet.
2. Bake at 350° for 9 to 10 minutes or until golden. Cool slightly on baking sheets; remove to wire racks to cool completely. Repeat procedure 5 times with remaining cheese mixture.

Bacon, Cheddar, and Ranch Pita Chips

make ahead • fast fixin's
MAKES: 4 DOZEN CHIPS; **PREP:** 6 MIN., **BAKE:** 15 MIN.

¼ cup olive oil
1½ Tbsp. Ranch dressing mix
3 (6-inch) pita rounds
⅓ cup real bacon bits
½ cup (2 oz.) shredded sharp Cheddar
    cheese

1. Preheat oven to 350°. Combine olive oil and dressing mix in a small bowl.
2. Split each pita bread into 2 rounds. Cut each round into 8 wedges. Place wedges on a lightly greased baking sheet. Brush rough side of each wedge with oil mixture. Sprinkle wedges with bacon bits and then cheese. Bake at 350° for 15 minutes or until crisp. Remove from oven; transfer to wire racks to cool.
Note: For testing purposes only, we used Hormel Bacon Bits.

Spicy Queso Dip

fast fixin's
MAKES: 7½ CUPS; **PREP:** 3 MIN., **COOK:** 9 MIN.

This is no ordinary cheese dip. It's chock-full of spinach, sausage, black beans, and green chiles.

1 (16-oz.) package mild ground pork sausage
2 (16-oz.) cartons refrigerated hot queso dip
1 (10-oz.) package frozen chopped spinach,
    thawed and well drained
1 (15-oz.) can black beans, rinsed and drained
1 (10-oz.) can diced tomatoes and green
    chiles, undrained

1. Cook sausage in a large skillet over medium-high heat, stirring until sausage crumbles and is no longer pink. Drain.
2. Meanwhile, heat queso dip according to package microwave directions in a 2-qt. microwave-safe bowl. Stir in sausage, spinach, and beans. Drain tomatoes and green chiles, reserving juice. Add tomatoes and green chiles to dip. Stir in enough reserved juice to get a good consistency (2 to 3 Tbsp.). Serve hot with tortilla chips.
Note: For testing purposes only, we used Gordo's Cheese Dip.

Creamy Chipotle-Black Bean Dip

fast fixin's • make ahead

MAKES: 1 CUP; **PREP:** 10 MIN.

Adobo sauce is a thick Mexican mixture made from chiles, vinegar, and spices that can be used as a marinade or as a sauce served on the side. Here, it packs a little punch into sour cream and prepared bean dip.

½ cup sour cream
½ cup prepared black bean dip
1 tsp. minced chipotle peppers in adobo sauce
1 tsp. adobo sauce from can
¼ tsp. salt

1. Combine all ingredients; stir well. Cover and chill up to 3 days. Serve with tortilla chips.

One-Minute Salsa

fast fixin's

MAKES: 2¾ CUPS; **PREP:** 1 MIN.

You control the consistency of this salsa by how long you process the ingredients.

1 (14½-oz.) can stewed tomatoes, undrained
1 (10-oz.) can diced tomatoes and green chiles, undrained
½ tsp. garlic salt
½ tsp. pepper

1. Combine all ingredients in a blender; cover and process 15 seconds or until smooth. Transfer mixture to a bowl; cover and chill, if desired. Serve with tortilla chips.

Quick Creamy Vegetable Dip

make ahead

MAKES: ABOUT 1½ CUPS; **PREP:** 10 MIN., **CHILL:** 2 HR.

½ cup mayonnaise
½ cup sour cream
1 (2-oz.) jar diced pimiento, drained
¼ cup chopped onion
¼ cup diced green bell pepper
½ tsp. garlic salt
⅛ tsp. pepper
⅛ tsp. hot sauce

1. Stir together all ingredients. Cover and chill 2 hours.

BLT Dippers

fast fixin's

MAKES: 4 CUPS; **PREP:** 20 MIN.

The bacon mixture also makes a chunky dressing for a salad.

1 cup mayonnaise
1 (8-oz.) carton sour cream
1 lb. bacon, cooked and crumbled
2 large tomatoes, chopped
Belgian endive leaves

1. Combine mayonnaise and sour cream in a medium bowl, stirring well with a wire whisk; stir in bacon and tomato. Spoon 1 Tbsp. onto individual Belgian endive leaves, or serve with Melba toast rounds.

Marvelous Main Dishes

Let these enticing entrées be the centerpiece of your meal.

Pork Chops With Shallot-Cranberry Sauce

fast fixin's

MAKES: 4 SERVINGS; **PREP:** 7 MIN., **COOK:** 13 MIN.

For an easy and impressive presentation, perch these skillet chops on a mound of mashed potatoes.

4 boneless pork loin chops (¾-inch thick)
¾ tsp. salt, divided
½ tsp. freshly ground pepper
2 Tbsp. butter, divided
2 shallots, finely chopped (¼ cup)
1 (12-oz.) container cranberry-orange crushed fruit
1½ tsp. chopped fresh thyme
Garnish: fresh thyme

1. Sprinkle both sides of pork with ½ tsp. salt and pepper. Melt 1 Tbsp. butter in a large skillet over medium-high heat. Add pork, and cook 4 to 5 minutes on each side or to desired degree of doneness. Remove pork from skillet; cover and keep warm.
2. Add remaining 1 Tbsp. butter to skillet, stirring just until butter melts. Add shallots, and sauté 1 to 2 minutes. Add crushed fruit and remaining ¼ tsp. salt to skillet; bring to a boil. Return pork and any juices to skillet; cook 1 minute or until heated. Sprinkle with chopped thyme, and serve hot. Garnish, if desired.

Slow-Cooker BBQ Pork
make ahead

MAKES: 6 SERVINGS; **PREP:** 5 MIN.,
COOK: 8 HR.

*This super-simple recipe delivers big
flavor. If you don't have a slow cooker,
place roast in a lightly greased Dutch
oven; stir together barbecue sauce and
cola, and pour over roast. Before placing
the lid on top of the Dutch oven, cover it
with a double layer of aluminum foil.
Bake, tightly covered, at 325° for 3 hours
and 30 minutes or until tender. Serve
on buns with slaw or over hot toasted
cornbread.*

1 (3- to 4-lb.) shoulder pork roast
1 (18-oz.) bottle barbecue sauce
1 (12-oz.) can cola soft drink

1. Place pork roast in a 6-qt. slow
cooker; pour barbecue sauce and cola
over roast.
2. Cover and cook on HIGH 8 hours or
until meat is tender and shreds easily.
Note: For testing purposes only, we
used Kraft Original Barbecue Sauce.

—**HAL RIDDLE**, TRUSSVILLE, ALABAMA
A TASTE OF TRUSSVILLE

Molasses-Grilled Pork Tenderloin

MAKES: 8 SERVINGS; **PREP:** 5 MIN.,
GRILL: 20 MIN., **CHILL:** 8 HR.

¼ cup molasses
2 Tbsp. coarse grained Dijon mustard
1 Tbsp. apple cider vinegar
4 (¾-lb.) pork tenderloins, trimmed

1. Combine first 3 ingredients, and
brush over tenderloins. Cover and chill
8 hours.
2. Preheat grill to medium-high (350°
to 400°). Grill tenderloins, covered
with grill lid, over medium-high coals
about 10 minutes on each side or until a
meat thermometer inserted into thickest
portion registers 160°.

Praline-Mustard Glazed Ham

MAKES: 12 SERVINGS; **PREP:** 5 MIN.;
BAKE: 2 HR., 30 MIN.; **STAND:** 10 MIN.

*The popularity of serving spiral-sliced
hams during the holidays can make them
hard to find. Shop early, or special order
your ham to be sure you get what you
want. You can purchase them at supermarkets and at specialty meat stores.*

1 (7- to 8-lb.) bone-in smoked spiral-cut
    ham half
¾ cup firmly packed brown sugar
¾ cup Dijon mustard
1 cup maple syrup
⅓ cup apple juice
Raisin Butter

1. Preheat oven to 350°. Place ham in a
lightly greased 13- x 9-inch pan.
2. Stir together brown sugar and mustard; spread over ham. Stir together
maple syrup and apple juice, and pour
into pan. Cover with aluminum foil.
3. Bake at 350° on lower oven rack 2
hours. Remove foil, and bake 30 more
minutes, basting every 10 minutes with
pan drippings until meat thermometer
inserted into thickest portion registers
140°. Let stand 10 minutes. Remove
from pan, and serve with Raisin Butter.

Raisin Butter:

MAKES: ABOUT 1 CUP; **PREP:** 10 MIN.;
COOK: 10 MIN., **CHILL:** 1 HR.,
COOL: 30 MIN.

½ cup golden raisins
¼ cup apple juice
½ cup butter, softened

1. Bring raisins and apple juice to a
boil in a small saucepan; reduce heat,
and simmer 10 minutes or until raisins
plump. Cool.
2. Process mixture in blender until
finely chopped. Add butter; process
until well blended, stopping to scrape
down sides. Cover; chill 1 hour.

Peppered Beef Fillets With Pomegranate Jus
fast fixin's

MAKES: 6 SERVINGS; **PREP:** 4 MIN.,
COOK: 12 MIN.

*The 1-inch thickness of the fillets is
important for uniform cooking. Press
fillets with the palm of your hand to
make fillet thickness consistent.*

6 beef tenderloin fillets (about 1 inch thick)
¼ tsp. salt
¼ cup au poivre marinade, divided
    (see Note)
⅔ cup minced onion or shallot
⅔ cup refrigerated pomegranate juice or
    red wine
3 oz. Gorgonzola or blue cheese

1. Sprinkle fillets evenly with salt. Rub
fillets with 3 Tbsp. au poivre marinade.
Place a large nonstick skillet over
medium-high heat until hot. Add
fillets, and cook 5 minutes on each side
or until desired degree of doneness.
Remove fillets from skillet, and
keep warm.
2. Add remaining 1 Tbsp. au poivre
marinade to skillet. Add onion, and
sauté 30 seconds, scraping browned
bits from bottom of skillet. Add pomegranate juice. Bring to a boil, and cook
1 minute.
3. To serve, pour pomegranate jus
over fillets, and top each serving with
cheese.
Note: We tested with LuLu Au Poivre
marinade from Williams-Sonoma.
You can otherwise use our similar
homemade marinade. Combine ¼ cup
extra-virgin olive oil, 1½ tsp. cracked
black pepper, 1 tsp. each dried parsley flakes and dried oregano, ¼ tsp.
fine-grained sea salt, and 1 large garlic
clove, pressed.

Beginner's Roast
make ahead

MAKES: 6 TO 8 SERVINGS; **PREP:** 5 MIN.;
BAKE: 3 HR., 30 MIN.

*The secret to this juicy, fall-apart-tender
roast is in the baking. Before placing
the lid on top of the Dutch oven, cover it
with a double layer of aluminum foil. An
eye-of-round roast has far less fat than
a chuck roast, but when tightly covered
and slowly baked with moist heat, it's
every bit as delicious.*

1 (3- to 4-lb.) eye-of-round roast
1 large sweet onion, sliced
1 (10¾-oz.) can cream of mushroom soup
1 (1.12-oz.) package brown gravy mix
1 garlic clove, minced

1. Preheat oven to 325°. Place roast in
a lightly greased Dutch oven, and top
with sliced onion. Stir together soup,
½ cup water, gravy mix, and garlic;
pour over roast.
2. Bake, tightly covered, at 325° for 3
hours and 30 minutes or until tender.
Note: For testing purposes only, we
used Knorr Classic Brown Gravy Mix.

Quick Mexican Dinner
fast fixin's

MAKES: 5 SERVINGS; **PREP:** 7 MIN.,
COOK: 12 MIN.

1 lb. ground chuck
1 (15-oz.) can Spanish rice
1 (15-oz.) can Ranch-style beans, undrained
10 (10-inch) flour tortillas
Toppings: shredded cheese, shredded
    lettuce, chopped tomato, sour cream,
    sliced jalapeño peppers

1. Brown beef in a large skillet over
medium heat, stirring until it crumbles
and is no longer pink; drain. Add rice
and beans, and cook until thoroughly
heated. Spoon evenly onto half of each
tortilla; fold tortillas over. Serve with
toppings.

Sensational Sides

Whether your gathering is planned or impromptu, you'll be set
with these tasty recipes.

Pepper Jack-Potato Casserole

MAKES: 4 TO 6 SERVINGS; **PREP:** 10 MIN.,
BAKE: 50 MIN.

1 (30-oz.) package frozen shredded hash
    browns
1 (8-oz.) package Monterey Jack cheese
    with peppers, shredded
1½ cups milk
1 (10¾-oz.) can cream of chicken soup,
    undiluted
2 Tbsp. butter, melted
1½ tsp. salt
½ tsp. pepper

1. Preheat oven to 350°. Combine hash
browns and cheese in a large bowl.
2. Stir together milk and next 4 ingredients; pour over hash brown mixture.
Pour into a lightly greased 13- x 9-inch
baking dish.
3. Bake at 350° for 45 to 50 minutes or
until bubbly.

Ranch Potatoes

MAKES: 4 SERVINGS; **PREP:** 10 MIN.,
COOK: 25 MIN.

*Yukon gold potatoes have been around for
centuries, but this variety is just beginning
to be widely available in supermarkets.
They're moist and sweet and good for
boiling or mashing.*

1½ lb. Yukon gold potatoes (about
    4 medium)
2 Tbsp. butter
¼ tsp. salt
½ tsp. pepper
⅓ cup Ranch dressing
2 bacon slices, cooked and crumbled

1. Bring potatoes and water to cover to
a boil in a large Dutch oven; boil 15 to

20 minutes or until tender. Drain; peel,
if desired.
2. Beat potatoes at low speed with an
electric mixer just until mashed. Add
butter, salt, and pepper, beating until
butter is melted. Gradually add dressing, beating just until smooth. Top with
crumbled bacon; serve warm.

Lighten up: Reduce calories with
no taste sacrifice by using light butter,
reduced-fat Ranch dressing, and turkey
bacon.

Roasted Broccoli With Orange-Chipotle Butter
fast fixin's

MAKES: 6 TO 8 SERVINGS; **PREP:** 2 MIN.,
BAKE: 17 MIN.

*Here's a high-flavored side dish worthy
of the finest dinner menu. Fresh orange
flavor and smoky chipotle pepper hit hot
roasted broccoli and sizzle with goodness. Chicken, beef, or pork make fine
partners.*

2 (12-oz.) packages fresh broccoli florets
2 Tbsp. olive oil
¼ cup butter, softened
2 tsp. orange zest
1 tsp. minced canned chipotle peppers in
    adobo sauce
½ tsp. salt

1. Preheat oven to 450°. Combine broccoli and oil in a large bowl; toss to coat.
Place broccoli in a single layer on an
ungreased jelly-roll pan. Bake at 450°
for 15 to 17 minutes or until broccoli is
crisp-tender.
2. While broccoli roasts, combine
butter and next 3 ingredients in a large
bowl. Add roasted broccoli to bowl,
and toss to coat. Serve hot.

Balsamic Beans

make ahead

MAKES: 10 SERVINGS; **PREP:** 6 MIN.,
COOK: 9 MIN., **BAKE:** 18 MIN.

*A quick-to-make balsamic syrup
enhances these roasted green beans.
The balsamic syrup's also good drizzled
over pork roast or even sliced fresh
strawberries.*

½ cup balsamic vinegar
2½ lb. green beans, trimmed
2 Tbsp. olive oil
1 tsp. salt
½ tsp. freshly ground pepper

1. Preheat oven to 475°. Cook vinegar
in a small saucepan over medium heat
9 minutes or until syrupy and reduced
to 3 Tbsp.; set aside.
2. Toss beans with oil in a large bowl.
Spread beans on a jelly-roll pan; sprinkle with salt and pepper.
3. Bake at 475° for 15 to 18 minutes
or until charred in appearance (do not
stir). Toss hot beans with balsamic
syrup. Serve immediately.
Fix It Faster: Purchase prewashed,
trimmed green beans available in the
produce department.
Note: The balsamic syrup can be made
a day ahead and stored at room temperature. Make a few extra batches of the
syrup and consider it for gift-giving.

Buttered Asparagus Spears

fast fixin's

MAKES: 8 SERVINGS; **PREP:** 2 MIN.,
COOK: 19 MIN.

3 lb. fresh asparagus*
¼ cup butter
½ tsp. salt
½ tsp. freshly ground pepper

1. Snap off tough ends of asparagus.
Bring 2 qt. water to a boil in a Dutch
oven. Add asparagus; cook 3 to 5 minutes or until crisp-tender. Rinse with
cold water to stop the cooking process;
drain. Cover and chill, if desired.

2. Melt butter in a large skillet; add
asparagus, salt, and pepper. Sauté until
thoroughly heated. Serve immediately.
***3 lb. fresh green beans can be substi-
tuted for asparagus, if desired.

Garlic Cheese Grits

fast fixin's

MAKES: 36 SERVINGS; **PREP:** 5 MIN.,
COOK: 20 MIN.

1½ tsp. salt
4 cups quick-cooking grits,
    uncooked
5 garlic cloves, minced
1 (2-lb.) loaf pasteurized prepared cheese
    product, cubed
1 cup half-and-half
⅔ cup butter

1. Bring 3 qt. water and salt to a boil in
a large Dutch oven; gradually stir in grits
and garlic. Cover, reduce heat, and simmer 10 minutes, stirring occasionally.
2. Add cheese, half-and-half, and butter; simmer, stirring constantly, until
cheese and butter melt.

Ranch Noodles

fast fixin's

MAKES: 4 TO 6 SERVINGS; **PREP:** 5 MIN.,
COOK: 10 MIN.

*Just drop the pasta in a pot of boiling
water, and heat up your desired add-ins
for a fast meal.*

1 (8-oz.) package egg noodles,
    uncooked
¼ cup butter
½ cup sour cream
½ cup Ranch dressing
½ cup grated Parmesan cheese

1. Cook egg noodles according to package directions; drain and return to pot.
Stir in butter and remaining ingredients. Serve immediately.
Note: Substitute 1 (8-oz.) package of
thin spaghetti for the egg noodles, and
add chopped cooked ham and steamed

broccoli, if desired. Sautéing the ham
in a lightly greased skillet over medium-
high heat gives it a crisp and smoky
baconlike flavor.

Maple Mashed Squash
With Candied Pecans

MAKES: 8 SERVINGS; **PREP:** 19 MIN.,
COOK: 37 MIN.

*Serve this delectable squash as an
alternative to sweet potatoes.*

1 (4-lb.) butternut squash
5 Tbsp. butter, divided
7 Tbsp. maple syrup, divided
1½ tsp. maple flavoring
1¼ tsp. salt, divided
1 cup chopped pecans

1. Microwave squash on HIGH 2 minutes to soften. Cut in half. Peel squash;
remove and discard seeds. Cut squash
into 1-inch squares.
2. Cook squash in water to cover in a
large Dutch oven 30 minutes or until
tender; drain.
3. Combine squash, 3 Tbsp. butter,
3 Tbsp. syrup, maple flavoring, and
¾ tsp. salt in a large bowl; mash with a
potato masher until smooth.
4. Cook pecans, remaining 2 Tbsp.
butter, remaining ¼ cup maple syrup,
and ½ tsp. salt in a medium skillet over
medium-low heat 7 minutes or until
syrup caramelizes and pecans begin to
brown; cool in a single layer on a plate.
Sprinkle pecans over squash, and serve
warm.

Sweet Endings

Complete your meal with the homemade goodness found in one of these impressive desserts.

Coconut-Sour Cream Cake

MAKES: 12 SERVINGS; **PREP:** 25 MIN.,
BAKE: ABOUT 27 MIN., **CHILL:** 9½ HR.

Butter-flavored cake mix gives you a head start on this elegant-looking 4-layer cake. The flavor gets better and the cake more moist the longer it chills.

1 (18.25-oz.) package butter-recipe cake mix
1 (16-oz.) container sour cream
2 cups sugar
4 cups sweetened flaked coconut
1½ cups frozen whipped topping, thawed

1. Preheat oven according to cake mix package directions. Prepare cake mix according to package directions, using 2 (9-inch) round cake pans. Let cool as directed. Slice each cake layer horizontally in half, using a long serrated knife.
2. While cake bakes, combine sour cream, sugar, and coconut in a bowl; stir well. Cover and chill 1½ hours. Reserve 1 cup sour cream mixture. Spread remaining sour cream mixture between cake layers.
3. Fold whipped topping into reserved sour cream mixture. Spread on top and sides of cake. Place cake in an airtight container. Cover and chill at least 8 hours.
Note: For testing purposes only, we used Pillsbury Butter-recipe Cake Mix.

Chocolate Éclair Cake

make ahead

MAKES: 12 SERVINGS; **PREP:** 15 MIN.,
CHILL: 8 HR.

One box of graham crackers contains three individually wrapped packages of crackers; use one package for each layer.

1 (14.4-oz.) box honey graham crackers
2 (3.4-oz.) packages French vanilla instant pudding mix
3 cups milk
1 (12-oz.) container frozen whipped topping, thawed
1 (16-oz.) container ready-to-spread chocolate frosting

1. Line bottom of an ungreased 13- x 9-inch baking dish with one-third of honey graham crackers.
2. Whisk together pudding mix and milk; add whipped topping, stirring until mixture thickens. Spread half of pudding mixture over crackers. Repeat layers with one-third of crackers and remaining pudding mixture. Top with remaining crackers. Spread with chocolate frosting. Cover and chill 8 hours.

Toffee Temptation

make ahead

MAKES: 10 SERVINGS; **PREP:** 15 MIN.,
CHILL: 2 HR.

1 (3.4-oz.) package vanilla instant pudding mix
2 cups milk
1 (12.75-oz.) package cream-filled sponge cakes
1 (8.4-oz.) package English toffee candy bars, crushed
½ (8-oz.) container frozen whipped topping, thawed

1. Prepare pudding with milk according to package directions.
2. Meanwhile, slice cakes in half horizontally. Line an 11- x 7-inch dish with bottom halves of cakes, cut side up. Sprinkle with ½ cup candy.
3. Spoon pudding over candy. Arrange tops of cakes over pudding, cut side down. Spread with whipped topping; sprinkle with remaining candy. Cover and chill 2 hours.
Note: For testing purposes only, we used Twinkies cream-filled sponge cakes.

Ambrosia Trifle

fast fixin's • make ahead

MAKES: 10 TO 12 SERVINGS; **PREP:** 7 MIN.,
BAKE: 8 MIN.

1 cup sweetened flaked coconut
1 (24-oz.) package prepared vanilla pudding*
1 (8-oz.) container frozen creamy whipped topping, thawed and divided
2 (24-oz.) jars refrigerated mandarin oranges
½ round bakery pound cake, cut into 1-inch cubes

1. Place coconut on a baking sheet. Bake at 350° for 8 minutes or until lightly browned; set aside.
2. Meanwhile, stir together pudding and 1½ cups whipped topping. Drain oranges, reserving liquid.
3. Layer half of cake cubes in 6 (2-cup) stemmed glasses or a 3-qt. glass bowl or trifle dish. Brush cake cubes with reserved liquid; spoon half of pudding evenly over cubes.
4. Top with half of oranges. Repeat layers, ending with oranges. Dollop with desired amount of whipped topping; sprinkle with toasted coconut. Chill until ready to serve.
*As an option, you can use 1 (5.1-oz.) package vanilla instant pudding that yields about 3 cups.
Note: For testing purposes only, we used Jello Pudding Snacks and Del Monte Sun Fresh Mandarin Oranges.

TennTucky Blackberry Cobbler

MAKES: 6 SERVINGS; **PREP:** 5 MIN., **BAKE:** 1 HR.

Scatter a handful of frozen berries over a buttery batter, and this melt-in-your-mouth cobbler will be ready for the oven.

1¼ cups sugar
1 cup self-rising flour
1 cup milk
½ cup butter, melted
2 cups frozen blackberries

1. Preheat oven to 350°. Whisk together 1 cup sugar, flour, and milk just until blended; whisk in melted butter. Pour batter into a lightly greased 12- x 8-inch baking dish; sprinkle blackberries and remaining ¼ cup sugar evenly over batter.
2. Bake at 350° for 1 hour or until golden brown and bubbly.

Rocky Top Brownies

MAKES: 32 BROWNIES; **PREP:** 10 MIN., **BAKE:** 25 MIN.

Former Executive Editor Susan Dosier came up with this fun recipe. Substitute an equal amount of your favorite chocolate-covered candy for the peanut butter cups, if desired.

1 (19-oz.) package brownie mix
½ cup butter, melted
3 large eggs
1 (13-oz.) package miniature chocolate-covered peanut butter cups, coarsely chopped

1. Preheat oven to 350°. Stir together first 3 ingredients until blended. Spoon batter into a greased and floured 13- x 9-inch pan.
2. Bake at 350° for 23 minutes or until center is set. Remove from oven, and sprinkle top of brownies evenly with chopped candy. Return to oven, and bake 2 minutes. Remove from oven, and cool completely on a wire rack. Cut brownies into squares.

Chocolate Panini

fast fixin's

MAKES: 10 SANDWICHES; **PREP:** 3 MIN., **COOK:** 1 MIN. PER BATCH

A slender loaf of rustic Italian bread is the ideal shape to use for these little dessert sandwiches. Get your dinner guests involved in making and serving these hot off the press.

1 (8-oz.) loaf ciabatta bread
2 to 3 Tbsp. olive oil
1 (4-oz.) bittersweet chocolate baking bar, coarsely chopped

1. Preheat panini press according to manufacturer's instructions.
2. Slice bread into 10 (1-inch) pieces; slice each piece in half. Brush crust sides of each piece of bread with olive oil. Turn bottoms of bread, oiled side down. Place chocolate evenly on bottom pieces of bread; cover with tops of bread oiled side up.
3. Place 5 sandwiches in panini press; cook 1 minute or just until chocolate begins to melt and bread is toasted. Repeat procedure with remaining sandwiches. Serve hot.
Note: For testing purposes only, we used Ghirardelli bittersweet chocolate.

Caramel-Chocolate Tartlets

fast fixin's • make ahead

MAKES: 30 TARTLETS; **PREP:** 14 MIN., **FREEZE:** 1 MIN.

Dulce de leche is a fancy name for caramel. It makes these bite-size sweets really rich. Make the tartlets ahead, and freeze them in the plastic pastry trays sealed in zip-top freezer bags.

1 (13.4-oz.) can dulce de leche*
2 (2.1-oz.) packages frozen mini phyllo pastry shells, thawed
1 cup double chocolate morsels or regular semisweet morsels
⅓ cup roasted salted peanuts, chopped, or coarsely chopped pecans, or both

1. Spoon 1 heaping tsp. dulce de leche into each pastry shell. Microwave chocolate morsels in a small glass bowl on HIGH 1 to 1½ minutes or until melted, stirring twice. Spoon 1 tsp. chocolate over dulce de leche. Sprinkle tartlets with peanuts or pecans. Freeze 1 minute to set chocolate.
*Find dulce de leche on the baking aisle or the Mexican food aisle or make your own. Pour 1 (14-oz.) can sweetened condensed milk into an 8-inch dish or pieplate; cover with foil. Preheat oven to 425°. Pour ½ inch hot water into a larger pan. Place covered pieplate in pan. Bake at 425° for 1 hour and 25 minutes or until thick and caramel colored (add hot water to pan as needed). Remove foil when done; cool.
Note: For testing purposes only, we used Nestle dulce de leche, Athens mini phyllo pastry shells, and Ghirardelli double chocolate morsels.

Caramel-Cashew Ice Cream

make ahead

MAKES: 1 QT.; **PREP:** 10 MIN., **FREEZE:** 8 HR.

You won't need an ice-cream freezer for this rich caramel ice cream—just an airtight container. It's a great make-ahead dessert: Just mix, freeze, scoop, and enjoy!

2 cups whipping cream
1 (14-oz.) can sweetened condensed milk
½ cup butterscotch-caramel topping
1 cup salted cashews, chopped
Toppings: butterscotch-caramel topping, chopped cashews

1. Beat whipping cream at high speed with an electric mixer until stiff peaks form.
2. Stir together sweetened condensed milk and ½ cup butterscotch-caramel topping in a large mixing bowl. Fold in whipped cream and 1 cup cashews. Place in an airtight container; freeze 6 to 8 hours or until firm. Serve with desired toppings.

Appendices

handy substitutions

ingredient	substitution
baking products	
Baking powder, 1 teaspoon	• ½ teaspoon cream of tartar plus ¼ teaspoon baking soda
Chocolate	
semisweet, 1 ounce	• 1 ounce unsweetened chocolate plus 1 tablespoon sugar
unsweetened, 1 ounce or square	• 3 tablespoons cocoa plus 1 tablespoon fat
chips, semisweet, 6-ounce package, melted	• 2 ounces unsweetened chocolate, 2 tablespoons shortening plus ½ cup sugar
Cocoa, ¼ cup	• 1 ounce unsweetened chocolate (decrease fat in recipe by ½ tablespoon)
Corn syrup, light, 1 cup	• 1 cup sugar plus ¼ cup water • 1 cup honey
Cornstarch, 1 tablespoon	• 2 tablespoons all-purpose flour or granular tapioca
Flour	
all-purpose, 1 tablespoon	• 1½ teaspoons cornstarch, potato starch, or rice starch • 1 tablespoon rice flour or corn flour • 1½ tablespoons whole wheat flour
all-purpose, 1 cup sifted	• 1 cup plus 2 tablespoons sifted cake flour
cake, 1 cup sifted	• 1 cup minus 2 tablespoons all-purpose flour
self-rising, 1 cup	• 1 cup all-purpose flour, 1 teaspoon baking powder plus ½ teaspoon salt
Shortening	
melted, 1 cup	• 1 cup cooking oil (don't use cooking oil unless recipe calls for melted shortening)
solid, 1 cup (used in baking)	• 1⅛ cups butter or margarine (decrease salt called for in recipe by ½ teaspoon)
Sugar	
brown, 1 cup firmly packed	• 1 cup granulated white sugar
powdered, 1 cup	• 1 cup sugar plus 1 tablespoon cornstarch (processed in food processor)
granulated white, 1 teaspoon	• ⅛ teaspoon noncaloric sweetener solution or follow manufacturer's directions
granulated white, 1 cup	• 1 cup corn syrup (decrease liquid called for in recipe by ¼ cup) • 1 cup honey (decrease liquid called for in recipe by ¼ cup)
Tapioca, granular, 1 tablespoon	• 1½ teaspoons cornstarch or 1 tablespoon all-purpose flour
dairy products	
Butter, 1 cup	• ⅞ to 1 cup shortening or lard plus ½ teaspoon salt • 1 cup margarine (2 sticks; do not substitute whipped or low-fat margarine)
Cream	
heavy (30% to 40% fat), 1 cup	• ¾ cup milk plus ⅓ cup butter or margarine (for cooking and baking; will not whip)
light (15% to 20% fat), 1 cup	• ¾ cup milk plus 3 tablespoons butter or margarine (for cooking and baking) • 1 cup evaporated milk, undiluted
half-and-half, 1 cup	• ⅞ cup milk plus ½ tablespoon butter or margarine (for cooking and baking) • 1 cup evaporated milk, undiluted
whipped, 1 cup	• 1 cup frozen whipped topping, thawed
Egg	
1 large	• ¼ cup egg substitute
2 large	• 3 small eggs or ½ cup egg substitute • 1 large egg plus 2 egg whites
1 egg white (2 tablespoons)	• 2 tablespoons egg substitute
Milk	
buttermilk, 1 cup	• 1 tablespoon vinegar or lemon juice plus whole milk to make 1 cup (let stand 10 minutes) • 1 cup plain yogurt • 1 cup whole milk plus 1¾ teaspoons cream of tartar
fat free, 1 cup	• 4 to 5 tablespoons nonfat dry milk powder plus enough water to make 1 cup • ½ cup evaporated skim milk plus ½ cup water
whole, 1 cup	• 4 to 5 tablespoons nonfat dry milk powder plus enough water to make 1 cup • ½ cup evaporated milk plus ½ cup water

ingredient	substitution
Milk (continued)	
sweetened condensed, 1 (14-ounce) can (about 1¼ cups)	• Heat the following ingredients until sugar and butter dissolve: ⅓ cup plus 2 tablespoons evaporated milk, 1 cup sugar, 3 tablespoons butter or margarine. • Add 1 cup plus 2 tablespoons nonfat dry milk powder to ½ cup warm water. Mix well. Add ¾ cup sugar, and stir until smooth.
Sour cream, 1 cup	• 1 cup plain yogurt plus 3 tablespoons melted butter or 1 tablespoon cornstarch • 1 tablespoon lemon juice plus evaporated milk to equal 1 cup
Yogurt, 1 cup (plain)	• 1 cup buttermilk

miscellaneous

ingredient	substitution
Broth, beef or chicken canned broth, 1 cup	• 1 bouillon cube or 1 teaspoon bouillon granules dissolved in 1 cup boiling water
Garlic	
1 small clove	• ⅛ teaspoon garlic powder or minced dried garlic
garlic salt, 1 teaspoon	• ⅛ teaspoon garlic powder plus ⅞ teaspoon salt
Gelatin, flavored, 3-ounce package	• 1 tablespoon unflavored gelatin plus 2 cups fruit juice
Herbs, fresh, chopped, 1 tablespoon	• 1 teaspoon dried herbs or ¼ teaspoon ground herbs
Honey, 1 cup	• 1¼ cups sugar plus ¼ cup water
Mustard, dried, 1 teaspoon	• 1 tablespoon prepared mustard
Tomatoes, fresh, chopped, 2 cups	• 1 (16-ounce) can (may need to drain)
Tomato sauce, 2 cups	• ¾ cup tomato paste plus 1 cup water

alcohol substitutions

alcohol	substitution
Amaretto, 2 tablespoons	• ¼ to ½ teaspoon almond extract*
Bourbon or Sherry, 2 tablespoons	• 1 to 2 teaspoons vanilla extract*
Brandy, fruit-flavored liqueur, port wine, rum, or sweet sherry: ¼ cup or more	• Equal amount of unsweetened orange or apple juice plus 1 teaspoon vanilla extract or corresponding flavor
Brandy or rum, 2 tablespoons	• ½ to 1 teaspoon brandy or rum extract*
Grand Marnier or other orange liqueur, 2 tablespoons	• 2 tablespoons unsweetened orange juice concentrate or 2 tablespoons orange juice and ½ teaspoon orange extract
Kahlúa or other coffee or chocolate liqueur, 2 tablespoons	• ½ to 1 teaspoon chocolate extract plus ½ to 1 teaspoon instant coffee dissolved in 2 tablespoons water
Marsala, ¼ cup	• ¼ cup white grape juice or ¼ cup dry white wine plus 1 teaspoon brandy
Wine	
red, ¼ cup or more	• Equal measure of red grape juice or cranberry juice
white, ¼ cup or more	• Equal measure of white grape juice or nonalcoholic white wine

Add water, white grape juice, or apple juice to get the specified amount of liquid (when the liquid amount is crucial).

equivalent measures

3 teaspoons	= 1 tablespoon		2 tablespoons (liquid)	= 1 ounce		⅛ cup	= 2 tablespoons
4 tablespoons	= ¼ cup		1 cup	= 8 fluid ounces		⅓ cup	= 5 tablespoons plus 1 teaspoon
5⅓ tablespoons	= ⅓ cup		2 cups	= 1 pint (16 fluid ounces)		⅔ cup	= 10 tablespoons plus 2 teaspoons
8 tablespoons	= ½ cup		4 cups	= 1 quart		¾ cup	= 12 tablespoons
16 tablespoons	= 1 cup		4 quarts	= 1 gallon			

metric equivilants

The recipes that appear in this cookbook use the standard United States method for measuring liquid and dry or solid ingredients (teaspoons, tablespoons, and cups). The information on this chart is provided to help cooks outside the U.S. successfully use these recipes. All equivalents are approximate.

METRIC EQUIVALENTS FOR DIFFERENT TYPES OF INGREDIENTS

A standard cup measure of a dry or solid ingredient will vary in weight depending on the type of ingredient. A standard cup of liquid is the same volume for any type of liquid. Use the following chart when converting standard cup measures to grams (weight) or milliliters (volume).

Standard Cup	Fine Powder	Grain	Granular	Liquid Solids	Liquid
	(ex. flour)	(ex. rice)	(ex. sugar)	(ex. butter)	(ex. milk)
1	140 g	150 g	190 g	200 g	240 ml
3/4	105 g	113 g	143 g	150 g	180 ml
2/3	93 g	100 g	125 g	133 g	160 ml
1/2	70 g	75 g	95 g	100 g	120 ml
1/3	47 g	50 g	63 g	67 g	80 ml
1/4	35 g	38 g	48 g	50 g	60 ml
1/8	18 g	19 g	24 g	25 g	30 ml

USEFUL EQUIVALENTS FOR DRY INGREDIENTS BY WEIGHT

(To convert ounces to grams, multiply the number of ounces by 30.)

1 oz	=	1/16 lb	=	30 g
4 oz	=	1/4 lb	=	120 g
8 oz	=	1/2 lb	=	240 g
12 oz	=	3/4 lb	=	360 g
16 oz	=	1 lb	=	480 g

USEFUL EQUIVALENTS FOR LENGTH

(To convert inches to centimeters, multiply the number of inches by 2.5.)

1 in				=	2.5 cm		
6 in	=	1/2 ft	=	=	15 cm		
12 in	=	1 ft		=	30 cm		
36 in	=	3 ft	=	1 yd	=	90 cm	
40 in				=	100 cm	=	1 m

USEFUL EQUIVALENTS FOR LIQUID INGREDIENTS BY VOLUME

1/4 tsp	=						1 ml
1/2 tsp	=						2 ml
1 tsp	=						5 ml
3 tsp	=	1 tbls			=	1/2 fl oz	=	15 ml
	=	2 tbls	=	1/8 cup	=	1 fl oz	=	30 ml
	=	4 tbls	=	1/4 cup	=	2 fl oz	=	60 ml
	=	5 1/3 tbls	=	1/3 cup	=	3 fl oz	=	80 ml
	=	8 tbls	=	1/2 cup	=	4 fl oz	=	120 ml
	=	10 2/3 tbls	=	2/3 cup	=	5 fl oz	=	160 ml
	=	12 tbls	=	3/4 cup	=	6 fl oz	=	180 ml
	=	16 tbls	=	1 cup	=	8 fl oz	=	240 ml
	=	1 pt	=	2 cups	=	16 fl oz	=	480 ml
	=	1 qt	=	4 cups	=	32 fl oz	=	960 ml
					33 fl oz	=	1000 ml	= 1 l

USEFUL EQUIVALENTS FOR COOKING/OVEN TEMPERATURES

	Fahrenheit	Celsius	Gas Mark
Freeze Water	32° F	0° C	
Room Temperature	68° F	20° C	
Boil Water	212° F	100° C	
Bake	325° F	160° C	3
	350° F	180° C	4
	375° F	190° C	5
	400° F	200° C	6
	425° F	220° C	7
	450° F	230° C	8
Broil			Grill

Menu Index

This index lists every menu by suggested occasion. Recipes in bold type are provided with the menu and accompaniments are in regular type.

Menus for Company

Easy Spring Supper

SERVES 8
(page 62)

Avocado Soup With Marinated Shrimp
Grilled Honey-Mustard Pork Tenderloin
Creamy Gruyère Grits
Grilled Fennel and Radicchio
Strawberry-Orange Trifle

Make-Ahead Lunch

SERVES 6
(page 75)

Spinach Lasagna Rollups
Three-Tomato Salad
Southern Sweet Tea

Bring-Your-Own-Meat Party

SERVES 8
(page 102)

Grilled Stuffed Peppers
Panzanella Salad
Grilled meat of choice or fish
Summer Vegetable Kabobs
Balsamic Strawberries or
Chocolate Mint Sundaes

Backyard Burger Bar

SERVES 4
(page 138)

Ginger Beer
Cajun Burgers or **Bacon-Wrapped Barbecue Burgers**
Choice of flavored condiments
Steak Fries
Frosted Sugar-'n'-Spice Cookies
Pineapple Iced Tea Punch

Rise 'n' Shine Breakfast

SERVES 4
(page 140)

Open-Face Ham-and-Egg Sandwich
Fresh Fruit with Lemon-Ginger Honey and Quick Stovetop Granola
Coffee and assorted sugar blends

Fish Fry Supper

SERVES 6
(page 144)

Stuffed Sweet-and-Spicy Jalapeño Poppers
Bayou Fish Fillets With Sweet-Hot Pecan Sauce
Shrimp and Okra Hush Puppies
Easy Blackberry Cobbler over
No-Cook Vanilla Ice Cream

Tex-Mex Menu

SERVES 6 TO 8
(page 156)

Sangría
Citrus Shrimp Tacos
Grilled Corn Salsa
Tortilla chips
Tres Leches Cake

Tasting Party

SERVES 8
(page 208)

Prosciutto-Wrapped Mango Bites
Cuban Black Bean Dip
Party-Style Pork Empanada
Lean Green Lettuce Tacos

Lunch Bunch

SERVES 6
(page 272)

Brandy Slush
Bacon-Wrapped Water Chestnuts
Ragoût of Mushrooms With Creamy Polenta
Citrus Salad
Quick Yeast Rolls
Cheesecake Squares

Menus for Family

Pork Chops Supper
S E R V E S 4
(page 30)
Savory Herb Pork Chops
Roasted Apples and Sweet Potatoes
Italian Tossed Salad
Dinner rolls

Mid-Morning Menu
S E R V E S 4 T O 6
(page 42)
Shrimp and Grits
**Baked Pears With Oatmeal
    Streusel Topping**
Cream Cheese-Banana-Nut Bread
Bloody Mary Punch

Easy Italian Supper
S E R V E S 4
(page 74)
Lemon-Basil Antipasto
Creamy Tortellini Primavera
Coffee
Carrot Cake Sandwich Cookies

Dinner on the Double
S E R V E S 4
(page 95)
Bacon-Wrapped Pork Tenderloin
Creamy Cheese Grits and Spinach
Sautéed Brown Sugar Pears or
    Ginger-Pear Shortcakes

Laid-Back Summer Supper
S E R V E S 6
(page 129)
Open-faced Turkey Joes
Corn-and-Lima Bean Salad
**Warm Blackberry Sauce Over
    Mango Sorbet**

Dinner on a Dime
S E R V E S 4 T O 6
(page 155)
**Chicken Thighs With Chunky
    Tomato Sauce**
**Mixed Greens With Toasted
    Almonds and Apple Cider
    Vinaigrette**
Bakery rolls
Raisin-Oatmeal Cookies

Creole Supper
S E R V E S 4
(page 199)
JoAnn's Jambalaya
Mixed greens salad
Garlic French Bread
Bananas Foster Ice-Cream Pastry

Healthy Morning
S E R V E S 6
(page 234)
**Over-the-Border Breakfast
    Sausage Wraps**
**Mixed Fruit With Vanilla-Apple
    Syrup**
Orange juice
Iced Coffee

Grilled Cheese Supper
S E R V E S 4
(page 243)
Extra Cheesy Grilled Cheese
Quick Turkey Chili
Tortilla chips
Iced tea

30-Minute Shrimp Supper
S E R V E S 4
(page 266)
Shrimp Scampi
Mixed greens salad
Cheesy Garlic Bread
Ice cream

Pizzeria Night
S E R V E S 4
(page 300)
Italian-style Pizza Pot Pie
**Iceberg Lettuce Wedge With Zesty
    Buttermilk Ranch Dressing**
Cinnamon Nuggets

Menus for Special Occasions

No-Fuss Entertaining

SERVES 6
(page 82)
Feta Cheese Truffles *(page 97)*
Chicken Scaloppine With Spinach
    and Linguine
Easy Three-Seed Pan Rolls
Sweet Dip With Cookies and Fruit

Passover Menu

SERVES 4 TO 6
(page 87)
Garlic-Herb Roasted Chicken
Sweet Vegetable Kugel
Lemon Roasted Asparagus
Chocolate Fudge Cake or Chunky
    Chocolate Brownies

Cinco de Mayo Fiesta

SERVES 6
(page 104)
Fiesta Dip
Scarlet Margaritas
Tortilla-Crusted Pork
Avocado Fruit Salad

Festive Fall Menu

SERVES 8
(page 196)
Guacamole-Goat Cheese Toasts
Sweet Potato Squares With
    Lemon-Garlic Mayonnaise
Grilled Pork Roast With Fruit
    Compote
Caramelized Onion-Potato Gratin
Mixed greens salad
Granola-Ginger Baked Apples

Fall Cookout

SERVES 4
(page 214)
Apple-Avocado Relish
Grilled Sausages
Orange-Sauerkraut Salad
Apricot Torte

Haunting (But Not Daunting) Menu

SERVES 8 TO 10
(page 222)
Onion-Bacon Dip
Assorted multigrain and
    vegetable chips
Monster Meatball Sandwiches
Barbecue Stew
Mummy Dogs
Cereal-and-Granola "Apples"
Chocolate Ghost Cakes

A New Orleans-Style Menu

SERVES 8
(page 260)
Roast Pork With Garlic-Onion
    Gravy
Oyster Dressing
Creamed Collards
Stuffed Mirlitons
Coconut-Almond Cream Cake

Thanksgiving Dinner

SERVES 8
(page 268)
Delta Roasted Turkey With
    Million-Dollar Gravy
Sweet Potato Cups
Cornbread 'n' Squash Dressing
    (page 285)
Basic Green Bean Casserole
    (page 288)
Fresh Fruit Tart With Mascarpone
    Cheese *(page 267)*
Grand Mimosas

Hanukkah Celebration

SERVES 6 TO 8
(page 270)
Golden Potato Latkes with
    Horseradish-Sour Cream Sauce
Spiced-Thyme Applesauce
Smoked Salmon-Avocado Salad
Mindi's Doughnuts and Easy
    Raspberry Sauce

Good-for-You Buffet

SERVES 8
(page 276)
Shrimp on Flats
Dan the Man's Pork Loin Roast
Sautéed Spinach
Power Salad
Hebni Banana Pudding

Christmas Eve Brunch

SERVES 2
(page 280)

Gentleman's Casserole
Winter Fruit Compote
Cranberry-Orange Tea Bread
  Muffins
Kane's Peppery Bloody Mary

Cozy Christmas Dinner

SERVES 6 TO 8
(page 294)

Goat Cheese-Pesto Crostini
Pork Loin With Carolina Apple
  Compote
Bacon-Brown Sugar Brussels
  Sprouts
Butternut Squash Risotto
Home-style Butterbeans
Christmas Shortbread Cookies

Last-Minute Gathering

SERVES 6 TO 8
(page 297)

Mini Caviar Parfaits
Andouille With Smoked Paprika
  and Red Wine
Warm Brie With Ginger-Citrus
  Glaze
Instant Italian Cheese Tray
Warm Fennel-Olive Sauté
Smoked Trout-and-Horseradish
  Spread
Bourbon Smash, Orange Lady, or
  Vicki's Dirty Martini
Beer and wine

Appetizer Buffet

SERVES 8
(page 302)

Marinated Shrimp
Black Bean-and-Mango Salsa
Spicy Southwestern Deviled Eggs
Chipotle Barbecue Meatballs
Southwest Fondue
Pomegranate Margaritas

Christmas Brunch

SERVES 6 TO 8
(page 305)

Breakfast Enchiladas
Hot Tomato Grits
Skewered Fruit With Rum
  Drizzle
Peppery Jelly Danish
Hot Chocolate With Almond
  Liqueur
Rudolph's Spritzer
Brunch Punch

Company's Coming

SERVES 8 TO 12
(page 308)

Maryland Crab Cakes With
  Creamy Caper-Dill Sauce
Caribbean Cashews
Bacon-Cheese Dip
Smoky Ranch Dip
Fresh Lemon-Basil Dip With
  Blanched Green Beans
Fresh Herb Sauce
Sun-dried Tomato Aïoli
Butternut Squash Parsnip Soup
Mock Tea Sangría
Frozen Sangría
Create-your-own cupcake station

January 1 Get-together

SERVES ABOUT 12
(page 313)

Red Roosters
Hot Roast Beef Party Sandwiches
Fruity Salad With Sugared
  Almonds and Sweet-Hot
  Vinaigrette
Grilled Herb Chicken Drumettes
  With White Barbecue Sauce
Warm Turnip Green Dip
Dixie Caviar Cups
Peel-and-Eat Shrimp With
  Dipping Sauces
Dressed Up Cheesecake Bars

Such a Delectable Dinner

SERVES 8
(page 318)

Beef Tenderloin With Henry Bain
  Sauce
Sweet Onion Pudding
Simple Roasted Asparagus
Baby Blue Salad
Creamy Bell Pepper 'n' Tomato
  Soup
Refrigerator Yeast Rolls
Cream Cheese Coconut-Pecan
  Pound Cake

Mix-and-Match Recipe Menus

Comfort Food Supper

SERVES 4
Red Wine Short Ribs *(page 35)*
Polenta
Sautéed Green Beans and Pears
(page 60)

Quick Weeknight Supper

SERVES 4
Nutty Turkey Cutlets *(page 111)*
**Sautéed Mushroom-and-Cheese
     Ravioli** *(page 111)*
Quick and Tasty Banana Pudding
     (make 4) *(page 34)*

Meat and Potatoes Dinner

SERVES 6 TO 8
Tomato-Basil Meatloaf *(page 115)*
**Buttermilk-Garlic Mashed
     Potatoes** (double recipe) *(page 106)*
English peas

Ultimate One-Dish Dinner

SERVES 8
King Ranch Chicken Casserole
     (page 58)
Guacamole salad

Healthy Dinner

SERVES 6
Chicken-fried Steak *(page 68)*
Mashed potatoes
**Baby Spinach Salad With Poppy
     Seed Dressing** *(page 90)*

Spaghetti Special

SERVES 4
**Spaghetti With Sausage and
     Peppers** *(page 57)*
Buttered broccoli
Crusty French bread

It's a Wrap

SERVES 6
Greek Beef Wraps *(page 93)*
Peanutty Coleslaw *(page 142)*
Fresh strawberries

Delta Dinner

SERVES 6
Buffalo Catfish *(page 110)*
Warm Purple and Potato Toss *(page 86)*
Collards With Red Onions *(page 34)*
Easy Blackberry Cobbler *(page 145)*

Veggie Plate

SERVES 8
Not Yo' Mama's Mac 'n' Cheese
     (page 154)
Summer Squash Casserole
     (page 114)
Fried Green Tomatoes *(page 107)*
**Green Beans With Caramelized
     Garlic** *(page 153)*
Cornbread

Winter Warm Up

SERVES 6
Peppered Beef Soup *(page 211)*
Toasted Bread Bowls *(page 211)*
Easy Spicy Caesar Salad *(page 59)*

Kabob Supper

SERVES 4
Choice of Kabob *(pages 238 and 239)*
Yellow rice
Cranberry-Nectarine Salad
     (page 213)

Make-Ahead Supper

SERVES 8
Easy Chicken Pie *(page 237)*
Mixed greens salad

Quick Company Supper

SERVES 8
**Creamy Chipotle-Black Bean
     Dip** *(page 329)*
Molasses-Grilled Pork Tenderloin
     (page 330)
Cheese grits
Buttered Asparagus Spears
     (page 332)
Coconut-Sour Cream Cake
     (page 333)

Recipe Title Index

This index alphabetically lists every recipe by exact title.

Month-By-Month Index

This index alphabetically lists every food article and accompanying recipes by month.

General Recipe Index

This index lists every recipe by food category and/or major ingredient.

Favorite Recipes Journal

Jot down your family's and your favorite recipes for quick and handy reference. And don't forget to include the dishes that drew rave reviews when company came for dinner.

Recipe	Source/Page	Remarks